"This translation—the first into English—of *The Life of Jesus Christ* by Ludolph of Saxony will be welcomed both by scholars in various fields and by practicing Christians. It is at the same time an encyclopedia of biblical, patristic, and medieval learning and a compendium of late medieval spirituality, stressing the importance of meditation in the life of individual believers. It draws on an astonishing number of sources and sheds light on many aspects of the doctrinal and institutional history of the Church down to the fourteenth century."

— Giles Constable
Professor Emeritus
Princeton University

"Milton T. Walsh has taken on a Herculean task of translating *The Life of Christ* by the fourteenth-century Carthusian, Ludolph of Saxony. He has more than risen to the challenge! Ludolph's text was one of the most widely spread and influential treatments of the theme in the later Middle Ages and has, until now, been available only in an insufficient late nineteenth-century edition (Rigollot). The manuscript tradition of *The Life of Christ (Vita Christi)* is extremely complex, and Walsh, while basing his translation on the edition, has gone beyond in providing critical apparatus that will be of significant use to scholars, as well as making the text available for students and all interested in the theology, spirituality, and religious life of the later Middle Ages. His introduction expertly places Ludolph's work in the textual tradition and is itself a contribution to scholarship. Simply put, this is an amazing achievement!"

— Eric Leland Saak
Professor of History
Indiana University

"Walsh has done pioneering work unearthing the huge range of patristic, scholastic, and contemporary sources that Ludolph drew upon, enabling us to re-evaluate the *Vita* as an encyclopedic compilation, skillfully collating a range of interpretations of the gospel scenes to meditational ends.

"This translation will hopefully stimulate further work on the late medieval manuscript tradition of the text, its circulation, use and readership. It will prove an invaluable tool for scholars researching the late medieval engagement with the humanity of Christ, while simultaneously catering for general readers and religious practitioners interested in learning more about a traditional and influential imaginative meditational practice."

— Christiania Whitehead
Professor of Middle English Literature
University of Warwick

CISTERCIAN STUDIES SERIES: TWO HUNDRED SIXTY-SEVEN

The Life of Jesus Christ

Part One

Volume 1, Chapters 1–40

Ludolph of Saxony, Carthusian

Translated and Introduced by
Milton T. Walsh

Cistercian Publications
www.cistercianpublications.org

LITURGICAL PRESS
Collegeville, Minnesota
www.litpress.org

A Cistercian Publications title published by Liturgical Press

Cistercian Publications
Editorial Offices
161 Grosvenor Street
Athens, Ohio 45701
www.cistercianpublications.org

Cover image: The Annunciation, miniature attributed to Jacques de Besançon (Paris: 1490s) in a French translation of the *Vita Christi* by Guillaume le Ménard, in the Special Collections of the University of Glasgow. Used by permission of the University of Glasgow.

1 2 3 4 5 6 7 8 9

Library of Congress Cataloging-in-Publication Data

Names: Ludolf, von Sachsen, approximately 1300–1377 or 1378, author. | Walsh, Milton T., translator, writer of introduction.
Title: The life of Jesus Christ / Ludolph of Saxony, Carthusian ; translated and introduced by Milton T. Walsh.
Other titles: Vita Christi. English
Description: Collegeville, Minnesota : Cistercian Publications, 2018. | Series: Cistercian studies series ; 267 | Includes bibliographical references.
Identifiers: LCCN 2017048107 (print) | LCCN 2018006386 (ebook) | ISBN 9780879070083 (ebook) | ISBN 9780879072674 (hardback)
Subjects: LCSH: Jesus Christ—Biography—Early works to 1800. | BISAC: RELIGION / Christianity / Saints & Sainthood. | RELIGION / Monasticism. | RELIGION / Spirituality.
Classification: LCC BT300.L83 (ebook) | LCC BT300.L83 M337 2018 (print) | DDC 232.9/01 [B]—dc23
LC record available at https://lccn.loc.gov/2017048107

Dedicated to the Memory of

ARCHBISHOP JOHN R. QUINN

1929–2017

Never have I known a truer friend, a more trustworthy brother, a more genuine father. In him there was no arrogance, no haughtiness, no putting on airs; but justice, humility, and prudence claimed the whole man for themselves.

Peter the Venerable, Letter 192

Contents

A cumulative index to the four volumes of Ludolph of Saxony's *The Life of Jesus Christ* will appear in the fourth volume, *The Life of Jesus Christ: Part Two; Volume 4, Chapters 58–59*, Cistercian Studies Series 284.

Abbreviations for Works Cited

Unless further identification is needed, *Sermo* or *Hom* refers to a sermon or homily by an author, followed by its number. When the citation is from a biblical commentary, *Com* is followed by the biblical reference, e.g., Com Matt 28:4. Bracketed references in this list refer to modern critical editions of the works.

Citations given in italics in the text are from sources Ludolph uses without attribution. Biblical texts that may come from a Latin Diatessaron are given in bold print. The bold letter **R 1**, etc., refers to section headings from L. M. Rigollot, *Vita Iesu Christi* (Paris: Palmé, 1865, 1870, 1878).

Allegoriae	Richard of Saint Victor (?), *Allegoriae in vetus et novum testamentum (Liber exceptionum).*
Amoris	*Stimulus amoris maior*; this is a fourteenth-century expansion of the *Stimulus amoris minor* written in the late thirteenth century by James of Milan; the material cited by Ludolph is not in the earlier version; in A. C. Peltier, *S. Bonaventurae, Opera Omnia*, vol. 12 (Paris: Vives, 1868).
Aquaeductu	Bernard, *Sermo in Nativitate Beatae Mariae,* "De aquaeductu" [SB 5]
Attr.	Attributed to
Brev in Ps	Ps-Jerome, *Breviarium in Psalmos*
Bruno	Bruno of Segni/Asti (biblical commentaries, homilies)

Burchard	Burchard of Mount Sion, *Descriptio terrae sanctae; Burchard of Mount Sion*, translated by Aubrey Stewart (London: Palestine Pilgrims' Text Society, 1896).
CA	Thomas Aquinas, *Catena aurea*
Caillau Aug	Caillau, *Augustini operum* (Paris, 1836).
Caillau Chrys	Caillau, *Chrysostomi opera omnia* (Paris: Mellier, 1842).
Chromatius	Chromatius of Aquileia, *Tractatus in evangelium S. Matthaei* [CL 9A]
CL	Corpus Christianorum Latinorum
CM	Corpus Christianorum, Continuatio Mediævalis
Cognitione	Ps-Bernard, *Meditationes piisimae de cognitione humanis conditione*
Compunctione	Chrysostom, *De compunctione cordis*
Conf	Augustine, *Confessiones* [CL 27]
Cons	Boethius, *De consolatione philosophiae* [CL 94]
Cratandri	*Tomus Operum Ioannis Chrysostomi* (Basel: Andrew Cratandri, 1523).
Creat	Ps-Isidore (seventh-cent. Irish), *De ordine creaturarum* (Monografías de la Universidad de Santiago de Compostela 10, 1972).
CS	Corpus Scriptorum Ecclesiasticorum Latinorum
CSP	Corpus Scriptorum Latinorum Paravianum
Cumm	Cummianus, *Commentarius in Evangelium secundam Marcam*
David	David of Augsburg, *De exterioris et interioris hominis compositione* (Quaracchi, 1899).
De civ Dei	Augustine, *De civitate Dei* [CL 47–48]
De cons	Augustine, *De consensu evangelistarum* [CS 43]

De doc	Augustine, *De doctrina Christiana* [CL 32]
De exc	Eadmer, *De excellentia Virginis Mariae*
De gen ad lit	Augustine, *De Genesi ad litteram*
De inst	Aelred, *De institutione inclusarum* [CM 1]
De iudicio	*De iudicio et compunctione; S. Ephraem Syri, Opera Omnia* (Venice: Gerardi, 1755).
De laud	Arnold of Bonneval, *De laudibus Beatae Virginis Mariae*
De moribus	Bernard, *De moribus et officio Episcoporum* (Ep 42) [SB 7]
De Trin	Augustine, *De Trinitate* [CL 50–50A]
De util trib	Peter of Blois, *De utilitate tribulationum*
De Vitry	Jacques de Vitry, *Historia Hierosolymitana: The History of Jerusalem*, translated by Aubrey Stewart (London: Palestine Pilgrims' Text Society, 1896).
Dial	Gregory the Great, *Dialogues*
Dialogus	Ps-Anselm, *Dialogus Beatae Mariae et Anselmi de passione Domini*
Drogo	Drogo of Ostia, *Sermo de sacramento dominicae passionis*
Durandus	William Durandus, *Rationale divinorum officiorum* [CM 140]
Elmer	Elmer of Canterbury, *De humanae conditionis*
Eluc	Honorius of Autun, *Elucidarium sive dialogus de Summa totius Christianae theologiae*
En Mark, Luke, John	Theophylact, *In quatuor Evangelia enarrationes*
En Ps	Augustine, *Enarrationes in Psalmos* [CL 38–40]

Ep	Epistle
Ep John	Augustine, *In Ioannis Epistulam ad Parthos tractatus*
Erasmus	Erasmus, *Origenis adamantii operum pars secunda* (Basel, 1545).
Ėtaix	*Opus imperfectum*, chapters not found in Migne: Raymond Étaix, *Revue bénédictine* 84 (1974).
Ety	Isidore, *Etymologiae*
Exp Acta	Theophylact, *Expositio in Acta Apostolorum*
Exp Luke	Ambrose, *Expositio Evangelii secundam Lucam* [CL 14]
Exp Or Dom	Jordan of Quedlinburg, *Expositio Orationis Dominice*, in Eric Leland Saak, *Catechesis in the Later Middle Ages I: The* Exposition of the Lord's Prayer *of Jordan of Quedlinburg, OESA* (d. 1380) (Leiden: Brill, 2014).
40 hom	Gregory the Great, *XL homiliarium in Evangelia* [CL 141]
Fratres	Ps-Augustine (early fourteenth cent.), *Ad fratres in eremo*
Fronton	Chrysostom, *Opera Omnia* (Paris: Fronton du Duc, 1687).
Gaufrid	Gaufrid of Clairvaux, *Declamationes de colloquio Simonis cum Iesu*
Gennadius	Gennadius of Marseille, *Liber de Ecclesiasticis Dogmatibus*
Gorran	Nicholas of Gorran, *Enarratio in Quatuor Evangelia et Epistolas B. Pauli* (Lyon: Annisonios, 1692).
Grimlaicus	Grimlaicus, *Regula solitariorum*
Guigo	Guigo de Ponte, *De contemplatione*
Habitat	Bernard, *In Psalmum 90, "Qui habitat," Sermones 17* [SB 4]

Haymo	Haymo of Auxerre, *Homiliarum sive concionum ad plebem in Evangelia de tempore et sanctis* (Migne wrongly attributes to Haymo of Halberstadt)
Henry	Henry of Friemar, *Explanatio passionis dominicae*; https://digital.library.villanova.edu/Item/vudl:234049.
Hiez	Gregory the Great, *Homiliae in Hiezechihelem prophetam* [CL 142]
Hist AA	Peter Comestor, *Historia libri Actuum Apostolorum*
Hist ev	Peter Comestor, *Historia evangelica*
Hist sch	Peter Comestor, *Historia scholastica*
Hom Acta	Chrysostom, *Homiliae in Acta Apostolorum*
Hom ev	Bede, *Homiliarium evangelii* [CL 122]
Homiliarius	Paul the Deacon, *Homiliarius doctorum*
Hom John	Chrysostom, *Homiliae in Ioannem*
Hom Matt	Chrysostom, *Homiliae in Mattheum*
Hugh	Hugh of Ripelin, *Compendium theologiae veritatis*; in A. C. Peltier, *S. Bonaventurae, Opera Omnia*, vol. 8 (Paris: Vives, 1866). The work is also attributed to Albert the Great and appears in vol. 34 of his collected works edited by Borgnet (Paris: Vives, 1895).
Int nom	Jerome, *Liber interpretationis Hebraicorum nominum* [CL 72]
Jordan	Jordan of Quedlinburg, *Opus Postillarum et sermones de tempore* (Strassburg: Hussner, 1483); sermons 189–254 are also known as *Meditationes de Passione Christi.*
Laon	Anselm of Laon (?), *Enarrationes in Evangelium Matthaei*
Laudibus	Bernard, *De laudibus virginis matris super verbi Evangelii: "Missus est angelus Gabriel"; homiliae quatuor* [SB 4]

Legenda	Jacobus de Voragine, *Legenda Aurea*
Lib de pas	Ps-Bernard, *Liber de passione Christi*
Lib specialis	Mechtild of Hackborn, *Liber specialis gratiae*
Lombard	Peter Lombard, *Liber sententiarum*
Lucilium	Seneca, *Ad Lucilium epistolae morales*
LV	Bonaventure, *Lignum Vitae*
Lyra	Nicholas of Lyra, *Postillae perpetuae in universam S. Scripturam; Biblia Sacra, cum Glossa Ordinaria, primum quidem a Strabo Fuldensi Monacho Benedictino Collecta, Tomus Quintus* (Antwerp: Keerbergium, 1517).
Mai	Mai, *Novae Patrum Bibliothecae* (Rome: Sacri Consilii, 1852).
Manipulus	Thomas of Ireland, *Manipulus florum*
Manuale	John of Fécamp, *Manuale*
Martin Braga	Martin of Braga, *Formula vitae honestae*
Massa	Michael de Massa, *Vita Christi* (Bayerische Staats Bibliothek: http://bildsuche.digitale-sammlungen.de/index.html?c=viewer&lv=1&bandnummer=bsb00082134&pimage=00082134&suchbegriff=&l=en).
Med	Anselm and others, *Meditationes*, in *S. Anselmi opera*, edited by Franciscus Salesius Schmitt, vol. 3 (Edinburgh: Nelson, 1946).
Med red	Anselm, *Meditatio redemptionis humanae*, in *S. Anselmi opera*, edited by Franciscus Salesius Schmitt, vol. 3 (Edinburgh: Nelson, 1946).
mor	moral: the Postilla of Nicholas of Lyra often presents moral interpretations in a separate category
Mor	Gregory the Great, *Moralium libri sive expositione in librum Iob* [CL 143–143b]

Moribus	Ps-Seneca, *De Moribus*
MVC	John de Caulibus, *Meditationes Vitae Christi* [CM 153]
Ogerius	Ogerius of Locedio, *Tractatus in Laudibus sanctae Dei genetricis*, in *De Mariaklachten*, edited by J.W. De Vries (Zwolle: Tjeenk Willink, 1964)
Opus Dan	Jordan of Quedlinburg, *Sermones de Sanctis* in *Opus sermonum patris Iordani Augustiniani* (Paris: Hichman, 1521).
Opus imperf	Ps-Chrysostom, *Opus imperfectum in Matthaeum*
Orat	Gregory Nazianzen, *Orationes*
Orthodoxa	John Damascene, *De fide orthodoxa*
Pelagius, Ad Dem	Pelagius? Prosper?, *Ad Demetriadem*
Peniteas	William of Montibus, *Peniteas cito*, in Joseph Goering, *William de Montibus (c. 1140–1213): The Schools and the Literature of Pastoral Care* (Toronto: PIMS, 1992).
Peraldus	William Peraldus, sermons. These were mistakenly attributed to William of Auvergne and are found in *Guilielmi Alverni, Opera omnia* (Paris: D. Thierry, 1674).
PG	J.-P. Migne, *Patrologia Graeca* (Paris, 1856).
PL	J.-P. Migne, *Patrologia Latina* (Paris, 1844).
Posteriorum	Richard of Saint Victor, *Posteriorum Excerptionum*
Prosper	Prosper of Aquitaine, *Sententiae ex Augustino delibatae*
Quaest 83	Augustine, *De diversis quaestionibus LXXXIII* [CL 44A]
Quaest Ev	Augustine, *Quaestionum Evangeliorum libri duo* [CL 44B]
Quatuor	Eadmer, *De quatuor virtutibus Beatae Virginis Mariae*

Quis dabit	Ps-Bernard (Ogerius?), *Meditacio de lamentacione beate virginis*; text in Thomas Bestul, *Texts of the Passion: Latin Devotional Literature and Medieval Society* (Philadelphia: University of Pennsylvania Press, 1996).
Radbertus	Paschasius Radbertus, *Ep 9 Ad Paulam et Eustochium, de Assumptione* [CM 56C]
Reg past	Gregory the Great, *Regulae Pastoralis*
Roland	*Chrysostomi opera* (Paris: Guillielmum Roland, 1546); (Venice: Pezzana, 1703).
SB	Sancti Bernardi Opera (Rome, 1957–1963).
SC	Bernard, *Sermones super Cantica Canticorum* [SB 1–2]
Sedulius	Sedulius, *Carmen paschale*
Selecta	Origen, *Selecta in Psalmos*
Sent	Isidore, *Sententiae*
Septem diei	Ps-Bede (thirteenth cent.), *De meditatione passionis per septem diei*
Sermone monte	Augustine, *De sermone Domini in monte* [CL 35]
SHS	*Speculum humanae salvationis* (Lutz and Perdrizet, *Speculum humanae salvationis*, Mulhouse, 1907–1909).
Spiritu	Ps-Augustine, *De spiritu et anima* (twelfth-cent. compilation of various authors)
St Cher	Hugh of Saint Cher, *Postillae in sacram scripturam, Tomus sextus*
Stim	Eckbert of Schönau, *Stimulis Amoris*
Suso	Henry Suso, *Horologium sapientiae*
Super unum	Peter Cantor, *Super unum ex quatuor*
Synonyma	Isidore of Seville, *Synonyma de lamentatione animae peccatricis*

Syrus	Publilius Syrus, *Sentences*
Tr John	Augustine, *In Evangelium Ioannis tractatus* [CL 36]
VC	Ludolph, *Vita Christi*
Vera et falsa	Ps-Augustine (eleventh cent.), *De vera et falsa poenitentia*
Voragine	Rudolphus Clutius, ed., Jacobus de Voragine, *Sermones Aurei in Omnes Totius Anni; Sermones de Tempore in omnes Dominicas* (Augsburg and Cracow: Bartl, 1760).
Vor Quad	Rudolphus Clutius, ed., Jacobus de Voragine, *Sermones Aurei in Omnes Quadragesimae Dominicas et Ferias* (Augsburg and Cracow: Bartl, 1760).
Werner	Werner of Saint Blase, *Liber Deflorationum*
Zachary	Zachary of Besançon, *In unum ex quatuor*

Introduction

Although Ludolph of Saxony, Carthusian, produced a very detailed *Life of Jesus Christ*, little is known of his own life. From his name it is inferred that his place of origin was the province of Saxony; he was born at the end of the thirteenth century. It is also believed that for many years he was a Dominican friar. Ludolph entered the Carthusian monastery near Strasbourg in 1340, where he clearly made a favorable impression on his fellow Carthusians, for he was elected prior of Coblenz in 1343, just three years after joining the Order. He resigned five years later, the reason being, according to the chapter of 1348, to settle a qualm of conscience. What this was is not known, but it has been suggested that he may have considered his election faulty because a prohibition announced at the chapter of 1319 barred anyone who transferred to the Carthusians from a mendicant order from holding office.[1] Following his resignation Ludolph lived at the charterhouse of Mainz and subsequently returned to Strasbourg, the house of his profession, where he died on April 13, 1378.

Ludolph has been credited with several works (even, incorrectly, the *Imitation of Christ*), but the two major writings that are surely from his pen are the *Expositio in Psalterium Davidis* and his most influential book, the *Vita Iesu Christi*. This magisterial work presents the entire sweep of the life of Christ, from the eternal generation of the Son through his incarnation, ministry, death, and resurrection, concluding with the Last Judgment. Drawing extensively on the fathers, later spiritual writers, and contemporary sources, Ludolph

[1] Sr. Mary Immaculate Bodenstedt, S.N.D., *The Vita Christi of Ludolph the Carthusian* (Washington: Catholic University of America Press, 1944), 3. Bodenstedt's doctoral dissertation, the most comprehensive examination of the *Vita Christi* available in English, has been reprinted in Ludolphus the Carthusian, *Vita Christi: Introductory Volume* (Salzburg: *Analecta Cartusiana* 241, 2007).

created an encyclopedic resource that proved to be an immensely popular spiritual text for several centuries. In the opinion of the noted Benedictine medieval scholar, André Wilmart, "It is one of the most beautiful and erudite works to have come down to us from the Middle Ages. . . . Almost all of the patristic literature can be found incorporated in it."[2]

The many surviving manuscripts of the *Vita Christi* testify to its popularity. The first printed edition was produced in 1472, and since then more than sixty editions have appeared. Like other works in the same genre, Ludolph's book was translated, and its popularity increased. Indeed, one scholar has noted that because of this translating impulse, "the fifteenth and sixteenth centuries were the great age of thirteenth and fourteenth century spirituality."[3] A Castilian translation of Ludolph's work read by Ignatius Loyola during his convalescence was instrumental in his conversion, and Teresa of Avila directed that every convent of her reform include "the Carthusian" in its library. The *Vita Christi* was read by Mary Magdalen de' Pazzi and Robert Bellarmine and was recommended to Jane Frances de Chantal by Francis de Sales.[4] Its influence was not limited to Catholic circles: Ludolph's book was a favorite among the followers of the *Devotio Moderna*, and it is probable that Luther and other reformers had been nourished by it. It is known that the great Protestant theologian Martin Bucer possessed a 1516 edition of the *Vita Christi*.[5] Finally, Ludolph's influence extended into the future through the

[2] "C'est l'un des plus beaux et savants ouvrages qui nous viennent du moyen age. . . . Presque toute la littérature patristique s'y trouve incorporée" (*Revue bénédictine* 47 [1935]: 268).

[3] Michael Sargent, "Bonaventure English: A Survey of the Middle English Prose Translations of Early Franciscan Literature," in James Hogg, *Spätmittelalterliche Geistliche Literatur in der Nationalsprach*, vol. 2, ed. James Hogg, *Analecta Cartusiana* 106 (Salzburg: Institut für Anglistik und Amerikanistik, 1984), 176.

[4] Ignatius of Loyola, "Reminiscences" 5, in *Saint Ignatius of Loyola: Personal Writings*, trans. Joseph A. Munitiz and Philip Endean (London: Penguin Books, 1996), 14; Teresa of Avila, "The Constitutions" 8, in *The Collected Works of St. Teresa of Avila*, trans. Kieran Kavanaugh and Otilio Rodriguez (Washington: ICS Publications, 1985), 3:321. For information about the influence of the *Vita Christi* on many saints and authors over the centuries, see Bodenstedt, 53–92.

[5] I. Backus, P. Fraenkel, P. Lardet, *Martin Bucer Apocryphe et Authentique: Ètudes de Bibliographie et D'Exégèse* (Geneva: *Cahiers de la Revue de Théologie et de Philosophie*, 1983), 46.

writings of later authors, such as Henry Herp and Francisco de Osuna, who drew on his *Vita Christi*. The Anglican writers Lancelot Andrewes and William Austin did the same. Sometimes sections of Ludolph's work were published under other names or anonymously. There is an element of poetic justice in this, for, as we shall see, Ludolph himself often used the writings of other authors without attribution.

The Genre of a "Life of Christ"

Why did "lives of Christ," culminating in Ludolph's book (which incorporated many previous works of the same type), appear in the fourteenth century? We might say that for the first thousand years of the Christian faith, "the life of Christ" was the gospels. This is patently true, but several important points must be made. First, the gospels were not read as a biography of Jesus as we understand the term. Before the modern era, history and biography were related more to rhetoric than to science: the intent was not so much to describe events and analyze their causes and consequences but to inspire virtue. This does not mean that authors were less conscientious or that readers were more credulous than people today, but it does mean that they had a different understanding of the value of history. Second, for Christians in the first millennium, the life of Christ was not only recorded in the gospels; it was found in the whole Bible. Every page, indeed every detail on every page, was understood to be about Jesus Christ; all of the events recorded in the Old Testament were considered part of his life story. Third, his "life" projected forward as well as backward: the biography of Jesus continued in his Body, the church, and in the lives of individual members of his Body, and it also offered hints about the world to come. These presuppositions are the basis of a spiritual reading of Scripture and foundational for what has been called the "four senses" of biblical interpretation (literal, allegorical, moral, eschatological).[6] In this understanding,

[6] The classic study on this topic is the four-volume work by Henri de Lubac, *Exégèse médiévale: Les quatre sens de l'écriture* (Paris: Editions Montaigne, 1959). Three of the four volumes have been translated into English as *Medieval Exegesis: The Four Senses of Scripture*, vols. 1–3 (Grand Rapids, MI: Eerdmans, 1998, 2000, 2009).

creation, salvation history, the church, and the life of every single human person are all part of "the life of Christ."

The primary place where this reading of the life of Christ went on was the liturgy. The great masters were the fathers of the church, who delivered their insights in sermons. For the most part they were not composing scholarly commentaries for the learned; they were teaching their people basic doctrines revealed by Christ's life, death, and resurrection and offering them moral instruction drawn from Jesus' example. Liturgical feasts and customs, the sacred images in churches, the association of Old Testament texts with the various events in the life of Christ—in all of these Christians experienced the life of Christ as a present reality. Public reflection on his life was complemented by a personal appropriation through meditation. The pattern of this reflection is described very simply by an early Carthusian writer: "Seek in reading and you will find in meditating; knock in mental prayer and it will opened to you by contemplation."[7] This mental prayer or meditation was a matter of ruminating, chewing over the word of God.

Beginning in the eleventh century there was a growing emphasis on the humanity of Christ, and especially on his sufferings, which blossomed with particular intensity two hundred years later in the life of Saint Francis. The Franciscans and other mendicants were great proponents of this spirituality, but they were the inheritors of a tradition that emerged first in the monastic context of meditation on the Scriptures. The prayers of Saint Anselm, for example, "introduced a new note of personal passion, of elaboration and emotional extravagance which anticipated some of the chief features of later medieval piety."[8] Every detail of Christ's behavior was seen as exemplifying various virtues and providing patterns for Christians to follow. Peter Damian wrote, "Clearly the life our Savior lived in the flesh, no less than the Gospel he preached, is proposed as the way of life we must embrace."[9] The great Cistercian figures of the twelfth century, such as Aelred of Rievaulx, William of Saint-Thierry, and Bernard of Clairvaux, continued to develop the practice of meditat-

[7] Guigo II, *Scala Paradisi*; PL 40:998.

[8] R[ichard] W[illiam] Southern, *Saint Anselm and his Biographer*, Birkbeck Lectures, 1959 (Cambridge: Cambridge University Press, 1963), 47.

[9] Letter 87, To Oldericus of Fermo 4.9; PL 144:314D.

ing on the humanity of Christ and encouraged the use of imagination in pondering the gospel scenes, inviting their listeners and readers to picture themselves as actually present at the event being considered. According to Giles Constable, "This 'mysticism of the historical event,' as it has been called, combined an ardent concentration on the human life of Christ with an effort to personalize and interiorize His experiences on earth, which occasionally came close to an assimilation or even an identification with Christ."[10]

Both a flowering and a radical shift in this spiritual current took place in the thirteenth century with the growth of the mendicant orders, especially the followers of Saint Francis. By his intense poverty, humility, and sufferings, the *Poverello* became a living icon of Christ. The mendicant way of life opened a new chapter in the history of meditation on Christ's life: no longer was the matrix the monastic community; it was the town square and the daily lives of ordinary Christians. Bonaventure translated the vision of Francis into words, and in his *Lignum Vitae* and *Vitis Mystica* he penned devotional reflections on events in Christ's life. Toward the end of the thirteenth century the Franciscan James of Milan wrote a book called the *Stimulus Amoris* containing several meditations on the passion, a work that circulated under Bonaventure's name.[11]

Michelle Karnes, in *Imagination, Meditation, and Cognition in the Middle Ages*, has suggested that an important shift occurred in the nature of meditations on the life of Christ because Bonaventure's spiritual writings, and those of his immediate followers, were based on a sophisticated theory of cognition that Bonaventure had developed.[12] He combined the thought of Aristotle, who taught that all

[10] Giles Constable, "The Ideal of the Imitation of Christ," in *Three Studies in Medieval Religious and Social Thought* (Cambridge: Cambridge University Press, 1995), 203.

[11] Bonaventure's *Lignum vitae* did much to popularize this affective form of meditation, but Marsha Dutton has demonstrated that the great Franciscan was inspired by a work of Aelred, *De institutione inclusarum*; thus the roots of this approach pre-date Bonaventure by nearly a century. Marsha L. Dutton, "The Cistercian Source: Aelred, Bonaventure, Ignatius," in *Goad and Nail: Studies in Medieval Cistercian History, X*, edited by E. Rozanne Elder (Kalamazoo, MI: Cistercian Publications, 1985), 151–78.

[12] Michelle Karnes, *Imagination, Meditation, and Cognition in the Middle Ages* (Chicago: University of Chicago Press, 2011).

knowledge is derived from the senses and that "species" (cognitive images) link sensory and intellectual cognition, and of Augustine's Neo-Platonic understanding that the Father contains the forms of all things, the Son is the expression of those forms, and the Holy Spirit is the link between them. For Bonaventure, this meant that (1) Christ is involved in every act of cognition, for it is by the divine light of the perfect "species" of the Father that the human mind is able to perceive the reality beneath the appearances of things, and (2) just as the mind can move from the material appearance of something to an intellectual apprehension of it, so in Christ incarnate we can move from the material creation of his body to the spiritual reality of his divinity. Therefore, human cognition is a journey from this world to God through Christ, and meditation is a journey from Christ's humanity to his divinity.

This affected the shape of meditations on the life of Christ, including Ludolph's, in several ways. Where the earlier meditations of the Anselmian type were marked by a sense of distance from the events being considered and expressed an ardent longing to be there, texts by Aelred and Bonaventure emphasized that by meditation we really *are* there, or, better, that Christ and the events of his life become present to us here and now by the power of imagination. These meditations reflect a greater intimacy than heretofore: we can truly enter into communion with Christ by meditating devoutly on his life. And this is important not only because, as Christians had always done, we should enter into the gospel stories and draw inspiration from them; rather, by our entering into communion with Christ, and especially by sharing in his passion, he can bring us through the cross to the resurrection and union with his divinity. (This may be why Ludolph includes a lengthy chapter on the assumption of the Blessed Virgin Mary: she was the human being who most deeply shared in her Son's passion, and by union with her Son she is carried up into glory. Thus her assumption encourages the reader of the *Vita Christi* to see how union with Christ in his humanity leads to his divinity.)

In order to foster the sense of intimacy with the Lord, meditations of this kind from Bonaventure on were lively, imaginative, and detailed, and they took liberties with the gospel text—adding figures that were not present and even describing scenes not found in the Scriptures. The purpose was not to entertain the reader; these meditations were not written scripts of passion plays (although in fact there was a symbiotic relationship between such texts and those dramas). They drew the reader into a relationship with Christ in order to assist in the journey from this visible world to heaven, rewarding the reader with intimacy with Jesus now and glory with him later.

This sacramental understanding of the visible world explains the wealth of detail found in Ludolph's *Vita Christi*. Not only the appearance, words, and actions of Christ speak of his divinity; the ceremonies of the church, the elements of this world, its seasons, plants and animals, places, names—everything in the visible world speaks of Christ. Ludolph's work offers a course in the training of our senses and imagination to enable everything to remind us of Christ, so that in time our meditation on him embraces all things.

There is one final, very important characteristic about coming into communion with Christ through meditation: it can be done by anyone, by ordinary Christians as well as monastics. This may be why several major lives of Christ appeared in the fourteenth century. Three were written by Augustinians: a *Vita Christi* by Michael de Massa, Jordan of Quedlinburg's *Meditationes de Passione Christi*, and the *De Gestis Domini Salvatoris* by Simon Fidati da Cascia. The Franciscan strain was represented by the *Meditationes Vitae Christi*, written by John de Caulibus but attributed to Bonaventure. And Ludolph wrote his *Vita Christi*. It is interesting to note that, with the exception of Ludolph, all of these authors were mendicant friars—and Ludolph had been a Dominican for many years before joining the Carthusians, so he too was shaped by that milieu. This meant that they were composed by men whose vocation was preaching, and the intended audience was not just cloistered monastics but also people living in the world. Ludolph had joined an eremitical community reputed to be the most austere of religious orders and the one most remote from everyday life, but in his *Vita Christi* he presents meditations on Christ's life that are intended not only for hermits, monks, and nuns but also for friars, secular clergy, rulers, and ordinary laypeople.

Along with this appeal to diverse audiences, what made Ludolph's book an immediate best seller was its comprehensiveness. I have briefly indicated several major monuments of Christian spirituality in the centuries preceding Ludolph's life: the biblical texts themselves, patristic homilies, liturgical practices, the works by Benedictine and Cistercian authors, and the writings of mendicant friars. All of these were incorporated by Ludolph into his magisterial life of Christ, which begins with the eternal generation of the Son of God and ends with the Last Judgment. The *Vita Christi* is a very long book, to be sure, but it is a kind of spiritual *Summa*, bringing together between two covers a wealth of prayerful reflection on the life of Christ.

The Structure of the *Vita Iesu Christi*

Ludolph's meditations on the life of Christ are arranged in two parts, containing ninety-two and eighty-eight chapters, respectively, with a prologue and brief conclusion. Part 2 begins with Peter's confession of faith (the event that many modern biblical scholars hold to be the turning point in Mark's gospel). It is likely that Ludolph chose to divide his work here because it was on this occasion that Jesus first spoke explicitly about his approaching passion, the central theme in the second half of the *Vita Christi*. The author blends the events found in the four gospels into a single narrative, generally following the chronology of the Synoptic Gospels. He occasionally adverts to differences between the gospel accounts, sometimes providing a symbolic meaning to explain the discrepancies. Ludolph generally avoids using material from the apocryphal gospels; when he does, or when he relates a legend, he often includes the caveat "It is said."

Before beginning the life of Christ proper, Ludolph offers a brief but important reflection on the first few verses in John's gospel, followed by a description of the fall of Lucifer and of Adam and Eve. The life of Jesus is a moving human drama, but for Ludolph the protagonist of the story is the Son of God incarnate, and the purpose of his coming was to restore a ruined creation and open the way to eternal life.

In a doctoral dissertation devoted to the *Vita Jesu Christi*, Charles Abbott Conway, Jr., has suggested that Ludolph offers a dynamic description of salvation history in five phases.[13] The drama opens in

[13] Charles Abbot Conway, Jr., *The "Vita Christi" of Ludolph of Saxony and Late Medieval Devotion Centred on the Incarnation: A Descriptive Analysis* (Salzburg: Analecta Cartusiana 34, 1976).

heaven with the eternal generation of the Son of God. This starting place is important, not only because it underscores the divine identity of Jesus Christ, but also because it establishes the connection between God the Son and creation even before his incarnation. The relationship between the Father and the Son is a mystery beyond human understanding, which is why, according to Ludolph, the fourth evangelist writes, *In the beginning was the Word*, rather than "In the beginning was the Son." The word *Son* concerns the relationship of the second Person of the Trinity to the Father, but *Word* concerns his relationship not only to the Father but also to creation. The universe begins as an idea in the Father's mind, but he expresses that idea through his Word. This fact affirms that creation in itself is good and, when rightly viewed, brings us into communion with its Maker.

The crucial words are "when rightly viewed." The second act of the drama, related briefly in chapter 2 of the *Vita Christi*, concerns the fall of the angels and of the first human beings. Because creatures have sought to usurp the place of their Creator, the world becomes a wilderness instead of a garden. Rivalries, pride, greed all serve to tear asunder the fabric of creation; Ludolph suggests that the elements themselves have been affected by this revolt. There is a need to restore harmony, and the Son of God becomes Man to bring this about.

The third act opens with the incarnation of the Son. It is precisely in the material world that redemption will be won, making the events in Jesus' life so important. Ludolph describes the world as variable, storm-tossed, and chaotic; it lacks meaning in itself and of itself can only lead to further ruin. But now that God the Son has come into this wilderness, a voluntary exile from heavenly glory, the world can become the way back to God. The light of God had not been extinguished in the world after the Fall, but it had become very faint and ambiguous. Christ came to endure freely the poverty, humiliation, and suffering of a fallen world and to bring light into that world. This divine light shines in the words and deeds of Jesus; occasionally Ludolph reminds his reader that what he said, did, or endured was the work of God the Son. But the light of the incarnation transcends history: it shines backward from the life of Jesus so that words and events in the Old Testament can rightly be seen as foreshadowing it, and it reaches forward into the present, so that the believer today encounters the incarnate Christ in the liturgy, in meditation, and in daily life and is reminded of him even by the material creation. This is why Ludolph continually associates gospel stories with events and figures in the Old Testament, makes allusions to liturgical practices, and applies the words and actions of Jesus to contemporary situations.

The fourth act includes the entire life of Jesus, but above all his passion and death. The Son of God voluntarily embraced poverty, fasting, obedience, and humiliation to heal a broken world. The final indignity, the signature key to meaninglessness, was his death. By freely accepting it in obedience to the Father's will, Jesus overcame death, and by his resurrection and ascension he brought the human nature he had assumed back to its true home, heaven. His exile became a pilgrimage.

The final act involves audience participation. Readers are invited to unite themselves to Christ in his obedience, humility, and charity and so to pass with him through the shame of the cross to divine life. Or they can choose to cast their lot with a world devoid of God's light, which can only lead to meaninglessness and despair. Ludolph, after all, lived in what Barbara Tuchman has called the "calamitous" fourteenth century: the era of the Hundred Years' War, the Black Death, and the Avignon Papacy.[14] She suggests that it serves as "a distant mirror" for people today, but the time of tremendous social upheaval in which Ludolph lived created but a distant echo in his writing. War, plague, and famine had a deleterious effect on religious life, intensified the love of luxury among the wealthy, and created a climate that fueled apocalyptic movements, but these were simply more intense expressions of the perennial human failings of pride, avarice, dissension, and lust.

Ludolph's vivid descriptions in the *Vita Christi* are meant to prompt vivid imitation: when meditating on the events of Christ's life, and especially on his passion, the reader is urged not simply to admire what Christ did, but to imitate him. In the words of Eric Saak, "Ludolph's work is neither one of personal, mystical vision, nor strictly one directed toward monastic piety; rather it is intended to

[14] Barbara Tuchman, *A Distant Mirror: The Calamitous Fourteenth Century* (New York: Alfred A. Knopf, 1978).

teach the believer how to live devoutly."[15] There is thus a homiletic quality to Ludolph's presentation of this divine/human drama.[16] His style is foreign to readers today, but Conway's description of it is illuminating:

> The nearest formal analogy is perhaps that of a musical work in which a theme is stated, and some of its permutations and combinations are explored, then the whole movement goes into a development of primary and secondary themes alike, allowing all the melodic, harmonic, rhythmic and tonal implications of the themes to be drawn out, then moving to a recapitulation of the material originally stated, with perhaps a coda appended at the end.[17]

Each individual chapter of the work follows the traditional progression of *lectio–meditatio–oratio*, although not always in a systematic way. Ludolph begins with an examination of the literal meaning of the passage under consideration; this examination may include historical, legal, or geographical background material. There follows a meditation on the moral and/or mystical implications of the text, which involves the etymology of names, symbolic meanings of the characters, places, and objects connected with the event, associations with the liturgy, and moral applications to readers of various kinds. The chapter concludes with a prayer, evidently written by Ludolph himself, which briefly summarizes the virtues and graces for which the reader should ask in light of the subject of the chapter. These prayers are succinct and lovely and have been published independently of the *Vita Christi*.[18] Ludolph does not address the fourth stage,

[15] Eric Saak, *High Way to Heaven: The Augustinian Platform between Reform and Reformation, 1292–1524* (Leiden: Brill, 2002), 597.

[16] Bodenstedt notes that the *Vita Christi* was prescribed for public reading in the charterhouse of Basle (Bodenstedt, *The Vita Christi,* 53). His work was also cited frequently in collections of texts assembled to assist preachers.

[17] Conway, *The "Vita Christi,"* 25–26.

[18] See Bodenstedt, *The Vita Christi*, 126. She herself produced an English translation of these prayers: *Praying the Life of Christ. First English Translation of the Prayers Concluding the 181 Chapters of the* Vita Christi of Ludolphus the Carthusian: *The Quintessence of His Devout Meditations on the Life of Christ* (Salzburg: *Analecta Cartusiana* 15, 1973).

contemplatio; this is a gift of God, for which devout meditation on the life of Christ is a good preparation. At the very end of the book he urges the reader not to abandon the humanity of Christ even when attaining contemplation and holds up Saint Bernard as a model to emulate in this regard.

Ludolph follows a more definite pattern in his exposition of the passion: he presents a scene (*articulus*), draws lessons (*documenta*), invites application (*conformatio*), and concludes with a prayer (*oratio*). This pattern is found in Jordan of Quidlenburg's *Meditationes de Passione Christi*, although Jordan has the prayer first; much of Ludolph's material and many of the short prayers in these chapters are from Jordan.

Conway likens each chapter of the *Vita Christi* to a painting in a chapel depicting a particular scene from the life of Christ:

> Surrounding each panel are the comments and precepts of the learned doctors of the Church, who appear to look upon the event with the reader (the analogous form of presentation in a chapel might be roundels portraying the Prophets and Fathers observing the scene and writing upon it). All this is drawn together by the author of the work, whose material gives the reader keys to understanding the meaning and symbolism of events contained in the Gospel.[19]

Ludolph's Sources

A closer examination of each of these literary panels reveals the brushwork of many artists, both writers whom Ludolph cites and others whose work he incorporates without attribution.[20] He was not an original theologian, but he was very adept at weaving a wealth of material into one narrative.

[19] Conway, *The "Vita Christi,"* 147.

[20] Walter Baier has written a thorough analysis of the sources used by Ludolph in his chapters on the passion: *Untersuchungen zu den Passionsbetrachtungen in der Vita Christi des Ludolf vons Sachsen: Ein quellenkritischer Beitrag zu Leben und Werk Ludolfs und zur Geschichte der Passionstheologie* (Salzburg: *Analecta Cartusiana* 44, 1977).

Ludolph's primary source is the Bible: the *Vita* contains 840 citations from the Old Testament and 2,200 from the New Testament. In his meditation on the events of Christ's life, he gives pride of place to Matthew's gospel (122 pericopes), followed by Luke (85), Mark (51), and finally John (44). Ludolph offers a thorough spiritual commentary on the biblical events, drawn from a multitude of patristic and medieval authors.

Sources Cited by Ludolph

The Paris edition of the *Vita Christi* published in 1865 tabulates sixty-two ecclesiastical and sixteen secular authors cited by Ludolph; this list is given in the appendix to this introduction. While Ludolph provided the names of authors, he omitted the titles of their works. Jean Dadré published an edition (Venice, 1581) in which he identified a great number of the titles. This translation of the *Vita Christi* is the first to identify correctly nearly all of Ludolph's citations.

By far the authors cited most frequently are John Chrysostom and Augustine, each nearly a thousand times. Then follow Jerome, Bede, Gregory, Bernard, Anselm, and Theophylact. Very often works by other authors were attributed to these men in the Middle Ages; for example, Anselm's *Meditations* were in fact written by several different people. Wherever the true authorship is known I provide this in the margin, but I retain the name given by Ludolph in the text. It has not been possible to locate all of Ludolph's citations; in some cases, the sentences may have come from glosses, and either the original work has been lost or the earlier attribution was erroneous. It is evident that Ludolph relied heavily on the *Catena Aurea* of Saint Thomas: it was his source for many quotations, including well over one hundred from the biblical commentaries of Theophylact, the Greek archbishop of Ohrid (d. 1107).[21] In some instances, a quotation

[21] Latin translations of the Greek fathers began to circulate in the West in the mid-twelfth century. Thomas Aquinas was commissioned by Pope Urban IV to compile a collection of patristic texts on the four gospels, including the Greek fathers whenever possible. Thomas had the commentaries of Theophylact translated, but this translation was lost; the only surviving texts were in the *Catena Aurea*.

has been located in the *Catena Aurea* but could not be traced back to its original source.

The citations from John Chrysostom come from several different sources. There are many excerpts from his biblical commentaries, but the vagaries of the Latin translations of these books in the Middle Ages create a challenge for anyone trying to find the original source. Around the year 420 Anianus of Celada translated Chrysostom's *Commentary on Matthew* into Latin, but only the first twenty-five of ninety homilies survive.[22] In 1151 Burgundius of Pisa produced a new Latin translation for Pope Eugenius III, which was difficult to find even in older times (this was the book that Aquinas said he would prefer having to all the beauty of Paris). Ludolph also relies heavily on a work of an Arian author in the fifth century attributed to Chrysostom, the *Opus Imperfectum*, which consists of fifty-five homilies on the first twenty-five chapters of Matthew. On occasion Chrysostom's name is attached to citations from the works of Chromatius of Aquileia or Peter Chrysologus, presumably because of the similarity of the three names in abbreviated form. Finally, it should be noted that many sermons were wrongly attributed to Chrysostom in the Middle Ages.

Sources not Cited by Ludolph

Just as remarkable as the wealth of credited citations in the *Vita Christi* is the array of other texts for which Ludolph does not give a source. Medieval notions of intellectual property were very different from our own; Ludolph was not plagiarizing. Jean Mabillon called Saint Bernard "the last of the Fathers," and that seems to have been Ludolph's notion too.[23] Ludolph cites Bernard and his predecessors because they were thought to possess a higher degree of authority than later writers. Of course, Ludolph often cites later works unwittingly because they had come to be attributed to one or another

[22] It was later thought that only the first eight were genuine. These appear in Migne; the remaining chapters of Anianus's translation can be found in an edition of Chrysostom's works published in Basel in 1523.

[23] Mabillon's opinion is found in the Preface to his edition of Bernard's works (PL 182:26).

of the fathers. The matter is more complex in that authors Ludolph cites have often themselves used other authors without attribution, especially in the genre of lives of Christ. Because Ludolph's unattributed sources are less familiar to the general reader than his patristic authors, some brief background on them may be helpful.

Glosses and postillae

Glosses began in Ireland in the eighth century, when phrases from the writings of the fathers were written near texts from the psalms to assist meditation. Gradually the practice spread to other books of the Bible: passages from the fathers and ecclesiastical authorities were written in the margins or between the lines to clarify or explain matters and to provide spiritual interpretations from the fathers. The *Glossa ordinaria*, which became the fundamental text for the study of Scripture in the twelfth and thirteenth centuries, is credited to the circle of Anselm of Laon (d. 1117).[24] Its materials were drawn from patristic authors and Carolingian interpreters, especially Rabanus Maurus. Much was taken from existing glosses and *florilegia*, which were often used instead of the patristic texts. Ludolph occasionally mentions the gloss, but he also cites it without attribution. Some of his texts can be found in the *Manipulus florum*, a collection of quotations from the fathers and other authors arranged by subject, composed by Thomas of Ireland at the beginning of the fourteenth century.

The great contribution of the schoolmen to this biblical enterprise was the creation of *postillae*.[25] These contained material from the

[24] Migne offers two glosses in his collection, the first of which he wrongly attributes to Walafrid Strabo, ninth-century abbot and student of Rabanus Maurus. But then the gloss he attributes to Anselm was not Anselm's work, either. One principal difference is that the first gloss was marginal, the second interlinear; these two texts combined represent the *Glossa ordinaria*. For the complex history of glosses, see Beryl Smalley, *Gospels in the Schools, c. 1100–1250* (London: Bloomsbury, 1985).

[25] The etymology of the word is uncertain, but may have been an abbreviation for *post illa verba* ("after those words"). The *postilla* had the biblical text and patristic interpretations from fathers and glosses, but also exegetical commentaries from the 12th–13th centuries.

fathers and glosses but also offered theological and moral commentaries on the text drawn from the principal exegetes of the twelfth and early thirteenth centuries. Two noteworthy *postillae* were composed in the thirteenth century by the Dominican Hugh of Saint-Cher and the Franciscan Alexander of Hales. Ludolph's contemporary, the Franciscan Nicholas of Lyra, produced a *postilla* of the entire Bible that emphasized the literal sense of Scripture and incorporated material from his study of Hebrew. The *Glossa ordinaria* and the *Postilla* of Nicholas were often published together. Ludolph relies heavily on the works of Gorran and Lyra, who in turn often cite texts of the *Glossa ordinaria* not found in Migne.

Gospel Commentaries

Along with glosses, the twelfth century also witnessed the emergence of biblical commentaries; these proved very useful to Ludolph. The first was written by a Premonstratensian canon, Zachary of Besançon, around 1145. Entitled *In unum ex quatuor* ("Into one from four"), it uses as its biblical text a sixth-century Latin translation by Victor of Capua of an earlier Gospel Harmony, that is, a text that blended the four gospel narratives into one account. Victor was not certain whether the text he translated was the *Diatesseron* of Tatian, a disciple of Justin Martyr. Whatever its provenance, he brought the text into line with the Latin of the Vulgate and had a scribe produce a beautiful manuscript. Saint Boniface gave it to the Abbey of Fulda, where it served as a basis for several vernacular Gospel Harmonies. Ludolph includes over five hundred excerpts from *In unum ex quatuor* in his *Vita Christi*.

In unum ex quatuor was also one of the many sources used by Peter Comestor (d. 1178) for his *Historia Scholastica*, an account of history from the creation up to the end of the Acts of the Apostles.[26] Comestor was a student of Peter Lombard, and toward the end of his life he became attached to the Abbey of St. Victor. Hugh of St. Victor was a strong advocate of the literal meaning of a biblical text; this fact prompted Comestor to undertake a historical approach. Some of his

[26] *Comestor* ("devourer") was a nickname given him because of his voracious appetite for knowledge.

sources for the literal meaning were liturgy, art, relics, and geography. The *Historia Scholastica* appears over a hundred times in Ludolph's work.

A contemporary of Peter Comestor, Peter the Chanter or Peter Cantor, thought that Comestor's *Historia* contained too many details and put too much emphasis on recent traditions, so he produced his own version of the *Super unum ex quatuor*, which Ludolph uses a few times and cites. But Cantor also produced a guide for moral behavior aimed primarily at religious, called the *Verbum abbreviatum*; this was a source for some of Ludolph's patristic citations.

The Scholastic Doctors

Ludolph mentions Thomas Aquinas on a few occasions but otherwise makes no reference to him, Albert the Great, or Bonaventure, although he does draw on their writings. He takes many texts from their biblical commentaries, and the *Lignum vitae* of Bonaventure is cited over forty times. As was mentioned above, Ludolph relies heavily on the *Catena Aurea* of Aquinas. He also employs many of the teachings found in the *Summa*. A less-renowned Dominican theologian, Hugh of Ripelin (d. 1270), was the author of the *Compendium theologicae veritatis*, a theological handbook popular for centuries; its authorship was often credited to others. Ludolph has many excerpts from this book. Although Jacobus de Voragine (d. 1298), a Dominican contemporary of Aquinas and Bonaventure, was not a theologian, mention should be made of him. Ludolph used some material from his sermons, but more from his renowned collection of the lives of the saints, the *Golden Legend*.

Ludolph's Contemporaries

Most of the material Ludolph uses from his contemporaries is taken from various meditations on the life and passion of Jesus, but there are two other noteworthy sources. The first is the *Horologium sapientiae* of Henry Suso, from which Ludolph borrows several passages. The other is a work called the *Speculum humanae salvationis*, which associates individual events in the lives of Christ and the

Virgin Mary with three prefigurations in the Old Testament. The text is written in rhyming couplets. Ludolph frequently uses this text and maintains its rhyme scheme in his prose work. In fact, some scholars have suggested that Ludolph himself was its author.

Lives of Christ

The fourteenth century was the heyday of meditations on the life and passion of Christ, and several of them found their way into Ludolph's *Vita Christi*. Scholars disagree about when particular books were written and who was borrowing from whom, so the following chronology is tentative. However, given the way excerpts from all these various texts are woven through Ludolph's account, it seems likely that he was drawing on these other authors rather than vice versa.

The precursor in this genre was a book written in the mid-twelfth century by Aelred of Rievaulx for his sister, *De institutione inclusarum*.[27] Aelred's sister was an anchoress, and he wrote her a rule for the eremitical life. In the course of the book he invites her to enter into various scenes in the life of Christ. The following century saw the publication of Bonaventure's *Lignum vitae*, which urged the reader to picture a tree with twelve fruits; these are events in Christ's life, and as the reader meditates on each fruit he climbs the tree of Christ's cross. Three other thirteenth-century texts should be noted: the *Liber de Passionis* of the Cistercian Oglerius de Tridino, abbot of Locedio (d. 1214), a work later ascribed to Bernard; *De meditationis Christi Passionis per septem diei horas*, attributed to Bede; and the *Dialogus Beatae Mariae et Anselmi de Passione Domini*, in which Mary describes the events of her Son's passion to Anselm. The latter two works were probably written by Franciscans.

At the end of the thirteenth century or early in the fourteenth, an extremely influential life of Christ was written by a Franciscan, probably John de Caulibus: the *Meditationes vitae Christi*. It was composed for a Poor Clare, and the text invited the reader to place herself in

[27] This came to be known as "Meditation 15" by Anselm, and Ludolph credits Anselm when citing it.

various scenes in Christ's life. Its authorship came to be attributed to Bonaventure, and its translation into various languages made it one of the most popular spiritual books in the late Middle Ages. Ludolph relied heavily on this work, both in his own writing and in the passages he took from the *Vita Christi* of Michael de Massa.

Michael de Massa (d. 1337) wrote a life of Christ in which he drew on the *De meditationis Christi* of Ps-Bede, the *Liber de Passionis* of Ps-Bernard, the *Meditationes vitae Christi* of Ps-Bonaventure, and other authors as well.[28] (Ludolph's Prologue is taken largely from this work, so it was Michael, not Ludolph, who so deftly combined the works of several authors there.) Often the citations from these other sources in Ludolph come via Michael's book, but not always; it seems that Ludolph used both his book and the other works independently.

Also at some time in the fourteenth century two other books were written from which Ludolph freely and frequently drew. Both were by Augustinians: the *Explanatio Passionis Dominicae* of Henry of Friemar (d. 1340), and the *Meditationes de Passione Christi* of Jordan of Quedlinburg (d. 1380).[29] As will be seen in the text, especially in the chapters dealing with the passion, Ludolph incorporated much material from Michael de Massa, Henry of Friemar, and Jordan of Quedlinburg.

Other Sources

A few other works used by Ludolph should be mentioned. One is the *Stimulus amoris*, or *Stimulus dilectionis*, of the twelfth-century Cistercian Eckbert of Schönau, which came to be known as "Meditation 9" of Anselm; Ludolph cites this nearly thirty times.

[28] Copies of this work are rare, but it is available online from the Bavarian State Library.

[29] Again, these works are scarce. The book by Henry of Friemar is available online from Villanova University, under the title *Passio Domini litteraliter et moraliter: ab Henrico de Firmatia explanata*. Jordan's writings are being prepared by Eric Saak for publication by Brill in the series Studies in Medieval and Reformation Traditions.

About forty *exempla* are scattered throughout the *Vita Christi*. These stories were drawn from legends, ancient pagan literature, and popular lore and were used to illustrate moral teachings. They circulated within monastic communities and were employed by the mendicant orders in their preaching endeavors. These *exempla* were gathered into collections; Ludolph drew on the collections available to him, and his book in turn became a resource for later such anthologies.

Ludolph occasionally includes geographical information about the Holy Land to help his readers understand the literal meaning of the text and also to facilitate their visualization of events. At times he has recourse to older chronicles, such as the *De locis sanctis* of Adamnan (d. 704), which was based on an account this monk received of a visit to the Holy Land by Bishop Arculf around 680. An abridgement of this work under the same name was composed by Bede. But Ludolph also relies on more recent information, primarily taken from Burchard of Sion's *Descriptio terrae sanctae* written in 1285.

As the appendix indicates, Ludolph quoted a number of ancient non-Christian authors, but none so frequently as Seneca, whom he cites well over sixty times. Seneca's reputation reached its pinnacle in the Middle Ages, when he was considered almost a Christian. Anthologies of his writings also existed, one produced in the sixth century by Martin of Braga, the *Formula honestae vitae*. Another work, *de Moribus*, was ascribed wrongly to Martin, and its author is now known as Ps-Seneca. Ludolph also attributes to Seneca the sayings of Publilius Syrus, a slave in the first century BC who organized a collection of sayings popular in the Middle Ages.

This Translation

There is no critical edition of the *Vita Christi*. In the opinion of James Hogg, who has devoted his life to publishing works by and about Carthusians, one is not likely to be prepared because of the vast number of extant manuscripts and extracts.[30] The text used for

[30] *Ludolphus the Carthusian* Vita Christi *Introductory Volume* (Salzburg: *Analecta Cartusiana* 241, 2007), 177.

this translation is the four-volume edition published in 1870, but I consulted older printed versions as well, including one printed at Strasbourg in 1474, the second oldest printed edition, which may have been made from the autograph text.[31] I have translated every sentence of Ludolph's work, although on a few occasions what he wrote as an aside has been relegated to a footnote. Occasionally a word or phrase from the Latin has been included marginally to help the reader understand Ludolph's meaning; sometimes, too, this has been done when there is a play on words or rhyme. Ludolph's style is somewhat repetitive (intentionally so, given the book's intended purpose for meditation), and his sentences can be lengthy and convoluted. My intent has been to convey as accurately as possible in ordinary English what Ludolph wrote. The experience of the reader of this text should be similar to that enjoyed by its original intended audience—people from all walks of life, possessing varying degrees of theological background. While I hope that this translation will be of service to scholars, I have produced it with the general reader in mind. For this reason, I provide explanatory footnotes when these help a modern reader understand the allusions of a fourteenth-century author.

Biblical citations are based on the Challoner revision of the Douay-Rheims translation of the Latin Vulgate, the text customarily used by Ludolph.[32] Often his interpretations are dependent on the Vulgate, which differs somewhat from the original Greek and Hebrew, as well as from modern English translations made from these languages. Occasionally a text differs from the Vulgate, and this is noted. Some of Ludolph's sources used Latin translations of the *Diatessaron*, and Ludolph himself may have done so. Gilles Quispel has proposed that a number of Ludolph's biblical texts came from such a source, but there is scholarly disagreement on the matter; in this edition, the

[31] L. M. Rigollot, *Ludolphus de Saxonia: "Vita Iesu Christi"* (Paris: Victor Palmé, 1870). The Bancroft Library at the University of California, Berkeley, possesses a copy of the 1474 edition, which was printed at the charterhouse where Ludolph spent his last years.

[32] The numbering of the psalms is that of the Vulgate, which follows the Greek Septuagint.

verses identified by Quispel are given in bold print with a note that the words may come from a Latin *Diatessaron*.[33]

There is one area where contemporary sensibilities have been taken into account in this translation: the many references to *the Jews*. Both Ludolph and his sources repeatedly refer to Christ's enemies in this way, especially in the chapters on the passion. The fourteenth century did witness increased hostility to the Jewish people, but other reasons may have been at work as well. Erik Saak suggests that one motive for this practice in the stories of the passion is that they were written in part to provide a spur to ethical living. While "the Jews" are frequently presented in a bad light, the authors of such books (including Ludolph) want to connect their behavior with that of their contemporaries who were considered be bad Christians: heretics, Simoniacs, and hypocrites. The texts were a mirror held up, rhetorically equating the reader with the text's antagonists, the Jews.[34] We should be on guard against reading back into the distant past more recent patterns of anti-Semitism. However, while there are some passages in Ludolph's book where "the Jews" as a collective must be retained in order to be faithful to his text (as, for example, when he contrasts the Jews with Gentile believers), whenever he uses the word to mean Jesus' enemies among the Jewish people and their leaders, the English translation renders it accordingly.

There is a school of thought in some translation circles that the same word in the original language must always be translated by the same word in the receptor language. That principle has not been followed here, because a word can have several different meanings in Latin, often suggested by context, and different words can justifiably be translated by the same word in English. The aim has been to provide a readable version of a great spiritual work, not the equally laudable aim of creating a critical, scholarly translation of an ancient text. Mention should be made of one word where it was felt necessary to have two English words serve: *salus*, which can mean

[33] Gilles Quispel, *Tatian and the Gospel of Thomas: Studies in the History of the Western* Diatessaron (Leiden, the Netherlands: E. J. Brill, 1975).

[34] See Saak, *High Way*, 554–58.

"health," "prosperity," "safety," or "salvation." Ludolph uses this word and its variants when describing the healing miracles of Jesus, and it is clear from the context that he understands the word to refer both to the physical state of the individual and to salvation in a theological sense. In this translation, the word is translated by *health/salvation*.

Conclusion

The *Vita Christi* of Ludolph is one of the most comprehensive and influential versions of the late medieval genre of a meditated life of Christ. An English translation of this seminal work will be useful to students of medieval history and spirituality. Given the tremendous advances in biblical exegesis, theology, history, and anthropology since the fourteenth century, what does it offer the ordinary Christian seeking spiritual nourishment? José García de Castro Valdés, a Spanish Jesuit, has recently suggested three qualities of this spiritual classic that give it a perennial value: he calls it prophetic, sapiential, and mystagogical. The *Vita Christi* is *prophetic*: in the face of the multiple programs in contemporary culture that guarantee happiness and even salvation, the *Vita* proposes the poor, humble humanity of Christ as the center of our human existence. It is *sapiential*: even with the cultural and linguistic limitations inherent in a text from six centuries ago, its message transcends the historical, exegetical ambience of the past to speak directly to the heart, inviting the reader to experience an encounter with the living Christ. Finally, it is *mystagogical*: the *Life of Jesus Christ* is above all a *life*; it challenges us to plunge deeply into the mystery of Christ's life as our own. This mystery is nothing less than the revelation of the Father in Christ and the power of that revelation to transform us by the love of the Holy Spirit.[35]

[35] José García de Castro Valdés, "La *Vita Christi* de Ludolfo de Sajonia (+1377) e Ignacio de Loyola (+1556): A propósito de un gran libro," *Estudios Eclesiásticos* 86, no. 338 (Madrid: Comillas, 2011): 545.

Appendix

Authors Cited by Ludolph

This list is given in the Rigollot edition of the *Vita Christi* published in 1865 (Paris: Victor Palmé). Bodenstedt points out that it omits Plato, Ptolemy, Quintilian, and the authors of the *Evangelium Nazaraeorum*, the *Itinerarium Clementis*, the *Passio Anastasiae*, and the *Vita St. Columbani* (Bodenstedt, *Vita Christi*, 24 n. 1). It also does not include the many authors Ludolph quotes without attribution.

Ecclesiastical Authors

Alain of Lille
Alcuin
Ambrose
Anselm
Athanasius
Augustine
Basil
Bede
Bernard
Boethius
Bridget of Sweden
Cassian
Cassiodorus
Chrysostom
Cyprian
Cyril of Alexandria
Dionysius the Areopagite
Ephrem
Epiphanius
Eusebius of Caesarea
Fulgentius
Gennadius
Greek catenae
Gregory Nazianzen
Gregory of Nyssa
Gregory the Great
Haymo
Hegesippus
Hilary
Hildebert of Lavardin
Hugh of St. Victor
Ignatius of Antioch
Innocent III
Isaac Abbas
Isidore
Jerome
John Abbas
John Damascene
Leo the Great
Maximus of Turin
Nicholas III
Origen
Papias
Paulinus of Nola
Peter of Blois
Peter Cantor
Peter Chrysologus
Peter Comestor
Peter Damian
Peter Lombard

Prosper
Rabanus
Remigius
Richard of St. Victor
Rupert of Deutz
Sedulius
Severianus
Sulpicius of Jerusalem
Theophilus
Theophylact
Thomas Aquinas

Secular Authors

Anaxagoras
Aristotle
Cato
Cicero
Hippocrates
Horace
Josephus
Juvenal
Lucan
Ovid
Priscian
Sallust
Seneca
Valerius Maximus
Virgil

The Life of Jesus Christ

Part One

Prologue[1]

For other foundation no man can lay, the apostle says, *but that which is laid, which is Christ Jesus.** Augustine tells us that God is the plenitude of abundance and we are an abyss of need, and God's goodness is such that nothing can go well when we turn away from him.* Because this is so, you must not forsake this foundation if you want to escape the ruin caused by your failings and replenish your spirit; here you will find every kind of remedy for your needs.* ***R 1**

*1 Cor 3:11

*Solil 1.3 approx; PL 32:870; De natura boni 7; PL 42:554

**Massa; Guigo 2.1*

*First, anyone who wishes to lay down the burden of sins and attain peace of heart should heed God's gracious invitation addressed to sinners, "*Come to me all you that labor* with the toil of vices *and are burdened* with the baggage of your sins, *and I will refresh you* by healing and reviving you; *and you shall find rest to your souls** here and hereafter." Listen, patient, to your loving and devoted physician; come to him with ***R 2**

*Matt 11:28-29

[1] Ludolph's Prologue consists largely of excerpts from the *Vita Christi* of Michael de Massa, who in turn drew on the works of other writers, especially the *Meditationes Vitae Christi* of John de Caulibus (MVC) and the *De exterioris et interioris hominis* by David of Augsburg. The first several pages are from the *De contemplatione* by the Carthusian Guigo de Ponte (English translation: Dennis Martin, *Carthusian Spirituality* [New York: Paulist Press, 1997]). This combination of perspectives shapes Ludolph's characteristic approach to meditating on the life of Christ: from Guigo, meditation as a path to contemplation; from the MVC, the role of the senses and imagination; from David, the moral implications of Christ's behavior.

heartfelt contrition, sincere confession, and the firm intention to avoid evil and do good.*

*Massa; Guigo 2.1

Next, the sinner who already faithfully believes in Christ and has been reconciled to him through penance should strive to stay close to this physician by devoutly meditating on his most holy life as much as possible. But take care to do this with deliberation and not hurry through the reading of Christ's life; rather, take a small selection in turn each day. With such devout reflections you can celebrate a daily Sabbath for Christ—your thoughts, feelings, prayers, praises, and all of your daily work will lead to this, and you will find delight in it. Here you will find a respite from the din of distractions and worldly preoccupations, and you will enjoy sweet repose. Wherever you may be, return often here; this is a sure and holy refuge to protect you from the manifold varieties of human weakness that constantly attack God's servants.*

*Massa; Guigo 2.1

Frequently consider the major events in Christ's life: his incarnation, birth, circumcision, epiphany, presentation in the temple, passion, resurrection, ascension, sending of the Holy Spirit, and second coming as Judge. Do this with an eye to definite spiritual recollection, self-discipline, and consolation. Meditate on the life of Christ with a thirst to put into practice what you read there—it does little good to read unless you seek to imitate. Bernard asks, "What does it profit you to read repeatedly the Savior's good name in books, unless you are trying to be good in your conduct?"* And Chrysostom writes, "Whoever reads about God wants to find God. Let us hasten to live in a way worthy of God. Our good behavior will be like a lamp shining before the eyes of our heart, showing us the way of truth."*

*SC 14.8; PL 183:843B; SB 1:81

*Chrysostom, Ps 45:5; PG 59:453; Massa; Guigo 2.1

*R 3

*There are many reasons that this way of living should be a sinner's greatest aspiration. First, for the forgiveness of sins: when we judge ourselves, accuse ourselves in confession, and freely undertake penance, we are already delivered in no small measure from the squalor of sin; we walk attentively with God and are meditating in the aforesaid manner. *For our God is a consuming fire,** purifying those who cling to him of their sins. Second, for enlightenment: the one who comes to our aid is *a light shining in the darkness.** Those who are illumined by this light learn to set proper priorities, giving themselves first to Christ and then to godly concerns: their own, their neighbor's, and those of the world. Third, for the gift of tears: these are so necessary for a sinner in this miserable valley. Christ, who is *the fountain of gardens and the well of living waters,** customarily gives these tears to one who stays close to him.*

*Heb 12:29
*John 1:5
*Song 4:15
**Massa; Guigo 2.2*

Fourth, for renewal after the sinful lapses of daily life: the Lord always lifts up those who cling to him, as he says, *Make a brazen serpent, and set it up for a sign: whosoever being struck shall look on it, shall live.** Fifth, because of the sweet and longed-for taste this practice holds for those who follow it, as the psalmist says: *O taste, and see that the Lord is sweet.** Sixth, for the knowledge of the Father's majesty, which can be had only through Christ, as he himself teaches, *Neither does any one know the Father, but the Son, and he to whom it shall please the Son to reveal him.** Seventh, for the sure deliverance from this world's dangers that it offers: faithful sinners who daily welcome Christ into their hearts and make a bower for him from these sweet meditations will in turn be sought out and welcomed by Christ after death. What they longed for and grew accustomed to here below they will enjoy forever: life with Christ.*

*Num 21:8
*Ps 33:9
*Matt 11:27
**Massa; Guigo 2.2*

*This is a blessed, well-irrigated way of life; it purifies and renews sinners who cling to it, making them fellow citizens with the saints and members of the household of God. To live like this is sweet and lovely: *her conversation has no bitterness, nor her company any tediousness, but joy and gladness.** This food is so agree-

***R 4**
*Wis 8:16

able and delicious that once a loving heart has tasted it, all other practices will seem bland. It nourishes and refreshes, for, as Ambrose observes, those who receive Christ into their inner dwelling feed on the greatest delights and abundant pleasures.* It is the consolation of the solitary, for whom it is the best of companions, giving joy, comfort, and solace; for the sinner it is *a tower of strength against the face of the enemy*.* This way of life offers an easy and thorough way to contemplate the Creator—a duty from which no one may excuse oneself—because there is no faster way to reach the heights of God's majesty than by meditating on the life of our Redeemer. Everyone can follow this practice, the young beginner as well as those advanced in the spiritual life, and all find here a pleasant home in which to nest like a dove, and a hiding place for the offspring of their chaste love.*

*Exp Luke 5.16; PL 15:1640B; CL 14:140

*Ps 60:4

**Massa; Guigo 2.3*

This meditation makes the saints loving, solicitous, and disposed kindly to those who invoke them because of the joy we share with them. For example, could the Blessed Virgin, the mother of mercy, tenderness, and grace, possibly despise you or turn her eyes from you, sinner though you are, when she sees you take her son—whom she loves above all—into your arms and hold him close to your breast, and this not just once a day, but frequently? Could she possibly desert you when she sees you holding her son each and every day, attending to every detail of his life, and offering him every service of devotion and affection? Certainly not. So it is with the other saints: they look gladly on those with whom God is pleased to dwell; this way of life turns their clients into their companions, because it is their way of life, too. Clearly this is the life of Christ's mother, who served him and cared for him for so many years. This is the life of the apostles, his intimate companions, who persevered faithfully with him. This is the life of the heavenly citizens who enjoy Christ, marvel at his wondrous works, and reverently attend him for all eternity.*

**Massa; Guigo 2.4*

Here we find what is truly the best part: to sit at the feet of Christ and listen to his words. Rightly, it is not taken away from one who by grace possesses it, for this is the reward promised to the good and faithful servant: a life begun here on earth but fulfilled in eternity. No tongue can sufficiently praise this way of life, which is truly good, holy, and more eminent than any other: it marks the beginning of that profound contemplation we long for in the angelic, eternal life of our true homeland. What can compare with abiding continually with Christ, *on whom the angels desire to look*?* If you wish to reign with Christ forever, begin to reign with him now; do not abandon him, for to serve him is to reign.*

*1 Pet 1:12

**Massa; Guigo 2.3*

***R 5**

*Draw near to him who descends from the bosom of the Father into the Virgin's womb. Come forward with pure faith as another witness with the angel to his holy conception. Rejoice with the Virgin Mother, who is made fruitful for your sake. Be present at his birth and circumcision as a good provider with Joseph. Go with the magi to Bethlehem and adore the infant king. Help his parents carry Jesus when they present him in the temple. In company with the apostles, follow the loving shepherd about as he performs remarkable miracles. Be present as he dies, sharing in the sorrows of his Blessed Mother and John and consoling them; with devout curiosity touch and caress each wound of the Savior, who died for you. Search for the risen one with Mary Magdalen until you deserve to find him. Marvel at his glorious ascension into heaven as if you were standing among the apostles on Mount Olivet. Sit with the apostles in conclave, removed from all external distractions, so that you may deserve to be clothed from on high with the power of the Holy Spirit. If you have followed him for a little while on earth with a godly, humble, and loving heart, he in turn will raise you up to sit with him at the right hand of God the Father in heaven, just as he promised the faithful sinner who clings to him: *If any man minister* *to me, let him follow me: and where I am, there also shall my minister be.**

*John 12:26; *Massa; Guigo* 2.3

Faithful sinners who lovingly embrace this way of life should never doubt that Christ adopts them as daughters and sons. As it says in the book of Proverbs, *I love them that love me.** Bernard writes, "God cannot please the person who is not pleasing to him; for if God is pleasing to someone, that one cannot displease God."* Let faithful sinners prudently beware of relying on their own merits, no matter what their condition; rather, let them approach the Lord to beg for alms with empty hands, conscious that they are merely paupers, possessing nothing. But do not do this out of false humility, concealing merits; rather, know with utter certainty that *in your sight no man living shall be justified.** The fact is, we cannot render an account for even a single thought should God choose to summon us to Judgment. Those who throw themselves devoutly and with reverent fear upon the good God who calls sinners will not be considered presumptuous. It is just like beggars in this world: they are thought to be more wretched, not more admirable, in proportion to their need; they are not held to be presumptuous or proud—on the contrary, generous benefactors view them with greater pity.*

*Prov 8:17

*SC 24.8; PL 183:899A; SB 1:162

*Ps 142:2

**Massa; Guigo* 2.4–5

***R 6**

*Saint Bernard meditated continually, collecting a bundle of myrrh, that is, an accumulation of bitter recollections from the life and sufferings of Christ, which he pressed between his breasts, that is, in his affectionate heart. He advises us,

> If you are wise, you will imitate the prudent bride and never let this precious bundle of myrrh be removed from your bosom for even an hour. Preserve without fail the memory of those bitter trials he endured for you, and meditate upon them frequently. Then you too can say, *A bundle of myrrh is my beloved to me, he shall abide between my breasts.** As for me, friends, I have been conscious of my

*Song 1:12

lack of merits from the early days of my conversion, so I have undertaken to collect a bundle from my Lord's anxieties and sufferings and hold it close to my breast. First there were the privations in his infancy; then his labors in preaching, his weariness in journeying, his vigils in praying, his temptations in fasting, his tears in compassion, his disputes in teaching; finally peril from false friends, insults, spitting, blows, mockery, and scorn; the nails and other torments that fill the pages of the gospel like trees in a forest—and all for the salvation of our race.

Among the many twigs of this fragrant bouquet we should not overlook the myrrh he tasted upon the cross and that which was used to prepare him for burial. In the first he took upon himself the bitterness of our sins, and in the second he proclaimed the future incorruption of our bodies: "*I shall publish the memory of the abundance of your sweetness** as long as I live; *your justifications* and mercies *I will never forget: for by them you have given me life.*"*

*Ps 144:7

*Ps 118:93

I have said that wisdom is to be found in meditating on these things. They are for me the source of perfect righteousness, fullness of knowledge, riches of salvation, and abundance of merit. Sometimes I take from them a bitter but healing tonic; at other times, a sweet and consoling ointment. These events support me in times of trial and humble me in times of prosperity. They offer sure guidance to one who travels on the king's way among the joys and sorrows of this life, warding off impending evils on every side. They draw to me the favor of the world's Judge, whom, despite his awesome powers, they describe as meek and humble; though he is beyond the reach of princes and fearful to kings, they portray him as kind and easily pleased. As you know, such thoughts are often in my mouth, and God knows that they are always in my heart—and it is clear that they are certainly no strangers to my pen. They express for me the most sublime philosophy: *to know Jesus*

*1 Cor 2:2

> *Christ, and him crucified.** Dear friends, you must gather this prized bundle for yourselves.
>
> Recall that Simeon took him in his arms; that Mary bore him in her womb, cradled him on her lap, and like a bride placed him between her breasts. I imagine that Joseph dandled him on his knees and smiled often at him. All these people kept Christ before them, not behind them. They are your models: do as they did. If you carry him in such a way that your eyes can rest on him, it is certain that the sight of the Lord's sufferings will make your own much lighter.*

*SC 43.2–5; PL 183:994B; SB 2:42-44; *Massa*

Because most people give little thought to these matters, they tire quickly; if they reflected on them, they would not grow weary of doing good.

Benefits of Meditating on the Life of Christ

***R 7**

The blessed virgin Cecilia was accustomed to read the life of Christ.[2] For among the many words in praise of her virtues and renown, it is said that she always carried a copy of the gospels close to her heart. I understand this to mean that from among the events of the life of Christ preserved in the gospels, she had chosen the ones that most moved her, and she meditated on these day and night with a pure and undivided heart, giving them particular and fervent attention. When she finished reading she would start again, pondering his deeds with sweet and gentle enjoyment and gathering them into her heart for conscientious consideration.

**Massa; MVC Prol; CM 153:7*

[2] The following pages incorporate almost the entire Prologue of the *Meditationes Vitae Christi* by the Franciscan John de Caulibus, a work long attributed to Saint Bonaventure; Ludolph removed specifically Franciscan references. English translation: Isa Ragusa and Rosalie Green, *Meditations on the Life of Christ* (Princeton, NJ: Princeton University Press, 1961).

I encourage you to do the same. Of all the many kinds of spiritual exercise, I believe this is the one that is the most necessary, the most beneficial, and the one that can lead you to the greatest heights. The life of our Lord Jesus Christ was perfect and blameless—you will find no better manual to help you deal with empty and passing delights, tribulation, adversity, vices, or temptations of enemies. Through frequent and assiduous meditation on his life, the soul learns to know him, to love him, and to have confidence in him; in this way we can resolutely resist foolish and passing things, scorning them and treating them with contempt. It is clear that Saint Cecilia's heart was so filled with the life of Christ that there was no room for trivial concerns. As she processed in on her wedding day, surrounded by the many distracting ceremonies of such an occasion, her heart was steadfast. As the organ sounded, she sang to God alone, *Let my heart be undefiled, that I may not be confounded.**

*Ps 118:80; *Massa; MVC Prol; CM 153:7*

Meditation on Christ's life also fortifies us to face tribulation and adversity, so that we feel and fear them less. This is shown by the martyrs, as Bernard teaches:

> Therefore they hear the words, *My dove in the clefts of the rock,** because all their devotion is centered on the wounds of Christ, and they dwell there continually by constant meditation. From these wounds flows strength for martyrdom; from them comes immense trust in the Most High. Our gentle commander wants his loyal soldiers to lift up their faces and eyes to his wounds; these emblems will strengthen their resolve and teach them how to bear up more courageously. While gazing upon the Lord's wounds, they will not feel their own. The martyrs leap for joy and triumph even as their bodies are being mangled and the sword slashes their sides; they watch the holy blood stream from them not merely bravely, but joyfully.
>
> Where is the martyr's soul at that moment? In a safe place, surely; in the rock, surely; in Christ's

*Song 2:14

heart, surely; without doubt, his wounds are open to receive them. Had they been focusing only on their own heart, they would have felt the piercing steel and been unable to bear the pain; they would have given in and denied the faith. But now that they dwell in the rock, is it any wonder that they stand firm like a rock? Nor should we marvel that, exiled from the body, they do not feel bodily pains. Lack of feeling does not do this, love does; feelings are leashed, not lost; pain is not banished, but scorned. The martyr's strength comes from the rock.*

*SC 51.7–8; PL 183:1074A; SB 2:152–53; *Massa*

*R 8

Confessors of the faith and others also learn from Christ's life not only to put up with their labors, trials, and infirmities but to do so cheerfully. By virtue of their loving meditation on the life and sufferings of Christ, their souls do not seem to be in their own bodies but in Christ. A person is prepared for the temptations and vices of the enemy so that it is not possible to err about what to do or avoid: in Christ's life is found the perfection of all virtues. Nowhere can you find the instruction and examples of poverty, humility, charity, gentleness, obedience, patience, and the other virtues to match the virtues in the life of Christ.

***Massa*

Indeed, whatever virtues the church possesses she has received from Christ himself by means of the lessons of his deeds. Bernard asks,

> What do you know about virtues, if you are ignorant of Christ, who is the virtue of God? Where, I ask, is true prudence, except in Christ's teaching? Where is true justice, except in Christ's mercy? Where is true temperance, except in Christ's life? Where is true fortitude, except in Christ's passion? Only those are prudent who have learned his doctrine, only those are just who have had their sins pardoned by his mercy, only those are temperate

> who strive to imitate his life, only those are courageous who firmly hold onto his lessons of wisdom and patience in trying times. You will labor in vain to acquire virtues if you hope to find them apart from the Lord of virtues, whose doctrine is the seedbed of prudence, whose mercy is the work of justice, whose life is the mirror of temperance, and whose death is the emblem of fortitude.*

*SC 22.11; PL 184:883D; SB 1:137

Gregory the Great writes, "Why does the bride call her beloved not myrrh, but a *bundle* of myrrh, unless it be that the holy soul, while devoutly pondering the life of Christ from every angle, is gathering together virtues of all sorts from him? By imitating these she can counter her faults and make for herself a bundle that prevents the everlasting putrefaction of the flesh."*

*Robert of Tombelaine, Exp in Cant 1.33; PL 79:493A

And Augustine observes,

> Although God heals souls in all sorts of ways through many gracious circumstances ordained by his marvelous wisdom, he has chosen none better than the Wisdom of God himself, that is, the only-begotten Son, consubstantial and coeternal with the Father, who deigned to take on our human nature completely: *And the Word was made flesh and dwelt among us.**

*John 1:14

> People were avidly seeking riches and paying court to selfish desires, and he chose to be poor; they coveted dignities and honors, and he refused to be made a king; they thought earthly progeny a great blessing, and he had no wife and family; they arrogantly shrank from insults, and he bore every kind of outrage. They judged injustices to be intolerable, but what is a greater injustice than the condemnation of the just and innocent one? They viewed bodily punishment with horror; he was scourged and tortured in many ways. They were afraid to die; he was sentenced to death. They held crucifixion to be the most shameful way to perish;

> he was crucified. He made everything that we are afraid to be deprived of worthless by depriving himself of it, and he overcame everything we are afraid to face by embracing it. Sin is simply wanting what he rejected or avoiding what he accepted.*

*De vera religione 16:30–31; PL 34:134; CL 32:205–6; *Massa*

*R 9

*So Christ's whole earthly life, which he chose to assume for us, offers instruction for our behavior. Again, Augustine: "We judge that people these days are not worthy of imitation. If you agree, apply your mind to the God who became Man to teach men and women how to live. Recall the words of John, *he that says he abides in him ought himself also to walk even as he walked,** and you will not lack someone to follow, because Christ's every action was done for our instruction. We encounter the same lesson again in the Lord's passion: *For I have given you an example, that as I have done to you, so you do also.*"* Bede says, "Those who claim they abide in Christ should walk as he walked: they should not amass earthly goods or run after perishable wealth; they should flee honors and welcome contempt in this world for the sake of heavenly glory; they should help everyone gladly; they should injure no one and bear injuries from others patiently, even asking the Lord to pardon them; they should always seek the Creator's glory and never their own, and encourage their companions to pursue noble goals. To do things like this is what it means to follow in Christ's footsteps."*

*1 John 2:6

*John 13:15; Sermo 351.4.11; PL 39:1547

*Ps-Bede, Hom 2.22; PL 94:252A

In the knowledge of Christ we possess salvation and all wisdom, as Ambrose writes: "We have all things in Christ, and Christ is everything to us. If you seek someone to heal your wounds, he is a physician; if you are burning with fever, he is a fountain; if you are weighed down by iniquity, he is justice; if you need help, he is strength; if you fear death, he is life; if you shun the darkness, he is light; if you desire heaven, he is the way; if you hunger, he is food."* An old saying expresses this truth very well:

*De virginitate 16.99; PL 16:291C

> If you do not know Christ, other knowledge is vain;
> If you know Christ well, this alone is all gain.[3]

Would that the worldly-wise might understand, and so exchange their empty knowledge for this!

Whoever follows Christ cannot go astray or be deceived: when we meditate frequently on his life, our heart is refreshed, enkindled, and divinely illuminated to imitate and obtain his virtues. Indeed, many who are simple and illiterate have come to know great and profound mysteries of God because they have found here an anointing that gradually purifies and elevates the spirit, teaching all things.* *Massa; MVC Prol; CM 153:9

***R 10**

In whatever concerns virtue and right conduct, always hold up before you that bright mirror and model of all holiness, the life and behavior of our Lord Jesus Christ, the Son of God.[4] He was sent from heaven for our sake, to blaze the trail of virtue, to give us by his example the law of life and discipline, and to instruct us in his person. We had been created in his image, but we defiled that image by sin; however, we can restore that image by imitating his virtues. The more you strive to conform yourself to him by following his example, the closer you will be to him in heaven and the more of his glory you will share. *Massa; David 1.20

[3] *Hoc est nescire, sine Christo plurima scire; Si Christum bene scis, satis est; si cetera, nescis.* The origin of this couplet is unknown, but it was popular from the Middle Ages on, sometimes being used as an epitaph. The idea can be traced back to Augustine's *Confessions*: "Surely someone is unhappy who knows all these things and does not know you, and the one who knows you is happy even without knowing all these other things" (Conf 5.4.7).

[4] Michael de Massa interpolates several passages here from book 1, chap. 20 of the *De exterioris et interioris hominis* by David of Augsburg, another work often attributed to Bonaventure. English translation: Dominic Devas, trans., *Spiritual Life and Progress by David of Augsburg* (London: Burns Oates & Washbourne, 1937).

How to Meditate on the Life of Christ

As Christ's faithful follower, examine in turn each phase in Christ's life, study all his virtues, and seek to imitate them to the best of your ability. In your exterior and interior efforts, call to mind Christ's hardships and labors; if you are heavily burdened, run to him, the gentle father of the poor, and throw yourself upon him like a child in its mother's lap. Tell him everything, entrust everything to him, cast all your cares upon him—he will calm the storm and relieve you. Do not simply yearn for the Lord Jesus when you keep vigil, but as you lie on your bed lay your head on its resting place and imagine yourself reclining with John on Jesus' breast, and as you recline, nurse at that breast, and you will peacefully slumber and rest in him.*

*Massa

In everything you say and do keep your eyes fixed on Jesus as your model: walking and standing, sitting and getting up, eating and drinking, speaking and keeping silence, alone or with others. In this way, you will grow to love him more, familiarity with him will increase your faith and grace, and you will become more perfect in virtue. Let this be your wisdom and your purpose: always to be thinking somehow about Jesus, so that you are striving to imitate him more closely or love him more deeply. You will use your time well by meditating on these subjects and devoting yourself to good and holy reflections about the Lord Jesus. By continually thinking about him,* the mirror and model of all perfection, you will change your behavior to resemble his as you go about your business. The more frequently you engage in these meditations, the more familiar they will become to you: they will come into your mind more spontaneously and refresh your spirit more delightfully.*

*Massa; David 1.20

*Massa

***R 11**

You have seen to what an eminent position meditation on Christ's life leads. Now I would like to say something about the meditations themselves; I will not treat everything written in the gospels but will pick out the more important events. Nor should you think that everything Jesus said and did, and upon which we can meditate, was written down. In order to make a greater impression on you I will describe events as they occurred, or might have occurred, employing imaginative representations that strike the mind in different ways. For we can consider, understand, and express the meaning of Sacred Scripture in as many ways as we find helpful, provided they are not contrary to the truth of life, justice, or doctrine; in other words, so long as they are not contrary to faith and morals.

*Massa; MVC Prol; CM 153:10

However, if people assert something about God that seems unreliable to you because it is not in accord with natural reason, the moral law, faith, or Sacred Scripture, they sin by presumption. So you will find me saying the Lord Jesus, or other persons, said or did something; if this cannot be demonstrated from Scripture, you should consider what I say to be no more than a devout reflection. That is, take it as if I had said, "Imagine the good Lord Jesus as he says this, or does that," and so with the other characters. If you want to gain the greatest benefit from this exercise, put aside all other concerns and tasks, and with your whole heart strive with diligence, delight, and determination to be present when Jesus speaks and acts.*

*Massa; MVC Prol; CM 153:10

As you read the narrative, imagine you are seeing each event with your own eyes and hearing it with your own ears, because the sweetest thoughts are born of desire—and these are much more pleasing to the taste. Although these accounts describe events that occurred in the past, you must meditate upon them as if they were taking place now: there is no question but that you will savor them with greater pleasure. Read what once happened as if it were happening here and now. Put past deeds before your eyes as if they were present; you will experience them more deeply and more happily.

*R 12

This is why sometimes I describe the locations where events took place: when we read in the gospel that this or that action happened in a certain place, it is very helpful to know something about where it occurred. Christian churches all over the world never cease to unite themselves day and night with the Holy Land, where the good Jesus lived and which he illuminated by his preaching and consecrated by his precious blood. We find it pleasing to think about these places, but it would be even more delightful to visit them in person, there to ponder in our hearts how the Lord labored for our salvation in each different locale.

**Burchard 3 approx*

Who can describe how the many devout pilgrims in the Holy Land travel from site to site, and with burning zeal kiss the ground and embrace the places where they hear that Jesus sat or performed some deed? Beating their breasts, weeping, groaning, and sighing by turns, they express outwardly in their bodies the devotion they doubtless feel in their hearts, and their emotion moves many to tears, even among the Saracens. What shall I say about the patriarch Jacob, or about Joseph and his brothers, who, although they could not dwell there in their lifetime, chose to be buried there after they died? What more? Well might we weep over the indifference of the Christian people in our time, who in spite of so many examples are slow to deliver the land Jesus Christ hallowed with his blood from the hands of the enemy.*

**Burchard 3–4 approx*

*R 13

Take it as a general rule that wherever you do not find material for reflection in following a narrative, it suffices to picture in your mind's eye something the Lord Jesus said or did, and simply talk with him so that you might become more familiar with him. For it seems that greater sweetness and more devotion is to be had in this way; in fact, almost all the efficacy of these reflections consists in always and everywhere attentively contemplating the deeds and behavior of Jesus. Picture him among his disciples and in the company of sinners, when he converses and preaches, when he walks and when he sits, when he sleeps and when he keeps vigil, when he eats and when he serves others, when he heals the sick and when he performs other miracles. **Massa; MVC 18; CM 153:93*

Ponder in your heart his conduct and his actions: how humbly he carried himself among the people and how gently he dealt with his disciples; how merciful he was to the poor, making himself like them in everything so that they seemed to be his special kin; how he despised or spurned no one, even the lepers; how he did not curry favor with the wealthy; how free he was of worldly cares, giving no thought to his bodily needs; how patient he was in the face of insults, and how meekly he responded to them; how he did not defend himself with biting and bitter retorts but instead countered malicious words with a humble response.* **Massa; David 1.20*

Observe how suitably he acted in all things and how concerned he was for the salvation of souls, out of love for those for whom he was willing to die, how he made himself an example of all goodness, how compassionate he was with the afflicted, how he patiently bore with the imperfections of the sick and did not scorn sinners, how mercifully he welcomed the penitent, how obedient he was to his parents, and how promptly he served the needs of all. As he himself said, *I am in the midst of you, as he that serves.** See how he shunned all boasting and ostentation and avoided giving any cause for scandal, how sparingly he ate and drank, how modest he was in appearance, how dedicated to prayer, how attentive at vigils, how willing to endure labor and want, and how calm he remained in all circumstances. Similarly, as you hear or read about what Jesus said and did, meditate on the

*Luke 22:27

way in which he did everything, or might have done it in your estimation, because he who was the best and most perfect of us always acted in the best and most perfect way.*

*Massa; David 1.20

What Jesus Looked Like

Jesus had a pleasing appearance and a gentle way of speaking, and he was kind in all he did. Above all contemplate his face, if you can picture it; this is probably the most difficult thing to do but is also perhaps the most pleasing. Let his countenance instruct you, and have recourse to it in the narratives that follow. If individual meditations are unclear or subjects for consideration are lacking, hasten back to picturing him, and it will suffice for you as regards what is written here. *To help you see Christ's face and appearance, or indeed his complete figure, I would like to include something that you may find useful while meditating on the narrative of his deeds. It is said that the following document appears in annals of the Romans:

*R 14

> Jesus Christ is proclaimed to be a prophet of truth by the people. He is rather tall, with a venerable countenance that inspires either love or fear. His hair is the color of a ripe hazelnut; it hangs down straight to his ears, but below the ears it is wavy and curly, with a bluish sheen, and fans out on his shoulders. It is parted in two at the top of his head, as is customary for Nazarenes. His brow is smooth and very serene, his face without spot or wrinkle, with a slightly ruddy complexion. His nose and mouth are flawless. His beard is full and youthful, of the same color of his hair, not long, but forked at the chin. His aspect is grave and mature, his bluish-gray eyes changeable and bright. He is formidable when reprimanding, sweet and amiable

> when teaching, and cheerful without being undignified. He sometimes weeps but never laughs. His stature is well developed and straight, and his hands and arms are beautiful to behold. His conversation is serious, reasonable, sparing, and modest.[5]

According to the description just given, he truly deserves to be called by the psalmist *beautiful above the sons of men.** *Ps 44:3; *Massa*

The Excellence of the Gospels

***R 15**

According to Augustine, among the entire collection of divine records contained in Sacred Scripture, pride of place should be given to the gospels. For this reason, see to it that you always hold them in your hands and carry them in your heart—they will best illuminate for you the life and deeds of our Lord Jesus Christ, and all that pertains to your salvation. Chrysostom teaches that the gospels provide a summary of the perfections of our rational nature,* and Jerome claims that in them we find the complete fulfillment of the Law and a digest of precepts and examples for life.*

*De cons 1.1; PL 34:1042; CS 43:1

*Hom Matt 1.12; PG 57/58:20

*Primasius, Com Ep S Pauli, Pref; PL 68:413D

[5] This description was probably written in Italy in the thirteenth or fourteenth century but purports to be a contemporary description of Jesus' appearance. The Byzantine historian Nicephorus Callistus (d. 1335) has a similar description, so it is possible that the Latin version was a translation from the Greek. Although Ludolph simply refers to it as a document from the annals of the Romans, it later came to be described as a letter from Publius Lentulus, governor of Judea before Pontius Pilate. No such person existed, nor was there a "Governor of Judea." In 1440 Lorenzo Valla demonstrated that the letter was spurious.

Chrysostom writes,

> It would be wonderful if we had no need for the Scriptures because by the grace of the Spirit we were living rightly simply because the Spirit has written in our hearts the same doctrine recorded with ink on paper. But because we have lost the grace to act in this way, and also to help us anticipate future blessings, we should attend to what has been written down.*
>
> *Hom Matt 1.2; PG 57/58:15
>
> The Scriptures were not given to us simply for us to preserve them in books but so that we could engrave them on our hearts. For if the devil will not dare to approach a house in which the gospels are kept, much less will he, or any demons, or any sinful nature, ever touch or enter a soul that bears about with it the ideas contained in the gospels. Sanctify your soul, sanctify your body, by always having the words of the gospels on your lips and in your heart. Just as foul language soils us and opens the door to demons, so it is evident that spiritual reading sanctifies us and draws down divine grace upon us.*
>
> *Hom John 32.3; PG 59:187

Beloved, let us devote ourselves to the Scriptures—if nothing else, let us assiduously study the gospels and have them always at hand. Once you open these books, provided you keep on to the end, you will hold worldly preoccupations in contempt and reject them. If you are wealthy, you will account riches as nothing; if you are poor, your poverty will not ruin you, you will not be grasping or avaricious. In fact, you will be greedy for more poverty and despise riches. If you act in this way, you will banish all wickedness. Many other benefits are to be gained, too many to be enumerated here; those who follow my counsel will learn them by experience.

Elsewhere Chrysostom says,

> What equals the gospels in excellence? God himself descends to speak to us on earth and mortals are

raised up to heaven; human beings converse with angels and the other supernal powers. By virtue of the Gospel the ancient struggle is concluded: demons flee, death is destroyed, Paradise is opened, the curse is broken, sin is banished, error is repelled, truth returns, the word of mercy is sown everywhere and everywhere springs up, heavenly powers speak with us as friends, angels make frequent visitations to earth. In all of this, our assurance regarding the certainty of all future blessings is strengthened. For this reason, the gospels alone should truly be called *Good News*, because all other words are empty, promising good things only in this present life. That message first proclaimed by the fishermen can rightly be described as good tidings, since it was freely and generously given to us. We have received these tremendous promises not by the sweat of our brow, or hard work, or great torment, but simply because of God's great love for us.*

*Hom Matt 1.3; PG 57/58:15

And Augustine explains, "The word *Evangelium* in Latin means *good message* or *good proclamation*. The word can be used for any good news but is properly applied to the announcement of the Savior. Therefore, those who narrated the birth, words, and deeds of our Lord Jesus Christ are called *evangelists*."*

*Contra Faust 2.2; PL 42:210; CS 25:255

***R 16**

Before beginning to read the gospel stories themselves, you should note that each of the evangelists, guided by the Holy Spirit, sometimes anticipated events that came later, or recorded events omitted in earlier accounts, or repeated events related elsewhere to improve their narrative. Their intention was simply to record the Gospel story in the most beneficial way; as Augustine suggests, it is likely that each of the evangelists was careful to record the story in exactly the way God had inspired him.

*De cons 1.2; PL 34:1044; CS 43:2

Lest the devotion of the beginner be unduly troubled, in this presentation I have laid out the sequence of events in a way that fidelity to the course of events seemed to require. This does not mean that what follows is necessarily the actual, certain order in which these events took place, because such a definitive presentation is not possible. Be that as it may, in the gospels themselves you will learn the life story of the Word incarnate, what he commands and what he promises, in which you have the way, the truth, and the life. Study carefully Christ's example: from his life, you will see that you *can* live rightly; from his commandments, you will know *how* to live rightly; from his promises, you will *desire* to live rightly. With these three weapons you can repel our three enemies—impotence, ignorance, negligence. The one who chooses to remain ignorant will be ignored, the negligent person will be neglected, the one who feigns lack of ability will be cast out.*

**Zachary, Praef 3 approx; PL 186:39C–40A*

***R 17**

So rouse yourself, O soul devoted to Christ! Be alert, Christian! Examine diligently, ponder attentively, tease out scrupulously every detail in the life of Jesus Christ, and follow in your Lord's footsteps. For your sake he came down to earth from his heavenly throne; for your own sake, flee earthly things and strive for those of heaven. If you find that the world is sweet, know that Christ is sweeter; if you find that the world is harsh, know that he endured all its pains for you. Arise and walk! Do not drag your feet on the path, lest you forfeit your place in your homeland.

**LV Prol approx*

✠

Lord Jesus Christ, Son of the living God, grant that I, a poor and weak sinner, may keep the eyes of my heart fixed on your life and deeds, and imitate you to the best of my ability. By this means enable me to attain perfect maturity and become a holy temple of the Lord. Shed upon my heart the light of your grace: may it continually precede me and follow me so that, with you as my leader in all my ways, I may do all those things that are pleasing to you and avoid those that displease you. O Most High, I beseech you to direct all my thoughts, words, and deeds according to your law and your counsels; by doing your will in all things, may I deserve to be saved by you here and for all eternity. Amen.

CHAPTER 1

The Eternal, Divine Generation of Christ

(John 1:1-5)

*R 1

Thirsting to savor each precious drop of the good wine of the Gospel that the Lord Jesus has stored up till this time of grace, let us begin with his divine generation, which the fourth gospel treats. John introduced this theme and explained it fully so that the divinity of the Word would be manifest, especially in answer to certain heretics who claimed that Christ was only human and consequently denied that he was eternal; they taught that he came into being only when he was born and did not exist before Mary. John, therefore, begins with the eternal existence of the Word, who existed before his mother in his divine nature. This evangelist teaches five things about the divine Persons, which we will review in order.

**Lyra John 1:1*

The Eternal Generation of the Word

*R 2

**in principio*
‡John 1:1

*First he proclaims the eternal generation of the Son from the Father, saying, *In the beginning** *was the Word.*‡ That is, the Word was in God himself, who is understood to be the ground of everything else. The first principle is necessarily the Word properly so called, as being in him of whom he is the Word. It is as if he were saying, "The Son was in the Father, co-eternal with the Father. He did not begin to be in Mary, but *in the beginning*,* that is, in the Father, who is the origin without origin, and the Son is the origin *from* the origin." **in principio*

John calls the Son of God the *Word*; our Lord Jesus Christ is called the Son of God, and also the Word of God, and the Power and the Wisdom of God. These all say the same thing, because the realities are one and the same: Son, Word, Power, Wisdom.* **Bruno John 1:1; PL 165:451B*

But John says *Word*, not Son, because that name is more suitable in this context. Recall that a meaningful articulation is called a *word*; this is true broadly speaking, but *word* more fundamentally signifies the interior concept of the mind. A face is said to be healthy because it indicates health: well-being is the reality expressed by the face.[1] Just so, the word is what is signified by the sound of the voice. The underlying reality is the interior concept in the mind; the sounds are vocal expressions of impressions that are in the soul, and these concepts also are properly speaking called *words* even before they are pronounced.* The term *word* signifies the vocal sound that comes from the mouth but also the mental idea that is born from the mind, and when this concept emerges in the spoken word, it still remains present in the mind. The Son can be understood in this way: he proceeds from the Father by an eternal birth, but he remains with him and in him by the unity of their divine essence—just as a thought or a concept remains in the mind from which it is born. This is why John prefers *Word* to *Son* here. The Word is in God's self properly and perfectly. A spoken word proceeds from the one thinking, and a concept from the one conceiving it; and, because the Word and the Son are one and the same, it follows that as there is a generation of the Son from the Father, so there is procession of the Word from the Speaker. **Lyra John 1:1*

[1] Lyra in fact says that urine, not the face, indicates health.

However, the evangelist chooses to describe the Son here as the *Word* rather than *Son* because Son can be used only in relationship to a Father, whereas *Word* can be used not only in relationship to the Speaker but also in relationship to what is spoken and what is brought about in others who hear what is said. Therefore, the Son of God is described here not only in terms of his relationship with the Father, from whom he proceeds, but also in terms of the creatures he made, the flesh he assumed, and the truths he taught. All of these aspects are most correctly and fittingly embraced by the term *Word*, nor could one find any more appropriate term under heaven.*

**Bonaventure John 1:1*

The Distinction of Persons

***R 3**

*Second, John indicates the personal distinction between the Father and the Son, saying, *and the Word was with God*.* In this phrase, the noun *God* is a personal term: the Word was with God the Father; the Son is always in the Father, and the Father is always in the Son. The preposition *with* refers to a relational distinction between two Persons, not their nature. Nothing is ever said to be "with itself," nor can anyone be said to be "in himself," so there exists a personal distinction between the Word and the Origin* with whom the Word abides. However, the Word does not come from the Father by an action that carries him out of the Father but remains within him. Therefore, the Word abides within the one whose Word he is but is personally distinct from him, as has just been said. *The Word was with God* as one is with another.*

*John 1:1

**Principium*

**Lyra John 1:1*

The Father and Son Are Consubstantial

***R 4**

*Third, John declares that the Father and the Son are consubstantial, that is, they possess a unity of essence, saying, *and the Word was God.** Thus the noun *God* is predicated of the Word: the Word is God. Subjects and predicates mean the same, though they be transposed.* In this phrase *God* refers to the divine essence: the Word is God, possessing the divine nature or substance. John does not say that he was with God but was not himself God. Nothing can be in God that is not God—he is totally and substantially the same. When John says that *the Word was with God*, this does not mean he was of an extraneous nature, as our word is to us. Rather, he was of the divine nature, which is indivisible and not manifold, for in no way could God be other than one and absolutely simple.* Therefore, the Word and the Origin from which he comes share the same inner nature, although, as has been said, they can be distinguished personally. All three Persons are implied in this clause: the Father by the noun *God*, the Son by the noun *Word*, and the Holy Spirit by the preposition *with*.

*John 1:1

*Aristotle, Peri Herm 10

**Lyra John 1:1*

The Father and the Son Are Co-eternal

*Fourth, he speaks of the co-eternity of the Father and the Son, saying, *The same was in the beginning with God.** This Word about whom he speaks is with God the Father from the beginning of eternity, that is, before all ages, eternally.* It was as if he were saying, "This Word of God never existed apart from God the Father: just as there was never a Father without the Son, so there could not be God without his Word, or without his Power, or without his Wisdom."* We speak of the Father because he has a Son; parenthood necessarily requires progeny. And because the Father who speaks and conceives the Word is from eternity, then the Word he brings to birth by speaking must truly be called the Word *in the beginning*. Not, understand, in the beginning of time, about which it was said, *In the beginning God created heaven, and earth,** but

***R 5**

*John 1:2

**Lyra John 1:1*

**Bruno John 1:1; PL 165:451B*

*Gen 1:1

from the beginning of eternity, about which it is said, "*With you is the principality in the day of your strength: in the brightness of the saints, from the womb*, that is, from my substance, *before the day star*, that is, before the creation of the world, *I begot you*."* Where it says, *This day have I begotten you*,* this is understood to refer to the day of eternity, which embraces every day.

*Ps 109:3

*Ps 2:7

The phrase *in the beginning* has a different connotation here than in the previous verse: there it referred to the Father, and here it refers to eternity. As to how the Father himself begets the Son, it is better not to inquire, because it cannot be understood. The divine generation is utterly indescribable; about it, the prophet asks, *Who shall declare his generation?** Even though it can be said that the Son is begotten of the Father, no prophet or angel comprehends how this happens.*

*Isa 53:8

**Lombard 1.9; PL 192:986B*

In a moral sense we can learn from the foregoing that God should be the beginning of everything we intend, because *in the beginning was the Word, and the Word was God*. Again, if you wonder if any of your actions, interior or exterior, are divine, and whether God is performing them in you, and they are done through him, ask if God is the goal of your intent. If so, then your action is godly because it has one and the same origin and goal: God.* Having spoken of the being of the Word, and his generation, John now moves on to speak of his actions and operations.

**Eckhart John 1:1*

The Works of the Father and the Son Are Inseparable

***R 6**

*Fifth, the evangelist tells us that the activities of the Father and the Son are indivisible, saying, "*All things were made by him*, that is, everything that exists was made by the Father; *and without him was made nothing*,* that is, both beings visible to the eye and

*John 1:3

those that are intelligible to the mind were made by the Father." Accordingly, God made everything with wisdom, and nothing was made without wisdom. God made creatures the way an artist creates a masterpiece; the Craftsman of the universe acts, as it were, through his understanding. Whatever is shaped by an artist, or in our understanding, begins in the intellect. For example, a real house begins as a concept in the mind. As was noted above, the Word in God is identical with an intellectual concept in God; therefore, everything was made *through him*, whether spiritual or material creatures. The word *by** here means the efficient cause, not an aid, or a servant, or an instrument.[2] The Son himself, with the Father, is the agent of all things, as is the Holy Spirit, because all of the actions of the Trinity are inseparable. *All things were made by him* in such a way that neither the Father nor the Holy Spirit is excluded.

*per

All things were made together and at one time, although the work of creation was spread over six distinct days. *All things were made by him*, but the Word could not become of himself or make himself, because he existed *before* all these things were made through him; so it follows that the Word himself is not created. According to Augustine, if he is not made, then he is not a creature; if he is not a creature, he is of the same divine nature as the Father.*

*De Trin 1.6.9; PL 42:825; CL 50:38

Every substance that is not God is created, and whatever is not created is God. This Word does not consist of a syllable, nor is he produced by the voice; he is always *in sinu*, that is, he abides secretly in the

[2] The efficient cause is primarily the agent that causes something to happen; the instrumental cause is the tool or agent through which it works. The sculptor is the efficient cause; the chisel is the instrumental cause.

Father's heart.[3] There he disposes, guides, and performs all things.* God acts not by speaking but by willing: for him, to will is to speak and to create everything through his Word, that is, his Son.

*Bruno John 1:1; PL 165:451D–52B

*R 7

*Having shown that the Word is the efficient cause of all things, John goes on to explain in what way he acts, saying, *"All things were made by him, and without him was made nothing that was made. In him* (that is, in the Word) *was life** and the living entity." When a carpenter makes a box, he first designs it in his mind and then constructs it out of wood. What is in his mind dwells with the builder; what is made changes over time. For not all things that are made have life, nor are they life in themselves, that is, in the nature in which they exist as created things. Rather, they live insofar as they are in God and by the divine art that is life itself, because it is there that they have their exemplar and living *raison d'être*. All things that exist in time or that have been made he in fact made from all eternity, that is, he ordained that they be made: he knew of them before he brought them into being, and they were living and flourishing in his mind and presence. All things that exist were imagined before the creation of the world by the Son of God himself and were ordained as they would afterward be; they were in a manner of speaking already existing and living in him.

*John 1:3-4

All things that are alive are part of the divine dispensation because it is impossible for them to come into being in any other way but as they were arranged.

[3] "In the bosom of the Father" is the traditional English translation of *in sinu Patris*, which is first used in John 1:18. Most modern translations render it as "closest to the Father's heart." Here is Ambrose's interpretation: "*The bosom of the Father* is to be understood in a spiritual sense, as a kind of innermost dwelling of the Father's love and of his nature, in which the Son always dwells. Even so, the Father's womb is the spiritual womb of an inner sanctuary, from which the Son has proceeded just as from a generative womb" (De Ben Patriarch 11.51; PL 14:689C).

Hence it is clear in what way creatures proceed from the Word: in the way that works of art emerge from the mind of their maker. For this reason Boethius says,

> You lead all things by a celestial example.
> Most beautiful yourself,
> You produce a beautiful universe,
> Shaping it by means of a similar image.[4]*

*Cons 3.9; PL 63:758B–59A; CL 94:52; *Lyra John 1:1*

Morally, we should note that a virtuous work is a work of life, just as wicked actions are called the works of death. If you want to know if an action of yours is living, that is, virtuous, and if it is good and divine, see if it is made in God: *what was made in him*, God, *was life*, that is, it is living and life-giving. What is done in charity is done in God; what is done apart from God or without him has neither a direction nor a goal.

The Word of God is the Light of Men and Women

*Having shown how the Word imparts life to all things generally, John goes on to speak about how he does so in a unique way to human beings, saying, *and the life was the light of men*.* Life, that is, the Word who is Life itself and in whom all creatures live, *was the light of men*. Rational beings require enlightenment if they are to attain beatitude.* He does not fail to shed this light on all people through his grace shining upon them. This assumes, of course, that people do what lies within their power by turning to God through knowledge and love. In a moral sense, *the light of men* is a good life: deeds do more than words to build up and enlighten others. As Jerome observes, "We understand much better what we see with our eyes than

***R 8**

*John 1:4

**Zachary 1.1; PL 186:48D*

[4] Ludolph's idea of the pre-existence of all things in the mind of God and the image of the artisan and his creation are taken from Augustine, Tr John 1.16-17 (PL 35:1387–88; CL 36:9-10).

*Ep 64.10; PL 22:613; CS 54:597–98
*Lucilium 6.5
*Acts 1:1

what we hear with our ears."* And Seneca says, "The path of precepts is long, the way of examples short and effective."* This is why we are told, *Jesus began to do and to teach.**

***R 9**
‡John 1:5

And the light shines in darkness,*‡ that is, on sinners. The Word by his very nature shines on them, but they are in darkness because they turn away from the influence of the divine light of the Word. Hence John continues, *and the darkness did not comprehend it. Sinners refuse to follow this light because of their own revolt, not because of the light itself. Augustine writes,

*John 1:5

> When a blind person is placed in the sun, the sun is present to him, but he is absent to the sun. In the same way, although Wisdom is present, those who are foolish, evil, or ungodly are blind in heart. He is present to blind persons, but absent from their eyes—not because Wisdom is absent from them but because they are absent from Wisdom. What must they do? They must be cleansed, so that they can see. Take away the sins and iniquities, and you will see the Wisdom that is present, because God is Wisdom itself. This is why we are told, *Blessed are the clean of heart: they shall see God.**

*Matt 5:8; Tr John 1.18; PL 35:1388; CL 36:11

According to Origen, *the light shines in darkness* because the Word of God, the life and light of men, does not cease to shine in our nature, although considered in itself that nature is dark and formless.*

*Scotus Eriugena, Hom Prol John; PL 12:291A

And because pure light cannot be comprehended by any creature, the text goes on to say, *and the darkness did not comprehend it*. There are three ways to *comprehend* something: by surrounding and enclosing it, by seeing it clearly, or by clinging to it by faith and charity. No creature can comprehend this light in the first sense; the blessed in heaven comprehend it in the second sense; holy people on earth comprehend it in the third sense. But the wicked cannot comprehend it in any way: because they refused to cling to it in faith and charity, *the darkness did not comprehend it.** Some-

**Bonaventure John 1:5*

thing is also said to be comprehended when it is known through and through, as perfectly as it can be known. Only the divine eye can comprehend the light in this way; no creature ever could.

Morally, *the light shines in darkness* because virtue shines and becomes evident in the midst of adversity and opposition: *Power* is made perfect in infirmity.*‡ Gregory the Great says, "No one makes progress unless he tastes adversity;* only with much testing is the inner self revealed."‡ Because no amount of hardship can overwhelm the saints and separate them from the love of Christ, we are told, *And the darkness did not comprehend it.* When good people experience adversity, they are not crushed or overcome by it; on the contrary, they rejoice in it and take delight in it. Or, *the light shines in darkness* when God's consolation shines on those who are enduring trials and tribulations, as we read, *The Lord is near to those that are of a contrite* heart,** and, *I am with him in tribulation, I will deliver him.** *And the darkness did not comprehend it* because *the sufferings of this time are not worthy to be compared with the glory to come.** God rewards us beyond our merits and punishes us less than we deserve.[5]

**virtus*
‡2 Cor 12:9
*Mor 23.XXVI.32; PL 76:284B; CL 143B:1185
‡Dial 1.5; PL 77:180D
**tribulato*
*Ps 33:18
*Ps 90:15
*Rom 8:18

Also, *the light shines in* the *darkness* of this world because the Creator appears in his creatures. In our heavenly homeland God is the mirror of his creatures: they all shine out in him, and we will see in him everything that brings us joy. In this life, on the other hand, creatures are the mirror of the Creator, and we see him in them. As the apostle said, *We see now through a glass*, creatures, *in a dark* and obscure *manner;** and, *For the invisible things of him*, God, *from the creation of the world are clearly seen, being understood by the things that are made.** Not only does faith rightly testify to

*1 Cor 13:12
*Rom 1:20

[5] In a commentary on the Mass Peter Damian says, "God does not reward strictly according to our merits: he punishes less than we deserve and rewards more than we deserve" (Exp canon missae 13; PL 145:888A).

God's existence, and Sacred Scripture speak of it, and the relationship of things to him indicate it, and right reason profess it—creatures themselves proclaim it:
*Ps 99:3 *He made us, and not we ourselves.** All things announce, each in their different way, that God exists, including the voice of nature: all beautiful things testify that he is unparalleled beauty; all sweet things testify that he is excelling sweetness; all sublime things testify that he is infinite profundity; all pure things testify that he is matchless purity; all strong things testify that he is
Hugh 1.1 unrivaled strength; and so on.*

The Generation of the Son of God Should Not Be Understood in a Carnal Way

***R 10** *You heard earlier that the Son is truly begotten of the Father, but you must take care lest some carnal, deficient understanding of this mystery suggest itself to your mind's eye. Rather, with the intuitive glance of the dove or the eagle believe simply, and contemplate intently, that from a light that is at one and same time immense and completely simple, brilliantly shimmering and yet deeply hidden, a co-eternal, co-equal, and consubstantial splendor shines forth, who is the highest Power and Wisdom, and in whom from eternity the Father disposed all things to be. *By whom also*
*Heb 1:2 *he made the world** and governs all things that were made and regulates them to his glory: partly by nature,
LV 1 partly by grace, partly by justice, partly by mercy.*

In this way, nothing in this world would be disordered. Augustine teaches,

> Just as brilliant light is produced from the substance of the sun, so we understand that the Son is begotten from the substance of the Father. Now the sun's flame does not exist before its light, even though the light is produced from it; rather, the splendor appears together with the sun. I cannot

say that the brilliance appears after the fire, even though, as I have said, the light is produced by it. If, therefore, we can find something in creation that is produced by but is not later than its source, why do you despair that such a thing is possible in the Creator?

The brilliance generated by the sun fills the whole earth, but it is not cut off from its source, nor does it recede from it; so the Son who is generated by the Father abides always and everywhere in the Father. The brilliance of the sun is substantially in the sun, and the sun is substantially in its light; so the Son is substantially in the Father, and the Father is substantially in the Son. The sun and its brilliance are substantially united, but they are not one person, because we do not say that the sun is its brilliance, or the brilliance is the sun itself; so although the Father and the Son share the same divine essence, they are not one Person. The sun warms, illuminates, dries, dissolves, bleaches, blackens, and performs all of the actions for which God made it by means of its brilliance; so we read that the Father has done all things through his Only-begotten Son.* *Ps-Augustine, Hom 246.4; PL 39:2199

According to this same Augustine, a certain Platonist said that the prologue of John's gospel should be displayed in letters of gold at a prominent place in every church.[6] ***R 11**

*De civ Dei 10.29; PL 41:309; CL 47:306

[6] Augustine says he was told this anecdote by Simplicianus, later bishop of Milan. Over time the prologue came to be used as a kind of blessing: it was read in the sickroom while conferring extreme unction, or at the baptism of children, or even as a prayer for good weather. In the mid-thirteenth century there is evidence of its being recited by the priest at the end of a private Mass, but the "Last Gospel" did not become a common feature of the public celebration of Mass until the end of the sixteenth century. It was never incorporated into the Carthusian liturgy.

✠

Lord God, all-powerful Father, in an ineffable way you brought forth your co-eternal, co-equal, and consubstantial Son before all ages. With him and the Holy Spirit you created all things visible and invisible, and you created me, a poor sinner. I adore you, I praise you, and I glorify you. Be merciful to this wretched sinner: do not despise the work of your hands, but save and help me for the sake of your holy name. Stretch out your right hand to what you have fashioned and aid this fragile flesh. You who made me, remake me who am stained by wickedness; you who formed me, re-form me who am corrupted by sin. Then will my poor soul be saved by your great mercy. Amen.

CHAPTER 2

The Remedy of Human Salvation; the Birth of Mary

In the beginning, when Lucifer was created, he revolted against God his Creator and in the blink of an eye was cast down from the heights of heaven into hell. Because of this, God resolved to create the human race, that through it he might repair the effects of the fall of Lucifer and his companions. The devil, envious of our first parents, lay in wait for them and labored to induce them to violate God's command. He chose for himself a certain kind of serpent that walked erect and had the head of a young woman. The fraudulent deceiver entered into this creature and with its mouth spoke lying words to Eve. By deceiving her, he brought death upon the whole human race. We were condemned to hell's prison, from which no mere human could set us free.[1] *R 1

*SHS 1

Finally, *the Father of mercies and the God of all comfort** looked with compassion on our condition of condemnation and resolved to set us free himself. The dove that held an olive branch in its beak and carried it to *2 Cor 1:3

[1] The idea that human beings would occupy the places left vacant by the fallen angels goes back at least to Augustine (Enchiridion 29; PL 40:246). The description of the serpent with a human head appears first in Comestor, who attributes the notion to Bede; his theory is that the tempter assumed the form of a young woman because this would encourage Eve to trust him (PL 198:1072).

the ark was a sign that in the future God would deliver those who were held in the chains of death. This emblem of deliverance was not intended solely for those who were in the ark; that olive twig presaged the salvation of the whole world. And God indicated his will for us with many other figures.*

*SHS 2

His compassion was evident from the very beginning: he formed our Adam out of the earth in the field of Damascus near Hebron, and brought him into a Paradise of delights, and drew Eve out of Adam's side as he slept in Paradise, and gave her to him as a companion, and established our first parents there to tend it. Then, although they were banished from Paradise by a strict divine decree for having eaten from the forbidden tree, his heavenly mercy never stopped urging people to seek the good by hidden inspirations, nor did he cease to call wandering humanity back to repentance, giving us the hope of forgiveness by the promised coming of a Savior.

***R 2**

Lest his loving condescension be put to naught by our ignorance or ingratitude, God never ceased, throughout the five ages of the world, to promise, to prophesy, and to prefigure the coming of his Son. Through patriarchs, judges, priests, kings, and prophets, from Abel the just to John the Baptist, down through thousands of years, he gave great and varied oracles to rouse our understanding to faith and inflame our hearts with great, lively desires.

*LV 1

Pope Leo says,

> Let those who object to the divine arrangement and the lateness of Christ's birth stop complaining—as if what happened in the final age of the world was not applied to the earlier ages as well! The mystery* of human salvation was not inactive in any earlier age, because the incarnation of the Word accomplished the same effect when it was about to take place as when it actually did so. What the apostles preached, the prophets had also an-

*sacramentum

nounced; nor was it too late in fulfillment, since it has always been believed. By this delay in his salvific work the wisdom and kindness of God made us better disposed to answer his call: what had been foretold through so many ages by numerous signs, numerous words, and numerous mysteries could not be open to doubt in these days of the gospel. In this way, the more often and the earlier the birth of the Savior had been proclaimed beforehand, the more constant would be the faith it engendered in us.

No, it is not that God has just now come up with a plan for attending to human affairs, nor that it has taken him this long to show compassion. Rather, from the very foundation of the world he had laid down one and the same cause of salvation for all. The grace of God—by which the entire assembly of saints has always been justified—was augmented, not inaugurated, when Christ was born. This mystery* of great compassion was so powerful even in its prefigurations that those who believed it when it was promised gained no less than those who received it when it was actually given.*

**sacramentum*

*Sermo 23.4; PL 54:202A; CL 138:106

Augustine points out that Christ did not come until the human race stood convicted before the tribunals of the natural and written law. If Christ had come immediately, people would say that it was possible to be saved by the natural law or the written law and believe his coming to be unnecessary. Because all were descending into the infernal region, it was evident that the law could not save us; when it became clear that mercy was needed, Christ himself then came. It had not been necessary for him to come earlier, because the efficacy of a spiritual medicine depends on the condition of its recipient. He did not come later, lest faith and hope in the promised incarnation be lost; had his advent been further delayed, faith and hope would daily have become more lukewarm and weak.

***R 3**

*cited in Hugh 4.5

According to the same Augustine, the people in ancient times had a great desire to see Christ. They knew he was coming; not just the patriarchs and prophets, but all who were living devout lives would say, with great longing, "O, that his nativity would come to me here! O, that I could see with my own eyes what I believe!"* If the faithful back then had such yearning and were so devoted to Christ even before he came, what must be done now that he has been received? But woe to us in our own day, who are less moved by grace present than the ancients were by grace promised! Bernard writes, "During my frequent reflections on the burning desire with which the patriarchs longed for the incarnation of Christ, I am stung with sorrow and shame. Even now I can scarcely restrain my tears: the lukewarmness, the cold unconcern of these miserable times make me blush. For who of us is filled with as much joy by the consummation of that event as the mere promise of it inflamed the desires of the holy people of ancient times?"*

*Ps-Augustine, Sermo 370.3; PL 39:1658

*SC 2.1; PL 183:790A; SB 1:8

The Dispute between Justice and Mercy

***R 4**

Thus it was that for nearly 5,200 years the human race lay prostrate in misery, and because of the sin of the first man no one could ascend to eternal beatitude. The angelic spirits were moved to compassion by the sight of such ruin, and they also desired to fill the places left vacant in their own ranks so long ago. When the fullness of time had come, they insistently and devoutly brought a humble petition before the Lord. So Mercy, with Peace at her side, appealed to the depths of God's compassion. But Truth, accompanied by Justice, contradicted her, and there ensued a lengthy debate between them.

**MVC 1–2; CM 153:11–12*

Bernard gives a full account of this in a sermon on the annunciation, which can be summarized as follows:

Mercy spoke to God: "The rational beings need divine mercy, for they are in a wretched and miserable state. *It is time to have mercy on it, for the time is come.** But Truth countered, "I ask you to execute the sentence you pronounced, that Adam and all who were in him should die if, transgressing your command, he tasted the forbidden apple." Mercy rejoined, "Why, then, Lord, did you create me? Truth knows I shall perish if you are never merciful again." But then Truth objected, "If the transgressor escapes your sentence, Truth will perish and not abide in eternity."

*Ps 101:14

The Father then referred this case to the Son. Truth and Mercy put their same arguments before him. It was not clear how both justice and mercy could be preserved in humanity's case. Then the King wrote his decision in these words: "One side says, 'I die if Adam does not perish,' and the other, 'I die if he does not receive mercy.' Let death become a good, and each will have what she desires: Adam will die, and mercy will follow."

Everyone marveled at this wise sentence, and agreed that Adam should receive mercy by dying. But they asked how death could be a good, because it is horrible even to hear about it. The King answered, "*The death of the wicked is very evil, but precious in the sight of the Lord is the death of his saints;** it is the gate of life. Let someone be found who does not deserve death but who will die out of charity. Death will not be able to hold the innocent, and he can make a breach through which the others will be liberated." This verdict pleased them, but they wondered where such a person could be found. Truth searched the earth but found no one free of evil, not even a newborn child. Mercy scoured heaven but could find no one with sufficient charity. Thus the victory was reserved for the one who was greater than any other and would lay down his life for useless servants.

*Ps 33:22; 115:15

Justice and Mercy returned on the appointed day, greatly troubled because they had not found what they sought. At length Peace took them aside and said, to console them, "Did you not know *there is none that does good, no not one*?* Let the one who made the decision provide the help." The King understood this and said, "*I repent of having made them.** It falls to me to bear the punishment for the human beings I have created." And, summoning the angel Gabriel, he said, "Go and say to the Daughter of Sion, *Behold your King will come to you*."* The angel made haste and said, "Adorn your bridal chamber and receive the King."* We learn from this scene how truly terrible sin is and how difficult it was to find a solution. The four virtues here spoken of consented to this resolution, and so the word of the prophet was fulfilled: *Mercy and truth have met each other, justice and peace have kissed*.[2]‡

*Ps 13:3

*Gen 6:7

*Zech 9:9

*Antiphon, Presentation of the Lord

‡Ps 84:11; Bernard, Sermo Annunciation 1; PL 183:383–90B; *MVC 2; CM 153:12–14*

***R 5** *Concerning this matter, Pope Leo says,

> Because the devil had not dealt so violently with the first man as to win him over to his side without the consent of free will, his voluntary transgression had to be destroyed along with the enemy's plan in such a way that the gift of grace would not violate the standards of justice. In the general downfall of the human race there was only one remedy in the hidden divine counsels that could help those who had been brought low: if a child of Adam was born who was innocent of any connection with the original betrayal and had no part in it. Such a one could profit others both by his example and by his merits. But because natural generation would not allow for this, David's Lord was made David's Son,

[2] The "Four Daughters of God" first appeared around the tenth century as a Jewish Midrash concerning the creation of humankind. Hugh of Saint Victor took it up and applied the story to redemption rather than creation, moving the action to just before the incarnation (*Adnotationes in quosdam psalmos* 63; PL 177:623–25). Bernard in turn used it in a sermon, placing Christ at the center of the dispute. Ludolph cites a shortened version of Bernard's sermon in the MVC.

and a faultless shoot sprang up from the promised stock.*

*Sermo 28.3; PL 54:223A; CL 138:140–41

And Anselm writes,

Our nature was created originally in the likeness of God so that it would ceaselessly find joy in God himself and possess his glory without any change or corruption. This great good was immediately lost by our first parents; unhappy humanity tumbled headlong into the miseries of this world, which in turn gave way to even greater unhappiness and eternal desolation in the next. Many ages passed, and the frightful condemnation only worsened as it swept away all the descendants of Adam and Eve. The wisdom of the supreme God could find nowhere in the whole of creation any way by which, as he had arranged, he could enter our world and repair this most lamentable loss. That is, until he came to that Virgin of whom we are speaking.

As soon as she came into the world through the line of human generation, she was so resplendent with all virtues and constancy that the Wisdom of God himself judged her to be truly worthy of being the means by which he might enter the world. By his coming, he would blot out not only the offense of our first parents but the sins of the whole world; he would utterly crush the diabolical enemies of his works, and, having rescued the human race from damnation, he would lead it back to its heavenly homeland. Who, pondering these things, can find fitting words to praise the only mediatrix who deserved to be the means by which such great goods would be bestowed?*

*Eadmer, De exc 9; PL 159:574B–75A

Mary's Predestination

*This Virgin was not discovered suddenly by chance—she was predestined from all eternity. John Damascene teaches, "The Mother of God was herself ***R 6** foreseen from all eternity in the divine counsels, and prefigured and foretold by many words and images of the prophets through the Holy Spirit."* Let us arise and give thanks for what God has deigned to do for us, saying with Anselm,

*Orthodoxa 4.14; PG 94:1155

> We adore you, Christ, the king of Israel, the light of the nations, ruler of the kings of the earth, Lord of hosts, power of the omnipotent God. We adore you, most noble price of our redemption, the sacrifice of peace, who alone exude a fragrance worthy to ascend to the Father who dwells in the heights. You caused him to look upon us in our humiliation and made us children of wrath pleasing to him. We proclaim your mercies, O Christ, and we burst into praise as we recall your abundant sweetness. We offer to you, O Christ, a sacrifice of praise for the bountiful goodness that you have lavished upon us, the offspring of wickedness and the children of depravity. Although we were as yet your enemies, Lord, and ancient death exercised iniquitous power over all flesh, the seed of Adam that shared in the guilt of his primordial offense, you remembered your generous mercy and looked down upon this valley of tears and misery from your sublime dwelling. Lord, you saw the affliction of your people and, moved to the core of your being by charity for our sorrow, you were inspired to think thoughts of peace and redemption for us.*

*Eckbert, Stim [Med 9 Anselm]; PL 158:749AC

***R 7**

*We will pass over in silence the many prophecies made about this Virgin from the beginning of creation to the coming of her holy Son, either by the just who lived before the Law or those who lived under it. We will speak about her birth. We know that she was descended through a human genealogy, and we believe that her birth was surrounded by certain great and wondrous signs that we will consider. The glorious Virgin in whom the incarnation of the Son of God took place belonged to the tribe of Judah and the line of

David.* For, as Augustine observes, it was fitting to the heavenly mystery that Mary, who was found worthy to be the Mother of God according to the flesh, should come from a family of regal stock and priestly origin, since the Son of God, who is king and eternal priest, took his human body from her.*

**Eadmer, De exc 2; PL 159:559D–60A*

*De cons 3.5; PL 34:1044; CS 43:5

The glorious Virgin Mary was born around the twenty-seventh year of the reign of Augustus, her father being Joachim of Nazareth and her mother Anna, who was from the town of Sepphoris, about two leagues distant from Nazareth. Both were just in the sight of God. They had been childless for twenty years, and they prayed earnestly for a baby, vowing that they would consecrate the child to God. When the priest Issachar observed Joachim assisting his fellow citizens with the oblation, he spurned his offering and reproached him for his sterility. Joachim was shamed by this taunt and went to stay among the shepherds of his flock. There an angel of the Lord appeared to comfort him, who said that his prayers had been heard and his alms had ascended into the sight of God. (Joachim gave a third of his possessions to the poor and a third to the temple and its ministers, and he and his household lived off the remaining third.) And the angel told him, "Behold, your wife will give birth to a daughter, and you will call her Mary. She will be consecrated to the Lord, as you vowed, and she will be filled with the Holy Spirit from her mother's womb, and she will dwell in the Lord's temple." The angel gave the same tidings to Anna. Having been advised by the angel, they went up together to Jerusalem, gave thanks in the temple to the Lord, and returned to their own home. Anna conceived and gave birth to a daughter, whom she named Mary.[3]

[3] Ludolph's sources for the stories of Mary's birth and childhood are the *Golden Legend* and the MVC. These in turn draw on the apocryphal *Gospel of Pseudo-Matthew*, a seventh-century

*R 8

*By a singular privilege, Mary was cleansed of original sin in her mother's womb. Bernard says,

> And so the Virgin Mary has accumulated so many distinctions of goodness that it is beyond question that she was holy before she was born. I hold that a more plentiful blessing descended upon her than on others who were sanctified in the womb, so that not only was she holy at birth, but from that time on she was free from all sin. It was evidently fitting that by a singular privilege she would lead a life free from sin and obtain the gifts of life and justice more than others because she was to give birth to the one who would destroy sin and death.[4]*

*Ep 174.5; PL 182:334CD; SB 7:390

And Augustine writes that Mary was sanctified before her conception of the Son of God but could commit venial sin, but that after conceiving him she could sin neither mortally nor venially.[5]*

*Ockham, Quaest in Librum Tertium Sent, Q. 5, Art. 1

Latin reworking of the second-century *Protoevangelium of James*. In the ninth century, letters were attached to the text suggesting that the translation was done by Jerome, and authorship is sometimes attributed to him in later medieval writings.

[4] This citation is taken from Bernard's famous letter to the canons of Laon Cathedral objecting to their celebration of a feast in honor of the Immaculate Conception. During Ludolph's lifetime this doctrine was fiercely debated; given his Dominican background, it is not surprising that he follows Aquinas's teaching that Mary was sanctified after her conception. The dispute was reflected in the Carthusian Order itself: in 1333 permission was given at the general chapter to celebrate the feast of Mary's *conception*; this was changed in 1341 to a commemoration of her *sanctification* and, several years later, back to her *conception*. It has been suggested that the change to *sanctification* may have been in deference to the position taken by Ludolph in the *Vita Christi*. By the mid-fifteenth century the Carthusians clearly professed the doctrine of the Immaculate Conception.

[5] Augustine himself did not teach explicitly that Mary was sinless but simply said, "We must except the holy Virgin Mary, concerning whom I wish to raise no question when it touches the subject of sins, out of honor to the Lord. From him we know

Mary in the Temple

At the age of three the glorious Virgin Mary was brought to the temple by her parents and offered to God. She lived in the temple precincts with other young girls, learning her letters and serving God until the age of fourteen. When her parents left her in the temple, Mary's use of reason quickly increased: from then on, she chose in her heart to have God as her Father, to set herself to learn his law, and to think constantly about how to please God so that he would deign to give his grace to her. She earnestly begged from him the grace to observe all of his laws and precepts and to enable her to love everything he loved and hate everything he hated. She also asked for all the virtues that would make her more pleasing in his sight, and she made greater and greater progress in the work of God. *R 9

*Massa; MVC 3; CM 153:15

She spent all her time in contemplation, prayer, divine reading, and good works; she prayed ceaselessly for the salvation of the whole human race and read frequently the Scriptures that spoke of the coming of the Messiah. Whenever she came to a passage concerning the incarnation of God, she would warmly embrace the scroll, kiss it, and read the sentence again.*

*SHS 5

Mary was earlier at vigils, wiser in divine learning, more lowly in humility, more mellifluous in singing the psalms, more gracious in charity, more chaste in purity, and more perfect in every virtue than others. Each day she became better. No one ever saw her angry or heard her raise her voice. Every word she spoke was so full of grace that God could be discerned in

---

what abundance of grace for overcoming sin in every particular was conferred on her who had the merit to conceive and bear him who undoubtedly had no sin" (*De Natura et Gratia*, 42; PL 44:267).

her speech. She was very attentive to her companions, lest any of them offend another by what she said, or laugh boisterously, or say anything hurtful or arrogant to her peers, or do wrong in any way. She blessed the Lord ceaselessly, and in order to avoid being drawn from her prayer when meeting people, she responded to their greeting with *Deo gratias*. In fact, it was she who initiated the custom among holy people of using *Deo gratias* as a greeting.* ‡She was also the first among young women to make a vow of virginity for life (unless God were to ordain otherwise), an offering no one had made to God from the very beginning of the world.[6]

**Massa; MVC 3; CM 153:17–18*
‡R 10

Mary conducted herself with such prudence, humility, and devotion that her life can serve as a model for everyone. Here is what Ambrose says of her:

> Let Mary's life be set forth as a likeness from which, as from a mirror, the appearance of charity and the form of virtue is reflected. She was a virgin both in body and mind, humble in heart, grave in speech, prudent in spirit, sparing in words, studious in reading. She did not put her trust in uncertain riches but in the prayers of the poor; she worked hard and was modest in conversation. She made God, not other people, the judge of her thoughts. She injured no one, did good to everyone, stood up in the presence of her elders, did not envy her equals, avoided boasting, followed reason, and loved virtue. When did she even by a glance pain her parents? When did she despise the

[6] The description of Mary's life in the temple reflects a monastic provenance, possibly drawn from the Rule of Saint Benedict. Another change from the *Protoevangelium* is that, although this work speaks of Mary's perpetual virginity, the *Gospel of Pseudo-Matthew* adds that she had taken a vow, an idea found as far back as Gregory of Nyssa (*Oratio in Diem Natalem Christi*, PG 46:1139). The description of her life in the temple also draws (via the MVC) on the *Revelations* of Saint Elizabeth of Schönau.

lowly? When did she ridicule the crippled? When did she avoid the needy? There was nothing stern in her look, nothing frivolous in her speech, nothing unseemly in her actions. Her gestures were controlled, her gait modest, her speech free of insolence: her outward appearance was the image of her soul, the very form of probity.* Such was Mary, and her life is a lesson for us all. If, then, the performer is not displeasing, let us show our approval for the performance: whoever desires the reward, imitate the example.*

**Massa quotes to this point*

*De virginibus 2.6–7, 15; PL 16:208D–9B; CSP 1:36–37, 40

And Anselm writes,

Notice how chastely, devoutly, and worthily Mary ordered her life toward God when she left childhood behind and how she lived out this determination in a way beyond human reckoning. There can be no doubt that, under the continuous protection of the angels, her body was entirely chaste and her soul entirely holy, and she was free from any taint of sin. This is because God the Creator was to dwell bodily in her as in his royal palace and, in an ineffable way, would take from her the human nature that he would unite to his person for our salvation.

Are we surprised? What is the practice in human society, if we may presume to compare earthly things with heavenly? When wealthy or important people go to stay somewhere, their staff goes ahead to find a lodging, make it secure, clean it, decorate it, and keep guard over it, so that when the masters come they find it a suitable place to stay. If all of this is done for the arrival of a mere human being, whose power is fleeting, what kind of preparation of all good things do we think was made for the arrival of the heavenly eternal King into the heart of the most holy Virgin, in whom he would not be simply a passing guest, but from whom he would take his humanity and be born?*

*Eadmer, De exc 3; PL 159:560C–61A

Pause here and consider attentively the virtues and behavior of the Virgin Mary, and strive to imitate them to the best of your ability.

Types of the Blessed Virgin Mary

*R 11

*Concerning Mary's conception and sanctification, we must realize how fitting it was that, because God had resolved to assume our human nature, this great event would be foreshadowed in the mother from whom he was to be born. She was prefigured by the daughter of King Astyages, of whom it is said in *Historia Scholastica* that in a dream he saw a luxuriant vine growing from the womb of his daughter that put out leaves and flowers and, heavy with fruit, overshadowed his whole kingdom. He was told that his daughter would give birth to a mighty ruler, and from her was born Cyrus, who freed the children of Israel from their captivity in Babylon.[7]* Similarly, Joachim was told that he would have a daughter who would give birth to the messianic king; this ruler would free us from our captivity to the devil and be the true vine and overshadow the whole world.*

*Hist sch, Dan 16; PL 198:1470C

**SHS 2–3*

Mary was also prefigured by the sealed-up fountain placed in an enclosed garden.* The Holy Spirit sanctified her while she was still enclosed within her mother's womb, and she was safeguarded by the seal of the Holy Trinity so that nothing impure could enter into her. She was prefigured by the star that Balaam prophesied would arise from Jacob.* This star symbolizes Mary, a singular and special leader and helper* amid the waves; without this star we could not cross the tempestuous sea or reach the harbor of our heavenly homeland.*

*Song 4:12

*Num 24:7

**ductrix et adiutrix*

**SHS 3*

[7] Herodotus 1.108 tells of the dream of Astyages.

Mary's birth was prefigured by the shoot that sprouted from the root of Jesse, David's father; from her in turn arose that most beautiful flower, Christ the Lord, upon whom rested the sevenfold grace of the Holy Spirit.* Moreover, the way she brought forth that flower was prefigured by the closed door that the Lord showed to Ezekiel; no one could open it, and only the Lord would pass through it although it remained closed.* Mary herself was prefigured by the temple that Solomon built for the Lord. This temple was constructed of brilliant white marble and decorated within with the purest gold; so Mary was distinguished by the purest chastity and adorned within with perfect charity.*

*Isa 11:1-2

*Ezek 44:1-2

**SHS 3–4*

The presentation of Mary in the temple is prefigured by the renowned "table of the sun in the sand."[8] The *Historia Scholastica* relates the following account of this table: some fishermen cast their nets into the sea and by an astonishing chance drew out a table made entirely of gold. Their people worshiped the sun as a god, so they dedicated this table to the sun in a temple they built on the sand of the seashore. That table offered to the material sun is a good image of Mary, who was offered to the true Sun, that is, God most high, in the temple of the eternal Sun. And the table is a beautiful symbol of Mary because heavenly food has been prepared for us through her: for our sake she gave birth to Jesus Christ, the Son of God, who revives us by his Body and Blood.*

**SHS 4*

Mary was also prefigured by Jephthah's daughter.* However, that girl was offered rashly and unwisely

*Judg 11

[8] The story does not appear in the *Historia* but in the SHS. Jerome reports in a letter that in his travels Apollonius of Tyre saw the famous "table of the sun spread in the sands of the desert," but this passage does not appear in the biography by Philostratus, nor is it clear to what Jerome refers (Ep 53.1; PL 22:541).

and was unable to serve afterwards. Mary, on the contrary, was offered with due observance and discretion, and after her consecration she served the Lord for the rest of her life. And the former was offered in thanksgiving for a victory over earthly enemies, whereas Mary offered herself beforehand to prepare the way for victory over earthly enemies.*

*SHS 4–5

Mary's manner of life and the way Mary served God in the temple can be illustrated by the famous hanging gardens that a Persian king planted in a high place for his queen, who loved to contemplate her homeland there. This can symbolize Mary's contemplative life: she persevered in her meditations in the Lord's temple, continually contemplating her heavenly home.[9]*

*SHS 5

✠

O Mary, Virgin of virgins, no one has seen the like of you before, nor has anyone since equaled you: you offered a glorious gift to God by being the first among women to make a vow of lifelong virginity. No mere mortal instructed you to do this, nor was there a model for you to imitate. Adorned with this and all other virtues, you were pleasing to God and bequeathed an example to all people. I implore your great goodness, you, who are my greatest consolation, that you will guide my life and help me to imitate your example of virtue as much as I can, and grant that your grace never fail me. Amen.

[9] According to legend, the gardens were built by King Nebuchadnessar II for his wife, who was homesick for her native country and longed for the plants of her homeland.

CHAPTER 3

The Blessed Virgin's Marriage

And so Mary, the Lord's Virgin, grew each day in virtue as she progressed in age; the Lord cared for her because her parents had left her at the temple. Daily she was visited by angels, daily she benefited from divine supervision; she was protected from all evils, and all good things were lavished upon her. This continued until she turned fourteen and the priest announced that girls who had attained this age were to return home and marry. The other young women readily obeyed, but Mary responded that she could not do this, for her parents had surrendered her into the Lord's service and she had made a vow of virginity to the Lord. *R 1 *Massa

The priest was confronted with a dilemma. On the one hand, he did not believe that a vow should be broken, for Scripture says, *To the Lord your God let your vows be made and paid.** On the other hand, he did not dare to introduce such a novel custom to the nation. He asked his superiors what was to be done, and they all agreed to seek God's counsel in this matter. As the other priests devoted themselves to prayer, the high priest went in to consult the Lord, as was customary. Immediately, a voice coming from the propitiatory could be heard by all, saying that anyone to whom the Virgin was commended in marriage must fulfill the prophecy in Isaiah, *And there shall come forth a rod out of the root of Jesse, and a flower shall rise up out of his root. And the spirit of the Lord shall rest upon him.** All those *Ps 75:12 *Isa 11:1-2 men from the house and family of David eligible for marriage were ordered to bring their staff to the altar.*

*Massa

*R 2

Among these was a man named Joseph, whose rod, when it was brought forward, produced a beautiful flower from its tip, and a dove descended from the heavens and came to rest upon it. From this it was clear to everyone that the Virgin should be betrothed to him.[1] This is why we read of Moses in the book of Numbers, *He returned on the following day, and found that the rod of Aaron for the house of Levi was budded, and that the buds swelling it had bloomed blossoms which, spreading the leaves, were formed into almonds.**

*Massa

*Num 17:8

We can understand from this that the blessed Virgin resembles the rod of Aaron in several ways: she is slender through poverty, flexible through humility, and straight through intention and charity. This Virgin produced a burgeoning bud when she conceived the Son of God in her womb, and this bud flowered and produced fruit when she gave birth to him while remaining a virgin. And just as flowers decorate a tree without harming it, so the Son of God did not violate the Virgin's integrity but adorned her with more gifts and graces. According to Chrysostom, Mary is the rod placed in the tent of meeting, which bore the fruit of the almond without coming into contact with the moist earth: she brought forth a Son without human seed, who was attached to the wood of the cross like an almond.* And it is fitting that he is first called the flower and then the fruit; for, as Ambrose observes, Christ as the fruit of a good tree now blooms for the increase of our virtue, now bears fruit in us, now is restored by renewed resurrection of the body.*

*Chromatius, Trac Matt 2.5; CL 9A:205–6

*Exp Luke 2.24; PL 15:1561B; CL 14:41

Sometimes Christ is called the flower, at other times the fruit. In the pages of both Testaments he is proclaimed as the flower in the letter, the fruit in the spirit;

[1] Massa's source is the ninth-century *Libellus de Nativitate Sanctae Mariae*, a work inspired by the *Gospel of Pseudo-Matthew.*

the flower in the law, the fruit in grace; the flower in the first tabernacle, the fruit in the second; the flower in the offering of animal sacrifices, the fruit in the spiritual understanding of the mysteries. Just as the appearance of the flower announces in advance the appearance of the fruit, so the ceremonies of old signified the future coming of Christ. It is evident that Christ is spoken of as the flower in prophecies promised in the Old Testament, and he is called the fruit in the perfection of grace in the New Testament. However, as the fruit does not appear while the flowers are still blooming, so the truth of Christ could not appear while carnal observance of the law continued. The fruit appears after the flowers wither: when the wilted blossoms of the law dropped away, the fruit of *grace and truth came by Jesus Christ.** *John 1:17

The Betrothal

The Virgin of the Lord returned to her parents' home in Nazareth, accompanied by some other young women who were sent with her by the priest as a kind of retinue on account of the notoriety of the miracle, to safeguard her modesty. It was customary for her to be surrounded by these guardians and witnesses to her purity, and she traveled nowhere without them. Jerome teaches, "Modesty was the companion to all her other virtues; this is essential to safeguarding virginity, and chastity cannot be maintained without it." Blessed Mary never went anywhere without modesty as her guardian. ***R 3**

*Radbertus, Ep 9; PL 30:140C; [16.105; CM 56C:157]

Joseph also returned to Nazareth and, having finalized the marriage contract, went home to make preparations for the wedding. The Virgin Mary was espoused to a man of her own tribe because a woman could not marry into another tribe when she stood to inherit from her father. As her father's only child,

Mary was required to marry a man of her tribe. They were both of David's tribe, because they were both descended from David: Mary was descended through Nathan, Joseph was descended through Solomon.*

Lyra Matt 1:15

Following the custom of his people Joseph had to contract marriage, but it was his set purpose to live a virginal life, although he had not taken a formal vow. He entered into marriage with the Virgin, entrusting himself to the divine will. Afterwards, Mary's intention in this regard was made known to him by a divine revelation, and by common consent the couple vowed to live a life of virginity. According to Augustine, before their mutual betrothal Mary and Joseph intended to live as virgins, and each of them only consented to the marriage thanks to a revelation by the Holy Spirit.* Nor would either of them have consented to marry the other unless, by the instruction of the Holy Spirit, they had been apprised of the other party's intentions. But afterwards they both made a solemn, spoken vow of virginity. *It is believed that Joseph himself was still a virgin, and one reason for thinking so is this: because, when he was dying, Christ would entrust his Mother only to a man who was a virgin, it is probable that before his conception, while Mary was still a young woman, he would do the same.[2]

*cited by Gratian, Decretum, Case 27 Q 2.3; PL 187:1393B

***R 4**

The Blessed Virgin was truly married to Joseph, and not just promised in marriage; the betrothal and consent were spoken in the present tense.* There was a true marriage between them; the ceremonial rites are not the essence of marriage, which is why Joseph was customarily referred to as her spouse and husband.[3]

**consensus per verba de praesenti*

[2] Eastern tradition, following the *Protoevangelium of James*, holds that Joseph had children from a previous marriage; Jerome and the Western tradition maintain that Joseph had no other children: "As for myself, I claim that Joseph himself was a virgin, through Mary, so that a virgin Son might be born of a virginal wedlock" (Adv Helv 19; PL 23:203B).

[3] Ludolph alludes here to the teaching of Peter Lombard that consent given in the present tense created a binding marriage,

Hugh of Saint Victor says that when the Blessed Virgin had taken a vow of virginity and then was commanded by her parents to marry, she feared disobeying her parents but did not want to forsake her vow. So she was led by the Holy Spirit to entrust herself entirely to God, believing that in his divine mercy he would enable her to obey her parents and keep her vow. And he draws a parallel with Abraham, who received the promise to his seed in Isaac but afterward was commanded to sacrifice him. He obeyed the command, absolutely certain that, although according to human calculation the command seemed to contradict the promise, according to that divine power through which all things are possible, God would keep his promise if he fulfilled God's command. And so it happened: by his obedience he gained merit, and the fulfillment of the promise followed. And this was also the case in regard to the Blessed Virgin's resolution.*

*De Mariae virginitate 1; PL 176:870AB

---

even if the marriage was not consummated (Sent 4, d. 27, c. 3.1). Lombard developed his idea of the centrality of consent in connection with the question of how Mary and Joseph were truly married although they remained virgins. Saint Ambrose held that marriage consisted not in the loss of virginity but in the marital agreement (En ev Luke 2.5; PL 15:155A). Aquinas teaches, "Now the form of matrimony consists in a certain inseparable union of souls, by which husband and wife are pledged by a bond of mutual affection that cannot be sundered. And the end of matrimony is the begetting and upbringing of children: the first of which is attained by conjugal intercourse, the second by the other duties of husband and wife, by which they help one another in rearing their offspring. Thus we may say, as to the first perfection, that the marriage of the Virgin Mother of God and Joseph was absolutely true: because both consented to the nuptial bond, but not expressly to the bond of the flesh, save on the condition that it was pleasing to God. . . . But as to the second perfection that is attained by the marriage act, if this be referred to carnal intercourse, by which children are begotten, this marriage was not consummated. . . . Nevertheless, this marriage had the second perfection, as to upbringing of the child" (ST III, q. 29, a. 2).

*R 5 *Anselm has this to say about Mary's espousal:

> She joyfully loved two things: virginity and fruitfulness. She loved virginity because she understood that this was more pleasing to God than anything else. And she loved fruitfulness because she feared that without this she would come under the curse of the law, which was still understood in carnal terms. There was in her heart a hidden but very real struggle between two emotions: love of virginity and fear of the law's condemnation. After a long and fierce conflict, love triumphed and fear was banished. The love of preserving her virginity won the day, and anxiety about the curse of the law left her. This gentle, delicate, and most beautiful Virgin, born of royal stock, devoted all her energy, all her love, all her zeal to this end: that she would consecrate herself body and soul to God in perpetual virginity. She understood that the more fully she dedicated herself in this way, the closer she would approach him who is more chaste than any creature, and indeed is purity itself.
>
> By embracing a way of life that she knew was more acceptable to the Lord of the law, she hoped and believed that she would completely evade the law's curse. God was so good and so wise that Mary felt sure she would incur no sin when he saw that she judged in conscience that there was nothing more generous than this, and that she could in fact do nothing better than what she was doing. Nor was she deceived in this. For who has ever hoped in the Lord and been abandoned?
>
> Indeed, when God beheld such holy intention, such pure desire, such firm faith, such constant hope, and such unfailing charity, he looked upon her with such infinite mercy that her holy intention would not be frustrated, nor would her chaste way of life be dishonored. And lest her firm faith, constant hope, and unfailing charity waver, he hastened to her aid, removing what she dreaded and by his sacred seal guaranteeing that what she loved

would not be taken away. He brought it about that she would remain a virgin, as she so greatly desired, and she would also be fruitful, so that no one could imagine that she came under the curse of the law. He granted her the double gift of being fruitful with child without forfeiting her virginity.*

*Eadmer, De exc 4; PL 159:563BD

Mary's Relatives

*R 6

Because the gospels often mention Mary's relatives, the following background may be helpful. Anne had three husbands in succession: first, Joachim; next, Cleophas, the brother of Joseph; and finally, Salomas. With each husband she had a daughter whom they named Mary. These three Marys in turn each had a husband: Joseph, Alphaeus, and Zebedee. The first Mary gave birth to Jesus; the second gave birth to James the Less, Joseph the Just (also known as Barsabbas), Simon, and Jude; the third gave birth to James the Greater and John the Evangelist. Although James, the son of Zebedee, was born later than the other James, he is known as "the Greater" because he was called earlier by the Lord, so James the son of Alphaeus is "the Less." Among these relatives James and his brothers were known as "brothers of the Lord," because they were not only the offspring of sisters but also (as it was thought) of two brothers, Joseph and Cleophas. James the Less was in particular nicknamed "the brother of the Lord" because he looked like Jesus.[4]

**Hist ev 47; PL 198:1563D*

[4] Ludolph refers to the medieval legend of the *trinubium* found in the *Golden Legend* (Nativity of Mary). "The Holy Kindred" was a popular theme for artists in the fourteenth and fifteenth centuries, but the depiction was prohibited by the Council of Trent. The earliest mention is found in the writings of the ninth-century Haymo of Auxerre (PL 118:823–24).

Why the Lord's Mother Was Married

*R 7

The Lord wanted his mother to have a husband rather than be single for many reasons: some pertain to the child, some pertain to the mother, and some have other causes. Five reasons concern the child. The first reason, according to Jerome, was for the sake of declaring his human ancestry: Mary's origin would be demonstrated through Joseph's genealogy, since they were related, and, following the biblical custom, the genealogy of Christ would be described through the male line. Ambrose says that a second reason was for the sake of removing suspicion, lest there be a shadow of illegitimacy regarding Christ's birth, because the law condemned those born out of wedlock.* This same father suggests another cause, for the sake of removing suspicion, lest it seemed that Herod and others persecuted Jesus justly as one born from adultery and unbelievers rejected him as illegitimate.* The fourth reason, Origen suggests, was for the sake of the child's receiving the care he needed, especially when he had to be taken into Egypt; this is why Joseph could be called "the nourisher of the Lord."* The fifth reason, according to Origen (and Jerome and Basil concur) was for the sake of keeping Christ's birth secret, so that the mystery of the birth of the Son of God would be concealed from the devil, who would suppose that he was born of a wife and not from a virgin.[5]*

*Jerome, Matt 1:18; PL 26:24A; CL 77:10

*En Luke 2.1; PL 15:1553A; CL 14:30

*En Luke 2.2; PL 15:1553B; CL 14:31

*Luke Hom 17.1; PG 13:1843A

*Luke Hom 6.4; PG 13:1815A

*R 8

Similarly, five reasons concern the mother. First, Ambrose suggests, was to ensure that Mary's pregnancy would not be a source of shame; the Lord preferred that there should be some doubt concerning his birth rather than concerning his mother's honor. A

*En Luke 2.1; PL 15:1553A; CL 14:30

[5] Origen in turn attributes the idea to Ignatius of Antioch, citing part of a sentence: "Mary's virginity escaped the notice of the ruler of the age" (Eph 19.1). The reasons given here are briefly presented in Massa.

second reason is proposed by Jerome and Bede: to avoid her being punished, for if the Jews had mistakenly believed that she was guilty of adultery, they would feel justified in stoning her.* The third reason, advanced by both Jerome and Origen, was to provide her with the care she needed, especially during the flight into Egypt and the return journey.* Fourth, the Gloss suggests that this was done to deepen faith in Mary's word: a young, unmarried woman who was found to be pregnant would hardly be believed if she claimed to be a virgin.* Fifth, this was done to embrace every state of life: the mother of the Lord would experience virginity, marriage, and widowhood.

*Jer, Matt 1:18; PL 26:24B; Bede, Matt 1:18; PL 92:12A

*Jer, Matt 1:18; PL 26:24B; Origen: Luke Hom 18.2; PG 13:1848A

*Laon, Matt 1:18; PL 162:1250B

There are five other reasons that Christ's mother was married. Ambrose suggests that it was to remove any excuse for sin, lest virgins who live immodestly or others leading a wicked life could claim that even the mother of the Lord was held in disrepute. Second, Origen teaches that it was to safeguard matrimony against later heretics who condemned marriage; further, the fact that Christ was born of a woman who was both married and a virgin defended both these states of life from heretics who denigrate either of them.* Third, it was to remove the curse that women of every condition had inherited from Eve: virgins, married women, and widows were all delivered by Mary from the opprobrium that was Eve's legacy.

***R 9**

*En Luke 2.1; PL 15:1553A; CL 14:30

*Luke Hom 17; PG 13:1844C

Fourth, to give an example to people who, although legally married, had not yet begun married life, showing that they are free to leave their spouse for the sake of a higher vow by entering religion, in which the soul is espoused to God, for this is what the Blessed Virgin did.

Finally, Chrysostom says that it was done to proclaim the mystery of Christ's own espousal of the church, an ever-virgin bride without stain or wrinkle; we are the offspring of this virgin bride in the faith of Jesus Christ.* As Pope Leo teaches, just as Christ was

*Opus Imperf 1; PG 56:630

*Sermo 29.1; PL 54:227B; CL 38:147
‡R 10

born of the Virgin by the power of the Holy Spirit, so the Christian is born from the womb of the church.* ‡Chrysostom also says that blessed Mary was espoused to a carpenter because Christ, the church's bridegroom, effected the salvation of all people through the wood of his cross,* and Augustine suggests that she married a working man to humble the boastful pride of human nobility. *

*Opus Imperf 1; PG 56:630–31

*De catechizandis 22.40; PL 40:339; CL 46:164

Types of Mary's Betrothal

Our Lady's marriage was prefigured by Raguel's daughter, the virgin Sarah, betrothed to Tobias, who kept her soul free of all lustful desires; how much more did Mary, betrothed to Joseph, do this, because she remained a pure virgin for ever. She was also prefigured by the invincible Tower of Baris described in the *Historia Scholastica*, which was so strong that two sentries could defend it from all attackers; Mary was even stronger and more invincible, because her especial guardian was the eternal Wisdom of God.[6]* Her life can also be compared with the Tower of David, which was protected by a thousand shields that hung from it.* A thousand virtues and more adorn the Virgin Mary; her life was so protected that she overcame all temptation and sin—and she repels these not only from herself but also from others by the outpouring of her grace.*

*Hist sch, Macc 6; PL 198:1527B

*Song 4:4

**SHS 6*

Reflect here on the many holy virgins who lived before and after this blessed Virgin Mary; she alone was found worthy to become the mother of the Lord. What a great and ineffable grace, that this one should be chosen from so many thousands. She was chosen instead of all others because she surpassed all others

[6] The Tower of Baris was built by John Hyrcanus in Jerusalem in the second century BC.

in holiness. Anselm writes, "God, *the searcher of hearts and reins*,* chose and consecrated her alone from among all virgins to be the one in whom he would dwell bodily. He had already favored her with the fullness of virtues and encompassed her spiritually.* I think that anyone who reflects on the matter will realize that she surpassed all other women in sanctity: they deserved to receive some graces, but she was hailed by the angel as *full of grace*."*

*Ps 7:10

*Eadmer, Quatuor 6; PL 159:583D

*Eadmer, Quatuor 7; PL 159:584B

✠

Hail, flowering and fruit-bearing rod of Jesse, most blessed Virgin Mary! You brought forth that unique flower and fruit from whom burst forth the seeds of spiritual virtues: a most fragrant flower, a most delicious and sweet fruit; a flower whose goodness banishes sorrow, a fruit whose taste gives perfect joy. Blessed shoot of the root of Jesse! Blessed blossom, sprung from such a root! Blessed tree, and blessed fruit of the tree! Revive me by your flower, Virgin Mary eternally blessed, and by your fruit deliver me from woe.

CHAPTER 4

The Conception of John the Baptist

(Luke 1:5-25)

*R 1

There was in the days of Herod, the king of Judea, a certain priest named Zachary, of the course of Abia; and his wife was of the daughters of Aaron, and her name Elizabeth. And they were both just before God,* not like hypocrites who feign justice in the world's sight, *walking in all the* moral *commandments and* ceremonial *justifications of the Lord without blame, living at peace with their neighbors. *And they had no son** because of sterility, a condition affecting women, and advanced years, which affects men and women alike.* From this it is clear that the conception of the Forerunner was miraculous: it was brought about not by nature alone, but by nature assisted by grace.

*Luke 1:5-6

*Luke 1:7

**Lyra Luke 1:5-7*

Herod's father was an Idumean, that is, a foreigner. Now that the scepter had been taken from Judah, the time for the Messiah's arrival had come. The patriarch Jacob, with prophetic inspiration, had foretold that the Christ would come when the kingdom of Judah had been transferred to a foreigner, saying, *The sceptre shall not be taken away from Juda, nor a ruler from his thigh, till he come that is to be sent, and he shall be the expectation of nations.**

*Gen 49:10

You should also know that, although Moses instituted only one high priest, to be succeeded by another at death, David wanted to add solemnity to divine worship, so he appointed priests from twenty-four families descended from Aaron. These twenty-four priests exercised their office under the greatest of their number, who was called the high priest.* David also determined that these priests would exercise their office by turns for a week, from Sabbath to Sabbath. During their time of service they remained chaste and did not go to their own homes; rather, they slept in dormitories near the temple, known as *exedrae*.* The weekly rotation was determined by lot, and the eighth week fell to Abijah, from whom this Zechariah descended.* There were also twenty-four Levites from the tribe of Levi who were chosen in the same way and ministered as the priests did.

*Hist ev 1; PL 198:1537B

*Bede Luke 1:8–9 approx; PL 92:310D; CL 120:23

*1 Chr 24:10

According to the custom of the priestly office, it was his lot to offer incense. Zechariah emerged from the room where he had put on the priestly vestments, *going into the temple of the Lord* on the tenth day of the seventh month. *And all the multitude of the people was praying outside, at the hour of incense;** they were not permitted to enter the temple, but only the courtyard. *From this description it is clear that Zechariah was an ordinary priest, not the high priest. It says that he went into the temple only to offer incense, which was the task of the lesser priests; the apostle tells us that these priests entered the first part of the tabernacle every day to offer sacrifices.* This daily sacrifice was offered at the vestibule of the temple on the altar of holocausts, where the lesser priests ministered; one of them then took coals from this altar and went into the first tabernacle, called the *Holy Place*, and offered incense on the altar. This was how the offering was consummated: sacrifices of the old law were accepted only because of the faith and devotion of the offerers, and this was signified by the burnt incense.*

*Luke 1:9-10

R 2

*Heb 9:6

*Lyra Luke 1:9 approx

The high priest alone entered that part of the temple called the *Holy of Holies*, and only on one day in the year, with the blood of goats and calves that had been sacrificed for the sins of the people; this he sprinkled toward the propitiatory. It does not say that Zechariah entered with such a blood-offering, but only to offer incense; hence we read that the angel of the Lord was

*Luke 1:11 *standing on the right side of the altar of incense,** which is also called the golden altar. This altar was not in the *Holy of Holies* but in the first chamber of the temple, where ordinary priests were allowed to go. The high priest alone was permitted to burn incense in the *Holy of Holies* on the Day of Atonement; this was not in the nature of a sacrifice, but to create a cloud enveloping the propitiatory while he sprinkled the blood of goats and calves. No historians who describe the Jewish priesthood make mention of the high priesthood of Zechariah.[1]*

**Lyra Luke 1:9 approx*

‡R 3 ‡Zechariah, whose name means *mindful of the Lord*, can represent a good pastor, who should carry the memory of God in his heart, both for his own welfare and for the sake of his subjects.[2] He enters the temple by his diligent attention to divine worship and offers incense through devout prayer, and the people pray through his guidance.*

**Lyra Luke 1:8 mor*

He should have a threefold memory of God: God's power, which pertains to creation; his wisdom, which pertains to re-creation; and his goodness, which pertains to reward and punishment. The first refers to the Father, the second to the Son, the third to the Holy Spirit.*

**Gorran Luke 1:5*

The Angel

*R 4 **And there appeared to him an angel of the Lord,* Gabriel, *standing on the right side of the altar of incense.* When Zechariah saw this, *fear fell upon him.** He was fright-

*Luke 1:11-12

[1] The *Protoevangelium of James* 23–24 did identify Zechariah as high priest.

[2] Jerome interprets *Zechariah* as *memory of the Lord* (Int nom; PL 23:1156; CL 72:138).

ened by the noble and mighty appearance of this being, but a good spirit can be distinguished from an evil one in this way: in the case of a wicked angel, the dread continues, and there is no better weapon to overcome this, Bede suggests, than an intrepid faith; but a good spirit immediately offers comfort and consolation.* Accordingly, the angel immediately reassured him, saying, "*Fear not, Zachary*, I have come for your consolation," and quickly added, "*for your prayer is heard*."* Zechariah had not been praying for a child: he and his wife were of such advanced years that they had given up any hope of this, so he did not believe that the angel meant this. Rather, he interpreted him to mean that his prayer had been heard for the sins of the people, and redemption, and the coming of the Messiah. But because the people's salvation was to come through Christ, the angel then told Zechariah he was to have a son who would prepare them for the Savior by preaching faith and repentance.*

*Com Luke 1:12; PL 92:311C; CL 120:24

*Luke 1:13

Augustine, Quaest Ev 2.1 approx; PL 35:1333A; CL 44B:41

He also told him that the boy was to be called John, a name meaning *in whom there is grace*. John himself would make Christ known, for *grace and truth came by Jesus Christ*.* Bede writes, "John is interpreted *in whom there is grace* or *the grace of the Lord*. This name refers first to the grace bestowed on the parents, who received the gift of a child in their old age; then to John himself, who would be great before the Lord and would be enriched by the gift of the Holy Spirit while still in his mother's womb; and finally to many of the children of Israel, who would be converted to the Lord their God."*

*John 1:17

*Bede Luke 1:13–16; PL 92:312A; CL 120:25

The angel said the father would experience inner *joy and* outward *gladness*.‡ The word *exsultatio* is used, meaning to "jump for joy" as it were, *extra saltatio*: when inner rejoicing is so great that it must find outward expression.[3] Gabriel promised that many others

‡Luke 1:14

[3] Albert attributes this etymology to Cassiodorus (*Com Matt 5:12*).

would also experience joy at John's birth, and this proved true—many *rejoiced with her** when Elizabeth's child was born. And we see the promise still fulfilled today, because the nativity of John the Baptist is a great feast not only for all Christians, but also for Saracens and some other peoples.[4]*

*Luke 1:58

**Lyra Luke 1:14*

Bede says, "Rightly did the father rejoice, either to have a son so late in life or to have received one so blessed with graces. Others were to rejoice when this child proclaimed what had formerly been unheard of: the coming of the kingdom of heaven."* And Ambrose writes, "There is a solemn joy in the birth and begetting of the just; a saint is not only the grace of the parents, but the salvation/health of many others.[5] Thus we are enjoined in this passage to rejoice in the birth of the saints."*

*Com, Luke 1:14; PL 92:312A; CL 120:25

*Exp Luke 1.29; PL 15:1545D; CL 14:21

‡R 5

‡There are moral lessons to be drawn from the story of Zechariah and his wife Elizabeth, who brought forth a child for him, whom they named John, a boy at whose birth they and many others rejoiced. Elizabeth, Zechariah's wife, can represent the flesh united to the spirit: just as a husband guides and directs his wife, so the spirit should guide and direct the flesh lest it become lascivious and fall into the sin of fornication. She brings forth for him a child when the spirit acting through the flesh performs the corporal works of mercy—giving alms, clothing the naked, feeding the hungry, visiting the sick, burying the dead, and so on. Then in truth is *your wife as a fruitful vine, on the sides of your house.** This child is called John, meaning *the grace of God,* because we should not ascribe any good

*Ps 127:3

[4] *Saracens* refers to Muslims, who revere John as a prophet; a variation of the account of Zechariah in the temple appears in the Quran 19:4–10.

[5] The Latin word *salus* means both health and salvation. Often Ludolph uses the word for both, so it is translated this way throughout the text.

actions to ourselves, but only to God's grace. This child brings joy and gladness to its parents, because our good works bring light and joy to our minds. And many others rejoice too, because virtuous people find joy in the good their neighbors do. Let us, then, keep special watch over ourselves, that while we rejoice outwardly and dance bodily, we are also rejoicing inwardly in our souls, so that the remnants of our thoughts may shape a feast day for the Lord. It is not for the impious to rejoice, says the Lord, nor sinners in the presence of sinners.* Therefore, let us purge our souls of the stains of sin so that we can worthily celebrate the joy of such a great solemnity.*

*Isa 57:20-21

**Innocent III, Sermo 19, in Festo S. Ioannis approx; PL 217:542D–44B*

John's Greatness

*The angel also predicted that the child would be *great before the Lord* * in virtue, holiness, and dignity. This greatness consists of four things, according to the four dimensions: in the height of his behavior, the depth of his humility, the breadth of his charity, and the length of his final perseverance. This is what the apostle prayed for: *You may be able to comprehend, with all the saints, what is the breadth and length and height and depth.** The Savior himself would later testify, *There has not risen among them that are born of women a greater than John the Baptist.** But the angel went on to specify John's manifold greatness, enumerating his numerous privileges in turn. He foretold a life of abstinence: he *shall drink no wine nor strong* inebriating *drink,** for it was not fitting that a vessel formed to receive heavenly grace should be given over to earthly enticements. From this the angel clearly indicated that John would be far removed from all the wickedness and worldly vice that customarily wreak havoc with the mind. The angel went on to say that *he shall be filled with the Holy Spirit even from his mother's womb,** that

R 6
*Luke 1:15
*Eph 3:18
*Matt 11:11
*Luke 1:15
*Luke 1:15

is, cleansed of original sin and capable of performing meritorious good works.[6] These words certainly show that when John came into the world he would be illustrious because of his many virtues.

Then he foretold that John *shall convert many of the children of Israel to the Lord,** that is, to Christ, by preaching and bearing witness to him. In addition, he predicted that John *shall go before him in the spirit and power of Elijah** in several ways: first, by a similar vocation, for just as Elijah would prepare the way for the second coming of Christ, so John prepared for his first coming; second, by their manner of life, because both were renowned for great austerity in food and clothing; third, by similar teaching, because both men rebuked vice even in the lives of powerful rulers.*

*Luke 1:16

*Luke 1:17

**Lyra Luke 1:17*

John had to go before Christ *that he may turn the hearts of the fathers to the children* by the understanding of Scripture, *and the incredulous to the wisdom of the just* by the obedience of faith, *to prepare unto the Lord a perfect people** by their accepting the grace of the Gospel and the New Testament, because the ancient law could not lead anyone to perfection. This is why it was known as the law of fear, because the imperfect are motivated to avoid evil by the fear of punishment; but the Gospel precept is called the law of love, because the perfect are moved to turn from evil by love of the good.

*Luke 1:17

Finally, just as such a remarkable child was born to a very elderly couple, so it is not uncommon that people who are advanced in years and sterile in good works can, by a gift of the Holy Spirit, at length bear

[6] On the basis of biblical texts that speak of their being sanctified in the womb, it has been devoutly believed by many that Jeremiah and John the Baptist were freed from original sin before they were born. This is theological opinion, not official church teaching. Aquinas discusses this briefly in ST III, q. 27, a. 6.

fruit in the church of God. Augustine and Dionysius are sterling examples of men who came to faith in Christ later in life.[7]* *Lyra Luke 1:36 mor

Zechariah Is Struck Mute; Elizabeth Conceives

Given his wife's sterility and their advanced age, Zechariah did not believe the angel's words, and so he was struck mute until the day of John's birth; this symbolizes that with the coming of Christ, the law and the prophets are fulfilled and become silent. Chrysostom says, "Therefore Zechariah, one of the Jewish priests, loses his speech because the sacrifices they had been offering for the sins of the people must now cease and become silent. The one true Priest was coming who would offer himself to God as the Lamb of sacrifice for the sins of all people." ***R 7**

*attr. to Chrys by Bede, Luke 1:20; PL 92:314D; CL 120:27

The fact that Zechariah became mute when he doubted signifies that the tongue of one who doubts the faith is silenced because his prayer is not acceptable to God. And the fact that he was speechless after experiencing an angelic revelation suggests that a person who experiences a vision or revelation should hold his tongue and not proudly boast about it.‡ ‡*Lyra Luke 1:18 mor*

And it came to pass, after the days of his office were accomplished, he departed to his own house, as the priests were not permitted to do while they were ministering. The priests observed chastity during their time of service, and, in accord with God's directive, they did not drink wine or any other intoxicating beverage. ***R 8** *Luke 1:23

[7] Lyra is probably referring to Dionysius the Areopagite, who was converted by Saint Paul in Athens (Acts 17:34). He was subsequently wrongly identified as the third-century bishop and martyr of Paris and with an influential Eastern spiritual author of the fifth or sixth century.

Now if the priests of the law observed such continence, abstinence, and reverence in relation to holy things, how much more should the priests of the Gospel do so, because they consecrate the sacrament itself. The Jewish priests served in the temple for an entire week, remaining there and devoting themselves completely to divine matters and not leaving to engage in external affairs.

From this practice there has arisen in some religious communities the holy and honorable office of the *hebdomadarian*, who remains within the cloister for an entire week. He does not go out to engage in business but gives all of his attention to divine matters, acting as a kind of intermediary between God and the com-

Lyra Luke 1:23 munity.* In some other communities it is customary for the *hebdomadarian* to abstain from community recreation, and, among some secular canons, to sleep in the common dormitory during his week of service.[8]

***R 9** **And after those days, Elizabeth his wife conceived* on Thursday, the twenty-fourth of September, and, because of her advanced years and modesty, *she hid her-*

*Luke 1:24 *self five months** until Mary conceived and her child could prophesy by leaping in the womb.[9] Although she rejoiced that the stigma of sterility had been removed from her, Elizabeth was a little embarrassed, lest it be thought that in advanced age she had given herself over to desires of the flesh. (It was not customary for elderly people to engage in sexual relations when they were beyond childbearing age.) Bede says, "Elizabeth shows us how careful holy people must be to avoid behavior that makes them ashamed, because

[8] The *hebdomadarian* (from the Greek word for *week*) is the person who presides over liturgical services for a week in a monastic or religious community.

[9] The Eastern Church has an ancient feast of the Conception of John the Baptist on September 23; in some Western martyrologies this is commemorated on September 24.

she blushed even when she received a gift that she greatly desired."*

*Com, Luke 1:24; PL 92:314D; CL 120:28

Reflect here on how Elizabeth was chagrined before others even regarding a permissible circumstance, and make certain that you avoid anything that would cause you to be embarrassed, not only in the sight of other people, but before God and his angels. According to Boethius, our lives should be marked by uprightness and probity, because all that we do is done before the eyes of a Judge who sees everything.* Augustine writes, "God attends to everything I do; he is the vigilant inspector of all my thoughts, intentions, and actions. When I reflect seriously on this truth, I am fearful and greatly ashamed. He is present everywhere, and he sees my most secret thoughts; there is much in me that causes me to blush in God's sight."‡ Anselm says quite simply, "You sin when you are not aware that God is present."* And a verse has it,

*Cons V prosa 6; PL 63:862C; CL 94:105

‡Ps-Augustine, spiritu 17; PL 40:793

*Ps-Anselm, Ad contemptum; PL 158:684A; Isidore, Synonyma 2.59; PL 83:859A; CL 111B:110–11

> When I see you sin, you turn red with shame;
> Should you not blush more when God sees the
> same?†

†Ps-Anselm [Roger of Caen], Carmen de contemptu mundi; PL 158:690D

It is a human trait to blush with embarrassment when we do something disgraceful. Shameless people are called incorrigible because in some way they have lost the dignity of reason and assumed the nature of pigs, acting brazenly among rational people.

✠

Holy John, your conception was announced by the same angel who announced Christ's, and he praised you before your birth; indeed, God himself said that there was no man born of woman greater than you. Uncertain of my salvation, I fly to your protection, O good, blessed, and great benefactor.

I know my faults are many, but I hope that your grace will be even greater. Blot out my iniquities before God, because your merits in his sight are surpassing. So abundant are your merits, great Saint John, that they suffice for both of us, and my profiting from them means no loss to you. Let your abundance supply my need so that, enriched and saved through you, I may rejoice for ever. Amen.

CHAPTER 5

The Savior's Conception
(Luke 1:26-38)

*R 1

**And in the sixth month* after the Forerunner's conception, the fullness of the most blessed and joyful of times had arrived, that is, the beginning of the sixth age, ordained by the most holy Trinity before all time for the restoration of the human race by the incarnation of the Word. The omnipotent God summoned *the angel Gabriel*, one of the foremost princes in his realm, and sent him *into a city of Galilee, called Nazareth, to a virgin espoused to a man* of her lineage *whose name was Joseph, of the house of David, and the virgin's name was Mary*.* They were both of David's house, of royal stock, noble lineage, and surpassing others in religious devotion, as Bernard says.* It pleased God to reconcile us by the same means and in the same order by which we had fallen. According to Bede, humankind fell through the devil's design, the serpent's deed, the ensuing dialogue, and the woman's consent; the repair was done by God's design, the angel's deed, the ensuing dialogue, and the Virgin's consent.[1]* He also says that the account of this mystery is so filled with meaning that we should attend to the words most carefully: the more deeply they are pondered, the more clear it

*Luke 1:26-27; *Massa*

**Bruno Luke 1:3; PL 165:340B*

*Hom ev 1.1; PL 94:9B [1.3; CL 122:14]

[1] The thought is Bede's, but the poetic expression is not: *diabolo destinante, serpente exequente, dialogo interveniente, muliere consentiente*.

becomes that the whole mystery of our salvation is contained in them.*

*Hom ev 1; PL 94:11C [1.3; CL 122:16]

So let us attentively examine the beginnings of our salvation. Notice first that the number six is not without spiritual meaning. Inasmuch as this number signifies perfection, Christ was conceived at the beginning of the sixth age, because all things were to be perfected through him; in the sixth millennium, because the number one thousand is the limit of all numbers and Christ is the limit and end of all things; in the sixth month, because the world was made in that month and it was to be remade through him who had first made it; and on the sixth day, because man and woman were created on this day, and after the Fall they had to be re-created through him who had made them. And, for the same reason, thirty-three years later he suffered in the same age, the same millennium, the same month, and the same day of the week. And perhaps (so that all things might be in harmony), it could be that he was conceived at the sixth hour: that was the hour when he suffered, and it was also the hour when the first man sinned. By a fitting congruence, Mary was instructed by the angel at the same hour that Eve had been seduced by the devil.[2]

[2] Ludolph presents the numeric symbolism of the ancient world and early Christianity. The number six was considered perfect because it was the sum of its factors (1 + 2 + 3 = 6), a point dwelt on at some length by Augustine in his interpretation of Genesis. The six ages were derived from the six days of creation, because to God a thousand years are like a day (2 Pet 3:8); Augustine associated these with Old Testament history: from Adam to Noah, from Noah to Abraham, from Abraham to David, from David to the Babylonian Captivity, from the Captivity to the birth of Mary, and the sixth age being ushered in by Christ. In Christian antiquity, Christ's death was said to have taken place on March 25, a date associated both with his conception and with the creation of Adam and Eve, because Creation itself was associated with the vernal equinox.

***R 2**

**The angel Gabriel was sent*, whose name means *strength of God*, to announce that the strength and the wisdom of God was appearing in humble form to vanquish the powers of the air; it was fitting that one from the ranks of the archangels announced such great tidings.* He *was sent from God*. The God who sent him was the whole Trinity, although this is attributed especially to the Father. The Father sent the angel, because his providence governed the Son, the bride, and the mother; but the Son also sent the angel, because he himself was to come to the Virgin; and the Holy Spirit sent the angel, because he was to overshadow and sanctify her. He *was sent into a city of Galilee*, a name that means *carrying away*, because Christ was to be taken away from the incredulity of the Jews and given to the belief of the Gentiles.[3] *Galilee* has a double reference: there is *Galilee of the Gentiles* adjoining Tyre, which Solomon gave to King Hiram,* and there is *Galilee of the Jews* on the Sea of Galilee; the latter is what is meant here. He was sent to a city *called Nazareth*,* a name meaning *flower*.[4]

**Zachary 1.3; PL 186:54A*

*1 Kgs 9:11

*Luke 1:26

This was an appropriate name because the true flower, Christ, was conceived *in* the flower (Nazareth), and *from* the flower (the Blessed Virgin), and *with* the flowers (in springtime). Jesus is called a flower on account of the beauty and grace of his conduct, the sweet fragrance of his good reputation, the fruit produced by his passion, and the usefulness of his example to the faithful. This bloom budded at his conception, blossomed at his birth, withered at his passion, and finally blossomed again at his resurrection. If you want to pick this flower, imitate the beauty of

[3] Jerome renders *Galilee* as *volutabilis* (roll, think over), *transmigratio perpetrata* (removal accomplished), *rota* (rotate, wheel); Int nom; PL 23:844; CL 72:140.

[4] Jerome renders *Nazareth* as *flower, shrubbery, clean, separated,* or *protected* (Int nom; PL 23:842; CL 72:137).

his behavior and spread abroad the fragrance of his actions—in this way you will possess the fruit of his passion. Unlike earthly kings, the Lord did not choose a great city as the site for the nuptials at which he was to unite himself with our human nature. No, he chose the modest village of Nazareth to give us an example of humility and instruct us always to choose the lowest place; but he chose to suffer in the metropolis of Jerusalem to teach us not to blush when we endure shame for his sake before the multitude.

Mary the Virgin

*R 3
‡Luke 1:27

*The angel was sent *to a virgin*‡—and not to just any virgin but to a woman who was pledged to virginity in mind and body by a vow. Christ chose to be conceived and born of a virgin. First, according to Bernard, because it was fitting that if God was to be conceived and born, he would be conceived and born of a virgin, and if a virgin was to conceive and give birth, she would conceive and give birth only to God.* Second, according to John Damascene, so that he who had a Father but no mother in heaven would have on earth a mother without a father.* Third, according to Augustine, because the members of his Mystical Body would be born of the virgin church according to the Spirit, it was fitting that the Head of the Body should be born of a virgin.* Fourth, so that just as the first Adam was formed from the virginal earth, so the second Adam would take flesh from the Virgin. Fifth, so that just as the ruin of the human race was brought about by the virgin Eve, so its restoration might be brought about through the Virgin Mary.

*Laudibus 2.1; PL 183:61D; SB 4:21

*Augustine Tr John 26.10; PL 35:1611; CL 36:264

*Virginitate 6; PL 40:399

*Luke 1:27

To a virgin, it says, *who was espoused to a man*.* Why Christ chose to be conceived and born of a woman who was engaged was considered earlier, when we spoke about the Virgin Mary's betrothal. Bernard says that he was called a man* not because he was married to her, but because he was strong and courageous, and thus a legitimate witness.[5]* His *name was Joseph,*‡ meaning *increase,* which suggests an increase of virtue, indeed, a constantly growing virtue.

*vir

*Laudibus 2.15; PL 183:69B; SB 4:32

‡Luke 1:27

Note that there are four illustrious biblical figures named Joseph. The first is Jacob's son, famed for his prudence because he wisely interpreted Pharaoh's dreams. The second is Joseph, Mary's husband, noted for his temperance because he honored Mary's virginity. The third is Joseph of Arimathea, renowned for his fortitude because he boldly went to Pilate and asked for Jesus' body. The fourth is Joseph Barsabbas, so celebrated for his justice that he was surnamed *Justus.** It was fitting that the man espoused to the Virgin should have a name that embraced the mystery of all the virtues. The evangelist adds *of the house of David** to indicate that Christ was descended from David's seed, as the prophets had foretold. True, Joseph was not the Savior's father, but the Virgin Mary, from whom he took flesh, belonged, like Joseph, to David's house.

*Acts 1:23

*Luke 1:27

*The evangelist rightly adds *and the virgin's name was Mary.** This venerable name has three meanings in three languages: in Hebrew, *star of the sea* or *illuminatrix;* in Latin, *bitter sea;* in Syriac, *lady* or *sovereign.** Mary was the *star of the sea* at the birth of her son, for then she brought forth a ray of light that illuminated the whole world; she was a *bitter sea* during her son's passion, for then a sword pierced her heart; but she was *sovereign* at her assumption, for then she was exalted above all the angelic choirs.

***R 4**

*Luke 1:27

**Gorran Luke 1:27*

Mary is also called *star of the sea* because of the guidance she offers sinners: she directs them through the sea of this world to the harbor of repentance and so

[5] The word *vir* can mean a man, a husband, or a courageous person.

leads them to her son. And just as a star appeared to the magi at Christ's birth that led them to the newborn child, so the eyes of all sinners are fixed on her, like the eyes of sailors on the lodestar. Bernard writes,

> Do not avert your eyes from the brightness of this star if you want to avoid being overwhelmed in the gale. O you, whoever you may be, if you feel that in the storms of life you have lost your footing and are tempest-tossed, gaze up at this star and call out to Mary. When you are buffeted by the waves of pride, ambition, slander, or jealousy, gaze up at this star and call out to Mary. When rage, or greed, or carnal desires batter the skiff of your soul, gaze upon this star and call out to Mary. When the sheer weight of your sins threatens shipwreck, when the loathsomeness of your conscience confuses you, when terror of infernal regions threatens to drown you, gaze upon this star and call out to Mary. In dangers, in hardships, in all doubtful matters think of Mary and invoke her; let her never be absent from your lips or your heart.
>
> Do not ignore the example of her life, so that you may receive the support of her prayers. When you follow her, you will never go astray; when you ask her help, you will never despair; when you think of her, you will never be wrong. With her holding your hand, you will not stumble; with her protecting you, you need not fear; with her guiding you, you will not weary: she will propitiously lead you to port. Then you yourself will know by experience how fitting it is that *the virgin's name was Mary*, the star of the sea.*

*Laudibus 2.17; PL 183:70D; SB 4:34–35

Again, her name is interpreted as *illuminatrix*, because the whole world is illuminated by the splendor of grace and the example of her most holy life. Hence the church sings of her, "whose renowned life illumines all the churches."* Apropos of this, Bernard asks, "Take away the sun, where is the day? Take away

*Antiphon, Nativity of Mary; PL 78:902C

Mary, this star of the sea, and what is left but dark clouds, the shadow of death, and impenetrable darkness?"* *Aquaeductu 6; PL 183:441B; SB 5:279

Clearly she is the star of the sea, of this dark ocean where *there are creeping things without number*.* The heavens are adorned with countless stars, the sea has but one—but she is far brighter and better than all the rest, gleaming with merits and enlightening by example. From her alone was born the Sun of Justice, who sheds his rays on all creation: *Whoever follows me walks not in darkness, but shall have the light of life*.* How can we gauge the splendor of the star who brought forth so great and mighty a Sun for this world? Whoever follows this star cannot go astray or be lost.‡ *Ps 103:25 *John 8:12 ‡*Bruno Luke 1:27; PL 165:340C–41A*

*Mary is also the *bitter sea* for the conversion of sinners as she intercedes for them to turn away from their sins, changing the water of earthly pleasures into the wine of compunction. This name is also appropriate to her inasmuch as it refers to this present age, which to her was bitter because of her desire to see her son in his kingdom. And her name derives from the Latin *mare*, in that in her is found the confluence of all graces, just as all rivers empty into the sea. ***R 5**

*Finally, she is *sovereign* in assisting us in temptation and liberating us from difficulties when they assail us. She is both ready and able to come to our assistance because she is Queen of Heaven and Mother of Mercy. She exercises her sovereignty not only over people on earth but also over the angels in heaven and the devils in hell: this is why Mary should be invoked not only in time of temptation but also when the demons assail us. According to Bernard, visible enemies do not fear a vast throng encamped against them in battle array so much as the powers of the air fear the name, the patronage, and the example of Mary.* Just as dust scatters before the wind and wax melts in the presence of fire, so the demons flee and perish when Mary's name is invoked. He says, "The demons take flight when ***R 6** *Attr. to Bernard in Conrad of Saxony, Speculum BVM 3

Mary's name is spoken. The guilty are pardoned, the sick are healed, the wavering are strengthened, the afflicted are consoled, and strangers are assisted."* The three interpretations of her name can also be understood in this way: the *bitter sea*, as a type of those living in the world; the *star* or *illumination*, as a model for those who follow the contemplative vocation; and *sovereign* as an example for leaders.

*Sermo in assumptione 4.9; PL 183:430A; SB 5:250

*R 7

The angel Gabriel was sent to Mary to announce that the Son of God was drawn by her beauty and had chosen her to be his mother, and to induce her to accept him joyfully as her son because God had decreed that the salvation of the whole human race was to be effected through her. So Bernard says,

**Massa*

> How blessed was Mary, who lacked neither humility nor virginity!* So that she might conceive and give birth to the Holy of Holies she was sanctified in her body by accepting the gift of virginity, and in her soul by accepting the gift of humility. This royal maiden, adorned with the jewels of these virtues, resplendent with matchless beauty in both mind and body, so captivated the citizens of the heavenly court that the heart of the king himself was drawn to her and he sent down from on high a heavenly messenger.‡
>
> *And the angel being come in.** Come in where? Into the private corner of her little room, I suppose, where, perhaps, behind closed doors she was praying to her Father in secret. There is no reason to think that the angel found the Virgin's door open—she clearly intended to flee from human company and avoid conversation, lest the silence of one given to prayer be disturbed and the purity of one vowed to virginity be tested. Surely that most prudent Virgin had closed the door of her private room to people, but not to angels.*

*Laudibus 1.9; PL 183:60; SB 4:20

‡Laudibus 2.2; PL 183:62A; SB 4:22

*Luke 1:28

*Laudibus 3.1; PL 183:71C; SB 4:36; *Massa*

Mary was not to be found in the village square or lingering in public places. She remained within, sitting by herself in the inner recesses of the house; but because she was surrounded by such a host of angels, she was hardly alone.*

Bruno Luke 1:28; PL 165:341A; Massa

John Chrysostom writes, "The angel did not find Mary wandering about outside, but given over to undistracted contemplation in solitude. Because she was not seeking the world's applause, she found God's grace."* And Ambrose, "When the angel went in he found her alone in the innermost part of the house, lest her prayer be interrupted. She felt no need for female companions because her good thoughts kept her company. She never felt less alone than when she was alone. How could she feel lonely in the company of good books, archangels, and prophets? In fact, Gabriel returned to her in her place of solitude."* And Jerome, "You have a room you can occupy by yourself, but you will not be alone there; a host of angels dwells with you. Read the gospels, let Jesus converse with you; re-read the apostles or the prophets. Could you have better companions than their words?"* And Bernard, "I am never less alone than when I am alone."‡

*Gottfried of Admont, Hom 27 approx; PL 174:750D; *Massa*

*De virginibus 2.10–11; PL 16:210A; CSP 1:39

*Ep 18.4; PL 30:186B

‡Ambrose, Ep 49.1; PL 16:1153D

It is certainly believable that she was then completely absorbed in devout prayer or intimate contemplation, and perhaps meditating particularly on the idea that a virgin would be instrumental in the salvation of the human race. In fact, there are those who say that at that very moment she was reading the words of the prophet Isaiah, *Behold a virgin shall conceive*.* It is reasonable that when the eternal Word wished to unite himself with her bodily, she was already spiritually one with him in contemplation.

*Isa 7:14

*And so the angel came to the Virgin as she was abiding in her bridal chamber behind locked doors. He appeared to her as a bodily vision in human form and said, *Hail, full of grace, the Lord is with you; blessed are you among women.** The angel appeared in human form to teach by example and to announce that by the working of the Holy Spirit, God was to become incarnate. It was fitting that he should appear in visible form to announce that the invisible God was to take

***R 8**

*Luke 1:28

a visible body from the Virgin. The angel made for himself a body of light; Augustine says that he appeared to the Virgin with a glowing countenance and shining vesture.* It was appropriate that the incarnation of the Word was announced to the Virgin, so that she could conceive in her heart before she conceived in her body. Then the angel, changing Eve's name, said to the Virgin, *Ave*, indicating that she was free of all woe.[6]

*Ps-Augustine, Sermo 195.2; PL 39:2108

And it is well that she is described as *full of grace*, because grace is given to all others according to some measure, but to her uniquely was given the grace that no other creature was worthy to receive, to carry the author of grace.* If she was full of grace even before conceiving him, who can imagine what grace of God she would receive after his conception? Accordingly, Jerome says, "It is right to say *full*, because to others grace is given piecemeal, but the fullness of grace is given all at once to Mary alone. Truly she through whom the Holy Spirit has poured down a shower of gifts upon all creatures is *full of grace*."* She has given glory to heaven, God to earth, peace to humanity, faith to the nations, an end to vice, an order to life, reform to morals.*

**Ambrose, Exp Luke 2.9; PL 15:1556A; CL 14:34*

*Radbertus; PL 30:127A [5.28; CM 56C:121]

*Chrysologus, Sermo 143; PL 52:583C

The Angelic Salutation

*The angel continued, *The Lord is with you*,‡ that is, "May he be in your body who is already in your soul; may the one who fills your heart now dwell in your womb. He is not only with you through his essence, his power, and his presence, as he is in all things; nor only through his grace, by which he dwells in holy

R 9
‡Luke 1:28

[6] Ludolph alludes to a verse in the ancient hymn, *Ave, Maris Stella*: "*Sumens illud Ave Gabrielis ore, funda nos in pace, mutans Hevae nomen.*" *A-vae* means "free from woe" in Latin.

men and women; but also through the flesh he assumes from your most pure blood."* Note here that, even though the angel's entire greeting was most pleasing to the Virgin, this short phrase, *The Lord is with you*, gave her especial delight, and so it must have been uttered with singular devotion; granted that he was already with her, the angel was sent with the novel tidings that the Lord was now to be with her in a unique way. **Lyra Luke 1:28*

Then he says in praise of her, "*Blessed are you among all women** and above all women." Every woman comes under the malediction of either God or the law: if she is not a virgin, she comes under the sentence of God, *In sorrow you shall bring forth children;** if she remains a virgin, she is condemned by the law for her sterility. But Mary evaded both curses: God's, by remaining a virgin; the law's, by bearing a child. Therefore, this first of consecrated virgins, by dedicating her virginity to God, rescinded the law's reproach; she through whom the world was delivered from malediction is deservedly called blessed. *Luke 1:28 *Gen 3:16

Here I must observe that no one could ever improve upon this salutation, nor is there a more excellent, sweet, or pleasing way to greet the Blessed Virgin than with these words that God the Father himself uttered and dispatched an angel to address to her. A host of mysteries is entwined in each and every word. God the Father, by virtue of his omnipotence, arranged that Mary should be immune from woe, as the word *Ave* suggests. God the Son in his wisdom so adorned her that she became a brilliant star illuminating heaven and earth, as her name, *Mary* (*stella maris*) indicates. And the Holy Spirit, imbuing her with all his divine sweetness, made her by his grace so highly favored that everyone seeking grace through her will find it, as the words *full of grace* attest. The words *the Lord is with you* call to mind the ineffable activity of union the Holy Trinity wrought in her, when the substance of the divine nature was united with her flesh in one Person, so that God might become Man, and we human creatures might become God. The clause *blessed are you among women* expresses the wonder of all creation at the realization that she is blessed and exalted above all creatures, both heavenly and earthly. Finally, in the words *blessed is the fruit of your womb*, the most excellent offspring of her virginal womb is blessed and extolled: he who gives life and holiness to every creature now and will bless them in eternity.[7]*

**Mechtild, Lib specialis 42*

‡R 10

‡Having heard the angel's greeting, Mary *was troubled** and did not respond. The source of her disquiet was not disbelief, as it had been for Zechariah, nor was it due to anything blameworthy. Nor was it the sight of the angel, because she was used to seeing angels.* Rather, she was troubled first, according to Chrysostom, by the splendor of this novel apparition: she was accustomed to angelic visitors, but this one appeared in a new form, in human shape and possessing remarkable brilliance.* This startled her, a reaction noted in the liturgy: "The Virgin was frightened by the light."* Second, because of the modesty of her virginal purity; for, as Ambrose says, it is customary for maidens to tremble every time a man comes in, and to shrink back when he addresses them.* Third, because of the novel form of his salutation, as Ambrose

*Luke 1:29

**Lyra Luke 1:29*

*source unknown

*Antiphon for Matins, Annunciation; PL 86:1297C

*Exp Luke 2.8; PL 15:1555C; CL 14:34

[7] The "Hail Mary" in Ludolph's day included only the phrases he comments on here; the name of Jesus and the second half of the prayer as we know it were added later. The combination of these biblical texts appears in liturgical antiphons as far back as the seventh century, and several medieval authors wrote commentaries on this prayer. The recitation of the "angelic salutation" grew in popularity throughout the Middle Ages, linked especially to meditation on the mysteries of Christ through the recitation of the rosary. The Carthusians and Dominicans both played an important part in the development of this devotion, and it is likely that the *Vita Christi* influenced the shaping of the rosary mysteries, at least indirectly.

also notes: "She marveled at the strange form of blessing, nowhere revealed before; this greeting was reserved for Mary alone."* Fourth, because of high praise addressed to her by the angel's words: such is the view of the humble that the more highly they are praised, the more uncomfortable they become.*

*Exp Luke 2.9; PL 15:1556A; CL 14:34

**Massa*

Mary's virtuous and sound modesty was thrown into confusion, but she was not perturbed. So, as one who was prudent and careful, and completely modest, she gave no answer,* pondering within herself the novelty of this greeting and carefully weighing its words; the angels were not accustomed to greet her in this way, nor had she ever heard such words before. Given the three things the angel said to her, it would be impossible for our Lady in her humility not to be troubled. He had told her that she was full of grace, that the Lord was with her, and that she was blessed above all other women. This humble maiden could not help but blush and be confused at hearing such things, because truly modest people feel embarrassed and ill at ease when they are praised and honored. According to Bernard, "That she was troubled is only virginal modesty. That she was not distressed shows courage; that she was silent and reflective shows prudence and discretion."*

**Massa; MVC 4; CM 153:20*

*Laudibus 3.9; PL 183:76A; SB 4:42; *MVC 4*; CM 153:20

‡Then the angel looked at the Virgin, and, discerning the thoughts running through her mind and knowing the cause of her disquiet, he sought to alleviate her dread and calm her fear. He called her by name to show that he was familiar with her and gently urged her not to be alarmed, saying, "*Fear not, Mary,* and do not blush at the words of praise I speak to you, for they are true. Not only are you full of grace, but you have restored grace abundantly to the whole human race, *for you have found grace with God* * that no other creature has obtained." It was as if he said, in Chrysostom's opinion, that anyone who had gained such grace from God need fear nothing.* How did she

‡R 11

*Luke 1:30

*CA Luke 1:30–33

come to deserve this grace? Certainly by her humility, her chaste modesty, and her pure conscience. About the first of these qualities Chrysostom says, "How can anyone find grace except through humility, for *God gives grace to the humble*."* Of the other two virtues, Gregory writes, "She found favor with God because she prepared a dwelling place pleasing to God by the splendor of the chastity that adorned her spirit. Not only did she retain her virginity inviolate, but she also kept her conscience free of stain."* Truly, Mary, *you have found grace*: peace between God and humankind, the destruction of death, the restoration of life; through you, God redeems the world, enlightens it, and calls it back to life.

*Jas 4:6; CA Luke 1:30–33

*CA Luke 1:30–33

Mary was already full of grace, but she found grace to dispense to others. Augustine says, "O Mary, you have found grace with God, and you have deserved to distribute this lavishly to the whole world."* Notice that the angel says *you have found*, not *you have* or *you have acquired*, because to have or acquire something justly means to safeguard what is one's own, whereas *to find* means to return something to those who had lost it. Thus Mary found grace, not as something to be held onto by her alone, but as something to be restored to others. Someone who finds something is bound to restore it to the person who lost it. The grace that Eve had lost, Mary found—not for herself alone, but for us, too; indeed on account of us, because if we had not been sinners, God would not have been born of her very flesh. Let all of us who have lost grace through sin confidently approach the throne of grace; there let us entreat Mary, the finder of grace, with fervent tears and devout prayers, that she might restore to us the grace that she found for us and on account of us. She is so lawful, just, loving, and well disposed that she refuses grace to no one who seeks it. Saint Bernard writes, "She has become all things to all people, she has opened the bosom of mercy to all, so that from her fullness they might receive all things: freedom to the

*Attributed to Augustine in Conrad of Saxony, Speculum BVM 3

prisoner, health to the sick, comfort to the sorrowing, forgiveness to the sinner, grace to the just, joy to the angels, and finally glory to the undivided Trinity."* And again, "My dear children, she is the ladder for sinners, she is my great source of confidence, she is the reason for my hope. I tell you: if you devoutly call out to her and invoke her, she will have compassion on you, she will never fail to assist you in your need. She lacks neither the power nor the will to do so, because she is the Queen of Heaven and the tender-hearted Mother of Mercy."* And again, "Consider carefully with what great devotion he wished us to honor her into whom he had placed the plenitude of all good things; whatever we have of hope, of grace, of salvation, we recognize it has overflowed to us from her. God wanted us to have nothing that had not passed through Mary's hands."*

*Sermo Sunday after Assumption, 2; PL 183:430D; SB 5:263

*Aquaeductu 7; PL 183:441D; SB 5:279

*Aquaeductu 6,7; PL 183:441A; SB 5:278–79

You Shall Conceive a Son

You have found grace with God, the angel said, meaning that she was about to conceive the author of all grace. For, "*Behold you shall conceive in your womb* without stain or sin *and shall bring forth a son** without pain or sorrow, remaining a virgin in giving birth as you do in conceiving." Rightly did the angel say *in your womb*, because Mary had already conceived Christ in her heart by her faith and devotion, and this is how we too should conceive him, by faith and devotion, and give birth to him through holy works. *"And you shall call his name Jesus*, that is, *Savior*."* He did not say, "You shall give him the name," because this name had been given to him by the Father from all eternity; the angel revealed it to Mary and Joseph, and they disclosed it to others. The name *Jesus* (which is interpreted as *salvation*) had been given to him because in the future the human race would be saved through him.*

***R 12**

*Luke 1:31

*Luke 1:31

**Lyra Luke 1:31 approx*

And so the angel went on to say, *"For he shall save from their sins*, not just anyone, but *his people* who cling to him by faith and imitate him by their good works."* From this it is clear that he is true God, because only God can deliver us from our sins, as Chrysostom observes.* The people of Christ would not be of the Jewish nation only; all those who come to him and are given knowledge of him are included. Lord Jesus, would that you would consider a poor sinner like me worthy to be numbered among your people, so that you would free me from my sins!

*Matt 1:21

*Rupert of Deutz, Super Matt 1; PL 168:1310D

***R 13**

*The angel then said, *He shall be great*.‡ His greatness, Ambrose explains, differs from John's, of whom the angel had said, *He shall be great before the Lord*,* because John was to be great as a human being before the Lord, but Jesus is great as God and the Son of God.* *He shall be great*, not because he was not great before he was born of the Virgin, for as God he is always great; rather he will be great as a human being because the greatness the Son of God eternally possesses by nature will be bestowed on the son of the Virgin in time by grace. This will be his forever after, so that the one Person is both God and Man.

‡Luke 1:32

*Luke 1:15

*Exp Luke 2.10; PL 15:1556B; CL 14:34

And he is rightly described as *great*, because he is worthy to *be called the Son of the Most High*,* as the angel went on to say. He is by nature *Son of the Most High*, that is, of God himself, who alone is the *Most High*: human beings rank above all other corporeal creatures, angels rank higher still, but God is the *Most High*.*

*Luke 1:32

**Lyra Luke 1:32*

***R 14**

**"And the Lord God shall give to him the throne*, that is, the kingdom, *of David his father*."* According to Bede, the fact that the angel had previously spoken of Christ as Son of the Most High but now calls David his father clearly demonstrates the two natures in the one Person of Christ: the divine nature, according to which he is the Son of the Most High; the human nature, according to which he is son of David.* He *shall give to him the throne of David*: not figuratively, but really; not in

*Luke 1:32

*Com Luke 1:32; PL 92:317D; CL 120:32

time, but eternally; not on earth, but in heaven. It is called David's throne because his earthly reign is an image of Christ's eternal reign.* Bede explains: "The Lord accepted the throne or kingdom of David so that the nation over whom he had once reigned and to whom he had given an example of just government, and whose faith and devotion he had inspired with spiritual hymns addressed to their maker would now, by Christ's deeds, words, gifts, and promises, be invited into a heavenly and eternal kingdom, and be led to the vision of God the Father himself."*

**Bernard, Laudibus 4.1; PL 183:79B; SB 4:47*

*Com Mark 3:11; PL 92:242D; CL 120:574

The angel is not speaking of an earthly kingdom. Christ himself rejected this in Pilate's presence: *My kingdom is not of this world*.* Nor did he exercise temporal power over the Jewish people, although the Jewish kingship was his rightful inheritance; rather, he spoke of the spiritual kingdom of his church triumphant, which was prefigured by David's earthly reign, just as the heavenly Jerusalem was prefigured by the earthly one. David held sway over an earthly kingdom; Christ rules a spiritual and heavenly realm, because he reigns in his church, both here on pilgrimage and in heaven. This is why the angel also said, *And he shall reign in the house of Jacob for ever*.*

*John 18:36

*Luke 1:32

Here, too, the *house of Jacob* must be interpreted in an eternal sense and not an earthly one, because he reigns *for ever*. *He shall reign for ever in the house of Jacob*, that is, over all the elect: in the houses of Abraham and Isaac there were some who were rejected, such as Ishmael and Esau; but all the members of Jacob's house, in the opinion of holy doctors, were counted among the elect, because even though some of them sinned, they did penance.* *Jacob* is interpreted as *supplanter*, and Christ reigns in those who uproot inordinate passions and vices; but the devil rules over those who are tripped up by these.* Therefore, *he shall reign* not only over David's house, that is, the tribe of Judah, but in truth *in the house of Jacob*, that is, over all of Israel, and in the whole church and in all the elect—not according

**Lyra Luke 1:32*

**Lyra Luke 1:32 mor*

to an earthly succession, but by faith. By this it is understood that his royal ranks include all those who imitate the faith and justice of David and Jacob. They comprise the eternal and spiritual throne of David and house of Jacob upon which the Lord Jesus sits and rules *for ever*, now through grace, and in the world to come through glory. Blessed are those in whom Jesus will reign eternally, for they will reign with him!

***R 15**

*Luke 1:33

*The angel concluded by saying. *And of his kingdom there shall be no end*.* Not only as God but as man Jesus will reign for ever, and not only over human beings but over angels as well. This reign is eternal and will not collapse; this kingdom will neither end nor be taken away, because *the Lord shall reign to eternity, indeed, for ever and ever*.* Bernard exclaims,

*Ps 9:37 [10:16]

> O, how glorious is that realm where the rulers have gathered and come together as one to praise and glorify him who is over all as King of kings and Lord of lords; the contemplation of his brilliance makes the just shine like the sun in their Father's kingdom! O, if Jesus would remember me, a sinner, in showing favor to his people when he comes into his kingdom! O, if on that day when he hands over the kingdom to his Father he would deign to visit me with his salvation, enabling me to behold the goodness of his elect and share in the rejoicing of his nation, so that even I could praise him together with his heritage! Come in the meantime, Lord Jesus: remove from your kingdom of my soul all inducements to sin, so that you may reign there as you should. You yourself are my king and my God, who orders deliverance for Jacob.*

*Laudibus 4.2; PL 183:80A; SB 4:48

The Mystery of the Incarnation

***R 16**

Mary was perplexed when the angel had recounted all these things. According to Ambrose, she could not disbelieve the angel, nor could she rashly seize upon such divine realities. Seeking his assurance about a

*Exp Luke 2.14; PL 15:1558B; CL 14:37

matter that troubled her greatly, the safeguarding of her virginity, she asked how this conception was to happen, saying, *How shall this, **your promise that I will give birth to a son,*** *be done, because I know not man?** That is, "I have promised in my heart that I would never know man, and have taken a vow." Although Mary had been betrothed, she had not married and was absolutely certain that she would not know man: she was a virgin in mind, in body, and by vow.

*Latin Diatessaron?

*Luke 1:34

It was as if she said, "I believe the fact, but I ask how this can happen because the Lord God knows, as my conscience bears witness, that his handmaid has promised not to know man. By what law, by what ordinance will it be pleasing to him that this should happen?"* Ambrose writes, "The fact that she asked how this was to happen did not mean that she doubted it would. Mary had read, *Behold a virgin shall conceive, and bear a son,*‡ so she believed it would take place in the future, but she had not read before how it was to happen. It had never been revealed, even to so great a prophet, how this was to be accomplished; so great a mystery was not entrusted to a mere mortal, but to the mouth of an angel."†

*Bernard, Laudibus 4.3; PL 183:81C; SB 4:49

‡Isa 7:14

†Exp Luke 2.15; PL 15:1558C; CL 14:38

*The angel answered. "This will come about in a divine manner, not humanly, not through man, but through the work of *the Holy Spirit,* who *shall come upon you.** As a divine fire inflames your soul and sanctifies your flesh by uniting it with the most perfect purity of God the Son, you will be made fruitful in a unique way, and by his working you will conceive even as you preserve your virginity." The Holy Spirit had previously come upon the Virgin to sanctify her, cleansing her of original sin; but in the conception of the Son of God *supervenit,* that is, he comes upon her again, conferring a greater plenitude of grace, so that not only her soul would be sanctified but her womb as well. The Holy Spirit came upon the Virgin as the energy of the sun descends upon a rose or a lily and enables it to conceive.

***R 17**

*Luke 1:35; *superveniet*

Although this ineffable conception is celebrated as the work of the whole Trinity, because the works of the Trinity are indivisible, it is appropriated especially to the Holy Spirit for several reasons. First, according to Augustine, to show that this came about by a completely unmerited grace: it is said, "He was conceived of the Holy Spirit," to indicate that this deed was effected by grace alone, and not from any human merit.* Grace is attributed to the Holy Spirit, as we read in the Gloss, "*Spirit* is the name of every grace inspired of God."* Second, according to Ambrose, to show the power of the deed: he was conceived by the power and working of the Holy Spirit, to whom are attributed the works of mercy and devotion.* Third, according to Peter Lombard, the Master of the *Sentences*, to show the magnitude of charity, which is attributed to the Holy Spirit: this deed shows that *the Word* of God *was made flesh* by ineffable charity, because *God so loved the world as to give his only begotten Son.*‡

*Enchiridion 40; PL 40:252; CL 46:72

*Martin of Leon, Sermo 4.4; PL 208:134A

*De Spiritu Sanctu 2.5.43; PL 16:752A; CS 79:103

‡John 1:14; 3:16; Sent 3.4.1; PL 192:763

***R 18**

*The angel continued, "*And the power of the Most High*, that is, the Word or the Son of God, who is called by the apostle the Wisdom of God, *shall overshadow you*,* that is, he will take a body from you as a shelter in which God will hide himself, like a hook within a morsel of food," because the power of God will be concealed in the Blessed Virgin under the bower of her flesh.

*Luke 1:35

Divinity overshadowed the Virgin by assuming a human nature, so that although it was impossible for a mortal woman, she could carry the presence of his majesty by the medium of a living body and bear the inaccessible light, just as we are able to gaze upon the sun when it is obscured by clouds.* Bernard says, "Because God is spirit and we are flesh, he hid himself for us under a veil so that we could look upon the Word made flesh in bodily form, like the sun in the clouds, a light in an earthenware vessel, or a candle in a lantern."*

**Bernard, SC 32.9; PL 184:945B; SB 1:232*

*Sermo for Ascension 3.3; PL 183:305D; SB 5:132

The church sings in the Preface of Blessed Mary, "For by the overshadowing of the Holy Spirit she conceived your only begotten Son,"* and this does not contradict what is said here, because the overshadowing took place when the body of Christ was brought into contact with the divine light.[8] The Son is, like the Holy Spirit, the *power* of the Father, and the power of both Persons cooperated in the incarnation: the Holy Spirit as the agent by whom Jesus was formed and the Son as the one to whom Jesus' body was united. So it is clear that this *overshadowing* was the work of both the Son and the Holy Spirit.

*Roman Missal; PL 78:133C

And notice here how the angel disclosed the undivided Trinity to the Virgin. First, the *Holy Spirit* is named explicitly; then the Son is spoken of, under the title *power;* and then the Father is alluded to as the *Most High.* The whole Trinity brought about the Incarnation: it is attributed to the cooperation of the Holy Spirit, where it says *the Holy Spirit shall come upon you;* it is attributed to the assumption of the flesh by the Son, where it says *and the power of the Most High shall overshadow you;* it is attributed to the authority of the Father where it says *of the Most High.*

For in fact the incarnation was the pre-eminent work of the whole Trinity because, like their Persons, their works are indivisible and inseparable. What is done by one Person is done by all, although only the Son became incarnate, and not the Father or the Holy Spirit.* God brought about the re-creation of the world by the same wisdom with which he had created it; he who was the Son of God in his divine nature became the Son of Man in his human nature, so that the name *Son* would not be given over to one who was not the Son through an eternal nativity. It is rather like three

**Hugh 4.6*

[8] This Preface is sometimes attributed to Pope Urban II, Saint Bruno's pupil, or even to Bruno himself, although it is older; Pope Urban added it to the Roman Missal.

persons working together to clothe one of their number, so that it could be said that they all work as one; what one does, another does, but only one of them is clothed. Augustine says, "The Trinity acts in such a way in the works of each Person that the other two cooperate in the work of the other one, and there is such concord among the three agents that the result cannot be attributed solely to one Person."*

*Sermo 71.16.27; PL 38:460

***R 19**

*Then the angel said, *And therefore also the Holy which shall be born of you shall be called the Son of God.** Son, not by adoption like others, but by his nature: although he was the Son from all eternity, he was not known to be or called that name by anyone until he appeared in time.

*Luke 1:35

It was as if he said, "Because you will be made fruitful by the power of the Holy Spirit, you will not give birth to a man's offspring, but to the Son of God; because you do not conceive in concupiscence, you will not bring forth a sinner, but the Holy One. Consequently, you will not experience birth pangs."*

**Bonaventure, Luke 1:35*

Bernard writes,

> What does this mean, but that you will conceive, not by man, but by the Holy Spirit? You will therefore conceive the *power of the Most High*, that is, the Son of God; *therefore that which shall be born of you*, that is, of your true nature, *shall be called Holy, the Son of God*. This means that not only will he who comes from the bosom of the Father overshadow you, but that he who is already the Son of God will even take to himself some of your substance. He who is begotten of the Father before all ages will be acknowledged to be your Son as well. Thus the one born of him will be yours and the one born of you will be his; however, they will not be two sons, but one. And although he receives one nature from the Father and another nature from you, yet you will not each have your own Son: he will be the one Son of both of you.*

*Laudibus 4.4; PL 183:81D; SB 4:50–51

And note that the angel says *the Holy* absolutely and substantively, without any qualification; if he had said *holy flesh* or *holy human being*, or some other similar term, it might seem that he had said too little, or had not expressed completely the Son's sanctity. He simply used the generic word *Holy*, because what was born of the Virgin was without doubt uniquely *Holy*.

*So that the Virgin would not view the idea of her giving birth as hopeless, and to confirm and increase her faith by an example, the angel told her of an elderly, barren woman who was now with child. He announced to the Virgin the fruitfulness of an aged woman who was thought to be sterile so that she would understand that all befitting things are possible to God, even things that are recognized to be contrary to nature. If, beyond the bounds of nature, he had made it possible for someone who was sterile to conceive, it should not be doubted that he could enable a virgin to do so. So, to make it easier for her to believe, the angel said, *"And behold your cousin Elizabeth also has conceived a son* through the power of God *in her old age; and this is the sixth month with her that is called barren."** ***R 20**

*Luke 1:36

This example, however, is not completely apt, because it is an even greater marvel for a virgin to conceive than for a woman who is barren to do so, and so he added that this was brought about by God's omnipotence, *because no word shall be impossible with God.** This meant either that God can fulfill the promise he has made by his word, or that God's word (meaning any work or deed) accomplishes what was foreseen in God's plan. For with God, to speak is the same thing as to do, as the psalmist wrote, *For he spoke and they were made.** So everything that does not contain a contradiction is possible with God, even a virgin conceiving; but it is impossible for inherently contradictory realities to be, such as for two opposing conditions to both be true (as for example that something could

*Luke 1:37

*Ps 32:9

Lyra Luke 1:37 approx

both exist and not exist at the same time).* However, this impossibility is not of God, but simply of the thing itself. According to the ordinary laws and powers of nature, neither a woman who is sterile nor one who is a virgin can conceive, but divine power can bring these things about. Bernard observes that the angel said *no word*, not *no deed*, to show that, however easy it is for human beings to say what they desire, it is incomparably easier for God to bring about whatever he expresses by his word.*

*Laudibus 4.7; PL 183:83A; SB 4:52

In addition, Bernard suggests that Elizabeth's conception was announced so that miracle could follow upon miracle, and joy would abound, or because what had been hidden would not remain hidden much longer, and it was fitting for the Virgin to learn of this event before others did so, or that she might know about the deeds of both the Savior and his Precursor so that she could teach those who were to record them later, or for the sanctification of the Baptist, whom Jesus wished to sanctify in his mother's womb, or so that in her humility she would assist her elderly relative.* Elizabeth and Mary were cousins, because they were the daughters of two sisters, Anne and Hismeria; like Mary, Elizabeth was of the tribe of Judah.[9]

*Laudibus 4.6; PL 183:82B; SB 4:51–2

***R 21**

*At this point, pause to consider and meditate on how the undivided Trinity is present here, awaiting the answer of this remarkable daughter of theirs, regarding her modesty and manner with love and devotion, and listening for her response. O, how blessed is that little room where such remarkable events took place! Although the holy Trinity is everywhere, now in this place it can be contemplated in a special way because of its extraordinary action. Ponder, too, the pleasing expression on the face of the angel as he gazes

[9] Hismeria (or Esmeria) appears in the *Golden Legend* in the account of the Nativity of the Blessed Virgin.

with reverence upon his Lady and carefully chooses his words so that he might accomplish the will of his Lord; contemplate how Mary maintains her reverence and humility, lowering her eyes modestly as if she could forestall these unexpected words from the angel. She is not swollen with pride; nor does she think about herself: when she hears astounding words spoken about her, such as no person had ever heard before, she gives no credit to herself, but ascribes it all to divine grace.*

**Massa; MVC 4*

Now, his embassy completed, the angel awaits the Virgin's answer. Here is how Bernard describes the scene:

> You have heard, O Virgin, that you shall conceive; you have heard that this will take place, not through human agency, but through the Holy Spirit. The angel is waiting for your reply, for it is time for him to return to the God who sent him. We, too, who are weighed down under the sentence of condemnation, await your word of mercy, Lady. Behold, the price of our salvation is being offered to you, and we will be set free immediately if you consent. Sorrowful Adam and his unhappy children, exiled from Paradise, beg this of you, gentle Virgin; David and your other ancestors ask this of you, and all those who dwell in the land of the shadow of death; the whole world awaits your answer, prostrate at your feet. O Lady, give the response that the earth, the netherworld, and the heavens await. Speak a word, and receive the Word; give a human word, and receive the divine Word; breathe out a fleeting word, and embrace the eternal Word.*

*Laudibus 4.8; PL 183:83C; SB 4:53

And Saint Augustine exclaims, "O blessed Mary, the whole imprisoned world entreats your consent; O Lady, the world has made you the surety of its faith. Virgin, do not delay; speak your answer quickly to the messenger and receive a Son."*

*Fulbert of Chartres, *Sermo* 9.3; PL 141:337D

The Virgin Mary's Response

*R 22

*At length the most prudent Virgin consented to the message she had heard from the angel. It is said that she knelt with fervent devotion and raised her hands and then joined them; lifting her eyes to heaven, with profound humility she spoke those so-desired words, words that must be heard with all our heart's devotion: *Behold the handmaid of the Lord: be it done to me according to your word.** *Behold* prompt obedience, devout willing, faith, and consent. "***I am**** *the handmaid of the Lord,*" she says, "so this is to be done by his power, not mine. *Be it done to me according to your word,* that is, in accordance with what you have told me." She who is chosen to be the mother of the Lord, mindful in all things of her condition and of the honor due to God, calls herself his handmaid and with all her heart desires that his will be done.

*Luke 1:38

*Latin Diatessaron?

Hearing these words, Augustine cries out, "O happy obedience! O eminent grace! When she humbly gave over her faith, she received within herself the Creator of the heavens!"* Anselm exclaims, "O faith accepted by God! O humility pleasing to God! O obedience more dear to God than all oblations! O sublime Virgin Mother of God! O humble mother and handmaid of the Lord! Who could imagine any position more exalted, and yet regard it with such humility?"* Ambrose writes, "See humility, see devotion: she who is chosen to be the mother of the Lord calls herself his handmaid, nor is she puffed up by the fulfillment of the promise. By calling herself his handmaid, she who would do as she was bidden claimed no prerogative from such a great grace: since she was to give birth to one who was meek and humble, she herself must also display humility."* And Bernard, "The virtue of humility is always found in the company of divine grace, for *God resists the proud and gives grace to the humble.** She responded humbly so that the throne of grace

*Fulbert of Chartres, *Sermo* 9.4; PL 141:338C

*Eadmer, De exc 3; PL 159:561B

*Exp Luke 2.16: PL 15:1559A; CL 14:38

*Jas 4:6

could be made ready: *Behold the handmaid of the Lord.* What is this humility so sublime that it resists honors and is a stranger to haughtiness in its glory? It is no great thing to be humble when we are cast down, but humility amidst honors is a rare and great virtue."* *Laudibus 4.9; PL 183:84C; SB 4:55

Therefore the Blessed Virgin, who was exalted above all other people in the world through the annunciation, humbled herself all the more profoundly at this moment; her humility is unparalleled and is commended before all other virtues. The Blessed Virgin's humility pleased the Son of God more than all her other virtues; this is what drew him down from heaven to take flesh from her, just as a piece of iron is attracted by a diamond.[10] Augustine writes, "O true humility, which caused God to be born for humanity, gave life to mortals, opened Paradise, and liberated the souls of the dead! Mary's humility was the heavenly ladder on which God came down to earth."* It was fitting, Bede points out, that just as death entered the world through Eve's pride, so life came in through Mary's humility.* The Virgin's voice was so pleasing to Christ when she said, *Behold the handmaid of the Lord*, that in the Scriptures he named himself as "the son of your handmaid" more often than "the Virgin's son."[11] From this it is clear that Mary's humility was more pleasing to God than her virginity.

*Ps-Augustine, *Sermo* 208.10; PL 39:2133

*Attr. to Bede in Zachary 1.3; PL 186:57D

*Although all the words in this gospel are full of mysteries, a particular virtue is to be found in this sentence with which the Virgin gave her consent. She used six words, each of which eloquently expresses a different virtue. *Behold*, prompt obedience; *the* ***R 23**

[10] The belief that diamonds exercised a gravitational effect upon iron was only disproved scientifically in the sixteenth century by William Gilbert. He suggests in *De Magnetate* 1.2 that the same name came to be used for the diamond and the magnet for philological reasons.

[11] Ludolph seems to include the Old Testament here.

handmaid, perfect humility; *of the Lord*, immaculate virginity; *be it done*, burning charity; *to me*, certain hope; *according to your word*, zealous faith. And the Virgin's faith was indeed zealous, because at the angel's word she believed that something would take place in her, the like of which had never been heard from the beginning of time, had never been reported or seen, and had never been imagined by anyone. Of this faith, Bernard says, "The Lord accomplished three miraculous events in the incarnation: he united God and humanity, motherhood and virginity, faith and the human heart. The last is less remarkable than the others, but not less powerful. It is amazing that the human heart could accommodate the first two mysteries and was able to believe that God became man and that his mother would remain a virgin. These realities could never be combined, unless the Holy Spirit held them together."*

*Sermo 3.7, Vigil of Christmas; PL 183:98A; SB 216–17

The Incarnation

*R 24

Immediately in that most sacred moment, as soon as Mary had uttered these words, the Holy Spirit overshadowed her and the glorious Virgin conceived the Son of God. Upon her word of consent, the Son completely entered into her womb and took flesh from her, even as he remained completely in the bosom of the Father. In that instant Christ's body was formed and his rational soul was created, and both were joined to divinity in the Person of the Son, so that he was completely God and Man, with each nature maintaining its own properties. Christ's body was formed from the blood of the Virgin Mary, not from her flesh, and in that moment the separation, consolidation, shaping, animation, and deification of the blood took place.

**in sinu Patris;* Massa

At that same instant Christ was fully and perfectly human in soul and body, possessing all the features of a body, but they were so tiny that it would be difficult to discern his members with the naked eye. Afterwards, he grew naturally in the womb like other infants, although the distinguishing of members and the infusion of a soul was not delayed, as it is with others. He was perfect God as well as perfect Man.[12]* In his human nature he possessed a true body and a rational soul, by virtue of his union with the Word he possessed a divine nature, and he united these two natures in the Person of the Word. **Massa*

In God there is one essence and three Persons; conversely, in Christ there is one Person and three essences: deity, soul, and body. The first is eternal, the second new, the third ancient: the divine nature is eternal; the soul is new, because it was created at the moment it was united to the body; the body is ancient, because its origin goes back to Adam. Christ is eternal according to his divine nature, created according to his soul, and made according to his body.* **Hugh 4.8*

*There is in Christ a threefold union: a unity between deity and his soul, a unity between deity and his body, and a unity between his body and his soul. The first two of these are permanent; the third was dissolved at the moment of his death. The union of his divinity with his humanity is not in its nature, but in his Person: there is no human person, only the divine Person. This divine Person assumes the human nature, and this is not just any person, but the Person of the Word himself. It is impossible for the divine nature to mingle with another to form a third nature, ***R 25**

[12] Saint Thomas Aquinas, relying on Aristotle, understood that in human generation the woman provided the matter and the man's semen exercised the active role of imparting form to this matter; this took about forty days or so, and the soul was created at the moment when this matter took human form. Because Jesus had no human father, he was formed, body and soul, at the moment of conception by the power of the Holy Spirit.

nor can it pass into this other nature, or vice-versa; therefore, the divinity and humanity are not united by nature, but by the Person. Furthermore, the divine nature is not able to subsist in an individual substance* besides its own proper hypostasis, so the union could not be in a human person, but in a divine Person: God assumed a human nature in one of his Persons. The unity of the Person, and his personality, derive from the one who assumed the human nature. Accordingly, Christ possesses a human nature but is not a human person.*

*suppositum

*Hugh 4.8

Hugh of Saint Victor writes,

> When God assumed man he assumed him entire, body and soul; that is, a human nature but not a human person, for he assumed the nature into his Person. That flesh and soul were not united into a person before the Word united them in his Person. There was one union, and the union was unto one, of the Word and flesh and soul: not the Word first and the flesh, or the Word first and the soul, or the soul and the flesh, but at the same time Word, soul, and flesh. Nor did the Word begin to be a person when he began to be a man; rather, he assumed the humanity in such a way that the man would become a person; nor did his humanity possess any personhood until the Word assumed it. The Person of the Word received not a human person, but a human nature, so that whom he received and what he received might be one Person in the Trinity.*
>
> Therefore, Christ's Person descended into the underworld, but only in his soul; Christ's Person lay in the tomb, but only in his flesh; Christ's Person was everywhere, but only in his divinity. What have some written, that when it is said that Christ lay in the tomb, the whole was stated for the part? Perhaps you are thinking that Christ is composed of three separate things: divinity, soul, and flesh. God forbid! Christ is not part Word and part human; Christ is wholly the Word, and Christ is

*De sacramentis 2.9; PL 176:394D

wholly man. Divinity was not a part of him, nor are there parts to divinity. In humanity only do we find parts, the body and the soul, and where these are, the whole human being is. So it is true to say that Christ lay in the tomb, but not that the whole human being was there, even though Christ was the whole man. His flesh and his soul were united to the Person of God by the Word. Therefore, where the flesh was present, the Word could not be absent. *

*De sacramentis 2.11; PL 176:401D

*Listen to what Anselm said to the incarnate Word: ***R 26**

Lord, you have seen the affliction of your people, and, moved to the depth of your heart by our sorrow, you have applied yourself to think thoughts of peace and redemption upon us. And although you are the Son of God, true God, God co-eternal and consubstantial with the Father and the Holy Spirit, dwelling in light inaccessible and sustaining all things by the power of your word alone, you have not disdained to lower your lofty eminence into this prison house of our mortality so you could taste and absorb our misery and restore us to glory. It would have been too little for your charity, good Lord Jesus, to dispatch a cherub, a seraph, or one of the angels to complete the work of our salvation. You, you yourself deigned to come to us by your Father's command so that we might experience his great love in you. You came, not changing your location, but making your presence visible in the flesh. You descended from the royal throne of your sublime glory to a young girl who was in her own eyes a lowly and common handmaid, and who had consecrated her virginal chastity to you by a vow. The ineffable power of the Holy Spirit alone brought it about that you would be conceived in her womb and born in our true human nature, in such a way that your birth would entail neither the lessening of your divine nature nor the loss of her virginity.*

*Stim [Med 9 Anselm]; PL 158:749C; Massa

And to his sister he wrote,

> First, enter with blessed Mary into her chamber and open the sacred books in which the coming of Christ and a virgin giving birth are prophesied. Wait there for the coming of the angel, so that you can see him enter and hear his greeting. Filled with wonder and ecstasy, you may salute your Lady, the most sweet Mary, with the angel's own greeting, crying out and exclaiming, *Hail Mary, full of grace!* Say these words over and over again, pondering what this fullness of grace might be by which the world became graced when the Word became flesh. Marvel at and contemplate how the Lord, who fills the heavens and the earth, confined himself in the womb of a young girl, whom the Father sanctified, the Son made fruitful, and the Holy Spirit overshadowed.
>
> O dearest Lady, with what floods of sweetness you were drenched, with what fires of love you were inflamed when you perceived the presence of such majesty in your soul and in your womb as he took flesh from your flesh, and from your members fashioned the members of a body in which the fullness of divinity could dwell.*

*Aelred, De inst 31 [Med 15 Anselm]; PL 158:785B; CM 1:662–63; *Massa*

***R 27**

O, if only you could experience how manifold and how surpassing was that fire sent down upon her from heaven, what refreshment gathered, what consolation infused! What exaltation for the Virgin, what nobility to the human race, what condescension of majesty! If you are able to hear the Virgin singing for joy, consider that you should begin to rejoice together with her for such a great benefit, and that you should never cease expressing your gratitude to God in song. In order to rekindle the Virgin's own joy and to recall it to your mind, greet her frequently with the words of the angelic salutation; greet her with affectionate kisses, at the very least kissing her feet and saying, *Hail Mary*. Bernard says, "Virgin Mary, for you it is like receiving a kiss to hear this angelic greeting, *Ave.*

**LV 3*

As often as you are lovingly hailed by the *Ave*, O most blessed one, so often are you greeted with kisses. So, my dear brothers, approach her image, kneel down, greet her with a kiss, and say, *Hail Mary*."* And again, "The heavens resound, the angels rejoice, the earth exults, the demons tremble, when I say, *Hail Mary*."*

*source unknown

*Alanus de Rupe, De psalterio seu rosario 30

Christ Conceived in Us

*Here we shall consider six moral qualities that are needed by holy souls who wish to have Christ conceived in them spiritually. First, you should dwell apart from all earthly attractions, making your home in Galilee, which is interpreted as *carrying away*. That soul lives perfectly in a place removed when she passes over all created delights and takes no pleasure in them except insofar as the image and perfection of the Creator shines out in them. Not only does she love nothing that is contrary to God, but she does not love anything except those things in which God himself is manifest, or that possess his image (such as our neighbor), or that can be beneficial to eternal salvation. Second, you should live where there is a flourishing of the divine operations that make us godlike, residing in Nazareth, a name meaning *flower, shoot, holiness*, or *consecration*. Such a soul will blossom and dwell among the flowers by her radiant innocence; she will send forth shoots under the influence of divine sweetness; she will be sanctified by the fervor of divine charity, and she will abide in a kind of consecration by the splendor of truth. Third, you should be virginal, carefully controlling not only your senses but also all the powers of your soul, so that nothing corrupting can enter in. Let nothing in through your five senses that could tempt you to impurity, or through your intellect that could incite vain curiosity. According to Augustine, the soul that acts in this way can truly be called virginal.*

***R 28**

*Sermo 93.4; PL 38:575

Fourth, you should be betrothed, so that you are bound by faith and love to the one good, which is God, lest you wander from one lover to another. And you should be espoused to Joseph, a name meaning *increase*, so that by exercising your faith and love these virtues may continually increase—for in such matters, not to gain is to lose. And with good reason it is added that Joseph was of the house of David, whose name means *with a strong hand*: in spiritual exercises only those advance who show courage in thought and deed.[13] Fifth, because Mary's name means *illuminata* you should be flooded with light: have God's face continually shining upon you, imparting spiritual joy to your heart. Sixth, because the angel who came to announce the good news to Mary was called Gabriel, a name that means *God my comfort*, or *strength of God*, you should be comforted by God's gift of fortitude.[14] When a contemplative soul is strengthened by God she is raised up by hope to seek the fullness of grace, the Lord's presence, and she receives a certain singular blessing among all creatures.

***R 29** *Something more should be said about the third point. The conception and formation of Christ in the womb of the Virgin by the working of the Holy Spirit signifies mystically that he can also be conceived and formed spiritually in a chaste mind by the working of the same Holy Spirit. In order for the mind to conceive the eternal Word it must be virginal, that is, removed not only from any sin but also immune to the attractive appearance and corrupting influence of created realities. Because every *creature was made subject to vanity*,* every idea derived from a created thing is also joined to vanity, and in this way the mind is distracted

*Rom 8:20

[13] Jerome renders *David* as *desirable*, or *with a strong hand* (Int nom; PL 23:840; CL 72:135).

[14] Jerome renders *Gabriel* as *God has comforted me*, or *the strength of God*, or *my strength* (Int nom; PL 23:843; CL 72:140).

from higher realities and is, in a manner of speaking, corrupted.[15]

In connection with this mental distraction, Dionysius the Areopagite exhorts Timothy, "You also, dear Timothy, should abandon with bold contrition the use of your senses and all operations of the intellect, and all sensible and intellectual realities, if you wish to attain quickly that union with him who is above all created realities and all knowledge."* This detachment is perfected in the beatitude *Blessed are the clean of heart,** understanding by these words a cleansing from all extraneous appearances. Such people will see God, here through internal contemplation and hereafter through everlasting enjoyment. These virginal souls *follow the Lamb* of total purity *wherever he goes, for they are virgins.** Of this kind of soul Bernard writes,

*Glossae in myst theol 1; PL 122:271C
*Matt 5:8
*Rev 14:4

> Once the soul has been taught by the Lord to enter into herself, to long for God in her inmost depths, and to seek his face continually, such a soul would not, I say, regard a temporary experience of Gehenna itself as worse than having to go out again among the enticements—or better, the troublesome demands—of the flesh, and the insatiable prurience of the bodily senses, after having once tasted the sweetness of this spiritual devotion. Therefore I tell you: nothing is more dreaded by a

[15] This paragraph translates Ludolph's text, but it should be noted that he is employing somewhat technical language: the "attractive appearances" are *speciebus creatarum rerum*, and "every idea derived from a created thing" is *omnis species a re create abstracta*. Medieval theories of vision were complex, but a basic element was the relationship between the object, the "sensible species," and the "intellectual species" produced in the mind by a process of abstraction by the agent intellect. By entering the soul, images exert an influence over it, hence both the need to be vigilant in controlling the images we allow in and the frequent exhortations for the reader to "see" this or that event in the life of Christ.

person who has once received this blessing than, abandoned by grace, to have to go out again to those carnal consolations, which are really desolations, and to endure again the tumult of sensual cravings.*

*SC 35.1; PL 183:962C; SB 1:249

***R 30**

*There are two churches in the town where the annunciation took place, Nazareth. One stands on the site of the house in which the angel came to Mary to make the annunciation. This church has two altars: one dedicated to Mary, on the spot where she was at prayer when the angel greeted her; the other is dedicated to Gabriel, where he stood when he made the annunciation. The other church is on the site of the house in which the Lord was nurtured as a child.[16]

Biblical Types

***R 31**

*Exod 3:2

Our Lady's conception was prefigured in the Burning Bush. The bush supported the fire but did not lose its greenness; Mary conceived a Son and did not lose her virginity; the Lord dwelt in the burning bush, and he himself in pregnant Mary's womb; he descended into the bush to free the Jews and lead them out of Egypt, he descended into Mary for our redemption, to deliver us from the realm of death. Although the Lord desired to become incarnate, only Mary was chosen from among all women.*

**SHS* 7

This event is also prefigured in Gideon's fleece, which alone was dampened by the dew while all the ground around it remained dry.* Thus no other creature was found worthy to be saturated with the dew of God's presence, only Mary. The soaking of the fleece

*Judg 6:38

[16] The seventh-century *De Locis Sanctis* mentions these two churches (PL 173:1127C). Recent excavations (2012) have found remnants of a cave church and later edifice from the Byzantine era that may be the site of the second church mentioned here, known as "the church of the nutrition."

was a sign given to the children of Israel that they would be delivered from their enemies; Mary's conception was the sign of our redemption. Gideon wrung out the fleece and filled a vessel from it; Mary brought forth a Son, who filled all creation with the dew of divine grace.* **SHS 7*

Her conception took place through Gabriel's annunciation, which is prefigured in Abraham's servant and Rebecca, the daughter of Bethuel.* Abraham sent his servant to find a bride for his son from among the maidens of his people, and when Rebecca gave the messenger water to drink, she was chosen to be the wife of her master's son. So the heavenly Father sent his angel to find a maiden to be the mother of his Son, and when he found that most worthy of virgins, Mary, she gave him refreshment, that is, her consent to his tidings. Rebecca did not give water only to the servant, but to his camels as well; Mary gives drink as the fountain of life to human beings and angels.*

*Gen 24

**SHS 7*

The Angel Departs

***R 32**

Then Gabriel, having completed the mission on which he had been sent, bowed reverently and bade his Lady farewell. He withdrew from her presence and vanished, rejoicing and exulting because he could report her positive response to God. The bridegroom had arrived and the marriage had been consummated, so his attendant could depart, leaving him in the sacred matrimonial chamber of his bride. The angel was gone, but the king of the angels, the Son of God, remained in her. Gabriel had departed as a visible presence, but a multitude of angels reverently surrounded Mary, out of respect for her and to show deference to their king. When the successful messenger returned to his homeland and related there all that had happened, new festivity and joy broke out, and great exultation.

**Massa*

Conclusion: The Great Solemnity of the Lord's Incarnation

*R 33

*You should contemplate how great is this day's solemnity, rejoicing in your heart and making a holiday of it. Such a solemnity was unheard of from all ages until that time. Today is the solemnity of God the Father, who has made a wedding feast by espousing his Son to our human nature, to which the Son on this day has inseparably united himself. Today is the solemnity of the Son's nuptials in the womb, but later they will take place outside the womb. Today is the solemnity of the Holy Spirit, to whom this wondrous work is attributed and who today began to manifest a singular liberality toward the human race. Today is the solemnity of our glorious Lady, who is selected and recognized to be a daughter by the Father, a mother by the Son, and a bride by the Holy Spirit. Today is a solemnity for the whole heavenly court, because their restoration now begins. Today is all the more a solemnity for the human race, because it marks the beginning of its salvation and redemption, and the reconciliation of the whole world; today our human nature is raised up and deified, *for nowhere does he take hold of the angels* to assume their nature in his Person, *but of the seed of Abraham he takes hold*.*

*Heb 2:16; *Massa; MVC 4; CM 153:23*

Today the Son undertakes a new obedience from the Father, to accomplish our salvation: going forth today from the highest heavens, *he has rejoiced as a giant to run the way** of our salvation and enclosed himself in the cloister of the Virgin's womb. Today he has become like one of us, our brother, and has begun to sojourn with us; today the true light comes down from heaven to scatter our darkness and dispel it. Today the living bread that gives life to the world is prepared in the Virgin's womb, to be baked later in the oven of the cross. For today *the Word was made flesh and dwelt among us,** who is called Emmanuel, *which being interpreted is God with us,** that is, God and man.‡

*Ps 18:5

*John 1:14

*Matt 1:23

‡*Massa; MVC 4; CM 153:23*

Today are fulfilled all the types of the Old Testament, all the lessons of Scripture, all the expectations of the prophets, who cried out for this day with inexpressible desire and awaited it with intense longing; for this reason, the coming of Christ is called the fullness of time. Today is the foundation and source of all our solemnities, and the beginning of all our blessings. Until now, the Lord had been angry with the human race on account of the transgression of our first parents; from now on, seeing his Son made man, that anger is dispelled for ever. You see what an admirable work and what a most solemn feast this is, totally delightful and totally pleasing; it is absolutely desirable and deserves to be celebrated with the most worthy devotion, accompanied by joy and exultation. Meditate on these mysteries, take delight and rejoice in them, and perhaps if you are vigilant the Lord will show you even greater things.*

**Massa; MVC 4; CM 153:24*

✠

O Jesus, Son of the living God, emerging from the bosom of the Father by his will and the cooperation of the Holy Spirit, you flowed down like a river cascading from Eden into the lowly valleys. Looking upon the humility of your handmaid, you descended into the Virgin's womb, where you were conceived and ineffably became flesh. Merciful Jesus, through the merits of your Virgin Mother may your grace eagerly descend upon me, your unworthy servant, so that I may yearn for you and conceive you within me by love, and, by that same grace working in me, I may bring forth the salutary fruit of good works. Amen.

CHAPTER 6

The Birth and Circumcision of the Lord's Forerunner

(Luke 1:39-80)

*R 1

*Reflecting on the words spoken by the angel about her cousin Elizabeth, Mary resolved to visit her, both to congratulate and to assist her. Jesus in her womb was hastening to sanctify John, who was in the womb of his mother. *Mary rising up in those days* from the place where she had been seated and praying in quiet contemplation (for she always prayed before undertaking any work), *went* with Joseph's leave south from Galilee *into the hill country** of Judea. She went, notwithstanding that the home of Zechariah was situated in a mountainous area in the Judean hills and that the road was steep and rocky. She went *in haste* because she did not want to appear in public for long, to show that a virgin should not linger in public places or engage anyone in conversation there.*

*Luke 1:39

**Massa; MVC 5 approx; CM 153:24–25*

And she came to Jerusalem, *a city of Juda*, that is, of the kingdom of Judea in the hereditary territory of the tribe of Benjamin. It seems she passed through this city and continued on to a town about four miles to the west of Jerusalem and a little to the south; this is where Zechariah lived, and where John was born. Mary, having conceived the eternal Word, went to visit Elizabeth. According to Ambrose, she did this not because she was incredulous of the angel's prophecy, nor had she any uncertainty about his message, nor was she doubtful regarding the example of Elizabeth; no, she went joyful in her prayer, determined to be of assistance, and hastening with happiness because she had conceived.* *Exp Luke 2.19; PL 15:1560A; CL 14:39

‡Observe how the Queen of heaven and earth travels: not on a horse, but walking on foot down a long and arduous road—thirty-four miles from Nazareth to Jerusalem and another four miles to Zechariah's town—accompanied by some young women who were staying in her home. She was also attended by modesty, humility, poverty, and honesty together with all the other virtues; even more, the Lord of all virtue himself was with her. Hers was a great and noble retinue, but nothing like the vain and pompous displays of this world. She was not weighed down by the son she had conceived, as pregnant women usually are; the Lord Jesus was no burden to his mother. O, how joyful it would have been to have met Mary on that road and received a word of greeting from her!* ‡**R 2**

**Massa; MVC 4 approx; CM 153:25*

And she entered into the house of Zachary and her cousin Elizabeth, which she approached with marks of gentleness and humility, like some religious shrine, and first, she *saluted Elizabeth*,* congratulating her upon the gift that God had given her, as Mary had been told. Mary spoke first for two reasons: as a sign of humility, because she was more humble, and as a sign of favor, because she was superior. The first reflects the custom of that land, where inferiors address superiors first out of deference; the second reflects the custom among us, where the superior speaks first to indicate that benefits come from her. *Luke 1:40

*Pause here and note that the Virgin did six things that have a moral significance; we ought to imitate her example. First, she *arose*: let us rouse ourselves from the torpor of sloth and distance ourselves from worldly desires, in which we linger by slumbering. Second, she *went into the hill country*: let us ascend the mountain, aspiring to a higher life, hungering for *R 3 heavenly things and drawing near to them. Third, she *went in haste*: let us also make haste to do good, and whatever we can do, let us do without delay. Chrysostom cautions, "Nothing is so able to ruin our lives as to ignore the performance of good works and continually to procrastinate; often that is enough to make us fall away from doing good at all."* Hence it has been suggested that a good deed should never be put off, lest something happen to impede it, but the urge to do evil should always be postponed, in the hope that something will interrupt it.

*Hom Matt 16:10; PG 57/58:252

Fourth, she came *to a city of Juda*: let us go into the city of Juda (a name meaning *praise* or *thanksgiving*), that is, into the church, to praise and adore, and into the city of contemplation, the heavenly Jerusalem, *to praise the name of the Lord*.* Fifth, she *entered into the house of Zachary*: let us also go into Zechariah's house, by calling to mind the Lord's commands in order to carry them out, rather than chasing after useless thoughts; for Zechariah is interpreted as *remembering the Lord*. Sixth, she *greeted Elizabeth*: let us also greet Elizabeth by disdaining created things and being saturated by the desire to ponder God alone, *who satisfies your desire with good things*;* for Elizabeth means *plenitude of my God*.[1] And in addition, let us share the grace we receive with others, as Mary did with Elizabeth and her child.

*Ps 121:4

*Ps 102:5

John the Baptist Rejoices

***R 4**

*As soon as the Virgin *greeted Elizabeth* John was filled with the Holy Spirit in her womb, just as the

[1] Jerome, Int nom, renders *Juda* as *praise* or *thanksgiving* (PL 23:781), *Zechariah* as *mindful of the Lord* or *memory of the Lord* (PL 23:843), and *Elizabeth* as *fullness of my God*, or *oath of my God*, or *seventh* (PL 23:843).

angel had promised. Sensing the nearness of the Lord, for sheer joy he danced and leaped and expressed himself by such signs; because he could not express himself by voice or tongue, he did so by his movement. He moved about in the womb as if he would like to stand up to greet his Lord, and if he could have gotten out of the womb he would have rushed to him. At the very beginning Jesus made the Forerunner his prophet; by leaping in the womb he began his office of Precursor,* almost as if he were already crying out in his mother's womb, *Behold the Lamb of God, behold him who takes away the sin of the world.** **Massa* *John 1:29

Chrysostom writes, "Christ prompted Mary to greet Elizabeth so that the word proceeding from the womb of his mother, where the Lord dwelt, would enter through the ears of Elizabeth, descend to John, and anoint him there as prophet. For as soon as the voice of greeting came to her ears, the rejoicing child prophesied, not by his voice but by his action."* And the same Chrysostom begs, "Speak, infant, speak, greatest of the prophets, worthy in fact to be called *more than a prophet*:* what is the cause of your joy? You are not even born, and already you preach. You know the Lord has come, and since you cannot greet him with your voice, you do so by leaping. How eagerly you would run to him if you were already born; knowing he is near, you attempt to reach him."* *Opus imperf 27.8; PG 56:775 *Matt 11:9 **Bruno Luke 1:41; PL 165:344C*

Then John's mother was filled with the Holy Spirit through her son and his merits. It was not that the mother was filled first and then the son, but the son first and then the mother. From that fullness of grace by which Christ became present in Mary, the grace of sanctification flowed to John by the Virgin's greeting and then overflowed to his mother. Rejoicing and exhilarated, and inflamed by the Holy Spirit, Elizabeth tenderly embraced the Virgin and gave a shout of joy. The son hidden within instructed the mother how to act without: the infant's spirit, unable to cry out with his own voice, caused his mother to exclaim with a loud voice.

She cried out for several reasons: as a sign of her great affection, because she had come to know the great gifts of God, and because she was carrying in her womb the one who was the voice of the Word. Elizabeth was moved by a deep emotion not simply to return the Virgin's greeting but to cry out—but this expressed devotion, not noise; it is not *clamor* but *amor* that reaches God's ears.[2] So the great intensity of this shout is to be attributed to interior devotion, not exterior noise, for piety is the sound loud enough to pierce the heavens. Even though Moses was silent, the Lord asked, *Why do you cry to me?** because Moses was crying out with the desire in his heart, not the words on his lips. According to Augustine, "The shout to God is the intention of the heart and the ardor of love, because it always begs for what it desires."*

*Exod 14:15

*En ps 30.3.10; PL 36:254; CL 38:220

‡R 5

†Luke 1:42

°Latin Diatessaron?

‡And Elizabeth said, *Blessed are you among women,*† that is, ***over all women,***° and among all who are blessed, with a singular blessing. No one had ever shared in such grace before, nor would anyone afterward. "*Blessed are you,* and you will accumulate even more blessings; *and blessed is the fruit of your womb,* through whom blessing comes to others. He is blessed as Man by the blessing of grace, because he is filled with the gift of all charisms; he is blessed as God by the blessing of glory, because he is God from eternity to eternity. The fruit of your womb is not blessed because you are blessed; rather, he *has gone before you with blessings of sweetness,** and so you are blessed."

*Ps 20:4

Blessed is the tree, and blessed is the fruit of the tree. Blessed is the shoot from the rod of Jesse, and blessed is the flower that blossoms from that shoot. Blessed is

[2] Ludolph cites a contemporary poem: *Non vox sed votum / Non musica chordula sec cor / Non clamor sed amor / Sonat in aure Dei.*

so excellent a mother, blessed is so excellent a son.* **Bruno Luke 1:42; PL 165:345A*
Mary was called blessed by the angel earlier, for the ruin of the angels was to be repaired in the church triumphant; now she is called blessed by Elizabeth, because the moribund church militant is raised up to life. Bede says, "Mary is hailed as blessed by both Gabriel and Elizabeth to show that she must be honored by humans and angels alike."* *Com Luke 1:42; PL 92:320D; CL 120:36

Note here that five fruits can be gathered from the Blessed Virgin. The first is the fruit of her womb, and this is the son she bore, for *through her we have tasted the fruit of life.** The second is the fruit of her heart, and this is compassion, which she extends to sinners and the afflicted. The third is the fruit of her mouth, and this is prayer. The fourth is the fruit of her works, and this is protection. The fifth is the fruit of her name, which is the devotion that comes from blessing her name (even by the wicked), so she should be invoked by everyone in any danger.

*Antiphon for Feasts of Our Lady; PL 78:799B

***R 6**

And why is it granted to me that the mother of my Lord should come to me? That is, "What is my claim, what are my accomplishments or merits, that to me, who am old, sterile, and thought accursed by people, that *the mother of my Lord*, the fruitful and blessed Virgin, should humbly, reverently, and lovingly come to me, her servant and handmaid?" This was as if she said, "Nothing. No sanctity, no religion, no kind of nobility has been accorded to me that I might be worthy of such a great honor and blessing; this is due to God's grace alone. I would rather have come to you, but your humility, and your son's, constrained you to come to me."*

*Luke 1:43

**Bruno Luke 1:42; PL 165:345A*

And consider here that the mother of the Lord comes to sinners with compassion, since she is the *bitter sea* who gives them the astringency of contrition; she comes to the downtrodden with protection, since she is the *sovereign Lady* who frees them; and she comes to those who mourn with consolation, since she is the *star* who gives them joy. Hence, Augustine prays, "Holy Mary, assist the wretched, support the fainthearted, refresh the sorrowful."*

*Ps-Augustine, *Sermo* 194.5; PL 39:2107

"Truly, *blessed are you and blessed is the fruit of your womb*, and, given the virtues that are apparent in you, I marvel at the humility with which you visit me. Behold, at your arrival and greeting not only I but the infant in my womb rejoiced, and because he could not speak, he leaped for joy." Thus Elizabeth knew about the miracle of the incarnation and understood that Mary was the mother of the Lord and that God had filled her. She understood because she herself had been filled with the Holy Spirit, and because the joy of her baby showed that the mother of him for whom John would be the Forerunner had come. She now blessed who earlier had blushed to learn that she was with child because she had not understood the mystery of religion; she who had concealed the fact that she had conceived a child now boasted because she had conceived a prophet.*

**Zachary 1.3; PL 186:57C approx*

***R 7**

*Now Elizabeth, who had come to this knowledge by a secret inspiration, proclaimed it openly to those who were present, saying, *"And blessed are you who have believed* what you heard from the angel when you conceived by faith, *because those things shall be accomplished* more greatly in the future *that were spoken to you by the Lord** through his angel and by the Holy Spirit illumining your mind and teaching you directly." This shows quite clearly that she knew what the Holy Spirit had said to the Virgin through the agency of the angel. *Blessed are you who have believed*, and blessed are all those who hear and believe. Pause here to consider what power there was in the Blessed Virgin Mary's greeting: it produced joy, it imparted the Holy Spirit, it revealed divine secrets, and it gave the gift of prophecy. Therefore we should greet Mary often, in the hope that we shall receive the blessings of her greeting in return.

*Luke 1:45

Mary's *Magnificat*

*Having heard Elizabeth's response, which called her the Mother of the Lord, proclaimed her blessed, and praised her strong faith, Mary broke out in prophecy. She could no longer keep silent about the gifts she had received; the time had come to make known what her virginal modesty and humility had up till now wrapped in silence. She broke out into a canticle of joy that the Lord taught her, saying, *My soul magnifies the Lord,** completing the entire paean with great exultation. It was customary among the Hebrews on great occasions to compose and sing hymns to the Lord when God had done wondrous things for them—and this Virgin was able to magnify the Lord more than anyone else. Out of humility she had not immediately publicized the great mystery that had been made known to her; she kept it hidden until it had been revealed to Elizabeth. But because her cousin had come to learn of the mystery through the Holy Spirit, she understood that at last the Lord wanted it to be made known, and so she proclaimed it. She magnified the Lord, that is, she praised and made known his works. She did not do great things, because of herself she could not; she could neither diminish nor increase what she had received. *R 8

*Luke 1:46; *Massa*

It was as if Mary were saying, "O Elizabeth, you magnify me because of the good things you see in me, but my soul praises my Lord and Creator, that is, God the Father, from whom all things come, attributing all to him by this canticle in which I praise his greatness."*

**Lyra Luke 1:46*

*"*And my spirit has rejoiced in God my Savior,*‡ that is, in my son, through whom all things were made and through whom salvation is restored to the world."* The Virgin has good cause to rejoice in this Savior, indeed better cause than all other creatures, because parents are in the habit of rejoicing in their children; *R 9

‡Luke 1:47

**Zachary 1.3; PL 186:58A*

and further, while he is the Savior of all people he has accorded an even greater gift of salvation to the Virgin because of the singular prerogatives he has bestowed on her.

Spirit can mean the same thing as *soul*, although sometimes the word refers specifically to the excellence and rationality of the soul. We live by the soul, we discern and understand by the spirit: *soul* and *spirit* include all our powers.* The soul embraces the lower faculties that control the body, while the spirit is the higher powers of the same substance, which can be snatched out of itself by the ecstasy of contemplation. Mary has consecrated all the powers of her soul and spirit to God, employing them all to praise and thank God for the many blessings he has showered upon her. Ambrose suggests that it is as if Mary were saying, "God has bestowed such great gifts on me that my tongue is not equal to the task of thanking him; I offer thanks with all the affection of my inner soul, and in fulfilling his precepts I give him all by which I live, all by which I understand, and all by which I discern."*

**Zachary 1.3; PL 186:57D*

*Exp Luke 2.27 approx; PL 15:1562A; CL 14:42

That person truly magnifies the Lord whose goodness glorifies and praises him. Teachers are praised and magnified in their students, and artists in their creations. Similarly, God is glorified in us when our soul, which was made in his image, is conformed to him through the justice of Christ, who is the Father's image; God is glorified in us when his image in our soul is magnified, that is, when by great virtue great things are done; God is glorified in us when we live in accord with the divine precepts and give light by our good works. Hence the apostle says, *Glorify and bear God in your body*.* Notice here that God can be magnified in three ways through the benefits he bestows: first, by attributing the blessings themselves to God; second, by giving thanks to him for them; third, by treating them as blessings.

*1 Cor 6:10

***R 10**

*You should also note here that in this canticle the Blessed Virgin expressed her praise and thanksgiving of God at length, whereas in the rest of the gospels she does not speak often, and then only in a few words. In all, she only spoke seven times, perhaps to show that she was filled with the sevenfold grace. She spoke twice to the angel: *How shall this be done?** and *Behold the handmaid of the Lord.** She spoke twice to Elizabeth: when she greeted her and when she said, *My soul magnifies the Lord.** She spoke twice to her son: in the temple, *Son, why have you done this to us?** and at the wedding feast, *They have no wine.** And she spoke once to the servants on the same occasion: *Do whatever he tells you.** From this it is clear that Mary talked rarely and then but little, except when she let herself go in this canticle, speaking with God.*

*Luke 1:34
*Luke 1:38
*Luke 1:47
*Luke 2:48
*John 2:3
*John 2:5
**Albert, De laudibus BVM 1.31 approx*

It should also be noted that she spoke these seven words on four different occasions, and with good reason. On each occasion, a great miracle took place: at the angelic annunciation, she conceived God; at the visitation, the child leaped in Elizabeth's womb; at the wedding feast, the water was changed into wine; in the temple: *and* then he *was subject to them.** Furthermore, on these four occasions she spoke to four people: the angel, her elderly cousin Elizabeth, her son, and the servants. Here is a beautiful example for young women, and especially for nuns, that they should say little, except to four kinds of people: to the angel, that is, to the priest in confession, for then he is acting as God's messenger; to holy Elizabeth, that is, to another woman who is mature and learned, for consolation; to the Son of God, in prayer and holy reading; or to reputable people when making necessary requests.*

*Luke 2:51
**Albert, De laudibus BVM 1.31 approx*

‡Ponder how happy both mothers are: each praises God for the conception of her child, and they pass their days by joyfully giving thanks. Truly blessed home, where two such mothers dwell, carrying two such remarkable sons! O, imagine if you could ascend those mountains with your Lady, and witness the loving embrace between the barren woman and the Virgin Mother and offer them assistance! I think you

‡R 11

would join your voice with Mary's in her sacred *Magnificat* and would leap for joy with the little child as you adored the marvel of the Virgin's conception! Anselm urged his sister,

> Now climb those mountains with your most sweet Lady, gaze upon the barren wife and the Virgin as they embrace and exchange those greetings in which the tiny servant recognized his Lord, the herald his Judge, the voice the Word, the one enclosed in the womb of his aged mother, the other in the Virgin's womb. Blessed wombs, in which the salvation of the world dawns, gloomy sadness is dispelled, and eternal happiness is foretold! Run, hurry to take part in such joy: prostrate before both women, and embrace your bridegroom in the womb of one, and in the other venerate his friend.*

*Aelred, De inst 29 [Med 15 Anselm]; PL 158:785D; CM 663

Pay attention and imitate this lesson of humility: Mary comes to Elizabeth, Christ comes to John, the Lady to the handmaid, the Lord to the servant.* Mary does not disdain to serve Elizabeth; do you want yet another spur to humility? Although Mary was filled with all virtues, in her canticle she recognized only one: *He has regarded the humility of his handmaid.** Join with Mary in stirring up feelings of humility in yourself, and like her attribute whatever good you have to God, not to yourself.

**Bruno Luke 1:39; PL 165:344B*

*Luke 1:48

***R 12**
‡Luke 1:56

**And Mary stayed with her about three months*‡ because she had come to offer Elizabeth comfort and assistance, helping her humbly, reverently, and devoutly in any way she could. So strong was her desire to realize the full measure of humility that it was as if she had forgotten that she was the Mother of God and Queen of the whole world.* In Mary, contemplation does not neglect action, nor does action diminish contemplation. This is why the gospel of Martha serving and Mary sitting at the feet of the Lord is read on the feast of Mary's Assumption: she was active, as we see

**Massa; MVC 5; CM 153:26*

here, but always also contemplative, because *Mary kept all these words, pondering them in her heart.** *Luke 2:19

Mary remained with Elizabeth until the time had come for her to give birth to the Lord's Forerunner. She had come to witness John's nativity,* to care for him and his mother (since she would not see much of them in the years ahead), so that during this time Elizabeth and John would grow in grace. They had been filled with the Holy Spirit when Mary and the Lord himself first came to them, but grace continued to be lavished upon them so long as they all remained together. **Massa*

The Birth of Saint John the Baptist

**R 13*

Now Elizabeth's full time of being delivered was come, and she brought forth a son on the twenty-fourth of June, a Friday. The Blessed Virgin humbly cared for the baby and his mother, although she stayed in another house, preferring to serve rather than be served. *And her neighbors and kinsfolk heard that the Lord had showed his great mercy towards her* by removing the stigma of infertility and giving Elizabeth such a remarkable child, who had been so wondrously announced and conceived. *And they congratulated with her** for this astounding gift, just as the angel had foretold to Zechariah: *Many shall rejoice in his nativity.** This rejoicing was a presage of John's future holiness. Their reaction reminds us that we should rejoice over the good fortune of others and congratulate them rather than imitate the envious, who rejoice over the misfortunes of others and are saddened when they prosper. *Luke 1:57 *Luke 1:58 *Luke 1:14; *Lyra Luke 1:57–58*

**R 14*

*Here it should be noted that on this same date Saint John the Evangelist was released from the prison of this world and gloriously entered the heavenly mansions, to the great joy of the angels. However, because the birth of John the Baptist is such a great solemnity, the church has determined that the feast of John the Evangelist is to be observed on the third day within the octave of Christmas; or this may be because December twenty-seventh is the anniversary of the dedication of a church in his honor or perhaps because on that day John the Evangelist was enthroned as patriarch of the churches of Asia. In any event, the solemnity of John the Baptist continues to be celebrated on June twenty-fourth, in accordance with the prediction made by the angel that *many shall rejoice at his nativity*. Therefore, dearly beloved, on this day let us devoutly honor both of these saints, who are equally God's friends and who shine out among the angelic choirs; let us send up prayers before the throne of grace, so that we may obtain mercy and find grace in time of need.[3]

But why do we celebrate the nativity of John the Baptist rather than the birthday of other saints? The reason, in Augustine's opinion, is that other saints only professed faith in the Lord after they were born and had attained the use of reason; none of them served under his standard from the moment of their birth.* But John's very birth foretold the coming of Christ, since he had even greeted him from his moth-

*Sermo 292.1; PL 38:1320

[3] The feast of the Birth of John the Baptist is one of the oldest celebrations on the Christian calendar; it is celebrated on June 24 because this is six months before the feast of Christ's nativity. The appropriateness of these two births being associated with the summer and winter solstices was noted as far back as Augustine's day; the fact that we have seven homilies preached by him on this occasion indicates how important the feast was in the early church. The *Golden Legend* relates the story of the death of John the Evangelist occurring on June 24 and includes a charming story that two eminent theologians argued about which Saint John should be honored on this day; each saint appeared to his particular champion and said, "We get along well together in heaven—don't start disputes about us on earth!"

er's womb. John's nativity is also celebrated because he was given the grace to be born at the beginning of the time of grace: he who was to announce the grace of the new covenant was himself purified in the womb. It is customary in many places to light bonfires to honor the man about whom the Lord himself said, *He was a burning and a shining light.** *John 5:35

*R 15 **And it came to pass that on the eighth day they came to circumcise the child,* in accordance with the precept of the law. And, because it was customary to give the boy his name then (as we do at baptism), *they called him by his father's name, Zachary.** It was a common practice to name a firstborn son after his father, especially when he was an only child. And it was fitting that the child be named on the occasion of his circumcision, for no one is worthy to be entered into the Book of Life without casting off the desires of the flesh, which is what circumcision symbolizes. *And his mother answering, said, "Not so;* he shall not be called Zechariah. *But he shall be called John."** This had certainly been revealed to her by God; she had not learned it from his father, who was mute. *Luke 1:59 *Luke 1:50

The father himself was asked by gestures what name he wanted the child to have, which suggests that he was deaf as well as mute. *And demanding* by signs *a writing table,** *he wrote, saying: "John is his name."*[4]‡ He did not say *will be*, but *is*: as if he were saying, "This is the name already given to him by God and the angel; I am not giving him this name, I am simply making known the name he already has." **pugillarem* ‡Luke 1:63; *Zachary 1.4; PL 186:60B*

*R 16 *Notice here how appropriate the name *John* was for him: first, because of the fullness of grace he possessed; second, for the season of grace, which had

[4] Ludolph adds an explanatory note from St Cher: "A *pugillus* is a tablet that can be held in the hand. In the everyday language of the Romans, a *pugilla* is a writing tablet; similarly, sometimes we speak of a tablet pen, pencil, or stylus."

begun in him; third, for the excellence of grace, that is, the forgiveness of sins and the giving of grace, which he was the first to preach.[5] *And they all wondered** at how the two parents were in agreement about the name, or at the marvelous way in which it had been given.

*Luke 1:63

Zechariah Speaks

***R 17**

*Luke 1:64

**Ambrose, Ex Luke 2.32; PL 15:1564A; CL 14:45*

*Luke 1:64

*Dan 3:84

*Luke 1:65

**Lyra Luke 1:65 approx*

And immediately* Zechariah's *mouth was opened and his tongue loosed, because belief untied what unbelief had bound.* He was found worthy to be liberated by the faith he evidenced by writing (because he was unable to speak), just as he had deserved to be bound by the word of doubt he had uttered. In this way the grace of the New Testament was revealed and made known. *And he spoke, blessing God** for the favors he had shown him. Nor should we be surprised that he spoke, since his "prior" (God) had given him the *Benedicite*: so he blessed God, according to the command, *O you priests of the Lord, bless the Lord.*[6]*

*And fear came upon all their neighbors.** This was either a sense of awe at all the marvels surrounding John's birth (an elderly, barren woman giving birth, the singular circumstances of his naming, Zechariah's recovery of speech), or it was a fear of punishment, because they saw a holy man chastised on account of his hesitation and they knew it was imprudent to offend God.*

[5] Jerome (Int nom) renders *John* as *the grace of God* or *the one to whom it is given* (PL 23:853).

[6] Ludolph employs a play on words here: the word *Benedicite* can refer to the Canticle of the Three Young Men in the book of Daniel; in liturgical contexts, it is sometimes used as an imperative, equivalent to, "Say the word of blessing."

And all these wondrous *things were noised abroad over all the hill country of Judea. And all they that had heard them laid them up in their heart*, considering the miraculous events that had taken place and silently awaiting their outcome, *saying among themselves: "What shall this child later be?"** This was as much as to say, "He will be very great and praiseworthy." Nor was it surprising that *they were saying that the hand of the Lord*, that is, divine power and God's virtue, *was with him** on account of the miraculous events surrounding John's birth. Thus they reasonably concluded that the boy would one day be great in God's sight. *And Zachary his father was filled with the Holy Spirit. And he prophesied, saying: "Blessed be the Lord God of Israel,"** and so on.

*Luke 1:65-66

*Luke 1:66

*Luke 1:67-68

***R 18**

*How great is the largesse of divine mercy and God's gifts, when we are prompt and ready to accept them! See how the gift of speech that had been taken away because of distrust is now restored to the believer, and with it the spirit of prophecy. *Where sin abounded, grace did more abound:** often God gives back more than he took away, and he heals in spirit those he has healed in body. Ambrose writes, "See how good God is, and how willing to forgive sins: not only does he restore what was lost; he also bestows what was unhoped for. He who was formerly mute now prophesies. This is God's greatest gift: that those who denied him confess him. Let no one distrust, let no one mindful of earlier transgressions despair of divine rewards. God can commute the sentence, if you know how make amends for your failings."*

*Rom 5:20

*Exp Luke 2.33; PL 15:1564B; CL 14:45

Mary Returns Home

***R 19**

*At last, bidding farewell to John and Elizabeth, and blessing John, Mary *returned to her own house** in Nazareth. It is commonly believed that she left once John was born; having completed her task of assisting

*Luke 1:56

them, she left as soon as her cousin had safely given birth. In this way she showed that it is shameful to stay in someone else's home without good reason.

It is agreeable to consider here what tears Zechariah and Elizabeth shed when the Virgin Mary left them, when the joy of the world and the star of the sea *returned to her own house*. John was not a little saddened, too, by her departure—after all, her arrival had brought him such great joy.* As she makes her way home, strive to recall her poverty. She was going to a house in which there was neither bread nor wine nor other necessities to be found. She had remained for three months with them in rather comfortable circumstances; now she was returning to her poor home, and to the need to provide food by the work of her hands. Be moved by compassion for her, and enkindle your own love of poverty.*

**Bruno Luke 1:56; PL 165:347B*

**Massa; MVC 5; CM 153:27*

John's Infancy

And the child John *grew* in body *and was strengthened in spirit,** increasing in grace and virtue; his bodily growth was matched by an increase of virtue. The flesh is weak, so it must be strengthened by a willing spirit. And to perfect his manner of living *he was in the deserts* because such places lent themselves to prayer and contemplation. He dwelt there from the time he was seven years old *until the day of his manifestation to Israel,** that is, until it pleased God to reveal him to the people of Israel. This was *in the fifteenth year of the reign of Tiberius Caesar, when he came into all the country about the Jordan preaching the baptism of penance.** Then he emerged from the desert to preach to the people. Reflect on John's greatness, both as it is demonstrated in all that has been presented here and in the other privileges of his that can be known.

*Luke 1:80

*Luke 1:80

*Luke 3:1, 3

✠

Saint John the Baptist, you were known fully to God before you were known outside the womb, and you knew God before you were known in the world. In my anxiety I fly to you; iniquity has made me so guilty before God, but grace has made you such a friend of his. O my great patron, be mindful of me: as God's grace has greatly exalted you, so may your compassion help raise up one whom guilt has cast down. My iniquity has made me what I am; what you are is not your doing, but the effect of God's grace in you. Obtain for me, a miserable creature, that just as you leaped with great joy at the first coming of our Savior, so I may be found worthy to rejoice at his second coming and exult with the saints in glory. Amen.

CHAPTER 7

The Savior's Genealogy

(Matt 1:1-17; Luke 3:23-38)

***R 1** *Having considered the birth of John the Baptist, the next subject for our meditation is the Savior's genealogy, because this preceded his nativity. Matthew speaks of this genealogy as follows: *"The book of the generation** in time *of Jesus Christ*, that is, the anointed Savior, *the son of David, the son of Abraham."** Matthew's work is entitled *The Book of the Generation* because he wrote in Hebrew, and it was customary for the Jews to call a book after its opening words or the first subject considered. Therefore, Matthew named his book after Christ's genealogy because this was the topic with which he began his narrative.[1]*

**liber generationis*
*Matt 1:1
**Lyra Matt 1:1*

In his prologue Matthew proposes two ancestors in particular, David and Abraham. Christ is spoken of as the son of these two especially, because one was the principal king and the other the principal patriarch, because only to these two figures in the Old Testament was the promise expressly made that the Messiah would be born from them, and to show that the priesthood (from Abraham) and the kingship (from David) were Christ's birthright. Why does he mention David first, although Abraham lived before him? Because royal dignity takes precedence over priority in time; because David was a great sinner, so that by mention-

[1] The Greek *genesis* and Latin *generatio* can mean either genealogy or birth; the words clearly mean the latter in Matt 1:18.

ing the sinner before the just man he could show that Christ's sole motivation for being born was for mercy; because the promise was made more often, more clearly, and more firmly to David; and because Matthew did not want to disturb the pattern of his genealogical list, in which the name that ends one clause begins the next.* **Lyra Matt 1:1 approx*

Starting the genealogy proper, he writes, *Abraham begot Isaac,** and so on until he comes to Joseph. He lists all the generations until he reaches the one in Mary's time, *of whom was born Jesus, who is called Christ.** About this more will be said later. And he says *the book of the generation*, singular, because although many generations are unrolled in order, there is only one generation sought, that of *Jesus Christ*, and the others are introduced here to reach that one. He is called *Jesus* on account of his divine nature, and *Christ* on account of his human nature. The name *Jesus* is proper, the name *Christ* is common; *Jesus* is a name of glory, *Christ* is a name of grace.

*Matt 1:2

*Matt 1:16

Pause here to reflect that Matthew carefully constructed Christ's genealogy in descending order to emphasize how Christ descended among us in his humanity and how God took on our mortal weakness. This is why he begins with Abraham, showing how God came into the world by assuming the flesh that came down through the ages from the patriarchs to the time of Joseph, the husband of Mary. Jesus is born of her only in a material way, being born substantially from the Father. Luke, on the other hand, presents his genealogy in ascending order to show that the children of grace ascend to the heavenly kingdom through Christ, and he describes how human nature returns into God. Thus he begins with Christ's baptism, where human beings become children of grace, and goes back from there to Adam; spiritual generation embraces all those who want to become the children of God in Christ. ***R 2**

**Lyra Matt 1:2*

Hilary says, "What Matthew related in terms of royal succession, Luke sets forth in order of priestly origin. While accounting for each order, both indicate the relationship of the Lord to each ancestral lineage. Each in his own way demonstrates the glory of our Lord Jesus Christ, who is both the eternal King and Priest, as seen in even the fleshly origin of his ancestries."* Augustine writes, "In those times only a king and a priest were anointed, and in these two personages the one King and Priest was prefigured. The one Christ holds both offices, ruling and interceding for us, and he makes us the members of his Body, so that we are in the anointed one and he is in us."*

*Com Matt 1:1; PL 9:918C–19A

*En Ps 26:1; PL 36:200; CL 38:154

*R 3

*Matthew begins his genealogy with Abraham and comes through the line of Judah to David, the first king of that line, and proceeds to enumerate all of the other descendants down to Joseph. Thus he shows that according to the flesh our Savior comes from the seed of Abraham, the greatest of the patriarchs, and from the progeny of David, the greatest king, and from the tribe of Judah, the most illustrious of the tribes. The Christ had been promised to Abraham and David, and it was prophesied that he would originate from the tribe of Judah.

*R 4

He delineates his genealogy in three sets of fourteen; some of these generations were before the law, some were under the law, and the last, that is, the generation of Christ, was in the time of grace that commenced with his conception. This suggests that some people were saved in each of those ages through faith in Christ. Chrysostom notes that at every fourteenth generation there was a change in the status of the Jewish people: from Abraham to David they were ruled by judges; from David to the exile they were ruled by kings; and from the exile to Christ they were ruled by priests. Just as at every fourteen generations there was a change in the human condition, so it changed again with Christ, who is in himself Judge, King, and Priest.

*Opus imperf 1; PG 56:629

This pattern also suggests that obedience to the Ten Commandments and the truth of the four gospels in the faith of the Trinity are fulfilled in Christ, through whom *he gave* us *the power to be made the sons of God.** When we observe these commandments, Christ, the Sun of Justice, will arise in us through spiritual illumination.

*John 1:12

Also, three times fourteen equals forty-two: the children of Israel advanced to the Promised Land through forty-two stages, and forty-two generations bring us to Christ, our promised reward.* ‡These three sets of fourteen mark three epochs: before the law, under the law, and in the time of grace. The first period stretches from Abraham to David, the second from David to the Babylonian captivity, the third from the captivity to Christ. The first was the age of the patriarchs, the second the age of the kings, and the third the age of the leaders. Finally, these generations consist of three groups: those born before the migration into Egypt, beginning with Judah; those born in Egypt, beginning with Perez; and those born after the exodus from Egypt, beginning with Nahshon.

*Num 33:1-49; *Christian Druthmar, Matt 1:17; PL 105:1271C*
‡R 5

A Spiritual Interpretation of the Generations

*The three sets of fourteen generations can be understood to represent the birth of Christ through grace in the penitent, the proficient, and the perfect. The spiritual generation of Christ in the penitent soul is manifested by the three stages of repentance: beginning, progress, consummation. The beginning of repentance in turn consists of three kinds of acts: preparatory, constitutive, and preservative. The preparatory acts are two: faith in God's goodness, signified by Abraham, and hope for pardon, symbolized by Isaac. The constitutive acts are three: sorrowful contrition and hatred for sins formerly loved, symbolized

***R 6**

by Jacob; confession, symbolized by Judah; and satisfaction, symbolized by his brothers. The preservative acts are also three: fear of offending, symbolized by Perez (*division*); love of glory, symbolized by Zerah (*dawn*); and fear of Gehenna, symbolized by Hezron (*arrow*).[2]

Next comes the spiritual birth of Christ in the soul that is progressing in penitence; there are four generations here, corresponding to four aids to repentance. The first is for the elect to do good rather than evil, symbolized by Ram (*elect*); second is a perfect will in doing good, symbolized by Amminadab (*spontaneous*); next comes the prudent discernment that enables us to avoid what is harmful, symbolized by Nahshon (*serpent*); fourth is finding joy and well-being in doing good, symbolized by Salmon (*perceptible*).

The generation of Christ in the soul through the consummation of penitence also contains four aids. The first is strength in resisting the temptation to sin, symbolized by Boaz (*strength*); next comes docility to the movement of grace, symbolized by Obed (*serving*); third is steadfastness in the face of persecution and punishment, symbolized by Jesse, that is, the *islands of Lebanon*[3] (because islands are pounded on every side

[2] The interpretations of the Hebrew names, given in parentheses, come for the most part from Jerome; Ludolph's principal source is Zachary 1.5 (PL 186:66D–68C). Medieval commentators sought to explain why these interpretations suited Christ's ancestors and drew allegorical and moral meanings from them. Two early examples are Ps-Bede, Hom 55 (PL 94:414A–19A) and Ps? Alcuin, *Interpretationes nominum Hebraicorum progenitorum* D.N.I.C. (PL 100:725A–34A). Ludolph's presentation is remarkable for its combination of medieval biblical exegesis and scholastic organization of the elements and stages of the spiritual life.

[3] Jerome has *insulae libatio* (offering of the island), not *insulae Libani*, but the meaning is not clear in either case.

by waves); fourth is the strength of final perseverance, symbolized by David, that is, *with a strong hand.*

*There follow the next fourteen generations, which symbolize Christ's spiritual birth in the proficient. There are four stages here: choosing good, avoiding evil, keeping the commandments, and fulfilling the counsels. Choosing to do good consists of three things: peace of heart within, which is symbolized by Solomon (*peaceful*); breadth of charity towards our neighbor, symbolized by Rehoboam (*breadth of the people*); and subjection of the will to God, symbolized by Abijah (*lord and father*), by which subjection of both fear and love is understood. *R 7

Similarly, there are three ways to turn away from evil: avoiding scandal, symbolized by Asa (*taking away*); avoiding perverse judgments, symbolized by Jehoshaphat (*judging*); not holding others in contempt, symbolized by Joram (*noble*). The first way pertains to deeds, the second to thoughts, and the third to feelings.

The third stage, keeping the commandments, consists of four generations, in which the commandments must be observed both in adversity and in prosperity. Two pertain to times of adversity: strength in approaching difficult matters, symbolized by Uzziah (*strength of the Lord*), and patience in sustaining adversity, symbolized by Jotham (*perfection*), because *patience has a perfect work.** Two generations pertain to times of prosperity: continence, so that we do not take delight in ephemeral goods, symbolized by Ahaz (*moderation*), and solace in lasting goods, symbolized by Hezekiah (*the Lord has comforted me*).

*Jas 1:4

The fourth stage, fulfilling the counsels, brings together four virtues: forgetfulness of worldly concerns, symbolized by Manasseh (*forgetfulness*); acceptance of the Lord's yoke as spiritual nourishment, symbolized by Amos (*nourished*), for, as Christ said elsewhere, *Come to me all you that labor and are burdened, and I will*

*Matt 11:28 *refresh you;** third, devotion regarding present merit, symbolized by Josiah (*incense of the Lord*); and fourth, preparation for future reward, symbolized by Jechoniah (*preparation*).

*R 8 *The last set of fourteen generations signifies the birth of Christ in the souls of the perfect according to four stages. The first concerns religious, then pastors, third those in the world, and finally all alike who strive to persevere. These generations were born after *the transmigration of Babylon,** that is, after leaving the state of imperfection and embracing the perfection of religious life. The three qualities needed here are prompt obedience, symbolized by Jechoniah (*preparation*); voluntary poverty, by which nothing is sought but God, symbolized by Shealtiel (*God is my petition*); and a disciplined regimen, symbolized by Zerubbabel (*master of confusion*), because regularity of religious observance conquers the confusion of sin.

*Matt 1:17

Four virtues pertain to the perfection of pastors: paternal solicitude for those under their care, symbolized by Abiud (*that one is my father*); teaching that provokes the lazy, symbolized by Eliakim (*reawakening*); wisdom that counsels the ignorant, symbolized by Azor (*seeing the light*); and holiness of life that influences others, symbolized by Zadok (*just*).

Four virtues pertain to those living in the world: perfect charity towards neighbors, symbolized by Achim (*my brother*); perfect love of God, symbolized by Eliud (*my God*); perfect trust in God in adversity, symbolized by Eleazar (*God is my help*); and perfect humility in prosperity, so that everything is seen to be a gift of God, symbolized by Matthan (*gift*).

Three virtues pertain to people of every state of life who are striving to persevere: overcoming vice, symbolized by Jacob (*supplanter*); continued progress in virtues, symbolized by Joseph (*increase*); and constant, immovable faith, symbolized by the words *the husband of Mary* (whose name means *star of the sea*, that is, the pole star). These three virtues are essential if we are to persevere. All of the personages listed here are figures of Christ, because the reality underlying the interpretations of their names is found in him.

Christ's Undistinguished Ancestry

*Let us pause here to reflect on the Lord's forbears. He did not consider it beneath him to come from poor and even sinful stock, nor did he desire to boast of his ancestry. We should not take pride in our lineage or, all the more, in our virtues or good works, lest by doing so we diminish our reward or even forfeit it completely. Chrysostom says, *R 9

> Christ's dignity shines out, not because he had renowned and powerful ancestors, but because he came from a poor and modest line. Great and admirable is the glory of one so high, that he should voluntarily abase himself so completely. Just as it is a cause for wonder that he not only died but was in fact crucified and buried, so we marvel that in speaking of his birth it can be said that he not only deigned to take on our lowly nature when he became Man, but that he also willed to have such undistinguished ancestors.
>
> Christ was not ashamed of our worthlessness: without doubt he was instructing us that we should never blush because of our ancestors' failings, but seek one thing only: to ennoble ourselves with the honor of our own virtues. People should not be praised or blamed for the virtues or the vices of their parents; in truth, no one is either renowned or belittled on that score. On the contrary, having given the matter more thought, I do not know anyone more illustrious than the person with splendid virtues whose parents were far from being virtuous themselves. So let no one boast of his or her family tree. Rather, reflecting on the Lord's ancestors, let

us put such haughty conceits out of our minds and glory only in our own virtues.

What am I saying? We should not take pride in these virtues either—this is how the Pharisee made himself inferior to the publican. Take care that the fruit you have harvested does not rot, that you do not pour out your sweat in vain or run your course foolishly and, after completing a thousand laps, forfeit the prize of your labor. Your Lord, who is much better than you, knows the reward your merits deserve. Let us not be swelled with pride, but say that we are only useless servants, so that we may cross over into a useful direction. If you say you should be congratulated, you will be rejected, even if you were praiseworthy before.

This is why we must forget our past good deeds: the safest bank in which to keep virtue is the forgetfulness of virtue. If we carry our deeds around in our memory, greedily counting them over and over, we are only buying weapons for our enemy and goading him to attack us, or tempting a thief to rob us. But if the only one aware of them is the one from whom nothing can be hidden, what is most precious to us is stored in a safe place. If we continually parade our goods, we only increase the likelihood that they will be stolen; the Pharisee had his good deeds on the tip of his tongue, and it was from there that the devil snatched them! Let us avoid boasting, which only makes us repellent to others and detestable to God. The more good we do, the less we should talk about ourselves; this is the best way to grow in the estimation of our neighbors and of God. Then we will receive not only praise from God, but our full reward as well. Doubtless, if we perform holy actions in this way, God becomes our debtor; and, when we view ourselves as useless servants, we earn a greater reward for our attitude than for our actions.

*R 10 *The benefit of humility far exceeds all other virtues, and if it is lacking, no other virtues are praiseworthy. If you want your good works to be great, do not think they are great; if you do, they will not be great. Remember the centurion: he said, *I am not worthy that you should enter under my roof,** and so saying, he became worthy and the wonder of him was praised above all the Jews. Paul said, *I am not worthy to be called an apostle,** and he became the greatest of them all. John the Baptist said, *the latchet of whose shoes I am not worthy to stoop down and loose,** and on that account he became the friend of the bridegroom, and the hand he thought unworthy to touch his sandal Christ raised over his own head. Peter said, *Depart from me, for I am a sinful man, O Lord,** and so he became the foundation of the church.

*Matt 8:8

*1 Cor 15:9

*Mark 1:7

*Luke 5:8

Nothing makes us friends of God more than thinking of ourselves as small and of little worth. Humility, more than any other virtue, is born and nourished when we look deep into our soul and see it for what it truly is. A heart that is bruised and humbled will not be lifted up by vainglory, or turn green with envy, or be shaken with violent anger, or harbor any other passion. The Lord says, *Learn of me, because I am meek, and humble of heart; and you shall find rest to your souls.** If we seek to enjoy great rest, both here and hereafter, let us plant humility, the mother of all good things, deep within our souls. In this way we will be able to cross the tempestuous sea of this world and find our way into that most tranquil port.*

*Matt 11:29

*Hom Matt 3.2–6; PG 57/58:998–1004

✠

Lord Jesus Christ, our hope and confidence, be mindful of what you took on for our redemption. Recall that you, the Creator of all things, assumed our weakness when you accepted our nature. Lord, you came for sinners, to wipe away the sins of all. What can I do for you in return? How to fittingly respond? I praise you and thank you with all my heart for the boundless kindness with which you came to save our fallen race. And I beg you, most gracious Lord: do not allow this human nature of ours to perish, that nature that you humbled yourself to take on for love of us. And make me serve you as I ought, in a way pleasing to you. Amen.

CHAPTER 8

Joseph's Wish to Send Mary Away

(Matt 1:18-25)

*Matthew had demonstrated the truth of Christ's humanity by recounting his genealogy; now he shows Christ's divinity by describing the miraculous nature of his conception. He writes, *Now the generation of Christ happened in this way.** This was as much as to say, "It should not be believed that God would be born as a result of the union of husband and wife, but rather in a miraculous way." He goes on to say that when Mary had returned home from visiting Elizabeth, and Joseph had at length come from Judea in Galilee, *as his mother Mary was espoused to Joseph,* he wanted to bring her into his home. But then Matthew adds, *Before they came together she was found with child.** *Before they came together* means before the wedding ceremony had been celebrated. *R 1

*Matt 1:18

*Matt 1:18

This does not mean necessarily that they came together afterwards, but only that the date for the wedding was approaching. This is a turn of phrase; for example, if I say, "He died before he repented," it means the person did not repent.* Or else *before they came together* can mean before they came together under the same roof: Mary was still living in her home and Joseph in his. The Jews did not think it right that a couple live together before the wedding celebration. Joseph found that Mary was with child, but what he

*Gloss Matt 1:18; PL 114:70C

had not found or discovered is what Matthew next says: that this was the work *of the Holy Spirit*.*

*Matt 1:18

*R 2

*Weighing the situation carefully, and being in ignorance of such a great mystery, Joseph was troubled and saddened. *Not willing publicly to expose* her*, he *was minded to put her away privately** and send her back to her parents, from whom he had accepted her. He was *not willing to expose her* publicly, ***lest she be stoned to death as an adulteress***; or ***he was not willing to lead her into his home**** to live with him because he felt unworthy to be her companion on account of the excellence of the mystery, even though he did not know how it had taken place.[1] He had read, *There shall come forth a rod out of the root of Jesse*,* and he knew that Mary came from this stock. But he had also read, *Behold, a virgin shall conceive*,* and he believed that this was true of Mary, especially because her face shone with such divine light after her conception that its brightness made him avert his eyes; he could not regard her without experiencing a kind of awe. For this reason he wanted to humble himself before such grace and believed he was unworthy to live with the Virgin.

**traducere*

*Matt 1:19

*Latin Diatessaron?

*Isa 11:1

*Isa 7:14

Jerome says, "It is a testimony to Mary that Joseph, knowing her chastity and perplexed by what had taken place, conceals in silence the mystery he did not know about."* Chrysostom exclaims, "O inestimable praise of Mary! Joseph believed her chastity more than her womb, and the work of grace more than the work of nature. He could see that she was pregnant but could not suspect fornication. He believed it was more possible for a virgin to conceive without a man than for Mary to sin."*

*Com Matt 1:19; PL 26:24C

*Opus imperf 1; PG 56:633

Mary herself was disturbed, for she saw that Joseph was troubled, and this caused her no little distress. But she humbly kept silent, preferring to be thought

[1] *Traducere* can mean either *to display* or *to lead over*.

wicked rather than advertise God's gift and, by speaking a word in her defense, be liable to anything that approached vainglory. She asked God if he would deign to apply a remedy to take away the tribulation she and her spouse were experiencing. Consider here how great their distress and anxiety were and how, for the sake of a future crown, God permitted his own to be tested and disturbed. But in the end he delivered them both.* **Massa*

Joseph Is Instructed by the Angel

Joseph reflected and deliberated about whether he should send Mary away, which teaches us that we should devote a great deal of thought to doubtful or uncertain cases, lest we sin by acting rashly. As Joseph was pondering this question, the Lord sent an angel to him—according to Augustine, the angel Gabriel. Chrysostom says he did this for three reasons: so that a just man would not do an unjust deed, albeit with a just intent; so that he could preserve the mother's honor, who would be suspected of indecent conduct if she were sent away; and so that Joseph would treat Mary with even greater reverence once he knew how she came to be pregnant.* The Gloss adds a fourth reason: so that a man so commendable for his righteousness should not be plagued too long with doubt.* ***R 3**

*Ps-Augustine, Sermo 195.6; PL 39:2109

*Opus imperf 1; PG 56:633

*St Cher Matt 1:19

The Angel of the Lord appeared to him in his sleep, not in an unmistakable vision, because he was overwhelmed with doubt in spirit, as in the sleep of unbelief, *saying: "Joseph, son of David."** By addressing him in this way, Chrysostom suggests, the angel was reminding him of the promise of the Messiah made to David.* This was as much as to say, according to the Gloss, "Remember the promise made to David, of whom Mary is a descendant, and see it fulfilled in her."*

*Matt 1:20

*St Cher Matt 1:20

*Matt 1:20; PL 114:71B

The angel continued, *"Fear not to take unto yourself* and into your home *Mary, your wife,** and to live with her, not for marital relations, but as her devoted servant, and indeed, to enjoy the union of your souls' affections, for this is the essence of marriage." Mary's example demonstrates that it is possible for a believing couple by mutual consent to embrace a life of continence; true marriage does not require sexual union but safeguarding the heart's affection. Hence Joseph is called Mary's husband, because there is a true marriage where love is maintained, and in Mary was found the fruit of marital love.[2]* It was as if the angel were saying, "Do not suppose that this child is the result of human action: *for that which is conceived* in her is of the Holy Spirit,** and this has come about by the Spirit's power."[3]

*Matt 1:20

*Gloss Matt 1:16; PL 114:70A

*natum

*Matt 1:20

Here the angel made a very clear revelation to Joseph. He had surmised implicitly that there was something divine about the Virgin's having conceived, as we noted earlier, but he did not know how this had taken place and was ignorant as to the mysterious manner of Mary's conception. Now these truths were revealed explicitly to him by the angel: *"*And she shall bring forth* from her womb *a son*, as a star gives out

***R 4**

[2] The Gloss cites a principle given by Augustine in De cons ev 2.1.2: "By this example an illustrious recommendation is made to married persons of the principle that, even when they maintain their continence by common consent, they are indeed married and can be called such; although there is no bodily sexual intercourse, the affections of the mind are maintained" (PL 34:1071).

[3] The Vulgate, in line with the Greek ("begotten"), reads *quod enim in ea natum est*. Ludolph gives the following explanation: "To be born *in* her is to be conceived, to be born *from* her is to be brought into the light. Therefore, we can speak of a twofold nativity: in the womb and from the womb. We are born in the womb at conception, and we are born from the womb when we emerge into the light." This idea expands on a line in Zachary 1.5 (PL 186:71D).

light, or a stem buds a flower, or the earth produces a shoot, *and you shall call his name Jesus*, that is, Savior, *for he shall save his people from their sins.** And this is no small matter, because there is no slavery worse than slavery to sin, and he will do this for their benefit." *Matt 1:21

Here the angel shows that Christ is true Man, because he is born of the Virgin, and true God, because he will save his people from their sins—and no one can save us from sin but God.* (This theme was treated at greater length earlier when we reflected on Christ's conception.) **Lyra Matt 1:21*

Joseph Obeys the Angel

*Having been assured about Mary's virginal conception, Joseph, *rising up from* the *sleep** of doubt, did as the angel commanded and took his bride in marriage; that is, he claimed Mary as his wife, although he lived as a virgin with the Virgin, obediently serving her as his Lady. From this we learn that we should immediately do whatever God tells us. If you have made a vow to God, fulfill it right away if you can; if you cannot, then do so as soon as you are able. If you make a promise that is not tied to a specific time, keep it as soon as you can. Chrysostom observes, "Once he had been instructed about the sacrament of the heavenly mystery by the angel, Joseph joyfully obeyed the angel's command, eagerly carrying out the divine decree. He received holy Mary and gloried in his vow, rejoicing that he deserved to have the angel call a Virgin Mother of such majesty his wife."* **R 5** *Matt 1:24 *Chromatius 3.1; CL 9A:208

Joseph, who had considered sending Mary away but then received her as his Lady once the mystery was explained to him by the angel, can represent a person experiencing doubts about a matter of faith or morals who is given assurance by a preacher or good confessor and obeys his admonition.* **Lyra Matt 1:18-20 mor*

*R 6
*Matt 1:25

And he knew her not till she brought forth her firstborn son; that is, he did not know how very great Mary's dignity was until Christ was born. Chrysostom writes, "Truly, he did not know her beforehand, that is, what honor she had been given. But after she gave birth he knew her, because she had been made more splendid and noble than the entire world. She alone received into the narrow confines of her womb him whom the whole world could not contain."*

*Opus imperf 1; PG 56:635

Or this phrase could mean that, because of what the angel had revealed to him, Joseph did not ever know her carnally, in which case *till* here means *never*, a brief period of time representing all time. Sometimes the word *till* can mean a set period of time, after which something happens: If I say, "He did not eat till noon," this means that he ate at noon. But at other times, the word can mean *always*. For example, *Sit at my right hand till I make your enemies your footstool,** means, "Always sit at my right hand." At other times the word can be understood to mean the negation of all time, hence *never*, as in this case.* For if Joseph had no relations with Mary before she gave birth, all the more would he not have had relations after she gave birth, having seen such miraculous signs surrounding Christ's birth and knowing after the Lord's nativity that the child who was born was God.

*Ps 109:1
*Lyra Matt 1:25

Others suggest that *he knew her not* refers to recognizing her face: they say that the presence of Christ in the Virgin's womb imparted such glory to her visage that Joseph could not look her in the face; such was the effect on her who had been filled with the Holy Spirit. We read that the children of Israel could not look upon the face of Moses after he had spoken with the Lord, so brilliant was its splendor. Similarly, Joseph could not look at his wife face to face until the child had left her womb.*

*Lyra Matt 1:25

So Joseph remained with his blessed wife, loved her with a chaste affection that defies description, and faithfully cared for her. Our Lady stayed with him with complete assurance, and they lived together joyfully in their shared poverty.

Jesus Teaches Us Patience and Humility

When the tribulation ended, great consolation returned. And so it happens to us when we are patient in time of trial. *Jesus also remained enclosed in his ***R 7** mother's womb for nine months, like any other child, so that those imprisoned in the miseries of this world or the realm of death might be restored to fellowship with the nine choirs of angels. He dwelled there benevolently, patiently awaiting the moment chosen for his birth. Feel compassion for him in such depths of humility. We should cherish this virtue profoundly—how can we vaunt ourselves or boast of our reputation when the Lord lowered himself so much? Because we cannot worthily make satisfaction to him who endured this lengthy period of enclosure to gain us this one virtue, let us at least acknowledge this in our heart and give fervent thanks to him who has chosen us from among so many others to make some recompense to him by embracing the cloistered life in his service. This is his gift, not our merit, a benefit that is acceptable, venerable, and very great.* **Massa*

We are sequestered for protection, not punishment: we are gathered together in the most secure citadel of religious life, beyond the reach of the poisonous arrows of this wicked world and the tempestuous waves of the sea, unless our own rashness exposes us to danger. Let us strive, then, to keep our minds free of all perishable things and so create a space for the Lord by purity of heart. Without mental discipline bodily seclusion affords little or no advantage.* Augustine **Massa* asks, "What good is bodily solitude if mental solitude is lacking?" And Gregory, "What advantage is there to keeping your body in the cloister if your mind is wandering through the world?"* *Mor 20.XVI.52 for both; PL 76:553A; CL 143B:1527

Let us make the effort to give thanks to God in all circumstances and bless him from our hearts. It is the noblest of virtues and a most splendid thing in God's sight when we bear the yoke of obedience, endure exile, poverty, derision, or illness, and sustain tribulations of mind or body—and still we want to praise God, know how to bless him wholeheartedly, render him thanks joyfully, seek to raise our desires heavenward, and honor him with our deeds.* *Massa* Bernard exclaims, "Happy those whose bodily passions are regulated by righteousness, so that they endure all their sufferings for the sake of God's Son! Discontented murmuring is uprooted from the heart, and on their lips are words of praise and thanksgiving."‡ ‡Sermo Wed Holy Week; PL 183:270B; SB 5:66

Let us attend well to the truth *that to them that love God all things work together unto good;** *Rom 8:28 if we do, we will attain great tranquility of spirit and experience what the sage said: *Whatsoever shall befall the just man shall not make him sad.** *Prov 12:21 According to Augustine, whatever befalls the just person is attributed to the divine will, not the enemy's power.† †En Ps 86, 2.4; PL 36:366; CL 38:350 And similarly, we can say with Job, *As it has pleased the Lord, so is it done: blessed be the name of the Lord.** *Job 1:21

***R 8** *Do not be wracked by doubt when affliction, trials, and scourges fall upon you; God does not permit them to come to his own unless it be to their advantage. And the advantages of trials are many:

First, they cause us to turn away from the world and reject temporal pleasures, and instead turn to God and long for eternal things. Augustine writes, "The soul only turns to God when she turns away from this world, and she is most likely to turn from this world when its trifling and dangerous pleasures are mingled with pains and labors.* *En Ps 9:10; PL 36:121–22; CL 38:63 If the Lord stopped mixing bitterness with the joys of this world, we would forget him."‡ ‡En Ps 93:24; PL 37:1212; CL 39:1326 As the psalmist says, *Their infirmities were multiplied; afterwards they made haste.*† †Ps 15:4

Second, they enable us to acknowledge our sins better, and we are washed and purified by correcting ourselves and doing penance. Augustine teaches that tribulation is to the just person what the file is to the iron, the furnace to the gold, and the winnowing tool to the wheat.* This is why Joseph's brothers said, *We deserve to suffer these things because we have sinned against our brother.*‡

*attr. to Augustine by Peter of Blois?, De util trib; PL 207:993C

‡Gen 42:21

Third, when help is taken away, we see our imperfections more clearly and know ourselves better. *In my abundance I said: "I shall never be moved."* But to show me to myself better, *You turned away your face from me, and I became troubled.**

*Ps 29:7-8

Fourth, they help us preserve humility and safeguard virtue, so that we do not presume on our merits and lift ourselves up by pride. Hence the apostle writes, *And lest the greatness of the revelations should exalt me, there was given me a sting of my flesh, an angel of Satan, to buffet me.**

*2 Cor 12:7

Fifth, we learn how bad it is to forsake God and to be forsaken by him. As Jeremiah says, *Know and see that it is an evil and a bitter thing for you to have left the Lord your God, and that my fear is not with you.**

*Jer 2:19

Sixth, they are a means by which God makes known a person's patience and by the example of his holy ones teaches others endurance. Job says, *And this may be my comfort, that he does not refrain from afflicting me with sorrow, nor do I contradict the words of the holy ones.*[4]*

*Job 6:10

Seventh, our tribulations teach others holy fear, and from them they learn how to live. We read in Proverbs, *The wicked man being scourged, the fool shall be wiser.**

*Prov 19:25

Eighth, they are an opportunity for God to manifest his glory and so lead us to praise his saving work; the infirmities of the man born blind and of Lazarus

[4] *Sermonibus sanctis* is a variant reading found in some of the fathers; the Vulgate has *sermonibus Sancti* (the words of the Holy One).

provided occasions for God's works to be manifest, and for them he is praised eternally.

Ninth, they can be signs of Christ's love for us, so that we will recall God's mercy in our regard. It says in Maccabees, *For it is a token of great goodness, when sinners are not suffered to go on in their ways* doing penance *for a long time, but are presently punished.** Jerome holds that it is a great tragedy not to obtain mercy from present misery, and Augustine suggests that God's wrath must be great indeed when he does not chastise a sinner but permits him to fall headlong into sin.*

*2 Macc 6:13

*Jer: unknown; Albert attr. to Gregory, Ps 98:9; Augustine, attr. by Lombard, Ps 9:25; PL 191:139C

Tenth, trials prompt us to place greater hope in God and grow in confidence on their account. Augustine says, "You should be fearful when all goes well with you. Is it not better to be tested and approved rather than not to be tested and condemned?"* And Bernard writes, "God is angrier when he is not angry. It is not when I am ignorant of your anger but when I feel it that I trust most in your goodwill: *indeed, when you are angry, you will remember mercy.*"*

*En Ps 144:4; PL 37:1871; CL 40:2090

*Habitat 3.2; SC 42.4; PL 183:989B; SB 2:35

Eleventh, in tribulations we can know that God is ready to come to our aid if we turn to him with our whole heart. As the psalmist says, *In my trouble I cried to the Lord, and he heard me.**

*Ps 119:1

Twelfth, God tests us by trials to see if we truly love him and to determine if there is virtue in us. Gregory says, "Adversity probes peaceful persons to see if they really love God."* And, "No one realizes his power in times of tranquility; if conflict is absent, virtue's advantage cannot be tested."‡

*Mor Praef 3: PL 75:520B; CL 143:13

‡Mor 23.XXV.51; PL 76:284A; CL 43B:1185

Thirteenth, and finally, it is when we are tested that we earn a greater crown by our patience and receive more merit, as is clear from Job and the martyrs. James says, *Blessed is the man who endures temptation, for when he has been proved, he shall receive the crown of life which God has promised to them that love him.**

*Jas 1:12; *Massa approx for these thirteen*

Likewise, according to Chrysostom, trials imply that great treasures and gifts have been entrusted to us: the devil would not assail us unless he saw that we were receiving much honor. He attacked Adam because he saw that he enjoyed great dignity, and he afflicted holy Job because he saw him wreathed with great praises by God.* *Hom Matt 13.1; PG 57/58:209

*In addition to all this, there are people who are worn down by trials and adversity, not so that they can find pardon and be cleansed of their sins, but for vengeance and punishment. Their tribulation is the beginning and growth of the eternal damnation that is the lot of the reprobate; this applies to figures like Antiochus and Herod. Up to our own time there are many whose sufferings correspond to the words of the prophet: *With a double destruction, destroy them.** For such as these, present difficulties are but the preview and beginning of the pains of Gehenna, showing by present affliction the perpetual sufferings they will endure in hell. ***R 9** *Jer 17:18; *Bede Matt 9:4; PL 92:46AB*

But in regard to his own, the Lord ordains all things mercifully and disposes everything for their benefit. The Lord acts with justice or mercy in all that he does and in all that he permits to happen. Augustine teaches, "The believer's true humility is shown by neither disdaining nor murmuring about anything, by not complaining or being ungrateful. Rather, the believer gives thanks for all God's judgments and praises him for them, because in all things God acts with either justice or kindness." ***R 10** *Prosper 83; PL 45:1866

By weighing these matters carefully, let us make it our business to rein in our hearts and make them firm in the face of adverse circumstances, bearing humbly, patiently, and indeed joyfully with what displeases us. May we so walk in the way of the spirit that we will be full of fervor and will long for such things out of love for the Lord Jesus: in his own life and in the lives of his disciples he walked this exalted path and pointed it out, leaving an example for all to follow in his footsteps.* He suffers and endures so that the chosen children of the kingdom might be afflicted here **MVC 36; CM 153:145* in body and spirit. As the apostle says, *But if you be without chastisement, then are you bastards and not sons.** Or, as Augustine puts it, "If you are spared the scourges,* then you are not numbered among the sons*."‡

*Heb 12:8
**flagellorum*
**filiorum*
‡Sermo 46.11; PL 38:276; CL 41:538

Elsewhere Augustine cautions,

> Do not promise yourself what the gospel does not promise. It is necessary for things to be as Scripture says right up to the end. Scripture guarantees us nothing in this world but tribulation, oppression, difficulties, an increase of sorrow, and an abundance of trials. Let us ready ourselves especially for these, lest we be unprepared for them and falter.* But sometimes in this life sinners are not scourged at all, or punished very little, because they are already beyond correction.
>
> Those, however, who are destined for eternal life must be scourged here, because *he scourges every son whom he receives,** that is, whom he will receive into eternal life.* Note that the apostle said *every son*, including even the only-begotten Son who was free of all sin. If he scourges this one Son who is without sin, will he spare the adopted son or daughter who is a sinner?*

*En Ps 39:28; PL 36:451; CL 38:445
*Heb 12:6
*En Ps 37:23; PL 36:409; CL 38:397
*Sermo 46:11; PL 38:276; CL 41:538

God had one Son without sin, but none without suffering; in this he gives us an example. When we see some holy person enduring the most burdensome and cruel afflictions, we will not be confounded if we do not forget what the most holy and just one endured.* He despised all worldly goods to teach us to despise them, and he endured every kind of evil that can be experienced here on earth so that we would not seek happiness in the first or fear unhappiness in the second.*

**Gloss Heb 12:6; PL 114:666D; from En Ps 31:26; PL 76:274; CL 38:243–44*
**Rabanus, De ecc disc 1.7; PL 112:1208D*

Thus it is advantageous for us to be troubled and afflicted here. We should not grow impatient or be broken; on the contrary, let us welcome trials and love them, because they frequently pull us back from evil and lead us to good. Let us view the opposite of tribulation as the real enemy and flee from it, because it can have the contrary effect.

✠

Lord Jesus Christ, the invincible wall protecting all who trust in you, be my refuge in adversity. See my tribulation and hardship, take pity on me, and in the fullness of your compassion come to my aid. Behold my weakness, and with fatherly solicitude protect me; upheld by your providence, may I never be deprived of your consolation and mercy. Remember your creature, Lord, and repel my insidious enemies. Safeguarded by your mercy, may I know the sweetness of your goodness toward me and perform fitting penance for my sins. Amen.

CHAPTER 9

The Birth of the Savior

(Luke 2:1-20)

*R 1

And it came to pass that in those days, during Mary's pregnancy, *there went out* everywhere *a decree* in writing *from Caesar Augustus that the whole world should be enrolled* ***to pay the census**** in their own cities. Pope Gregory observes, "Why was the whole world enrolled just before the Savior's birth, except to show that he was coming in the flesh to enroll his elect in eternity?"* O Lord Jesus, would that you might count me, a miserable sinner, among your elect, so that I might be enrolled for eternity! We should declare the value of our faith and justice to him, our king, by hearts, mouths, and works. We should pay him the *denarius*, that is, our soul stamped with the light of his visage (the Ten Commandments of the law), in which we discern the face of our Redeemer (his will). Just as no one was exempt from taxation, so no one is excused from following his commandments.

*Luke 2:1; Latin Diatessaron?

*40 Hom 8.1; PL 76:1103D [7.1; CL 141:54]

Here it should be noted that the first Roman Emperor was Julius Caesar. According to Isidore of Seville, he was called *Caesar* because he had been removed from the womb of his dead mother by cutting,* or because he was born in Caesarea, or because he hacked* his enemies to pieces.‡ The emperors who came after him were called *Caesar*. When Julius died, he was succeeded by his nephew Octavian Augustus, the second emperor, who was called Augustus because he greatly enlarged the Republic and the Roman

**caeso*

**caedebat*

‡Ety 9.3.12 for the first; PL 82:343A

Empire; emperors who followed him used the title Augustus. This second emperor kept his predecessor's last name and combined it with his own, so he was known as Caesar Augustus. The month of August (formerly the sixth month) was called after him, either because he was born in that month or because he returned from a victorious campaign then. He began then to exercise imperial rule (which in Greek was called the monarchy), and he reigned for fifty-seven and one-half years. He ruled in peace for a period of twelve years around the birth of Christ.

This time of peace served Christ, who chose to be born at this time: he greatly sought peace and deigned to visit those who love peace and charity. It was fitting that there should be a time of peace just before the arrival of him who was to be born as the peacemaking King and Prince of Peace, as a kind of presage; he himself taught peace to the world and bequeathed peace to his disciples when he left the world. In a moral sense we can understand that the eternal Word is only born in a peaceful heart. As the psalmist says, *And his place is in peace.** *Ps 75:3

*Before the reign of Caesar Augustus there had been many upheavals, but now the whole world, in all its regions, was at peace. Augustus wanted to maintain the Republic and foster peace, so he gave an edict *that the whole world should be enrolled*. He desired to know the number of regions in the world that were under Roman sovereignty, and the number of cities, and the population in each city, so that he could determine a fair amount for them to pay in tribute. To accomplish this he ordered that the residents in each province should come in from the small towns and villages where they were living to the cities where they had property, or where they had originally come from; there they were to give to the Roman official a denarius (this was a silver coin worth ten copper asses, hence *denarius*), to show that they were under Roman ***R 2** rule and acknowledged that they had to pay tribute. This coin was stamped with Caesar's image and had his name inscribed on it.*

*Massa

This practice was called a *declaration,* because when people presented the coin to the officials, they were to hold it over their head and by their own mouth declare themselves subjects of the Roman Empire. It was also called an *inscription* because there was a head count, and the name of each person was written down.* So there was a threefold declaration: in fact, because they paid tribute to the Roman Empire; in word, because they stated by their own mouths that they were subject to Rome; and in writing, because their names were recorded.

*Hist ev 4; PL 198:1539B; Legenda 6

*This enrolling was first made by Cyrinus, the governor of Syria,** who had been sent there by Caesar Augustus as both ruler and judge. Judea did not have its own governor but was included in the territory of Syria. This enrollment was first carried out by Quirinius, because Judea was practically the center of the inhabited world, so the census was begun in Quirinius's territory and from there was carried out by the rulers of other provinces. Or it was the first in a universal sense, because previous censuses had only been undertaken in specific regions. Or it was first because the census was carried out first on a local level by the governor; the second stage would be conducted by legates of Caesar for all the cities of a region; the third stage, of all the regions of the world, before Caesar himself. This was the first time Judea was required to pay tribute to Rome.* That this enrollment was subsequently required annually is made clear later in the gospel, where we read, *Does your master not pay the didrachma?*‡

*Luke 2:2

*Hist ev 4; PL 198:1539C; Legenda 6

‡Matt 17:23

Mary and Joseph Journey to Bethlehem

*R 3

And all went to be enrolled, every one into his own city* of origin. *And Joseph also went up from* where he was residing in *Galilee, out of the city of Nazareth, into Judea, to the city of David, which is called Bethlehem, to be enrolled with Mary his espoused wife, who was* in her ninth month *with child. Bethlehem was considered David's city because he had been born there and anointed king there; both Joseph and Mary were of his house, that is, of his tribe and family, so they went there to register for the census along with many others. See how the Lord allows himself to be inscribed in this earthly census for your sake, so that your name may be written in heaven. In this way the Savior gave an example of humility at the very beginning of his life, and he would continue to do this until death, *when he humbled himself, becoming obedient unto death, even to the death of the cross.** Bede says, "No one should miss the opportunity to contemplate such remarkable and gentle humility: Christ not only became incarnate for us; he chose to become incarnate when he would be registered under Caesar's census as soon as he was born. He was born in servitude to free us."*

*Luke 2:3-5

*Phil 2:8

*Com Luke 2:4; PL 92:330B; CL 120:48

‡Consider here how the Blessed Virgin Mary herself, even though she had conceived the King of heaven and earth, wanted to fulfill the imperial edict with her husband Joseph. Then she could say with her son, *For it is fitting for us to fulfill all justice,** and give us an example of compliance to all those in authority. Our Lady made the effort to undertake this arduous journey for a second time: it was thirty-five miles from Nazareth to Jerusalem and then another five miles or so south from Jerusalem down the mountainside to Ephrata, where Bethlehem was situated. Here we should remember that although the Blessed Virgin was about to give birth, she did not feel burdened by her child as she journeyed from province to province. According to Augustine, although Mary was pregnant, she felt buoyant and energetic because the light she bore within her did not weigh her down.*

‡R 4

*Matt 3:15

*Ps-Augustine, Sermo 123.1; PL 39:1991

In describing this journey in a literal sense, we would say that Joseph, desiring to pay the census tax to the earthly emperor, went up from one province to another (from Galilee to Judea), and from one city to another (from Nazareth to Bethlehem). *But spiritually we can interpret it as follows: Joseph, whose name means increase, teaches us that if we want to grow spiritually and pay our levy of devotion to the eternal king, we should take to the road of virtue, ascending from the worldliness and kaleidoscopic confusion of Galilee to the profession of divine praise in Judea. (Recall that *Galilee* means *removal to another place*, or *rotate*, or *whirl*, but that *Judea* is interpreted as *praise*.) Going in this way we climb from the flowering of the active virtues in Nazareth to the pasture of inner contemplation of Bethlehem, where our souls find true refreshment. *Nazareth* means *flower*, and *Bethlehem* signifies *house of bread*, and thus *house of refreshment*. Joseph went up with Mary, which reminds us that we should always have repentance as our companion: until the end of his life Joseph was with Mary, whose name signifies *bitter sea*.

*R 5

The Birth of Jesus

*R 6

Mary and Joseph could not find any lodging when they reached Bethlehem; they were poor, and the town was thronged with people who had come for the census. Pause here and share in our Lady's difficulties: she was a young woman of around fifteen years, tired out from a long journey, trying to make her way modestly through crowded streets, looking without success for a place to rest. Everyone dismissed them and their companions and sent them on their way. They were finally received into a public accommodation in a communal passageway*; this was inside the city, near one of the gates, under a concave cliff. There was no roof above it other than the overhanging rock, as can still be seen today.

**Massa; MVC 7; CM 153:31*

**diversorium*

According to Bede, a *diversorium* is a passageway between two streets that has walls on two sides and doorways on each end opening onto the two streets, with a covering to provide protection in inclement weather; people gather here on festive occasions for conversation and comfort. This serves as an image of the church, situated between Paradise and this world, in which we find shelter from the deceptions of this world.* People who had come to that city on business also sheltered their animals there from the elements, so it was also called a *diversorium* because people drove their animals in there.

*Ps-Jerome, Exp ev de brevi prov; PL 30:569B

Joseph was a carpenter, so perhaps he made a manger there for the ox and the ass they had brought with them: his pregnant wife rode on the ass, and he may have brought the ox to sell in order to pay the tax for himself and the Virgin and live off the remainder.* Or perhaps someone else had led the ox there, which then began to feed from the manger with their donkey; or both animals may have belonged to someone else. Chrysostom writes, "Let whoever is poor draw consolation from this: Joseph and Mary, the mother of the Lord, came alone from Nazareth in Galilee. They had neither servants nor maids; they owned no beast of burden. They were both masters and servants. A new thing! They resided in the stalls of animals rather than go into the city. Timid poverty dare not associate with the wealthy."*

**Lyra Luke 2:7*

*attr. to Chrysostom in Zachary 1.5; PL 186:74B

‡The hour came for Mary to give birth, at midnight on the Lord's Day. This was the day on which *God said, "Be light made." And light was made;** when *the night was in the midst of her course,** *the Orient from on high has visited us*:* the Virgin *brought forth her firstborn son.*‡ He is called her *firstborn* not in relation to others who followed, but because she had not given birth to any children before him. Bede comments that Jesus was described as firstborn, not because any came after him, but because none had come before him, and further,

‡R 7

*Gen 1:3

*Wis 18:14

*Luke 1:78; *Massa*

‡*Luke 2:7*

that that only-begotten is necessarily also firstborn, and the firstborn is only-begotten.* The Son of God had chosen to be born in time from a mother according to the flesh, so that he might receive a multitude of brothers and sisters through their spiritual rebirth; so it is preferable to call him firstborn rather than only-begotten. Accordingly, Bede says that Christ is only-begotten in his divine nature and firstborn in the human nature he assumed.*

*Com Luke 2:7; PL 92:331A; CL 120:49

*Com Luke 2:7; PL 92:331B; CL 120:49

He was born secretly under cover of darkness to lead back into the light of truth those who were living in the night of error.* As soon as her son was born, his mother immediately adored him as God and then *wrapped him up* herself *in swaddling clothes*, that is, in strips and pieces of cheap cloth, *and laid him*, not in a gilded crib, but *in a manger*, between the aforementioned ox and ass, *because there was no* **other*** *room for them in the inn*.*

**Werner, Sermo Christmas; PL 157:791A*

*Latin Diatesseron?

*Luke 2:7

Behold the great poverty and destitution of Christ: not only was he not born in his own home, but he could not even find any space in the common caravanserai and in his great want had to be laid in a manger. This illustrates what he himself later said: *The foxes have holes, and the birds of the air nests, but the Son of man has nowhere to lay his head*.* Note also that this stable was crowded with animals, so that even here he was pressed in on every side by brutish beasts; as the psalmist said, *I am become as a beast before you*.* Look at what meager resting places he had: first, enclosed in the Virgin's womb; next, laid in a common trough; then, stretched out on the gibbet of the cross; and finally, placed in another man's tomb!

*Luke 9:58

*Ps 73:23

***R 8**

*From what has just been said, you can see that Christ is already teaching by example that the state of perfection consists in humility, austerity, and poverty. With the psalmist he can truly say, *I am poor, and in labors from my youth*.* In this way he condemns the honors and pomp of this world, luxuries and effete-

*Ps 87:16

ness, carnal delights, and above all riches and excessive possessions.

Anselm exclaims,

> O dignity worthy of love and admiration! God of ineffable glory, you deigned to become a worthless worm; Lord of creation, you appeared as our fellow slave. You became little so that you could be like us and be our brother. You rule the universe and lack nothing, but you chose to taste the most abject poverty from the very moment of your birth. As Scripture says, when you were born *there was no room in the inn* and no crib to receive your tender body. Rather you, who hold the earth in the palm of your hand, were wrapped in bits of cloth and laid in the common feeding trough of a dirty stable, borrowed by your mother from rough animals.
>
> Be consoled, be consoled, all you who live in squalid poverty: God himself shares your destitution. He was not cushioned in a luxurious bed, nor was he *found in the land of them that live in delights*.* And you rich, how can you who are really nothing more than clay and mire boast of your delicate gilded beds when the King of kings preferred to lay his head upon a pile of straw? How can you, with your silk sheets and down comforters, reject a hard bed when that tender little infant, whose tiny hand wields power over all kingdoms, chose to sleep on the prickly straw that served as fodder for beasts?*

*Job 28:13

*Eckbert, Stim [Med 9 Anselm]; PL 158:750A; *Massa*

Bernard for his part says, "The silent infancy of Christ will not console the talkative, his tears will not console the boisterous, his swaddling clothes will not console those who parade about in elegant garments, the stable and manger will not console those who love the best seats in synagogues. The joy of the new light, the birth of the Savior, was announced to shepherds who kept watch over their flocks, poor, hard-working men, not to you rich, who have your consolation here below."* And elsewhere he writes,

*Sermo Christmas 5.5; PL 183:130B; SB 4:269; *Massa; MVC 7; CM 153:33*

> The Son of God, in whose power it remained to do whatever he willed, when the time came for him to be born chose the time and also chose to be born in distressing circumstances, especially for a little child, and of a mother so poor that she barely had sufficient material to clothe him and no crib in which to lay him. And though his need was so great, we hear no mention of even an animal hide to warm him. Christ, who cannot be deceived, chose what was troublesome to our human nature. This, therefore, is the best, the most useful, and the preferable way to live; whoever seeks to persuade you otherwise should be avoided as a seducer. This is what Isaiah prophesied long ago: "The little child *will know to refuse the evil, and to choose the good.*"* The pleasures of the body are the evil he refuses, affliction the good he chooses. Assuredly, the one who embraced the latter and rejected the former is a wise child, the infant Word, the tender newborn, whose body can perform no labor and is incapable of effort.
>
> "Fly from pleasures, you who are worldly, for death comes in on the heels of sensual delight. Do penance, for the kingdom is at hand"— that is the sermon preached to us by the stable and the manger; that is what the tiny members of the infant make clear; that is the gospel he announces with crying and with tears. O, the hardness of my heart! Lord, would that just as *the Word became flesh,** so you might give me a heart of flesh. This is what you promised through your prophet: *I will take away the stony heart out of your flesh and will give you a heart of flesh.*‡

*Isa 7:15

*John 1:14

‡Ezek 36:26; Sermo Christmas 3.1–3; PL 183:123B; SB 4:258–59

***R 9**

You have witnessed the nativity of the most holy prince, who was born of the heavenly queen. You have been able to see in each of them the most extreme poverty. This virtue is the pearl of the gospel, for whose sake you should be willing to dispose of all you possess. This is the foundation of the whole spiritual edifice. This is the road to spiritual health, the basis for humility, and the root of that perfection whose fruits are numerous, although hidden. You have also been able to see in each of them the most profound lowliness. In order to give us an example of perfect humility they did not think the stable beneath their dignity, nor the manger, the hay, or the squalid surroundings. There is no salvation where this virtue is lacking, because none of our works is pleasing to God if they are accompanied by pride.

Massa; MVC 7; CM 153:32

It is certain that humility attracts other virtues, watches over them, and perfects them, and where it is missing, the other virtues are not to be found. You have been able to see in each of them, and especially in the infant Jesus, no little amount of bodily affliction. To mention just one among many, when his mother placed him in the manger she did not even have a pillow or cushion to place under him; with great bitterness of heart, she had to rest his head on a little stone, upon which she may have put some straw borrowed from the animals. It is said that this stone has been preserved to the present day and can still be seen. Let us ponder carefully this poverty, humility, and bodily mortification and seek to grow in these virtues, taking Christ as our model.*

Massa; MVC 8; CM 153:37

Saint Bernard urges us to do this: "He has shown us the road we must take to follow him by exemplifying three virtues. First, the example of poverty, because he did not wish to possess earthly riches; this allows us to run after him easily, because we are unencumbered. Second, the example of humility, because he scorned worldly glory; this makes us small, so that we escape the notice of others. Third, the example of patience, because he endured evil things; this makes us strong and able to persevere."* Anselm says that our Redeemer applied the salve of his incarnation to

*Hugh of Saint Victor? Eluc var 1.48; PL 177:496C

our blinded eyes: because we could not look upon the majesty of divine glory shining in secret, God appeared in human form so that we could look upon him. By seeing, we would come to know; by knowing, we would come to love; and by loving him intensely, we would be able to approach his glory. He became incarnate to renew us spiritually: he made himself a sharer in our mutability so that we could share in his immutability.* And Chrysostom writes that he who is by nature the Son of God deigned also to become the Son of David so that we might become the sons and daughters of God. He allowed his servant to become his father so that God might become our Father. It was not for nothing or in vain that he abased himself to such humility, but to raise us out of our debased condition. He was born according to the flesh so that we could be born again according to the Spirit.‡

*Elmer 8 [Med 1 Anselm]; PL 158:716C

‡Hom Matt 2.3; PG 57/58:25

***R 10**

*You should also notice that, as birth follows conception just as fruit succeeds to flower, so it was fitting that Christ's conception in Nazareth (a name meaning *flower*) bore fruit when he was born in Bethlehem (*house of bread* or *refreshment*).

The Lord is conceived in Nazareth and born in Bethlehem every day whenever those who receive the flower of the Word make themselves a home of the bread eternal. And it is also appropriate that Christ was born in a town called the *house of bread*, because he himself is *the living bread that came down from heaven*,* who refreshes the souls of his elect with spiritual nourishment.* And he was born in Bethlehem, the smallest of the cities of Judea, because he did not want any to boast about the eminence of their earthly city.*

*John 6:51

**Zachary 1.5; PL 186:73C*

**Augustine, De catechizandis 22.40; PL 40:339; CL 46:164–65*

He was born on the road, not in the family home, to show that he was a sojourner whose kingdom was not of this world. He also said, *I am the way*,‡ by which we journey to our homeland. He was received at a humble inn to teach us not to seek palaces in this world, but modest dwellings. He chose to be born in a stable to condemn worldly glory and sumptuous

‡John 14:6

buildings. He became a small child to make us great and perfect human beings, and so that we would avoid self-aggrandizement. He became weak to make us strong and powerful in doing good. He became poor to enrich us by his poverty, and so that none of us would boast of our earthly riches.

He was wrapped in strips of common cloth to free us from the chains of death and clothe us in the robe of original innocence. His hands and feet were bound up to free our hands for good works and direct our feet onto the path of peace. He went without room at the inn to prepare many mansions for us in his Father's house. He was laid in a narrow manger so that we would disdain delicate beds and spacious buildings, and to fill us with the joy of his heavenly kingdom, and so that we might enlarge our hearts to create a space for him, just as he said, *My son, give me your heart.** He was also laid in the manger so that he might nourish us, like sacred animals, with the grain of his flesh; to be in fact food for beasts of burden, for sin turns us humans into beasts, as it is written, *And man when he was in honor did not understand; he is compared to senseless beasts, and is become like to them.** Thus the Lord became hay, the food of beasts, because *the Word became flesh,**and *all flesh is grass.*‡

*Prov 23:26

*Ps 48:13

*John 1:14
‡Isa 40:6; *Bede, Com Luke 2:7; Ludolph expands*

The ox (symbolic of the Jews) and the ass (symbolic of the Gentiles) had their Lord placed in between them; miraculously, they recognized him and knelt before him, incessantly adoring and praising him, as if with their voices. Ambrose says, "You hear the infant crying, but you do not hear the lowing of the ox who recognizes his Master. *The ox knows his owner, and the ass his master's crib.*"[1]* And Gregory Nazianzen

*Isa 1:3;
Exp Luke 2.42;
PL 15:1568B;
CL 14:49

[1] The ox and ass are familiar figures in the *mise en scene* of the nativity, but as far back as the third century they were seen as symbolic of the Jews (the ox being a clean animal, fit for sacrifice, carrying the yoke of the law) and the Gentiles (the ass being an unclean animal); Origen is the first to make the connection with the passage from Isaiah (Hom in Luke 13.7; PG 13:1832).

urges us, "Venerate that manger from which, like a mute animal, you feed now on the Word and Reason of God. Like the ox, know your owner; like the ass, your master's crib. Be counted among those clean animals who know how to ruminate, that is, who constantly go over in their memories the word of God, and who are thus acceptable as divine sacrifices on the altars. Do not be among the unclean animals that are fit for neither table nor altar."*

*Orat 38.17; PG 36:331

Mary can be seen as a type of the church, and Joseph her spouse represents the bishop. This is why the bishop wears a ring, as a kind of wedding band, and, just as Mary was made fruitful by the Holy Spirit and not by her husband, so it is God's grace that makes the church fruitful.* The church and her spouse ascend by striving to reach their own city, the heavenly Jerusalem, even as they offer due obedience to earthly rulers. And truly, the church gives birth to a child whenever a virtuous person puts into effect a good deed formerly conceived in the mind; this newborn is wrapped in swaddling clothes when we hide the good deed from human praise; he is placed in the manger when we are humbled rather than inflated with pride by the good we have done. Angels also surrounded the infant Lord, adoring him as soon as he was born.

*\textit{Zachary 1.5; PL 186:73D}

Tidings Announced to the Shepherds

***R 11**

*Luke 2:8

And there were in the same country shepherds watching and keeping the night watches over their flock. They were about a mile from Bethlehem, near a monument called "the tower of the flock": this was where Jacob, returning from Mesopotamia, halted with his sheep, and where Rachel died and was buried.* There is also a church here where pilgrims are shown the tombs of three of the shepherds.

*Gen 35:21; *Comestor, Hist ev 6; PL 198:1541A*

And behold, around the fourth watch of the night* *an angel of the Lord stood by them** in brilliant vesture, his face radiant and joyful. It is generally believed that this was Gabriel, who had announced the conception of the Word to the Virgin; he was more joyful than any others at the fulfillment of what he had earlier foretold, and to be the first to proclaim the birth of Christ. *And the brightness of God shone* both within their hearts and *round about them** as a sign that the Sun of Justice had been born, and light now shone in the darkness for the righteous, and the brightness of glory had drawn near. The angel shone to proclaim that the true Light had come into the world to illuminate every person.

*three to six a.m.
*Luke 2:9
*Luke 2:9

*The angel appeared to shepherds rather than to any other class of people for several reasons. First, because they were poor, and it was to these especially that Christ came, according to the psalmist: *By reason of the misery of the needy, and the groans of the poor, now will I arise, says the Lord.** Second, because they were simple, in accord with the book of Proverbs: *His communication is with the simple.** Third, because they were vigilant, as Proverbs also says: *They that in the morning early watch for me, shall find me.** Fourth, in a mystical sense, to show that doctrine should come from pastors and prelates to their subjects.

***R 12**
*Ps 11:6
*Prov 3:32
*Prov 8:17

*And they feared with a great fear** because of the unexpected and sudden brilliance of the angelic appearance. *And* to comfort them *the angel said to them: "Fear not; for, behold, I bring you good tidings of great joy that shall be to all the people*, that is, the church, which unites Jews and Gentiles. *For this day is born to you* to benefit the whole human race *a Savior*, that is, a lover and dispenser of salvation, *who is Christ* as Man and *the Lord* as God, *in* Bethlehem, *the city of David."** By *this day* the angel meant first the natural day, calculating from sunset to the day following, but he also said *day* instead of *night* because the news he came to announce

*Luke 2:9
*Luke 2:10-11

was so wonderful that the divine brilliance had turned the night into day.*

Lyra Luke 2:11

The Greek word *Christos* means *anointed*. Under the old Law, kings and priests were anointed; but Christ is the true King and High Priest, and so he is rightly called *anointed*. He was not anointed by human beings, but by God, because in the human nature he assumed for our sake he was anointed by the Father, or more precisely, by the entire Trinity, with the fullness of grace. Bede observes that the angel instructed Mary, Joseph, and the shepherds in different ways: Mary was told she would conceive, Joseph was told that she had conceived, and the shepherds were told that she had given birth. Thus the angel continually fulfills his service to God and instructs us according to our need.*

*Com Luke 2:8; PL 92:332C; CL 120:50–51

"*And this shall be a sign unto you* (for, as the apostle observes, the Jews seek signs): *You shall find* by seeking, because he is hidden and does not show himself, *the infant*, who is the Word, although he cannot speak, *wrapped in swaddling clothes*, not silk sheets, because he is so poor, *and laid in a manger*,* not in a gilded bed, because in his humility the Lord of lords rests in a trough for feeding animals."

*Luke 2:12

Note here that the shepherds were poor, simple, and lowborn—in other words, held in contempt. So that they would not fear to approach, the sign they were given was a silent, poor, and lowborn infant.* These were the signs of Christ's first coming; those announcing his second coming will be very different.

Bonaventure, Com Luke 2:12

***R 13**

*The moral lesson to learn here is how Christ is to be found, and by whom. Only those who are pure and simple respond to his infancy; only those who are poor respond to his swaddling clothes; only those who are humble and common respond to his manger. These three conditions are embraced by the three vows of religion: chastity, poverty, and obedience. And it is well that the angel announced the birth of the supreme shepherd to shepherds who were keeping watch, which suggests that pastors in the church should be humble and vigilant.

According to Bede, in a spiritual sense these shepherds represent the teachers and rulers of the faithful, who keep watch over the lives of those entrusted to them lest they wander off, and they protect their flock by night lest the wolves of hell tear them to pieces. Night symbolizes the dangers of temptation, from which vigilant leaders never cease to safeguard themselves and their charges. God's angel stands near these pastors to protect them, and God's brightness engulfs them and those under their direction.* *Hom ev 6 approx; PL 94:35B [1.7; CL 122:46]

Furthermore, in Bede's opinion, the word *shepherd* does not apply only to bishops, priests, deacons, or abbots; all of the faithful who keep watch over the little ones in their homes are rightly called pastors insofar as they are vigilant in safeguarding their houses. Those who give daily guidance to just one or two others and are directed to provide a banquet of the Word to the best of their ability are also exercising the pastoral office. In fact, even those who live in solitude act as shepherds, feeding the flock and keeping watch over it by night, if, gathering a multitude of pure thoughts and good acts to themselves, they seek to govern them with prudent moderation and nourish them in the heavenly pastures of Scripture and, by vigilant shrewdness, to ward off the attacks of unclean spirits.‡ ‡Hom ev 6; PL 94:37AB [1.7; CL 122:49]

*And as the shepherds marveled at what they were seeing and hearing, *suddenly there was with the angel* who was sent to proclaim Christ's birth *a multitude of the heavenly army,** to confirm his testimony, lest the authority of one angelic witness be judged insufficient.* They are described as a *heavenly army*, either because they fight against the demons for our salvation,† or because the heavenly king had arrived who had been born to do battle, and they were marshaled as his soldiers. ***R 14** *Luke 2:13 **Bede, Hom ev 6; PL 94:35B [1.7; CL 122:46] †Zachary 1.6; PL 186:75A*

They were *praising God* with one voice for Christ's birth, because they knew this meant salvation for the human race and repair for the angelic ranks, *and saying* a blessing in God's honor: "*Glory to God in the highest*, that is, in the heavens, because although God's glory shines out everywhere, it is especially brilliant in the empyrean, where saints and angels dwell, since God is glorified by every creature there, whereas here below there are those who despise him; *and on earth peace to men of good will.*"*

*Luke 2:13-14; *Lyra Luke 2:13 approx*

This peace is not for everyone, but only for those *of good will*, that is, those who welcome Christ's birth with a good will and do not attack him, for *there is no peace to the wicked,** *but much peace have they that love your law.** As Pope Leo teaches, "True peace for a Christian means not being separated from the will of God, and taking delight only in those things that God loves.* What it means to have peace with God is to desire what he commands and to reject what he forbids."* Therefore peace is announced to *men of good will*, that is, to good people. That person is good who is motivated more by goodness than by any other quality; the will directs the other powers to act, so that actions themselves are the result of a good or an evil will. This is why *there is no peace to the wicked.*

*Isa 57:21

*Ps 118:165

*Sermo 29.1; PL 54:227B; CL 38:147

*Sermo 26.3; PL 54:214B; CL 38:128

The angels' words also make it clear that the peace foretold by the prophets at Christ's coming was the inner peace of good will. As it says in Proverbs, *Whatsoever shall befall the just man shall not make him sad.** The *Pax Romana* that held sway over all the nations at the time of Christ's birth was but a figure of this inner peace. It is fitting that the angels sang, *Glory to God and peace to men*, because the Father was glorified through Christ, and peace was made between God and the human race, between human beings and angels, and between Jews and Gentiles. The rest of the words of this hymn (*Laudamus te*, etc.) were added by Saint Hilary, and Pope Anastasius II directed that this

*Prov 12:21

canticle should be sung on Sundays and feast days because it is a song of rejoicing and exultation.[2]

*About the joy of this day, in commenting on the Psalm verse, *This is the day which the Lord has made,** Cassiodorus says, "Although it is true that God has made every day, it may be said that he made this day in a particular way, because it is made holy by the birth of Christ the Lord; it is right that we come together to celebrate and rejoice, because this is the day when the devil was vanquished and the world was saved."*

***R 15**

*Ps 117:24

*Com Ps 117:24; PL 70:833A

Note that a multitude of the heavenly host joined the angel who announced the glad tidings to confirm his message. According to Bede, as the one angel announced the glad tidings, a multitude broke out in praise of the Creator, fulfilling their duty to God and instructing us by their example, so that every time we receive sacred learning from the mouth of a companion, or holy thoughts return to our minds, we should immediately praise God with our hearts, our lips, and our actions.* This angelic manifestation also shows that Christ's birth should convert all people to the same faith, hope, and love, and to the praise of divine glory.*

*Com Luke 2:13; PL 92:333B; CL 120:52

*Bede, Hom ev 6; PL 94:35B [1.7; CL 122:46]

Then the angels returned to heaven, still singing canticles of joy, to announce these same tidings to their fellow citizens there. The whole heavenly court then

[2] The *Gloria* was originally a Greek hymn from the second or third century used at Morning Prayer. Hilary of Poitiers became acquainted with the tradition of liturgical hymns while exiled in the East and introduced them to the West, where formerly only biblical texts were used in the liturgy. He is the author of the Latin translation of the Greek hymn. Gradually the *Gloria* was introduced at Masses celebrated by a bishop, and, from the eleventh century on, at all Sunday and feast day liturgies. According to the sixth-century *Liber Pontificalis*, it was not Anastasius II but his successor Pope Symmachus (d. 514) who directed the use of the *Gloria* at all Sunday Masses.

erupted into festal celebration; with praise and thanksgiving to God the Father, they descended in their proper orders to behold the human face of their Lord God, to worship him, and to glorify him and his mother. Who among them, on hearing the good news, could remain in heaven and not visit their Lord now born humbly as a creature on earth? No, none of them could have fallen into such pride. As the apostle says, *When he brings in the first begotten into the world, he says: "And let all the angels of God adore him."**

*Heb 1:6; *Massa; MVC 7; CM 153:34–35*

Augustine writes,

> He is born in a stable, wrapped in strips of cheap cloth by his mother Mary, and laid in a manger. There was no house of cedar in which to give birth to the Creator, no ivory bed upon which she could lay the Redeemer of all. No, it was as an exile and an alien that she gave birth to the Lord of the world in a strange house, and as a poor woman that she had to wrap him not in silk, but in shreds of common cloth, and place him in a manger. As soon as she gave birth, she adored her God.
>
> O happy stable in which Christ was born, O blessed manger in which the Lord of all creation was laid! Angelic powers and comforting angels were like midwives there; thousands upon thousands of spirits rejoiced. Christ wailed in the stable while the heavens resounded with joyful paeans; he was crying in the manger, but the multitude of the heavenly host proclaimed glory to God in the highest and proclaimed peace to those of good will on earth, because heaven's goodness had been born on earth.
>
> True peace came down from heaven, and from there the festive singing of the angels gave glory to God in the highest. The angels exulted, and Mary trembled because she had become the Mother of God. The angels danced and rejoiced around Christ's manger; Mary stood before it and with great awe and trembling gave thanks, and diffidently continued to rejoice.*

*Ogerius 278–79

The Shepherds Go to the Manger

After the angels departed from them into heaven, the shepherds said one to another: "Let us go over to Bethlehem and let us see with our own eyes *this word*, or event worthy to be recorded in words, *that is come to pass, which the Lord* has done—for none other could do such a thing—and *has showed* or revealed *to us*."* It was as if they said, "Let us see this child whose birth the angel called a notable sign for us," because in Scripture the term *verbum* or *sermo* may be used for something noteworthy, as in Isaiah, *For there was nothing in his house,* nor in all his dominion that Hezekiah showed them not.** *R 16 *Luke 2:15 **non fuit verbum* *Isa 39:2

Or, "Let us see how this Word who was with the Father in the beginning has become flesh," because when our Lord's flesh is seen, the Word who is the Son is also seen. And *which the Lord has done*, because the whole Trinity brought about the Son's incarnation as a mortal man; *which he has showed us*, because he could not be seen as God.* **Zachary 1.6 approx; PL 186:75C*

And they came with haste,‡ principally because of their joy and intense desire to see the newborn babe, but also so that they could return quickly to their flocks and not leave them unprotected.* Notice that they sought Christ with determination and devotion; no one who seeks Christ in a casual way deserves to find him. Bede suggests that to go in haste does not mean to accelerate one's pace, but to advance continually in faith and virtue.* ‡Luke 2:16 **Lyra Luke 2:16* *Com Luke 2:16; PL 92:334C

*And they found Mary and Joseph, and the infant lying in the manger.** Because of the abundant peace that people then enjoyed and because large numbers of visitors were coming to the inn, the doors were not closed and the shepherds could come to the child at night. They found him in the manger with Mary the Virgin and Joseph the just man nearby, from which we learn that if we want to find Christ we should have a pure heart in relation to ourselves, signified by Mary; justice in our relations with our neighbors, signified *Luke 2:16

by Joseph; and humility and reverence in our relationship with God, signified by the humble manger.* Christ is found between Mary and Joseph, that is, contemplation and action. This is also symbolized by Jacob, called Israel (meaning *seeing God*), who had two wives, Rachel and Leah.[3]

**Bonaventure, Com Luke 2:16 approx*

And seeing with their bodily eyes *the child* in the flesh, *they understood* with their minds and interior faith *of the word that had been spoken to them concerning this child** that he was the Son of God. By knowledge of his humanity they came to the knowledge of his divinity; they were illuminated both outwardly and interiorly by acquaintance with the Word incarnate. *And all that heard wondered* at the mystery of the incarnation, *and at those things that were told them by the shepherds.**

*Luke 2:17

*Luke 2:18

***R 17**

What the shepherds did contains moral lessons for us. If we desire to find Christ spiritually, three things are required: to converse by meditating on the Scriptures, to go over by contemplating created things, and to hasten by savoring divine grace. Or, to converse by confessing our sins; to go over by rejecting earthly, ephemeral concerns; to hasten by stirring up our fervent desires; and to go as far as Bethlehem, *the house of bread*, to taste divine things. Then we shall find Christ in the manger of our heart, known by the wonderful signs of his presence, for *his delights are to be with the children of men.**

**Bonaventure, Com Luke 2:16*

*Prov 8:31

In a mystical sense, Bethlehem stands for our heavenly homeland, because there is found the blessed bread about which it is said, *Blessed is he that shall eat bread in the kingdom of God.** There are three crossings over to be made to this Bethlehem: from vice to virtue,

*Luke 14:15

[3] Jerome, Int nom, renders *Israel* as *seeing God* (PL 23:1184), *Rachel* as *seeing the source*, and *Leah* as *laborious* (PL 23:1174). Jacob's two wives have symbolized the contemplative and active lives at least as far back as Gregory the Great: Mor 6.XXXVII.57 (PL 75:764B; CL 143:326-28).

from virtue to greater virtue, and from this world to the Father, that is, from death to life.* *St Cher, Luke 2:12

The Venerable Bede urges us to follow the example of the shepherds and go over in thought to Bethlehem, the city of David, by recalling it with love and celebrating the Lord's incarnation with due honor:

> Having put aside worldly attractions, let us go over with our mind's whole desire to that heavenly Bethlehem, the house of the living bread, not made by hands but eternal in heaven. Let us recall that the Word who was made flesh ascended there in the flesh, where he sits at the right hand of the Father. Let us follow him to that place, spurred on by all our virtues and solicitously chastening both our hearts and our bodies, so that we may have the privilege of beholding enthroned in his Father's glory the infant they saw crying in the manger. Such blessedness is not to be sought idly or carelessly; Christ's footsteps must be followed briskly. And just as the shepherds understood by seeing, so let us hurry to perceive with devout faith and embrace with full love those things that have been said about our Savior, so that we will be able to comprehend him in that future vision, which is perfect recognition.* *Hom ev 1.6; PL 94:35C–36C [1.7; CL 122:47–48]

Mary, the Model Disciple

*R 18

But Mary kept all these words, pondering them in her heart* ***and memory*.* She reflected on the annunciation by the angel, John leaping in his mother's womb, the Savior's birth, the song of the angels, and the shepherds' belief and their visit, in light of the prophecies contained in Scripture. See, she was the best of disciples, commending to her memory everything she had heard, consigning none of it to oblivion, contemplating all that she had witnessed. Mary was like the ark of the covenant, containing all the hidden mysteries of the divine word. She *kept all these words*, committing

*Luke 2:19; Latin Diatessaron?

them to memory, so that afterwards she herself could hand them on to those who were to preach the Good News to the world and commit the Gospel to writing. She personally told the apostles many things that the Lord had done, especially events that had taken place before he called them, and they had frequent recourse to her as their teacher.

*Massa

‡Radbertus, 4; PL 30:125D [4.19; CM 56C:118]; *Lyra Luke 2:19 approx*

*Contra Rufinum 2.25; PL 23:449D; CL 79:63

Because she had read the holy Scriptures and was well versed in the prophets, she reflected on what the Lord had done with her and how this related to what the prophets had written about him,* carefully noting how their prophecies were fulfilled in her child. She *pondered them* as she watched her son's life unfold in light of what she had read of the biblical oracles, as much because she truly believed that he was God as because she could discern all the prophecies finding their fulfillment in him. This comparison gave her great delight and proved very useful for the church. Jerome suggests that Mary was left on earth with the apostles for a time after her Son's ascension so that she could fully enlighten them: she had the most intimate experience of what she had seen and touched and so was in the best position to explain everything.[4]‡ And, Jerome says, "We can speak best about what we know best."*

With virginal modesty Mary reflected on these things to herself, for she was as chaste in speech as she was in body. The Virgin did not wish to reveal the secrets she had learned about Christ to anyone until the time came when God wanted them to be revealed, and in the way he wanted them made known; she waited patiently, silently pondering in her heart what

[4] A letter about Mary's assumption (purportedly by Jerome) speaks of her in company with the apostles. It was in fact written by Paschasius Radbertus, but its attribution to Jerome gave it great authority in the Middle Ages. A passage from *De Excellentia Mariae* by Eadmer (PL 159:571C) is closer to the idea expressed here.

she saw taking place around her and what the Scriptures had said must happen. She had read, *Behold a virgin shall conceive, and bear a son,** and she saw that she was a virgin, had conceived, and had brought forth a son. She had read, *The ox knows his owner, and the ass his master's crib,** and she had seen the Son of God, and her son, crying in the manger between these two animals. She had read, *There shall come forth a rod out of the root of Jesse,** and she had seen that she was born of Jesse's stock. She had read, *He shall be called a Nazarene,*[5]* and she saw that it was in Nazareth that she had conceived by the Holy Spirit. She had read, *And you, Bethlehem Ephrata of Juda, out of you shall he come forth unto me that is to be the ruler in Israel,** and she saw that she had given birth in Bethlehem. Therefore she compared what she had read in the prophets with the events that she had seen and heard, and this mother of wisdom discerned the agreement between them, and found sure evidence for belief.*

*Isa 7:14

*Isa 1:3

*Isa 11:1

*Matt 2:23

*Mic 5:2

**Zachary 1:6; PL 186:76AB*

O, how great a cause for joy it must have been for her to know that she was the Mother of God! Anselm says, "Only of holy Mary the Virgin can it be said that she is the Mother of God, and this surpasses any dignity that can be spoken or even thought, saving that of God alone."*

*Eadmer, De exc 2; PL 159:559B

The Shepherds Return to Their Flocks

R 19

**And the shepherds returned* with great rejoicing to protect and care for their flocks, *glorifying* in their hearts *and praising God* with their lips *for all the things*

[5] Matthew does not specify the source of this prophecy. Along with the place where Jesus lived, biblical scholars see it as referring to the Messianic branch (*neser*) of the house of David, and to Jesus as the Holy One dedicated to God's service from birth (*Nazir*). In the latter case, Matthew may be referring to Isa 4:3 and Judg 16:17.

they had heard from the angels *and seen* in Bethlehem with their own eyes, *as it was told to them** by the angel. They glorified God that upon arriving they had found everything exactly as it had been described to them. They praised God and broke out into great rejoicing because such a great blessing had been given to the whole world, and because they in particular had been shown such favor. They also showed their dedication by returning to their labors after contemplating the Savior.

*Luke 2:20

In this they can serve as a model for the church's pastors: while others sleep, they should keep vigil and sometimes go to the Bethlehem of contemplation by studying the Scriptures.* Then, having fed there on heavenly bread, they should go back and feed their flocks with the bread of nourishing doctrine. As Ezekiel says, *And the living creatures ran and returned.**

**Lyra Luke 2:8 mor*

*Ezek 1:14

A Meditation on these Events

***R 20**

You too should now go to see the Word made flesh for you; kneel and adore the Lord your God, and reverently greet his mother and the holy old Joseph. Then kiss the feet of the child Jesus lying in the manger and ask the Lord to reach out to you or allow you to pick him up. Take him in your arms and hold him close to you. Gaze lovingly into his face and reverently kiss him; find your heart's delight in him. You can do this with confidence because he has come to save sinners, to dwell humbly among them, and finally to give himself to them as food. The kindly Lord patiently allows you to touch him if you wish; he does not accuse you of impudence because you are moved by love. But you should do all this with great reverence, because he himself is the Holy of holies.

**Massa; MVC 7; CM 153:35*

Then give him back to his mother and carefully observe how wisely and lovingly she feeds him and takes care of him, and all the other things she does for him. Stand by and be prepared to take care of him and assist her if you can. Find delight and happiness in doing these things, and reflect seriously on all of this. To the extent you can, join the family of our Lady and her child Jesus, and look on his face often, *on whom the angels desire to look*.* But, as I have already said, do these things with awe and reverence, lest you suffer a rebuff because of your presumption; you should consider yourself unworthy of such great and wonderful exchanges.*

*1 Pet 1:12

**Massa; MVC 7; CM 153:35*

Saint Anselm urges us,

> Accompany this mother devoutly to Bethlehem. Take shelter with her in the inn; be present and help her when she gives birth, and when the little child is laid in the manger, break out in words of exultant joy and cry out with Isaiah, *A child is born to us, and a son is given to us*.* Embrace that sweet and divine manger; let love banish shame and affection repel fear. Press your lips to the feet of that most sacred infant and kiss them repeatedly. Then contemplate the patient vigilance of the shepherds and the rushing choirs of angels. Mingle your prayers with their heavenly melodies, singing with both heart and voice, *Glory to God in the highest, and on earth peace to men of good will*.*

*Isa 9:6

*Aelred, De inst 29 [Med 15 Anselm]; PL 158:756A; CM 1:663–64

Augustine says,

> When the gospel was read, we heard the words by which the angelic voices proclaimed to the shepherds that the Lord Jesus Christ was born of the Virgin, *Glory to God in the highest, and on earth peace to men of good will*. These joyful words of congratulation were not addressed only to the individual woman whose womb had given birth to the child, but to the whole human race for whom the Virgin had given birth to a Savior. Let us too say, with all the joy we can muster, with faithful hearts and devout voices, *Glory to God in the highest, and on earth peace to men of good will*. Let us give ourselves over

completely to considering these divine words, these praises of God, this joyful Gospel, and meditate on them with faith, hope, and charity.*

*Sermo 193.1; PL 38:1013

And, finally, Gregory Nazianzen: "Adore the boy along with the shepherds, sing the hymn with the angels, prolong the archangels' praises. Leap for joy! If you cannot do it like John in his mother's womb, you certainly can dance like David in the presence of the ark. Venerate that nativity that frees from earth-born chains."* May you come daily to see Jesus in his spiritual manger, that is, the altar, so that you may be worthy to be fed with the grain of his flesh with the holy animals.

*Orat 38.17; PG 36:330

***R 21**

*Realize that Christ is born in three ways: in his divinity, in his humanity, and by grace. He is born eternally from the Father, in time from his mother, and in our hearts spiritually. These three births are related to Christ's three substances: deity, flesh, and spirit. He is born of the Father as God, of his mother as Man, and in the soul through grace by the Holy Spirit. He is eternally begotten of the Father, born once of his mother, and born in us often. In his divine birth Christ has a Father but no mother; in his human nature he has a mother but no father; in his birth in us by grace he has both a father and mother, as he himself says, *For whosoever shall do the will of my Father that is in heaven, he is my brother, and sister, and mother.** These three births are commemorated in the church by our Christmas liturgies. His first birth is symbolized by the Midnight Mass, because the divine nativity is hidden from our eyes. His human birth is symbolized by the Mass at Dawn, because that birth was partly hidden and partly seen—hidden as to its manner, but known in its effect. The Mass of Christmas Day represents his birth in our souls by grace: Christ is conceived in us through love, born through the effect of grace, and fed through good works.*

*Matt 12:50

**Innocent III, Sermo Christmas 3; PL 217:439C–61B; and Hugh 4.11 approx*

Praise of Bethlehem

*Venerate and honor little Bethlehem, in which the way back to Paradise and our heavenly home was first opened for us. This small village, originally called Ephrata, had been practically abandoned because of a great famine. A time of plenty followed, and so the town came to be called Bethlehem, *house of bread*. This city is *not the least among the princes of Juda*[6]* in dignity, because people are conscious of the great mysteries that occurred there before the coming of Christ. There David was anointed as king* and offered a solemn sacrifice;* there the marriage of Ruth and Boaz was celebrated.* This last prefigured the wedding between humanity and divinity in Christ, our true sacrifice and eternal king. People are also conscious of the joyful events there surrounding the birth of Christ: O, who can worthily conceive the joy of angels praising, shepherds seeing, kings adoring, people believing! And they are conscious of the martyrs there after the coming of Christ, when Herod ordered the slaughter of the Innocents.*

*R 22

*Matt 2:6

*1 Sam 16:13

*1 Sam 20:6

*Ruth 4:13

*Gorran Matt 2:6

But above all this city is blessed because it has put forth a noble shoot, that is, a ruler and Lord who has appeared to guide the people of Israel. Bernard exclaims, "O tiny Bethlehem, how the Lord has magnified you! He who was born in you magnifies you, he who though great became little in you. What city on hearing of your good fortune would not envy that precious stable and glorious manger? Everywhere *glorious things are said of you, O city of God*; everywhere it is sung, *This man is born in her, and the Highest himself has founded her!*"*

*Ps 86:3, 5; Sermo Vigil Christmas, 1.4; PL 183:88D; SB 4:200

Bethlehem is situated on a long, narrow ridge that runs from east to west. At the eastern end, under a

[6] Matthew cites Mic 5:1 but reverses the meaning of the verse, which spoke of Bethlehem's insignificance.

cliff, there was a kind of stopping place from which arose for us *the Sun of Justice, Christ our God.** Four or five paces to the west was a trough for feeding animals, in which that dear child was placed. In this city there stands a holy, venerable, and beautiful cathedral church consecrated in honor of the Blessed Virgin Mary,* built by Blessed Helena, the mother of the Emperor Constantine, about which she wrote.[7] Inside there is a lovely marble altar on the spot where Mary gave birth and Christ chose to be born. There is also a chapel in which the venerable divine manger stood.

*Resp Vesp Nat BVM; PL 78:802B; Burchard 87

*de Vitry 37

The church also contains the tomb of the Holy Innocents, and those of Saints Jerome, Paula, and Eustochium. There is also a cistern, into which it is said that the star that had guided the magi plunged.*

*Burchard 89

Blessed Jerome loved this city, so holy and dear to God, and chose to serve the Lord there. Blessed Paula and Eustochium, and many other holy virgins, lived there in a community devoted to the service of God and divine contemplation. They scorned earthly kingdoms and riches out of love for Jesus Christ and devotion to the holy places.*

*de Vitry 38

***R 23**

*Many others have imitated them, leaving their native land, home, and family to live in the Holy Land. Even though the turbulent crowds thronging the streets are a distraction to religious concentration, they prefer to dwell amid this great din rather than be deprived of the opportunity to live in those cities that were so dear to Christ and where the memory of his

[7] As far back as the third century Origen spoke of a particular grotto near Bethlehem that was venerated as the birthplace of Christ. Helena built a church on this spot, which was replaced in the year 530 by a magnificent basilica erected by Justinian. This was one of the few churches spared by the Persians in the seventh century, according to legend because the magi depicted in a mosaic wore Persian dress. The medieval guide books speak of the splendor of this house of worship, which still stands.

words and actions lingers like a perfume: Jerusalem, Bethlehem, and Nazareth.* The Lord was conceived of the Holy Spirit in the Virgin Mary at Nazareth, he was born in Bethlehem, and he was crucified, died, and was buried in Jerusalem. *de Vitry 32

The second Adam was born in Bethlehem, and about seven miles to the south is the city of Hebron, where in the Field of Damascus the first Adam was formed out of the red clay. A bowshot beyond this field there is a double cave, where Adam and Eve were buried. Here too are the tombs of the three great patriarchs Abraham, Isaac, and Jacob, and their wives.[8]* *Burchard 91–92

Prefigurations of Christ's Nativity

Christ was born to set us free. We can see his birth prefigured in the story of Pharaoh's cup bearer's dream. While in prison, he saw a vine grow out of the earth that had three branches; these began to blossom and then produced grapes, which he squeezed into Pharaoh's cup and gave him to drink. According to Joseph's interpretation of the dream, this meant that the cup bearer would be released from prison within three days. Similarly, while the human race was enduring harsh captivity, a vine grew out of the bare earth, Mary, having three branches. These could represent Christ's body, soul, and divinity, or the three Persons of the Holy Trinity. On the third day after the wine of his blood was squeezed out of him on the cross and offered to the King, the human race was led out of its captivity. This wine so captivated the heavenly King that he forgave all the offenses of the human race. Christ left us this wine under the form of the ***R 24** *Gen 40:9-13

[8] Burchard says that the clay in the Field of Damascus could be molded like wax and that he, like other pilgrims, took a great quantity of it away with him.

Eucharist so that it might be offered daily to the heavenly King, because the world offends him daily by sin. At the birth of Jesus the vine of Engaddi blossomed, to testify that Christ, the true Vine, had come.*

*Song 1:13; *SHS 8*

The manner of Christ's birth was prefigured by the rod of Aaron, which blossomed and brought forth almonds.* Just as it was contrary to nature for that lifeless stick to blossom, so it was above the order of nature for Mary to give birth miraculously to a son. Aaron's staff produced fruit without being planted in the ground, and Mary gave birth to her Son without man's seed. The sweet almond lies hidden within its hard shell, and the sweet divinity of Christ was hidden within the shell of his humanity. Aaron's staff brought forth the green leaf, the fragrant flower, and abundant fruit; similarly, Mary possessed the freshness of virginity, the fragrance of devotion, and the fruit of perfect abundance.*

*Num 17:8

**SHS 8*

***R 25**

*Christ gave a presage of his birth to the pagans as well as to the Jews, because he *will have all men to be saved.** Octavian, who ruled the whole world and accordingly was regarded by the Romans as a god, consulted Sibyl the prophetess to learn if there would be an even greater ruler in the future. On the same day that Christ was born in Judea, the sibyl, who was in Rome, beheld a golden circle around the sun, and within this a beautiful young virgin holding a splendid child on her lap. She described this vision to Octavian Caesar, intimating that a Ruler more powerful than Augustus had been born.[9]*

*1 Tim 2:4

**SHS 8*

[9] Ludolph refers to the *Fourth Eclogue* of Virgil, written in the year 40 BC, which speaks of the birth of a boy who will usher in a golden age of peace and prosperity. Several fathers associated this figure with Christ, and Virgil was highly revered in the Middle Ages (witness his role in Dante's *Divine Comedy*, and the linking of pagan sibyls with biblical prophets in medieval and renaissance art). The story of the meeting between Augus-

The Great Solemnity of Christ's Birth

*You should meditate with joy on the greatness of today's solemnity. Today Christ is born, so this truly is the birthday of the eternal King, the Son of the living God. Today *a child is born to us, and a son is given to us.** Today the Sun of Justice emerges from behind the clouds to shed his rays. Today the church's bridegroom, the head of all the elect, comes forth from his nuptial chamber. Today he who is *beautiful above the sons of men** shows his longed-for face. Today is the day of our redemption, the repair of the ancient transgression, the joy of eternal life shining out for us. Today peace is proclaimed for us; that peace of which the angel sang has now come to pass. *Today the heavens distilled honey throughout the whole world*, as the church sings.‡ Today *the goodness and kindness*† *of God our Savior appeared.**

*R 26

*Isa 9:6

*Ps 44:3

‡Responsory for Christmas; PL 78:7784A

†Vulg: *humanitas*

*Titus 3:4; *Massa; MVC 7; CM 153:36*

For this reason Bernard said, "His power was made manifest in the creation of the world and his wisdom in its governance; but now his goodness and his mercy are more specially made known in his humanity."* Today God is adored in the likeness of sinful flesh. Today we are born together with Christ because his nativity is the origin of the Christian people. Today two miracles occur that are infinitely beyond our understanding and can only be grasped by faith: God is born and a Virgin gives birth. Today a whole host of miracles is made known. All that had only been hinted at about the incarnation now becomes clear as day: the outline is filled in, and we can see how past prophecies and present realities meet. This is truly a day that calls for happiness and exultation, and the greatest expressions of joy.*

*Sermo Christmas 1.2; PL 183:115D; SB 4:245

**Massa; MVC 7; CM 153:36*

---

tus and the sibyl came to be associated with the church of Santa Maria in Aracoeli on the Capitoline Hill.

✠

Sweet Jesus, you chose to be born in humility of a humble handmaid, who humbly wrapped you in the swaddling clothes of humility and laid you in a manger. Most merciful Lord, grant that the holiness of new life may be reborn in me through the ineffable mystery of your nativity. Thus may I be wrapped in the swaddling clothes of the religious habit and strive to live within the constraints of Christian discipline—placed as it were in the manger—to lead me to the summit of true humility. And as you deigned to share in our humanity and mortality, grant that I may share in your divinity and eternity. Amen.

CHAPTER 10

The Lord's Circumcision

(Luke 2:21)

And after eight days were accomplished from the Lord's birth, *the child should be circumcised* according to the precept of the law, and, as was customary on the occasion of the circumcision, *his name was called Jesus*, that is, Savior, *which was called by the angel before he was conceived in the womb** of the Virgin by the Holy Spirit. The rite of circumcision originated with Abraham, on which occasion his name was lengthened.* With the sign of circumcision he deserved to have his name changed and lengthened: he had previously been called Abram (*exalted father*), but because of his faith he was worthy of the name Abraham (*father of many races*). And his wife deserved to have her name changed from Sarai (*my princess, the princess of her house*) to Sara (*princess of everyone*), that is, of all women who believe rightly.*

*R 1

*Luke 2:21

*Zachary 1.7; PL 186:76C

*Jerome, Quaest in Gen 17; PL 23:963B–64A; CL 72:21

Hence the custom arose of naming boys on the day of their circumcision, and so Jesus was given his name on this occasion. He accepted the mark of circumcision at the beginning of his life out of humility, the root and guardian of all virtues. Furthermore, he did not want to delay pouring out the price of his blood for you to show that he was most truly your Savior, promised to his ancestors by both word and deed, and like them in all things, ignorance and sin excepted.*

*LV 5

The First Mystery of This Day: The Naming of Jesus

*R 2

Two great mysteries took place on this occasion. The first was that Jesus' name was made known, the name he had been given from all eternity and that the angel had announced before he was conceived in the womb. When the angel Gabriel was sent to Mary, he said, "*Behold you shall conceive in your womb and shall bring forth a son; and* at his circumcision *you shall call his name Jesus,** the name given to him by God the Father." As we read in the prophet Isaiah, *And you shall be called by a new name, which the mouth of the Lord shall name.** According to Origen, *Jesus* is a name of such sweetness and glory, *a name which is above all names,** that it was not fitting for it to be given first by mere mortals or brought into the world by them, but by a creature possessing a greater and more excellent nature.*

**Massa*

*Luke 1:31

*Isa 62:2

*Phil 2:9

*Hom Luke 14.2; PG 13:1833

The Hebrew word *Jesus* means *Savior*. This name was innate to him because he is *Savior* by his very nature. True, others before him had received this name; but it was new in his case because he is the Savior of all people, unlike his predecessors who were saviors in some limited way. He is called Savior first by virtue of his saving power, so that this name was given him fittingly from all eternity; second, because of the saving plan he put into effect from the moment of his conception, and so it was given fittingly on that occasion by the angel; third, because of the saving act he accomplished by his passion, which was foreshadowed by his circumcision, and so he received it fittingly then as well. Chrysostom says that the name of God that Jesus was called in the womb of Mary was not new, but old: he was called Jesus (Savior) according to the flesh, who had always been Savior in his divinity.*

*Chromatius, 2.4; CL 9A:203

Pause to consider the great dignity of this name: first, it was preordained and consecrated from all eternity; second, it was spoken by the mouth of God; third, it was longed for by patriarchs and prophets from of old; fourth, it was foretold by the prophets; fifth, it was prefigured by Joshua, the son of Nun; sixth, it was proclaimed by the angel to Mary and to Joseph; seventh, it was made known by Mary; eighth, it was given by Joseph on this day; ninth, it was spread abroad by angels; tenth, it was glorified by the apostles; eleventh, it was borne witness to by the martyrs; twelfth, it was praised by confessors; thirteenth, it was savored like a sweet perfume by holy virgins; fourteenth, it is venerated by all the faithful.

Augustine distinguishes between the name *Jesus* and the name *Christ*: the first is his personal name whereas the second refers to his sacred office.* Also, Christ is a name of grace, while Jesus is a name of glory: here below, people are called Christians, from Christ, because of the grace of baptism; but in the glory of heaven Jesus himself will call us *Jesuitae*, that is, those who have been saved by the Savior.[1] As great as the difference is between grace and glory, so great is the difference between the names *Christ* and *Jesus*. In a spiritual sense, Bede suggests that just as Christ received the name *Jesus* at the time of his bodily circumcision, so his elect share in this name by virtue of a spiritual circumcision: as they are called *Christians* by Christ, so they will be called *Saved* by the Savior. This name was given to them not only before they were conceived in the womb of the church by faith, but by God himself from all eternity.*

*Ep John 3.6; PL 35:2000

*Com Luke 2:21; PL 92:338B

This is *the name which is above all names, for there is no other name under heaven given to men whereby we must be saved*.* Bernard describes the name of Jesus as honey in the mouth, music in the ear, and a song in the heart; like oil, it illuminates, it nourishes, and it heals: "When

*Phil 2:9; Acts 4:12

[1] It seems that Ludolph is the first writer to use the term *Jesuit*. His source is St Cher's *Postilla* on the book of Revelation, but Hugh uses the word *Jesuani*.

preached it gives light, when meditated on it nourishes, when invoked it relieves and soothes."* Peter Chrysologus writes, "This is the name that gave sight to the blind, hearing to the deaf, healing to the lame, speech to the mute, life to the dead. By this name all demonic power was expelled from the bodies of those who were possessed."* And Anselm says, "Jesus is a sweet and delectable name, and a name of blessed hope, bringing comfort to sinners. Jesus, be Jesus to me!"*

*SC 15.6, 5; PL 184:847A, 846C; SB 1:85–86

*Sermo 144; PL 52:586B

*Med 2; PL 158:725A

The name of Jesus has great power, as the apostle says: *You are washed, you are sanctified, you are justified in the name of our Lord Jesus Christ.** Jesus' name has the power to wash as regards the stain of sin, the power to sanctify as regards the offense of sin, and the power to justify as regards the guilt of sin. Stain, offense, and guilt are all aspects of sin, so it is clear that that all of these are remitted through the power of Jesus' name. Hence John writes, *Your sins are forgiven you for his name's sake.** At this name *every knee should bow, of those that are in heaven, on earth, and under the earth.** And Paul also says, *Whosoever shall call upon the name of the Lord shall be saved.** In fact the Lord himself told us, *Whatsoever you shall ask of the Father in my name, he may give it you.**

*1 Cor 6:11

*1 John 2:12

*Phil 2:10

*Rom 10:13

*John 15:16

This is why we should make all of our prayers in his name, and for this reason the church concludes all of her prayers with *through Christ our Lord* or similar words. Those who ask for something contrary to the will of God, or not beneficial to their own or another's salvation, do not pray in this name and should not expect their prayer to be answered, even though it is made in the name of Jesus. Truly and rightly is he called Jesus, because only in this name may we be saved. This is why he himself said, *I am Alpha and Omega, the beginning and the end.** Just as all things were created through the eternal Word, so all things are repaired, advanced, and perfected by the Word united to the flesh of Jesus.

*Rev 1:8

The Second Mystery of This Day: The First Shedding of Christ's Blood

On this day the Lord Jesus began to shed his blood for us when his flesh was cut with a stone knife. He took this opportunity to suffer for us, and, although he had not sinned, he began on this day to bear the punishment for our sins. He wanted to pour out his blood for us not only in adulthood but also in infancy. The pain he felt in his flesh today caused the boy Jesus to cry, for he had a real body and could suffer like us. When he cried, do you imagine that his mother could contain her tears? She wept along with him. You, too, should share in his pain and cry with him because he wept so loudly today. True, we should all rejoice greatly on this solemn occasion, because he obtained our salvation, but we should also be sorrowful and compassionate when we witness the suffering he endures for our sake. We will find encouragement to bear the punishment for our own sins when we see him accepting punishment for the sins of others. Hence Bernard asks, "Who would not blush to evade many small punishments meted out for their own transgressions, when they know that the sinless Christ bore so many great sufferings for the sins of others?"* ***R 3**

**Massa; MVC 8; CM 153:37–38*

*Sermo Circumcision 1.1 approx; PL 183:133A; SB 4:274

Notice that Christ shed his blood six times for us: first, at his circumcision, to begin our redemption; second, at prayer in the garden, to show his desire for our redemption; third, at the scourging; and fourth, at the crowning with thorns, to gain our redemption, *for by his bruises we are healed*;* fifth, at the crucifixion, to pay the price for our redemption, for he made amends for what he had not stolen; sixth, when the lance pierced his side, to give the sacrament of our redemption, since we must be cleansed of our sins by baptism, and baptism gains its efficacy from the blood of Christ.* The first occasion teaches us to be circumcised spiritually and cast off sin; the second teaches

*Isa 53:5

**Massa*

us to bear with mental anguish for the sake of our salvation; the third teaches us to subdue the flesh; the fourth teaches us to crown our soul with virtues; the fifth teaches us to hold ourselves fast by God's commandments; the sixth teaches us to have a heart wounded by love of God.

You see how often Christ poured out his blood for our salvation, but where are our tears, our groans, our weeping, our thanks for such a copious shedding of blood? *Come, let us adore and fall down and weep before the Lord that made us** and so generously redeemed us. Bernard writes, "One drop of that most precious blood would have sufficed to redeem the world, but he gave it lavishly to show his love and enliven our gratitude. Truly *with you there is merciful forgiveness*!"*

*Ps 94:6

*Ps 129:4; Damian, Sermo 47; PL 144:762B

The Spiritual Meaning of Circumcision

*R 4

*It should be explained that the religious ritual of circumcision began with Abraham. He was the first to profess faith in the one God, and as a sign of this he accepted circumcision to distinguish believers from unbelievers. He also believed God's promise that he would have a son and accepted circumcision for this reason as well, so that it could be understood that he was justified by his faith.

The rite of circumcision was given for many reasons. First, because of the merit of Abraham's faith; just as that faith distinguished him from other nations, so did the mark of circumcision. Second, so that his descendants would know that their unique relationship with God made them different from other nations; they received this sign to mark them as the children of Abraham, who believed. Third, so that when soldiers fell in battle it would be evident that they were not Gentiles, but descendants of Abraham's holy stock, and so be accorded proper burial. When the Jews lived in the wilderness, far away from Gentiles, they were not circumcised.* Fourth, as a remedy for original sin and a curb to carnal desires.*

*Josh 5:5

**Haymo, Hom 14 approx; PL 118:91C–92A*

Circumcision was also mandated to prepare the way for faith: the rite professed obedience to the law of Moses, just as baptism entails acceptance of the law of the Gospel. The former prepared its recipients for the latter. Therefore, circumcision was mandated in ancient days as a sign of the promised Messiah, and it remained in force until the birth of the one promised to Abraham. Once Christ was born and the promise was fulfilled, the necessity for a sign of the promise was not needed, and the obligation of circumcision ceased.‡ The rite of circumcision had to be performed with a knife made of stone, because *the rock was Christ*.†

‡*Ambrosiaster, Quaest 50; PL 35:2250*

†1 Cor 10:4; *Haymo, Hom 14; PL 118:95C*

***R 5**

*Christ chose to undergo circumcision for several reasons, as if he were subject to the law. First, to show that he was of the seed of Abraham, to whom had been given both the commandment regarding circumcision and the promise of the Christ. Second, so that by associating himself with his ancestors he would do what was required by the Jewish people, in order to remove any cause for scandal or excuse for not accepting him and believing in him. Third, to approve the old law and the rite of circumcision that God had instituted, and to show that it was holy, just, and good. Fourth, so that he could commend to us the virtues of obedience and humility by his observance of a law to which he was not subject. Fifth, to obey himself the law that he had given to others, and to show that even though he had not come in sinful flesh, but in the likeness of sinful flesh, still he did not refuse the remedy that had been laid down to cleanse the flesh from sin. Sixth, so that by shouldering the burden of the law in himself he could free others who were unable to carry this burden, for he was *made under the law that he might redeem them who were under the law.** Seventh, so that he might shed his blood for us not only in adulthood but in infancy as well, and begin to suffer at the first opportunity. Eighth, to show that he possessed a true

*Gal 4:4-5

body of flesh, and so refute those heretics who maintain that his body was but an appearance, and not real. Ninth, to commend chastity and reprove carnal concupiscence, since circumcision is performed on that member of the body that is especially under the sway of such desires. Tenth, to end the rite of physical circumcision and initiate spiritual circumcision, to urge us to be circumcised in a spiritual way, as the apostle said: *For the end of the law is Christ unto justice to everyone that believes.*‡

‡Rom 10:4; *Aquinas, ST III, q. 37, a.1; Ludolph expands*

***R 6**

In our day we have baptism instead of circumcision, a ceremony that involves less pain and imparts more grace; the coming of the grace of baptism has emptied the circumcision of the flesh of its meaning, just as blossoms fall and wither when the fruit appears. Gregory teaches, "What the water of baptism accomplishes in us was in former times achieved for little children by the faith of their parents, in adults by the offering of sacrifice, and to those of Abraham's stock by the mystery of circumcision."* Bede adds that while it is true that under the law circumcision healed the wound of original sin, it could not open the gates of heaven, whereas the grace of baptism does both.*

**Massa*

*Mor 4.Pref.3; PL 75:635B; CL 143:160

*Hom ev 1.10; PL 94:54BC [1.11; CL 122:74]

Baptism does not do this of itself, but by virtue of its association with the passion; the rite of circumcision would have accomplished the same had it been associated with the passion. Circumcision was performed on that member of the body most dominated by concupiscence, and the means by which original sin was propagated. It was fitting, therefore, that the remedy for sin should be associated with the means of sinning.*

**Zachary 1.7; PL 186:77A*

***R 7**

Physical circumcision signifies spiritually the circumcision of the heart, by which the soul is purified of defects; we should be circumcised without and within, and freed in every way from spiritual faults. Christ underwent circumcision to teach us that we should cut away all sins and vices. Bernard says, "We should perform a twofold spiritual circumcision, exterior and interior. Exterior circumcision consists of three things: our habits should not be notorious, our actions should not be reprehensible, and our words should not be meaningless. Similarly, interior circumcision consists in three things: our thoughts should be holy, our affections pure, and our intentions proper."[2] *Sermo de div 32.2; PL 183:625BC; SB 6/1:219

Accordingly, let us cut out of our hearts all poisonous and unclean thoughts, all false and rash judgments, all unkind intentions and desires. We should shudder to contemplate in our hearts before God what we would blush to say or do before other people, because what words and deeds are to people, thoughts are to God. We should also be circumcised in our speech, avoiding any words that are base, slanderous, lying, idle, or unnecessary, because on the Judgment Day we will have to answer for even the smallest thoughts and every idle word. Finally, we should be circumcised in our senses and all the members of our body, shunning all prohibited and illicit matters, as well as luxuries and excesses. We must avoid not only sin, but the near occasions of sin.* Unless we avoid these, we can hardly escape falling into sin itself. **Massa*

By such a spiritual circumcision all faults and sins are taken away and removed. For this reason, it was fitting that the rite was carried out on the eighth day after Christ was born, because on the eighth day the final resurrection will take place, when every human being will rise to life immortal with sins and defects cut away, cleansed of all excesses, and completely renewed. This eighth day is in fact the first day: this was the day the world began, this was the day Christ rose from the dead, and this will be the day of the general resurrection.* There are six ages in this world, during which we must persevere in our labors for God, and it is necessary to work to attain everlasting **R 8**

**Bruno Luke 1:59; PL 165:348C*

**Bruno Hom 15; PL 165:766B*

[2] Only the final clause, without a mention of circumcision, comes from Bernard; the citation in its entirety is taken from Ps-Aquinas, *De humanitate Christi* 5.

rest. The seventh age is not here on earth, but is found in the next life, a time of rest awaiting the resurrection of all things; and the eighth age is the day of resurrection itself, a blessed age without end.* Then not only the circumcised but all who have had their sins taken away and have become clean and immaculate will receive the name and the inheritance of the Holy One.*

*Bede, Hom ev 10; PL 94:56C [1.11; CL 122:77]

**Bruno Hom 21; PL 165:769D*

Whoever is free from sinful thoughts, words, and deeds—such a one is perfectly circumcised, both within and without. It does little good to be only partly circumcised, for, as Pope Pius I teaches, "It is not useful to fast, pray, and perform other religious exercises unless you refrain from thinking evil thoughts or speaking disparaging words."* That is, not useful for eternal life, although these practices can bring earthly benefits. And Bede writes,

*Gratian, Decret 2.33.3.21; PL 187:1598B

> No one will fully credit the idea when circumcision is concerned with only one part of the body—be that by the avoidance of fornication, or a temperate and proper use of the marital act, or even the glorious state of virginity—and this is unrelated to the other virtues, and we do not recognize how it calls for self-control over all of our powers of heart and body. Those are cleansed by true circumcision who close their ears lest they hear of bloodshed and their eyes lest they look on evil, who keep guard over their ways lest they sin with their tongue, who are careful not to burden their hearts with drunkenness, who wash their hands among the innocent and keep their feet from evil paths, who above all things chastise their bodies and subject them, and keep close watch over their hearts, because it is from the heart that life comes. Yet it is no less important to circumcise good deeds by keeping them hidden, so that when I fast, or pray, or give alms, I seek only inward glory. This is why the apostle was careful to commend the hidden circumcision of the heart, *whose praise is not of men, but of God.**

*Rom 2:29; Com Luke 2:21; PL 92:340A; CL 120:60–61

We must shun every kind of wrongdoing, external and internal, and be spiritually circumcised in every way. And we undergo circumcision every time we do penance after sinning.

*Here we might consider eight spiritual illuminations of divine grace preceding circumcision, by which the eight days leading up to spiritual circumcision are understood: the sinner's conversion to God, recognition of sin, contrition, confession, satisfaction, hatred for sin, precaution for the future; then on the eighth day comes the justification of the sinner, when sin is expelled and grace pours in. On that octave day the spiritual circumcision of the repentant soul is celebrated in the justification of the sinner. In fact, circumcision is simply the cutting away of wickedness with the knife of repentance. Just as physical circumcision entails the removal of a useless bit of flesh, so spiritual circumcision is the removal of sins and faults; only these are useless to us, because everything created for us is very good. ***R 9**

We are children of perdition unless we accept this spiritual circumcision, as we read in the book of Genesis: *The male whose flesh of his foreskin shall not be circumcised, that soul shall be destroyed out of his people.** Those eight days might also be understood as an eightfold illumination by the Holy Spirit: the seven gifts of the Holy Spirit, with final perseverance as the eighth. And because sins can only be taken away by Christ, who is himself *the Lamb of God who takes away the sins of the world,** so it is said that circumcision was performed with a stone knife, and *the rock was Christ.**

*Gen 17:14
*John 1:29
*1 Cor 10:4

This is what the Jewish circumcision signifies, and apart from this it is unprofitable. For this reason Christ was circumcised, so that he could entrust the meaning of circumcision to us. Just as he was born for us, was baptized for us, and died for us, so he was circumcised for us, not for himself. Let us strive to have within us that spiritual circumcision of which the visible rite was a sign, so that, cleansed from all sin and guilt, we may be found worthy to take part in that joyful octave of the resurrection awaiting us in the future.

There are three elements in this circumcision: one is the *sacramentum** of bodily circumcision; the other two are the *res** signified by the visible sign: circumcision from sin, which takes place daily in the soul, and circumcision from sin and all punishment due to sin, which in the resurrection will be in both the soul and the body.*

*the visible sign

*the realities

**Werner, Sermo Octave Christmas 1; PL 157:801C*

✠

Gentle Jesus, born of the Virgin, you willed to be circumcised according to the law. Merciful Jesus, circumcise the thoughts, words, and deeds of your servant so that nothing may be found in them that is contrary to your will. May my thoughts be in the spirit of God, my speech in harmony with the precepts of the Most High, and all my actions be directed by your commands. See, Lord, they are all before you: my heart, my words, my senses, and my limbs. They strive, but of themselves they can do nothing. May you accomplish what they cannot, and as you ever fulfill the desires of the just, so may you bring to a good fruition the desires of this poor sinner. Amen.

CHAPTER 11

The Epiphany of the Lord to the Three Magi

(Matt 2:1-12)

The boy Jesus manifested himself to the Gentiles, that is, to the pagan magi, on the thirteenth day after his birth. A prediction had been made by a Gentile prophet that a star would arise out of Jacob and a man would appear from Israel; from this it is clear that the rising of a new star would herald the birth of the Messiah. When these men beheld the new star, they knew by divine inspiration that what Balaam had foretold had now taken place; they immediately started out from home and came to venerate the newborn child. *R 1

*Num 24:17; *Massa*

They were descendants of Balaam's clan, his heirs in faith as well as in race. They were called magi, not because they dabbled in magical arts, but because of the great breadth of their learning: they possessed great wisdom and were experts in astronomy. Such people were called scribes in Hebrew, philosophers in Greek, sages in Latin, and magi in the Persian tongue.* They were *magi*, not *malefici*,‡ learned in the beginnings of our faith. They were also spoken of as kings, because it was customary in their day for philosophers and sages to be rulers.

**Comestor, Hist ev 7 approx; PL 198:1541C*

‡*sorcerers*

Seneca wrote about the happiness of those ancient times: "The greatest happiness was found among those peoples in which people could be more powerful only if they were also more virtuous. In the time they held to be the golden age, ruling was a service, not an expression of royalty. It was enough for a ruler to find some modest place of shelter without great difficulty or artistry."* Then he added a word about a certain philosopher then reigning: "When Diogenes the cynic saw a boy drinking water in his cupped hands, he immediately took a goblet out of his bag and smashed it, upbraiding himself with these words: 'Fool that I am! I have been carrying around this unnecessary baggage!' And then he curled up in his tub and went to sleep."* O how different our times are from those! Now it is all the reverse: leaders seek only riches, honors, and pleasures. It may be that their future fate will be worse than that of the pagans.

*Lucilium 90.4, 5, 8

*Lucilium 90.14

***R 2**

‡Matt 2:1

**Behold, there came wise men from the East,*‡ that is, from lands east of Judea and Jerusalem. Chrysostom observes that it was fitting that the beginning of faith should come from the place where the sun rises, because faith is the light of souls.* Bernard agrees that it was right that those who announce that the new Sun of Justice had been born for us should come from the East, and with this joyful news illuminate the whole world.*

*Opus imperf 2.1; PG 56:637

*Sermo Epiphany 3.3; PL 183:150B; SB 4:305

More precisely, these magi came from the frontiers of the Persians, the Medes, and the Chaldeans, through which the Saba River flows; the region is called Sabaea. This is near Arabia, where it is said that the magi were their kings.* The name *Arabia* is given to two different locations; one borders on the territory of Judea, and it seems that this is where the magi came from. (The other location is adjacent to India, and since this is a year's journey from Jerusalem they could not have arrived in thirteen days.) Remigius writes, "It is said that some believe that the child who had been born was able to bring them from the ends of the earth very quickly. But if they were descendants of Balaam, their kingdom was not far from the Promised Land, and so they would be able to make the journey in a short

**Innocent III, Sermo 8; PL 217:485C*

period of time."* Having seen the star, they were soon enlightened by the Holy Spirit to understand its significance. Therefore they sought Christ, God and Man, in the star, having been divinely inspired as to the star's meaning. *Hom 7; PL 131:900D–901A

*This star differed from ordinary stars in many ways. First, in substance: while other stars are composed of celestial matter and the fifth essence, this was made of a perishable substance. Second, in its efficient cause: other stars were created by God through his Word alone, without assistance from nature, but this was brought into being by the Word through the ministry of an angel. Third, in duration: other stars were created at the beginning of the world and will exist forever, whereas this one was made when Christ was born and ceased to exist soon after. Fourth, in location: others are situated in the heavens, while this one was not in the firmament, but in the air not far from the earth. Fifth, in magnitude: according to Ptolemy, the stars visible to us in the firmament are larger than the earth, whereas this one was not more than two or three cubits in diameter. ***R 3**

Sixth, in motion: other stars travel in a circular pattern from east to west, while this star was carried in a direct line from east to south. Seventh, in resting: other stars are in constant motion and never stand still, while this star moved when the magi traveled but stood still when they rested. Eighth, in the alterations of its appearance: when the magi arrived at Jerusalem, it disappeared and showed itself again when they left Herod's presence. Ninth, in time: while other stars only shine at night, this one could be seen in daylight, when the sun was shining; according to Chrysostom, its brightness was greater than the sun's rays.* Tenth, its meaning: other stars mark the distinctions between times and years, while this star signified the birth of Christ. Eleventh, in its effects: while other stars exercise a certain power to change things beneath

*Hom Matt 6.2, and for much of this list; PG 57/58:64

them, this one exercised no influence apart from announcing the Savior's birth. Twelfth, in its service: God created the other stars to serve all people, while this star showed itself only to serve Christ. Thirteenth, in the uniqueness of its appearance: any other star can be seen by everyone within its hemisphere, but this was seen only by the three magi. Fourteenth, in the agency of its motion: other stars are moved according to the laws of nature, while this star was moved by the angel who had announced Christ's birth to the shepherds.

***R 4**

Many great and wonderful things were done on this day through the Lord Jesus, most especially in regard to the church. The first is that today, in the persons of the magi, he welcomed his bride the church, which is made up largely of the Gentiles. On the day of his birth he received in the persons of the shepherds the Jewish people, not a few of whom accepted the Word of God. Today he appeared to the Gentiles, who were to make up the rest of the church; the splendor of the star prefigured the light of grace, and the three magi the call of the Gentiles. They symbolize all the nations who were to come to faith in Christ, so today's feast is rightly a celebration for the church and for all the faithful.

**Massa; MVC 9; CM 153:40*

Next, on this day the church is made holy by her bridegroom and is truly united with him by the baptism he will receive when he is thirty years old. This is why we joyfully sing, "Today the church is joined to her heavenly bridegroom, since Christ in the Jordan has washed away her offenses."* The soul is married to Christ in baptism, who obtained virtue by his own baptism, and the congregation of the baptized is called the church.*

*Antiphon for Epiphany; PL 78:743B

**Massa; MVC 9; CM 153:40*

Finally, on the same day one year after his baptism Christ performed his first miracle at the wedding feast, and this too can be understood to refer to the church's nuptials,* as will be seen in a later chapter. Hence the

**Massa; MVC 9; CM 153:40*

church sings, "We celebrate a day adorned with three miracles."* The bishop Maximus of Turin writes, "In the ancient liturgical books that day is spoken of in the plural, 'day of *epiphanies*, or *manifestations*.' These three manifestations are distinguished by different names: *Epiphaniam* refers to appearance of the star *from above*; *Theophaniam* refers to the manifestation made *by God* at the baptism, that is, the voice of the Father; *Bethphaniam* refers to the appearance made *in the house* (*Beth*) at the wedding feast. Quite rightly we celebrate these three mysteries all on the same day, because we profess the mystery of the Trinity under the name of the one God."‡

*Roman Breviary, Antiphon for Vespers on Epiphany

‡*Innocent III, Sermo 7; PL 217:485B; Comestor, Hist ev 7; PL 198:1558C*

Also, according to Origen, Jesus fed the four thousand with seven loaves and a few fish on this day in a different year.[1]* You can certainly see how august this day is on which the Lord chose to perform so many great and marvelous signs. As she ponders all the blessings bestowed upon her by her spouse, the church has good reason to feel great joy and exultation and desire to celebrate this occasion with much festivity. Let us now speak of the first great sign, and consider the other events in their proper places.*

*source unknown

**MVC 9; CM 153:40*

The Arrival of the Magi

*In accordance with the prophecy of Micah, *Jesus therefore was born in Bethlehem of* the tribe of *Juda* (to

***R 5**

[1] The association of the miracle of the loaves and fishes with these other signs is ancient. Saint Ambrose's sister, Marcellina, received the veil of a virgin on Christmas Day; Pope Liberius mentioned both the wedding feast of Cana and the multiplication of the loaves for the four thousand in his sermon De virginibus 3.1 (PL 16:219C). A hymn erroneously attributed to Ambrose by Cassiodorus, *Illuminans Altissimus*, also connects this miracle with the other three events, although it speaks of the five loaves.

distinguish it from another Bethlehem in Galilee, in the territory of the tribe of Zabulon), *in the days of King Herod*.* Specifically, this occurred in the thirtieth year of Herod's reign and shows that the time foretold for the Messiah's birth had arrived. The patriarch Jacob had prophesied that the Savior would come when the scepter had been taken away, that is, there would be a ruler in Israel who was not Jewish, and this was fulfilled in Herod of Ashkelon, who was an Idumaean, and the first foreign king.

*Matt 2:1

Behold, there came wise men from the East, representatives of the future church of the Gentiles, *to* the royal city of *Jerusalem* inquiring as to the birth of Christ and *saying: "Where is he that is born king of the Jews?"** See, the magi proclaim the title that the Jews will reject—*Write not: The King of the Jews*—*but that was confirmed by Pilate, *What I have written, I have written*.* *"For we have seen his star* (and it was uniquely his, because it was created to make him known) *in the East, and are come* in person *to* humbly *adore him* alone."* We saw earlier that the shepherds came to ascertain the truth; here we see that the kings came to adore; later we shall see that the old people came to give thanks. These can serve as types of pastors, the active, and the contemplative: the first see and proclaim, the second venerate and worship, the third embrace and hold.

*Matt 2:1-2
*John 19:21
*John 19:22
*Matt 2:1-2

Some people believe that the star disappeared when the magi entered Judea, and with their guiding light gone they had to go into the royal city of Jerusalem to ask about the newborn king.* Others are of the opinion that the magi forfeited the guidance of the star when they went into Jerusalem to make inquiries about the boy; by seeking human aid they justly lost divine assistance, because it is only right that those who prefer human direction to God's rightly lose the latter.* Here we can see the star as a symbol of divine grace: when good people seek counsel from wicked people they

*Chrys, Hom Matt 7.3 Anianus; PG 58:1045
*Legenda 14

forfeit true enlightenment.*Whether it happened before or after they entered Jerusalem, the star did vanish. *R 6

God did this for several reasons. First, for the sake of the magi themselves, so that what had first been communicated to them by a heavenly sign would also be confirmed by the words of the prophets and answers given by the learned doctors resident in the city. Second, for the sake of Christ, so that his birth would be announced in the royal city, and it would be seen that the prophecy regarding the Messiah's birthplace had been fulfilled. Third, so that the energy of the magi would put to shame the indolence of the Jewish priests, because the Gentiles made a great effort to find Christ, while they would not take a single step to do so.* Fourth, so that those Jews who did not welcome Christ could not plead ignorance, since the magi had made known to them both the time and the place of his birth. This also is an image of the fact that the faith of Christ would be eagerly embraced by many Gentiles, whereas a good part of the Jews would reject it.*

**CA Matt 2:1–2 approx*

**Lyra Matt 2:1*

These magi were firmly grounded in their awe of Christ and strong in their faith: they remained steadfast in their confession of Christ even though they knew that there was an imperial edict that anyone who swore allegiance to a king other than the Roman emperor would be punished severely. Chrysostom asks, "Who did not know that Herod reigned in Jerusalem? Who could be ignorant of the fact that to hail and adore another as king instead of the reigning monarch would be to invite terrible punishment? But as they contemplated the future king, they did not fear the present one. They had not even seen Christ yet, and they were prepared to die for him. O blessed magi, who became confessors of Christ in the presence of a most cruel despot even before they had seen Christ!"*

*Opus imperf 2.1; PG 56:637

Herod's Reaction

*R 7
‡Matt 2:3

And King Herod hearing this, was troubled‡ at the birth of such a boy, fearing that he would depose him as a foreigner and usurp his throne. Augustine asks, "What will the tribunal of Christ the Judge be like, if his infant's crib terrified proud kings? Let kings now fear him who is seated at the right hand of the Father, whom the impious king feared while he was still nursing at his mother's breast."†

†Sermo 200; PL 38:1029
*Matt 2:3
**Comestor, Hist ev 7; PL 198:1541D*
**Gloss Matt 2:3; PL 162:1255C*
*Opus imperf 2.1; PG 56:637

Not only did he tremble, but *all Jerusalem with him,** struck by these novel wonders* and wanting to placate Herod, whom they feared and to whom they were subject. Often the populace is most flattering to those rulers who are the cruelest;* unjust kings are surrounded by wicked and obsequious servants. According to Chrysostom *all Jerusalem was troubled* either from fear or from flattery: the arrival of the just brings no joy to the wicked.*

Or, *all Jerusalem* can be understood as taking a part for the whole, meaning all those in Jerusalem who curried favor with Herod. It is commonly said when a majority in a city does something, the city does it; in this case the high officials and ministers of his court all shared in their king's discomfort.*

**Lyra Matt 2:3*
*R 8
*Matt 2:4
*Matt 2:5

And assembling together all the chief priests and the scribes of the people,* who were the most learned among the Jews, *he inquired of them where Christ should be born. He was eager to know his birthplace because he was anxious to murder him, and so he consulted those who knew what the prophetic Scriptures had said about the Messiah and experts in the genealogy of David's descendants. *But they said to him: "In Bethlehem of Juda,"** that is, in the town in Judea, as the prophet Micah had written. Augustine observes that these Jewish scribes, who teach others where Christ is to be born but do not go there themselves, are like the men who helped Noah build the ark that carried others to safety while they themselves drowned, or like the milestones that point the way for others but do not travel the road themselves.* He also writes that it can be said of them that they show others the way to the fountain of life yet die of thirst themselves.* These scribes and priests who made known the birthplace of Christ but, far from adoring him themselves, persecuted him all the more, symbolize those who teach good doctrine but live wicked lives: they proclaim Christ with sound teaching but attack him by their evil behavior.

*Sermo 373; PL 39:1665

*Sermo 199; PL 38:1027

Then Herod, privately and secretly *calling the wise men, learned diligently of them the time of the star which appeared to them.** He had ascertained from the Jewish scribes the place of Christ's birth; he wanted to learn from the magi themselves the time of his birth; then, if they returned to him, he would know both the time and the place, and he could kill Christ. As a foreigner, Herod did not trust the Jews, which is why he met privately with the magi.*

*Matt 2:7

**Lyra, Com Matt 2:7*

And sending them into Bethlehem, he cunningly *said,* to deceive them, *"Go and diligently inquire after the child, and when you have found him, bring me word again, that I also may come and adore him."** To deceive them more easily, he feigned a desire to adore and in this way induce them to return to him.* Certainly his promise was counterfeit, for, as Chrysostom says, he pledged devotion even as he was sharpening his sword, camouflaging his wicked heart with the hues of humility.* This is a stratagem often employed by evil people: to simulate friendship and humility towards those they plan to wound mortally in secret. Rabanus Maurus suggests that by his words and facial expressions Herod pretended he wanted to worship the very child he intended to kill out of envy: he did this both so that the magi would hurry back to him and so that those Jews who wanted Christ to be their king in the future would not hide him from Herod. He is the very likeness of hypocrites who only pretend to seek God and so never deserve to find him.*

*Matt 2:8

**Lyra Matt 2:8*

*Opus imperf 2.9; PG 56:641

*Com Matt 2:8; PL 107:758C; CM 174:58

And just as Herod wanted to kill Christ under the cloak of religion, so hypocrites murder him to the extent they can, as the apostle teaches, *crucifying again to themselves the Son of God.** Pope Gregory says, "Feigned holiness is a double iniquity."[2]* And Chrysostom teaches that those who receive Holy Communion unworthily are like Herod: they pretend to worship, but in fact do their utmost to slay him, as the apostle warned: *Whosoever shall eat this bread, or drink the chalice of the Lord unworthily, shall be guilty of the body and of the blood of the Lord.**

*Heb 6:6

*Guerric of Igny, Sermo Epiphany 4.3; PL 185:60C

*1 Cor 11:27; Hom Matt 7.5; PG 57/58:78

The Magi Go to Bethlehem

*R 9

Having heard the king*, and unaware of his evil intentions, *they went their way*, leaving Jerusalem and heading toward Bethlehem, directed by the prophecy. *And behold, the star which they had seen in the East* reappeared to them; since they had forsaken human help, they were deserving of divine assistance. (A church has been erected to commemorate the place where they saw the star again.) The star *went before them* to show them the way, *until it came and stood* **over a place near the house* *where the child was.** It came to rest over the child's head, as if to point him out and say, "Here is the newborn King about whom I have been giving testimony." The star could not speak, but it witnessed by its very presence. And so, led by the star, the magi arrived with great joy at the little shed in which Jesus had been born.

*Latin Diatessaron?

*Matt 2:9

There is some disagreement as to whether the magi had seen the star standing motionless over Judea from their location in the East or the star had appeared in

[2] Guerric cites without attribution. The phrase *Simulata sanctitas, duplex iniquitas* has also been attributed to Jerome and Augustine.

the East and then led them to Judea. Chrysostom
favors the latter explanation, and it is the one more
commonly held.* Fulgentius, however, is of the opin- *Hom Matt 6.3;
ion that they first saw it standing motionless over PG 57/58:65
Judea, beckoning them there. Upon their arrival they
entered Jerusalem, the capital city of the region. With
a remarkable motion the star then went before them, ‡*Comestor, Hist ev 7;*
and, having fulfilled its purpose, it disintegrated.‡ *PL 198:1542A*

And entering into the house, they found the child with* ***R 10
Mary his mother;‡ perhaps at that moment she was ‡Matt 2:11
seated, holding the child on her lap. They rejoiced
greatly because they had not been deceived in their
desire, nor had they labored in vain. Chrysostom says,
"They rejoiced for several reasons: that they had found
what they had been so desperately seeking, that they
were proven to be heralds of the truth, and that their
arduous journey had not been in vain, so great was
the longing they had for Christ."* *Hom Matt 7.4;

And Blessed Mary! Without Mary, Jesus would not PG 57/58:77
have been born, for she herself was the servant of the
incarnation; without Mary, Jesus would not have been
found, because she herself was the handmaid of his
rearing; without Mary, Jesus would not have been
crucified, for she herself was the partner in his passion. Joseph is not mentioned. Chrysostom suggests
that this was because nothing was recorded of his
service as a foster father.* Hilary and Rabanus hold *Werner, Sermo
that it was by divine dispensation that he was absent Epiphany;
at that moment, lest he be thought to be the father, or PL 157:807A
the Gentiles be given any cause to wonder whether
this newborn Savior, to whom they were about to *Rabanus, Com Matt 2:11;
make their offerings, was not God.* PL 107:759B

‡*And falling down they adored him*† with both their **‡R 11**
hearts and their bodies, kneeling before the child Jesus †Matt 2:11
and adoring him reverently with the *latria* due to him
as God. **They did him honor as a King*** and gave him *Latin Diatessaron?
worship as God;‡ they saw the human being and knew ‡*Massa*
God. They fell down as a sign of humility, without

which virtue there is no true adoration: a worshiper must put aside all haughtiness and self-reliance, bearing in spirit the sentiments he expresses bodily by prostrating in God's sight, offering to God the sacrifice of a humble and contrite heart, and trusting in his care. What was the joy you felt, O most blessed Virgin, who can even imagine it, when you saw them adoring as God the infant you held on your lap?

O how great was the faith of the magi! Who could believe that this baby boy dressed in rags in the company of his poor little mother, and in such a squalid place, bereft of family and friends, without possessions, was in fact the King and true God? And yet they believed both these things. They would not have honored and worshiped the little child if they had believed he was just a little child. It was becoming for us to have such leaders and antecedents,* from which it is clear that they knew of Christ's divinity by divine revelation. When they saw this poorly clothed infant cradled in his mother's lap, lacking all outward signs of regal or divine power, it is not credible that they would have shown him such signs of reverence unless they had come to know of his identity through some more than human way.*

*Massa; MVC 9; CM 153:41

*Lyra Matt 2:11

Bernard writes, "The magi adore and offer gifts to the infant at his mother's breast. But where, O magi, is the royal purple? Do you not see the cheap swaddling clothes? If this is a king, where is his crown? But you see him *in the diadem with which his mother crowned him*,* the sack of our mortality, about which at his resurrection he will say, *You have undone my sackcloth and have robed me with gladness*."* And again,

*Song 3:11

*Ps 29:12; Sermo Epiphany 3.4; PL 183:147D; SB 4:306

> What is this to you, O strangers, that Christ is adored by you? We have not found such faith in Israel. The squalor of the stable and the poverty of the manger-crib do not shock you. The sight of the poor mother with the infant at her breast does not scandalize you.*

*Sermo Epiphany 3.4; PL 183:151A; SB 4:306

> What are you doing, magi, what are you doing? You adore a nursing infant wrapped in rags in a wretched hovel! Is this really God? *The Lord is* certainly *in his holy temple, the Lord's throne is in heaven,** and you look for him on his mother's lap in a poor stable! What are you doing, offering him gold? Is he then a king? If so, where is his palace, his throne, his royal entourage? Is the stable his palace, the manger his throne, Mary and Joseph his retinue? Have these wise men become so foolish that they worship a mere infant, contemptible alike for his age and his condition? Yes, these wise men have become fools, so that they might become truly wise. The Holy Spirit has taught them the lesson that the apostle would later proclaim: *Let him become a fool, that he may be wise.**
>
> Was it not to be feared that such men, upon seeing this poverty, would be scandalized and believe themselves deluded? They were expecting to find the king in the royal city, but they are directed to the poor little hamlet of Bethlehem; they are led to a stable; they find an infant in swaddling clothes. The sordid surroundings do not scandalize them, nor the rags, nor the infant at the breast. They fall down prostrate, honoring him as a king and worshiping him as God. Immediately the one who brought them there instructs them, and he who had led them outwardly by a star now teaches them secretly in their hearts.*

*Ps 10:4

*1 Cor 3:18

*Sermo Epiphany 1.5; PL 183:145A; SB 4:296–97

Augustine asks, "How did he draw those men to him from such a vast distance, humbly beseeching him with such offerings? He was not resting under a royal canopy, swathed in purple, with a diadem on his head, surrounded by a princely retinue; he had neither an awe-inspiring army nor fame for military triumphs. Lying in the manger was a newborn babe, tiny in stature and living in poverty. But there was hidden within this child a greatness that had been revealed to those men not by earth but by heaven."*

*Ps-Augustine, Sermo 132; PL 39:2008

Chrysostom comments,

> *And entering into the house, they found the child with Mary his mother*. She was not crowned with a diadem, bedecked in gold, or reclining on a gilded bed; she had barely one garment, for covering and not for display, the kind of the thing a carpenter's wife would wear on a journey. Had they come looking for an earthly monarch, they would have been more confounded than joyful, thinking their great efforts a waste of time. But because they were searching for a heavenly king, even though they did not see any royal trappings they were content with the solitary witness of the star; their eyes rejoiced to see this unassuming infant, because the Spirit revealed his awesome majesty to their hearts.*

*Opus imperf 2.11; PG 56:642

And finally, Pope Leo:

> Not inappropriately, when the brightness of a new star led the three wise men to worship the child, they did not find him expelling demons, raising the dead, giving sight to the blind, healing the lame, restoring speech to the mute, or evincing any other manifestation of divine power. They saw him as a child, silent, at rest, in the care of his mother. There appeared no sign of great power, but a great miracle was presented by this lowliness. For the whole of the Savior's life, by which he overcame the devil and the world, began in humility and ended in humility. Its appointed days began and ended under persecution. The child was not exempt from suffering, nor did the Man of Sorrows lose his childlike gentleness.
>
> Consequently, the whole of Christian wisdom consists not in an abundance of words, in cleverness in argumentation, or in the desire for fame and glory, but in that true and willing humility that Jesus both chose and taught by enduring with courage everything from his mother's womb till his final agony on the cross.*

*Sermo 37.2; PL 54:257C; CL 38:200–201

So if you also want to overcome the devil and the world, strive with all your strength to follow Christ's example of patience and humility: with these safeguards you can conquer your enemies, seen and unseen.

The Gifts of the Magi

*The magi opened their treasures when they found the child. A moral lesson for us in this is that we should not bring out our treasures on our journey until, having bypassed our enemies, we can offer them to God alone from the secret treasury of our heart. *They* each *offered him gifts: gold, frankincense, and myrrh.** It was the custom among the ancients that no one would come into the presence of God or a ruler empty-handed and without gifts. Among the Arabs gold and various spices were to be found in abundance; these were customary gifts, and accordingly the magi had obtained them. ***R 12** *Matt 2:11

Granted that they were following the usual practice of their people in gift giving, it was also by divine inspiration that they did this: by their choice of gifts they revealed mysteries and in a mystical way declared their faith. They showed faith in the mystery of the Trinity by adoring the Trinity in Christ, they indicated that Christ was both mortal and King, Lord, and God, and they venerated Christ's regal power, divine majesty, and human mortality. The magi knew these three things about Christ, as their earlier words suggest: "*Where is he that is born*, that is, one who is human, *king of the Jews*, that is, possessing royal power, for we *are come to adore him*, because he is God." Christ's royal dignity was symbolized by gold, a noble metal whose regal eminence made it a fitting tribute for rulers; this gift showed that the child was indeed a king. The gift of frankincense signified divine majesty because it is burned in sacrifice to God, and thus it showed that the child was God; it was also a priestly offering, proclaiming that the boy was a priest, whom no other priest could equal. Human mortality was symbolized by the myrrh, because it was customary to preserve the bodies of the dead with this spice, and Christ, the King and Priest, wished to die for the salvation of all people.

Augustine says, "Gold is given as tribute to a king, incense is offered as to God, myrrh is provided to one who will die for the salvation of all."* Each of them presented all three gifts, because it is thought that this was fitting to the mystery. No one can truly be called a Christian who does not profess Christ to be God, King, and mortal Man, which is what these three gifts signify. As Remigius teaches, "The magi did not each offer one of the gifts; they each offered all three, so that by their gifts they could proclaim their belief that Christ is King, God, and Man."* The Christian who professes Christ to be true God, true Man, and true King imitates them. So let us offer him gold, because we believe he is truly Lord of all creation; frankincense, because we profess that he is God and Creator of all things; and myrrh, because we do not doubt that he whom we profess to be true God really became Man for our sake.

*Ps-Augustine, Sermo 131.6; PL 39:2007

*Hom 7; PL 131:906C

Holy faith never ceases to offer these three gifts to Christ, believing that one and the same is true God, true Man, and him who truly died for us.* We also have in these gifts no little knowledge of great mysteries, according to Hilary: Christ's death as Man, his resurrection as God, and his returning to judge as King.* Lord Jesus, I who am the very least of your servants adore you enthroned at your Father's right hand and reigning over all creation, and I offer to you the splendor of the faith by which I profess that you are the King of all ages, God from God, Man from the Virgin, who died for our sins.

**Haymo, Hom 15; PL 118:114B*

*Com Matt 1.5; PL 9:923A

Bernard suggests that the magi gave the gold to assist the mother and child in their poverty, the incense as a perfume to counteract the fetid odor of the stable, and the myrrh as an unguent for the infant, to soothe and strengthen his weak limbs.‡

‡Sent 15; PL 183:751A; SB 6:2:11

***R 13**

*Since we have offered to Christ what is his, let us also offer what is ours. The fact that we believe he is King, God, and Man is his gift to us; but there are three things we have received from God that can be our gift to him. We have within us three gifts that are pleasing to God, and these we offer him. The first is our soul, symbolized by gold: there is nothing more precious and noble than gold, and there is nothing more valuable, fine, and beautiful than the soul considered in the presence of God. The second is our body, symbolized by myrrh: myrrh is bitter, and the body is made bitter by self-discipline and suffering. The third is holy and honorable conduct in both soul and body: this is symbolized by incense, for as incense only releases its aroma when it is burned by fire, so our manner of living cannot send up its fragrance to God unless it is burned by the fire of tribulation.

Let us also offer to Christ the gold of our love, because he submitted to the sufferings of the passion for us, the frankincense of grateful praise by our thanksgiving, and the myrrh of compassion by the recollection of his death.*

**SHS 9*

In a spiritual sense the church possesses the gold of perfect wisdom, doctrine, and right faith; the incense of loving prayer, good thoughts, and holy conduct, which makes a pleasing aroma for God; and the myrrh of bitter penance, mortification of the flesh, and good works. Therefore theologians offer gold, martyrs and confessors offer incense, penitent sinners offer myrrh. Every oblation is included in these three gifts. Such were the presents the magi offered, which symbolize the truth of the faith and the whole of ecclesiastical discipline.*

**Bruno Com Matt 2:11; PL 165:81CD*

Bernard says,

> We offer gold to the Savior when we give up entirely all worldly possessions for the sake of his name; but along with forsaking earthly goods, it is necessary for us ardently to desire heavenly ones. Likewise, we offer to God the fragrant aroma of incense, which is undoubtedly the prayers of the saints. It is also required of us not only to disdain the attractions of the present age, but to discipline our flesh and bring it into subjection. Prayer has two wings, contempt for the world and affliction of the heart, and it cannot be doubted that it reaches the heavens and comes into God's presence like incense only when myrrh is offered to him along with the gold and incense.*

*Sermo Epiphany 3.5–6; PL 183:151B; SB 4:307

***R 14**

*The magi honored Christ in three ways from their resources: bodily, because they prostrated; spiritually, because they adored; and from their possessions, because they presented gifts. A person has nothing more to give than body, soul, and possessions.

And it is appropriate that it is said that there were three magi, because those who come to faith must confess the undivided Trinity, or because those who adore God ought to have the three principal virtues of faith, hope, and love, or because those who want to see God should avoid evil and do good in thought, word, and deed, or in memory, intellect, and will.* Gregory says that holy people are sometimes called kings because they are not ruled by their carnal passions; ruling them well, they know how to take charge of them.‡ And, as Isidore points out, kings are called such because they reign rightly,* so it follows that those who act rightly hold the title of king, while those who sin forfeit it.† These three kings left the Orient behind, which can be understood to mean human prosperity, and this, too, is threefold: riches, pleasures, and honors.

**Haymo, Hom 15; PL 118:111BC*

‡Mor 26.XXVIII.53; PL 76:381B; CL 143B:1307

**reges a recte regendo vocantur*

†Ety 1.29.3; PL 82:105C

*The star that appeared to the magi can be understood to symbolize Mary, who is *the star of the sea*. Moreover, this star appears to magi, or kings, deigning to show herself to those who are devout and control themselves; she guides them through the turbulent sea of this world to the port of safety, who is Christ. When they reach him they worship, offering him the gold of charity, the incense of devoted prayer, and the myrrh of bodily mortification.* ***R 15** **Lyra Matt 2:2 mor*

On the same day that Christ was born in Judea, this messenger appeared in the East. For they saw a new star, in the midst of which a boy appeared, above whose head a golden cross shone. And they heard a voice say to them, "Go to Judea, and there you will find a newborn King." Therefore, they hastened to Judea and, boldly entering that land, offered their gifts to the heavenly King who had been born.* **SHS 9*

Prefigurations of the Magi

The Magi were prefigured by the three strong men who carried water to King David from the well in Bethlehem. These three soldiers had no fear of their enemies but bravely broke through their camp and drew out the water; similarly, the three magi were not cowed by Herod's power but courageously entered Judea and inquired about the new king. The three strong men went to Bethlehem for water from the well, which they drew out of an earthly cistern; the three magi came to Bethlehem for the water of eternal life, which they received from the heavenly cup bearer. The well symbolized that this heavenly cup bearer was to be born in Bethlehem, who would serve the water of grace to all who thirst and the water of life to all who lack it.* ***R 16** *2 Sam 23:16 **SHS 9*

This new King and his offering were foreshadowed in the reign of King Solomon.* He sat upon a throne *2 Kgs 10 of brilliant white ivory that was overlaid with the purest gold. All the kings of the earth wanted to look upon Solomon and brought to him most precious gifts. Indeed, the Queen of Sheba brought so many and such wonderful gifts that the like had never been seen in Jerusalem before. In truth, Solomon's throne is the Blessed Virgin Mary, upon whom is seated the true Wisdom, Jesus Christ. His throne, too, is of ivory and pure gold. The cool, brilliant whiteness of ivory signifies the purity of virginal chastity, and the rosy hue that ivory develops over a very long time suggests that chastity lived over many years is a kind of martyrdom. Gold, the most precious of metals, signifies charity, which is the mother of all virtues. Mary is described as ivory on account of her virginal chastity, and she is robed in gold on account of her matchless charity: she unites charity to the beauty of virginity, because in God's sight virginity without charity counts for nothing. Solomon's throne was raised up on six steps, and Mary is pre-eminent over six ranks of the blessed: patriarchs, prophets, apostles, martyrs, confessors, and virgins. The six steps of the throne were decorated with twelve small lions, because the twelve apostles ministered to the Queen of Heaven, or because the twelve patriarchs were her progenitors. The top of the throne was round, because Mary was totally spotless, without unswept corners. There were two hands on either side for holding the seat, because the Father and the Holy Spirit never left the Son's Mother.[3]*

*SHS 9

[3] The description of Solomon's throne is taken from the Vulgate, which differs slightly from the Hebrew version: see 1 Kgs 10:18-21.

The Magi Return Home

Finally, after reverently and devoutly kissing the baby's feet, adoring the Lord, and having performed every kind of obeisance, the magi received a blessing with bowed heads and joyfully departed. As they were deliberating about their journey, *they received an answer in sleep* by divine revelation *that they should not return to Herod,** because once the truth is known it is not permitted to go back. In this incident we are admonished not to seek out the society of the wicked and to shun error when it becomes known. Seneca teaches, "There is no inconsistency in giving up an intention when we discover it is wrong, and there is no disgrace in altering our plans after due consideration."* They sought within their consciences to know what God's will was regarding their return to Herod, and just as Moses cried out silently in his heart, so these magi inquired about the divine will with devout piety. Accordingly, they deserved to receive an answer, either through some interior revelation or through the agency of an angel.

*R 17

**Massa*

*Matt 2:12

*De beneficiis 4.38

And going down to the coast they boarded a ship headed for Tarshish in Cilicia and *went back another way into their country** so that, according to Jerome, they would not be associated with the infidelity of the Jews.* Herod was furious when he heard of this and set fire to the ships of Tarshish, as David had prophesied, *With a vehement wind you shall break in pieces the ships of Tharsis.** Chrysostom says, "See the faith of the magi: they were not troubled within themselves, saying, 'If this boy is so great, what need is there to flee and return secretly?' True faith does not ask the reasons for any commands but is persuaded by the commands themselves."*

*Matt 2:12

*Com Matt 2:12; PL 25:27A

*Ps 47:8

*Hom Matt 8.1; PG57/58:83

*The magi provide an example to believers that we should come devoutly to God and wait upon his will in all our actions. In this way we will not return to the

*R 18

devil, but we will return to our homeland through Christ, who is *the way, the truth, and the life,** and through the paths of virtue. We are admonished to find all of our hope and salvation in Christ and, leaving behind the roads we traveled before conversion, travel by another route. Augustine counsels, "The road has changed: we do not return on the same way we came, nor do we retrace the steps we made before our conversion."* And Gregory says, "The magi show us something important by returning to their country by another way. Our true country is Paradise, and once we know Jesus, we are forbidden to return there by the way we came. We left our country by being proud, disobedient, and captivated by passing things; we must return by weeping, obeying, despising worldly delights, and curbing our bodily appetites. And so we return by another way: pleasures led us away from the joys of Paradise; sorrows summon us to return."*

*John 14:6

*Sermo 202.3.4; PL 38:1035

*40 Hom 10.7; PL 76:1113C [8; CL 141:71]

Another illustration of the idea that we should return to our country by another route is that in processions the Holy Father follows a different route when he returns home from the one taken when he went out.* The magi went home more earnestly than before, glorifying God by their praise and instructing many by their preaching.

**Comestor, Hist ev 113; PL 198:1596B*

Mary and Her Child

***R 19**

It may be piously believed that our Lady—a lover of poverty, a strong advocate for this virtue, and knowing her Son's will—distributed the gold to the poor within a few days. When she went to the temple she did not have enough money to purchase a lamb to offer for her Son, but bought a couple of doves or pigeons, which was the offering of the poor. See how poverty is praised in two ways: first, on this day the child Jesus and his mother accepted alms because they were poor; second, not only did they not seek these alms, but they refused to keep what had been given to them. If you reflect well on this, your desire both for poverty and for deeper humility will grow. There are some people who in their hearts consider themselves to be base and worthless and do not exalt themselves in their own eyes—but would not want to be appraised as such in the eyes of others! *Massa; MVC 9; CM 153:43

Jesus, the Lord of all, was not like this. He willingly showed his mean estate and reduced circumstances to others, and not only to a few others in similar circumstances, but also to kings and their associates, the entourage that they had led to him. And he did this in a situation where such poverty could create much consternation: they had come to see the King of the Jews, whom they also believed to be God, and it is very likely that finding him in such squalor they would have thought themselves deluded and gone away lacking in faith and devotion. But not even on this account would the lover of humility renounce it. He showed us by example that even for an apparently good reason we must not forsake humility, and taught us to wish to appear worthless and poor in the eyes of others.* *Massa; MVC 9; CM 153:43

*Once the magi had left and returned to their own country, the Queen of the universe remained patiently and humbly with her child Jesus, and Joseph his foster father, near the crib in that modest stable for forty days, as if she were simply like any other woman of the people, and the boy Jesus were merely human, and that they needed to fulfill the dictates of the Law. Our Lady stood by vigilantly, attending to the care of her beloved Son. O, with what concentration and solicitude she tended him, not neglecting the least of his needs! With what reverence, care, and holy fear she caressed him, knowing that he was her God and Lord! Kneeling down, she lifted him from his crib *R 20 and put him back there. With what joy, confidence, and maternal solicitude she took him in her arms, kissed him, sweetly hugged him, and took delight in him whom she saw and most certainly knew to be her son! How carefully and prudently she wrapped his tender limbs! Just as she was most humble, so she was most prudent. In all of her service and care she was most attentive, when he was waking or sleeping, and not only in infancy, but also as he grew. O, how willingly she nursed him! It is hardly possible that other mothers could have known the great and unique sweetness she experienced in feeding such a Son!*

**Massa; MVC 10; CM 153:44–45*

This Virgin had conceived her infant without shame, had given birth to him without pain, and now nursed him with heavenly dew.* She was a virgin before his birth, in conceiving him; a virgin at his birth, in bringing forth her child; and a virgin after his birth, in feeding her boy with the sweetest milk.

**concepit sine pudore, peperit sine dolore, lactavit coelesti rore*

Augustine tenderly addresses the Virgin Mother in these words: "Suckle Christ, your Lord and ours, mother; give milk to the bread that came down from heaven. Nurse him who did such a marvel for you that he came to be in you. He gave you the gift of fruitfulness by being conceived in you, and he did not take away the gift of virginity by being born of you."* And Anselm asks, "As she turned this real little boy in her arms, held him to her breast, and noticed him crying—as infants will do when their tender little bodies hurt—who, I ask, could be so moved as her most loving soul, and anxious to take away any discomfort she feared his most pure body felt?"* And Bernard says of that holy old man Joseph that he often smiled at Jesus as he held him on his lap.*

*Ps-Aug, Sermo 128.2; PL 39:1988

*Eadmer, De exc 4; PL 159:564C

*SC 43.5; PL 183:994D; SB 4:43–44

As our Lady stands near the manger, you should stand there with her, and be beguiled by the child Jesus, because virtue comes from him! Any faithful soul, and especially a religious, should visit the manger at least once a day from Christmas to the Purification to adore Jesus and his mother. Meditate with affection on their poverty and affliction, their humility and kindness. You have seen how the Blessed Virgin patiently abided in that sordid stable for many days with the boy Jesus and Joseph; it should not seem such a terrible thing for us to remain sequestered in the monastery.*

**Massa; MVC 10; CM 153:45*

The Magnitude of the Solemnity of Epiphany

*Consider now how great is today's solemnity, and rejoice in it, because today the beginnings of our faith first appeared. Pope Leo says, ***R 21**

> Let us recognize, dearly beloved, the first-fruits of our calling and the beginning of our faith in the magi who adored Christ, and with joyful hearts celebrate the dawning of blessed hope. Let us honor this most sacred day when the author of our salvation appeared! Let us worship the All-powerful in heaven, whom the magi worshiped in the manger. And as they offered to the Lord mystical gifts from their treasure, let us bring forth from our hearts offerings worthy of God.* The mystery of the present feast ought to be with us perpetually; undoubtedly it will be celebrated without end if the Lord Jesus Christ is made manifest in all our actions.*

*Sermo 32.4; PL 54:239D; CL 38:168–69

*Sermo 38.4; PL 54:263A; CL 138:208

*You have also seen how many new realities appeared concurrently at Christ's nativity to sanction his birth. Chrysostom lists them: ***R 22**

> All kinds of new things take place at the birth of the Lord in a manner beyond human imagining: an angel speaks to Zechariah in the temple, he promises him that Elizabeth will have a son, not

believing the angel, the priest is struck mute, the sterile woman conceives, John leaps in his mother's womb, the Virgin gives birth, the birth of Christ the Lord is announced by an angel and the salvation of the world is proclaimed to the shepherds, the angels rejoice, the shepherds exult, great joy arises in heaven and on earth because of this wondrous birth, the new sign of a heavenly star appears to the magi, by which it is known that the newborn child is the King of the Jews and the Lord of heaven and earth.*

*Ps-Chrysostom, Hom Epiphany 1; Fronton 2:465B

✠

O good Jesus, when you were born of the Virgin you revealed yourself to the magi by the guidance of a star and inspired them to return to their own country by another route. May the light of your grace, merciful Jesus, illumine the darkness of my conscience and by your joyful epiphany grant me full knowledge of you and of myself. May I behold you within and come to you within, there to offer to your majesty the myrrh of inner compunction, the incense of devout prayer, and the gold of godly love. With you as my guide, may I who departed from my native land of supernal joy by the gloomy road of sin return there by the path of truth and grace. Amen.

CHAPTER 12

The Presentation of the Lord in the Temple

(Luke 2:22-39)

*Mary left the stable with Joseph and the boy *after the days of her purification were accomplished,** ***that is, on the fortieth day,**** to fulfill the requirements of the Law.‡ In truth, Mary did not need purification, because she had conceived without sin. A boy was cleansed by circumcision from the original sin he had inherited from his parents; by the rite of purification a mother was cleansed of sin contracted by the passion involved in conceiving—but none of this was present either in this boy or in his mother. *They carried him* from Bethlehem *to Jerusalem according to the Law, to present him* and offer him to the Lord ***in the temple,**** *and to offer a sacrifice of a pair of turtledoves or two young pigeons*‡ for him.

***R 1**
*Luke 2:22
*Latin Diatessaron?
‡*Massa*

*Latin Diatessaron?
‡Luke 2:22-24

*As background, it should be understood that there was a twofold precept regarding the birth of a child. The first was a general rule applicable to all: when the days of a mother's purification were completed, the boy was carried to the temple and a sacrifice was offered for him. The law of purification concerning the mother was that if she had given birth to a boy she was unclean for a period of seven days, during which she was not allowed to associate with people, enter the temple, or touch sacred objects. On the octave, the baby was circumcised and the mother was considered

***R 2**

to be purified as regards association with people, but not as regards the temple or sacred objects; this condition would continue for another thirty-three days, during which time she remained at home. On the fortieth day the mother entered the temple and presented her newborn son, offering sacrifice for him and for herself. Had she had given birth to a girl, the intervals of seven days and thirty-three days would have been doubled.*

**Legenda 37 approx*

In addition, there was a second precept pertaining to the firstborn, of animals as well as children, that they were sacred to God because they had been consecrated to the Lord. Ever since the Lord had delivered the children of Israel by slaying the firstborn of the Egyptians, God claimed all the firstborn of Israel for himself and commanded that they be offered to him: this included, along with their offspring, the firstfruits of the land and of all clean animals. And what does this mean, if not that we should offer to the Lord what is first, especially those things that are best and most dear?[1]

***R 3**

*Christ wanted to fulfill the law because he was born of a woman and was her firstborn, and these observances were followed in his regard. It was not enough for the teacher of perfect humility, who was the Father's equal in all things, to submit to being born of a humble virgin—he also submitted to being born under the law. There were several reasons that he did this: first, to approve the old law; second, to show that it had been promulgated for his sake: by obeying it he would both fulfill it and conclude it in himself; third,

[1] Luke combines two distinct and unrelated rituals: 1. The consecration of the firstborn son to the Lord (Exod 13:1, 11-13); the child was "redeemed" for five shekels (Num 18:15-16); 2. The purification of a mother after the birth of her child (Lev 12:1-5). Luke does not mention the ritual of buying the firstborn back, although Ludolph will comment on it later.

to remove any cause for calumny by the Jews; fourth, to free all people from servitude to the law; and fifth, to give us an example of humility and obedience.* *Aquinas, ST III, q. 40. a. 4 resp.

Similarly, the Blessed Virgin was not bound by the law regarding women: she did not need to be purified, because she had not conceived from human seed but by a mystical exhalation of the Holy Spirit. However, she submitted to the rites of purification for several reasons. First, so that in this she might conform herself with other women, just as her son wished to be like his brothers and sisters in all things. Bernard says to her, "Truly, Blessed Virgin, you have no cause or reason for purification. But what need did your son have to be circumcised? Be among the women like one of them, because your son was like that among the other boys."‡ Second, according to Bede, like Christ the Blessed Virgin voluntarily subjected herself to the law in order to free us from it. Third, to avoid an occasion for scandal: since it was not yet known that she had given birth without human seed, she would have caused scandal and invited criticism among the Jews if she had not observed the days of her purification. Fourth, to bring the laws of purification to an end, because our purification has come with Christ, who purifies us through faith. Fifth, to give us an example of humility. To teach us this virtue, she humbly obeyed laws that did not pertain to her. Thus the mother of all theologians, indeed, the Doctor* herself emerges: her gender impeded her from teaching publicly by word, so she wished to teach by example. *R 4

‡Sermo Purification 3.2; PL 183:370B; SB 4:342

*Com Luke 2:22; PL 92:341C; CL 120:62

*Doctrix

Prefigurations of This Mystery

*Granted that Mary did not require cleansing, still she chose to carry out all the rites of purification because she was most diligent in observing the law, and therefore she herself is prefigured by the ark of the *R 5 covenant in which the mandates of the law were kept. These were the two tablets upon which the Ten Commandments were inscribed, which Mary assiduously obeyed. The ark also held the books of the law, and Mary gladly read the Sacred Scriptures. It contained Aaron's staff that had bloomed, and Mary had blossomed and brought forth the blessed fruit of her womb. Within the ark there was also a golden urn containing some of the heavenly manna, and Mary offered to us the true heavenly manna. The ark was made of incorruptible setim-wood, and Mary's body never decayed or was reduced to dust. The ark had four golden rings on its sides, and Mary lived according to the four cardinal virtues, which are the root and beginning of all virtues. The ark was carried with two poles, which represent Mary's twofold charity. The ark was overlaid with gold inside and out, and Mary was resplendent with virtues within and without.[2]* *SHS 9*

For this reason Mary is wonderfully prefigured by the golden candelabrum that shed light in the Lord's temple in Jerusalem, upon which seven lamps burned; these symbolize the seven works of mercy, and thus Mary herself, who is the queen of mercy and the mother of goodness. We honor this candelabrum and its tapers by carrying lighted candles on the feast of the Purification. Mary truly offered a candle to the Lord at her purification, when Simeon sang, *A light to the revelation of the Gentiles*.[3]* Christ, the Son of Mary, *Luke 2:32

[2] The ark of the covenant is described in Exod 25:10-15. It was originally made to contain the two tablets of the law, and this was all that was in it when Solomon placed it in the temple (Deut 10:5; 1 Kgs 8:9). The manna and Aaron's rod were placed near it, but some Jewish traditions, and the Letter to the Hebrews, hold that they were placed in the ark (Heb 9:4). The "book of the law" was also placed near it (Deut 31:26). The seven-branched lampstand is described in Exod 25:31-39.

[3] Ludolph alludes to the procession with candles on the feast of the Presentation, when this phrase is sung as an antiphon.

is the lighted candle because a candle consists of three things, a wick, wax, and a flame, and in Christ are to be found soul, body, and true divinity. This candle illuminating the night of our gloom is offered to the Lord for the human race.* *SHS 9

The offering of this most blessed candle was prefigured in the boy Samuel.* Contrary to the law of nature, *1 Sam 1-12
God gave a child to Hannah, who was sterile, and, above the course of nature, he breathed into the Virgin Mary a son. Hannah bore a son who fought for the Jews; Mary gave birth to a son who protected the world. Hannah's son was later rejected by the Jews; Mary's son was most wickedly condemned to death by them. This is what Simeon prophesied to Mary, predicting that her son's sword had to pass through her soul.[4]* *SHS 9

The Holy Family Goes to the Temple

*The parents of Jesus went to Jerusalem to fulfill the precepts of the law. *R 6
Although they feared Herod they did not presume to transgress the law, and so they brought their child to the temple. In the event, all was quiet because Herod was still awaiting the return of the magi and had not yet revealed the malice in his heart. The Lord Jesus and his mother, in their observance of this and other laws, show us with what solicitude and care we should fulfill the precepts of the Gospel, because they gave themselves over so completely to a diligent observance of the law.

[4] Several other details of the Samuel story resonate with the Presentation: he was presented in the sanctuary of Shiloh and greeted by the aged priest Eli, who blessed his parents; women were ministering at the door of the sanctuary, like Anna; and it concludes with a statement that the child grew in stature and favor with the Lord and with the people.

***R 7**

*They carried the temple's Lord to the temple *to offer a sacrifice* for him, *according as it is written in the law of the Lord*.* And when they had entered the temple they bought *a pair of turtledoves or two young pigeons* to offer for him, as was customary for the poor. It is believed that they bought two young pigeons because they were very poor: these animals were less expensive, which is why they were last on the list of offerings allowed by the law. The evangelist says nothing about a lamb, because this was the offering of the wealthy.*

*Luke 2:24

**Massa; MVC 11; CM 153:45–46*

See what impoverished parents the Lord chose: they had no lamb to offer for him but had to make do with a pair of turtledoves or two young pigeons. The Lord had laid down in the law that on the day when a mother presented her baby in the temple, she should offer an immaculate yearling lamb as a holocaust to purify herself and her offspring and also offer a turtledove or young pigeon as a sin-offering, because she had conceived in lust. If they could not afford a lamb, they offered two turtledoves or young pigeons: one would be substituted for the lamb and was completely burned; the other would be the sin-offering, and part of it was given to the priest, who prayed for the woman's purification. The Lord chose to give this holocaust and offering of the poor for himself. Although he was rich, he deigned to become poor for our sake to enrich us by his poverty, and by allowing us to share in his riches to make us rich in faith and co-heirs in his heavenly kingdom.* Just as he took on our mortality in order to give us immortality, so he chose to assume our poverty so that through it he could bestow everlasting wealth on us. Let us imitate our Lord by loving voluntary poverty: *having food and wherewith to be covered, with these we are content*!*

**Zachary 1.7; PL 186:78BC*

*1 Tim 6:8

Now, why *young* pigeons* were stipulated for sacrifice to the Lord, and not just pigeons, is explained by Bernard:

**pulli columbarum*

And though elsewhere the Holy Spirit is usually designated by the dove, yet because it is a lustful bird, it is not a fit offering for the Lord except when it is young and ignorant of lust. But no age is stated for the turtledove, for its chastity at any age is acknowledged. She is content with one mate; if he is lost she does not take another, thus arguing against the human tendency to marry more than once. During her bereavement you may see the turtledove fulfilling the duties of holy widowhood with unflagging zeal. Everywhere you see her alone, everywhere you hear her mourning; you never find her perched on a green bough—a lesson to you to avoid the green but poisonous shoots of sensual pleasure. Rather, she haunts the mountain ridges and the tops of trees, to teach us to shun the pleasures of earth and to love those of heaven.*

*SC 59.7; PL 183:1064D; SB 2:139

Simeon

R 8

And behold there was a man in Jerusalem*, renowned and notable among the priests, *named Simeon: and this man was just and devout. He was *just* in doing good works and *devout* in avoiding evil. Or he was *just* in acting rightly in relation to his neighbor and *devout* in what pertains to God, because it is difficult to act justly without maintaining a filial and chaste fear of God. Fear of the Lord is the guardian of justice and all other virtues; the more ardently just people fear God, the more careful they are not to offend him. The psalmist testifies that justice always shapes the actions of those whose souls are illuminated by the fear of the Lord: *Blessed is the man that fears the Lord: he is merciful, and compassionate and just.** And Solomon says, *He that fears God neglects nothing.**

**timoratus*; Luke 2:25

*Ps 111:1, 4

*Eccl 7:19

It is fitting that Simeon is called just: he acted rightly toward his neighbors because he was seeking salvation not only for himself but for the whole people by

*Luke 2:25

*waiting for the consolation of Israel.** He possessed the rectitude of faith and hope that waits in hope for the fulfillment of good promises. Lesser people anticipated only earthly consolation; they understood the promise of a Savior to mean that they would be freed from Herod's yoke when the Savior appeared. Great figures like Simeon cherished a hope for spiritual consolation as well, and awaited deliverance from the devil. Consolation would come from seeing God, that is, when the Lord came in the flesh. The holy patriarchs and ancestors, who wept in fear because of the Fall, believed that they would be consoled by the incarnation of the Lord.* Simeon, whose name means *obedient*, was awaiting this consolation; his advanced years were compelling him to leave this world, but he stayed in the flesh because of his desire to see the Lord.[5]

**Haymo, Hom 14; PL 118:103C*

And the Holy Spirit, the Sanctifier and the presence of the Highest Good, *was in him** to the extent that he had the fullness of grace: he not only possessed the grace of justification, as all just people do, but he had also received divine illuminations and special consolations.* The evangelist who says of Simeon that the Holy Spirit was in him had said earlier that he was just and devout, because God dwells in the hearts of those who fear the Lord and act justly. God himself asks through the prophet, *Upon whom shall my Spirit rest, but on the humble and tranquil who fear my words?*[6]*

*Luke 2:25

**Lyra Luke 2:25*

*Isa 66:2

***R 9**

*Luke 2:26

And he had received an answer* in his earnest prayers *from the Holy Spirit through grace dwelling in him. This answer about the advent of Christ came invisibly into his mind through a secret inspiration, and he

[5] Jerome, Nom int, renders *Simeon* as *hearing*, or *hearing sad tidings* (PL 23:844; CL 72:141).

[6] This is the wording of Isa 66:2 found in many patristic authors, but it differs from the Vulg, which does not speak of "my Spirit."

understood that before he ended his earthly life he would behold with his own eyes the Messiah he saw in his mind. From this it is clear that he had been praying about this; he was hoping for this as he *was waiting for the consolation of Israel*. At that time it was commonly held by sages, on the basis of the signs given by the patriarchs and prophets, that the Messiah's arrival was imminent. Simeon was fervently praying to God about this; *and he came by* a revelation of *the Spirit*, and at the Spirit's command, *into the temple*,* so that just as the same Spirit had promised and vowed, he would see the Christ, that is, the Lord's Anointed, before he died.*

*Luke 2:27

**Lyra Luke 2:27 approx*

O, what an ardent desire to see the Lord burned in the heart of this most blessed old man! He knew that because of his advanced years the time had come for him to leave this world, but God's pledge held him here: *he should not see death before he had seen* and experienced *the promised Christ of the Lord** with his own eyes. This is what he yearned for, this occupied his thoughts* and was always on his mind: "I know he will come, I know that I will see him. But when will he come? When will I see him? Come, Lord Jesus, break these bonds and permit me now finally to go in peace." As he was meditating in this way, and fueling his longing, the Holy Spirit spoke to him: "Behold, the one whom you await, the one whom you seek, is here. Now you will see him. Get up, hurry, go to the temple."‡

*Luke 2:26

**Bruno Prolegomena 2.5; PL 164:45BC*

‡Bruno Com Luke 2:26; PL 165:359B

***R 10**

Arriving in haste Simeon entered the temple, and as soon as he saw Jesus he knew who he was by a prophecy of the Holy Spirit. The same grace of the Spirit that had enlightened him about the future birth of Christ now revealed that he had come. Simeon recognized the Savior at a glance.

**Zachary 1.7; PL 186:79C*

Quickening his pace, he ran up and fell on his knees to adore the infant in his mother's arms. Stretching out his hands, he said to the parents, "Give him to me; he is destined for me! This is my duty, for this I have been sent, this service has been reserved for me!" His mother, knowing her son's will, handed him to Simeon.* His heart overflowing with joy, Simeon took the child in his arms with jubilation.

**Massa*

O, how blessed were those hands that touched the Word of life, and those arms that embraced him!* As soon as he had taken the boy in his arms he got up; the burden of age immediately vanished, and Simeon was filled with the vigor and strength of youth.* Great is the Lord's power here, but no less great is his humility. He whom the heavens and the earth cannot contain is now carried in the arms of an old man. Formerly this aged man could only move with difficulty; now he exults as he carries the child with such ease. He was carrying the one who was supporting him, and indeed *upholding all things by the word of his power*:* he was carrying Christ in his humanity, but Christ was upholding him by his divinity. As the phrase so neatly has it, "The old man carried the boy, but the boy guided the old man."* The old man carried the newborn Christ; Christ was reigning over the man living on into old age.

**Gregory of Nyssa? CA Luke 2:22–24*

**Bruno Com Luke 2:28; PL 165:359C*

*Heb 1:3

*Responsory, feast of the Purification; PL 78:745C

How blessed was Simeon, who was permitted not only to see Christ, but to hold him in the flesh! Greatly blessed indeed, because he merited a consolation that the patriarchs and prophets had longed for but had not received! There can be no doubt that he received many consolations and singular graces from holding Jesus Christ. The Greek Doctor* says that the ineffable brilliance shone on the old man so powerfully that events yet to come were made known to him.† No less blessed *are they that have not seen and have believed*.*

*John Damascene

†Greek catena? CA Luke 2:28–32

*John 20:29

*Simeon *blessed* and praised *God*‡ and gave thanks for the great gift of a promise fulfilled by the appearance of salvation. Having beheld the Redeemer, he now made known what had been revealed to him in secret, saying, *Now you may dismiss your servant, O Lord, according to your word in peace, because my eyes have seen your salvation, which you have prepared before the*

***R 11**

‡Luke 2:28

*face of all peoples: a light to the revelation of the Gentiles and the glory of your people Israel.** In other words, "I bless you, Lord. Your promise is fulfilled, and so are my desires: I have seen Christ, who is your salvation—for *Jesus* means *Savior*—and my Lord."* His physical eyes saw the child in the flesh, but with the eyes of his heart he knew he was God. "You may now dismiss (here Simeon expresses a wish) your servant to go in peace from this world to peace of heart in the bosom of Abraham. I can die securely because he is now present who will soon endure his passion to redeem me."

*Luke 2:29-32

**Bruno Com Luke 2:29; PL 165:360A*

He knew how blessed those eyes would be that looked upon Christ, and until he did so he had no wish to die. But as soon as he saw him he wanted to leave this world and dwell in the peace of Abraham's bosom.* He joyfully longed to descend into the limbo of the ancestors now that the Savior had been born. But how could he go in peace to the place where they all reclined on beds in the darkness? The peace of which he spoke was the stillness of repose, not the serenity of enjoying God. See how Simeon had become perfect: he lived patiently and died longing for God. In some ways, Bede observes, the Old Testament fathers were perfected like those in the New.‡

**Zachary, 1.7; PL 186:79C*

‡Com Luke 2:21; PL 92:339C; CL 120:59

***R 12**

*If you wish to hold and embrace Jesus in your arms, and be dismissed in peace, you must strive in every work to be led by the Spirit: come to Jerusalem, pondering heavenly things; enter the temple, imitating the example of those in whom God dwells, sighing and asking only that you might dwell for ever in the house of the Lord; long for the Lord's coming. Then you will be worthy to take the Word of God himself into your arms and be embraced by faith, hope, and charity. You will be dismissed, but you will not see eternal death, for you have seen the Lord.

If you have sought to contemplate Christ the Lord in your heart in this way, you will be happy to undergo bodily death.* Bernard says, "Those who have Christ

**Bede, Com Luke 2:26; PL 92:344C; CL 120:66*

*Eph 2:14

in their heart will depart in peace, *for he is our peace.** But where will you go, miserable soul, if you do not have Christ as your guide on the road?"*

*Sermo Purification 1.2; PL 183:366D; SB 4:335

In a spiritual sense, Simeon (whose name means *obedient*) signifies good religious: they stay in Jerusalem (which means *peace*) by maintaining both inner tranquility and concord in the community. They are just to others, have fear of the Lord, and wait for the consolation of Israel (which means *seeing God*), that is, the vision of God. The Holy Spirit is in them by the blessings of his grace. It is to such as these that Jesus is given to be held; along with Simeon, they bless God for this great gift and desire to leave this world so that the perfect fulfillment of his desires may be given to him, as the apostle says, *I desire to be dissolved and to be with Christ.** There are other spiritual lessons to be drawn: first, that Jesus is held in the arms of good works; second, as the old man received the infant, so we should lay aside the burden of old sins and be clothed in new life; third, we learn humility from the Lord, who upholds all things and yet allowed himself to be carried; fourth, that as Simeon blessed God, so we should thank God for all the good we possess.

*Phil 1:23; *Lyra Luke 2:25 mor*

***R 13**

We can say that Christ is magnified in four ways in Simeon's canticle, according to the four names he calls him: peace, salvation, light, and glory. Christ is peace as Mediator, salvation as Redeemer, light as Teacher, and glory as Rewarder. As the praise of Christ is captured perfectly in these four words, so the whole Gospel narrative is summed up in them. All that pertains to the incarnation is summed up by the word *peace*: *he is our peace, who has made both one,** uniting two natures in one substance, forging two peoples into one, making peace between those who are near and those who are far off, and reconciling humanity with God. His entire public life—his preaching, his conduct, and his miracles—is summed up in the word *light*; as he himself said, *I am the light of the world.** Everything pertaining to his redemptive passion is

**Bonaventure, Com Luke 2:29–32*

*Eph 2:14

*John 8:12

expressed by the word *salvation*, and his resurrection and ascension are captured by the word *glory*. This canticle combines a perfect expression of praise for Christ with the consolation of an aged person about to die, so it is fitting that we sing it late in the evening at the end of the office of Compline.

And his father*, that is, his putative father Joseph, ***R 14 who deserved to be called his father because he was raising him, *and his* real *mother* Mary *were wondering at those things which were spoken concerning him;** won- *Luke 2:33 dering, not in the sense of doubting, but marveling and rejoicing. Mary marveled about what the angel had spoken at the annunciation, what Elizabeth had spoken when John leaped in her womb, and what Zechariah had spoken at John's birth. She and Joseph both marveled at the angelic rejoicing and the new hymn they sang at Jesus' birth, the visit of the shepherds, the adoration of the magi, and the arrival and praise spoken by Simeon—for surely all these events were worthy of admiration and wonder. Ambrose writes, "The Lord's birth is attested not only by the testimony of the angels and the prophets, by the shepherds and his parents, but also by the aged and the just. Every age, each sex, and miraculous happenings contribute to faith: a virgin conceives, a sterile woman gives birth, a mute man speaks, Elizabeth prophesies, a child in the womb leaps, a sage adores, a widow *Exp ev Luke confesses, a just man awaits."* 2.58; PL 15:1573B; CL 14:56

And, drawing strength from the child he carried in his arms, *Simeon blessed them*,* that is, Mary and *Luke 2:34 Joseph, with joy and gladness, giving thanks to God. While it is true that Mary and Joseph surpassed Simeon in sanctity, he had precedence in this regard because of his priestly office, which called for blessing people.* It was customary in the law for the priest to **Lyra Luke 2:34* bless parents and children when they were presented in the temple; so Simeon blessed the parents who were presenting Christ, that is, calling them blessed, or asking God to bless them. We do not have the exact words of this blessing, but it can be assumed that they were expressions of praise and thanksgiving; when we say that a creature blesses God, we mean giving thanks and praise. He blessed the parents on account of their child, while ordinarily children were blessed on account of their parents. Note that Joseph was included in this blessing, even though he was only the foster father of Jesus; but the Virgin Mary really *was* his mother, so the blessing brought by the child pertained especially to her. This is why Simeon went on to speak particularly about her, foretelling hidden things.

Simeon's Prophecies

***R 15**

*Simeon addressed Mary because he had been taught by the one he carried in his arms that he was not Joseph's son but had been born by divine power. He did not simply bless her; he also prophesied future events: "*Behold this child* who has come *is set* by God's ordinance *for the fall and for the resurrection of many in Israel and for a sign which shall be contradicted*."* He is *set for the fall* of the proud and self-reliant; of them, Jesus said, *If I had not come and spoken to them, they would not have sin*.* And Simeon added *and for the resurrection of many*, meaning for the humble, who do not trust in themselves but believe in him and believe that they will rise above their sins through him.

*Luke 2:34

*John 15:22

Then he said *in Israel*, because many of the Jews, turning away from the truth, became blind, while many who were simple and ignorant were enlightened.* He is *a sign* of the covenant and reconciliation between God and humanity, *which shall be contradicted*: first by the Jews, then by the Gentiles or pagans, and afterwards by heretics and unbelievers.

**Lyra Luke 2:34*

Origen observes that there is nothing said about Christ by believers that is not contradicted by unbelievers.* As Christ himself said through the psalmist, *Unjust witnesses have risen up against me, and iniquity*

*Hom Luke 17.4–5; PG 13:1845A

*has lied to itself.** They can fight against Christ, but they cannot conquer him. Bad Christians contradict him by their behavior and actions, even if they do not do so by their belief and words: *they profess that they know God, but in their works they deny him.** The Savior came for the fall of unbelievers and the proud, but only as an occasion; he came as the cause of the resurrection of believers and the humble. Nor did he come only to bring about the fall of some people and the rising of others; in each individual he brings about both a fall and a resurrection: the collapse of vices and the resurrection of virtues. Bernard teaches, "Virtue and vice cannot prosper together; if the one is to flourish, the other must be weeded out. Remove the superfluous, and the wholesome will thrive."*

*Ps 26:12

*Titus 1:16

*SC 58.10; PL 183:1061A; SB 2:134

Notice that Christ destroyed the reign of sin and built the reign of virtue; this is why it is said he *is set for the fall and for the resurrection*. He destroyed pride by his humility, greed by his poverty, extravagance by his chastity, envy by his gentleness, gluttony by his sobriety, anger by his patience, laziness by his labors and vigils. Christ brought down the kingdom of vices by constructing a kingdom of virtues; in this way he brings about both a fall and a resurrection in the same person. According to Chrysostom, when the proud person becomes humble, the lustful person becomes chaste, the greedy person becomes generous, and so on, then in that person vices have fallen and virtues have risen.* Christ was set in this world as a target, so to speak; whoever wishes may shoot his arrows into him.*

*Com ad Rom 10.4; PG 60:480

*see Lam 3:12

*Then, prophesying about Christ's passion, Simeon said, *"And your own soul a sword shall pierce** with compassion, **that is, by the sorrow of the passion itself**."* Even though Mary hoped he would conquer death and rise again victorious, her mother's heart suffered greatly as she watched her son being crucified. Jerome says that Mary was more than a martyr because she suffered in spirit.* Anselm writes, "Now the terrible

***R 16**

*Luke 2:35

*Latin Diatessaron?; *Massa*

*Radbertus, Ep 9; PL 30:138B [3.14; CM 56C:115–16]

force of nature reclaims with interest the debt owed it since your painless birthgiving, increasing and prolonging the pangs that are the common lot of mothers."‡

‡Ps-Anselm, Med de gestis Christi; PL 149:598C

Simeon added, *that out of many hearts thoughts may be revealed.** Christ's passion did reveal the thoughts of many hearts: the words and reflections of the prophets and hidden mysteries came to light and were accomplished there. The temple veil symbolized this: when Jesus died it was torn open, revealing the holy of holies to everyone. Or, the thoughts of many hearts, good and evil, were revealed, because when Christ died some believed and others refused to believe.

*Luke 2:35

Bede says that before the passion it was uncertain which of the Jews would accept him and which would not; afterwards it was clear.* He goes on to speak of the sword in a spiritual sense as applying to the church: "The sword of tribulation will pierce the soul of the church until the end of time: when the sign of faith is contradicted by the impious and the reprobate, when she sees the fall of many, when the thoughts of hearts are revealed and tares are seen to be growing where the good seed had been sown."*

*Com Luke 2:35; PL 92:346D

*Com Luke 2:35; PL 92:347A; CL 120:69

That thoughts may be revealed should not be understood in a causative sense: Christ did not choose to suffer principally so that thoughts might be revealed; rather, the meaning is consecutive, and the revelation of hearts followed after Christ's passion.* It would be like my saying, "I went out into the battlefield, so I was captured by the enemy." It was not my intent to be captured, but it followed upon my going out. A similar mode of speaking is used often in the gospel: *This was done that the scriptures might be fulfilled*. Christ's main reason for doing or suffering something was not to fulfill the Scriptures; but once it was done, it was clear that the Scriptures had been fulfilled. Prophecy does not cause something to happen; the event itself inspires the prophecy. Origen gives a different explanation of these words, referring them to the revelation

**Lyra Luke 2:35*

of secret sins in confession: when evil thoughts that were hidden are made known in confession, they are healed through the efficacy of Christ's passion working in the sacrament of penance.* *Hom Luke 17.8; PG 13:1846A

Anna the Prophet

***R 17**

*****Now Anna, a prophetess, at the same hour* when Simeon was holding Christ in his arms and speaking about him, *coming in*, not by chance, or human arrangement, but like Simeon by a revelation of the Holy Spirit, adored the child and *confessed to the Lord*.* She *Luke 2:36, 38 praised God and gave thanks with great rejoicing for the many benefits he had bestowed through Christ's incarnation and birth. Giving testimony about the Son **and instructing the people**,* she *spoke of him to all that* *Latin Diatessaron? *looked for the redemption of Israel*.* She announced to *Luke 2:38 them that the Redeemer and Savior of the human race had been born, the one who had been long desired to redeem them and set them free. All of the faithful who were oppressed under the yoke of the foreigner Herod longed for the liberation of the city and its people, and also for spiritual deliverance; Anna promised that with the coming of Christ redemption from the tyranny of both Herod and the devil was near at hand.

This august woman was suitable, indeed very worthy, to bear witness to the incarnation of the Son of God because she was venerable both in age and bearing, noble, renowned for her piety and honored for her chastity. And she is described as a prophet because her word carried authority: prophetic utterances are inspired by revelations from God. Origen writes, "The holy woman justly deserved to receive the spirit of prophecy, because by a long life of chastity and many fasts she had risen to this high estate."* *Hom Luke 17.9; PG 13:1846B

Because the Lord had come to redeem people of both sexes, of every age, of every state in life, and of every profession, it was fitting that all these should bear witness to his birth. Three conditions of both men and women are designated: virgins (Mary and Christ), widows (Anna and Simeon), and married couples (Elizabeth and Zechariah). So there is no state of life among the Christian faithful that does not have its representatives to bear witness to him who is the Savior of all. Anselm writes, "He was offered in the temple and received by a holy widow to teach his faithful ones to frequent the house of God and exert themselves in the pursuit of holiness. He was received and praised by the old man Simeon to show that a dignified life and mature conduct were prized by him."*

*Elmer [Med 1 Anselm]; PL 158:716D

You too should rejoice with old Simeon and aged Anna! Hasten to meet the mother and child! Let love conquer modesty and affection cast out fear! Take the child in your arms and say with the bride: *I held him, and I will not let him go!** Rejoice with that most holy elder and sing, *Now you may dismiss your servant, O Lord, according to your word in peace*!*

*Song 3:4

**LV 7*

***R 18**

*Note that there is a spiritual meaning to be found in the unexpected meeting of these people; their coming together by divine inspiration is not lacking in mystery. A similar procession of figures should joyfully take place in our hearts: Simeon, whose name means *hearing*, and who *had received an answer from the Holy Spirit* by divine revelation, signifies an attentive listening to the word of God; Anna, whose name means *grace*[7] and who never left the temple, signifies constant prayer; Joseph, whose name means *increase* and who lavished attentive care on the Christ child, signifies a continual growth in good works; and Mary, whose name means *illuminata*, and who carried Christ in her womb, signifies union with God and perfect conformity to his will.

[7] Jerome, Nom int, renders *Anna* as *his grace* (PL 23:1162; CL 72:139).

These four persons who offer Christ suggest four figures who ought to carry candles in our hearts: Simeon carries the light of holy meditation, Anna bears the light of inner devotion, Joseph brings the light of progress in virtues, and Mary carries the light of heavenly contemplation. The psalmist speaks of these four things when he says, *I remembered God, and was delighted, and was exercised, and my spirit fainted away.** The reference to each of the four in this verse is evident. Notice, too, that five persons took part in the Lord's presentation: Jesus himself, representing the innocent; Mary, *the bitter sea*, representing the penitent; Joseph, *increase*, representing the proficient; Simeon, representing the perfect in the active life; and Anna, representing the perfect in the contemplative life. They symbolize the people who are worthy to be presented before the face of God in the temple of the heavenly Jerusalem.

*Ps 76:4

The Procession

At last Simeon returned the baby Jesus to his mother, who joyfully received him. Then they walked in procession to the altar, an event that is imitated solemnly today all over the world. The two elders, Simeon and Joseph, went first, exulting with great jubilation. The mother followed, carrying King Jesus with ineffable joy of heart, and Anna accompanied her, walking at her side, giving thanks to God with indescribable happiness. They formed a venerable procession, few in number but great in meaning, representing as they did every kind of human being. There were among them women and men, young and old, virgin and widow.

***R 19**

**Massa; MVC 11; CM 153:46*

Mary and Joseph, as the parents, presented their child in the temple, while Simeon and Anna offered praise with prophetic proclamations. And so on this day at Mass we carry in our hands lighted candles that symbolize the boy Jesus; going in procession to the altar, we lay them down and offer them to God, recalling the ineffable light that Mary and Simeon carried on this occasion. There are three elements in a candle, signifying three things in Christ. The wax stands for his body, which was born incorrupt from the Virgin Mary, just as bees make honey without mingling with each other. The wick within the wax stands for the most pure soul of Christ, hidden in his body. The flame, or light, stands for his divinity, for *the Lord your God is a consuming fire.** These three elements also suggest the Trinity, as the verse has it: "Wax, fire, wick—these three show tri-unity."[8]

*Deut 4:24; *Legenda 37 approx*

When they had reached the altar, his mother knelt reverently and offered her most beloved Son to God his Father on the altar.* The Blessed Virgin herself presented her child to the Lord, giving thanks to God the Father for such wonderful gifts: she, a virgin, had conceived and given birth, and she and God the Father both had such a remarkably noble offspring.

**Massa; MVC 11; CM 153:47*

***R 20**

*Parents were commanded to present a boy in the temple for three reasons: to consecrate the child to the Lord from infancy, to commend him to God's care, and to express thanks to God for the gift of their baby. The first two reasons did not apply to Christ because he had been completely consecrated to God from the first moment of his conception and was commended to God's care in virtue of his perpetual divine union with the Father. But the third reason certainly did apply to Christ, because his mother had greater cause than all other women to give thanks for the singular grace of her conceiving and giving birth to Christ.

[8] *Cera, focus, lichnum, tria sunt monstrantia trinum.* This is a variation of a verse in the Textus Sacramentorum, a rhymed commentary on the liturgical year written in 1098: *Cera, focus, lumen, tria sunt, monstrant Numen.* The wax symbolizes the Father, the wick the Son, and the flame the Holy Spirit.

We have no written record of the prayer she spoke, but perhaps words like these arose from her heart: "Behold, Lord, holy Father, I present to you your Son, eternally begotten of you and born in time from me; I present to you the one who is always with you. I give you thanks for the great gift of allowing me miraculously to conceive him and ineffably give birth. O holy Father, I offer to you a new oblation, your Son and mine, God incarnate, who will offer himself to you for the salvation of the world! O, how great will be that offering; none such has been known from the beginning of time." Bernard asks Mary, "Offer your Son, holy Virgin, and show to the Lord the blessed fruit of your womb. Offer *a living sacrifice, holy, pleasing to God,** for the reconciliation of us all."* *Rom 12:1 *Sermo Purification 3.2; PL 183:370C; SB 4:342

Christ wanted to be presented to God the Father, from whom he is never in truth absent, to give us an example. God did not become Man for his sake but for ours, so that through grace we could become gods. Similarly, he was circumcised in the flesh not for his sake, but so that we could be circumcised spiritually; and he was held up in the Lord's presence so that we might learn to present ourselves to God.* **Athanasius? CA Luke 2:22–25*

Then the priests came forward, and the Lord of all was bought back as if he were a slave; the price was five silver shekels, because he was a firstborn. A shekel was a coin equivalent to twenty obols. It was laid down in the law that the firstborn male, whether of man or beast, was called holy to the Lord, that is, it was presented and said to be dedicated to the Lord like a priest. The firstborn sons of the tribe of Levi were not redeemed but were perpetually set apart for service in the house of David, the temple. The firstborn sons of the other eleven tribes were ransomed, and once the price had been paid they were free to return home with their parents. The firstborn of clean animals was offered in sacrifice; the firstborn of unclean beasts could be purchased back at a price, or a clean animal could be sacrificed in its place, or it was killed. **R 21** **Massa*; about one dollar

A clean animal fit for sacrifice was any species of animal considered suitable for eating. Among unclean animals some were considered clean by nature but unfit for sacrifice, such as a donkey, which could be ransomed for a price or by substituting a clean animal like a lamb. Other unclean animals, such as dogs, were considered unfit either for sacrifice or for being redeemed; being considered worthless, they were killed and their bodies thrown out of the temple.

Because Christ belonged to the tribe of Judah, it was evident that he had to be redeemed, and so he was. His mother received from Joseph the two birds mentioned earlier and, kneeling, offered them on the altar to God the Father. As a poor woman the Blessed Virgin offered *a pair of turtledoves or two young pigeons*, one as a holocaust for her son and the second as a sin offering. In this she submitted to the law for sinners, although she was without sin. Once the offering had been made and the buying back completed, the mother received back her son and carried him home.

The Spiritual Significance of the Presentation

Bernard says, "The offering was very pleasant, brethren, that was made by two such parents, and redeemed with two birds, and immediately carried home. The day will come when he will not be offered in the temple or carried in Simeon's arms: he will be offered outside the city and held in the arms of the cross. The day will come when he is not redeemed by another creature but will redeem other creatures with his own blood, because God the Father sent him to redeem his people. This is the morning sacrifice; that will be the evening sacrifice."‡

‡Sermo Purification 3.2; PL 183:370C; SB 4:342–43

*R 22

*In a mystical sense the firstborn of animals symbolize him who was worthy to be born as God's Only-Begotten, *the firstborn* in dignity *of every creature*,* who is truly the holy Lord, because he is without sin.

*Col 1:15

In a moral sense the firstborn signifies the beginning of a good act, to which we give birth in the heart, as it were, by God's grace. So we are urged here to offer all of our firstborn to God; whatever we find in our works to be just or good, we credit to his grace and not to our merits, saying, *Not to us, O Lord, not to us, but to your name give glory.** Should we give birth to something unclean, that is, if we commit sin in our deeds, let us kill the evil thing by pulling it out, roots and all, or let us redeem it with the five shekels of good works and by bringing forth the good fruit of penitence through our five senses.* And, if we find in the flock of our works a lamb of innocence, or the great virtues such as charity, chastity, humility, and patience, we are exhorted to offer them to God by living upright lives and giving the credit for this not to ourselves, but to him who said in the gospel, *Without me you can do nothing.* For it is God who works in you, both to will and to accomplish.**

*Ps 113:9

Haymo, Hom 14; PL 118:100AB approx

*John 15:5

*Phil 2:13; *Haymo, Hom 14; PL 118:101CD*

If we are so poor that we can find among our works no innocent lamb, or the riches of an unstained life, or any great virtue, let us at least offer two turtledoves or two young pigeons, that is, the twofold compunction of fear and love. Let us make this offering not only for the forgiveness of our sins, but for an increase in virtue, and let us weep daily with longing for our heavenly home.‡ We make a sin offering when we shed tears for the evil we have done; we offer a holocaust when we are aflame with heavenly love.†

‡*Haymo, Hom 14; PL 118:101D–2A approx*
†*Hildebert of Lavardin, Sermo 57; PL 171:617C*

*In a moral sense, three things should be carefully considered here: the mystery of Mary's purification, the mystery of Christ's being carried, and the meaning of the oblation that was offered. As regards the first, know that Mary, whose name means *star of the sea* or *bitter sea*, represents the soul, be it in the light of the contemplative life or the bitterness of the active life. Purification is required in either state: the contemplative soul must be cleansed of pride by holy fear; the active soul must be cleansed of negligence through

***R 23**

*Bonaventure, Com Luke 2:22
‡which means *vision of peace*

rigorous labors.* No one can be brought into the Jerusalem‡ of the beatific life unless the day of purification is fulfilled. Unless we are completely purified and are as pure as the moment we emerged from the baptismal font, we cannot enter the temple of the heavenly Jerusalem. Such purification must be performed, either here by penitence, tribulations, and similar things, or hereafter in the chastisement of purgatory.

***R 24**

*Touching on the second mystery, we read here that Jesus was carried into Jerusalem, and we are told later that he was carried into Egypt. This teaches us that the offspring of our mind, our intelligence, must be raised up at one time to the contemplation of eternal realities, symbolized by Jerusalem, the *vision of peace*, and at another time must be plunged down to the consideration of our own failings, symbolized by Egypt, whose name is interpreted as *darkness*.[9]*

*Bonaventure, Com Luke 2:22

We can list five places into which Jesus was carried or led: Jerusalem, Egypt, the wilderness, the high mountain, and the pinnacle of the temple. These five places signify the five places where Christ is found. Jerusalem stands for the contemplative life, where the vision of peace is; Egypt symbolizes the active life, where there is grief and hard struggle; the wilderness symbolizes the religious life, with its prolonged fasts; the high mountain symbolizes eminent positions of leadership; the pinnacle of the temple symbolizes the teacher's rostrum. Jesus is found in these five places, because in every position in the church one can find salvation, that is, Jesus. But also reflect on who carries Jesus: he is carried into Jerusalem and Egypt by Mary and Joseph, in other words, by faith and charity. He is led into the wilderness by the Holy Spirit. But he is carried up to the high mountain and to the pinnacle of the temple by the devil. Prelates and teachers ought to be fearful, lest it be the devil who carries them to the episcopal throne or the doctoral chair.*

*St Cher, Luke 2:22

[9] Bede, *Com Matt 2:13* interprets *Egypt* as *darkness* (PL 92:13D).

*As to the third point, it is noteworthy that the offering could be either turtledoves or pigeons. The turtledove, which is solitary and chaste, represents the contemplative life; pigeons, which are prolific and fly in flocks, stand for the active life. Both these kinds of birds do not sing, but sigh—for different reasons. The sighing of the turtledove expresses the redoubled longing of the contemplative life, signified by a pair of turtledoves. The first is the sigh of love, of which the apostle speaks: *We ourselves groan within ourselves, waiting for the adoption of the sons of God.** The second is prompted by devotion, as the same apostle writes: *The Spirit himself asks for us with unspeakable groaning.** The moaning of the pigeon, representing the active life, is twofold, as the text speaks of two young pigeons. The first is caused by one's own sins, as the prophet Isaiah writes: *We shall lament as mournful doves.** The second is elicited by the sins of others, as we read in Jeremiah's Lamentations: *All her gates are broken down; her priests sigh.** This fourfold groaning should be made by all those who do not have the lamb of innocence to offer.* *R 25

*Rom 8:23

*Rom 8:26

*Isa 59:11

*Lam 1:4

*Bonaventure, Com Luke 2:22

We can sum up what has been said about the purification, the carrying, and the offering by saying that the perfect fidelity of a soul devoted to God consists in this: having been purified of pride and negligence, we are disposed to ascend to the heights of the contemplation of God and descend to the consideration of sinful failings. Rising again, we sigh from love and devotion; returning to earth, we weep from contrition and compassion.* Because both ways of life, contemplative and active, are pleasing to God, the text does not specify whether doves or pigeons were offered for the Lord; it simply reads *a pair of turtledoves or two young pigeons.*

*Bonaventure, Com Luke 2:22

*You see the poverty of Christ and his parents in this mystery, because they made the offering of the poor. If you want to learn about humility, you can see at once how they observed the law, offered sacrifice, *R 26 and went through the ritual of redeeming the child. Notice, too, how the sequence of events unfolds the mystery of Christ's humility: he was a poor man in his birth; he was a poor and sinful man in his circumcision; and in today's mystery he is poor, a sinner, and a slave. As one of the poor, he chose to make the offering of the poor. As a sinner, he wanted to have the sin offering made for him and his mother. As a slave, he submitted to the rite of redemption.*

**Legenda 37 approx*

***R 27**

*As we have seen, *they carried him to Jerusalem to present him to the Lord* after the son's circumcision and the mother's purification. Pay close attention: these three events, understood in a moral sense, instruct the faithful that we should imitate Christ and his mother when we wish to enter God's earthly temple, the church building. We should be purged of the dregs of sin by a spiritual circumcision, we should be borne in the arms of our mother, the church, and we should have a proper intention.

First, therefore, before entering the church we must be cleansed of the remnants of sin. After giving birth to her immaculate son, the Blessed Virgin completed the days of purification before she entered the temple; her son wished to be circumcised before being brought there. The mother did not need to be purified, and the son had no need to be circumcised: she had not conceived from human seed, and he had been born of an intact virgin. But they both wanted to observe this law to give us a model of purification and spiritual circumcision. We ought to be cleansed and cut off from sins before we come to church and make our offering to God, if we want that offering to be pleasing to him. As Bede says, we are not worthy to look upon God unless we are purified and circumcised from sin.*

*Com Luke 2:22; PL 92:341A; CL 120:61

From this we learn that we should not come into church with mortal sin on our conscience, without having first gone to confession or, if there is no opportunity to do so, at least being profoundly contrite; and we should be cleansed of sin, at least by means of general contrition, even if we do not have specific sins on our conscience. It is a sign of a good conscience to be apprehensive of sin even when no actual sin may be present, in imitation of the Blessed Virgin, who underwent purification although she did not need to. This is why we have the custom of blessing ourselves with holy water before going into church so that, even when we are not conscious of mortal sin, we may be purified from venial sins. This cleansing is prefigured in the water basin that stood at the entrance of the tent of meeting, in which Aaron and his sons washed their hands and feet before entering the tent.* *Exod 30:18-19

Second, we must be carried in the arms of our mother, the church, just as Christ was carried into the temple in the arms of his mother. So that the faithful will be worthy to enter the church, Holy Mother Church herself says through the prophet Hosea, *I carried them in my arms*.* Those outside the unifying embrace of the church are the heretics, who err in faith; the schismatics, who err in charity; and the excommunicated, who are cut off from the unity of the church. Whoever is not carried in the arms of Mother Church is not worthy to enter the church building: as Cyprian says, no one can have God as Father who does not cling to the unity of our mother, the church.* It is useless, and indeed unfitting, to go into the material church if you are not held in the arms of the mystical church. *Hos 11:3 *De unitate 6; PL 4:503A

Third, we must be motivated by the proper intention when entering church, prompted by devotion and a desire to pray. Not for the sake of vain simulation, like hypocrites; not for showy display and ostentation, like those who attract attention to themselves by their fine clothes; not out of wantonness, like those who go to church to see women or men, to desire and be desired; not to be amused, like those who go to church and engage in idle chatter, boisterous laughter, and levity; not for greedy gain, like those priests who only show up to get some of the offerings, or to carry out business and make money. All who do not come to church with a good intention are not worthy to cross its threshold: they are not coming to present themselves to the Lord, nor are they led by the Spirit to the temple. Therefore, they do not see Christ, nor are they worthy to hold him spiritually in their arms.

Pay attention to what Bede writes:

> After his circumcision he was carried to Jerusalem and offered to the Lord. About him the psalmist said, *Decline from evil and do good,** and as soon as he left sin behind, he began to abound in good works. He could in truth say, *My eyes are ever towards the Lord,** *that I may hear the voice of your praise.** And further, *We are the good odor of Christ,** and *I lifted up my hands to your commandments,* and turned my feet unto your testimonies.** For whether he ate or drank, or did anything else, he did all for the glory of God, and said, *How sweet are your words to my palate!** and, finally, *My heart and my flesh have rejoiced in the living God.**

*Ps 36:27

*Ps 24:15

*Ps 25:7

*2 Cor 2:15

*Ps 118:48

*Ps 118:59

*Ps 118:103

*Ps 83:3; Com Luke 2:21; PL 92:340BC; CL 120:60–61

‡R 28

‡There are other reasons that the Savior wanted to be carried into the temple. One of these was to sanctify the temple by his presence, just as he was baptized in order to sanctify the waters. All waters were made holy by Christ's baptism, not just the water that touched his body; similarly, by being carried into the Jerusalem temple he consecrated all houses of worship dedicated to his name. This is why we are required to reserve the sacramental Body of Christ in churches; there also the relics of the saints are preserved, and there the angels themselves minister. Therefore it is fitting to maintain a spirit of recollection in churches and only visit them with the greatest reverence and devotion. As the psalmist says, *Holiness befits God's house.*[10]*

*Ps 92:5

[10] The phrase is a reworking of the psalm, used as the antiphon in the Office for the Dedication of a Church: *Domum Dei decet sanctitudo: Sponsum ejus Christum adoremus in ea* (Holiness befits God's house; let us adore in her Christ her bridegroom).

*These reflections may also be applied to the temple of the mind, into which the eternal Word is brought daily by devout believers, as the apostle said: *The temple of God is holy, which you are.** Now the worth of anything is derived from its causes, and the nobility of this temple flows from four causes: the dignity of the cause that brought it into being, the value of its matter, the beauty of its form, and the loftiness of its purpose. The nobility of the first cause is patent, because the mind of the rational soul is created immediately by God himself. This shows how utterly great is the soul's value: in creating the soul, God did not call on the help of any creature; the holy Trinity summoned its very self, saying, *Let us make man.** As Augustine notes, God did not say this to the angels, but the Father himself addressed the other divine Persons.* By this it is shown that this was a singular work of the Trinity itself. ***R 29**

*1 Cor 3:17

*Gen 1:26

*De civ Dei 16.6.1; PL 41:484; CL 48:506

Second, it is evident that the soul is not made from any pre-existing matter, but is created *ex nihilo*. Among all created things, none could be found worthy enough that the rational soul would be made from it. Not among earthly things or any of their constitutive elements, nor among those in the heavens, like the sun, the moon, and the stars, or any heavenly bodies, was any matter found worthy to be employed in making the rational soul; its existence far exceeds all these in eminence and nobility. So it was made *ex nihilo* to give it the greatest excellence.

Third, it is clear that the form of the rational soul is also most noble because it is marked with the image of God himself. God did not impress upon the soul the image of any created thing, but his own form, so that the form of the rational soul is nothing other than a kind of effulgence of the Blessed Trinity. The triune God could not make the rational soul more majestic than by assimilating the soul to himself and impressing the image of his own form upon it. Because similitude is the cause of love, the soul returns all her loving affection to God since she finds nothing in created things similar to herself.

Fourth, it is clear that God created the soul to have as its goal or end nothing other than his very self, so that she may be his dwelling-place, as the psalmist says, *For the Lord has chosen Sion*, that is, the watching soul; *he has chosen it for his dwelling.*[11]* And because he has chosen her for this, he greatly loves his dwelling, as he says in Proverbs, *My son, give me your heart.** And elsewhere, *My delights were to be with the children of men.** Therefore, wherever God finds a soul worthily prepared, he possesses her almost by a vow, as the psalmist said: *This is my rest for ever and ever: here will I dwell, for I have chosen it.**

*Ps 131:13

*Prov 23:26

*Prov 8:31

*Ps 131:14

***R 30**

And so, O faithful soul, mindful of your high nobility from all that has been said, may you never sin! Bernard says, "If you know your nobility, O soul, you will detest sin." And it is true that consideration of the nobility of the soul can lead to a hatred for sin even when the thought of the reward of heaven and the pains of hell does not keep one from sinning, because the noble soul views such base things to be vile and worthy and does not want to be soiled by them. Here is a kind of holy and noble pride of the generous soul, about which the pagan Seneca wrote, "Even if the gods would pardon it, and people would be ignorant of it, I would avoid sin because of the vileness of sin itself."*

*Ps-Bernard, De interiori domo 79 approx; PL 184:547A

*Zachary 99 approx; PL 186:315D

The mind as God's temple should be decorated with the colors of the various virtues: the white of chastity, the red of voluntary suffering for Christ, the yellow of spiritual joy, the green of virtuous labors, the blue of heavenly desires, the gold of charity, and finally the black of humility. Into the temple so adorned we should bring the eternal Word, the child Jesus, and there offer for him *a pair of turtledoves or two young*

[11] Jerome, Nom int, renders *Sion* as *watch-tower*, or *watcher*, or *boulder* (PL 23:819; CL 72:108).

pigeons: the twofold love of God and neighbor, or solitary contemplation and social action, or (because turtledoves are chaste) chastity of mind and body, or (because they produce many young) a multitude of good works. Let us carry him in our arms with Simeon, embracing him with true devotion. And let us likewise bless him for all the benefits he bestows in giving our souls a foretaste of divine sweetness. Dissolved with ardent longing, let us look forward to the enjoyment of the eternal Word, singing with Simeon his joyful canticle: *Now you may dismiss your servant, O Lord, according to your word in peace.*

The Greatness of Today's Celebration

*This solemnity is great for many things that hap- *R 31
pened on this occasion, of which three might be especially noted: The first is that Christ is brought to the temple to be presented, the second is that his parents make the required offering for him, and the third is Simeon's consolation at seeing the Savior. These three events are reflected in the three names given to this feast. In honor of the first it is called in Greek *Hypapante*, or "Presentation," because on this very day Christ was presented in the temple.[12] In honor of the second, it is known as the feast of the *Purification*; on this day the Blessed Virgin offered the sacrifice required by the law for her purification although she did not need to. In honor of the third it is called *Candlemas*, or the feast of light, because on this day we carry

[12] The Greek name means *Meeting (of the Lord)*, and was simply transliterated into Latin on liturgical calendars. The emperor Justinian decreed in the sixth century that the feast should be celebrated throughout the empire; in the seventh-century Roman *Gelasian Sacramentary* the feast was called the Purification of the Blessed Virgin Mary. The blessing of candles seems to have been added around the eleventh century.

lighted blessed candles in our hands, representing Simeon and imitating his devotion.

In Praise of the Jerusalem Temple

*R 32

The holy temple of the Lord was built on Mount Moriah, where Abraham was willing to sacrifice his son Isaac; on this same spot, Jacob beheld in a dream the ladder reaching from earth to heaven.* On this mountain David saw the angel stand and smite the people; falling to the ground, he won God's clemency by the rigorous penance he inflicted on himself.* On this mountain David purchased the threshing floor of Araunah the Jebusite to build the Lord's house, in order to beseech his mercy in that place.* On this same holy spot, a cloud filled the house when Solomon had completed his work and offered sacrifices to the Lord; God's glory appeared, *and fire came down from heaven, and consumed the holocausts*.* When this happened, Solomon knelt down and, with hands lifted to heaven, begged that whoever came there to ask a blessing from God would receive an answer to their prayer. The Lord appeared to him, saying, *I have heard your prayer. I have chosen, and have sanctified this place*.* Heliodorus was sent by King Antiochus to violate and ransack the holy place, and he was scourged continuously with many blows.*

*Gen 22:2
*Gen 28:10-17
*1 Chr 21:15-16
*2 Sam 24:17-25
*2 Chr 7:1
*2 Chr 7:12, 16
*2 Macc 3:21-28

This was called the Lord's temple because sacrifices were offered to him here, but now it is consecrated to the Savior of the world and to his mother Mary. This temple was destroyed by the Babylonians and later by the Romans, but it has been rebuilt magnificently by religious and faithful people in the form of a rotunda.[13]

[13] The site of the Jewish temple had been left desolate when Jerusalem was rebuilt as a Christian city in the fourth century. In the late seventh century the Muslim conquerors built an

It is said that the Virgin Mary and other virgins served in this place, weaving the temple veil and vestments for the priests, and devoting themselves to reading the Scriptures, fasting, vigils, and prayer. In this place the angel appeared to Zechariah when he was offering incense to the Lord, proclaiming that his prayer had been heard and announcing the future birth of John the Baptist. In this same place, as we have related, our Lord Jesus Christ was presented by his parents, welcomed by Simeon, and spoken of by the holy widow Anna *to all that looked for the redemption of Israel*. In this temple Jesus was found when he was twelve years old, sitting and debating with the doctors of the law.* *de Vitry 43–44*

The devil carried Jesus to the pinnacle of this temple, saying that he would give all this to Jesus if he would worship him. It was from this temple that Jesus drove out the buyers and sellers, overturning the tables of the moneychangers and expelling those who were selling pigeons. Whenever Jesus stayed in Jerusalem it was his custom to teach the Jews here, although some were jealous of him. In this temple he delivered the adulterous woman from her accusers. When his passion drew near Jesus taught daily in this temple, withdrawing to Bethany in the evening. At the moment of Jesus' death the veil was torn in two from top to bottom in this temple, to reveal the entrance to the holy of holies. Blessed James the Apostle, the first bishop of Jerusalem, was thrown down from the pinnacle of this temple at mid-day while preaching and struck with a fuller's pole, and so was crowned with martyrdom.* Between this temple and the altar that stood in the courtyard before it Zechariah, the son of Barachiah, was slain as a martyr. *de Vitry 43–44*

---

octagonal shrine (inspired by the Church of the Holy Sepulcher) on the temple mount. For a time in the twelfth century this was converted into a Christian church known as the *Templum Domini*.

The exterior of this rotunda is octagonal, and the interior is shaped like the dome of a furnace, supported by massive marble columns. At the summit of this dome these words are inscribed: *Lord, hear the hymn and the prayer that your servant prays before you today, so that your eyes may keep watch over this house by day and by night*. There are texts written in large letters on the outer walls, visible to the whole city. Facing the city itself: *Peace eternal, from the eternal Father, be to this house*. Facing the building of the Knights Templar: *The House of the Lord is well founded upon solid rock*. Facing Bethany: *This place is nothing other than the House of God and the Gate of Heaven*. Facing Mount Olivet: *Blessed are they that dwell in your House, O Lord*. Facing the Valley of Jehoshaphat: *Blessed be the glory of the Lord from this place*. Facing the cloister of the temple: *In your Temple they all cry, "Glory!"* Facing Mount Sion: *The Temple of the Lord is holy; it is in God's care and is God's building*. And again, facing the city: *Let us go rejoicing to the House of the Lord*.[14]

This temple is in the lower part of the city, near the eastern wall, situated not far from the wall to the south. It was formerly in the care of the Augustinian canons who served the Lord there with their abbot.[15]

[14] Ludolph is citing a description of the Dome of the Rock written about the year 1165 by John of Wurzburg (PL 155:1064D). In the year 1141 the crusaders consecrated the building to Christian use and adorned it with the phrases recorded here, taken from the Scriptures and the Office for the Dedication of a Church. In the year 1220 the Dome of the Rock reverted to its former use as a mosque. The "Temple of Solomon" was the Al-Aqsa Mosque, which in crusader times was the headquarters of the Knights Templar.

[15] Ludolph may be conflating two sentences: the twelfth-century pilgrimage account of Bishop Thietmar relates that before the Crusader Kingdom fell there were Augustinian canons with their prior serving in the Church of the Holy Sepulcher, and an abbot and Canons Regular in the Lord's Temple.

Not far from this building is a very spacious and high edifice, known as *the house of the forest* of the cedars *of Libanus,** called Solomon's Temple, because Solomon taught there and rendered judgment, to distinguish it from the building known as the Lord's Temple.*

*2 Chr 9:20

**de Vitry 45*

Joseph and Mary Leave Jerusalem

R 33

And after they had performed all things according to the law of the Lord,* even those rites that were not really required of them, *they* departed from Jerusalem and *returned into Galilee, to their city Nazareth. Theophylact notes that Bethlehem was truly their paternal city, but Nazareth their place of residence.*

*Luke 2:39

*En Luke 2:39–41; PG 123:722B

✠

O longed-for Jesus, Simeon the just man ardently desired to see you, and in the temple you graciously allowed him to take you in his arms. Come to me, sweetest Jesus, and in your mercy give yourself to me, who longs for you with such great desire. Cleanse me of my impurities with your cleansing grace and make my heart your temple by deigning to dwell therein. There may I embrace you and hold you tenderly. May I ever long for you, the fountain of light who are with the Father. May I not depart from this life without gazing upon you with the eyes of my heart, you who are the love and desire, the life and the prize of those who long for you. Amen.

CHAPTER 13

The Flight into Egypt and the Slaughter of the Innocents

(Matt 2:13-18)

*R 1 *As Mary and Joseph set out for Nazareth, ignorant as yet of God's purpose and with growing apprehension about their child, *an angel of the Lord appeared in sleep to Joseph, saying: "Arise, and take the child and his mother, and fly into Egypt; for it will come to pass that Herod will seek the child to destroy him."** For humility to be perfect, it must be accompanied by three other virtues: poverty, by fleeing the riches that foster pride; patience, by enduring contempt with tranquility; and obedience, by yielding to the command of another.

*Matt 2:13; *Massa*

So it came to pass by a divine revelation that Jesus was taken away to Egypt to live as a poor foreigner, that in the children who were killed because of him he himself was in a certain way butchered, and that when he returned to his homeland he was obedient to his parents and did not rebel even for a moment, with the exception of the occasion when he remained behind in Jerusalem at the age of twelve and was sought with great sorrow and found with great joy by his mother.*

**LV 8*

When Joseph awoke, he in turn awakened Jesus' mother and recounted to her what the angel had told him. Without a moment's delay she arose and, picking up her child, prepared to set out. Joseph's words penetrated to the core of her being, and she did not want to be found wanting in anything that pertained to the safety of her baby.

Watch this scene and meditate upon it: when the mother picked up the sleeping child Jesus, he was startled and began to cry.* Enter into their emotions, if you have any devotion in your heart! Think, too, how you can console this mother, a delicate young woman who has only recently gotten up from giving birth, how she must undertake a long journey by strange and difficult roads to a distant land, carrying a tender newborn babe on this arduous trek, where they would be compelled to live among idolaters.*

*Massa

*Vor Quad, Sermo 2 Sat 4th Week of Lent, 118

Why Did They Flee to Egypt?

*They set out in the dead of night for the land of Egypt. Night was preferable to daytime for making their escape because the journey could be carried out in greater secrecy, lest anyone see them escaping and report them to the king. Even though they had received a heavenly warning in this matter, they did not neglect to follow the dictates of human prudence. See the way Christ fled, and how he fled by night: flight is never easy, but the darkness of night made it an even greater challenge. He fled to Egypt so that he might heal and enlighten that nation before any others.

***R 2**

Augustine says, "Listen to a wondrously great mystery: when Moses was in Egypt, he brought darkness over the unbelievers; when Christ came there, he restored light to those sitting in darkness."* Chrysostom asks, "But why Egypt? Remember that the Lord, whose anger does not last forever, had visited much evil upon Egypt. Therefore he sent his Son to them, giving them a sign of reconciliation and a pledge of perpetual friendship, healing the ten plagues of Egypt with one medicine. *This is the change of the right hand*

*CA Matt 2:13–15

*Ps 76:11

*of the most High,** that those who had earlier persecuted the firstborn people now become the guardians of the only-begotten Son!"*

*Opus imperf 2; PG 56:643

And again,

> He sent the child into Egypt so that the flame of faith might be ignited in the very land where the fire of impiety had blazed most brightly. By doing this he gave hope to other parts of the world, and also taught us to be prepared for temptation and treachery from the very beginning of life. For when we hear about such things happening to Christ virtually in his cradle, we will not be thrown into confusion when we find ourselves beset by a thousand different tribulations; rather, we learn from his example to bear with them, knowing that great adversity is the companion of true virtues.*

*Hom Matt 8.2; PG 57/58:84

He also chose to flee into Egypt rather than any other land to show that he was the true Moses: just as Moses freed the people of God from Pharaoh and the Egyptians and led them into the Promised Land, so Christ frees his faithful people from the devil and hell, leading them with him into the kingdom of heaven.*

**Eluc 1.20; PL 172:1124C*

***R 3**

*There are many good lessons to be learned from this event. First, notice how the Lord accepted the bad along with the good. At his birth he was lauded by the shepherds as God; soon after, he was circumcised like any sinner. Then the magi arrived, showering him with honors; nonetheless, he remained living in that stable among the beasts and cried like any other child. Next, he was presented in the temple to the great joy of Simeon and Anna, but then the angel warned him to flee to Egypt. And we see this same pattern repeated throughout his life, which can greatly redound to our instruction. Chrysostom says,

> The merciful God mingles hardships and pleasant things. This is certainly his way with the saints:

> neither dark dangers nor bright refreshments are continual, but the lives of all the righteous are woven with both colors. Reflect that he does the same here. When Joseph saw that the Virgin was with child, it caused him great anxiety; but straightaway the angel was at hand to remove his fears. Then, seeing the great sign of the newborn babe, he was filled with joy; but this was followed by great danger, when the king was filled with rage and the whole city thrown into consternation. But this trouble was again succeeded by another joy: the appearance of the star and the adoration of the magi. Again, after this pleasure, fear and danger return: Herod seeks the child's life, and they must flee to a distant land.* *Hom Matt 8.3; PG 57/58:85

When you are enjoying consolation, anticipate tribulation, and vice versa. Do not be carried away by blessings or crushed by adversity: God sends us consolations to strengthen our hope and trials to preserve our humility, so that the knowledge of our wretchedness will help us persevere in fear of the Lord.* **Massa; MVC 12; CM 153:49*

Second, consider how those who receive consolations and blessings from God should not vaunt themselves in comparison with those who have not received them, nor should those who do not receive them feel dejected in spirit or jealous of those who have. The angel's words were addressed not to the mother, but to Joseph, who was greatly inferior to her. Likewise, those who have received such things unbidden should not grumble or be ungrateful, since even Joseph, who was close to God, did not receive these words openly, but in his sleep. ***R 4** **Massa; MVC 12; CM 153:49*

*Third, reflect on how God permits his own to be plagued by persecutions and trials. The boy's mother and Joseph were very fearful when they saw that Herod sought to kill Jesus. They were also troubled at the prospect of journeying to an unknown land over difficult roads—difficult for the mother on account of ***R 5** her youth, for Joseph because of his age, and because they were carrying a tender newborn babe. They had to travel to a foreign country and live there as penniless paupers. All of this caused them great affliction. When you are thrown into confusion, be patient and do not believe that you should receive from God a privilege that he did not give to himself or his mother.*

*Massa; MVC 12; CM 153:49–50

***R 6**

Fourth, meditate on God's goodness. You see how soon he has to endure persecution and flee from his native country, and how quickly he gives way to the fury of a man whom he could destroy in an instant. Ponder, too, on the Lord's humility, which is as great as his patience. He upon whom angels wait flees from before the face of his persecutor. He is God, the refuge of everyone, but he runs away from Herod as a poor mortal. How deep his humility, how wondrous his patience! He does not take vengeance on his tormentor but strives to evade his blows by flight. In this he gives us an example: we should learn not to resist our enemies or persecutors, or to seek revenge. Rather, we should wait patiently, give way to their anger, and, as he teaches elsewhere, pray for them.

*Massa; MVC 12; CM 153:50

By being carried off in secret to Egypt to avoid being killed, the Lord shows that often his elect will be cast out of their positions and sent into exile by the wickedness of evil people. He also gives an example to the weak and offers comfort to them.* By fleeing he encourages his anointed not to be fearful, and he shows by example that the flight and protection of pastors may be beneficial to the church when they do not put the flock at risk, as it was in Paul's case.

*Bede, Hom ev 1.9; PL 94:51B [1.10; CL 122:69]

***R 7**

*In a moral sense the flight into Egypt symbolizes the just person's flight from the danger and destruction of sin into the state of penitence, there to remain until Herod's death, that is, until the enemy ceases his hostility.

Also, the Lord fled from the presence of his servant (or, better, the devil's servant),* not because he feared

*MVC 12; CM 153:50

death, but so that he could endure it at a more fitting time. The one who came to die did not flee from death, nor did he who came to reveal the devil's cunning snares tremble before his plots.* **Haymo, Hom 12; PL 118:76C*

The Arduous Journey

The elderly Saint Joseph and the mother carrying her tender young child made the long trek to Egypt through uninhabited, overgrown stretches of forest. It is said that it took them two months or more to make a journey that could ordinarily be accomplished in about two weeks. It is also said that they traveled through the wilderness in which the Israelites had sojourned for forty years. How were they able to take with them the food they needed? How and where did they find lodging for their night's rest? Only rarely did they come across houses in that desert land. Enter into their sufferings: their exertion was great, difficult, and prolonged—as much for the boy as for them. Go with them, help to carry the baby Jesus, and offer them help to the best of your ability. The effort of doing penance for our own sins will not seem so daunting to us when we consider the tremendous discomfort these august persons embraced for the sake of others. ***R 8** **Massa*

Anselm urges us,

> In your meditation, do not fail to accompany the Holy Family on the flight into Egypt. With the eyes of devotion gaze upon the little Jesus nursing at the sweet breasts of the glorious Virgin, his mother. A child being fed by his mother—what sight could be more pleasing and delightful? See him, who is infinitely great, with his tiny arms clasping his mother's neck, and say, "How fortunate I am, how much more blessed to see him *whom kings have desired to see and have not seen him.*"* How worthwhile is the sight of him who is *beautiful above the sons of* *Luke 10:24

*Ps 44:3

*men.** Ponder, and ponder yet again, what thoughts filled the mind of that sweetest mother as she joyfully held the Lord, so great and yet so little, in her arms. How often she gave sweet kisses to that infant crying in her lap! How she sought to comfort him with those tricks a mother knows, dandling him and cooing to relieve his distress.

***R 9**

*It is also worthwhile to think about Mary and her child being set upon by robbers on their journey. Imagine that the story is true that relates how they were waylaid by thieves and owed their escape to a young man. It is said that he was the son of the leader of the brigands; just as he was about to rob the travelers, he looked upon the child seated on his mother's lap and saw such majesty shining from his beautiful face that he realized he was more than human. Filled with love, he embraced the infant, saying, "O most blessed of children, if ever the occasion arises for you to have pity on me, remember me and do not forget this moment!" They say that he was the thief crucified at God's right hand, who rebuked his blaspheming companion: *Do you not fear God, seeing you are under the same condemnation? And we indeed justly: for we receive the due reward of our deeds. But this man has done no evil.** Then, turning to the Lord, he perceived the majesty he had seen in the little infant. Mindful of their agreement, he said, *Remember me when you come into your kingdom.** I recall this story for the sake of enkindling love, without making any assertion as to its authenticity.[1]*

*Luke 23:40-41

*Luke 23:42

*Aelred, De inst 30 [Med 15 Anselm]; PL 158:756BD; CM 1:664

The Slaughter of the Innocents

***R 10**

*When Herod realized that the magi had left by a different route without returning to him or sending him any report, he assumed that they had been deceived

[1] The legend of the thief appears in chap. 23 of the apocryphal *Arabic Infancy Gospels* and was popular with Christians of both East and West.

by the vision of the star and were ashamed to come back to him, and so he suspended his inquiry concerning the child. Or perhaps he was so preoccupied with important affairs of state that he was distracted or kept from following up on the investigations. However, when he later heard about what had happened in the temple, and what Simeon had said and Anna prophesied, and learned that the fame of the child was growing, he was disturbed and grew fearful.*

Zachary 1.10 approx; PL 186:85A

Perceiving that he was deluded by the wise men **when they did not return to him**,‡ *Herod was extremely angry*,† either by their disregard for him or from fear of losing his kingdom. He then gave thought to having all the little boys in Bethlehem killed, so that the one whose identity was unknown to him would die among them. He presumed that the one he sought would not escape if all the boys were slaughtered. The wretched man did not realize that *there is no wisdom, there is no prudence, there is no counsel against the Lord*.*

‡Latin Diatessaron?
†Matt 2:16
*Prov 21:30

While he was planning the massacre of the children, Herod received a letter from Caesar Augustus ordering him to come to Rome. Passing through Cilicia, he learned that ships from Tarshish had transported the magi; overcome by a gust of fury, he burned the vessels that it was believed the magi had secretly used, fulfilling by this act a prophecy of David: *With a vehement wind you shall break in pieces the ships of Tharsis*.*

*Ps 47:8; *Comestor, Hist ev 11 approx; PL 198:1543BC*

Upon returning to Jerusalem he dispatched executioners **and ordered them**‡ to *kill all the male children that were in Bethlehem, and in all the borders thereof, from two years old and under*, even to those born that very day, *according to the time which he had diligently inquired of the wise men** at the star's appearance. Neither the place nor the time of the child's birth had been kept secret; the greater number of the slain were buried about three miles south of Bethlehem.*

‡Latin Diatessaron?
*Matt 2:16
Comestor, Hist ev 11 approx; PL 198:1543CD

The term *two years old* (*bimatu*) comes from *bis* and the Greek *ymatos*, meaning *year*, and is used of an animal of two years, as *trimus* is used for one of three

Gorran Matt 2:16 years. Among the various interpretations, the more common and probable one is that a year had passed since Christ's birth, which Herod calculated on the basis of when the magi had seen the star. From this he judged that the child was probably just over a year old, and so he set the upper limit of the massacre at two years. But Herod also feared that—because the stars themselves were at the child's service—he could have changed his age or bodily appearance, which is why even newborn infants had to be killed. Thus it is likely that the massacre of the Innocents took place one year and four days after the Lord's nativity.[2]‡

‡*Comestor, Hist ev 11 approx; PL 198:1543CD*

***R 11**

Then was fulfilled that which was spoken by Jeremiah the prophet, saying, "A voice in Rama was heard, lamentation and great mourning; Rachel bewailing her children, and would not be comforted, because they are not." *Rama* here is not the proper name of a place, but a common noun meaning *high*.[3] The sense is *a voice was heard on high*,* that is, far and wide throughout the surrounding countryside, because of the great crowd of mourners. There was much *lamentation* from the cries of the children being slaughtered, and *great mourning* by their mothers and by everyone else, relatives and neighbors of both sexes; witnessing such cruel barbarity, they could not have refrained from crying out even if they had wanted to. In the case of the children, death put an end to their sufferings; but for the mothers, the memory of this horror never left them—this is why the text says *great mourning*. Or *a voice was heard on*

*Matt 2:17-18

*Jer 31:15

[2] Comestor also offers an alternative interpretation, which he attributes to Chrysostom, that the text means "starting with children age two up to five" because the magi had seen the star for a year before they arrived in Jerusalem. With the exception of the Armenians, who celebrate the feast on May 11, churches of East and West all commemorate the Holy Innocents a few days after Christmas.

[3] Jerome, Int nom, renders *Raama* as *high* or *exalted* (PL 23:842; CL 72:138).

high from heaven at the death of babes, whose blood cried out in testimony against their slayers, as it says: *The prayer of the poor shall pierce the clouds.** *Sir 35:21; *Opus imperf 2; PG 56:645*

Bethlehem was of the tribe of Judah, descended from Leah; Jerusalem was of the tribe of Benjamin, descended from Rachel. Why does it say that Rachel was bewailing the children of Judah (Bethlehem) as if they were her own? One explanation is that Rachel was buried at Ephrata, on the outskirts of Bethlehem, and she was called the mother of the inhabitants of Bethlehem because of the presence of her tomb nearby. Another explanation is that the tribes of Judah and Benjamin had very close ties with one another on account of their geographical proximity, because the border of Judah's territory reached the very gates of Jerusalem. For this reason Herod's decree called for killing the babies in the area surrounding Bethlehem. If this be so, as the evangelist's words suggest, then indeed many of Rachel's children, members of the tribe of Benjamin, were also slaughtered.* This makes Herod's crime even more enormous. Rabanus Maurus writes, "His cruelty knew no bounds: he laid waste not only to Bethlehem, but to all the neighboring villages as well."‡ **Zachary 1.10; PL 186:85C* ‡Com Matt 2:16; PL 107:762D; CM 174:65

***R 12**

**Rachel bewails her children, and would not be comforted, because they are not* in this world any more because they had died; but she knew that they were victorious in eternity. Rachel, whose name means *sheep* or *seeing the origin*, mystically represents the church, whose sole purpose is to contemplate God and who is herself that hundredth sheep that the shepherd carries on his shoulders to the sheepfold.[4] She mourns for her children because she is grieved by the persecution of the faithful. She does not refuse consolation because *they are not*, but because they are *not* dead (for by death

[4] Jerome, Int nom, interprets *Rachel* as *sheep* or *seeing God* (PL 23:842; CL 72:138).

they would conquer this world), and so they remain in the combat of this world and must endure persecutions; she would much rather rejoice that they are happy reigning with Christ as crowned martyrs. The church mourns for the good, because she sees them tormented unjustly, but she knows they are blessed, so she is consoled—not in this world, to be sure, but eternally. But she also mourns for those wicked who are unrepentant, for she knows they will be damned; because she sees them irremediably lost, she does not seek consolation.*

*Bede Matt 2:18 approx; PL 92:14D

*R 13

Touching on this subject, we should note that there are three kinds of martyrs: those who suffer both in fact and by their willing it, like Stephen; those who suffer by their willing it, although not in fact, like John the Evangelist; and those who suffer in fact, although they do not will it, like the Holy Innocents. Christ, in whose stead they suffered, supplied what was lacking in their ability to choose. This is why their feasts follow in an ordered progression according to the degrees of martyrdom: first Stephen, second John, and third the Innocents. Hence the church says of her bridegroom, *My beloved is white and ruddy, chosen out of thousands*:* white in John, red in Stephen, and chosen out of thousands in the Innocents. Even though the Holy Innocents did not have the use of reason and so were unable to bear witness, Christ in whose place they died made good their deficiency; they themselves bore witness *not by speaking, but by dying*.‡ Using the term loosely, they are called *martyrs* or *witnesses of Christ*. They are called *witnesses* (*martyres* in Greek) of Christ not because, strictly speaking, they died for the faith* or for the cause of justice, but because they were killed for loyalty* to Christ, that is, in Christ's place. Christ's death was sought in their murders, so they bore witness by dying, not by speaking.

*St Cher Matt 2:27–28

*Song 5:10

‡*non loquendo, sed moriendo*; Gelasian Sacramentary, Collect; PL 74:1060C

**pro fide*

**pro fide*

One can be a martyr for many different causes: for justice, like Abel; for God's law, like the Maccabees;

for proclaiming the truth, like Isaiah and Jeremiah; for denouncing sin, like John the Baptist; for the salvation of the people, like Christ; for faith and the name of Christ, like Stephen; for the liberty of the church, like Thomas;* for Christ, or in Christ's place, like these infants.* This is why the church celebrates them with great solemnity and allows joyful hymns, even though they descended to the realm of the dead.

*Becket

**St Cher Matt 2:27-28*

Chrysostom says, "All the infants in Bethlehem were killed, who as innocents died for Christ; they stand out as the first martyrs and have created a perfect hymn of witness. It is fitting that they should singled out for special blessings, because they deserved to be the first to die for Christ."* And Augustine: "O blessed infants, newly born, never tempted, not yet struggling, but already crowned!"[5]* And elsewhere, "No one could bestow such advantages on these children with solicitude as the impious foe did with his hatred. The more iniquity he rained down upon them, the more the grace of divine blessing shone out. And as he sought to hunt down Christ, he gained for him an army decorated with the emblems of victory."*

*Chromatius 6.2; CL 9A:222

*Sermo 373; PL 39:1664

*Ps-Aug, Sermo 220; PL 39:2152

R 14

*Consider here how Christ, although still a tender baby, began to bear suffering in himself and in his own; enter into his sufferings as intensely as your devotion allows. Anselm writes, "The sword of persecution is not absent, Christ, even in your tender infancy. You were still nursing at your mother's sweet breast when the angel appeared to Joseph in a dream, saying, *Arise, and take the child and his mother, and fly into Egypt; and be there until I shall tell you. For it will come to pass that Herod will seek the child to destroy him.** And then, good Jesus, you began to suffer. You suffered upheaval not only in your infant soul, but also from the deaths

*Matt 2:11

[5] *O parvuli beati, modo nati, nunquam tentati, nondum luctati, iam coronati!*

of your little ones and the sorrow that Herod's cruel butchery prompted in so many mothers' hearts."*

*Eckbert, Stim [Med 9 Anselm]; PL 158:750C

In King Herod we find an image of the cruelty of the impious who seek to destroy the Christian religion, and in the Holy Innocents the martyrdom of all the little ones, that is, the humble and innocent who are put to death by wicked oppressors. But this is not the way to extinguish the religion founded by Christ, for, as Pope Leo observes, the church is not destroyed by persecution; on the contrary, she grows.* Bernard says that Babylonian cruelty and Herodian malice seek to destroy religion in its cradle and slaughter the children of Israel. Those who impede what is beneficial to salvation, or to the growth and holiness of religion, its progress and fulfillment, or who attack it, are clearly in the same camp as those Egyptians who murdered the children of the Israelites and Herod who attacked the newborn Savior.*

*Sermo 82.6; PL 54:426A; CL 38a:516

*Sermo Epiphany 3.4; PL 183:150C; SB 4:306

The fact that the shadow of persecution fell upon the Lord at the very beginning of his life serves to remind us that God's elect will be persecuted throughout all of this present life. The Lord himself warns us in the gospel, *If they have persecuted me, they will also persecute you.** And the apostle teaches, *All that will live godly in Christ Jesus shall suffer persecution.** That little children were killed for the Lord signifies that it is through humility that one attains the crown of martyrdom, as the Lord says, *He that humbles himself shall be exalted.** The innocence of the babes symbolizes the lowliness of the simple, about which the Lord says, *Suffer the little children to come unto me, for of such is the kingdom of God.** The fact that they were killed and Christ escaped suggests that the wicked can kill the bodies of the martyrs but can never take from their hearts the Christ for whom they suffer: *whether we live or whether we die, we are the Lord's.*‡

*John 15:20

*2 Tim 3:12

*Luke 14:11

*Mark 10:13

‡Rom 14:8; *Haymo, Hom 12; PL 118:78D–79A*

***R 15**

In a moral sense, the many children meet death in various ways: they are drowned by Pharaoh, cut in pieces by Herod,# hanged by Antiochus,† shot with

*Exod 1:22

#Matt 2:16

†1 Macc 1:64

arrows by the Medes.* Drowning in the river signifies captivation by worldly pleasures; the cutting sword, being struck with present adversity; arrows shot from afar, fear of future harshness; hanging, the hunger for future prosperity. Thus the devil is *Pharaoh, squandering through envy*; he is *Herod, boasting through pride*; he is the *Mede, estimating* the penalty for wrongdoing *through evil intent*; and he is *Antiochus, silencing poverty through fraud*, for he conceals poverty and suggests riches.[6] He slays the children according to four affections: happiness in present prosperity, hope for future prosperity, sorrow at present tribulations, and fear of future tribulations. It is noteworthy that children are slain, symbolizing folly; in Bethlehem, meaning abundance; two years old and younger, signifying superabundance. And the church laments this, moved with compassion.*

*Isa 13:18

**Gorran Matt 2:16*

The Idols Fall

When Mary, Joseph, and the child Jesus entered the land of Egypt, all the idols in that territory collapsed in their temples, just as the prophet Isaiah had foretold. They say that just as when the children of Israel left that land there was not a household in Egypt where the firstborn did not die at the Lord's hand, so now as Jesus entered there was not a temple in Egypt where the idols did not fall to the ground.* Something similar happened when the idol of Dagon fell to the ground before the ark of the covenant when the ark had been placed near it.* In a spiritual sense vices crumble when the Lord enters the temple of a heart that had formerly been left forsaken through sins.

***R 16**

*Isa 19:1

**Massa*

*1 Sam 5:2

[6] Jerome, Int nom, renders *Pharao* as *dissipating* (PL 23:1198), *Herodes* as *ostentatious furs* (PL 23:1162), *Medi* as *estimating* (PL 23:848; CL 72:147), and *Antiochiam* as *silence of poverty* (PL 23:853; CL 72:155).

It is related in the *Historia Scholastica* that when Jeremiah had been led into captivity in Egypt, he prophesied to them that in the future a certain virgin would give birth, and then all the idols and gods of the Egyptians would fall to the ground.[7] The Egyptians then carved a statue of a virgin and child and paid honors to it. This prophecy was fulfilled when the Virgin did give birth as foretold, and all the idols in Egypt collapsed when the mother and child came to Egypt.*

*Hist ev 10; PL 198:1543A

This event was also prefigured in the story of Moses, the Pharaoh, and the breaking of a diadem bearing an image of the Egyptian god Amun. It is also related in the *Historia Scholastica* that the Egyptian ruler possessed a royal crown on which was carved an image of Amun, an Egyptian deity. Pharaoh's daughter, who had adopted Moses as her son, decided on a certain occasion to present him to her father. While playing with the child, Pharaoh placed the diadem on Moses' head; he threw it to the ground, and it shattered. The king was furious and wanted to kill the child, but they pleaded that the little boy did not understand what he had done.* By God's will Moses was spared from death at Pharaoh's hand; by God's will Christ evaded Herod's sword. Moses was born to lead the children of Israel out of Egypt; Christ became Man to deliver us from hell. Moses shattered Pharaoh's crown that bore an image of his god; Christ reduced all the idols of Egypt to rubble.*

*Hist sch Exod 5; PL 198:1144A

**SHS 11*

This destruction of the idols was also prefigured in the statue in Nebuchadnezzar's dream. A stone was cut from a mountain without human hand, and when this stone struck the feet of the statue (or idol, or image), it collapsed into a pile of dust; the stone became a great mountain.* That stone stands for Christ, who was cut from a mountain without human hand, that is, born of Mary, who had been untouched by man in marriage. That stone, Christ, brought down all the

*Dan 2:31-35

[7] Comestor does not mention Jeremiah but cites Isa 19:1.

Egyptian idols, of whatever material they were made. Once the statue was shattered, the stone became very great indeed: when idolatry ended, faith in Christ spread throughout the world. And Christ grew into such a great and wondrous mountain that he filled the heavens as well as the earth.* *SHS 11*

The Spiritual Meaning of the Flight into Egypt

Jesus' journey to Egypt to avoid Herod's persecution symbolizes the apostles' mission to the Gentiles, which was prompted by their persecution by the Jewish rulers. The Lord's return to Judea signifies the enlightenment of the Jews at the end of the world. Remigius writes, "Joseph represents preachers; the child, faith and knowledge of the Savior; Mary, the church and the Scriptures; Herod's persecution, the persecution by the Jews; Joseph's flight into Egypt, the mission of preachers to the Gentiles, by which they are brought to the faith of Christ and the church, leaving behind Herod, that is, the unbelief of the Jews; the time spent in Egypt, the period between the ascension and the coming of the Antichrist; the death of Herod, the death of ill will in the hearts of the Jews at the end."*

*R 17

Lyra Matt 2:14 mor

*CA Matt 2:13–15

At that time the Lord scattered the darkness of ignorance covering Egypt and, the vain worship of idols destroyed, he revived the veneration and worship of the true God. Where the flame of faith had been so wondrously enkindled its light filled the wilderness. With the coming of the Lord the Egyptian desert soon was found worthy to be better than a paradise, suffused with a light brighter than the heavens. Chrysostom writes, "Indeed, if you were to visit the solitary wilderness of Egypt today, you would see in that desert something more splendid than Paradise and a company of angels in resplendent human bodies. You would find Christ's army bivouacked throughout the whole region, the king's admirable flock making the earth sparkle with heavenly virtues. All the choirs of stars that fill the sky do not shine more brilliantly than the countless dwellings of monks that adorn and illumine that desert. The monks pass their nights in vigils and hymns, their days in prayer and manual labor, imitating the apostolic way of life."*

*Hom Matt 8.4 (Anianus); Cratandri 1:44–45; PG 57/58:87

The Holy Family at Heliopolis

*R 18

They went to a certain city of the Thebaid called Heliopolis, where they rented a small cottage in which they lived for seven years in poverty and want as destitute foreigners.[8] But how did they survive through all this time? Surely they did not beg, did they? We read that our Lady sought to support herself and her child by plying the distaff and the needle. The Queen of the universe took in sewing to earn money, and out of a love and zeal for poverty.

**Massa; MVC 12; CM 153:51*

O, how great and numerous were the injustices these strangers had to endure! But the Lord had come to experience such hardships, not avoid them. Were there times when the son felt hungry and asked for bread, but there was none to be had? Did not happenings like this shake Mary to the core? She comforted her son with words as best she could, and at the same time worked to get food, perhaps taking something from her own meager store for him. And if she had to work with her hands to provide food, what can we say about clothing, or utensils, or furniture? Did she have duplicate items, or superfluous things, or delica-

[8] Ludolph's sources confuse Heliopolis, in the Delta, with Hermopolis in the Thebaid, the upper valley of the Nile that was the cradle of Christian monasticism. The association of the Holy Family with Hermopolis is attested as far back as the late fourth-century *Historia Monachorum* (PL 21:410B).

cies? Such things are contrary to poverty, and she, the lover of poverty, would not have had them if she could. Might we imagine that she would have sewn or woven articles of clothing for others that were showy or luxurious? God forbid! These things are a danger and a sin for many reasons, as will be shown later.[9]* **Massa*

Contemplate our Lady absorbed in her various labors: sewing, weaving, mending—how she carries them out diligently, reliably, and modestly. And all the while she is keeping an eye on her son, taking care of the house with the greatest care, and not neglecting her vigils and prayers. Share her difficulties with all your heart, and reflect that even the Queen of Heaven did not have the kingdom of heaven completely *gratis*. Give a thought to holy Joseph plying his trade as a carpenter. When sufficient matter for compassionate reflection has come to mind, remain in their company for a time. And then on bent knee ask permission to leave, receiving a blessing first from the child Jesus, then from his mother, and last from Joseph. Bid them a compassionate farewell with tears, for they are banished from their homeland without cause and as exiles must dwell as strangers in a strange land for seven years, earning their food by the sweat of their brow.* **Massa; MVC 12; CM 153:55*

✠

Lord Jesus Christ, while still a babe you endured persecution and exile, and you allowed the infants to be killed for your sake. Grant to me, your poor servant, that I may patiently endure all things, even death itself if need be, for your sake; may I disdain all of the world's allurements and fear none

[9] Ludolph calls these things *opera curiosa* and speaks at some length about *curiositas* in Part One, chap. 68.

of its trials. And you, O most holy Innocents, the flowers and first fruits of martyrdom, who cling to the infant Son of God through innocence and the palm of martyrdom, deign in the fullness of your grace and innocence to obtain pardon for my sins and grace from the same most kind Son of God. Amen.

CHAPTER 14

The Lord's Return from Egypt and the Beginning of John the Baptist's Penance

(Matt 2:19-23)

After the Holy Family had sojourned in Egypt for seven years, the Lord was called back out of Egypt because Herod had died. The histories tell us that Christ was born in the thirtieth year of Herod's reign, and the king died during his thirty-eighth year on the throne. This happened to fulfill what the Lord had said through the prophet Hosea, *I called my son out of Egypt,** that is, God's consubstantial Son. In a literal sense this text refers to God calling Israel out of Egypt, because Israel is also called *child* and *son* by the Lord. *R 1 *Massa *Hos 11:1

Here it can be said with authority that the phrase has two literal meanings: it refers historically to the people of Israel, called out of Egypt by God, but it refers even more literally to our Lord Jesus Christ, because he is God's Son by nature, whereas the Israelites were God's sons and daughters by adoption.* *Lyra Matt 2:15*

In the year AD 8, in the first year of the reign of Herod's eldest son, Archelaus, *an angel of the Lord appeared in sleep to Joseph in Egypt, saying: "Arise, and take the child and his mother, and go* to Judea *in the land of Israel. For they are dead that sought the life of the child."** *They are dead* refers to Herod himself and his accomplices, those scribes and Pharisees who encouraged *Matt 2:19

*Zachary 1.11; PL 186:86A

*Antiquities 17.6.5

*Com Matt 2:20; PL 26:28B; CL 77:15

*CA Matt 2:19–20

*Matt 2:21

the idea of killing Jesus.* Josephus tells us that Herod gave orders that many Jewish leaders were to be killed after his death; he knew that the Jews hated him, and he wanted many tears shed at his passing.* Or, *they* may mean that Herod was literally dead and that the power of the others died with him. Jerome says that from this wording we can surmise that not only Herod, but also the scribes and priests in his time were planning Jesus' death.* Remigius writes that the angel appearing to Joseph in a dream suggests that those who rest from earthly cares and worldly preoccupations will deserve to enjoy angelic visitations.* Joseph *arose* as one who was prompt in obedience, *and took the child*, as a solicitous parent, *and his mother*, as a most attentive spouse, and began to go back *to the land of Israel*.*

***R 2**

*Ps 87:16

*Massa

*They departed and made their way back through the desert along the route they had come. Travel with them on this journey, providing help and assistance to them, devoting yourself to them as best you can. Enter into their weariness, see them worn out by their strenuous walking, getting little rest by day or by night. O, how much this noble and sensitive boy, the King of heaven and earth, labored for us, and how soon in life those labors began! The prophet had spoken his own words when he foretold that *I am poor, and in labors from my youth*.* Great want, hard work, much bodily pain—all these he bore without interruption, almost hating himself for love of us. To be sure, just the grueling journey that we are considering here could have sufficed to redeem us entirely.*

Young John the Baptist Begins His Life of Penance

***R 3**

*It is said that near the edge of the desert through which the Holy Family traveled the boy John the

Baptist had already adopted a penitential life, even though he was without sin himself. They say that at the age of seven he had asked permission to go into the wilderness to do penance at the place where the Israelites had crossed the Jordan when they came from Egypt through that same desert; this was where John himself later baptized.[1] As soon as he could, the future preacher of repentance asked leave and chose to dwell in harsh solitude, and there spent his boyhood.* **Massa*

Dwelling in the desert, John led a life of austerity so that he and his hearers could more easily forsake an attachment to worldly pleasures, and so that he would be more free there for contemplation, drinking in the divine wisdom that he would later pour out in his preaching. By his example he teaches that *it is good for a man, when he has borne the yoke from his youth*:* it is good to become accustomed to virtue in tender years, and to carry out first in deed what one later preaches to others. One who has not been perfected should not be put into the position to teach. John remained in the desert, where the air is purer, the heavens are more open, and God is more familiar. Because the time had not yet come for preaching and baptizing, he spent his days in prayer, conversing with angels and being nourished, away from the wickedness of the multitude. He did not need to fear criticism from others, and his conscience was clear, so he was worthy of credence when he preached about Christ and bore witness to him. *Lam 3:27

No one is worthy to bear witness to another without first being able to bear witness about himself. John shunned the companionship of the crowd to avoid the contagion of wickedness; his life was free of any stain

[1] Luke ends his story of the infancy of John the Baptist, *And the child grew and became strong in spirit, and he was in the wilderness till the day of his manifestation to Israel* (Luke 1:80). Ludolph's source refers to a legend of John going into the desert as a boy.

of scandal or transgression. Had he remained in the world, it is possible that he would have been perverted through his interactions with others. He fled the world to safeguard his holiness, and not the least hint of sin was associated with his name. For, as Chrysostom observes, just as it is impossible for a tree planted next to a road to keep its fruit to maturity, so it is impossible for those who are planted in midst of the world to maintain their innocence.* Some trees are planted in an enclosed garden, and passersby cannot pick their fruit—but they can pluck fruit from the branches that grow out over the road; so it is with those religious who engage in business with the world around them.

*Opus imperf 39; PG 56:815

John the Baptist, the Father of Monks

*R 4

*That boy John is truly marvelous and illustrious: he was the first hermit, the earliest model for those who desire to embrace religious life. Peter Damian has written,

> Blessed is that boy who, at tender years, was led by the Spirit into the desert: God's power compensated for the frailty of his youth. John left the world, fled from human society, was a stranger to his homeland, spurned his parents, all to gaze upon the heights of divinity alone. Behold a remarkable conversion: a man flies from the glory of the world at the very threshold of life! John did not desire to forget worldly temptations; he wanted never to know them and to establish a permanent relationship with God. Remote mountains, deep forests, inaccessible valleys became the dwelling places of the Boy-Patriarch when nightfall made shelter necessary. Overcoming the limitations of his youth, forgetting the excellence of his noble lineage, he gave himself entirely to God alone, and

> so by his way of life he became the pattern for monks, the inspiration for solitaries, and the vindication of religious life.*

*Sermo 23.1; PL 144:631C

Chrysostom says,

> Just as the apostles are the source of holy orders, so John the Baptist is the origin of monks; the Hebrew writings counted him among the priests, and this has been handed down to this day. Monastics, consider your dignity: John is its source. He was a monk almost from the cradle, he lived and grew in the desert, he waited in solitude for Christ, he chose not to live among people, but preferred to converse with angels in the wilderness. Blessed is this way of life: to disdain human company and seek out angelic, to abandon the city and find Christ in solitude. John did not look for Christ in the temple, but in the wilderness, and drew apart from the crowd. Since his eyes were straining to see Christ, only Christ was worthy of his attention. How blessed are those who follow John, for *among those that are born of men, there* was *not a greater prophet than John.**

*Luke 7:28; Jerome, Trac in Matt 1.1–12; CL 78:453–54; *Massa*

***R 5**

How wretched are those monks who do not follow their model, John, and abandon their solitude to mix with people; they think that the city is paradise and their cell is a prison. That was not Jerome's estimation: "Others may see it differently, and everyone follows their own taste, but for me the city is a prison, and solitude Paradise." Reflect that the word *monachos* comes from the Greek *monos* (one, or alone) and *achos* (sorrowful); so *monachos* means alone and mourning. The monk should weep in solitude, carrying out the tasks requested, but not taking on any others.* Hugh of Saint Victor counsels, "Let your cheap habit, simple demeanor, and holy conduct instruct others; you teach better by fleeing the world than by following it."* Pope Gregory advises monastics that their actions,

*Ep 125.8; PL 22:1078; CS 56.1:127

**Gratian, Concordia 16.1.8; PL 187:993A*

*Didascalion 5.8; PL 176:796D

speech, and thoughts should always be a credit to their way of life; they should leave behind completely the things of this world, and what their habit proclaims to human eyes, their conduct should manifest in the sight of God.* So do not boast that you have passed so much time in solitude or spent so many years in the monastery or in religious life, unless you have lived that life well. You will suffer greater condemnation if you have been called to the solitary or religious state but have not truly lived it. As Jerome's adage has it, "It is not praiseworthy to be in Jerusalem unless you live virtuously there."*

*40 Hom 17.18; PL 76:1149B; CL 141:133

*Ep 58.2; PL 22:580; CS 54:529

Augustine wrote to his eremitical brothers,

> It is not enough to desire this vocation if we live the same way we did in the world. What use is it to dwell apart from the world when wickedness reigns in us with tyrannical power, when resentment is in the saddle, when human praise is a greater spur to victory than divine approval, and when we think that our solitary life is praiseworthy and that the world will be blessed through our prayers, whereas in fact we cling to so many vicious passions that we hold the world within our heart, and it seems that it is we who need the prayers of those living beyond our walls? There can be no doubt that a soul held in thrall to selfish desires and living in a worldly manner cannot bring about the kingdom of God.
>
> *See your vocation, brethren.** It is the summit of perfection to embrace the solitary life, but if you do not live perfectly in solitude, it becomes the worst damnation. What good is it for your body to be in a place of tranquility if your heart is restless? What, I ask, does it benefit you to dwell in a place of silence, if you are inwardly seething with passions and wicked designs? To cling to our serene way of life externally, whereas all is stormy within? Therefore, we have not come here to be waited on by the world and to enjoy in peace an

*1 Cor 1:26

> abundance of goods, and certainly we have not come for leisure and security. No, we have come here to fight, to enter into the arena, to make war on the passions, to blunt the sword of the tongue, and to be sure that we not only avoid injuring others but also immediately brush off those injuries done to us by them.*

*Eusebius Gallicanus, Hom 4 ad monachos; PL 50:841C

Alas! How few religious in our day are found to be progressing from good to better, or ascending from virtue to virtue. Bernard complains, "It is much easier to find a worldly person who converts to goodness than it is to find a religious who advances to a better condition. The rarest bird on earth is that religious who has advanced even a step beyond the fervor he or she felt in the novitiate."* And elsewhere, "You must of necessity get better or worse; to stay in the same place will be your ruin. To be sure, a person will not be very good who is not striving to improve; where you do not try to become better, you will cease to be good."*

*Ep 96; PL 182:229B; SB 7:246

*Ep 91.3; PL 182:224A; SB 7:240

Joseph Crosses the Jordan

*Joseph and Mary crossed the Jordan with the boy Jesus and entered the land of Israel, as the angel had commanded. But the angel had not said where they were to go, nor had he named a specific city. Because Joseph was uncertain what to do, the angel returned to him often and by his appearances and messages gave Joseph comfort and assurance. Jesus' return to his homeland should encourage us to hasten to our heavenly home. ***R 6**

*Hearing that Archelaus reigned in Judea in the place of Herod his father, Joseph was afraid to go there.** Archelaus had inherited his father's cruelty along with his crown and continued to vent his rage on Bethlehem and its

*Matt 2:22

environs. *Judea* is sometimes used to designate the whole territory inhabited by the twelve tribes—*In Judea God is known*—*sometimes, the territory occupied by the tribe of Judah—*Juda and Jerusalem, fear not**—and sometimes for the land dwelt in by the two tribes of Benjamin and Judah, as in this case: *Archelaus reigned in Judea.*

*Ps 75:2

*2 Chr 20:17

***R 7**

Herod's realm had been divided up and apportioned among several rulers. The commonly held opinion is that when Herod was dying he wrote a will in which he directed that his son Archelaus was to inherit his kingdom. However, he could not receive his crown without the approval of the Roman emperor. In order to secure the crown Archelaus came to Rome, but so did his two brothers, Herod Antipas and Philip. They were the only surviving brothers, because their father had had his other three sons (Antipater, the eldest, Alexander, and Aristobulus) brutally murdered before he died. So these other two sons also came to Rome and asked for a part of their father's inheritance.

**Lyra Matt 2:22*

The emperor and senate, wanting to break Jewish pride and remove any pretext for rebellion, took away the title of king and divided Herod's kingdom into four parts, or *tetrarchies*. They gave two of these, Judea and Abilene, to Archelaus, who was the eldest; the third part, consisting of Galilee and the Transjordan, they awarded to Herod Antipas, under whom John was beheaded and the Lord suffered; the fourth part, consisting of Iturea and the region of Trachonitis, they apportioned to Philip, whose wife Herod Antipas took from him. Archelaus was a *diarch*, and his brothers *tetrarchs*.[2]

[2] Herod the Great intended Archelaus to rule the entire kingdom, with his brothers administering the regions later given to them in the disposition determined by Rome; Archelaus was called *ethnarch*, not *diarch*.

In addition to Herod the Great and Herod Antipas, there was a third Herod who ruled for a time: this was Herod Agrippa, the son of Aristobulus; it was he who had James, the brother of John, slain with a sword and imprisoned Peter. Archelaus had been his father's choice to succeed him as king, so it was natural that he continued to enforce his father's policies; this is why Joseph was afraid to go into Judea.

***R 8**

Being warned in sleep* by the angel, Joseph *retired* with the child and his mother *into the quarters of Galilee. Joseph felt safer here because this territory was under the control of Herod's other son, Herod Antipas, who had received this region from his father and lived there privately before his father's death. This was itself the land of Israel, because Israel was dwelling there. *And coming he dwelt in a city called Nazareth;** so Jesus grew up in the place where he was conceived, although he was born in Bethlehem. It was much safer for him to live here, rather than in Bethlehem or Jerusalem, which was under Archelaus's rule. Chrysostom says, "Jesus came to Nazareth not only to avoid danger, but also moved by affection for his homeland; he could live both more securely and more happily there."*

*Matt 2:22

*Matt 2:23

*Hom Matt 9.5; PG 57/58:180

This occurred *that it might be fulfilled which was said by the prophets: That he shall be called a Nazarene.** *That* should be interpreted as consecutive, not causative: the prophecy does not make an event happen; the event causes the prophecy to be made. Christ is called a *Nazarene* either from the name of the place where he was conceived and grew up, or from the sacramental meaning of *Nazarite* in the law, according to which the word is interpreted to mean *holy*, and all the books of sacred Scripture speak of and bear witness to our Lord's holiness. Just as Christ chose the village in which he was born, so he also chose the town where he would grow to manhood. This name suggests that he himself who is essentially the fountain of holiness grew up in holiness, that is the *holy of holies*, or, it could be said, the *Nazarene of Nazarenes*.

*Matt 2:23

Nazareth can be interpreted as *flower of the field*, or *tender sprout*, or *holiness*; so the name suggests that the holy of holies grows from this tender sprout.[3] Because Christ was known as the *Nazarene*, it was originally customary for his followers to be called *Nazarenes*. Later, when Peter established his see at Antioch, by common consent they were called by the Greek name *Christians*, from *Christ*.* Christ wished to be conceived and raised in Nazareth so that we might know that he blossomed both in his conception, which was without original sin, and in his conduct, because he was free of actual sin. This is why, Bernard says, the flower from the root of Jesse loved his flowering homeland.* By leaving Egypt, coming to Galilee, and living in Nazareth, Christ gives us an example: we should abandon the state of sin, pass over from vices to virtues, and bloom by persevering in good works, and in this way we can reach our heavenly homeland.

*see Acts 11:26

*Sermo Annunciation 3.7; PL 183:396B; SB 5:39

Jesus' Childhood

***R 9**

See, we have escorted the child Jesus back from Egypt. Upon his return, our Lady's sisters and other relatives and friends hastened to meet them. The Holy Family stayed in Nazareth, living a life of poverty. There, as was their custom, Joseph contracted to do carpentry and Mary worked at her sewing, mending, and other chores, and likewise cared diligently for her son. Anselm writes, "No wisdom is able to comprehend, no eloquence can describe, the loving devotion she lavished on her little boy, the diligent service she gave the youth and carried on into his young man-

**Massa; MVC 13; CM 153:59*

[3] Jerome, Nom int, renders *Nazareth* as *flower*, or *brushwood*, or *clean*, or *separated* (PL 23:842; CL 72:137). In his commentary on Matthew Jerome renders the Hebrew of Isa 11:1 as *Exiet virga de radice Iesse, et Nazaraeus de radice eius conscendet* (PL 26:29A).

hood. And, as she herself revealed to a certain person, how many times she held him in her lap and, moved by tender devotion, rested her head on that of her son; she wept such copious tears of love that his head and face were bathed in them, and she would say, 'O health and joy of my soul!' Who of us can hear these things, or picture them, and keep back our tears?"[4]*

*Eadmer, Quatuor 8; PL 159:585C

*From this time until the boy Jesus was twelve years old, nothing is recorded in Scripture either of him or of his family. There is a story, and it has the ring of truth, that to this day a little fountain is pointed out in Nazareth that our Lady visited, and that Jesus often drew water from it. He certainly did chores for his mother, since he *was subject to them*.* It is charming to picture him, *who gives food to all flesh*,* carrying water to his mother now and then. Here he also gathered greens in the fields that his mother used in preparing meals. The humble Lord performed other tasks for his mother because they had no servant or hired help. He began to carry out at a young age this virtue that later he would praise above all others: *Learn of me, because I am meek, and humble of heart*.* Anselm says, "Do not think it folly to contemplate the boy Jesus among the other children of Nazareth, and to watch him obeying his mother and helping his foster father in the workshop."*

***R 10**

*Luke 2:51

*Ps 135:25

*Matt 11:29; *Massa; MVC 13; CM 153:59–60*

*Aelred, De inst 30 [Anselm Med 15]; PL 158:786D; CM 1:664

✠

O most gentle Jesus, after you were born of the Virgin you withdrew into Egypt and returned to Israel when you were summoned. Call me back, Lord, your servant, from the Egypt of this earthly

[4] The recipient of the revelation was Mechtild of Hackborn, *Liber specialis gratiae* 1.12.

exile that has banished me from your sight. Lead back my body from the darkness of worldly living, lead back my mind and my heart as well. Make me forsake wickedness and pass over to virtue. May you deign to guide me into the Promised Land, here by faith, hope, and charity, and hereafter in reality by beauty, glory, and truth. Amen.

CHAPTER 15

The Boy Jesus Remains Behind in Jerusalem and Is Found in the Temple

(Luke 2:40-52)

***R 1**

******And the child* Jesus *grew and waxed strong*. And, lest someone imagine that he grew in soul as well as in body, the evangelist adds that he was *full of wisdom* as regards his soul, *and the grace of God was in him** in both body and soul. Bede teaches, "Because all the fullness of divinity was present in Christ bodily, that child was full of wisdom and had no need for increase or strengthening as God and the Word of God, but only as regards his human nature, by grace. For great was the grace given to that man: from the very beginning of his human life he was perfect, and God."* And Bede adds that the fullness of divinity identified by Luke as wisdom, the evangelist John described as truth *full of grace and truth*.*

*Luke 2:40

*Com Luke 2:40; PL 92:348B; CL 120:71

*John 1:14

Christ possessed the fullness of all the virtues and gifts of the Holy Spirit, with the exception of faith and hope, in place of which he had sure knowledge and certain possession, with which he was blessed from the moment of his conception. Whenever we read that Christ grew or became stronger, this and similar language should be understood as referring only to his body. As to his soul, this was perfect from the very moment of his conception, but he did not show this until the opportune time. Bernard writes,

> Jesus was a man even before his birth: not in age, but in wisdom; not in the maturity of his body, but in the vigor of his soul; not in the greatness of his members, but in the integrity of his senses. Jesus did not have less wisdom at his conception than when he was born, or when he was a child than when he was an adult. Whether he was hidden in the womb, crying in the manger, questioning the doctors in the temple as a boy, or teaching the people as an adult, he was always equally filled with the Holy Spirit.*

*Laudibus 2.9; PL 183:65D; SB 4:27

More will be said about this topic at the end of this chapter.

***R 2**

*And his parents, as devout and religious observers of the law, *went every year to Jerusalem, at the solemn day of the pasch** to hear the law, take part in the sacrifice, and participate in the solemnity. They continued to serve the shadows of that truth they already possessed.

*Luke 2:41

Here it will be useful to note that some Jewish festivals were decreed to be held commonly and continually, others annually. Of the former, there were two: the *Sabbath,* on which everyone rested from work because it was on this day that God rested from all his work of creation, and the *New Moon,* at the beginning of each month, to praise the Creator who created all times. There were five annual feasts. The first was the *Passover,* celebrated on the fourteenth day of the first lunar month, to commemorate the deliverance from Egypt. Second was *Pentecost,* which was held on the fiftieth day after Passover, to celebrate the giving of the Law to the Jews on Mount Sinai. Third was the feast of *Trumpet Blast,** on the first of September, when the ram's horn was blown to commemorate the day Isaac was spared from sacrifice and a ram offered in his place. Fourth was the *Day of Atonement,* celebrated on the tenth day of September to commemorate the occasion when Moses turned back God's wrath

Rosh Hashanah

against the people who adored the golden calf. Fifth was the feast of *Tabernacles*, celebrated on September fourteenth; during that celebration the people dwelt in tents to recall the forty years that their ancestors spent living in tents in the wilderness.

Of these five feasts, three were the most solemn and were observed for an entire week: Passover, Pentecost, and Tabernacles. According to the law, on these feasts the men of every tribe were to go up to Jerusalem to appear before the Lord. Those who lived at a great distance could for a reasonable cause excuse themselves from the pilgrimages of Pentecost and Tabernacles, but no one was exempted from the Passover celebration unless prevented by ill health. Women were not bound by the law to take part, but many did so out of devotion.

Therefore the Virgin went up to Jerusalem every year, not wanting to leave her boy unguarded because Archelaus still ruled. Even though the parents feared Archelaus, they went to Jerusalem every year for the feast: they judged that they could escape detection in such a large throng of pilgrims. Also, if they did not go it would be thought that they were non-observant, and their absence would have aroused suspicion.‡

‡*Aug, De cons 2.10.23; PL 34:1087; CS 43:120*

***R 3**

And when he was twelve years old, they went up into Jerusalem, according to the custom of the feast. Christ teaches us here that it is good for people to be accustomed to divine realities from childhood, and the fact that he stayed behind in the place of worship after the others had left teaches us the same lesson. Jesus made this long journey to honor his heavenly Father on the feasts; the Lord of the law humbly observed its precepts.*

*Luke 2:42

**Massa*

The Lord came to give us an example of humility and perfection, so he chose to observe the law so long as it was in force. Bede says, "He himself kept the law that he had given to show us, who are merely human, that whatever God commands must be done. Let us follow his pattern of human living if we desire to take delight in looking upon the glory of his divinity."* Following his example, let us devote ourselves seriously to doing good works, assiduously following the commandments, and preparing for and properly observing feasts. There was a certain brother who was so devoted to the feasts of our Lord, the Blessed Virgin, and the feast of All Saints, that he would prepare for these solemnities with fasting, prayer, and ascetical practices, and during the celebrations themselves he occupied himself completely with prayer and meditation.

*Hom ev 1.12; PL 94:64D [1.19; CL 122:135]

***R 4**

*The spiritual lesson here is that above all on feast days Christians should frequent the Lord's chosen place, the church, not taverns or theatres; we should attend to God's praises, not dances or frivolities; we should give alms, not lend money at interest or defraud others; we should devote ourselves to good works, not gluttony and drunkenness. The Lord says through Isaiah to those who act otherwise, *My soul hates your new moons and your solemnities*.*

*Isa 1:14

Having reached his twelfth year, Jesus began to manifest his wisdom and reveal the two natures he had received from his heavenly Father and his earthly mother.* The age of twelve was symbolic of the twelve apostles, through whom Christ's divinity and humanity were proclaimed to the whole world. He began to manifest the brilliance of his perfection with the number twelve, because the twelve tribes and twelve apostles signified the universality of those to be saved.

**Zachary, 1.12; PL 186:87D*

***R 5**

**And having fulfilled the days* of celebration, *when they returned* at the end of the eight days of the solemnity, *the child Jesus remained in Jerusalem*.* This was not by chance nor due to the neglect or thoughtlessness of his parents; no, this happened by his will and set purpose, so that he could show from childhood his zeal for spiritual things. As he had demonstrated his devotion to his parents by going up with them to offer sacrifice to God, as one human being among many, so

*Luke 2:43

he would show his devotion to his heavenly Father by giving himself over to spiritual doctrine. *And his parents knew it not, thinking that he was in the company **of those with whom they were traveling**.** Jesus chose to remain behind in secret and not inform his parents in order to avoid a dilemma: if he had obeyed them and departed, he would not have been able to manifest his wisdom to the doctors; if he had remained behind against their instructions, he would have been guilty of disobedience. *Luke 2:42-43; Latin Diatessaron?

From this we learn that it is permissible, where due prudence is observed, for sons or daughters to consecrate themselves to God's service in religious life and embrace the state of perfection without the knowledge or approval of their parents, provided the parents do not rely on them for support.* The Lord says to those who would try to stop such a one, *Suffer the little children to come unto me, for of such is the kingdom of God.** *Massa *Mark 10:14

Here someone might ask, "How could parents who were so attentive to raising their child forget him or leave him behind?" It might be helpful to know that it was customary among the children of Israel, when making these pilgrimages, for the men to travel with the men and the women with the women. This was partly a matter of prudence, to safeguard chastity; and also to foster that purity of spirit the law demanded. Children, however, could travel with either of their parents. When Joseph saw that the boy Jesus was not with him, he assumed he was with his mother and the women, and Mary assumed he was walking with Joseph and the men.* *Massa

R 6

**They came a day's journey*‡ without the child, mistakenly believing that he was traveling with the men or with the women. And when in the evening they came to the place where they were to stop for the night, our Lady saw Joseph without the boy whom she had believed to be returning with him; she was struck with a pang of sorrow and tearfully went to various dwellings looking for him. Elderly Joseph ‡Luke 2:44

Massa followed her, weeping. Go with them, and look for the child Jesus until you find him.

When his parents could not find him, give some thought to how little rest they could have, especially the mother who loved him so ardently. Although her relatives tried to comfort her, she could not be consoled: what must it have been like to lose Jesus? Watch her closely, and feel yourself the anguish of spirit that she felt. Never, from the moment of her birth till this hour, had she experienced such suffering. We should not be distraught when trials come our way, if the Lord did not shield even his mother from them. The Lord permits such tribulations to come to his own as a sign of his love for them.* *Massa; MVC 14; CM 153:61

At last our Lady withdrew into a room where she passed the whole night praying and weeping with great anguish on account of her son. First thing next morning they left the house and began to search for him in the surrounding neighborhood, because the pilgrims were returning by various routes. Circulating from group to group, they made repeated inquiries about him, especially *among their kinsfolk and acquaintances** who were journeying home in the groups of men and women. When they still could not find him, Mary gave up hope and could not be comforted.* *Luke 2:44 *Massa; MVC 14; CM 153:62

Pause here and consider attentively how many wounds and pains pierced the heart of the Blessed Virgin, what sighs, laments, and anxieties she felt when she did not find the son she so desperately sought! Then she began to experience the true nature of the sorrows Simeon had foretold when he had said to her, *Your own soul a sword shall pierce.** The Virgin did not know what to do: she had lost the treasure that had been lovingly entrusted to her care by God. She could in sorrow make her own the words of Reuben when he discovered that Joseph was not in the pit: *The boy is not to be seen; where will I go?** Reflect here that the Blessed Virgin had not lost her son when she was driven from her homeland and fled into Egypt *Luke 2:35 *Gen 37:30

with much tribulation; it happened when she had gone up to the feast. From this we can understand that often Jesus is kept safe in adversity but lost in prosperity.

*On the third day *they returned into Jerusalem seeking him,** having spent one day looking for him and another making their way back there. I picture the Virgin tearfully making the difficult trek back to Jerusalem. She could repeat in her own heart those words in the Song of Songs, *"I sought him whom my soul loves; I sought him, and found him not* among my kinsfolk and acquaintances. *I will rise, and will go about the city* from place to place: *in the streets and the broad ways I will seek him whom my soul loves."** ***R 7** *Luke 2:45 *Song 3:1-2

*And *after three days* of his being lost, which prefigures his three days in the tomb when he was thought to be lost, early in the morning of the fourth day *they found him in the temple.** Ambrose suggests that this was a sign that he who would later be thought dead would be found to have risen again with immortal glory three days after his triumphal passion.* *They found him in the temple*, in a place of devotion, in the holy place of God. They did not find him in the places boys were ordinarily to be found—the theater, the town square, the playing field—but in a place set aside for sacred learning and for prayer.* The Son gladly stayed in his Father's house. When we willingly stay in church, it is a sign that we are God's sons and daughters, because we remain in our Father's house; but if we readily hang around the tavern, this is a sign that we are the devil's children, because we are staying in our father's house. ***R 8** *Luke 2:46; *Massa* *Exp Luke 2.63; PL 15:1575B; CL 14:58 **Lyra Luke 2:46*

Jesus in the Temple

They found him in the temple, not playfully running about here and there as children usually do, but *sitting* gravely like a fountain of wisdom *in the midst of the* *doctors, hearing them and,* as an exemplar of humility, *asking them questions,** not teaching them.‡ The one who teaches the angels in heaven was asking the doctors questions in the temple;† he who had himself imparted the word of knowledge to his doctors wanted to learn by asking.° He did not ask because he was lacking in knowledge or had to add to his store of learning, but to give us a model of how to be zealous to deepen our understanding of sacred Scripture, and so that we will not blush to ask questions about what we do not understand. Sadly, many proud people are ashamed to admit their lack of understanding and choose to remain in ignorance by not asking questions, rather than being instructed. He also provides an example of humility by listening before instructing, teaching us that even learned people should be more ready to listen than teach; someone who answers first, before listening, is manifestly foolish. To show that he was also God, Jesus questioned these men acutely and responded in turn with such wisdom that those who heard him were amazed.

*Luke 2:46
‡*Massa*
†*Greg, Hiez 1.2.3; PL 76:796C; CL 142:18*
°*Greg, Reg past 3.25; PL 77:98D*

And all that heard him were astonished at his wisdom in putting questions *and his answers,** because it was unheard of for a boy of this age to discourse so wisely. Astonishment is a strong sense of wonder in the presence of something truly unusual, and that was the case here: he listened humbly, asked prudently, and responded wisely, even though he was just a boy. He himself asked, he himself answered, and he himself resolved his own questions and theirs, following the method of the most learned teachers, who instruct their students now by asking questions, now by giving answers. As Bede says, to show that he was truly Man, Jesus listened humbly to the doctors; to prove that he was God, he responded in a sublime way to them when they were speaking.* They were astonished to hear a mere child speak with such probity; his body and age were small, but his questions and answers

*Luke 2:47
*Hom ev 1.12; PL 94:65C [1.19; CL 122:136]

were great. Thinking him only human, and not God, the contrast between the frailty they saw and the majesty they heard threw them into confusion.

Unlike those Jewish elders, we are not amazed or astonished by his wisdom and his answers, because we believe that Jesus is both true God and true Man. All wisdom is from him, and was with him always from all eternity, and we know from the prophecy that in just this way a little child was to be born for us, who would still be the omnipotent God.

***R 9**

And seeing him in the temple*, sitting in the midst of the doctors, *they wondered greatly*,* because the like of such a thing had never been seen before. His mother, as it were restored to life, joyfully offered great thanks to God. As soon as the boy Jesus saw his mother he came to her, and she took him in her arms and lovingly kissed him. Looking into his handsome face, she said to him, *Son, why have you done this to us?

*Luke 2:48

It was as if she said, "My most-desired son, why have you done this, remaining behind here without telling us? Why have you given the mother who tenderly and devotedly loves you so much cause for grief?* I ask you, son, to tell me why, so that the great anxiety this event has given me can be mitigated." The Virgin Mother had just passed through three days of anxious distress, and now that she had found her son she was suspended between sorrow and joy and rebuked him with loving correction.

*Luke 2:48; *Massa; MVC 14; CM 153:62–63*

**LV 8*

Joseph, although he was reputed to be Jesus' father, did not dare to accuse him because he was firmly convinced that he was the Son of God; but his mother, impelled by the great love she bore for the son she had been seeking, did complain to him, because great love knows no measure.* She spoke to him, but Joseph did not, because she had experienced greater sorrow.

**Lyra Luke 2:48*

Gregory says, "Mary, moved by a mother's feelings, asks this question as if in tears; for in everything as a mother she acted with fidelity and humility. And so she showed her affection for him by asking, *Son, why have you done this to us?"** And Anselm: "What if you were searching for that twelve-year-old with his mother for three days? O, what abundant tears you would shed when you hear the mother gently scolding her son with the reproach, *Son, why have you done this to us?"** It could be that these words were not spoken as a reproach but simply expressed sadness at his absence, because she adds, *"Behold, your* foster *father and I have sought you sorrowing** because of your absence, and because your presence is our greatest joy."

*CA Luke 2:42–50

*Aelred, De inst 31 [Anselm Med 15]; PL 158:787A; CM 1:664–65

*Luke 2:48

***R 10**

From this incident we learn that we should be sorrowful when we lose Jesus, that is, eternal salvation, which happens when we sin. Then we must look for him through the three days of repentance: contrition with sorrow, confession with shame, satisfaction with effort, and then we will find him again. But alas! Many shed more tears over the loss of passing things than they do over the loss of eternal salvation, their own or someone else's. As Bernard observes, "If a donkey falls into a pit, someone will pull it out; a soul is destroyed, and no one lifts a finger."* The holy Virgin calls Joseph the boy's father, either to avoid raising suspicions among the Jews, or because he was bringing him up, or on account of his legal genealogy. Note here that we never read that Joseph said anything, but he left this to the Virgin; since she was truly his mother, it was more her responsibility.

**Lyra Luke 2:45 mor*

*De consideratione 4.6.20; PL 182:786B; SB 3:464

When we look for Jesus, it should be in the company of Mary and Joseph, which is suggested by the words *your father and I. Joseph* means *increase* and symbolizes that good works should be increased continually; *Mary* means *illuminata*, symbolizing the faith that illumines the mind, and *star of the sea*, symbolizing charity: just as this star remains shining when the others have set, so even if other virtues fail, charity remains. If we look for Jesus in the company of good faith, assiduous good works, and glowing charity, then he will be found. But if any of these are missing, we will search in vain. And we should search in tears, as the Virgin said, *We have sought you sorrowing.*

And he said to them,* not to upset his mother but to instruct her, "*How is it that you sought me among my relatives and friends, when you should have looked for me in the temple, in my Father's house, employed in spiritual matters?" He did not say this in a resentful tone of voice, but humbly, to reveal spiritual truths. Jesus did not chide or reproach those who sought him as a son, but to correct his mother; to remind her and us who his eternal Father is, he adds, "*Did you not know that I must be about my father's business** in the temple, teaching and doing works that manifest my Father?"* In other words: "I would rather look upon him of whom I am the eternal Son by nature than you, of whom I am the son in my human nature, and Joseph, whose son I am by adoption. You should not be surprised if I forsake you for the eternal Father, to whom I cling more completely." ***R 11** *Luke 2:49 *Luke 2:49 **Zachary 1.12 approx; PL 186:88C*

Jesus gave preference to the nature he shared with his eternal Father over the nature he shared with his created mother and adoptive father.* He loved his human parents and obeyed them, but he chose to give the place of honor to God. **Lyra Luke 2:49*

From this we learn that devotion to God takes precedence over devotion to parents: we must love and honor our parents, and obey them, but in all things God must come first. There is another moral here. Christ answers his mother's question as if to correct her for looking for him sorrowing among their friends and relations; this suggests the sundering of family ties, because we will not attain perfection when we remain preoccupied with earthly things; affection for family can impede us from reaching our goal.* This is implied in his words, "*How is it that you sought me* among my relatives and friends? *Did you not know that I must be about my father's business?*" And so he exhorts us to keep the eyes of our heart fixed on the higher things, not on those of earth. ***R 12** **Bonaventure, Com Luke 2:49* **CA Luke 2:42–50*

We can also learn a lesson from the fact that when his mother reproached him, Jesus excused himself with gentleness and humility, but when later she asked him to perform a miracle at Cana, he answered her sternly; in this he gives us an example and model of humility, urging us to prefer correction to praise.‡

‡*Bonaventure, Com Luke 2:49*

*R 13

*These are the first words spoken by the Savior in the gospels, and he proclaims his divinity in them. They were so profound that Mary and Joseph could not comprehend their meaning, which is why the evangelist adds, *And they understood not the word that he spoke to them** about the Father and what he wanted them to infer. He wanted them to understand that the care of the temple and the management of all spiritual matters were as much his concern as the Father's: they share the same majesty, glory, and activity, as well as the same throne and house, both materially and spiritually. Although Mary and Joseph believed that Jesus was the Son of God, they did not attend carefully to what he said; nor did they understand the hidden mystery of the divine nature, because they were not yet accustomed to hear him speak about his divinity. Or they may have understood what he said, but not so fully as they would later.

*Luke 2:50

But at his mother's request, and for her consolation, he did return with them to Nazareth, where he had been conceived and brought up, which is why he was called a *Nazarene*. Because Jesus is both God and Man, he reveals to us here both his natures, sometimes the greatness of his divinity, at other times his human frailty. As a man he went up to Jerusalem with his parents, as God he remained behind in the temple without their knowledge. As a man, he asked questions of the elders, but as God he gave answers that astounded them. As the Son of God, he remained in his and his Father's temple; as the Son of Man he returned home with his parents when they told him to.*

**Massa*

*R 14

‡Luke 2:51

**And he was subject to them*‡ for our instruction, to confound our pride because we often refuse to submit ourselves to our superiors.* He was subject in that nature in which he is less than the Father. For, as Augustine teaches, Christ took on the form of a servant for his parents also.* Let us be subject for his sake, so that as we have drifted away from him by the slackness of disobedience, we may return to him by the labor of submission. Here Christ gives us a great example and a model of humble obedience: he is himself the Lord of Creation and the whole world is under his sway, but he chose to submit humbly to his parents and obey them.

*Lyra Luke 2:51 mor

*Tr John 78.2; PL 35:1836; CL 136:524

Those who are under obedience should not despise their position, because Jesus did not hesitate to submit to those placed in authority over him. And those in authority should not boast, because the fact that Christ was obedient to Joseph's authority reminds us that often more merit is found in subjects than in superiors: those in authority will understand from this that they should not let a higher office lead to pride, because they will recognize that the one subject to them is actually better than they.*

Bruno Com Luke 2:51; PL 165:365BC

Notice, too, the great dignity of the Virgin, since the one to whom all creation is subject was himself subject to her. Augustine says, "The Virgin possesses this very great privilege: he whom not only human creatures but the angelic hosts revere made himself subject to her."* And Bernard, when treating the phrase *he was subject to them*, observes,

*Fulgentius, Fide 1.2.17 approx; PL 40:759

> Marvel at both things and choose which is more wondrous: the remarkable condescension of the Son, or the eminent dignity of the mother. Both are amazing, both are miraculous! That God should obey a woman is humility unequalled; that a woman should command God is dignity unparalleled. Learn, O human, to obey; learn, O earth, to be subject; learn, O dust, to be submissive; blush with shame, O ashes, for your pride. God humbled himself, and you exalt yourself; God bows before mortals, and you seek to rule over them and so

> prefer yourself to your Maker! As often as I seek distinction among people, so often do I seek precedence over God, and then truly I do not savor the things of God.*

*Laudibus 1.7; PL 183:60A; SB 4:19

Notice that children owe their parents many things: first, their hearts' love; second, the esteem of their deeds; third, support in need; fourth, solicitous service; fifth, respect in addressing them; sixth, obedience in worthy acts; seventh, pardon for their offenses; eighth, support in adversity.

*R 15

What did the boy Jesus do during these three days? Watch him, and see how he was reduced to the level of a beggar: Jesus shamefacedly had to seek lodging in a common shelter, and slept and ate with paupers. Some suggest that in company with other indigents he went begging door to door. Bernard asks, "Who took care of you during these three days?" and answers his own question in these words: "Lord Jesus Christ, in order to conform yourself to our poverty in all things, did you ask for alms door to door with a crowd of beggars? Who will obtain for me a share in those crusts you obtained by begging, or at least give me the leftovers of that sacred food?"*

*Massa

*Aelred, De Iesu Puero 6; PL 184:853D; CM 1:254

Observe him also in the midst of the doctors, with his placid, wise, and reverent demeanor: he asks questions and listens to them as if he were ignorant, and by his modesty he prevents the doctors from being put to shame by his remarkable answers.*

*Massa

Lessons from this Event

*R 16

We can learn three lessons from the event just described. The first is that those who want to cling to God should not dwell with their family members, but rather should distance themselves from them. The child Jesus withdrew from his most beloved mother when he wanted to carry out the works of his Father, nor was he later found to be among his relatives and acquaintances when they went looking for him: flesh and blood did not reveal him, nor was he found in worldly society. Bernard says, "The boy Jesus was sought among his relatives and acquaintances but was not found there. You also should distance yourself from your family if you want to find your salvation."* *Forget your people and your father's house, and the king shall greatly desire your beauty.*‡ And elsewhere, "O good Jesus, if you were not found among your own relatives, how can I expect to find you among mine? Can I find you in joy, when your mother barely found you sorrowing?"* Nor can he be found among throngs of people: he will not be discovered in a multitude of worldly distractions, but in the depths of the heart, which is God's temple.

Massa; MVC 14; CM 153:63

*Ep 107.13; PL 182:249A; SB 7:276

‡Ps 44:10-11

*source unknown

Second, if we live in a spiritual way we should not be surprised to find ourselves experiencing aridity sometimes, so that it seems that we have been abandoned by God—this happened even to the Mother of God.* Do not give way to this mental lassitude: continue to persevere in prayer and meditation, persist in seeking him by doing good works; if you are solicitous, you will find him again. Origen says that Jesus should not be sought halfheartedly, as he is by many who look for him languidly and so do not find him: we must search with labor and effort.* And Bernard writes, "If we do not want to seek him in vain, we must seek him in truth, not looking for anything but him; we must seek him fervently, not looking for anything else along with him; we must seek him persistently, not accepting anything instead of him. It would be easier to transverse the heavens and the earth than for those who seek in this way not to find, for those who ask in this way not to receive, or for those who knock in this way not to have the door opened to them."*

Massa; MVC 14; CM 153:63

*Hom Luke 18; PG 13:1848D

*Sermo de div 37.9; PL 183:643D; SB 5:228

Third, we should not cling to our own preferences or our own will: Jesus had said that he must be about his Father's business, but he then altered his intention and, following his mother's desire, returned with her and his foster father *and was subject to them*.* Let us weigh carefully how ardently we human beings should obey God, since God himself obeyed human beings: if the Lord has given us an example of how mere men must be obeyed, how much more should God be obeyed? Let us, then, obey both God and others, since the Son of God obeyed not only his heavenly Father, but also his earthly parents.

*Massa; MVC 14; CM 153:64

R 17

**R 17*

*Luke 2:51

**And his mother kept all these* sublime *words* and others she heard from him, locked away under a seal, as it were, *in her heart*.* Had she not kept them, we would not have received them from her: she is the treasury who safeguarded them for our sake. Everything about the Lord, all that he said and did—whether she understood it or not at the time—Mary stored in her heart and memory, lovingly pondering them and reflecting upon them; at the fitting time she came to comprehend their meaning and so could adequately explain them to the evangelists and others who questioned her.*

**Zachary 1.12; PL 186:88D*

In this behavior she teaches us a rule and a law to follow throughout life: setting aside worldly distractions, we should repeatedly meditate upon what the Lord said and did, and strive to share this knowledge with others. If you need an inspiring word, have recourse to our Lady, because she has preserved Christ's words and deeds. Her example teaches us how we should listen to God's word: do not let it go in one ear and out the other, but safeguard it in your heart and reflectively ponder it.

How Jesus Grew

*R 18

*Luke 2:52

**And Jesus advanced in wisdom and age and grace with God and men*.* Age pertains to the body, wisdom to the soul, grace to the well-being of both. Jesus certainly advanced in age, which is marked by bodily growth: like other people, Jesus went from infancy to boyhood, and from boyhood to adolescence. However, advancing in wisdom and grace can be understood in two ways. The first way is by an increase in the *habitus* of wisdom, augmented by grace: Christ did not advance in these, because he was full of grace and wisdom from the moment of his conception. The second way is through effects, that is, by exercising wisdom it is possible to perform works more wisely and more virtuously, and it was in this way that *Jesus advanced in wisdom and grace*, as well as *age*. As he grew older, he did greater deeds for God and others, which is why the words are added, *with God and men*.*

**Zachary 1.12; PL 186:89A; Aquinas, ST III, q. 2, a. 1*

Or else, in Ambrose's interpretation, he advanced in wisdom as regards his manifestation and use of wisdom, because he chose to reveal his wisdom and grace little by little.* Gregory for his part suggests that Jesus advanced through those who themselves advanced because of his teaching and example, just as a teacher is said to make progress when the students under his care advance; and so this was *with God*, that is, for God's glory, *and men*, that is, for their assistance.‡ Theophylact holds that *with God and men* means that we should please God first, and then human beings.*

*De incar 7.72; PL 16:837A

‡Attr. in Lombard, Sent 3.13; PL 192:782; also Bede, Hom ev 1.12; PL 94:68A [1.19; CL 122:139–40]

*En Luke 2:51–52; PG 123:735

Jesus could not advance in habitual knowledge or wisdom, because he possessed the fullness of these from the moment of his conception; he could, however, grow in experimental knowledge gained from sense perceptions, as he directed his senses to various things. This is why the apostle could write, *He learned obedience by the things which he suffered.** This does not mean that he learned something new that he had not known before, because what he learned humanly he already knew by divine wisdom and inspiration. Bernard writes,

*Heb 5:8

Another person's miseries are only truly experienced by those who have misery in their own heart; you will know how to come to the aid of your neighbor from your own experience.‡ The Son of God was incapable of suffering before he *emptied himself, taking the form of a servant.** He had no experience of misery and subjection, he did not know by experience mercy and obedience. He knew by virtue of his nature, but not by experience. But when he had lowered himself to take that form in which he was able to suffer and to be subject, then he experienced misery in suffering and obedience by being submissive.

‡De gradibus 3.6; PL 182:945A; SB 3:21

*Phil 2:6

This experience did not increase his knowledge—but it did increase our trust in him, when we see him from whom we had strayed draw close to us to know our misery by shared experience. Had he remained in the state of divine impassibility, would we dare to approach him? Now, however, we are encouraged to draw near to the Throne of Grace himself: because we know that he has borne our weakness and sorrows, we cannot doubt that he who has tasted these realities will have compassion on us.*

*De gradibus 3.9; PL 182:946C; SB 3:23

In a spiritual sense Jesus himself *advanced in wisdom and age and grace with God and men*, and suffered, and rose again, and so entered into his glory: may he show his followers how we can advance in virtues and pass through sufferings to eternal joys.‡

‡*Bede, Hom ev 1.17; PL 94:90D [1.17; CL 122:120–21]*

***R 19**

*This holy and beloved city of Nazareth, in which *the Word was made flesh*,* is rightly interpreted as *flower*, because here that blossom whose fragrance is unequalled sprouted in the Virgin's womb. This town can boast a unique and great privilege: in her the Lord who is our salvation was begotten; here, too, he was raised; here the Son to whom the Father subjects all things in heaven and on earth was himself subject to his human parents.*

*John 1:14

**de Vitry 37*

✠

Lord Jesus Christ, Son of the living God, your sorrowing parents sought you for three days, and at last they found you in the temple. Grant that I, a poor sinner, will desire you, and in desiring seek you, and seeking, find you, and finding, love you, and loving you, make reparation for my sins, and making reparation, will not return to them again. You give to those who ask, you show yourself to those who seek, you open to those who knock: do not deny to the least what you have promised to all. Returning to Nazareth in obedience to your parents, you were subject to them, giving us a model of obedience. Grant that, stubborn as I am, I may overcome my self-will so that I may be subject to you, and to every human creature for your sake. Amen.

CHAPTER 16

What the Lord Jesus Did between the Years of Twelve and Thirty

(Luke 2:51-52)

*R 1

*Luke 2:51

*The Lord Jesus left the temple and went back with his parents to Nazareth, *and was subject to them*.* He continued to live with them until he was thirty years old. The Scriptures tell us nothing of what he did during all that time, and this is truly remarkable. How can we meditate on what took place during those years? Was the Lord Jesus idle all that time, so that he did nothing worthy of being recorded in the gospels? If he did do things, why were they not written down, as his later actions were? This is something altogether amazing. Perhaps the Scriptures remain silent lest the activities of his youth be made too much of. But attend very carefully to a truth that is very evident: by doing nothing, Jesus did great things. None of his actions is devoid of spiritual meaning; his words and deeds were virtuous, and so were his silence and hidden life.*

**Massa; MVC 15; CM 153:64–65*

We must believe, as the learned Gregory affirms, that until he reached man's estate Jesus did not perform any great signs and wonders but was content to live an ordinary life.* This is why John the Baptist could say of him, *There has stood one in the midst of you, whom you know not*.* And Luke sums up all these years in one short phrase: *And he went down with them and was subject to them*.* Thomas Aquinas writes, "During

*Graecus? CA Luke 2:51–52

*John 1:26

*Luke 2:51

the time between his birth and baptism Christ did not perform any miracles but lived a life like others, and his powers were hidden from everyone. He did no wonders because the mystery of the incarnation might be thought illusory if he had comported himself differently from other people his age. Jesus delayed the manifestation of his knowledge and power until the stage of life when mature human beings customarily display these traits."* *Com John 1:31

At length this greatest of masters would teach a virtuous way of life, but he began to perform virtuous acts from his youth in a wondrous but unknown way, hitherto unheard of: he appeared in the eyes of others to be useless, unimportant, and simple. This is how we might picture Christ's hidden life and meditate upon it devoutly, although I would not be so bold as to assert that this was necessarily the case. This is how I will present the details of Christ's life for which the Scriptures themselves give no information, a principle I enunciated in the Prologue of this work.* *Massa; MVC 15; CM 153:65*

Jesus distanced himself from the company of other people and their distractions, devoting himself intensely to contemplation. He went frequently to the synagogue and stood there in prayer, customarily taking the last and most humble place. He returned home and helped his mother and foster father, and in coming and going he passed among people as though they were not there. *Everyone marveled at seeing ***R 2**
such an impressive young man doing nothing that seemed worthy of special praise. They had expected him to perform great signs and the works of a proven man; after all, when he was a boy *Jesus advanced in wisdom and age and grace with God and men.** But as he *Luke 2:52
reached the age of twenty, and then twenty-five and beyond, and had done nothing remarkable, they were very surprised; they ridiculed him and generally held him in contempt. He had spoken truly of himself through the words of the prophet in this way: *I am a*

*worm, and no man, the reproach of men, and the outcast of the people. All they that saw me have laughed me to scorn, they have spoken with the lips, and tossed the head.**

*Ps 21:7-8; *Massa; MVC 15; CM 153:66*

He presented himself as abject and worthless to everyone. Does this strike you as unimportant? He himself was not in need, but in fact nothing is held to be greater or more difficult to achieve by our labors than this. It seems that he attained the highest and most challenging level of human existence: heart and soul, he was in truth so much the ruler of his own life and had such complete control over his body that he was indifferent to the fact that he was held in no esteem and everyone looked down on him.*

**Massa; MVC 15; CM 153:66*

Were you to reach this level, nothing would be lacking to you. As the Lord himself said, we are only useless servants even when we do good;* if we have not attained this degree of humility, we are not standing in the truth but are lingering and walking in folly. Let us not lead ourselves astray: as the apostle says, *For if any man think himself to be something, whereas he is nothing, he deceives himself.** In whatever we do that pertains to our salvation, there is no service or medicine more useful than for us to consider ourselves to be useless and contemptible. Whoever treats us like this is our helper because he does what we have been doing, or should have been doing, for our salvation. When others do us an injury, let us treat them with courtesy and friendliness; if we injure another, we should be ashamed and beg forgiveness.* We should see our enemies and those who hurt us as our friends and helpers, view the harm they do us as a great blessing, and never cease to give thanks to God for them.

*Luke 17:10

*Gal 6:3

**Massa; MVC 15; CM 153:66*

R 3

*Someone has suggested that the humble rejoice when despised and mourn when honored, weep in prosperity and celebrate in adversity, fear riches and grieve over luxuries, are tormented by abundance and glory in poverty, disdain fleeting praise and consider themselves unworthy of honor, abhor hypocrisy and are strangers to posing. They love the truth, forget temporal gains and long for eternal ones, choose to ignore worldly benefits in order to gain heavenly ones; they never presume on their own abilities, and, should they possess abilities or graces, they do not attribute them to themselves. They ascribe nothing to their own merits or powers but give the credit to divine mercy. They would prefer to hide their virtues if this could be done without harm to their neighbor, so as to avoid the temptation to vainglory. *Who is* such a one, *and we will praise him*?* Bernard writes, "To seek praise for humility is to destroy the virtue in it. Truly humble people prefer to pass unnoticed rather than have their humility extolled in public. They are happy to be overlooked; if they have any pride at all it consists in despising praise."*

*Sir 31:9

*SC 16.10; PL 183:853B; SB 1:95

If you ask me why the Lord lived like this, I answer that it was not from his necessity, but for our instruction; there is no excuse for our not learning the lesson. It is utterly abominable for mere grubs, who will soon be food for worms, to exalt themselves when the Lord of majesty humbly debased himself. If someone objects that it is absurd to think that Jesus lived such an unproductive life, or that the evangelists omitted to record his many deeds, or makes similar claims, the correct response is that, far from being useless, his lowly behavior provides a great example of virtue: in fact, it is the foundation of all virtues. Saint Bernard agrees with me on this point, as we shall see at the end of the chapter on the Lord's baptism.* Whatever the actual condition of our Lord's life in Nazareth may have been, it is helpful to meditate on it in this way.‡

*Part 1, chap. 21

‡*Massa; MVC 15; CM 153:66–67*

*You see how *Jesus* first *began to do and* then *to teach*.† He himself would later say, *Learn of me, because I am meek, and humble of heart*.* He wanted to illustrate this saying by his own behavior, and to show that whatever he did truly came from a heart that was meek and humble. Jesus was a stranger to all pretense: the

***R 4**

†Acts 1:1

*Matt 11:29

foundation of his life was a profound self-abasement, and so he appeared useless in the sight of others. This is why when he later began to preach, delivering the most divine and elevated discourses, and to perform miraculous signs and wonders, his townsfolk refused to believe it and dismissed what they heard by remarking, *Is not this the carpenter's son?** and making other mocking and disrespectful comments. This understanding of Christ's hidden life echoes what the apostle said about the incarnation—*He emptied himself, taking the form of a servant**—and not just any kind of servant, but a useless servant by his humble and lowly behavior.‡

*Matt 13:55

*Phil 2:7

‡*Massa; MVC 15; CM 153:68*

R 5

*Study each of his actions: humility shines out in them all. He lovingly fashioned this virtue, that is, he showed us how to acquire it by humbling and lowering himself constantly in his own estimation and that of others, by continually carrying out the most humble, degrading labors. If you want to advance in humility, you must be humiliated and take on the most menial tasks. Bernard writes,

> Humility, to which humiliation certainly leads, is the foundation of the whole spiritual edifice. Humiliation leads to humility as surely as patience leads to peace and study leads to wisdom; if you hunger for humility, do not turn away from the path of humiliation. If you cannot bear to be humiliated, you will never attain humility. It is useful that my foolishness become known, and for me to be rightly confounded by the wise, I, who have often been unjustly praised by the foolish. In truth, it is dangerous for me to hear something about myself that is greater than what I perceive about myself.
>
> Who will do me the service of humbling me as I truly deserve before others, when I am falsely praised for the virtues I do not possess? I could make my own the words of the prophet, *Being*

*exalted, I have been humbled and troubled.** And also, *I will play and make myself meaner.** I will play and so become ludicrous. It is good sport when Michal is angered and God is delighted! It is good sport that provokes ridicule from people but offers a beautiful spectacle to the angels! It is good sport when we become *a reproach to the rich, and contempt to the proud.** He took part in this chaste and holy playfulness who said, *We are made a spectacle to the world and to angels and to men.** Let us for now enter into this game to be ridiculed, confounded, and humiliated—until he returns who will cast down the proud and raise up the lowly. Then he will give us joy and glory, and exalt us for ever.*

*Ps 87:16
*2 Sam 6:22
*Ps 122:4
*1 Cor 4:9
*Ep 87.11–12; PL 182:217AD; SB 7:230–31; *Massa; MVC 15; CM 153:69–70*

Elsewhere Bernard says,

Those who strive toward the spiritual heights must have a low opinion of themselves; otherwise, when they are raised up they may lose their hold on themselves unless they keep a firm grip through true humility. It is only when humility warrants it that great graces can be obtained; hence those to be enriched by them are first humbled by correction, that by their humility they may merit them. So when you see that you are being humiliated, take it as a sure sign that grace is on the way. Just *as the spirit is lifted up before a fall,** so it is humiliated before being honored.

*Prov 16:18

You read in Scripture of these two modes of acting, how *God resists the proud and gives grace to the humble.** Did he not decide to reward his servant Job with generous blessings after the outstanding victory in which his great patience was put to the severest test? The many onerous trials that humbled him prepared him for blessings. But it matters little if we willingly accept the humiliation that comes from God himself if we do not adopt a similar attitude when he humiliates us by means of another.

*Jas 4:6

I want you to take note of a wonderful instance of this in holy David, that time when he was cursed by a servant and paid no heed to the repeated insults, so sensitive was he to the influence of grace. He merely said, *What have I to do with you, sons of Zeruiah?** Truly this was a man after God's own heart, who chose to be angry with the one who would avenge him rather than with the one who reviled him! Hence David could say with a clear conscience, *If I have rendered to them that repaid me evils, let me deservedly fall empty before my enemies.** He would not allow them to silence this abusive scoundrel; to him the curses were gain. While the wicked tongue raged against him, his mind was intent on discovering the hidden purpose of God. The voice of the reviler sounded in his ears, but in his heart he disposed himself for blessings. Hence he says, *It is good for me that you have humbled me, that I may learn your justifications.**

*2 Sam 16:10

*Ps 7:5

*Ps 118:71

You see that humility makes us righteous. I say humility and not humiliation. How many are humiliated who are not humble! Some people meet humiliation resentfully, others patiently, still others willingly. The first kind are culpable, the second are innocent, the last just. Innocence is indeed a part of justice, but only the humble possess it perfectly. *God gives grace to the humble,** not to the humiliated. The person is truly humble who turns humiliation into humility and can say to God with David, *It is good for me that you have humbled me.*‡

*Jas 4:6
‡SC 34.1–3; PL 183:960A–61A; SB 1:245–47; *Massa; MVC 15; CM 153:70*

***R 6**

*Many are the exercises of humility and humiliation available to us, and of these Bernard writes,

There are five things that can assist us to experience humility. First, a love of lowliness, so that we seek out those circumstances that seem adverse. Second, the constant practice of subjection, so that we always want to be with someone we respect and fear in order to learn how to break our own will. Third, comparison with a better person, so that we should always be a companion to one in whom we find a grace lacking in ourselves; forgetting those things we have left behind, we should always strain toward those that lie before us. Fourth, constant meditation on our condition, so that at the first stirrings of pride these words will come to mind: *Why are earth and ashes proud?** Fifth, remembrance of the one who watches us secretly. If we frequently confess speaking words out of arrogance, how can we help but be thrown into confusion if we notice our confessor is in earshot when later we say something of the same sort? Similarly, when we remember that there is one who watches secretly and to whom our thoughts make confession, we cannot but be ashamed if we engage in prideful thoughts. And it is extremely beneficial, not only against pride but against all the vices, for us to realize that God is always watching us, to give heed to his gaze in our heart, and to consider what we should do as if it were of concern only to God.*

*Sir 10:9

*Sent 3.16; SB 6:2:74–75

We must continually strive for humility, without which we cannot make progress in the spiritual life or develop any other virtues. Again, Bernard counsels us, "Humility is so essential to the life of virtue that without it the other traits do not seem to be virtues at all. If you have charity, or any other virtue, you have earned it by your humility, because *God gives grace to the humble.** You preserve the virtues you have received by humility, because *the Spirit rests only upon one who is tranquil and humble.*[1]* The virtues you have preserved reach their perfection by humility, *because power is made perfect in infirmity,*‡ that is, humility."†

°First, humility wins grace for us. Hence the psalmist says, "*You send forth springs in the vales*, that is, you

*Jas 4:6

*Isa 66:2
‡2 Cor 12:9
†Ep 42.5.17; PL 182:821A; SB 7:113–14
°**R 7**

[1] *Super quem requiescet spiritus meus nisi super quietum et humilem corde?* This differs from the Vulg but is found as far back as John Cassian, Institutes 12.31 (PL 49:473A).

give grace to the humble; *between the midst of the hills the waters shall pass."** These hills represent two kinds of pride: the first is born of temporal blessings, the second of spiritual ones; the valley of humility is nestled between these two mountains, and the waters of grace avoid these and flow down.

*Ps 103:11

Second, humility earns an increase of grace: those who desire to receive further graces from God do not think that they are important; they humble themselves. Three signs indicate that we have not been made proud by graces received: we do not want more deference paid to us than to another because of these graces or virtues, we are prepared to endure contempt, inconvenience, and labors just like everyone else, and we do not consider such misfortunes to be an injury, but our just reward.

Third, humility conserves the graces received: just as ashes shelter a fire, so humility protects the spiritual embers of grace. A fire can also be kept going by adding wood, and grace increases when good works are added to it. Also, a fire is kept alive by blowing on it, and grace is kept alive by the breath of fervent meditation. Finally, a fire is kept going by keeping away anything that can extinguish it, and grace is kept burning when we avoid the occasions of sin and evil company.

Christ Works with His Own Hands

*R 8

*But let us return to our examination of the life and deeds of our model, the Lord Jesus, which is the purpose of our study. Let us be present to and contemplate in every way the poor, lowly existence of that small but highly exalted family. The blessed old man Joseph exercised the carpenter's trade to the best of his ability; our Lady worked with needle and thread, prepared meals for her husband and son, and performed all the household chores herself, since they had no servants. Unite yourself with her in her tasks, having to work with her own hands. Enter, too, into the labors of the Lord Jesus, who helped her in every way he could; as he himself said, *The Son of Man has not come to be ministered to, but to minister*.* Watch him carefully as he performs the humblest household chores, and study our Lady and elderly Joseph working to support themselves.*

*Matt 20:28

**Massa; MVC 15; CM 153:70–71*

Basil writes, "Obedient from his first years to his parents, he reverently and humbly endured all bodily labors. His parents were honest and just, but they were also very poor and lacked many necessities of life (as the manger bears witness), and so they had to earn what they needed by the sweat of their brow. Jesus showed himself completely obedient to them even in his labors."*

*Const Ascet 4.6; PG 31:1356D

Observe the three of them eating together daily at one table, not dining sumptuously or luxuriously, but sharing poor and simple fare. After dinner they talk together, not engaging in foolish and empty chatter, but speaking words imbued with the wisdom of the Holy Spirit, conversation that refreshes the soul as well as the body. After their recreation, we see them retire to pray in their small bedrooms. Picture those three modest beds, and watch the Lord Jesus taking his rest late at night after prolonged prayer. This was his nightly custom for many years; he lived in a humble, self-effacing way and persevered in this lifestyle like his poorest neighbors. Every night let us picture him resting on his bed after his day's labors, share his feelings, and commend ourselves humbly and devoutly to him.*

**Massa; MVC 15; CM 153:71*

***R 9**

*In the midst of such affliction and poverty, his loving mother's heart overflowed with joy because of the presence of such a son. Anselm asks,

> Who can imagine with what joy her whole being was suffused, when he whom she loved so deeply, and whom she knew to be the Creator and Lord of

all things, lived with her, and ate with her, and who with sweet words taught her all she could desire to know?* Who is able to comprehend what wondrous, ineffable, loving affection such a mother must have lavished upon such a son, and such a son gave to such a mother? Perhaps those who can concentrate all their love on one object, as a mother does her child and a child his mother, might be able to gain some idea of this. But let no one think that even this degree of affection can begin to equal the love this mother felt for her son. Whoever is worthy to understand this love, in my opinion, can never be a stranger to its sweetness; whoever tastes this love need never doubt that one day he will share in the recompense that is his reward.*

*Eadmer, De exc 4; PL 159:566A

*Eadmer, De exc 4; PL 159:565A

***R 10**

*You have seen what poverty, abasement, and harsh conditions the eternal Lord and King of Kings embraced for many long years in his vigils, his sleep, his abstinence, and all his labors for our sake. Where are the seekers of leisure and comfort, luxuries and ornaments, vanities and opulence? Those who long for such things have not been instructed by this teacher. Surely we are not wiser than he? He himself has taught us lowliness, poverty, and hard work. Let us follow in the footsteps of this greatest Master, who neither wishes to deceive nor can be deceived, and, according to the teaching of the apostle, *having* sufficient *food and* what is necessary *wherewith to be covered, with these we are content.** Let us persevere as well, vigilantly and ceaselessly, in our pursuit of virtues and our study of spiritual truth.*

*1 Tim 6:8

**Massa; MVC 15; CM 153:72*

Inspired by what the Lord has done, let us review frequently the lesson of our own insignificance: may we not only appraise ourselves in this way, but lower ourselves in the sight of others by assuming the most menial and degrading tasks. Keep before you your defects and your sins, and bear their weight to the best of your ability. As to others' defects, cast them behind your back and pay them no heed. Should you see them, take pains to excuse them and be lenient; feel compassion for those who have them and help them, mindful always that you would do worse things yourself, did not the grace of Jesus Christ prevent it. Turn the eyes of both your body and your soul from others, so that you can see yourself in the light of God's holy countenance. There is no more effective means of humbling yourself than to examine well your own life.

Bernard writes. "I wish therefore that before everything else you should know yourself, because this knowledge gives humility rather than self-importance and provides a basis on which to build. Unless there is a solid foundation of humility, the spiritual edifice has no hope of standing. And there is nothing more effective, more adapted to the acquiring of humility, than to learn the truth about oneself. There must be no dissimulation, no attempt at self-deception, but a facing up to one's real self without flinching and turning aside."*As Augustine observes, the knowledge of our own misery is the broad highway to beatitude.‡

*SC 36.5; PL 183:969D; SB 2:7

‡Sermone monte 1.12.36; PL 34:1247; CL 35:39

Let us examine ourselves constantly and judge ourselves honestly. If we hold up for scrutiny each of our actions, our words, and our thoughts, we will find plenty of material for compunction; even the good we have done has been half-hearted and lacking in conviction or fervor, and of no more value than a filthy rag. *We should also reflect often, and with trepidation, on the fact that any aptitude we enjoy for doing good, any grace we possess, any solicitude we feel for gaining virtue, is not due to us: Christ in his mercy has given them to us, and he could just as easily bestow these gifts on some other rogue and leave us wallowing in the miserable mire. ***R 11**

How can we possibly take the credit for such things, as if we were their author, when we know by experience how often we of ourselves are unable to do good, in small things as well as great, and recognize that frequently we are incapable of doing the good that we wish to do? And would we even conceive of doing such good deeds, except because a sudden divine inspiration imparts a wondrous fervor in us to carry out these works that, with all our knowledge, we would otherwise not be able to accomplish? God allows this sense of impotence to hold sway over us for long periods of time so that we will learn to humble ourselves: in this way, we will not foolishly boast about ourselves but attribute all the good to God—and not only with the lip service that is customary, but in the depths of our hearts.

Let us reflect further that there is no scoundrel or sinner who would not have served his God better, or been more grateful, than we if he had received the graces that we have received, graces bestowed because of God's goodness, not our merit. Such thoughts help us to see ourselves as more base and lowly than others. And, lest Christ drive us from his presence because of our ingratitude, we might with cause tremble and take the sins of others onto ourselves to awaken our sleeping consciences: "See, that man is a murderer; but how often have I murdered my soul? This one is an adulterer and a fornicator; but I commit adultery and fornication all day long, by turning my eyes from God and putting the devil's suggestions in his place," and so on.

We should foster two attitudes about ourselves. First, to see ourselves as a fetid, rotting cadaver, devoured by worms, the kind of corpse from which people avert their eyes in order to avoid seeing such a horrible sight, and hold their noses so as not to smell such a terrible stench.[2] And, if someone were to do

[2] This sentence jars on our modern sensibilities. However, when we recall that Ludolph lived during the time of the Black Death, we realize that the sight he describes was commonplace.

justice to our body, we would consider it just to have our eyes plucked out, and our ears and nose cut off, along with the other members of our body, because we have offended God with these senses. Far from resenting such treatment, we would gladly welcome all the insults, reproaches, and attacks that can be imagined; we would drink them in like wine, and receive them with the greatest joy, with a smile on our lips, our faces beaming. All who see us behaving like this would marvel, and examine their own lives, and know that such things could not be done without God.

Second, we must banish self-reliance completely, turn away from our good works, indeed our whole way of life, and rest in the arms of Jesus Christ, who became the poorest, the humblest, the most taunted, the most despised of people, and who died for our sake; there we must die to all human attachments, so that Jesus Christ crucified may live in our hearts and souls, totally transformed, transfigured, and alive. Welcoming these sentiments in the depths of our souls, we will see and hear nothing but Jesus hanging on the cross, dead for our sake. Following the example of the Blessed Virgin, we will die to the world but live by faith. In that faith we shall live our entire lives up to the day of resurrection, when God will send spiritual joy and the gift of the Holy Spirit into our hearts, and into the hearts of *all them also that love his coming*.* *2 Tim 6:8

*By reflecting on our Lord's hidden life we can ***R 12**
deepen our humility, which is the mother and source of all other virtues: the eyes of our souls will be fixed on God and our hearts purged of all superfluous thoughts. Let us call to mind our insignificance, despise ourselves, reprove ourselves, and think ourselves to be of no account; when we occupy ourselves with such meditations, all useless and vain ideas wither and die. Pushing away the daily distractions that we see and hear, we can consign them to oblivion and begin to turn our attention to ourselves and reflect

on our true state of affairs; we can begin to draw near to our original justice and spiritual purity. As we reflect on ourselves in this way our contemplative eye will open, and we can set up within ourselves the ladder that leads to the contemplation of angelic and spiritual realities. Just as those who want to look at the sun must avert their eyes from all other visible things, so the soul must turn away from material things. By means of such contemplation the soul is inflamed by a love of spiritual goods, viewing earthly concerns from a distance and appraising them to be worthless by comparison. Then the fire of charity can be lit, and this will burn away the rust of the vices. When love fills such a soul, there is no way for foolish pride to slip in; whatever is thought, or said, or done, will be dictated by charity.

In order to stay the course, we must retain a spirit of awe, recognize that all comes from God, and beg him for the gift of perseverance. And, if we are not to fall, we must not judge others or angrily rebuke them. If we see them erring in any way, let us feel sorrow for them in our hearts, pray earnestly for them, and sincerely excuse them as best we can, mindful that neither they nor we can do anything unless the gracious Christ stretches out his hand, as he does because of his generous good will, not on the basis of our merits. If we think in this way, we will stand firm.

Why do many begin to fast strictly or engage in other mortifications only to find that their bodies become listless and their fervor grows cold, so that they do not persevere? Doubtless this is due to their self-exaltation and pride: secure in themselves, they condemn others and judge them in their hearts, so God takes away his gift from them, and they become worse than those whom they had earlier condemned. When someone judges another for some failing, it often happens that God eventually allows that person to fall into the same sin, or one even worse. Let us, then, serve the Lord in holy fear, and if the recollection of some benefit bestowed by the Most High tempts us to pride, let us *embrace the discipline* of rebuke and self-correction, *lest at any time the Lord be angry, and we perish from the just way** and fall. *Ps 2:12

In brief, let us heed Anselm's useful advice: "Examine very carefully your interior dispositions and external acts, and see where they lead. And I believe, unless you are insane, you will undertake those things that lead to happiness and joy and reject those that gain for you only sadness and torment."* *Ralph of Battle? Med 4; PL 158:730D

✠

O gentle Jesus, model of patience and example of humility, take from me all arrogant pride, all hunger for vainglory, and all the evil plagues that attend these vices. Lord, may there not be, or even appear to be, such great evils, such signs of perdition in your servant: in your presence, may they be banished from my conduct, my thoughts, my words, and my deeds. Ground me in true and sincere humility, so that I may give no foothold to the wiles of my enemies. May I be small in my own sight, so that I may be found full of grace in the eyes of your majesty. Amen.

CHAPTER 17

The Mission and Life of John the Baptist

(Matt 3:1-10; Luke 3:1-4)

*R 1

*Passing over in silence all the other deeds from the Savior's childhood, the evangelists devoted themselves to describing the words and acts of Christ when he reached the age of perfect adulthood, and the first of these was the baptism he received from John. Before considering this, however, let us meditate on the mystery and office of John the Baptist and the baptism of repentance he proclaimed.

*R 2
*Matt 3:1
*in illo tempore
*procurante
*Luke 3:1

And in those days Jesus was still living in Nazareth. The initial words set the stage for what follows, like the words *at that time,** which introduce the proclamation of the gospel in church. So that time was *the fifteenth year of the reign of Tiberius Caesar*, who had succeeded Octavian Augustus, under whom Christ had been born; *Pontius Pilate being governor** and ruler *of Judea, and Herod* still *being tetrarch of Galilee, and Philip his brother* still *tetrarch of Iturea and the country of Trachonitis, and Lysanias still tetrarch of Abilina.**

Here we should recall, as was explained earlier, that the Jewish kingdom had been divided into four *tetrarchies*. Archelaus had been given charge of two of them, Judea and Abilene, and Philip had been given the other two. Archelaus ruled ruthlessly and was denounced to Augustus as a tyrant. Augustus deposed Archelaus and exiled him after he had reigned for ten years. It was at this time that Roman officials and procurators began to govern part of his territory, Judea. The fifth such was Pontius Pilate, so called because he resided on the island of Ponza. He was not an ordinary governor, but a vicar or delegate; hence his title of *procurator*. If at times the word *governor** is used of him, this should be understood as procurator. Vitellius was the governor of Syria, which took in the region of Judea. It may be that Pilate was sometimes referred to as governor because he carried out some of the governor's functions. Lysanias was given the other part of Archelaus's realm and became tetrarch of Abilene. Some think that this Lysanias was the son of Herod of Ascalon, under whom Christ was born, but Josephus says that he was Herod's nephew, the son of his sister Alexandra, and that his father was Ptolemy of Lebanon, and this seems more likely.[1]

**praeses*

The evangelist adds, *Under the high priests Annas and Caiphas*.* These two men were relatives and exercised the high priesthood in turns; Annas held the office in the year the Lord was baptized, and Caiaphas in the year he died. Three others held the office in the intervening three years, Ishmael, Eleazar, and Simon, but the gospels are silent about these men, mentioning

*Luke 3:2

[1] The title of procurator is slightly anachronistic in Pilate's case; the term did not come into use until the reign of the Emperor Claudius, ca. AD 44. An inscription found in 1961 confirms that Pilate held the title of prefect (*praefectus*). Bede, following Eusebius of Caesarea, believed that Lysanias was Herod's son (PL 92:351B). Josephus mentions a Lysanias, son of Ptolemy, who was killed by Mark Antony in 36 BC, and on this ground some have questioned Luke's historical accuracy. But Josephus also speaks of a later Lysanias and refers to "Abila, which had been the Lysanian tetrarchy" (Ant 20.7.1); two inscriptions also make reference to a later Lysanias. His exact identity remains mysterious, as does Luke's reason for mentioning the ruler of a small tetrarchy in Syria.

only who was high priest when John began to preach and when Christ died.[2]

The mention of the emperor, high priest, and governor provides a certain solemnity to the description of John's preaching, in order to designate the excellence of the man he had come to announce, inasmuch as Christ is the greatest emperor and high priest, and the governor of all that exists.‡

‡*Lyra Luke 3:2 mor*

***R 3**

The word of the Lord was made to John, the son of Zachary, in the desert. The communication was a heavenly inspiration that was called a *word* because it was spoken within John's mind, similar to what we read in the psalm, *I will hear what the Lord God will speak in me.** John was in his thirtieth year, the time of life appropriate for preaching, because he was in the full flower of manhood: the moment had come for him to baptize and proclaim the coming of the Christ and announce the consolation of salvation.

*Luke 3:2

*Ps 84:9

John heard the word of the Lord through an inner inspiration, a divine revelation spoken to his mind from above.* Chrysostom points out that here the word of the Lord was in fact a command: John did not take on this ministry by his own initiative, but by God's order.* This is why he himself said, *He who sent me to baptize with water.*‡ John emerged from the wilderness where he was doing penance and had already begun to preach, so that his preaching would have greater effect and those who were converted by his message would not have to delay baptism because of the scarcity of water. *And he came into all the country about the Jordan*, where both water and people were plentiful, baptizing and *preaching the baptism of penance for the remission of sins*.*

**Zachary 1.13; PL 186:90A*

*Hom Matt 10.1; PG 57/58:185

‡John 1:33

*Luke 3:3

In this way John gave an example to preachers that they should seek out places to preach because the

[2] Josephus (Ant 18.2.2) locates the high priesthood of Ishmael, Eleazar, and Simon later in the first century.

word of God will bear more fruit there, and not because they find the location pleasing.* *Lyra Luke 3:3 mor

John's Baptism

*The baptism of John prepared people to receive Christ, so only Jews were baptized because the promise of a Messiah had been made primarily to them. Women were not baptized, because they had to be instructed by their husbands, and children were not baptized because they did not yet possess the intelligence and understanding necessary for this mystery. Christ's baptism, on the other hand, is given to everyone regardless of race, age, or sex, for the forgiveness of sins. The phrase for *the remission of sins* refers not to John's baptism, but to the repentance associated with it, because only this repentance brings about forgiveness. The baptism of John was indeed a baptism of repentance, because he admonished those who sought baptism to repent, and he only baptized adults who he saw were repentant. Although their sins were not taken away by the baptism itself, their reception of it was a kind of declaration that they were doing penance, and it was through this means that their sins were forgiven. *R 4

John's baptism was for *the remission of sins* not efficaciously, but inasmuch as it prepared the way for Christ's baptism, which does bring about the forgiveness of sins. John's was a baptism of repentance to the extent that it involved doing penance for one's sins, but it could not take away sins. Christ's is a baptism of grace because it is given in Christ and removes sin. According to Chrysostom, the first baptism was given in penance, the second in grace; the first for pardon, the second for victory.[3]* It should be noted, according *Jerome, Trac in Mark 1:4; CL 78:453

[3] Jerome understood any forgiveness associated with John's baptism to be dependent on the sanctification coming from Christ: Contra Lucif 7 (PL 23:162B).

to Gregory Nazianzen, that there are five different kinds of baptism. The first is figurative, in water only: the baptism of Moses in the cloud and in the sea. The next is preparatory: the baptism of John, which we are considering here. The third is perfect: the baptism of Christ given in the Spirit. The fourth is the baptism of blood through martyrdom, which goes beyond the call of duty and is more noble than the others because, once received, it can never be soiled by sin. The fifth is the baptism of tears, shed daily to wash away actual sins, and this is more difficult than the others.‡

‡Orat 39.16; PG 36:354C

*R 5

John's baptism was preparatory because it was necessary for people to be prepared for Christ by his baptism; in relation to Christ's baptism, it can be understood to be a kind of catechesis by which those to be baptized are instructed in the faith and prepared for the true baptism. Remigius of Auxerre writes, "John's baptism was a kind of figure of catechumens. Just as children are catechized to prepare them to receive the sacrament of baptism worthily, so those baptized by John lived so devoutly afterwards that they were worthy to approach Christ's baptism." Chrysostom says, "Rightly then after saying that he came *preaching the baptism of penance*, Luke adds *for the remission of sins*. It was as if he were saying, 'The reason he was persuading them to repent was so that they would receive pardon more easily later by believing in Christ,' wherefore John's baptism had no other purpose than as a preparation for faith."*

*Hom 3; PL 131:884B

*Hom Matt 10.2; PG 57/58:186

This is why John baptized in the Jordan, a word meaning *descent*, because this signified those who were putting off the old self by descending from the pedestal of pride to humble confession and amendment, thereby being found worthy to be renewed in Christ.[4] It was also fitting that John baptized in the Jordan River as a kind of declaration of undertaking

[4] Ps-Jerome renders *Jordan* as *their descent* (PL 23:1228).

penance to approach the kingdom of heaven and pass over into the land of the living, just as the children of Israel crossed the Jordan to enter the Promised Land.

John baptized for many reasons. First, according to Augustine, to signify Christ's baptism, and thus in this way it was sacramental;‡ second, according to Chrysostom, to draw many people to him, so that he could speak to them about Christ;* third, according to Gregory, so that people would be familiar with Christ's baptism by means of John's;* fourth, according to Bede, so that people would be humbled and prepared by John's baptism to receive Christ's;† fifth, according to John himself, so that the Christ could be made manifest in Israel by John's baptism, the Father's voice, and the Holy Spirit.*

‡Contra Petiliani 2.37.87; PL 43:289–90

*Hom Matt 10.2; PG 57/58:186

*40 Hom 20.2; PL 76:1161A; CL 141:155

†Hom ev 1.3; PL 94:23A [1.1; CL 122:2]

*John 1:31-33

John's Preaching

*First in the wilderness, and afterward in the area of the Jordan, John said to those who came to him, moved by a desire to change their lives, *Do penance, for the kingdom of heaven is at hand*.* That is, "Let each one do penance for past wickedness, because the kingdom of heaven is near for those who do." According to Remigius, *the kingdom of heaven* has four meanings: Christ himself, for *the kingdom of God is within you;** sacred Scripture, for *the kingdom of God shall be taken from you and shall be given to a nation yielding the fruits thereof;** holy church, for *the kingdom of heaven can be likened to ten virgins;** and the heavenly realm, for *many shall come from the east and the west, and shall sit down in the kingdom of heaven*.* And all four meanings are intended here.*

***R 6**

*Matt 3:2

*Luke 17:21

*Matt 21:43

*Matt 25:1

*Matt 8:11

*Hom 3; PL 131:880A

Penance must not be undertaken too late, as with the damned; or under coercion, like thieves; or fictitiously, as by hypocrites, or desperately, as by those who are lost. It must be done sincerely: genuine penance, in Chrysostom's opinion, purifies the heart, illumines the mind, and prepares us at the core of our being to welcome Christ.* Jerome for his part says, "John the Baptist is the first to preach the kingdom of heaven, so that the Lord's forerunner should be honored by this privilege."‡

*Chrysologus, Sermo 42 approx; PL 52:318A
‡Com Matt 3:1; PL 26:29A; CL 77:16
†Damian

Peter† of Ravenna points out that after Adam's sin and the terrible catastrophe of the Flood, God chose many just persons with whom he deigned to speak face to face. He names many patriarchs, fathers, and prophets of the Old Testament, but then he notes that none of them ever mentioned the eternal dwelling place of the kingdom of heaven—none of them remembered, or named, or heard about, or prophesied this glorious kingdom. He goes on,

> What more? Call to mind all the elect from the beginning of the world to John, and in none of their words or works can you discover the sweetness of that heavenly kingdom. When I come to John, I hear that voice of exultation and joy, that word of mercy, that discourse of glory, that abundance of grace concealed by God, unspoken by angels, hidden by patriarchs, and unknown by prophets: *Do penance, for the kingdom of heaven is at hand*. A sweet word calling to repentance, a joyful word announcing the kingdom of heaven; it is fitting that this word should be proclaimed by the one who laid the foundations for the New Testament.
>
> From the days of Adam up to John, our organ of speech became an instrument of mourning: the abundance of sin and the absence of repentance provided a double incentive for weeping. But with John's coming we discover medicine for our wounds, penance for our sins, forgiveness for our iniquity. His voice, the voice in the wilderness, was the first to proclaim it. *The voice of the turtle dove is heard in our land*,* and *he put a new canticle into my mouth, a song to our God*;* a voice of praise and thanksgiving resounds from our lips. Mercy triumphs, sinners are pardoned, piety reigns, the sword of justice is sheathed, and the compassion-

*Song 2:12
*Ps 39:4

ate Lord seeks occasion to bestow clemency rather than wounds."* *Sermo 23; PL 144:633AD

John's Holiness

The evangelist described John's mode of life to show that he was worthy to bear witness to Christ. First he mentions his coarse clothing: John wore a rough *garment of camel's hair*.* This teaches us to wear uncomfortable clothing to check the desires of the flesh. Jerome writes, "It says he wore a garment of hair, not wool; the former is an indication of austerity, the latter of luxury and softness."* And Chrysostom says, "It befits the servants of God to use clothing to cover nakedness, not to make an elegant appearance or to cosset the body. Thus John does not wear a soft and delicate robe, but one that is rough, heavy, and uncomfortable, a garment that chafed rather than caressed the skin. The very clothing of his body proclaimed the virtue of his mind."*

***R 7** **Lyra Matt 3:4* *Matt 3:4 *Com Matt 3:4; PL 26:29C; CL 77:17 *Opus imperf 3; PG 56:648

Next the evangelist commends John's continence, noting that he wore *a leather belt*, that is, a rough belt made from the dried skins of animals, *about his loins*,* the dwelling place of luxury, to mortify his flesh. *They that are Christ's have crucified their flesh, with the vices and concupiscences*.* Again, Chrysostom: "It was customary among the Jews to wear a belt made of wool; but he wanted something rougher, so his belt was leather."* And this father elsewhere offers an allegorical interpretation of John's garment and belt:

*Matt 3:4 *Gal 5:24 *Opus imperf 3; PG 56:648

> John, that is, the law embodied by John, wore a *garment of camel's hair*. It would not be fitting for him to wear a lamb's tunic, he who was to say, *Behold the Lamb of God. Behold him who takes away the sin of the world*.* And he wore *a leather belt around his loins* because the Jews held that sin could be imputed only to sinful actions. It is otherwise with our Lord Jesus Christ, who is seen in John's Apocalypse standing among seven candlesticks wearing

*John 1:29

*Rev 1:13

a golden belt, not around his loins, but around his breast.* The law controls actions only, but Christ and his Gospel go deeper: the virtue of monks consists not only of conduct, but of thoughts. The law condemned the act of fornication as a sin, but Christ also condemns the thought.*

*Jerome, Trac in Mark 1.4; CL 78:453

Third, the evangelist speaks of John's abstinence: *his meat was locusts*, that is, plants with that name, *and wild honey*,* the food of the poor in that part of the world. Note that the word *locusts* can refer to many things, as this verse suggests:

*Matt 3:4

> Say that locusts are roots, grasses, and birds.[5]

There are small insects in the Judean wilderness that fly by jumping; these are fried in oil and eaten by the poor.* But it does not seem that John ate the flesh of these insects: he had also given up eating bread and had no implements for cooking. It is more likely that the word refers to something else. A plant called *langusta* grew in that region, and it is said that this is what blessed John ate.[6] *Wild honey* made by bees is found in tree trunks, or, according to Rabanus Maurus, this refers to white, tender blossoms from trees that, when crushed in the hand, taste like honey. Small reeds* also grow in the region containing a sweet sap;* these are also called by the name sugar cane.*‡

*Lyra Matt 3:4

**calamellae*

**calami pleni melle*

**cannamelle*

‡Com Matt 3:4; PL 107:768C; CM 174:75

[5] *Radices, herbas et aves, dic esse locustas*. The source of the verse is unknown. Over the centuries some interpreters have maintained that John did in fact eat insects (locusts were considered a clean animal in the law), and others have suggested that the word meant a kind of plant or the tips of plants.

[6] The thirteenth-century pilgrim Jacques de Vitry reports visiting a Syrian monastery and asking a monk what John ate. "He straightway replied that in his refectory a herb was often set before the monks which they called *langustae*, or locust-bean, whereof a great quantity grew round about their monastery, and he added that this was what Saint John used to eat" (De Vitry 28).

By his poor clothing and meager diet of uncooked food John clearly teaches us to give no thought to this world and all its luxuries; he ordered his conduct so as to seek only what was necessary for life. His imitators are those who can say, *But having food and wherewith to be covered, with these we are content.** Since he was preaching repentance, John wanted to show how penitents should live, so that as a good teacher he could offer others an example and rule by his own mode of life. The ground was his bed, a cave his house, camel skin his clothing, leather his belt, water his drink, locusts his food. And he not only teaches us to avoid luxury; he also bequeaths to his followers a useful example of weeping for the sins of the entire human race. *1 Tim 6:8

Everything about John proclaimed penance: his name, which means *the grace of God;* his dwelling place, the desert; his clothing, a rough pelt; his food, locusts; his speech, a message of repentance; and his work, a baptism that trained others to goodness.* **Gorran Matt 3:4*

*John is the model for a preacher of the Gospel. First, as regards doctrine: following John's example, the preacher should call people to repentance so that they will turn away from sin and follow the path that leads to the kingdom of heaven. Second, as regards continence: just as it is said that he girded his loins with a leather belt, so the preacher should possess the virtue of chastity, as the Lord said when he commissioned Jeremiah to preach: *Therefore gird your loins.** Third, as regards his way of life, and this in two ways: the preacher should follow John's example in dress and diet. ***R 8** *Jer 1:17

One who preaches penance and enjoins austerity should live a penitential life, dressing poorly and eating sparingly; this in itself will be a rebuke to those who live lavishly. The preacher of the Gospel must be marked by austerity. This is why the apostle says, *But I chastise my body and bring it into subjection: lest perhaps, when I have preached to others, I myself should become a castaway.** *1 Cor 9:27; *Lyra Matt 3:4 mor*

Jerome counsels, "Preachers should embrace an austere lifestyle in matters of clothing, food, and drink."* And Chrysostom writes,

*Cumm Mark 1:6; PL 30:593A

> It was fitting that the Lord's Forerunner, the prophet and apostle of Christ, should be totally devoted to God and heavenly realities, and gave no thought to earthly pleasures. Not without reason did the Lord himself call him an angel, for he lived a truly angelic life in this world. Now he was so pure, so much brighter than the heavens, and so much greater than the prophets that it could be said that no one born of woman was greater than he; yet even he who rejoiced to hold such familiar converse with God undertook hard labors with great patience, despised the whole flood of riches and earthly pleasures, and embraced such a rigorous way of life. Then what excuse can we offer if, after having received so many blessings from Christ, and having been freed from an infinite number of weighty sins, we do not imitate even in some small way his self-denial? If, on the contrary, we devote ourselves to gluttony and drunkenness, and surround ourselves with the fragrance—or better, the stench—of exotic perfumes, and pamper ourselves by easy living, are we not readying ourselves to be the devil's prey and making ourselves his prisoners?*

*Com Matt 10.5 approx; PG 57/58:189

People Come Out to John

***R 9**

*****_Then_, as John's fame grew, *the citizens of Jerusalem went out to him and all* those living in *Judea, and all* the two and one half tribes dwelling in *the country about Jordan*.* (*All* here is a hyperbole, meaning that a great many people went out to him from all these places.) *And were baptized by him in the Jordan* with John's baptism, *confessing their sins*,* which was preparing them for Christ's baptism. John's baptism was ordained as

*Matt 3:5

*Matt 3:6

a kind of pre-figuration and preparation for Christ's baptism, which was fast approaching. John did not only preach, he also baptized: as his preaching announced the proximity of Christ's coming, so his baptism prepared people to receive Christ's baptism willingly. Therefore, John's baptism was a kind of profession of faith in the Messiah who was about to come, so that by doing works of penance the people could receive him with greater devotion when he arrived. We read in Acts, *John baptized the people with the baptism of penance saying: That they should believe in him, who was to come after him, that is to say, in Jesus.** It says *confessing their sins,* which were to be obliterated by Christ's coming; John could not wipe them away but proclaimed that this would be done by Christ.*

*Acts 19:4

**Lyra Matt 3:6*

R 10

And seeing many of the Pharisees and Sadducees,* not confessing their sins, but *coming* with the crowds *to* receive *his baptism,* not for religious reasons but as a pose for fear of the crowd, *he said to them, "You brood* and *offspring of vipers* (that is, progeny of venomous snakes), *who has taught you to flee from the wrath to come and evade severe judgment in the future although you are not repentant?" This was as if to say, "No one, unless you forsake your evil ways and do penance. Although you can conceal your deceit from the eyes of the people, you cannot hide it from God's Judgment, for then the secrets of your hearts will be made manifest."* Thus did he try to persuade them to turn from evil, so that by doing fitting penance they could avoid the retribution of future Judgment. For, according to Gregory, *the wrath to come* is the final punishment of God: the sinner who does not have recourse to sorrow and repentance now will not be able to flee the wrath later.*

*Matt 3:7

**Final sentence: Lyra Matt 3:7*

*40 Hom 20.7; PL 76:1163B; CL 141:159

Pharisees were so called from the word *Phares,* meaning *division,* because they were separated from others, or separated themselves from others. That is, they were the Jewish priests, who signified that they were more religious than others by their dress, their diet, and their deeds. Sadducees were so called from the word *Sadoch*, meaning *the just* or *those who justify themselves*; they accepted only the first five books of Moses, rejected the prophets, and did not believe in angels or the resurrection.[7]*

Zachary 1.13; PL 186:94C; Isidore, Ety 8.4.3–4; PL 82:297B

When John beheld these men who were regarded as the leading parties of the Jews coming for his baptism, he rebuked them and boldly accused them of wickedness. He called them both the *brood* and *offspring of vipers* because they had inherited the venom of hypocrisy and error from their forebears: imitating them, they envy the good and persecute them and so are brought forth as the poisonous children of poisonous parents.* Remigius observes that it is customary in Scripture to give names from the imitation of deeds, so these men, from following vipers, are called a *brood of vipers*.* John rebuked them because they were in great need of penance and correction.

Zachary 1.13; PL 186:94C

*Hom 3; PL 131:885A

They had not expelled their venom before coming to be baptized, so John added, *Bring forth therefore fruit worthy of penance*.* That is, "Produce here and now a worthy and fruitful repentance through contrition, confession, and satisfaction, so that you can flee the wrath to come—for that is the only way to escape it." Chrysostom writes, "It is not enough for penitents to leave off sinning. They must also bring forth the fruits of repentance, as it is written, *Turn away from evil and do good*.* It is not enough to remove an arrow: for healing to take place, we must also apply a salve to the wound. But he does not say just *fruit*, but *fruits*,

*Matt 3:8

*Ps 33:15

[7] Jerome interprets *phares* as *division* (PL 23:1176); the Pharisees were in fact not priests. The etymology of *Sadducee* is more difficult: some say the name derives from their identification with the priesthood of the temple in Maccabean times, symbolized by the name Zadok, high priest in the time of David and Solomon; the Hebrew word *tsadaq* means *to be just*.

signifying abundance."* And he did not call for just any kind of fruit, but *fruit worthy of penance*, that is, proportional to the gravity of the sin. According to Gregory, the more seriously one has sinned, the more severe should be the penance undertaken, and the advantages sought by good works should be in proportion to the harm inflicted on oneself by sinning.* As it says in the book of Revelation, *As much as she has glorified herself and lived in delicacies, so much torment and sorrow give to her.**

*CA Luke 3:6–9, based on Hom Matt 10.6; PG 57/58:190–91

*40 Hom 20.8; PL 76:1164A; CL 141:160

*Rev 18:7

On this point, Peter Cantor of Paris asks,

> What should a confessor do with penitents who confess many grave sins but refuse to undertake the effort of producing a *fruit worthy of penance*? Should he impose a lighter penance, lest a heavier penance weigh them down and extinguish the love of God in their heart? Better that they make up in purgatory for their lack of penance here, rather than be punished eternally in hell. Either God or other people extract retribution. And what if a confessor does not assign us a *fruit worthy of penance* for the number of our sins? Let us voluntarily supply what is lacking, because the penance should be proportioned to the quantity and seriousness of our sins. In such matters, discretion is as important to the penitent as it is to the confessor.*

*Com in Rev 18:7

*The Jews prided themselves on their nobility and holiness because they were Abraham's descendants; on account of the promise made to him, they presumed that they could be saved without doing good works. So John went on to say, *"And think not to say* or imagine *within yourselves,* making a false estimation, *'We have Abraham for our father,'** and for that reason think that you are just, and believe that you can be saved without doing penance. None of the saints can save sinners without the fruits of repentance."

***R 11**

*Matt 3:9

We find the same thing among many Christians, who believe that because they have a devotion to one of the saints, this holy person's merits will save them without good works.* And there are religious who boast about the goodness and sanctity of their founders or holy members; to these, one could say: "If you are the children of Abraham, do the works of Abraham." Then there is the foolish boasting of some miserable people who vaunt their high birth. Of such people Chrysostom says,

Lyra Matt 3:9 mor

> What does a noble ancestry benefit those who defile their own character? Or how does a lowly ancestry harm those adorned with good character? Gold is born from the earth, but is not of the earth; the gold is chosen, and the earth despised. It is better for people of lowly background to become illustrious than it is for those of noble origin to make themselves contemptible. It is better that parents can take pride in character of their children than it is for children to boast of their pedigree. So do not brag, *We have Abraham for our father,* but blush that although you are his children you are not the heirs of his holiness. The person who does not resemble his father is like an illegitimate child; whoever does not imitate the parent's sanctity forfeits the parent's status.*

*Opus imperf 3; PG 56:651

Therefore, your confidence must come from spiritual imitation, not human reproduction; your pride should come from faith, not bloodline. Not all of Abraham's seed are his children, but only those who imitate his faith. Holiness comes from the power of divine grace, not natural propagation. To be sure, the Jews were Abraham's children according to the flesh, but not according to faith: when they rejected Abraham's faith in Christ, they forfeited the title *children of Abraham*. On the other hand, the Gentiles became Abraham's children when they joyfully embraced the faith of

Christ at the preaching of the apostles. And this is why John goes on to say, "*For I tell you that God is able of these stones* (which signify the Gentiles) *to raise up children to Abraham*,* by their imitating Abraham's faith." *Matt 3:9
Whoever imitates Abraham's faith and deeds deserves to be called Abraham's child. *God is* also *able of these stones to raise up children to Abraham* by making hard-hearted sinners devout. Would that he might do this to me!

Some interpret these words literally and suggest that as John spoke he pointed to those twelve stones that Joshua had ordered the leaders of the twelve tribes to carry from the middle of the riverbed of the Jordan and set up on the shore; then they carried twelve stones from the land and laid them in the bed of the Jordan. The first stones symbolize the dryness and blindness of the Jews, the second the faith of the Gentiles through baptism; or the first symbolize the Gentiles rising up out of the water into the light of faith, the second the Jews being submerged in unbelief. ***R 12** *Josh 4:1-9; Gloss Matt 3:9; PL 114:80C

It is fitting that stones should represent the Gentiles: either because they worshiped idols made of stone (for, as the psalm says, *Let them that make them be like to them*),* or because they had hearts of stone and were unable to understand the things of God. And children were raised up to Abraham from these Gentiles: when they believed in Abraham's seed, Christ, they became his children by virtue of being united with his seed. It was to these Gentiles that Paul wrote, *And if you be Christ's, then are you the seed of Abraham, heirs according to the promise*.* Children were raised up to Abraham from the stones when Jews forfeited the title "children of Abraham" through their lack of faith and Gentiles, professing faith in Christ, took their place. Also, according to Rabanus Maurus, because this great preacher of the truth wanted to incite the Jewish people to produce *a fruit worthy of repentance*, he challenged them *Ps 134:18; *Lyra Matt 3:9* *Gal 3:29

to humble themselves, for without this virtue no repentance is possible.*

*Com Matt 3:9; PL 107:770D; CM 174:78

The Axe Is Laid to the Root of the Trees

*R 13

*Because the doctor of truth sought not only to condemn vice boldly but also to proclaim repentance, John gave a motivation for his hearers to do penance quickly in the present age: *For now the axe is laid to the root of the trees*.* That is, "The severity of divine justice is poised to cut away obdurate sinners from this present life and cast them into the fires of Gehenna." Or, "From birth, the passage from this life for us and trees alike is at work; from the first moment of life, we advance toward death." For, according to Augustine, to live is simply to journey from life toward death.* Night and day are two carpenters who take turns sawing: the more days and nights a person lives the less time is left, and at last the tree must fall. As the tree falls, so shall it lie. As we read in Sirach, *If the tree fall to the south*, paradise, *or to the north*, hell, *in whatever place it shall fall, there shall it be*.* Naturally, the tree falls in the direction that is most weighed down with branches and fruit; so we fall in the direction toward which we are most inclined by affection and actions. Bernard writes,

*Matt 3:10

*Gregory, Mor 11.L.68; PL 75:984C; CL 143A:625

*Sir 11:3

> *If the tree fall to the south, or to the north, in whatever place it shall fall, there shall it be*. In Scripture, the warmth and gentleness of the south signifies good, *while from the north shall an evil break forth*.* We are like the trees: when a tree dies, it stays where it falls; and when we fall, God judges us according to where he finds us. There we stay, immutably and irrevocably. Let us see where we will fall before it befalls us, for once we have fallen *we shall rise no more*.* If you want to know which way a tree will fall, study its branches: when the tree is

*Jer 1:14

*Amos 5:1

> chopped down, it falls in the direction where there are the most numerous and heavy branches. Our branches are our desires: we will extend them to the south if they are spiritual, and to the north if they are carnal. The whole body will fall in the direction of the preponderant branches, and there it will remain.*

*Sermo de div 85; PL 183:702BC; SB 6:1:326–27

*And John continued, *Every tree therefore that does not yield good fruit shall be cut down, and cast into the fire.** In other words, "Every human being, without exception, who does not produce simple goodness, without any admixture of sin, will be cut off from the assembly of the faithful by a sentence at the moment of death and cast into the eternal flames without hope of redemption, which is the punishment for sin." From this it is clear that we can be damned even for sins of omission. A good example of this is the parable of the lazy servant, and at the Last Judgment it will suffice to cite what the wicked neglected to do.* It is not enough to avoid evil; we must also do good. God detests unfruitfulness: he wants there to be nothing barren in his garden or in his vineyard or in his field. Furthermore, it is clear that there was no unfruitful tree in Paradise, because our first parents were enjoined to eat from every tree in Paradise, except the tree of the knowledge of good and evil.

***R 14**

*Matt 3:10

*Matt 25:26, 42-43

If the person who simply does not bear good fruit is cast into the fire, what will be done to the one who produces evil fruit? This tree is the human race and individual members of it. Some trees are dried up and sterile: pagans and unbelievers. Christians are green trees, but of diverse kinds. Some are lazy and slothful, producing no fruit at all. Others, hypocrites, may produce fruit, but it is useless, neither good nor meritorious. Others produce fruit that is not so much useless as evil: these are the heretics, who do indeed produce fruit by their preaching, but it is deadly; fruits such as these can be worthily consigned to the flames. Finally, there are good Catholics who by obedience to the word of God produce good fruit.*

*Gloss Matt 3:10; PL 114:81AB

The roots of the tree are our thoughts, which either plunge into depths of the underworld or reach up to heaven.* Or the roots are our desires, good and bad: from these come good or evil words and deeds, which reveal what is rooted in the will. For this reason, Ambrose says, "Let the one who can, produce the fruit of grace, and the one who must, the fruit of penitence. The Lord is present who seeks fruit, vivifies the fertile, and condemns the sterile."*

*Gloss Matt 3:10; PL 114:81A

*Exp Luke 2.76; PL 15:1580B; CL 14:64

Almsgiving

***R 15**

*****_And the people_, frightened at the prospect of Gehenna for performing wicked deeds or neglecting to do good ones, _asked him, saying_: _"What then shall we do_* to avoid perishing and being cast into the flames?" This was as much as to say, "We are ready to amend our lives." _And he answering, said to them: "He that has two coats, let him give to him that has none; and he that has food, let him do in like manner."_* In other words, we should share with others our superfluous clothing, or food, or indeed any other possession, provided that the necessities of our own state in life are met. Basil writes, "Here we are taught that we must give to those who have nothing what we possess over and above what is necessary for daily support, and to do this for the sake of God, who has himself given liberally whatever we have."[8]* And Gregory says, "It is written in the law, _You shall love your neighbor as yourself._* Those who do not share with one in need even what is need-

*Luke 3:10

*Luke 3:11

*CA Luke 3:10–14

*Lev 19:18

[8] These words are taken from a Greek _catena_, but the idea is found in Saint Basil's writings, e.g.: "The bread you hold back belongs to the hungry; the coat that you keep locked away belongs to the naked; the shoes moldering in your closet belong to those who go barefoot. The silver that you keep hidden in a safe place belongs to the one in need" (PG 31:278A).

ful to themselves prove that they love their neighbor less than themselves."*

*40 Hom 20.11; PL 76:1165B; CL 141:162

We should understand *has two coats* to mean "surplus clothing," and *has none* can mean either "living in extreme destitution" or else "living in straitened circumstances." What is said here is that if you enjoy a superfluity of goods you *must* share what you have with those who are extremely destitute; otherwise, you are guilty of robbing the poor of their possessions and indeed their very lives, because the surplus is owed to those who would perish without it. (This presumes, of course, that you have provided first for your own dependents, because charity begins at home.) If, however, the needy person's condition is difficult but not desperate, then the directive to share is not a commandment, but a counsel. Here a person's character is revealed: how we respond to lesser needs shows how we will respond to greater ones.

Pope Gregory asks, "Will the person who does not give away a tunic in time of peace for love of God give away life in time of persecution? Cultivate the virtue of charity by being merciful in tranquil times, so that you will be invincible in times of upheaval. Learn first to give up your possessions for almighty God, and then your very self."* And Augustine teaches, "Charity is born so that it might be perfected. When it is nourished, it is strengthened. When it has been strengthened, it is perfected. And when it comes to perfection, what does it say? *For to me, to live is Christ, and to die is gain. I desire to be dissolved and to be with Christ.** This charity begins, brethren, when you, from your own surplus, give to another who is needy and in narrow straits. If you nurture the charity begun in this way with the word of God and the hope of future life, you will reach such perfection that you will be willing to lay down your life for your brothers and sisters."*

*40 Hom 27.3; PL 76:1206B; CL 141:231

*Phil 1:22, 23; Ep John 5.4; PL 35:2014

*Ep John 6.1; PL 35:2019

The wealthy should not grumble about helping the poor: God made the poor to help the rich, so that as the rich show mercy to the poor they in turn may receive mercy. Chrysostom says: "Do not think that God made the rich to be useful to poor, whom he could also sustain without wealth. Rather, he made the poor to help the rich, who would be fruitless and sterile unless the poor had been created."*

*Opus imperf 46; PG 56:892A

Accordingly, John did not yet impose demanding practices, fasts, and vigils upon this unlettered crowd; he enjoined them to bring forth fruit worthy of repentance by performing works of mercy. It is these whom the Lord will later judge, and about whom he himself says elsewhere, *Give alms, and behold, all things are clean unto you.** Bede writes,

*Luke 11:41

> It is a most suitable order in preaching to follow up a call to repentance by an exhortation to give alms, that is, to perform works of mercy. The repentant can legitimately beg to receive mercy from God if they have not been slow to show mercy to a neighbor in need. But those who close their ears to the cry of the poor will find that their prayer is detested. Hence when John was seeking to persuade the crowd to produce the fruit worthy of repentance, lest by their sterility they be consigned deservedly to the fire, he promptly added this counsel to those who were seeking salvation: *He that has two coats,* let him give to him that has none; and he that has food, let him do in like manner.**

**tunicas*

*Com Luke Proem. 16:1, Proem; PL 92:528D–29A; CL 120:296

The great value of works of mercy as fruit worthy of repentance is underscored here, as Gregory notes, by the fact that they are mentioned in preference to any other deeds.* And John does well to specify a tunic and food: the tunic is the basic garment with which we are covered, which is more necessary than a cloak, and food is even more essential.[9] So the fruit

*40 Hom 20.11; PL 76:1165B; CL 141:162

[9] The Douay and KJV, and versions that follow them, translate the word *tunica* (Greek: *chiton*) as *coat*, although that word has now come to mean an outer garment.

worthy of repentance does not refer to sharing extraneous and less necessary things with our neighbor, but those that are really essential: the food that keeps us alive and the most basic clothing.

If it be true that the person with two tunics must share with the person who has none, how much more true it is that a cleric holding two benefices should share with the one who has none, and even more that a priest cannot serve at two altars. And if the person with superfluous food is commanded to give to the one who has none, it follows that if you have two cooked dishes (which are more than what is necessary), you should give one to the person who is hungry, or at least make a plate from these two for the other person.

Tunics can also be interpreted as the virtues that adorn the soul, which their possessors should dedicate to the good of their neighbor. And by *food* we can understand the sacred Scriptures, which are spiritual food, from which we should feed our neighbor spiritually.* **Lyra Luke 3:11 mor*

Tax Collectors and Soldiers Come Out to John

**And the publicans also came to be baptized.*‡ These people were called *publicans* because they concerned themselves with business that pertained to the public, such as the collection of taxes, tolls, duties, and tribute, or the fiscal concerns of the community; among them were others who earned their living through trade and business. So, in the wake of lesser sinners, the greater ones *came to be baptized and said to him: "Master, what shall we do* to have eternal life?" *But he said to them: "Do nothing more* in exacting tribute or taxes from others *than that which is appointed you*, that is, what is lawful or customary."* He said this because the publicans often collected more taxes than they were permitted or commanded to, and kept the excess.*

***R 16**
‡Luke 3:12
*Luke 3:12-13
**Last sentence: Lyra Luke 3:12*

Notice that he did not first advise them to be generous in almsgiving, but warned them against taking what belongs to others, which suggests that we must first turn away from evil and then do good. We need to make restitution for what we have stolen before we give alms. Bede says, "He keeps the tax collectors from committing fraud. They should first rein in their appetite for the property of others, and eventually be moved to share their own possessions."* The publicans can be understood to represent today the agents of lords and rulers, who should not tax the people more than is established according to the dictates of justice.

*Com Luke 3:12-13; PL 92:355A; CL 120:79

***R 17**

******And the soldiers also asked him, saying: "And what shall we do,* that we might be saved?" *And he said to them: "Do violence to no man, neither calumniate any man; and be content with your pay."** That is, "Do not, under the pretext of carrying out your office, do violence to the poor who cannot defend themselves, harming them bodily or unduly frightening them; do not trump up false charges against the rich and mighty and deliver them up to justice in order to extort from them the wealth and possessions you cannot take from them in some other way; and be content with what you are paid to defend your country and do not seek further gain by oppression, false accusations, accepting bribes, or demanding protection money."*

*Luke 3:14

**Lyra Luke 3:14 approx*

John said these things because soldiers are prone to exact plunder from the very people they are armed to protect. Peter of Blois complains,

> Military discipline has completely disappeared today. In times past soldiers bound themselves by an oath to stand firm in the defense of their homeland, not to run from the battlefield, and to put the common good ahead of their own. Today they receive their sword from the altar to proclaim that they are sons of the church who take up the sword

> to honor the priesthood, protect the poor, punish evildoers, and safeguard the liberty of their country. But they do just the opposite! As soon as they are invested with their military insignia they rise up against the Lord's anointed servants, wreak havoc against the patrimony of the Crucified, rob and plunder their poor subjects, and mercilessly afflict the unfortunate. They bring great grief to others as they satisfy their illicit appetites and immoderate desires.* *Ep 94; PL 207:94BC

Formerly the rulers and governors of the earth, from the ordinary soldier up to the king or emperor, put the needs of the republic ahead of self-interest and protected the poor who could not defend themselves. But today, alas! They give no thought to their homeland or the poor but go off to invade and occupy foreign lands, and for one purpose only: to enrich and enlarge their own homes. They allow the poor to be miserably afflicted—and what is worse, they themselves afflict them without mercy. They should tremble for fear that in the world to come they will be alienated from the land of the living and be excluded from the kingdom of heaven, which belongs to the poor.

Augustine warns, "Any leaders or clerics who seek more for themselves than is ordained are condemned as calumniators and extortionists by John's sentence, because we are all soldiers of Christ."* We can interpret *soldiers* to refer also to preachers, whom the apostle equips with armor, saying, *Therefore, take the armor of God, and the sword of the Spirit (which is the word of God).** You should *do violence to no man* by preaching with such harshness that you cause your listeners to despair. Nor should you *calumniate any man* by refusing to preach because you think the people are unworthy to hear the word of God. And *be content with your pay* that is assigned to you and, if you are able, give alms yourselves to beggars.*

*Attr. to Augustine by Zachary 1.13; PL 186:96B

*Eph 6:13, 17

**Lyra Luke 3:14 mor*

An Exhortation to Heed John the Baptist's Warning

*R 18

O, how blessed would be that crowd of merchants, tax collectors, and soldiers had they embraced John's teaching! But where are the people with two tunics—and many more—who give one to the person who has none? Where are the people who engage in trade without deceit, or refrain from snatching the goods of those entrusted to their care? Where are the powerful who do not falsely accuse one who is weak, or strike their servants, or who are content with their pay? It is certainly a rare thing to find such.

Bonaventure, Sermo de sanctis 31

And note how John adapted his preaching to the needs of his hearers, so that after succeeding in smaller matters they could later accomplish greater ones. Chrysostom says, "When speaking to the tax collectors and soldiers, John wanted to bring them to higher perfection, but because they were not yet worthy of this, he reveals lesser things first, lest they should not strain to attain higher things when he proclaims them, and lose the lesser also."*

*CA Luke 3:10–14

The greater part of John's message to the crowds was applicable to the tax collectors and soldiers as well, and what he said to the latter was intended in some way for everyone. Ambrose makes this point:

> The holy Baptist fittingly gave one answer to everyone, but an answer adapted to the condition of each: tax collectors should not exact payment above what was allotted and soldiers should not falsely denounce others or seek plunder. But these and other precepts are appropriate for all occupations, and the exercise of compassion is shared. Thus it is a common precept that the necessities of life should be given by everyone to anyone regardless of his age or position. The tax collector and soldier are not exempted—but neither is the farmer or the city-dweller, the rich person or the pauper.

All are enjoined to give to those in need. Mercy is the fullness of all the virtues, and so the form of perfect virtue is proposed to all, lest they be stingy about sharing their food and clothing. Yet the measure of compassion is gauged in relation to the human condition, so that each person does not take all for himself or herself, but shares what they have with the poor.*

*Exp Luke 2.77; PL 15:1580CD; CL 14:64

✠

Most blessed John the Baptist, Forerunner of Christ and virgin most holy, you preached penance to sinners not only in word but by your example of austerity in food and clothing and by avoiding the enticements of this world. I ask that through your holy prayers the Lord will give me fitting abstinence in food and drink, as well as in thoughts, words, and deeds. May he safeguard me from any defilement of soul and body and grant that I may be kept from wickedness and serve him as his soldier as long as I live in this world. By producing fruits worthy of penance may I be able to receive pardon for all my sins and arrive at life everlasting. Amen.

CHAPTER 18

John's Mission Is from God, Not Himself

(John 1:6-18)

*R 1 *John the Evangelist testifies that John did not assume the office of baptizing on his own authority but had been commissioned to bear witness to the majesty of Christ: *There was a man sent from God, whose name was John.** Luke had written, *The word of the Lord was made to John, the son of Zachariah, in the desert.** John confirms this here by saying *there was a man*, that is, a person living according to the dictates of right reason, *sent from God*, that is, sent from the desert to baptize and give testimony about Christ. Here John's virtue of obedience is commended: he did not presume to come of his own will, but had been *sent from God*. His *name was John*, a most apt name, meaning *one in whom there is grace*; for he was to be the forerunner of the author of grace. *This man came for a witness, to give testimony of the light*, that is, Christ, *that all men might believe through him.**

*John 1:6

*Luke 3:2

*John 1:7

Note carefully that the evangelist sometimes uses the word *lux* and at other times (as here) *lumen*. The difference is that *lux* refers to brightness in its utter purity, not combined with any other nature, but *lumen* refers to light united to something else; thus the brilliance of the sky is not *lux*, but *lumen*. Because John was sent to bear witness to Christ, in whom a human nature is united to the Word, the evangelist says that he came *to give testimony to the light.*[1]* *lumine

John Was Not the Light

*Because the Jews may have thought that John himself was the Christ, the evangelist corrects this erroneous opinion: *He was not the light,** that is, true light by essence, shedding light by his very nature to illuminate others with the light of grace. John was light by participation, himself being illuminated by the true light *who inhabits light inaccessible,** that is, the sun of justice, the Word who shares the substance of the Father. He was illuminated by that light in whom there is no darkness *to give testimony to the light*. John, and all the holy ones, do not shed their own light, but enlighten by reflecting the light they receive.* There is light that illumines of its very nature, essential light; only God is light in this sense. Then there is light that illumines by participation; the saints are light in this sense, illumining by word and example.

*R 2

*lux; John 1:8

*1 Tim 6:16

**Lyra John 1:8 approx*

The light to which John was sent to bear witness *was the true* eternal *light*, without shadow, or falsehood, or mere participation, *which enlightens* by the light of grace *every man that comes into this* dark *world*.* When it says *every man*, Augustine interprets this to mean that there is no person illuminated who has not been enlightened by God.* Or, in Chrysostom's opinion, the text means that God enlightens *every man* to the

*John 1:9

*Enchir 103; PL 40:280

[1] Scholastic thought distinguished between *lux*, a self-luminous body, such as the sun, and *lumen*, the ray shining from such a body through the atmosphere. According to Bartholomew the Englishman in *De proprietatibus rerum* (ca. 1240): "*Lumen* is a certain emission, or irradiation, by the substance of *lux*. *Lux* is the original substance from which *lumen* arises" (De prop 8.40). This distinction is briefly referred to by Zachary 1.14 (PL 186:91C).

extent he is permitted to do so: if some people are not enlightened, it is because they have removed themselves from the influence of this light. If some deliberately close the eyes of their mind and do not wish to receive these rays of light, the darkness is not because of the nature of the light, but because of the wickedness of those who set up an obstacle to keep it out and, turning away from it, choose to deprive themselves of the gift of grace.* There is no excuse for those who do not prepare themselves to receive grace.

*Hom John 8.1; PG 59:65

***R 3**

He, the Word, the light, the Wisdom of God, *was in the world*.* The world, which means everything that exists, was made through this Word, so *he was in the world* from its very beginning, as a cause is present in its effect.* The skill of the omnipotent God, through whom in reality all things were made, was shining upon all creatures by bringing them into being and maintaining them in existence. God is present everywhere by virtue of his power, for it extends to all things, as the sway of an earthly monarch reaches to the limits of his realm. He is everywhere by his presence, because *all things are naked and open to his eye*,* just as everything is open to a monarch's inspection when he is in his throne room. And he is present everywhere by his essence, because he not only brings everything into being, but he keeps everything in existence by his being; he would not have made them unless the presence of his essence everywhere gave them existence, just as a monarch is present in a place determined by the location of his body.[2]

*John 1:10

**Zachary 1.13; PL 186:91C*

*Heb 4:13

[2] Thomas Aquinas writes, "But how he is in other things created by him may be considered from human affairs. A king, for example, is said to be in the whole kingdom by his power, although he is not everywhere present. Again, a thing is said to be by its presence in other things that are subject to its inspection, as things in a house are said to be present to anyone, who nevertheless may not be in substance in every part of the house. Last, a thing is said to be by way of substance or essence in that place in which its substance may be. Now there were some*

*the Manichees

And the world was made by him, and by his goodness, so that there would be some creatures to whom he could impart his grace; *and the world knew him not*.* That is to say, human beings living in the world knew him not, so it was necessary for the Creator himself to come into the world in the flesh, so that they would come to know through him. Or, the world, that is, worldly people and lovers of the world, did not know him because their preoccupation with mundane things impeded their knowledge of divine realities. However, those who were the friends of God knew him even before he came into the world bodily. Yet even though *he was in the world* inasmuch as God is present in everything created, this did not suffice to enable the ignorant and worldly to know him. *John 1:10

Those Who Accepted Jesus and Those Who Rejected Him

*So that he could be perceived by the senses of everyone, the Word took on flesh through the incarnation *and came unto his own**—his own because they *R 4 *John 1:11

---

who said that spiritual and incorporeal things were subject to the divine power, but that visible and corporeal things were subject to the power of a contrary principle. Therefore against these it is necessary to say that God is in all things by his power. But others, though they believed that all things were subject to the divine power, still did not allow that divine providence extended to these inferior bodies. . . . Against these it is necessary to say that God is in all things by his presence. Further, others said that although all things are subject to God's providence, still all things are not immediately created by God, but that he immediately created the first creatures, and these created the others. Against these it is necessary to say that he is in all things by his essence. Therefore God is in all things by his power, inasmuch as all things are subject to his power; he is by his presence in all things, as all things are bare and open to his eyes; he is in all things by his essence, inasmuch as he is present to all as the cause of their being" (ST I, q. 8, a. 3).

were in the world he had created, for through him all things were made. He who had made the world in his divine nature appeared in the world in a human nature. He came more particularly to Judea, the land of God, and to the Jewish people, from whom he was to arise, as they had been chosen by God before all others to be a people peculiarly his own: because *of the seed of Abraham he takes hold*.* He issued from the Father and came into the world when he assumed flesh.

*Heb 2:16

He was already in the world by virtue of his divinity but came into the world in his humanity. As Man he could come and go; as God, he always remains.* The sense of the evangelist's words is that he came, that is, he appeared visibly, and he came not for his sake but for ours: because the world could not know sublime divinity, he appeared in humble humanity.

**Haymo, Hom 9; PL 118:61A*

*And his own received him not** by faith and approbation. That is, a great part of the human race, whom he had made in his image and likeness, did not believe in him. Or, *his own* people, the Jews, *received him not* in faith and charity. It is the same today: a great part of the clergy, who, in relation to the rest of Christians, are particularly the Lord's own allotted portion, do not receive him; they abandon him, and their behavior is more corrupt than the laity's.*

*John 1:11

**last sentence: Lyra John 1:11 mor*

In a moral sense, we can understand the words *he came unto his own* to mean that he comes to those who dedicate themselves completely to God: denying themselves, such people give themselves to God wholeheartedly, living for God instead of themselves. **His own received him not*; they were his own, but they sought their own things, and not the things of God. Such as these *received him not*, nor did he come to such minds.

***R 5**

But if you want God to come to you, you must become a son or daughter of God. The Word of God, who is properly speaking the Son, comes only to those who are his own, that is, all those who are sons and daughters of God, who believe in his name, the name

Son. Some of his own, a comparatively small number, did receive him through a faith fashioned by charity: they believed and confessed that he was the Son of God sent from the Father, true God and true Man, and they held fast to him by charity. But what benefit did they gain by receiving him? A great benefit indeed. Without discrimination on the basis of status, condition, sex, age, or personal distinction, *as many as received him* by faith, *he gave them power to be made the* adopted *sons of God* through the grace of adoption and the rebirth of baptism, *to them that believe in* the truth and reality of *his name*.* That name is *Christ*, meaning God *anointing* and Man *anointed*, and *Emmanuel*, meaning *God with us*. Therefore, to believe in his name is to believe that he is God and Man, and the true Son of God. As the evangelist writes elsewhere, *Whosoever believes that Jesus is the Christ is born of God*.* *John 1:12 *1 John 5:1

Note that he does not say *he made them sons of God*, but *he gave them the power to be made the sons of God*. This signifies several things, according to Chrysostom: first, it shows that we must expend great effort to keep unsullied the image of sonship impressed upon us at baptism; second, that no one can wrest this power from us unless we surrender it ourselves; third, that this grace is not given at random, but only to those who want it and strive for it. The power of grace and the power of free will are both at work: it is God's part to give grace, and our part to provide faith.* *Hom John 10.2–3; PG 59:76

The power to be made the sons of God is given only to those who either profess faith in Christ themselves, in the case of adults, or through others, in the case of children.* This sonship does not come from physical propagation, but by believing in the one who is the Son by nature. See what fruit the coming of the Son of God produces: mere human creatures become through the grace of adoption what he alone is by nature! This is a great fruit indeed, as the apostle teaches: *And if sons, heirs also; heirs indeed of God and joint heirs with Christ*.* God's magnanimous mercy is **Lyra John 1:12* *Rom 8:17

shown in the fact that we, who do not even deserve to be his servants, are called, and indeed become, the sons and daughters of God. Augustine exclaims: "What great benevolence! He was the Only-Begotten but did not want to remain the only one. He was not afraid to have co-heirs: his inheritance does not diminish if many share it."‡

‡Tr John 2.13; PL 35:1394; CL 36:17

*R 6

*And, lest someone imagine this birth to be physical and not spiritual, the evangelist adds a few words about how this filiation comes about: *not of blood,** that is, the seminal matter of the father and mother (for, according to the Greeks, the plural *sanguinibus* demonstrates the equal participation of the father and mother).[3] This mutuality is also suggested by what follows: *nor of the will of the flesh,* which refers to concupiscence of the woman, because the flesh has less strength and needs to be supported by the bones, so that *flesh* here refers to the weaker sex; *nor of the will of man,** which refers to the concupiscence of the male, *but of God.**

**sanguinibus*

**viri*

*John 1:13

Thus we become adopted sons and daughters through the sacrament of baptism and spiritual rebirth. People receive grace from God by spiritual generation, not physical generation, being drawn, in a manner of speaking, to the divine nature: through the gift of grace, we become *partakers of the divine nature.** In a moral sense, we can infer from this passage

*2 Pet 1:4; *Lyra John 1:13*

[3] Scholastic thought relied on ancient and rather primitive understandings of biology. One question debated in the schools concerned the woman's role in the conception of a child. Aristotle held that the male semen was the active agent that imparted form to the passive matter of the female menstrual blood. Galen (who, unlike Aristotle, knew of the existence of the ovaries) taught that the woman, too, produced a "seed" and that the parents each contributed both form and matter in the act of conception. Zachary 1.13 (PL 186:92A) speaks simply of the *matter* of the father and the mother; he also has the idea that *flesh* refers to the female sex.

that we should not allow anything human to come to birth in us (and, consequently, nothing worldly or created), so that we will be born only of God, and not of such things.

In the next place it will be shown how the Word comes into the world and in what way he manifests himself. It is not by coming into a place from which he had been absent before; rather, he undertakes to be there in a new way. A ruler can be present in a certain city simply by virtue of his authority, but when he comes there in person, he is present in a new way. So the Son of God, who was already in the world by virtue of his power, his presence, and his essence, came there in a new way, by humbling himself and taking on our weakness. And he does this so that we could be sons and daughters by adoption through the one who is Son by nature.*

**Lyra John 1:14*

The Incarnation of the Word

***R 7**

*This is what is said: *And the Word was made flesh,*‡ that is, he united himself to flesh or assumed it; in other words, he took on humanity and united it to himself in one Person. *Flesh* here means *humanity*, a synecdoche by which the part signifies the whole: *the Word was made flesh*, that is, human. *The Word was* assuredly *made flesh*—not that the Word was turned into flesh, but that the flesh, animated by a rational soul, was taken up in such a way that one Person is made from divinity and humanity. Thus there are in the one Person two natures that remain unmingled, integral, and united without separation: one nature is not changed into the other, but both are in one Person, God and Man. Human nature was taken up by the Word, not in a unity of nature, but in the unity of an individual subject or Person. Thus, *the Word was made flesh* means *God became human*.

‡John 1:14

Augustine writes, "The Son of Man has a soul, has a body. The Son of God, who is the Word of God, has humanity, as the soul has a body. As a soul having body does not make two persons but one human being, so the Word, having humanity, does not make two persons but one Christ. What is a human being? A rational soul having body. What is Christ? The Word of God having humanity."* The Lord demonstrated that he possessed a complete human nature because he came to save the whole person. As Chrysostom says, "Long ago humanity incurred the sentence of death in soul and body on account of sin. It was necessary for the Lord to assume both in order to save both."*

*Tr John 19.15; PL 35:1553; CL 36:199

*Chromatius 7.1; CL 9A:224

The evangelist chose not to use the all-embracing word *human* so that he could underscore the singular and great union between the Word and Christ's humanity: it is not just that the Word is Man, and Man is the Word, but the Word is united to the separate parts of his humanity, his body and soul. And, although the soul is the more excellent and noble part, he speaks of the *flesh* rather than the soul to give us greater certainty, because it would be harder to believe that the Word was united to the lesser part than to the greater.

The evangelist chose to speak of the *flesh* rather than the soul to emphasize the ineffable condescension of God's humility and goodness by specifying the less noble part of the human being, and there is a moral lesson to be learned here. This is a rebuke to the many people who, when questioned about their relatives, boast about those who were eminent—even if they lived long ago—and say that they are the descendants of such and such a bishop, or general, or dean, but keep silent about other persons to whom they are more closely related. They are like the mule in the fable who, when asked who his father was, responded that his uncle was a warhorse—but with shame passed over in silence the fact that his father was an ass!

*And so *the Word dwelt among us,*‡ that is, was united to our human nature inseparably in such a way that he could never be disjoined from it. This should not be interpreted to mean that he dwells in each of us with the same personal unity as he did in Christ, where the human nature was united to the Person of the Word; rather, he began to dwell among us by being perpetually united to the human nature that he shares with us. Or, he *dwelt among us* can mean he lived among us in the world, as we read in the prophet Baruch: *Afterwards he was seen upon earth, and conversed with men.** In a moral sense these words can be taken to refer an indwelling in the mind, by which God inhabits the mind by grace. This spiritual indwelling of the Word follows upon that incarnate dwelling whereby *the Word was made flesh*, as an effect follows from its cause. From the incarnation of the Word we have received the good gift of having the same Word dwelling within us spiritually.

***R 8**
‡John 1:14
*Bar 3:38

The Manifestation of Christ's Glory

***R 9**

And we saw his glory*, that is, we recognized the glorious majesty of his divinity, *the glory as it were* in truth *of the Only-Begotten of the Father, that is, of the one Son who uniquely shares the Father's nature. *To see* can mean either to receive through bodily sight or to perceive through cognition, and John and the other apostles gained knowledge of the Word incarnate through both ways of seeing. They kept company with him bodily and beheld with their senses the works he performed that far exceeded natural human powers, and with the eyes of the mind they perceived and understood the excellence of his divinity concealed in his flesh.*

*John 1:14
**Lyra John 1:14*

The proud, however, refused to believe because of the frailty of Christ's visible flesh. The disciples recognized the glory of the Word in the wisdom of his

*Matt 7:29

doctrine, *for he was teaching them as one having power** and spoke with his own authority; in his miraculous deeds, and because creatures were obedient to his will as their Lord and Creator, and above all in his transfiguration, passion, resurrection, ascension, and sending of the Holy Spirit. This is why when the evangelist says *we saw his glory*, he adds as if to explain this glory, *as it were of the only begotten of the Father*, that is, not a son by adoption but as he truly is, the Only-Begotten by nature, coming from him naturally and consequently sharing the Father's nature.

Note that the words *as it were* are not placed here to signify a mere likeness or analogy to filiation, but as an expression of the truth. Chrysostom explains that the words suggest, "We saw glory such as it was fitting and likely for the only-begotten Son to have." And he goes on to explain that this is a mode of speaking:

> If someone saw a king splendidly robed and riding in state, when he began to relate what he saw to others he might not want to describe in detail the brilliance and variety of the ornaments and trappings. He would say, "Why is it necessary to say many things? He was as a king." That is, he was adorned as a king should be. This is what the evangelist does here, when it was not possible to summarize in a few words all that he had come to recognize about the glory of the Word. Think of the angels glorifying him as his servants, the shepherds, the magi led by a star, the demons he drove out, the dead he raised, the sick he healed, and all the other deeds recalled elsewhere, and in brief how all creatures recognized him and cried out that the King of the heavens had come, and more, how the Father from heaven and the Holy Spirit coming upon him bore witness to him. These wonders, and infinitely more that attested to the glory of the Word, John captured in a few words when he said, *We saw his glory, the glory as it were of the only begotten of the Father*. That is, he had the glory befitting the Only-Begotten of God.*

*Hom John 12.1–3 summarized; PG 59:82–84

He is the Son of God by virtue of the excellence of his divinity, *the only begotten of the Father*; he is the *firstborn* in grace by virtue of his kinship with us. Hence he is called both brother and Lord: the *firstborn* as brother, the *only begotten* as Lord.* The knowledge that the apostles and believers possessed of the Word incarnate embraced both his natures, divine and human. As to the divine nature, *we saw his glory, the glory as it were of the only begotten of the Father*. As regards his human nature, the evangelist adds *full of grace*, that is, charisms, because he received all the gifts of the Holy Spirit without measure, *and truth*, because he fulfilled all the promises. He says Christ is *full of grace* to take away all sins, and *full of truth** in fulfilling the promises; indeed, truly full, *for in him dwells all the fullness of the Godhead corporeally*.*

Zachary 1.13; PL 186:92CD

*John 1:14

*Col 2:9

*It should be noted that this part of the gospel is distinguished by its eminent insight and the profound mysteries it contains, especially where it says *the Word was made flesh*, but as to how this mystery was accomplished, even the most holy John admits he is unworthy to explain it. Unquestionably, these words possess great power, and it is a laudable custom to have this part of John's gospel read at the end of Mass.[4] ***R 10**

Here are a few brief *exempla* to illustrate the efficacy of these words. There were once two beggars in Aquitaine who were possessed by demons. When one of them noticed that his companion was obtaining more alms than he, he went in secret to a priest and said, "If you do what I say, and speak the words of the gospel, *In the beginning was the Word*, into my companion's ear, the demon possessing him will certainly be driven out—but make sure I do not hear the words." Knowing the demon's cunning, the priest proclaimed the gospel in a loud voice, and when he said, *the Word was made flesh*, both demons fled away and the two beggars

[4] Regarding the liturgical use of this gospel, see part one, chapter one n. 6.

were liberated. It is also said that a devil once told a holy man that there were certain words of the gospel that made the demons tremble greatly, but when asked what they were, he said nothing. The man read one passage after another, but every time the devil said, "That's not it." Finally, he asked, "Is it *the Word was made flesh*?" The demon said nothing, but with a loud cry he vanished.

Again, it is said that the devil appeared to a certain abbot in the guise of a beautiful woman, tempting him to have relations with her; they were alone in the garden. Recognizing the devil's malice, the abbot made the sign of the cross on himself and said, "*The Word was made flesh and dwelt among us.*" With a deafening scream the demon immediately disappeared. Again, it is said that there was once a monk who heard the gospel *In the beginning was the Word* being proclaimed, and when he heard the words *the Word was made flesh*, he did not genuflect or make any other kind of reverence. The devil gave him a slap, saying, "If we heard the words, 'The Word was made a demon,' we would never stop genuflecting!"

From His Fullness We Have All Received

***R 11** *That we have seen him *full of grace and truth* is proven by experience, *for of his fullness we all have received, and grace for grace.** It was as if the evangelist were saying, "*We all*, the Twelve and all the faithful both now and in the future, *of his fullness have received*, and for this reason we can say that he was *full of grace and truth*." Let us consider that *fullness* has many meanings. First, there is the fullness of universality, or number, or of the body, which is found in diverse persons throughout the church, for she is lacking in no gift. Then there is the fullness of sufficiency, found in Stephen and in the other saints and in each of the just, present in each according to their capacity. Third,

*John 1:16

there is the fullness of abundance or prerogative, which was in the Blessed Virgin, who excels all the saints in the gifts of grace. Just as God put the excellence of all the stars into the sun, so he put the excellence of all the saints into Mary. It would not have been enough for her to possess with others the fullness of sufficiency, unless she also enjoyed the prerogative of the fullness of abundance, and such abundance that it could overflow onto sinners, although the source of the grace is Christ. Fourth is the fullness of consummation, or excellence and superabundance, which was in Christ, and of this John is speaking here.

*Christ has not only the fullness that is found in others, but also a fullness that overflows into others. *Of the fullness* of the gifts he possesses, *we* all, the elect, *have received*, as members from the head, *grace for grace,** flowing like small streams beyond our merits. We receive the grace of reconciliation and salvation* in the wake of the grace of faith by which we believe in him, the grace of eternal life in the wake of prevenient grace, the grace of justification, and the grace of reward in the wake of the grace of merit. Indeed, he gives us this grace so that through it we may attain glory, which is the consummation of grace. In a word, whatever grace is added to prevenient grace is *grace for grace*. As the old axiom has it, ***R 12**

*John 1:16

**Zachary 1.13 approx; PL 186:93B*

> All your merit from prevenient grace flows;
> God crowns only what his own gift bestows.[5]

Augustine asks, "What grace did we receive first? Faith. It is called grace because it is given *gratis*. Thus the sinner received this first grace so that sins were forgiven."* And he goes on, "*Grace for grace*, that is,

*Tr John 3.8; PL 35:1400; CL 36:24

[5] *Quidquid habes meriti, praeventrix gratia donat; Nil Deus in nobis, praeter sua dona coronat*. This was a popular axiom, appearing in works as disparate as the *Ancrene Riwle* and *Carmina Burana*. It is sometimes attributed to Albert the Great, but he refers to it as an old axiom (Albert, ST Part 2, Tr. 16, Q. 100).

for this grace in which we live by faith we are going to receive another* in eternal life. For eternal life is, as it were, a reward for faith. But because faith itself is a grace, eternal life is a grace for grace."‡

*Tr John 3.10; PL 35:1400; CL 36:25
‡Tr John 3.9; PL 35:1400; CL 36:25

It says that *from his fullness we all have received* grace. When a vessel is plunged into a full fountain, it can take in the amount of water its capacity allows. If it receives only a little water, this is because of the limitation of the container, not that of the fountain. Similarly, we receive grace from Christ, the full fountain of life, according to the capacity of our hearts. We see that a low and wide vessel holds more than a tall, narrow one, and a heart made low by humility and wide by charity receives more and has a greater capacity for grace than a heart that is tall with pride and narrow from avarice. The defect lies in us, not in the giver, if we do not accept as much as we can through humility and love. According to Isidore, "Nothing earns us greater grace in the eyes of God and others than to strive for heartfelt humility in charity."*

*source unknown

***R 13**

Augustine teaches that this grace was not in the Old Testament: "The law threatened, but it did not bring relief; it commanded, but it did not cure; it exposed weakness, but it did not remove it. However, it did make ready for that physician who was to come with grace and truth."

*Tr John 3.14; PL 35:1402; CL 36:26

To describe how this grace is received, the evangelist adds, "*For the law was given by Moses*, as a prophecy of salvation; *grace*, however, which is given in the virtues, gifts, and sacraments that save us, *and truth*, that is, the fulfillment of figures and promises, *came by Jesus Christ*,* that is, sufficiently in him and through him, the Savior anointed by the Holy Spirit." As Augustine says, "Your Lord's death killed both temporal and eternal death. This is the grace that the law promised but did not possess."* And Chrysostom writes, "Those things that were to be fulfilled in the New Testament were prefigured in the Old, Christ at his coming

*John 1:17

*Tr John 3.13–14 approx; PL 35:1402; CL 36:26

executing the design. The figure *was given by Moses; grace and truth came by Jesus Christ.*"‡ ‡Hom John 14.3–4; PG 59:95–96

*The evangelist goes on to explain how this grace and truth are revealed to us: *No man*, that is, no creature, *has seen God* with the vision of comprehension *at any time*; for, as Chrysostom says, neither the angels nor the seraphim themselves behold God's essence.* Or, *no* mortal *man has seen God at any time*. Pope Gregory teaches, ***R 14** *John 1:18; Hom John 15.1; PG 59:98

> So long as we live a mortal life, God may be seen by certain semblances, but the actual appearance of his nature cannot be seen. The soul, being inspired by the grace of the Spirit, can behold God through various figures but not attain to the actual power of his essence.* But it does not contradict the words of the evangelist to say that the eternal brightness can be seen by those still living in this corruptible flesh: those who behold Wisdom, which is God, die so completely to this life that they can no longer be mastered by love of it.* *Mor 18.LIV.88; PL 76:92B; CL 143A:951 *Mor 18.LIV.89; PL 76:93A; CL 143A:952

And Augustine says, "For unless in a manner of speaking we die in this life, we cannot be snatched up and conveyed into that vision."* *De gen ad lit 12.27.55; PL 34:478

John goes on to say by whom God is comprehended: *the only begotten Son who is* and remains *in the Bosom*, that is, the innermost being, *of the* eternal *Father, he has declared him*.* According to Chrysostom, *in the Bosom* signifies the familiarity and co-eternity the Son enjoys with the Father.* *He has declared* what he sees to believers: Christ taught the secrets of divinity, setting forth the mystery of the Trinity and many other things that had not been handed down in a clear way by the law and the prophets. He also established his disciples in faith, and in the grace of faith. He showed all people the way to salvation and opened up that way in himself. In the words of Bede, "Having become Man, he declared the doctrine of the Trinity in unity, and how *John 1:18 *Hom John 15.2; PG 59:99

and by what acts we should prepare ourselves for the contemplation of it."*

*Com John 1:18; PL 92:645D

✠

Lord Jesus Christ, Son of the living God, you are the true light enlightening every person who comes into the world. I, a miserable sinner blinded by intense darkness, adore you and beseech your mercy to enlighten my soul, fashion my mind, regulate my thoughts, control my senses, and direct my words and actions so that the author of iniquity and the lover of darkness may not seize me or set his seal on me. Rather, struck by the brightness of the most true light, may he withdraw far from me, and may I, by striving along the clear and straight path that leads to you, the author of light, reach your eternal glory. Amen.

CHAPTER 19

John States That He Is Not the Messiah but His Forerunner

(Matt 3:11-12; Mark 1:7; Luke 3:15-17; John 1:19-28)

*What with John's wondrous conception and birth, the example of his holy life, the effectual wisdom of his teaching, and the novelty of his baptism, *the people were of the opinion, and all were thinking in their hearts of John, that perhaps he might be the Christ** promised in the law. When the Pharisees learned of what the crowd was thinking about John, they were stirred up against him. He had taken upon his own initiative the office of baptizing, contrary to the law and their traditions, and they doubted that he was the Christ. Because he was of a priestly line, *they sent from Jerusalem priests and Levites* who were well versed in the law to him *to ask him: "Who are you?"** and to inquire why he was baptizing. The sages and scribes knew that he could not be the Messiah, because the promised Christ was of the tribe of Judah and John belonged to the tribe of Levi.

*R 1

*Luke 3:15

*John 1:19

They asked John, who had been sanctified in his mother's womb, the provocative question, *Who are you?* We should pause and consider that this question calls for four different answers: What is his nature? What is his person? What is his character? How great is his stature? But you should pose these questions first to yourself, so that you can answer if God asks them. The first question is: What is your nature? There is a threefold answer to this. You are a human being, so by reason of your body formed from the earth you should be humble, contrary to pride; by reason of your immortal soul you should seek the things that are above, contrary to avarice; by reason of your intelligence you should exercise prudent moderation, contrary to luxury. And if God *were* to ask, *Who are you?* O proud and unnatural man! You are not earth, humbling yourself, but air, exalting yourself. You are not spirit, seeking spiritual things, but flesh, savoring earthly ones. You are not a human being exercising reason, but a wild animal, living like a beast.

The second question is: What are you as a person? This is the question you will be asked when you are knocking on the door, pleading, *Lord, Lord, open to us*.* Perhaps you will answer, "I am a Christian." But, as Ambrose observes, it is a lie to say that you are a Christian if you do not do the works of Christ.* Or perhaps you will say, "I am a friend." But attend to what he answers: *You are my friends, if you do the things that I command you*.* If, however, you are neither, you will hear, *Amen I say to you, I know you not*.*

*Matt 25:11

*Ps-Augustine, Sermo 30.3; PL 17:666B

*John 15:14

*Matt 25:12

The third question is: "What kind of person are you?" That is, what is your character, what are your interior and exterior actions? You should attend diligently to see if you are making progress here or falling away.

The fourth question is: "How great is your stature, spiritually?" How little do you make yourself by humility, so that you will know if you can enter into life through the narrow gate? How wide is the reach of your charity, so that you will know how great a place is reserved for you in heaven?

John's Response

***R 2**

*When John was asked who he was, *he confessed* the truth *and did not deny*, for this would be to deny Christ, who is Truth itself; *he confessed: "I am not the Christ."**

*John 1:20

This was more a response to the thoughts and intentions of his questioners than to their words.* They had asked who he was so that he would tell them whether or not he was the Messiah. True, they did not ask him this explicitly, but in Chrysostom's opinion this was what they were thinking, as is apparent from John's answer.* He confessed himself not to be what in fact he was not, but he did not deny what he was. He confessed that contrary to what the crowd believed he was not the Christ, but he did not deny that he was the Messiah's Forerunner, which he was. He confessed that he was not the Judge, but he did not deny that he was the Judge's herald. He confessed that he was not the church's bridegroom, but he did not deny that he was the friend of the bridegroom. He confessed that he was not the Word, but he did not deny that he was the voice. He chose to stand solidly on the foundation of who he was, lest empty human opinion raise him above himself. He preferred to be recognized in his human frailty as humbly numbered among the members of Christ's Body, rather than usurp an undeserved title and be cut off from the Body of Christ.

Lyra John 1:20

*Hom John 16.2; PL 59:103

Here John commends to us that most important virtue, humility. He enjoyed so much power and authority among the Jews that they believed him to be the Christ, but he did not let himself be raised up by pride to seize a title and honor that were not his. As Chrysostom says, "It is the character of a devoted servant not only to refuse to usurp his master's glory but even to reject it when the crowd offers it."* Lucifer was lacking in this humility of John's and sought to seize God's glory for himself. Our first parents did not possess this humility either, for they wanted to usurp the semblance of divine wisdom to themselves. That malignant one, who extols himself and seeks the honor due to God, does not have this humility. And in our own day there are some who imitate Lucifer, such as tyrants, who with fierce violence seize power, or the ambitious, who wickedly seek to raise themselves

*Hom John 16.2; PG 59:103

to high office. Others imitate the first-made man and woman, such as heretics and the worldly wise who want to know more than they should. And there are others who imitate the Antichrist, such as the hypocrites who feign sanctity but are crafty liars who do not speak the truth.

*R 3

*Many Jews believed John to be the Messiah promised in the law because prophecies were being fulfilled, such as the one that foretold that *the sceptre shall not be taken away from Juda . . . till he come that is to be sent,** so it was known that the time had come for the Lord's incarnation.[1] We can only marvel at the blindness of those Jews who believed that John was the Messiah but refused to believe that Christ was the Savior, although he performed many powerful signs that testified to him—and John himself bore witness to him!* And because it was expected that the Messiah would come from among the Jewish people, it was thought that Elijah would precede him. The coming of both Elijah and Christ had been promised to the Jews. So when those who had been sent saw that John did not claim to be the Messiah, they asked if he might be Elijah. They asked this for two reasons: first, John was similar to Elijah in his austere way of life and manner of dress; second, he was like Elijah in his office of preparing the way for the Messiah.

*Gen 49:10

Zachary 1.13; PL 186:96C

*R 4

John responded that he was not Elijah. Just as John was an angel, not by his nature or in his person but by his life and mission, so he denied that he was Elijah in his body or in his person, but elsewhere Christ said that John was Elijah by his life and mission. Therefore he was not Elijah in the flesh but in his spirit and power: he bore a likeness to Elijah in his deeds. Just as Elijah will precede the second coming of the Lord, so John precedes the first coming. Elijah will come as

Lyra John 1:21 approx

[1] In chapter four Ludolph suggested that this prophecy foretold that Israel would be ruled by a foreigner when the Messiah came, and it was fulfilled by the Idumean Herod.

the Precursor of the Judge, and John was the Precursor of the Savior. Like Elijah, John dwelt in desert places, took little food, and clothed himself in rough garments: both lived in the wilderness, both ate sparingly, both wore coarse clothing. Elijah was full of zeal, and John was killed because of his zeal for the truth. Both struggled with kings and suffered from royal madmen. Elijah petitioned heaven to divide the Jordan before he ascended there, and by his baptism John converted many who sought the way to heaven.

John denied that he was Elijah, who they knew was to come before the Messiah, so they then asked if he was a prophet, specifically that prophet who was to precede the Christ of whom Moses had spoken. It was rumored at that time that one great prophet was to come before the Messiah, of whom it was written, *The Lord your God will raise up to you a prophet of your nation and of your brethren like me: him you shall hear.** Correctly understood, this verse refers to Christ himself; however, the Jews thought it meant another prophet. Accordingly, they asked John if he was that prophet, and he replied, "No." He denied that he was the prophet referred to in that passage, but he did not deny absolutely that he was a prophet, or the prophet sent ahead of the Messiah.*

*Deut 18:15

**Lyra John 1:21*

If John was more than a prophet,* it follows that he was a prophet, because the lesser is contained in the greater. John was so renowned that he could have let people believe he was the Christ had he wished, but he not only did not want them to think he was the Messiah; he also denied that he was Elijah or another prophet. This is in stark contrast to those who boast about their ancestry, way of life, learning, and so on.

*Matt 11:9

A Voice in the Wilderness

*When they insisted that John say something about himself, lest they return to those who had sent them **R 5** without an answer, he responded by giving testimony to Christ, asserting that he was his Forerunner: "*I am the voice*, not in person and body, but in office and likeness; *the voice*, I say, of the Word, of the Christ, *of one crying in the wilderness* through me, *make straight the way of the Lord, as said the prophet Isaiah*."* In other words, "I am that one of whom the text from Isaiah said, 'He must cry out in the desert of Judea, so that people will prepare themselves for Christ's coming into the world.'" Christ's herald cries out in the desert because he is announcing the solace of redemption to Judea, which is deserted, abandoned, and destitute of God's grace.

*John 1:23

It is fitting that John is designated as the *voice*, because he was the herald of Christ, the divine Word, who, in his divinity, is the Word of the Father. Just as a human voice expresses a mental word, so John is called the voice because Christ is called the Word. The voice goes before the word; John precedes Christ. As soon as a sound comes from a speaker's mouth, this is the voice, but it is not the word, because every word signifies some thing. And as a voice makes known a word, so John makes Christ known, and this is why he came, to make him known in Israel. Again, the voice is closer to a word than to a sound: first the sound is heard, then the voice is perceived, and finally the word that is spoken by the voice is understood. Thus John is closer to Christ than the other prophets, whose prophecy was mere sound in comparison with his. They pointed out the Messiah from afar, but this man indicated that Christ was at hand, saying, *Behold the Lamb of God*.*

*John 1:29

Deservedly, then, John is called the Forerunner of the Lord: by his birth, baptizing, preaching, and death—and even by the title of his name—he was running ahead to prepare the way for Christ the Lord.*

**Bruno Com John 1:23; PL 165:456C*

***R 6**

*Another evangelist tells us what John was proclaiming: "*Prepare the way of the Lord* by fulfilling his commandments, *make straight his paths** by going fur-

*Luke 3:4

ther and following his counsels, so that he will deign to come to you and dwell among you." The Lord knows no way to come among us other than by straight paths. As the psalmist says, *Show, O Lord, your ways to me, and teach me your paths*.* First John cried out to everyone, and next to those who were more advanced.

*Ps 24:4

These ways that lead so quickly to our heavenly homeland are best traversed in solitude, that is, by distancing ourselves from temporal concerns and worldly preoccupations; otherwise we might find ourselves wandering off the path among the hills of earthly distractions. Some people feign sanctity and wear the habit, but they do not walk straight in the way of religious observance, nor do they stay on the path of the evangelical counsels. Alternatively, we can understand the more suitable *ways* to mean actions, and *paths* (because they are more hidden) to mean the intentions of the heart. Thus, "*Prepare the way of the Lord* by avoiding evil and doing good; *make straight his paths*, that is, make straight your hidden intentions so that they are not twisted, and you can act for eternity and not just for this world."

To transform the mind's image we need to stop staring at the ground through delight in mundane matters, raise our eyes heavenward, and be guided by the consideration of spiritual realities. We read in the Song of Songs, *The righteous* love you*.‡ Bernard interprets *recti* to mean those who stand erect: they are pulled away from earthly things and contemplate and desire what is lofty. Hence he says, "To pursue and enjoy what is on earth makes the soul crooked, while, on the contrary, to meditate on or desire the things that are above constitutes its uprightness."* He adds that this spiritual uprightness is suggested by the fact that we human beings stand erect: "What is more unbecoming than to bear a warped mind in an upright body? It is wrong and shameful that this body shaped from the dust of the earth should have its eyes raised on high,

**recti*
‡Song 1:3

*SC 24.7; PL 183:897D; SB 1:159

scanning the heavens at its pleasure, while on the contrary the heavenly and spiritual creature lives with its eyes, that is, its inward vision and affections, focused on the earth beneath."‡

‡SC 24.6; PL 183:897B; SB 1:157–58

*R 7

*John continued, "*Every valley*, that is, the Gentiles or whoever is humble, *shall be filled* with the spiritual gifts of grace here and glory hereafter, *and every mountain and hill*, that is, the chosen people and whoever is proud, *shall be brought low** and purged by forfeiting grace and glory." *God resists the proud and gives grace to the humble;** and *every one that exalts himself shall be humbled: and he that humbles himself shall be exalted.** *Mountains* can be taken to mean greater persons, and *hills* to lesser ones.

*Luke 3:5

*Jas 4:6

*Luke 14:11

"*And the crooked* hearts distorted by injustice *shall be made straight*, rectified by the equity of justice and guided by the rule of justice, *and the rough ways plain*, that is, minds seething with inexorable wrath will be converted by an infusion of grace, and hearts hardened against Christ will be softened. *And all flesh*, Jew and Gentile alike, *shall see the salvation of God*,* that is, Christ the Son of God."

*Luke 3:5-6

In those days the human family was divided into two parts, Jews and Gentiles, and many people from both these groups saw Christ keeping company with people in the world. Or these words can refer to seeing spiritually, meaning that people who see him from every race in the world convert to the Catholic faith. Again, they can mean that every human being, the lost and the elect alike, will see him in human form at his second coming on the Day of Judgment.*

**Lyra Luke 3:6*

John's Baptism

*R 8

*When those who had been sent from the Jewish leaders heard that John was none of three illustrious figures whom they were expecting, *they asked him and* *said to him*: "*Why then do you baptize*, introducing a novel rite and usurping a function that is not your own, *if you are not Christ*, who will baptize by his own authority, *nor Elijah*, who symbolized baptism by passing through the Jordan, *nor the prophet*,* whose office it is to baptize, as is evident from Elisha, who sent Naaman to be baptized?" This was as much as to say, "How do you dare to usurp the office of baptizing when by your own lips you have confessed that you do not hold the position of the three figures mentioned to whom Scripture concedes the right?" We should note that, although John was not the Christ, he was able to baptize because he was the Messiah's Forerunner and had to prepare his way; although he was not Elijah in person, he was so in power; and, although he was not that particular prophet, he was more than a common prophet, and therefore he could baptize. *John 1:25

John answered them, again bearing witness to Christ. Just as his sermons and warnings heralded Christ's preaching, so his baptism preceded Christ's baptism; in this he was like the prophets of old, who foretold future events in deeds as well as in words. He said, "*I indeed baptize you in water unto penance*, not in the Holy Spirit for the remission of sins; I teach you to do penance, not having the power to absolve you. *I baptize you in water** as a preparation, washing the body only, to symbolize the one who will come and baptize you in the Holy Spirit with authority, cleansing your soul as well." In other words, "Do not impute audacity to what I do, or marvel that I baptize even though I am not Christ, or Elijah, or that particular prophet. My baptism is not complete or perfect. For baptism to be complete, there must be a cleansing of both body and soul; by its nature, the body can be washed with water, but the soul cannot be washed without the Spirit. Therefore, *I baptize you in water* only *unto penance*, as a sign of the cleansing of your souls by penance. Body washes body: I practice the rite of

***R 9**

**Lyra John 1:26*

*Matt 3:11

baptism to prepare the way for one who is greater than I, until he comes to cleanse your souls with the Spirit."

Ambrose writes,

> He quickly showed that he was not Christ, who performs an invisible service. Because a human being is of two natures, that is, we subsist from soul and body, the visible mystery is sanctified by visible things, the invisible by invisible ones. The body is washed by water, the soul is cleansed of sin by the Spirit. The baptism of penance is one thing, the baptism of grace another, the former being from both and the latter from one. When the offenses are common to mind and body, the purification, too, must be common. And it was fitting that he declared that he was not the Christ by deed rather than word: it is the work of the human being to undertake penance for sins, it is the gift of God to fulfill the grace of the mystery.*

*Exp Luke 2.79; PL 15:1581BC; CL 14:65

John's baptism was a shadow and figure of a better baptism because it signified and prepared what was to come. This is why we read in Acts that the pattern of John's baptism was in the name of one who was to come after him.* However, we should not think that John's baptism accomplished little: although it did not take away sins, all those who were baptized by him recognized that they were held fast by the chains of sin, and they felt the need to seek out, as soon as he appeared, a Redeemer and Purifier who could forgive sins.* John's was a baptism of repentance, to incite people to do penance. As he washed them externally with water, they were washing themselves interiorly by doing penance, so that, as soon as Christ came, they were ready to receive his baptism—for those whom John baptized were baptized again. John's baptism was a kind of profession of faith in the Christ who was coming; those who received it did works of penance so that they could welcome him more devoutly. The baptism of John was useful as a preparation for

*Acts 19:4

**Haymo, Hom 7; PL 118:45C*

Christ's baptism and as a means of amending one's life: those who were baptized confessed their sins because the Messiah was at hand.

The Messiah Is Already Here

*John continued, "*But there has stood one in the midst of you,* that is, the one whom I am proclaiming is already present among you, the Mediator between God and man; *whom you know not** and do not recognize—and I am preparing you to recognize him by baptizing you with water." These words carry more than one meaning. In regard to Christ's humanity, in a literal sense they mean that Christ was *in the midst* of the Jews because he was dwelling among them as one of them, but they did not know that he was present because they believed he was coming in the future. In regard to Christ's divinity, he is invisibly present everywhere; in this sense, he is *in the midst* of all created things, but no one knows him because no one can comprehend him. ***R 10** *John 1:26

Note here that we read often that Christ chose to be *in the midst* because this is the position of humility, as he himself said, *I am in the midst of you, as he that serves.** It is also the heart of the community because everyone is on an equal footing, as the points of the circumference are all equidistant from the center. As Peter teaches, *In very deed I perceive that God is not a respecter of persons.** The midst is also the focal point of unity because the extremes are brought together in the middle; as the apostle says, *He is our peace, who has made both one.** It is also the source of stability because the middle of the world is fixed; again, the apostle: *For other foundation no man can lay, but that which is laid, which is Christ Jesus.** Finally, it is the place of proximity, because it is approached by all parts, as we read in Acts, *If perhaps they may feel their way toward him, although he be not far from every one of us.**

*Luke 22:27
*Acts 10:34
*Eph 2:14
*1 Cor 3:13
*Acts 17:27; *Bonaventure, Com John 1:26*

*R 11

*John then said about Christ, *The same is he that shall come*, or who is to come, *after me*, and before whom I go as herald, *who is preferred before me*.* Although Christ had already come by being born, nevertheless John says he is yet to come: Christ has not yet come to be baptized, to manifest himself by preaching and miracles, and to fulfill the mystery of our redemption. John preceded Jesus in birth and death, but not in resurrection or ascension. According to Remigius, Jesus came after John in five ways: by his birth, his preaching, his baptizing, his death, and his descent among the dead.*

**ante me factus est;* John 1:27

*Ps-Maximus of Turin, Sermo 6; PL 57:655B

When John says, *He was made before me*,[2] this cannot be understood of Christ's divinity, for as God he was not made; nor can it be understood of his humanity, because Christ was conceived after John. So this must be interpreted as referring to honor and dignity: John follows Christ as his Lord and goes after him. *Before* in this context signifies order, not time, and marks the priority of divinity, not birth. Chrysostom suggests that it is as if John were saying, "Do not think that because I came to preach ahead of him that I am greater than he. He came after me in time, because he was born after me; but he ranks ahead of me in dignity, as one who is more illustrious and honorable, possessing higher rank."* We use a similar turn of phrase when we say of someone, "He was once my subordinate or my equal, but lately he has gone before me in honor and surpassed me." Or another takes precedence by virtue of sincere conscience, innocence of life, or great reputation.

*Hom John 13.3 approx; PG 59:89

John explains the reason for Christ's precedence when he adds, *because he was before me*.* In other words, "He *is preferred before me* in rank and dignity because, although born later in time, he precedes me in eternity.

*John 1:30

[2] This is the literal meaning of the Latin (followed in English by Wycliffe and the 1582 Rheims New Testament); the rest of the paragraph explains the interpretation of the words given in the Douay-Rheims and KJV.

He was before me, not in the humanity he took on in time, but in the divinity that he shares from all eternity with the Father. *He was before me* because he is from eternity and I am from time. The one who was born after me from a mother without a father was eternally begotten of a Father without a mother before all creation.* He, the strong and powerful God, *is mightier than I*,‡ a weak and powerless human being. He is the Lord, I am the servant; he is the commander, I am the soldier." Rabanus Maurus writes, "John, who was found worthy to receive the Holy Spirit, is mighty; but the one who can give the Spirit is mightier. He who proclaims the kingdom of heaven is mighty; he who bestows it is mightier. He who baptizes for the confession of sins is mighty; he who forgives them is mightier."*

**Haymo, Hom 7; PL 118:45D–46A*
‡Matt 3:11

*Com Matt 3:11 approx; PL 107:772C; CM 174:81

John's Humility

*John demonstrated Christ's greatness with these words, *the latchet of whose shoes I am not worthy to stoop down and loose**—a humble and lowly service. In other words, "He is so much greater than I that I am not worthy to serve him; I am not called to perform the most menial service, such as the lowly task of loosening his sandals."* ***R 12**

*Mark 1:7

**Chrys, Hom John 3.16; PG 59:89*

John was speaking metaphorically, inasmuch as Jesus did not wear shoes; he was using a common figure of speech to indicate his unworthiness to render even the lowliest service to Christ. In our own day, when we want to express our own unimportance and another's greatness, we might say something like, "I'm not worthy to kiss his boots."[3] Nor is it surprising that John would say this: any human being, however great, is nothing but dust and ashes compared to God;

[3] Literally, "I am not worthy to touch his shoes": *Non sum dignus tangere sotulares eius.*

nor is any creature worthy to serve God, unless taken up by grace. John's words also show the Pharisees that he did not arrogate an undeserved office to himself by baptizing, but was in fact carrying out his mission as Forerunner.*

**Lyra John 1:27*

Gregory suggests that allegorically the sandal symbolizes Christ's humanity, the foot his divinity, and the strap the union of Christ's soul and body with his divinity, which defies understanding.* Neither John himself nor anyone else can explain or plumb the ineffable mystery of the union of the two natures, human and divine, by which the Word became flesh, a union so great that God became Man and Man became God. As Isaiah asks, *Who shall declare his generation?** Gregory goes on,

*40 Hom 7.3; PL 76:1101D; CL 141:50

*Isa 53:8

> We must ponder and consider with all our attention how holy people who possess wonderful knowledge strive to bring before their inner eyes what they do not know in order to safeguard the virtue of humility. On the one hand, they consider their weakness; on the other, their hearts are not lifted up in regard to that at which they excel. It remains, then, that the mind should abase itself in regard to everything it knows, lest the wind of pride blow away what the virtue of knowledge gathers. When you do good deeds, brethren, call to mind the evils you have done; when you attend to your fault, your heart is never heedlessly happy because of your good deeds. Those of you in authority over others, pay special attention to your neighbors, because you do not know what good lies even in those you see doing something wrong . . . .* Whatever good works may be present, they are worth nothing unless they are seasoned with humility. A person who gathers virtues without humility is like one carrying dust in the wind.*

*40 Hom 7.4; PL 76:1102BC; CL 141:51

*40 Hom 7.4; PL 76:1103A; CL 141:52

***R 13**

*John then said, "*He shall baptize you*, not only in water, but *in the Holy Spirit and fire*,* bestowing the

*Matt 3:11

grace of the Holy Spirit and charity, as no one but God can do." Indeed, the grace of the Holy Spirit is given in Christ's baptism, and through him the fire of charity, if it is duly received and no obstacle is put in the way; John's baptism could not confer this grace, but it signifies Christ's baptism and prepares for it. Chrysostom writes, "John's baptism was one thing, the Lord's is another. That was a baptism of repentance, this of sanctification and grace, in which the Holy Spirit comes to every believer to melt away sins, acting like a purifying fire to burn away transgressions and purge the flesh and spirit of its impurities."* And Bede says, "We are baptized by the Lord in the Holy Spirit, not only on the day of our baptism, when we are washed in the fountain of life for the remission of sins, but in truth daily, when through the grace of the same Spirit we are enflamed with a desire to do what is pleasing to God."* There is baptism of flowing in water, of the spirit or wind in penance, and of blood in martyrdom.[4]

*Chromatius 11.5; CL 9A:241

*Com Mark 1:8; PL 92:138A; CL 120:442

[4] *Est ergo Baptismus fluminis in aqua, flaminis in poenitentia, sanguinis in martyrio.* Ludolph mentions these three kinds of baptism in the context of his presentation of John's baptism of water and Christ's baptism of water and the Holy Spirit. The Latin name for "baptism of desire" may have come from the similarity of the words *fluminis/flaminis*. Thomas Aquinas speaks of baptism of water, of blood, and of the Spirit: "Baptism of water has its efficacy from Christ's passion, to which a person is conformed by baptism, and also from the Holy Spirit, as first cause. Now although the effect depends on the first cause, the cause far surpasses the effect, nor does it depend on it. Consequently, a person may, without baptism of water, receive the sacramental effect from Christ's passion, in so far as he or she is conformed to Christ by suffering for him. . . . In like manner a person receives the effect of baptism by the power of the Holy Spirit, not only without baptism of water, but also without baptism of blood, when the heart is moved by the Holy Spirit to believe in and love God and to repent of sins: wherefore this is also called baptism of repentance" (ST III, q. 66, a.11).

Christ's Second Coming

***R 14** *After bearing witness to Christ's first coming, John went on to speak about his final one, warning the people that he would return with the authority and office of a Judge *whose fan* is in his hand*.‡ The word *ventilabrum* comes from *ventilandis paleis*, meaning, "chaff blown in the breeze."* It was customary in Palestine to use this kind of shovel to separate the wheat from the chaff: the grain was tossed into the air, the lighter chaff was blown away, and the heavier grain fell to the ground. John is speaking metaphorically.

**ventilabrum*
‡Matt 3:12

*Isidore, Ety 20.14.10; PL 82:726A

By *ventilabrum* he understands the discernment of a just examination, or divine justice, and the power to distinguish the good from the evil, the fruitful from the unproductive, just as a winnowing fan separates the wheat from the chaff.* The power and arbitration are *in his hand*, because the office of judging has been entrusted to him by his Father, who *has given all judgment to the Son*.*

**Zachary 1.13; PL 186:98BC*

*John 5:22

John continues, "In the future *he will thoroughly cleanse and purge his floor*, that is, his church, of the chaff. For now the wheat and the chaff, the good and the wicked, are mixed together; but they will be separated by him at the Judgment. He *will gather the wheat*, the good and the just who are dispersed in many places, *into his barn*, that is, his heavenly habitation. *But the chaff he will burn with unquenchable fire** of Gehenna and its torments."

*Luke 3:17

The just resemble wheat in many ways: white within by their purity; red without by their patience; weighty in their behavior, useful in their speech, fruitful to others in their example. The wicked and reprobates, on the contrary, are like chaff: blown aloft by pride, pale green with envy, brittle from anger, parched with avarice, unproductive through laziness, worthless because of their inordinate desires.* In the present age the Lord purifies his church when, because of their

**Gorran Matt 3:12*

manifest sins, the perverse and wicked are judged deserving of excommunication, or by death are cut off from this life. But this final purification will be total, when by the ministry of angels all the scandalous will be uprooted from his kingdom.

Or we could say that he cleanses his church now by distinguishing the good from the evil by merit but not by number; at the end they will be distinguished both by merit and by number.* **Gorran Matt 3:12*

And many other things exhorting did he preach and teach *to the people*.* From these words it is clear that not everything John said and did has been recorded. In fact, very few things have been written down, just as John the Evangelist says of Christ in the final chapter of his gospel. *Luke 3:18

John as a Model

*In a moral sense John stands as a model in his way of life, his preaching, and his ministry. His austere life: harsh diet, rough clothing, dwelling in the desert. His true preaching: about God, about himself, about his neighbor. His fruitful ministry: calling, baptizing, and improving the multitude. In the first, he is a model for religious; in the second, for teachers; in the third, for pastors. He was such a remarkable preacher that people were coming from Jerusalem (the cloistered), Judea (the clergy), and the region about the Jordan (the laity), confessing all their sins, mortal and venial. And Jesus was coming to be with them to sanctify them by his words, his example, and his cures. ***R 15**

Conclusion

*And to where were they coming? *These things were done in Bethany, beyond the Jordan, where John was baptizing*.* Chrysostom comments, "He did not proclaim ***R 16** *John 1:28

Christ in a house or in the corner, but, crossing the Jordan, he did this in the midst of a great throng who came to be baptized by him."* The text says that John baptized *in Bethany*, which means *house of obedience*.[5] This signifies three things. First, that it was in obedience to God that John had come to announce that Christ would offer himself in sacrifice for the redemption of the world. Next, that people should realize that if they seek deliverance from the original sin our first parents had contracted by disobedience, they ought to receive the sacrament of baptism, submissive in body and heartfelt in faith; in obedience to faith, all should come to be baptized. Finally, that obedience is a fitting virtue for the baptized.

*Hom 17.1; PG 59:107

There are two towns named Bethany: one is on this side of the Jordan about two miles from Jerusalem on the slope of Mount Olivet, where Lazarus was raised from the dead; the other, of which we are speaking here, is across the Jordan in the region allotted to the two and a half tribes, about a day's journey from Jerusalem. John was baptizing at a place where the Jewish and Gentile territories were contiguous, demonstrating that Christ's baptism is available to Jew and Gentile alike. And it is fitting that he did this *beyond the Jordan*, because in the event more Gentiles than Jews would receive Christian baptism.[6]

[5] Jerome, Int nom, renders *Bethania* as *house of affliction* or *house of obedience* (PL 23:839; CL 72:135).

[6] Ludolph draws on Aquinas, Com John 1:28, for some of his symbolic interpretations of Bethany and the idea that there were two villages. Aquinas comments that Origen and Chrysostom were of the opinion that the biblical text had corrupted the original name of this latter town, which was Bethabora.

✠

O John, blessed Forerunner of Christ, herald of the Judge, friend of the bridegroom, voice of the divine Word, you merited the grace to proclaim the consolation of our redemption. By your most holy prayers in the presence of our Lord Jesus Christ obtain for me, a poor sinner, that, with my heart cleansed of sin and adorned with virtues, I may heed your teachings and prepare the way of the Lord and make straight his paths. At the Last Judgment, when the Lord cleanses the threshing floor of his church and separates the wheat from the chaff, may I deserve to be found among the grains of wheat, his elect, and to be placed with them in the granary of the heavenly habitation. Amen.

CHAPTER 20

The Need to Do Penance

*R 1

*In the preceding chapters we have touched on the subject of repentance, by which the kingdom of heaven draws near and the way of the Lord is prepared; now we will consider this subject in greater depth. True repentance, which produces love of God and hatred for sin, requires two things: the sinner must be sorry for offenses committed and be resolved not to sin again. There is no real repentance without these two conditions; if they are lacking, God cannot forgive the sinner and the priest cannot absolve us.

Bernard teaches, "True penitence consists in grieving without delay over past offenses and weeping for them in such a way that the sinner would not commit them again. If we continue to do the deeds for which we repent, we are not penitents but scoffers. Cease from sinning and do not sin again if you want truly to be repentant. That repentance is empty that subsequent offense defiles."* And Gregory: "Repentance means both weeping for the evil we have done and not doing again what we have bewailed. A person who weeps bitterly over some things in such a way as to commit others either does not know how to repent or is just pretending to do so."* Augustine says, "That repentance is empty that subsequent offense defiles. There is no use crying over sins if they are repeated. It does no good to ask pardon for your evil deeds and then commit them again."* And elsewhere he pleads, "Penitents, penitents! If you really are

*Ps-Bernard, Cognitione 4.13; PL 184:493D

*40 Hom 34.15; PL 76:1256B; CL 141:314–15

*Isidore, Synonyma 1.76; PL 83:845A; CL 111B:61

penitents and not mockers, change your life and be reconciled. You do penance, you kneel, but you are laughing—and so you mock God's patience. If you are repentant, do penance; if you do not do penance, you are not repentant. If you are sorry, why are you doing the evil you did? If you were truly repentant, you would not sin; if you continue to sin, you are not repentant."* *Aug?, Sermo 393; PL 39:1714

Forms of Repentance

*The same Augustine informs us that penitence takes several forms: ***R 2**

> There are three kinds of repentance. One is the sort that is in labor to give birth to the new person until, through saving baptism, we are cleansed of all past sins. When we who are able to make free decisions for ourselves approach the sacrament of the faithful, we cannot begin the new life until we repent of the old. Only very little children who are baptized are exempt from this kind of repentance, because they cannot yet exercise free will. However, the faith of those who present them for baptism avails them for sanctification and the remission of original sin; whatever defilement of wrongdoing they contracted through others, from whom they were born, they can be cleansed of through others, from whom the responses come to the questions asked at baptism. Aside from little children, no others can cross over to Christ and begin to be what they are not unless they have repented of what they were.* *Sermo 351.2; PL 39:1537
>
> There is another kind of repentance that we should practice with the humility of perpetual supplication throughout our whole life. This is true first because no one longs for eternal life who is not dissatisfied with this passing one. Who can doubt

that whatever kind of temporal well-being we enjoy, we ought still to be regretting this life so that we will hasten with all eagerness to that life of incorruptibility? Who would pine for their homeland and hasten to return there unless they mourned their exile? . . . And who in their right mind would not weep and regret their unhappiness at being like this? . . . There are many sins, and, although none of them taken singly is felt to inflict a mortal wound, when taken together they are lethal unless they are cut out by the medicine of daily repentance. . . . Whoever gives the matter sufficient thought will recognize the danger of wandering away from the Lord.*

*Sermo 351.3–6; PL 39:1539–41

The third sort of repentance is the kind that must be undergone for those sins named in the Ten Commandments. We should exercise greater severity on ourselves in this kind of penance; if we judge ourselves we will not be judged by God. Let us take our seat on the bench in the tribunal of conscience and face ourselves in the dock. With court convened in our heart, let self-examination appear for the prosecution, conscience be called as a witness, fear act as an executioner. Next, let a kind of blood of the spirit flow in the form of a tearful confession. Finally, our mind itself should pass the sentence that we are unworthy for the time being of sharing in the Lord's Body and Blood. Fearful of being cut off from the kingdom of heaven by the final sentence of the supreme Judge, let us embrace the discipline of the church and temporarily refrain from receiving the Bread from heaven.* Let us pass judgment on ourselves on these things voluntarily and change our behavior for the better while we can, lest when we no longer can, we be judged against our will by the Lord.*

*Sermo 351.7; PL 39:1543

*Sermo 351.9; PL 39:1545

But what if by now, despairing at being healed, you are piling sin upon sin, as it is written, *The wicked man feels contempt when he comes into the depths of sins*?* Do not despise and do not despair; cry out to the Lord even from the depths. It was

*Prov 18:3

> from such depths that the people of Nineveh cried out, and they found mercy; the prophet's threats were more easily discounted than the humiliation of repentance. Whatever you have done, whatever sins you have committed, you are still in this life, from which God would certainly remove you if he did not want to heal you. So why ignore the fact that God's patience is inducing you to repent?*

*Sermo 351.13; PL 39:1548

From what Augustine says it is clear that we should do penance daily not only for our major sins but for our minor ones as well; although they seem small, they are not for that reason negligible. Gregory observes, "No sin is so small that it will not grow if it is neglected."‡ And, "A sin that is not washed away by penance pulls us by its own weight to another sin."* Ambrose suggests that the smallest sin, committed with full knowledge, weighs more than the whole world.* Augustine writes, "Do not esteem lightly those sins we call 'light.' If you esteem them lightly when you weigh them, fear them when you add them up. Many light sins make a heavy one, just as many drops fill a river and many grains make a heap."* Let us neither ignore minor sins nor despair of great ones; for, according to the same Augustine, no sin is criminal that displeases, and no sin is unimportant so long as we take pleasure in it.*

‡Ps-Augustine, Vera et falsa 20; PL 40:1119

*Mor 25.IX.22; PL 76:334B; CL 143B:1247

*Honorius, Eluc 2.2; PL 172:1135B

*Ep John 1.6; PL 35:1982

*Richard of Saint Victor, Posteriorum NT 2.16

Do Not Delay

Let us repent without delay while we still can, lest, suddenly snatched away, we look for an opportunity to repent and not find it. Augustine warns, "The remedies of conversion to God should on no account be postponed; do not let the season of amendment be wasted through your slowness to act. He who promised pardon to the sinner did not promise tomorrow to the negligent." And again, ***R 3**

*Prosper 71; PL 45:1865

Those who find themselves in the final throes of illness and wish to receive penance do receive it and straightaway are reconciled, and then they depart from here. I have to admit to you that we do not deny them what they requested, but we cannot take it for granted that they made a good departure from here. I do not take it for granted; no, I will not deceive you, I do not take it for granted. The faithful who live good lives depart from here safely; those who are baptized at the last moment depart from here safely. But whether those who defer penance to the end and only then are reconciled depart from here safely, I myself cannot feel sure. Where I am sure, I can give assurances. Where I am not sure, I can give penance, but I cannot give assurances.

I am not saying, "They will be damned." Nor am I saying, "They will be saved." Do you want to avoid the uncertainty? Do penance while you are still healthy. If you are doing genuine penance while still in good health, and your last day comes suddenly upon you, hasten to be reconciled. If you do that, you will have nothing to fear as you depart from this life because you have done true penance during the time when you could also have gone on sinning. But if you want to do penance only after you no longer can sin, then you have not gotten rid of your sins—your sins have gotten rid of you! There are two possibilities: either you are forgiven or you are not forgiven. Which of these two will happen to you, I do not know. So put away what is uncertain, and cling to what is certain.*

*Augustine, Sermo 393; PL 39:1714

Augustine harbors doubts about those who repent *in extremis*: their repentance is dubious because they seem to be motivated more by a fear of punishment than by a love of justice. Do not neglect or delay; do penance while you are in good health, and quickly lay aside the burden of your sins. As Augustine observes, it is foolish to live in a state in which you would not want to die, and it is more reckless to go to sleep with one mortal sin than among seven enemies.* People often promise themselves a long life because they are young, healthy, or strong, but they do not know what tomorrow will bring, nor do they consider how rare a natural death is. They should rather reflect on fevers, abscesses, and similar ailments, or on sudden fortuitous deaths of various kinds. Nevertheless, they imagine they will die at the moment when they are at their best.

*Attr. to Augustine in Hugh 3.7

Hugh of Saint Victor says, "We must know that none of us, whether just or wicked, young or old, is released from the body before we reach that point of goodness or malice that we would never surpass if we were to live for ever."* Many people deceive themselves with the hope of a long life, but the repentance they anticipate never materializes. In Chrysostom's opinion, "Nothing so deceives people as the vain hope for a longer life."* And Augustine warns, "In my experience, many have breathed their last while waiting to be reconciled."*

*De arca Noe morali 3.14 approx; PL 176:661C

*source unknown

*Augustine, Sermo 393; PL 39:1714

‡R 4

‡Even if we could be assured of a long life, still it would not be a good idea to put off repentance until old age—our ability to exert ourselves will be lessened, and it is not likely that we will uproot by penance the sins to which we have grown accustomed. The best counsel, the highest prudence, and the greatest foresight consists in this: that while we are hale and hearty we dispose ourselves by true contrition, an unadulterated and integral confession, and appropriate satisfaction to banish all the harmful things that divert us or hinder us from eternal salvation; in this way, we will be ready to leave this world today, tomorrow, or next week. It is certainly possible to repent at the very end of life: after all, it is possible to sin to the end, and so it is also possible, through God's mercy, to obtain forgiveness from sin; divine mercy excels human malice. However, such belated penance is rarely genuine and fruitful because there may not

be adequate, characteristic hatred for sin. Sufficient contrition is necessary for the forgiveness of sins, but the suffering and pain that assault the sensitive part of the soul when we are *in articulo mortis* impede the penitent's use of reason, so we cannot deliberate well on our sins.

Therefore, rejoice when a penance is imposed or, better still, freely take it on, giving thanks to God, who has determined to await you with mercy at this hour. Do not be ungrateful: you have this very day an opportunity to reform. Yesterday you were bad; today, be good. Think about what many dying people would do if they were granted just this one hour that has been given to you for repentance. How they would hurry without delay to the altars, there to kneel or even prostrate themselves on the ground, and remain for a long time sighing, weeping, and praying until they were found worthy to receive the full pardon of God for all their sins. But you waste the time God has given you to seek grace and earn glory by eating, drinking, joking, laughing, and enjoying a leisurely life. Think, too, about the souls suffering in hell without hope of mercy. If the love of God cannot detain or delight you, at least be held and deterred by the fear of Judgment, the dread of Gehenna, the chains of death, and all those terrible punishments.*

**Ps-Bernard, De interiori domo 34; PL 184:543C*

But, alas! Many today abuse God's patience, giving little thought to such important matters; they waste time, that most precious of gifts, and wretchedly fritter it away on frivolous things. Bernard writes, "Today people neglect the care of their soul and devote themselves thoroughly to the desires of the flesh. They are not afraid to sin—they are only afraid of being punished. Their concern is not to develop the virtues of the heart, but the soundness of the body, and even its enjoyment. They learned these lessons at the school of Hippocrates and Epicurus. But this is a time for souls, not bodies; these are days of salvation, not salaciousness."* And again, "There is nothing more precious

*Gaufrid 30.36; PL 184:457BC

than time, but alas! Today nothing is considered more worthless. The days of salvation pass by, and they are not given a thought. No one reflects that these moments have slipped away, never to return."* *Gaufrid 44.54; PL 184:465C

‡In truth, there is no gift more precious than time: ‡R 5 we have a brief hour in which to obtain pardon, grace, and glory, and to merit more than the whole world can offer. The time is short, but in it we can acquire spiritual wealth that far exceeds in worth all the passing things of this world. Reflect, too, on the fact that one day of suffering here has more value than a year of suffering in purgatory; as we read in Ezekiel, *A day for a year I have appointed to you.** *Ezek 4:6 The punishment in purgatory exceeds all the temporal punishments in this world. Augustine says that the fire of purgatory is harsher than any pains we can feel or see or even imagine in this world.* *Caesarius of Arles, Sermo 179.5; CL 104:726–27 Therefore, it is better for us to undertake to live a good life than a long one. In the words of Seneca, "The important thing is not how long you live, but how well you live;* *Lucilium 77.20 life is measured by performance, not duration."[1]* *Lucilium 93.4

The First Element of Penance: Contrition of Heart

*Penance consists of three things: contrition of heart, *R 6 confession by the mouth, and satisfaction by works. Scripture says, "*Rend your hearts, and not your garments;** *Joel 2:13 *confess therefore your sins one to another,** *Jas 5:16 and *bring forth therefore fruits worthy of penance.*"* *Luke 3:8 Inasmuch as every sin is committed in our heart, in our words, or in our deeds, it is right that each sin be cured by its contrary: sinners should detest sin in their heart, confess it with

[1] The first phrase, *Quam bene vivas refert, non quamdiu*, give Seneca's words reduced to a maxim; the original sense was, "Life is like a play. What matters is not how long it lasts, but how well you play your part."

their words, and do penance in their deeds. These three parts are symbolized by the three days' journey to the Promised Land, spoken of in Exodus: *The God of the Hebrews has called us, to go three days' journey into the wilderness, and to sacrifice to the Lord our God; lest a pestilence or the sword fall upon us,** that is, either present fault or future punishment. The Virgin Mary sought her Son for three days and found him. If you seek Jesus, you will also find him in three days, and with him eternal salvation. A third image of penance is the ladder with three rungs that Jacob saw reaching from earth to heaven. The Lord supported the ladder for three reasons: first, to hold it steady; second, to stretch out a hand to help those climbing it if need be; third, so that if the climbers grew weary from the labor, they needed only look up at the Lord and cast all their care upon him. He is not so cruel as to let someone fall.*

*Exod 5:3

**Raymond of Penyafort, Summa de poen 3.24.7*

‡R 7

‡The first stage of penance is contrition of heart. Contrition can be defined as sorrow freely felt for sins committed, with the intention of confessing them and making satisfaction for them; contrition is not sincere if this intention is lacking. In contrition, we lead all our sins one by one before the tribunal of our conscience, there accuse ourselves with bitter, heartfelt regret, and afterwards confess them. Each mortal sin should excite its own contrition. Different diseases call for different medicines. It is true that contrition is the one medicine to be applied to each mortal sin; however, it is not enough to feel some vague sorrow for all your sins; you should experience grief for each individual mortal sin, if you can recall distinct offenses. Chrysostom says that just as tiny particles in the air can be seen in a sunbeam although they are otherwise invisible, so our smallest defects become visible when properly illuminated by a ray of mental introspection; they remain undetected to darkened or lazy minds.*

*source unknown

How long should you grieve for your offenses? When God frees us from the fetters of sin or from our faults and their eternal punishment, he binds us to an everlasting hatred of sin. For this reason it is useful for the priest to impose some small but perpetual penance, so that by this means the penitent can recall past sins with a contrite spirit.

Perpetual hatred for sin can take two forms: actual contrition and habitual contrition. The first is illustrated by Saint Peter, of whom it is written that he wept ceaselessly, or by holy David, who said, *My sin is always before me*.* This is a more perfect form of contrition, and those who strive to be perfect will seek to perform it; but it is not binding on anyone. The second form, habitual contrition, is binding on everyone, even after the complete remission of sin. Augustine says of this second form, "Penitents should regard all the fruit of their penance to be a small thing, never sufficient. They should always feel sorrow, and draw joy from their sorrow; they should feel sorrow because they have not always felt sorrow. Let them blush continually before God, in whose sight they sinned, and end their sorrow only when this life ends."* And again: "Either grief will torment my body continually in this life, or punishment will torment my soul eternally in the next."* The penitent's contrition should never cease, and it is never completed in this life: we have sinned against God, who is eternal, so we should repent "eternally," that is, so long as our earthly life lasts.

*Ps 50:5

*Ps-Augustine, Vera et falsa 28; PL 40:1124

*Ps-Augustine, De contrit cordis 4; PL 40:945

Yet many people weep for their sins, not because their sins displease them for God's sake, but from fear of punishment. Others only regret their sins because their behavior has been shameful. Fruitful contrition consists in feeling sorrow because you have offended God by your sins, and your tears and inner turmoil flow from this; your love of justice makes your iniquity detestable to you. The more deeply you experience genuine repentance, the more God forgives your sins, and the more disposed he is, by his grace in the present, to deliver you from the eternal punishment they deserve. Through a quickening of the mind, the eternal punishment due for your actual sins is commuted into temporal punishment so that you are purified from the illicit desires of your heart or from sins of the flesh by the bitterness of a fitting penalty. In this way you will avoid a more severe punishment in the future, because no evil goes unpunished. Finally, we have two reasons to weep: we should experience contrition for the sins we have committed and for the good we have failed to do.*

**Zachary 3.98 approx; PL 186:315D–16B*

The Second Element of Penance: Confession by the Mouth

*R 8

*The second part of penance involves confession by the mouth, that is, making known a hidden sickness with the hope that it will be pardoned. Such confession takes two forms: the first is mental, making sin known before God; the second is vocal, making sin known to a human being; the first is of natural law, while the second is not. Before the incarnation of Christ it sufficed to make a mental confession to God alone, because God had not yet become Man. But after God became Man, it became necessary to confess one's sins to him as Man. Christ could not be everywhere in his human body, so he appointed people to be his vicars—first, Peter and the other apostles, and subsequently his priests. He himself said to them, *Whatever you shall bind upon earth shall be bound also in heaven: and whatever you shall loose upon earth, shall be loosed also in heaven.** By giving his ministers the sacramental powers to bind and to loose, Christ implies that confession should be made to them as judges. Christ tacitly instituted confession, and it was expressly promulgated by the apostles.[2]* Therefore, confession

*Matt 18:18

**Hugh 6.25*

[2] Hugh of Ripelin associates the apostolic promulgation of confession with James 5:16, *Therefore confess your sins to one another.* Far from relying on simple proof texts regarding the

should be made to a human being who acts as Christ's vicar; in this way, our sins are hidden from the devil.

Augustine writes,

> Throughout the divine Scriptures, dear friends, we are admonished that it is a useful, wholesome practice to confess our sins frequently and humbly, not only to God, but to holy and God-fearing people. It is not that God wants us to confess our sins because otherwise he would not know them. Rather, the devil wants us to keep silent about our sins so that he can have accusations to hurl at us before the tribunal of the eternal Judge. God, on the contrary, being kind and merciful, wants us to confess our sins in this age so that we will not be confounded by them in the age to come. The devil knows the power of a thorough confession, and he will make every effort to keep us from confessing our sins. Just as he first tempts us to fall into sin, so he tries to keep us from rising again afterwards, and he knows that we cannot rise again without confession.*

*Ps-Augustine, Sermo 253.1, De confessione; PL 39:2212–13

It is worse to refuse to confess than it is to disregard the law; it is worse to refuse to make amends to God than it is to offend his goodness by sinning.* Even though sins are forgiven where there is contrition, vocal confession is still necessary either in fact, when it is possible, or at least in intention, when a person is prevented from going to confession by force of

**Ps-Chrysostom, de confess; Fronton 6:430*

institution of the sacraments, scholastic theologians spoke of their "institution" in dynamic terms: the sacraments had a foundation in natural law, adumbrations in the Old Covenant, and their full realization in the time of Christ and the apostles. In his commentary on the Sentences (IV Sent, d. 22, a.1, q.1 ad resp) Bonaventure writes, "clear and open confession was instituted by the apostles, or, to put it better, it was promulgated when the Lord taught the apostles, and they, once instructed by the Lord and having received authority, promulgated it on his authority. For they handed on to us nothing but what they had received either from the Lord or from the Spirit of the Lord."

circumstance and not simply out of contempt for religion. In the situation of a person who is unable to go to confession, the need to confess after contrition is not required for the sake of healing, but to fulfill the precept.*

*Hugh 6.25

*R 9

Sacramental confession was instituted with great wisdom: we have turned away from God by placing ourselves under our own power; we return by submitting with humility and devotion to the power of another. For this reason God established the priest to act in his place, almost as a physician who can lay bare the wounds of sinners, and sinners, for the sake of greater humility, receive the medicine of satisfaction from another person and not from themselves. The sacraments function as a kind of medicinal dressing.

*Abelard, Epitome 36; PL 178:1756D

Augustine teaches,

> Therefore, sinners hold nothing back and put themselves entirely under the authority of the priest who acts as judge. They are prepared to follow the priest's instructions in order to receive life in their soul, just as they follow a doctor's orders to avoid bodily death.* People are more prone to commit sin if they think that they will not have to reveal their shameful actions. Since confession is the beginning of good deeds, it is very useful to confess our bad deeds frequently.* It can happen that a heart already contrite and humbled is confirmed in confession. And while many times sinners present themselves to the priest motivated only by fear or by the church's precept, through the priest's exercise of his office they can experience true compunction of heart and leave full of charity. True, there are not a few who do not experience this heartfelt contrition, but the practice of going to confession regularly can nourish humility and charity in them.* And do not stop going to confession because you are embarrassed: the shame, anxiety, and humiliation of confessing are themselves a very significant penance to undertake.*

*Ps-Augustine, Vera et falsa 30

*De Vitry, Hist Orient, 76

*Zachary, Hist ev 3.99–100; PL 186:316C

*De Vitry, Hist Orient 76

Chrysostom says, "The confession of sin is a sign of a good heart and a God-fearing conscience; perfect fear removes all shame. On the other hand, confession is considered shameful where there is no belief in the punishment of future justice. But as the embarrassment itself is a heavy punishment, God commands us to confess our sins so that we endure shame as punishment; that itself is part of divine judgment."* And Valerius Maximus teaches, "The person who does not make excuses for sins is deserving of pardon. Where there is confession, there is remission. The next best thing to innocence is a modest confession."[3]* Augustine writes, "Because it is very embarrassing to confess our sins, the person who is shamefaced for love of Christ deserves mercy. The more often we confess our disgraceful wrongdoing, the more easily the grace of remission follows."* And elsewhere, "O foolish one, why do you blush to say to a human being what you do not blush to do in God's sight? Put aside your sense of honor, hasten to the priest, reveal your secret, confess your sin. Otherwise, your heartfelt contrition will avail you nothing, unless it is followed by going to confession if you can."* And again, "Confession is the health/salvation of souls, the destroyer of vice, the restorer of virtues, the scourge of demons. What more? It blocks the mouth of hell and opens the gates of Paradise."* Pope Gregory also commends the practice of confession when speaking of Job: "Let those who wish to do so admire his self-control in chastity, his integrity in justice, the depth of his compassion; I

*Opus imperf 3; PG 56:650

*Albertanus, Consol chap. 49

*Ps-Augustine, Vera et falsa 25; PL 40:1122

*Hildebert of Lavardin?, Sermo 42; PL 171:553A

*Ps-Augustine, Fratres 30; PL 40:1289

[3] Ludolph credits Valerius Maximus, a first-century Roman historian and moralist, but these lines come from *de Moribus 94*, and *Proverbia 52*, of Ps-Seneca, an anthology of writings by Seneca, Publilius Syrus, Ausonius, and Lactantius. They were brought together in the *Liber consolationis et consilii* by Albertanus of Brescia. Chaucer drew on material from Albertanus, including these lines, in "The Tale of Melibee," in *The Canterbury Tales.*

*Mor 22.XV.34; PL 76:344B; CL 143:1116
‡R 10

admire him no less for his most humble confession of sin than for the sublimity of his virtuous deeds."*

‡It is very useful and salutary to repeat the confession of the same sins frequently and to more than one priest. Although repeated confession is not necessary for salvation, it is beneficial, whether because we are unsure that we were sufficiently contrite when we first confessed, or because our greater humility and mortification is meritorious, or because in every confession some of the penalty due to sin is removed and some grace conferred by virtue of the sacrament. The priest frees a penitent from some of the punishment due to sin by the power of the keys, so a person might confess so many times that no punishment remains at all. Some maintain that the power of the keys is exercised only in the first absolution, because there is no need for absolution in subsequent confessions. Others hold a more generous opinion, that a person could confess the same sin several times with a contrite heart, be absolved of it, and so do away with the whole punishment of purgatory and go straight to heaven. The power of the keys always frees somewhat, and although there is no guilt requiring absolution, there remains the need for punishment.[4]*

**reatum poenae*

[4] Thomas writes in his *Summa contra Gentiles*: "In the later spiritual healing we are conjoined to Christ in accord with our own operation informed by divine grace. Hence we do not always entirely, nor do we all equally, achieve the effect of remission by this conjunction. For there can be a turning of the mind toward God, and to the merit of Christ, and to the hatred of sin that is so vehement that a man perfectly achieves the remission of sin, not only with regard to wiping out the fault, but even with regard to remission of the entire punishment. But this does not always happen. Hence, after the fault is taken away by contrition and the guilt of eternal punishment is relieved (as was said), there sometimes persists an obligation to some punishment to maintain the justice of God, which requires that fault be ordered by punishment" (IV.72.8). The "obligation to some punishment" is the *reatus poenae*; this connects contrition and confession to the third element of penance, satisfaction. Our

Even if no need for punishment remains, there is still an increase of grace brought about by the power of contrition. Nor does a * sin ordinarily remain without some punishment attached to it: the sorrow of contrition and the shame felt by the penitent in subsequent confessions form no small part of that punishment. Therefore, what could be better than frequently to confess our sins until, at the hundredth or thousandth confession, the one confessing is freed from all need for punishment? Note here that the general confession that is made in church before Mass cleanses us from venial sins and wipes away mortal sins that we have forgotten. *forgiven

*The confessor must be careful to protect the seal of confession and never reveal what he has been told, even if the penitent gives permission. The penitent may want to renounce the right to privacy and allow the priest to tell others what he heard in confession, but the penitent does not have the power to dispense from the precept of divine law, under which the seal of confession falls. And so, if the confessor judges that *R 11

sins have harmed others, and ordinarily there is some need to make reparation. This should not be understood merely in a juridical sense: the punishment we undergo by "doing penance" is also intended to free us from selfish attachments so that we can deepen our friendship with Christ. But the principal focus for scholastics is on contrition; as Thomas notes, this might be so intense that a person "achieves the remission of sin, not only with regard to wiping out the fault, but even with regard to remission of the entire punishment." In the first millennium, forgiveness was associated with doing penance: absolution and reconciliation took place after the penance was performed. In the Middle Ages, contrition came to the fore and absolution was given after the penitent expressed contrition by confession. Ludolph's idea of confessing the same sin frequently is not born of scrupulosity; as he says, the guilt of sin is removed the first time the sin is confessed. Rather, he sees this as a way of expressing ever more deeply one's contrition, even about past sins that have been forgiven. The shame associated with revealing one's sins is itself a purifying penance.

he does not have the authority to absolve or needs to seek more prudent counsel, he must have the penitent speak to him about the matter again outside of confession, but only so that he can consult his superior or some other advisor. A priest should never reveal to another person what he has heard in confession, even when threatened with death or when he himself is speaking to another priest under the seal of confession. Nor should the priest reproach penitents for their sin after confession or pressure them to speak about their sin to make it known.

The Third Element of Penance: Satisfaction by Works

*R 12

*The third part of penance is to make reparation by works; this is done by accepting a punishment commensurate with one's sins. In the words of John the Baptist, *Bring forth therefore fruit worthy of penance.** Here is Gregory's explanation: "He advises us to bring forth not merely the fruit of penance, but fruit *worthy* of penance. Good works should not bring the same reward to one who has sinned less seriously and to one who has sinned more seriously, nor to one who has not fallen into wicked deeds and to one who has. John's words apply to the conscience of each individual. Each of us should seek through repentance the advantages done by good works in proportion to the seriousness of the harm we have done ourselves by sinning."* And elsewhere, "We must keep in mind that people who remember having committed unlawful actions must strive to refrain even from some that are lawful, since they make satisfaction to their Creator in this way. Those who have done things that are prohibited should cut off from themselves even what is allowed."* Bernard says, "Let us abstain from what is lawful for the sake of the unlawful things we have done and for which we have been forgiven. It is evi-

*Matt 3:8

*40 Hom 20.8; PL 76:1153CD; CL 141:159

*40 Hom 34.16; PL 76:1256C; CL 141:315–16

dent that we should undertake forms of penance that are contrary to the sins we have committed."* *Sermo in Lent 4.1; PL 183:176C; SB 4:368

Chrysostom's interpretation is as follows:

> By repentance I mean not only to forsake our former evil deeds, but also to produce good ones. *Bring forth,* John says, *fruit worthy of penance*. But how shall we bring it forth? If we do the opposite deeds. Have you taken the goods of others? Henceforth give away even your own. Have you been guilty of fornication for a long time? Abstain for a time from lawful relations with your wife and meditate often on perpetual continence during those few days of abstention. Have you done injury to another by word or deed? Henceforth bless those that insult you and persecute you, and strive now to please them by your services to them. We will not regain our health simply by pulling out the dart; we must also apply remedies to the wound.
>
> Have you lived in self-indulgence and drunkenness? Compensate by fasting and drinking only water to overcome your cravings. Have you looked with lust upon a woman? Henceforth do not look on anyone at all; be more vigilant after having been wounded. It is said, *Turn away from evil and do good: seek after peace and pursue it*.* This is not peace with other people only, but also peace with God. And he says well, *pursue it*. For peace has been driven away and cast out; she has left the earth, and is gone to sojourn in heaven. Yet we can bring her back again if we wish, by putting away boasting and anger, and whatever else stands in the way of peace, and by following a pure and modest way of life.* *Ps 33:15 *Hom Matt 10.6; PG 57/58:190–91

Satisfaction should be made through works of penance. The wound of sin must be healed perfectly through satisfaction, but punishment is the medicine for sin, so it is necessary for satisfaction. Although it is impossible to take anything away from God, we sinners have stolen, to the extent we can, the honor *R 3 **ST Suppl., q. 15, a. 1 sed contra* due to God by our sin. Satisfaction represents a kind of recompense: we deprive ourselves of something that we give up for the honor of God. What is done must be a good work if it is to be done for the honor of God, and it must be a penitential work if it is to be done as reparation by the penitent. Thus it both makes amends to God and also discourages future malice and wickedness, inasmuch as it is a punishment.

A satisfaction should be something of our own we surrender for God's honor. Now in fact we only possess three goods: those of the soul, those of the body, and those of fortune, that is, material possessions. We can give up material goods by almsgiving and bodily goods by fasting. As regards diminishing the goods of the soul, it is not right to give up any of these, because through them we become acceptable to God, but we can give our soul entirely to God, to the extent it is good, and we do this through prayer. This threefold ordering of the works of satisfaction corresponds to the sources of sin: *the concupiscence of the flesh and the concupiscence of the eyes and the pride of life.** Fasting combats concupiscence of the flesh, almsgiving opposes concupiscence of the eyes, and prayer counters the pride of life.*

*1 John 2:16

**Aquinas, ST Suppl., Q. 15, concl.*

To reiterate, *the fruit of penance* should be produced in a way corresponding to the seriousness of the sin. This is said to correct those whose sins are many and whose penitence is modest. People who undertake a penance proportionate to the gravity of their crime and perform more penance if they sin more can be said to *bring forth fruit worthy of penance*. To the degree that you took pleasure in sin, to that degree offer a holocaust of repentance; if you parted from God by delight in wrongdoing, seek him now by detesting sin, reflecting through the rest of your years *in bitterness of soul.**

*Job 3:20

***R 14**

*Therefore, when the priest does not assign an appropriately weighty penance, or, if he does assign one but we do not fulfill it, we are not freed from all the punishment due for our sin, but only from that amount for which we did penance. Bernard warns, "Do not delude yourself: if you have sinned seriously and are given a light penance because you concealed something, whatever is lacking will be made up for in the fires of purgatory, because the Most High seeks *fruit worthy of penance*."*

*Damian, Sermo 58.2; PL 144:831A

But worthy penance does not consist so much in wearing down the body or protracted chastisement, but rather in heartfelt contrition. With God, the measure is depth of sorrow, not length of time; putting to death vices is more important than abstaining from food. This is why the canons of the church make allowance for a wise priest to vary the time that a person does penance, shortening or lengthening the duration according to the penitent's ardor or tepidity.* Contrition may be so great that it removes entirely the debt of punishment, because God accepts the affection of the heart more than exterior actions. We can be freed from guilt and punishment by actions, but we can also be freed by the heart's affection, which is contrition. The force of this contrition is manifested in two ways. The first way is by charity, which provokes hatred for sin; by means of this charity someone can deserve to be freed not only from guilt but from punishment as well. The second is by perceptible sorrow, which the will stirs up in contrition. And because that sorrow is itself experienced as a punishment by the penitent, it could be felt with such intensity that it suffices to do away with both guilt and punishment.*

**Zachary 3.99; PL 186:316D*

**ST III Supp., q. 5, a. 2 Resp*

‡R 15

‡If we cannot make satisfaction by ourselves for our sins, we can do so with the help of others. It may be that the punishment due to sin is greater than we can endure. For this reason, God in his great mercy has ordained that, with him and for him, satisfaction can be made first through the merits of Christ's passion: through that passion Christ not only redeemed the world; he also made satisfaction through his merits for all sinners. Second, the merits of the whole church

can make satisfaction for the sinner. Augustine teaches that the alms and prayers offered in the church come to the aid of those who are converted and seek pardon.[5]* Third, there is our own effort to make amends. From these three—the merits of the Lord's passion, those of the whole church, and our own penitential acts—is amassed the wealth that more than pays the debt for sins. Jerome warns, "Satan tempts some sinners with despair in the face of a hard penance, and others with presumption with a light one. Hence Solomon says, *Decline not to the right hand, nor to the left.*"*

*source unknown

*Prov 4:27; Ps-Jerome, Com 2 Cor 2:11; PL 30:777B

The Gravity of Sin

In order to stir up a greater desire to perform fitting penance, reflect that Adam was severely punished for one sin: he had to lament the misery of this life for ninety years and more, lacking the many supports and mechanical conveniences we enjoy, and then spend nearly four thousand years in the darkness of the underworld. How, then, will our transgressions be punished, which are so many and great? When we are delivered over to the supernal Judge, we will have to render an account of the number and kind of our sins, their gravity and their duration! What tears, what prayers, what fasting will be needed to offer fitting penance for sins that are deserving of eternal death!

[5] Augustine does teach, contra the Pelagians, that the prayers of the church help unbelievers come to faith and believers grow in faith: *De Haeresibus* 88 (PL 44:107). The first half of this paragraph is from Jordan of Quedlinburg: Sermo 104, Opus Jor Sermonum de Tempore. The Opus Jor was never printed and is very rare. The text here is cited in Saak, *High Way*, 398 n. 179; the source document is Opus Jor [Sermones de Tempore], Vatican City, Bibliotheca Apostolica Vaticana, MS. Pal Lat 448, fol. 180.

Let us consider as well what we lose through sin, what we gain, and whom we offend. We lose the friendship of the Trinity, the angels, the apostles, and all the saints, the soul's glory, the prayers of the church. We gain a very strong snare, most cruel enemies, a perilous condition, a terrible danger, a loss of grace, the death of the soul. We offend the one who created us, who endured death for us, who showered benefits upon us, and who promised eternal rewards to us. If we take this all to heart, we will certainly mourn and weep for our sins.

Rare indeed is the penitent who knows how to do penance, and few who actually do it in truth. For, according to Ambrose and Gregory, it is easier to find someone who has safeguarded innocence than it is to find one who really does penance.* This is why there are few who are not in need of the fires of purgatory. Bernard says, "Let others perceive and appraise the matter as they wish, but I am sure that to date I have not known a single penitent who in my estimation will not require the purifying flames. I will count myself extremely fortunate if I am cleansed in the crucible of purgatory right up to Judgment Day, so that I can dare to meet the Judge purified."[6]* What hope can the many poor sinners have, if so holy a man feared and trembled for himself?

*Ambrose, De poen 2.10.96; PL 16:520B

*source unknown

If you want to do true penance and so receive the grace of perfect remission of sins, you must exercise great care. When you have been purged through confession and circumcised, as it were, you should follow

[6] A similar sentiment is found in the sixth sermon on the Purification by Guerric of Igny: "But who are the people so perfect, so holy, that when they depart hence they owe nothing to the fire, who have so thoroughly burned out all the dross of sin in themselves that they can boast they have a pure heart? . . . Few are chosen, but in my opinion even among them there are very few indeed who are so perfect" (PL 185:89D).

Joshua's directive and stay at your place in the camp until you are fully healed.* Eat the bread of sorrow and repentance in silence away from the crowd; absent yourself from games, worldly spectacles, fellowship, and every occasion of sin.* Cut away every reason, every occasion, every hint of sin, and persons, places, and gatherings with whom you associated as a sinner. Cut away your senses, by which you were a transgressor; enter the chamber of your mind and, with the door closed against all the small streams of sins, pray in secret to your Father who is in heaven. Stay in one place, spending your time in penance; do not wander about or run off to banquets or shows. This is especially important at the beginning of penance, when the wounds of your circumcision are still fresh. This is why Joshua would not allow the Israelites to leave the camp before they were completely healed. Mary stood at the Lord's feet, watering them with her tears and drying them with her hair until she heard the words, *Your sins are forgiven you.**

*Josh 5:8

**Cantor, Verbum abbrev 146; PL 205:349D*

*Luke 7:58

The Example of the Saints

So that the labor of penance will weary you less, I commend to you the figure of Saint James the Less. Although he had received the Holy Spirit as a pledge and was confirmed in the certainty of eternal life, he nonetheless lived a life of penance and hardship, persevering in this right up to the end. He was a true *supplanter* of carnal desires, and he enjoyed such merit that everyone called him *just.* He was deservedly called the son of Alpheus, meaning *learned.*[7] When Paul traveled to Jerusalem to confer with the other

[7] Hegesippus calls him "James the Just" (Eusebius, Eccl Hist 2.23.4). Jerome renders *Jacob* as *supplanter*, or *supplanting*; *Alphaeus* as *fugitive*, *the best thousand*, or *learned* (PL 23:340, 341; CL 72:134, 136).

apostles about the truth of doctrines, he went immediately to see James. This apostle wrote a canonical epistle. According to Chrysostom and Hegesippus, a historian who lived shortly after the time of the apostles, James was so remarkable that he received the position of Bishop of Jerusalem by order of the apostles immediately after the Lord's passion.* He was proclaimed as holy from his mother's womb. He drank no wine or strong drink, ate no meat, never cut his hair, and neither bathed nor anointed himself with oil. Day and night he prayed on his knees, so much so that he developed calluses that were said to be as hard as those of a camel. And they say that he gave so little thought to his body and exerted himself to live such an austere life that all his members were weakened and, while he was still alive, it was as if they had died. He was so assiduous in prayer, and lay prostrate so much on the floor, that the front of his body was also covered with calluses almost as hard as the knees of a camel.*

*Chrys, Hom Act 3.2; PG 60:36

**Hegesippus, Fragmenta 1; PG 5:1307–10; Bede, Com Matt 10:3 approx; PL 92:399B*

Diligently call to mind as well the garment of camel's hair and locusts of John, the labors of Paul, the vigils of Bartholomew, the sack and bread of Jerome, the coarse garment and thorn bush of Benedict, the napkin and tears of Arsenius, the rush mat of Eulalia, the column and maggots of Simeon, the nakedness and herb roots of the penitent Mary of Egypt. Also, how King David came down from his throne and sat abjectly on the earth in sackcloth and ashes to do penance until he heard from the Lord through Nathan the prophet, *The Lord also has taken away your sin.** By his posture he showed humility; by the ashes, his contemplation of death, for the whole human race must return to dust; by the sackcloth, which is woven from hair, the bitter remembrance of sins that prick us. Gregory says, "For by sackcloth is set forth the roughness and piercing of sin, in ashes the dust of the dead. It is customary to employ these objects in doing penance, so that by the piercing of sackcloth we may know what we have

*2 Sam 12:13; *Cantor, Verb abbrev 145; PL 205:348D–49A*

done through sin and in the dust of the ashes we may consider what we have become through judgment."*

*Mor 35.VI.7; PL 76:753C; CL 143B:1777–78

Conclusion

Draw comfort from these things and drill yourself in them: sackcloth and ashes are the penitent's weapons. The work of penance consists primarily in food and clothing. These verses express what we have been talking about:

Let your drink be water, your bread be dry, your
 clothing rough;
Take the discipline, sleep but little and on a hard bed.
Pray bareheaded on your knees; beat your breast.
As you kiss the ground, may your mind be in heaven
And your tongue speak what your heart dictates.
Fast often, with open hands. May your mind be
 humble,
Your eye simple, your flesh pure, your heart devout.
With right faith and firm hope let your love always
 offer fervent prayers
From a mouth that is just. Do these things, O sinner,
To produce worthy penance now for your sins,
Lest the Judge sentence you to perpetual
 punishment.*

*William of Montibus, Peniteas 132

Listen also to Bernard, who says, "True penitents waste no time: they make reparation for past sins by contrition, master the present by good works, and face the future with firm and constant resolutions."*

*Sermo de div 106.1; PL 183:732D; SB 6/1:378

Those who do penance vigorously and do not flag will also not falter when harvest time comes, for *going they went and wept, casting their seeds, but they shall come back with joyfulness, carrying their sheaves.** Let those who are doing penance be consoled in their hearts, trusting that they share in the lot of the martyrs; for, according to Chrysostom, those who live a life of pen-

*Ps 125:6-7

ance can be compared to the martyrs. A long exile is more painful than a quick death. But the Lord himself proclaims them blessed and promises them consolation: *Blessed are they that mourn, for they shall be comforted.** The Lord compensates the mourning penitent with the consolation of eternal joy. Cyprian, too, praises penance: "O penance, what new can I say about you? You loose all that is bound, you open all that is closed, you alleviate all that is adverse, you heal all that is contrary, you enlighten all that is confused, you revive all who despair."*

*Matt 5:5; Chromatius 3.3 approx; PL 20:334B

*Haymo, De amore coelestis patriae 2.64; PL 118:928D–29A

✠

A careful scrutiny of my life frightens me. It appears to me either sinful or barren and unfruitful. What fruit I see is artificial, unripe, or spoiled in some way. What remains for me, a sinner, but to lament my entire life as long as I live? I am certain, Lord, that my sins merit eternal damnation; I am more certain that my penance is not sufficient to make amends; but I am most certain that your mercy surpasses every offense. Be merciful to me and grant me forgiveness for all my sins, because my merit is your mercy, O Lord my God. Amen.

CHAPTER 21

The Lord's Baptism

(Matt 3:13-17; Mark 1:9-11; Luke 3:21-22)

*R 1

*Latin Diatessaron?

*Matt 3:1

The Lord Jesus passed twenty-nine years in humble, hard circumstances. At the beginning of his thirtieth year, *in those days John the Baptist came preaching** and baptizing, before his imprisonment, and Jesus told his mother that the moment had come: he was to leave behind his hidden life and show himself to the world. In this way he would glorify his Father by making him known and carry out the mission of saving souls for which the Father had sent him. Reverently taking leave of her and his foster father Joseph, he *came from Nazareth of Galilee,** where he had been reared, north of Jerusalem, and went to the place at the Jordan River near Jericho, east of Jerusalem, where John was baptizing.*

*Mark 1:9

**Massa; MVC 16; CM 153:72–73*

Two miles east of Jericho stands the chapel of Saint John, at the place where it is said the Baptist lived, and a mile beyond that is the spot where he baptized. Some, however, maintain that Christ was baptized between Aenon and Salim, not far from Mount Gilboa at Bethany on the far side of the Jordan, four miles from the chapel of Saint John.* Remigius notes that Galilee means *passing over* and Jordan *descent*, and he suggests that the fact that Jesus travelled from Galilee to the Jordan teaches us that if the members of his Body wish to be baptized and so be washed in grace, they must pass from vice to virtue and descend to be humbled.*

**Burchard, 57–58*

*CA Matt 3:13–15

*Bede tells us, *R 2

> Jesus was baptized at thirty years of age, and only then did he begin to teach and perform miracles; by this he showed us the proper age at which priestly or teaching offices should be assumed, in answer to those who suggest they can be held by a person of any age. Someone might counter that Jeremiah and Daniel received the spirit of prophecy while they were still children, but miraculous occurrences should not be taken as normative. It was fitting for the Savior to be baptized at the age of thirty, and it has a meaning for us because the number is associated with the mystery of the Trinity and the observance of the Ten Commandments. Those who are baptized or, better, rejoice in having been baptized should attain the maturity of thirty years so that they might grasp the mystery of the Trinity and fulfill the Ten Commandments of the law.* *Com Luke 3:23; PL 92:360A; CL 120:85–86

According to Rabanus Maurus, Christ's example teaches that one should not be ordained a priest, be given license to preach, or be put in charge of a church until he has reached adulthood.[1]* But alas! Nowadays the care of churches is entrusted to men who cannot govern themselves, and the patrimony of the Crucified is given to those who cannot safeguard their own possessions. They want to be in command, yet they still need a tutor themselves. Chrysostom says, *Gloss Matt 3:13; PL 114:82C

[1] In the Middle Ages the age of thirty was generally mandated by local councils for priestly ordination, although dispensations were granted to meet the need for priests. The issue was complicated by benefices, which were often given to laymen, and sometimes children, *in commendam*. This meant that the person named received the revenues, although he did not exercise any spiritual office. The abuse was very common in Ludolph's lifetime, when the popes resided in Avignon.

> Jesus came to be baptized at the age of thirty because he was to abolish the old law after this baptism. Until reaching this age, during the years when it is possible to transgress against all of the commandments, he faithfully observed the law and fulfilled it, lest someone were to say, "He abolished the law because he could not keep it." For this reason he waited until the fullness of adulthood, all the while fulfilling all justice, and at length he came to be baptized, adding it as something that follows upon the complete keeping of the commandments.*

*Hom Matt 10:11; PG 57/58:184

***R 3**

*So the Lord of creation undertook this long journey alone and barefoot. Watch him with love and devotion, and enter into his travels with all the compassion in your heart. He did not take with him a retinue of soldiers, or cavalry, or any sort of entourage; nor did he have disciples or women accompanying him. He had no one to send ahead to prepare a lodging for him. Here were none of the pomps and displays that we, mere grubs, delight to employ. In his kingdom he has tens of thousands of angels to minister to him and countless throngs of spirits to assist him, but he made his way alone, his bare feet treading the earth, his body tiring from fatigue. His *kingdom is not of this world*,* he who refused a crown because he *emptied himself, taking the form of a servant*.* He became a servant to make us kings; he became a sojourner and an alien so that he might lead us to his homeland. Jesus set before our eyes the road that leads to his kingdom.*

*John 18:36

*Phil 2:7

**Massa; MVC 16; CM 153:73–74*

Why then do we ignore him? Why do we not humble ourselves? Why do we seek honors, vanities, and passing wealth with such avidity and cling to them so tenaciously? Simply because *our* kingdom *is* of this world: we do not see ourselves as sojourners here, so we chase after these disastrous things. O foolish mortal children! Why do we accept false things instead of true, unsteady things for certain, transient things for eternal, and so assiduously amass them?

Why do we not spurn these passing things and appraise them to be practically gone already?* *Massa; MVC 16; CM 153:74

And so Jesus humbly pressed on, the giver of salvation who did not need salvation himself, journeying day in and day out until he reached the Jordan River. *When he arrived there he found John baptizing, surrounded by a large crowd that listened spellbound to his preaching, because they were half-convinced that he was the Messiah. When the Lord came to be baptized with his servants, the Judge with sinners, it was not because he desired to be cleansed by the waters; rather, he wanted to cleanse the waters themselves. Indeed, Jesus came to John, the greater to the lesser, God to John, the Lord to the servant, the King to the soldier, the Light to the lamp, the Sun to the morning star. He came to confirm the Baptist's preaching, to accept John's testimony, and to receive the external washing of baptism; the fountain was baptized by a stream, the fullness by a single drop, the author of baptism by the minister of baptism.* He did not need to be cleansed but became the source of cleansing for us: although he did not need to be washed, he accepted baptism for the remission of sins to set his seal on John's baptism and show that it was ordained by God. ***R 4** *Hugh 4.13 approx

He underwent this rite to teach us the meaning of baptism, and, as one who was truly born as Man, he humbly fulfilled all justice according to the law, and by this fulfillment he taught us. He was baptized to reveal the mystery of the Trinity. He accepted baptism so that no one, no matter how holy, would consider baptism to be superfluous.* He first did what he would later command others to do: his servants would realize with what eagerness they should hasten to the Lord's baptism, when the Lord himself did not disdain to receive the servant's baptism; no one would refuse the bath of grace when Christ had not refused the bath of repentance.* *Gloss Matt 3:13 approx; PL 114:82D *Ambrose, Exp Luke 2.91 approx; PL 15:1669A; CL 14:73

He was baptized to *crush the heads of the dragons in the waters*,‡ to wipe away sins, and to bury the old ‡Ps 73:13

Adam. He was baptized so the waters would be sanctified by contact with his most pure flesh and body, thereby imparting to them the power to regenerate and cleanse, and to bequeath these powers to the blessed water that would be used later for baptism. He was baptized so that, by the descent of the dove, he might show forth the coming of the Holy Spirit on those who receive the baptism of believers. He was baptized so that the people would attend to John's preaching about the Christ and hear also the voice of God the Father. The Son of God received baptism so that all those born again in baptism might become, and appear to be, sons and daughters of God, and brothers and sisters to him. Let us, his faithful who have been regenerated in Christ, attend carefully to his sacraments and assiduously study all his actions.

Desiring our salvation, the Lord *Jesus began* first *to do and* then *to teach*,* and, because he was to make baptism the gateway to the sacraments and the foundation of virtues, he wanted to be baptized by John.*

*Acts 1:1

**LV 9*

The Humble John Demurs, the Humbler Jesus Insists

***R 5**

**Massa*

As John was baptizing sinners, Jesus said to him, "I ask you to baptize me along with them." But John, looking at him, recognized by a revelation of the Holy Spirit that Jesus was true God and true Man, and being sinless he had no need of this cleansing bath—had, indeed, come to cleanse others from sin—and he became frightened. As a soldier imitating the humility of his king, he reverently refused, saying, "Lord, *I* who am of earth *ought to be baptized by you*, who are of heaven and whose generation is immaculate; *and you come to me** to be baptized? You are the great Lord, I am the little servant; you should not be coming to me, I should be coming to you. You are pure and you

*Matt 3:14

cleanse all things; you should not be coming to me, I should be coming to you for the cleansing baptism.* I am a man, you are God; because I am a man, I am a sinner, because you are God, you are without sin. Why do you want me to baptize you? I am not refusing the service, but I do not understand the mystery. I baptize sinners in need of repentance; you who are without sin, why do you want to be baptized? How can you, who have come to pardon sins, want to be baptized like a sinner?"*

**Bruno Com Matt 3:14 approx; PL 165:89C*

**Chromatius 1.1; PL 20:329A*

Bernard asks, "Lord Jesus, you wish to be baptized? What need have you of baptism? Do the healthy need medicine, or the pure cleansing? What is your sin, that you need to be baptized? What stain can the lamb without blemish have?"* Chrysostom imagines John's thoughts to be, "Were you to baptize me, that would make sense: then I would be made just, and worthy of heaven. But what reason is there for me to baptize you? Every good gift comes down to earth from heaven; it does not go up to heaven from earth."* And Pope Leo:

*Sermo Epiphany 1.6; PL 183:146A; SB 4:298

*Opus imperf 4; PG 56:657

> Lord, what are you doing? Look, they will stone me as a liar! I have proclaimed great things about you, and you appear as a simple stranger. You are the King's Son above, you are the King's Son here below, but your royal scepter is never displayed. Reveal your august dignity! Why have you come as a solitary, humble figure? Where is your cohort of angels? Your entourage of six-winged cherubim? Your winnowing fan? You glorified Moses in the pillar of fire and shining cloud, and you bow your head to me? Lord, decline to do this; you are the Head of all. You have shown your lowliness; show your eminence! Baptize everyone here, beginning with me. Why do you desire baptism, since you are without stain? And if I were to agree to baptize you, I believe the Jordan itself would not permit it: recognizing in you its Maker, it would flow back upon itself.*

*Chrys, Orat in Theophania; Fronton, 6:449–50

It is no cause for wonder that the Baptist should tremble all over when the one before whom every knee bends in the heavens, on the earth, and under the earth* should himself bow beneath his hands. As Bernard says, "The head bowed under the Baptist's hands is adorable to the angels, venerable to the powers, terrible to the principalities. What wonder if a mere man trembles and refuses to touch the holy head of God? Who does not shudder at the very idea? This head that is now bent, how exalted it will be on the Day of Judgment! It is seen to be humble now, but how eminent and sublime it will appear then!"‡

*Phil 2:10

‡Sermo Octave Epiphany, 4; PL 183:154A; SB 4:311

***R 6**

*The Lord certainly approved of the attitude of lowly submission adopted by his faithful servant, but he made known the mystery of his plan, saying, *"Allow it to be so now*:* baptize me in water; later I will baptize you in the Spirit, for what I am now doing is a mystery." This suggests, according to Chrysostom, that Jesus baptized John later.* *"Allow it to be so now*, so that I, who have assumed the form of a servant, may perform a servant's humble task." And then Jesus added, "*It is well for us*, although I am your superior and do not need this washing, for me to receive baptism and for you to administer it, *to fulfill all justice*,* and to give an example of this fulfillment." Here *justice* is not to be understood as a particular virtue, in opposition to avarice, but more generally to embrace all the virtues, or the perfection of all virtues. Chrysostom pictures Christ as saying, "We have fulfilled all the requirements of the law and have not transgressed in a single commandment. This alone remains to be done. We must do this so that all righteousness may be fulfilled by us."*

*Matt 3:15

*Opus imperf 4; PG 56:658

*Matt 3:15

*Hom Matt 12.1; PG 57/58:203

Here Jesus speaks of justice as fulfilling all the commandments, indicating that he himself is the true justice, the Lord and Master who fulfills all the mysteries pertaining to our salvation. There was a commandment that people should be baptized by the prophet.* Or, *all justice* can mean giving all persons their due.

*This sentence attr. to Opus imperf in CA Mark 1:9–11

Those who receive Christ's baptism show a pity for their own soul that is pleasing to God and receive the medicine of salvation; by humbly submitting themselves to their Creator and what he ordains, they edify their neighbors and encourage them to do good. They *fulfill justice* by doing what they should in regard to God, their neighbor, and themselves.* Or, Jesus *fulfills all justice* by doing first what he will later command others to do, as if he were saying, "I now submit myself to you although you are less, so that the great ones of the earth will not think it beneath them to be baptized or guided by their inferiors."

**Zachary 14; PL 186:99B*

Ambrose asks, "What is justice, but that you undertake to do what you want others to do, and you encourage others by your example?"* Chrysostom says, "The Lord did not want to be baptized for his sake, but for ours, to fulfill all justice. It is just that we first do ourselves what we will later instruct others to do. Because the Lord had come as the teacher of the human race, he wished to teach by example what must be done, so that the disciples would follow their teacher and the servants their master."* Augustine concurs: "He wished to do what he was commanding everyone else to do, so that the Lord and Master would impart his doctrine not so much with words as with deeds."* Rabanus Maurus suggests that it was fitting for him to teach us that all justice is fulfilled by baptism, and that without it the kingdom of heaven is closed to us, so that we would learn that no one can be made perfect apart from the waters of baptism.* Finally, we can interpret *all justice* to mean abundant humility, for humility is the main ingredient of justice.

*Exp Luke 2.90; PL 15:1586B; CL 14:72

*Chromatius 1.1; PL 20:329B

*Maximus of Turin, Sermo 8; PL 57:547A; [100.1; CL 23:398]

*Gloss Matt 3:15; PL 114:82D

*There are three degrees of humility. The first is required of any just person and is sufficient: to submit to superiors for God's sake and not to vaunt yourself over your equals. It is greater humility to submit yourself to your equals and not prefer yourself to your inferiors. Perfect humility is to submit to your inferiors and not give preference to yourself over anyone; this

***R 7**

is what Christ did, and thus he fulfilled all humility.* Bernard writes,

Massa; MVC 16; CM 153:75

> There is justice in the narrowest and strictest sense, and when we fail in this is we fall into sin by lording it over our equals or acting as if we are the same level as our superiors. The definition of this justice is to give each person his or her due. Then there is a broader and more generous form of justice: this entails acting as though inferior to our equals and not commanding those subject to us. Just as it is a form of pride to prefer ourselves to our equals or to consider ourselves the equals of our superiors, so it is an expression of humility to see ourselves as inferior to our equals and on the same footing with our inferiors. The most egregious form of pride is to think ourselves equal to our superiors, and the greatest and fullest expression of justice is to make ourselves subject to our inferiors.
>
> When John said, *I ought to be baptized by you,* he exemplified the first form of justice. But what Christ did when he bowed his head beneath the hands of his servant was an example of the third and fullest form of justice. Let us strive to imitate Christ rather than *the son of perdition, who opposes and is lifted up above all that is called God or that is worshipped.**

*2 Thess 2:3-4; Sermo Octave Epiphany 4–5; PL 183:154AC; SB 4:312

And again,

*Ps 61:2

> *Shall not my soul be subject to God?** Does it matter if you are subject to God, unless you are also subject to every human being for God's sake? As Christ said, *It is well for us to fulfill all justice.* Justice finds its perfection in humility. If you desire to be completely righteous, seek out those who are unimportant; defer to those who are subject to you.*

*SC 42.8–9; PL 183:991D; SB 2:38

Since just people give others their due, those who are truly humble show justice by not taking what belongs to another or claiming what they should not for themselves. They do not steal honors for themselves, but give glory to God and view themselves as worthless.* Such people do not harm others or judge them or think themselves superior by comparison; on the contrary, they see themselves as being less than others and desire the lowest place. *Massa; MVC 16; CL 153:78

We can see how the Lord's humility has increased by considering what preceded this event. Then he was subject to his parents, but now he is subject to a mere servant; he demeans himself while justifying and magnifying the servant. But his humility has also grown in another way: up till now, he was thought to be of low estate, poor and useless, but now he chose to be manifested before others as a sinner. John was preaching to sinners a message of repentance and baptizing them; the Lord Jesus asked to be baptized along with them. *R 8 *Massa; MVC 16; CM 153:75

True, he identified with the sinful condition of humanity at his circumcision, but that was a private occasion, whereas the baptism took place before a large throng of people. Given that he was about to inaugurate his public ministry, was not Jesus afraid that people would not heed him because they considered him to be a sinner? No. Because he was to be the teacher of humility, he would humble himself all the more. He wanted to appear to be what he was not, an abject sinner, for our instruction; we, on the contrary, want to appear to be what we are not, people deserving of adulation and praise. If there is anything about us that appears to be honest, we advertise it, while we are careful to hide our defects.* *Massa; MVC 16; CM 153:76

We should study Christ's humility very carefully: even though he is the Lord of the law and is above the law, by submitting to baptism and the other requirements of the law he acted like other people and did not wish to enjoy any special privileges. Not many people follow his example in our communities; rather, all too often we love to insist on our prerogatives.* *Massa

Jesus Is Baptized

*R 9

*When, by a revelation of the Holy Spirit, John came to see that all justice was to be fulfilled in this way, he relented and *allowed him** to receive baptism from him. He set aside his objections and did what Jesus asked. John's reverence had held him back up to that point, but now his spirit of obedience overcame his hesitations. True humility has obedience as its companion, so the office that his awe and reverence prevented him from performing, he now gladly and obediently carried out. Bernard writes, "John acquiesced and obeyed; he baptized the Lamb of God, and the waters themselves were purified. We were purified, not he, and the need for our purification was made known by the cleansing of the waters."*

*Matt 3:15

*Sermo Epiphany 1.6; PL 183:146B; SB 4:298

Let us attend very carefully to what the Lord is doing here. Out of love for us he strips himself of his divine majesty and appears like any human creature, and the Lord of the elements makes himself subject to the elements, entering those frigid waters on a winter's day. For the sake of our salvation he purifies and consecrates the waters by contact with his sacred flesh, conferring on them the power of regeneration. In this way he established the sacrament of baptism to wash away our sins and sanctify us. He also took the church to himself as his bride and espoused all Christian souls to himself. We are each espoused to our Lord Jesus Christ by baptismal faith, as the Lord himself affirms, speaking through the mouth of his prophet: *I will espouse you to me in faith.** This solemn work is truly great and very beneficial to us, and so the church joyfully sings, "Today the heavenly Bridegroom is united to his church, for Christ has washed away her sins in the Jordan."*

*Hos 2:20

*Resp for Epiphany; PL 78:743B; *Massa; MVC 16; CM 153:82–83*

Anselm addresses these words to Christ:

> When you reached the age at which your strength was at its greatest and you were about to stretch

> out your hand to perform powerful deeds, you went out to save your people like *a giant running the way** of all our miseries. And first, so that you might be like your brethren in all things, you approached your servant who was baptizing sinners and asked him to baptize you, too, as if you were a sinner. You received baptism, the innocent Lamb of God whose purity is not marred by the slightest speck of sin. The waters did not sanctify you; rather, they were made holy by you, so that in turn they could sanctify us.*

*Ps 18:6

*Eckbert, Stim [Med 9 Anselm]; PL 158:751A

Chrysostom teaches:

> Christ received John's baptism so that from the very nature of the event you might know that he was not baptized because of his sins or because he was lacking the gifts of the Holy Spirit. Here, Jewish baptism ceases and is abolished, and Christian baptism begins. Just as later he will celebrate the Jewish Passover and, in celebrating it, change it, so he does the same here with baptism. When the Lord celebrated the Passover, it marked the end of one institution and the beginning of another. So here by receiving Jewish baptism Jesus annulled it and threw open for ever the gates of the church. As at the paschal table, so now in the river, Jesus received the shadow and bestowed the reality. The grace of the Holy Spirit is given by Christ's baptism, whereas John's could not impart this gift.*

*Hom Matt 12.3; PG 57/58:206

And also,

> Since the new baptism was to be given for the salvation of the human race and the forgiveness of sins, he did not disdain to receive baptism first, not to take away sins, because he alone was sinless, but so that he alone could sanctify the waters and empower them to wash away the sins of believers. The waters of baptism could never take away the sins of believers if they had not come into contact

with Christ's most holy body. He received baptism so that we could be cleansed of our sins. The water washed him so that we could be cleansed of the filth of our wickedness. He underwent the bath of regeneration so that we could be born again of water and the Holy Spirit. Christ's baptism is the washing away of our sins and the renewal of salvific life. Through baptism we die to sin but live with Christ; we are buried in the first life but rise into the new life; we strip off the error of the old person and put on the garment of the new one.*

*Chromatius 1.1–2; PL 20:329BC

***R 10**

It was fitting that the Lord chose to be baptized in the Jordan: he opened the gates to the kingdom of heaven at the spot where the children of Israel had entered the Promised Land. Just as the Israelites forded that river to enter the territory promised to them by the Lord, so through baptism the faithful cross over into the land of the living. Furthermore, the Jordan River flows between the land of the Jews and the land of the Gentiles, and baptism is common to Jews and Gentiles who come to faith and to Christ.

**Remigius, Hom 3; PL 131:884C*

The Lord's baptism in the Jordan was prefigured by Elijah, Elisha, Joshua, and Naaman, who were prefigurations of baptism.* He was baptized in water because this is the opposite of fire. Sin is fire and is punished by fire; the water of baptism douses the flames of passion and of punishment. Water also washes away dirt, quenches thirst, and reflects our image; similarly, in baptism the grace of the Holy Spirit washes away the filth of sin, slakes the soul's thirst for the word of God, and restores the image of God lost by sin.*

**Zachary, 1.13 approx; PL 186:97B*

**Eluc 1.20; PL 172:1124D–25A*

And, because the Lord was baptized with water, we understand that no other liquid can be used for baptism. It is the universal practice that baptism be administered with water: water flowed from Christ's right side. No other liquid is as effective for washing, and none is more easily found anywhere, so that no one could ever plead that it was lacking.* And, al-

**Zachary 1.14; PL 186:101C*

though the Spirit performs an interior cleansing, the washing with water is also necessary. Just as the human person has a twofold nature, body and soul, so there is a twofold rebirth, of water and the Holy Spirit.

The Heavens Open and the Spirit Descends

***R 11**

Now it came to pass, when* the crowds representing *all the people* of that region *were baptized* by John, *that Jesus, also being baptized*, emerged from the waters *and* was *praying* that the newly baptized would receive the Holy Spirit, and *heaven was opened*.* **An indescribable splendor surrounded Christ, and such a brilliant radiance shone about him* that it seemed as if the empyrean heaven could be seen and the celestial splendor that lights the stars in the firmament had descended to earth.* It is not that heavens were literally torn asunder; the opening was not in the heavenly bodies, but in the air—rather like what we experience when the clouds part above us and we can see the sky above.[2] By this prodigy God indicated that the glory of heaven is opened to those who believe in Christ and that the gates of Paradise, closed to the human race on account of sin, are now opened for those who are born again.

*Luke 3:21

*Latin Diatessaron?

**Massa*

Chrysostom says, "The heavens were opened at his baptism to teach you that this also takes place invisibly at our baptism, when God calls you to your heavenly home and persuades you to have nothing to do with

[2] Ludolph and his contemporaries envisioned the universe as made up of concentric spheres, the tenth and outermost being the empyrean heaven. This was an immaterial realm, not composed of any of the four elements, but of a "quintessence" of pure light. It was the home of blessed and the angels. The concept is found in the *Divine Comedy* and is reflected in the great Gothic cathedrals, which sought to express something of this paradise of light through the medium of stained glass.

*Hom Matt 12.2; PG 57/58:204

*CA Luke 3:21–22

*Com Luke 3:21; PL 92:358B; CL 120:83–84

mundane concerns."* And elsewhere, "He says *the heavens were opened* as if till then they had been shut. But now the upper and lower sheepfolds were brought together, and the whole flock had one Shepherd; *the heavens were opened*, and earthbound humanity was brought into the angelic fold."* Bede writes, "*Jesus also being baptized and praying, heaven was opened.* While the Lord's body was submerged humbly in the waters of the Jordan, his divine power was throwing wide the gates of heaven for us. His innocent flesh felt the tingling of the frigid waters and extinguished the flaming sword once unsheathed to punish our crimes."*

The words of the evangelist also suggest that the prayer of a holy and sinless person pierces the heavens. Christ prayed at this moment to instruct us how we should pray after we have been baptized and to show us both the nature and the need of prayer: its nature, because if prayer is to be pleasing to God, it must come from a heart that strives to maintain its baptismal innocence; its necessity, because prayer is required to preserve baptismal grace. His example serves to remind us that we must raise our minds to God whenever we receive the sacraments. Hence Bede also says,

> Jesus, who shares all things with the Father, was mindful to pray after his baptism in order to teach us an important lesson: just because the heavenly palace now lies open to us, this does not mean that we henceforth live a life of ease; on the contrary, he insists that we pray, fast, and give alms. All our sins are taken away in baptism but our human frailty remains. We give thanks that the hostile Egyptians drowned when we passed through the Red Sea, but there are other foes to be fought as we journey through the desert of daily life. Christ's grace leads the way, but still we can only vanquish these enemies with great effort as we make our way to the Promised Land.*

*Com Luke 3:21; PL 92:358C; CL 120:84

***R 12**

And the Holy Spirit descended* visibly *in a bodily shape, as a dove, upon him, **and rested upon him,**‡ alighting on his head. He *descended,* but not by grace, since Christ had been filled with the Holy Spirit from the first moment of his conception. Rather, he descended in visible form, and this for three reasons: first, to reveal to others that in Christ is found the fullness of grace; second, to instruct us that the Holy Spirit is in truth given to those who accept baptism; and third, to show that Christ himself is the one who baptizes with the Holy Spirit to take away sins.* The Spirit appeared in the bodily form of a gentle and meek dove, a creature in whom there is no bitterness or rancor,* to teach us that he comes to draw us to himself with great gentleness and to dwell in hearts that are humble and tender. He also appeared in this form to show that the Holy Spirit lives in those who possess the charity of God, of which the dove is certainly a fitting symbol.

*Luke 3:22
‡Latin Diatessaron?

**Gorran Matt 3:16*

**Bruno Com John 1:33; PL 165:458B*

Chrysostom writes, "The Holy Spirit was pleased to appear in the form of a dove because this bird is pre-eminent among animals as a cultivator of charity. The evil demons can simulate the appearance of all the other virtues that God's servants possess in truth; only the charity of the Holy Spirit eludes their false art. So the Spirit reserves this virtue of charity to himself: it is the infallible sign of the Spirit's dwelling place."* Chrysostom also suggests that this corresponds to a figure in the Old Testament. Just as the dove carrying a green olive shoot proclaimed God's mercy for those who had survived the flood and the return of tranquility to the earth, so now at the Lord's baptism the Spirit appears in the form of a dove proclaiming God's mercy for those who are baptized, washing away their sins and bestowing grace upon them.* The Spirit shows himself to be our Liberator, carrying not an olive branch, but the divine adoption of the human race.*

*Opus imperf 4; PG 56:560

**Aquinas, Com John 1:33*

*Chrys, Hom Matt 12.3 approx; PG 57/58:205

Likewise, all the baptized should be filled with and perfected by the seven qualities found in the dove.[3] Whoever is perfect must be perfect in relation to self, neighbor, and God—and we can find all these virtues exemplified by the dove. We should emulate two characteristics of the dove as regards ourselves: she does not sing, but moans, and she is without gall. Similarly, we should feel true contrition for our sins, weeping and mourning over them, and we should be free of the bitterness of sin or irrational anger. As regards our relationship with others, the dove can teach us three lessons. She does not attack other birds with her beak, and the good person should not speak ill of others; she does not grasp things with her claws, and the good person should not take what belongs to another; she cares for the young of other birds along with her own, and a good person should care for everyone in need.

Finally, as regards our relationship with God, here too the dove can teach us a couple of lessons. The dove hovers over rivers, and, if she sees the shadow of a predator reflected in the water, she dives in to avoid capture; so the good person should sail over the rivers of Holy Scripture, always on the lookout for the attacks of the evil one, and be ready to evade his wiles. Also, just as the dove chooses the best grain and feeds only on what is clean, so the good person should choose the most nourishing lines in Scripture and find rest only in God, the highest purity. Finally, just as the dove makes a nest for herself in the cleft of a rock, so the good person should find hope and refuge in the wounds of Christ crucified, who is a solid rock.

[3] Wolbero of Cologne lists the seven qualities in his commentary on the Song of Songs: "The dove has no gall, hurts no one, gathers the best grain, feeds the young of others, nests in the cleft of a rock, moans instead of singing, and hovers over the water to keep an eye out for predators" (PL 195:1086D). This list goes back at least to Bede, Hom ev 11; PL 94:62B–63B [1.12; CL 122:86].

The Father's Voice Is Heard

*And behold a voice of the Father bearing witness to his Son was heard *from heaven saying, "This is my beloved Son,** beloved more than all others, for he is my Son by nature, not simply by adoption." Chrysostom says, "He is certainly not his Son through the adoption of grace or the election of a creature, but because of the special character of his generation and the truth of his nature."* And Jerome, "The dove rested upon Jesus' head so that no one would think that the Father's voice was referring to John and not the Lord."*

*R 13

*Matt 3:17

*Chromatius 2.2; PL 20:331A

*Com Matt 3:17; PL 26:31A; CL 77:19

The voice went on, "*In whom I am well pleased*,‡ that is, in whom my desire to save the human race is accomplished."† Another evangelist records the words in this way: *You are my beloved Son; in you I am well pleased.** That is, "In you and through you I have arranged to do what is pleasing to me, to do what must be done to save the human race." Or, "I am well pleased with him because he entirely and completely pleases me." For there was nothing displeasing to God in him, as there is in us, who were formerly *by nature children of wrath.**

‡Matt 3:17

†*Lyra, Mark 1:11*

*Mark 1:11

*Eph 2:3

Bernard comments, "Truly, there was nothing in him displeasing to the Father, nothing to offend the eyes of divine majesty. As he himself said, *I do always the things that please him.*"* May the Lord Jesus, who always pleased the Father, grant that through him we too may deserve to please the Father in all things. Bede suggests that the splendor surrounding Christ lasted only so long as the Father's voice was heard, and then it disappeared.[4]* ‡The Father admonishes us to heed his Son, to believe in him and obey him: *Hear him.*[5]†

*John 8:29; Sermo Epiphany 1.7; PL 183:146C; SB 4:299

*Comestor, Hist ev 34; PL 198:1555D

‡R 14

†Matt 17:5

[4] The light at Jesus' baptism is not mentioned in the gospels; its origin may be in the extracanonical *Gospel of the Ebionites*, though Justin also makes allusion to it (Dial 88.3).

[5] These words were spoken at the transfiguration, not the baptism; Ludolph reflects Bernard's addition of them here.

In whom should we believe, if not him who is wisdom, justice, and truth?

Bernard says,

> *Hear him.* Lord Jesus, behold, you have been given leave by the Father: begin to speak. How long shall the Power and Wisdom of God remain hidden and unknown among the crowd? How long, noble king of heaven, will you allow them to think that you are only a carpenter's son? O sublime humility of Christ's virtue! How you confound my foolish vanity! I possess a little knowledge—or rather, I think I do—and I cannot keep quiet: both imprudently and impudently I put myself forward, showing that I am all too ready to speak, to lecture; but I am slow to listen.
>
> Did Christ, after so long a silence in his hidden life, still fear vainglory? Why should the Father's true glory fear vainglory? He feared it greatly—not for himself, but for us; he feared it so that we would learn to fear it. He kept silent for our sake to teach us. His lips kept silence, but his actions taught, and he proclaimed by example what he would later express in words: Learn of me, because I am meek and humble of heart.* I hear stories of the Lord's infancy, but from then until this event the record is silent. Now that the Father has openly pointed him out, he can no longer remain hidden.*

*Matt 11:29

*Sermo Epiphany 1.7; PL 183:146D–47A; SB 4:299; Massa; MVC 16; CM 153:83

This is my authority for the assertion I made in an earlier chapter that the Lord Jesus kept silent for our instruction, and that what he did not speak with his lips he demonstrated by his actions.*

*part one, chap. 16

Let us diligently study the lesson of his silence, because whoever is silent with everyone is at peace with everyone. Let us not only study this lesson but also put it into practice. As Ambrose says, "The virtue of keeping silent is rarer than the virtue of speaking."* We see that Christ's humility was a fragrance that spread everywhere, a virtue that is excellent, very

*Exp Luke 9.10; PL 15:1796A; CL 14:335

necessary, deserving to be ardently pursued and affectionately embraced. The Lord assiduously sought to act humbly so that his every deed could serve as an example for others.* **MVC 16 approx; CM 153:83*

The Manifestation of the Holy Trinity

*In this event the undivided and excellent Trinity appeared in a manifestly singular way (understanding *appeared* in its broadest sense) and consecrated baptism by this presence. The Father appeared in a voice, the Son in human flesh, the Holy Spirit in the form of a dove. There is an important difference, however: the Person of the Son was truly and substantially united with the human being Jesus, but in the appearance of the other two Persons, the union was only in the nature of a sign.* The human being Jesus was truly God the Son, but the voice and the dove were only symbolic manifestations of the Father and the Spirit. The Spirit appeared in the form of a dove, but the Spirit was not the dove; nor was the dove united to the Spirit, because only a human nature is capable of being united to a divine Person. The Spirit was not united to the dove by grace, but only by appearance to serve as a sign; when its symbolic purpose was fulfilled, the dove returned to the prime matter from which it had been taken, like other figures in which the Lord appeared. ***R 15** **Lyra, Com Mark 1:10*

The Trinity did not appear while Jesus was being baptized, but afterwards; because he did not need cleansing grace, he received John's baptism and not his own. The baptism of John was given in the name of the one who was to come, but Christ's baptism is given in the name of the Trinity. Thus it was fitting that the Trinity was revealed not during the baptism but afterwards, to distinguish John's baptism, which was not given in the name of the Trinity, from Christ's, which is.

The manifestation of the Trinity after Jesus' baptism signifies that baptism should be administered in the name of the Father, and of the Son, and of the Holy Spirit. There was a period of time in the primitive church when baptism was conferred in the name of Christ. This was done to increase reverence for the Savior's name and to combat the error of those who attributed the power of the sacrament to its minister, saying, *I am of Paul; and I of Cephas,** and so on. When these problems had abated, the church reverted to the trinitarian form.*

*1 Cor 1:12

**Lyra, Com Mark 1:10*

Baptism causes three effects, especially since Christ's passion: the opening of heaven, because the kingdom of heaven is accessible to those who have been reborn; the sending of the Holy Spirit, whose gift and grace is given by it; and the fulfilling of the Father's word that those who are born as adopted sons and daughters are pleasing to him, because through baptism the children of wrath become the children of grace, regenerated in the hope of eternal life. Let us meditate on each of these points at great length, and, now that the Trinity has opened heaven, let us lift up our souls and carry them to God. We should do this with a humble spirit, so that we may be worthy to hear the Father's voice and receive the Spirit's gift.

Anselm writes,

> Bowing beneath John's hands in the Jordan for baptism, he heard the Father's voice and received the Holy Spirit coming in the form of a dove. This he did to teach us humility (which is also signified by the word *Jordan*, meaning *descent*), and there he was honored by the Father's voice, of which it is said, *His communication is with the simple*.* He was lifted up by the presence of the Spirit, who rests upon the humble, and this took place under the hand of *John*, whose name means the *grace of God*. To that same grace we should attribute everything we receive from God, not ascribing it to our merits.*

*Prov 3:32

*Elmer [Med 1 Anselm]; PL 158:716D

Types of Baptism

Baptism was prefigured by the Sea of Bronze, which stood before the entrance to the temple in Jerusalem. Just as the priests had to wash themselves with the water contained in this vessel before entering the temple, so those who wish to enter the heavenly temple must first be washed by baptism. That basin was supported by twelve bronze oxen, and the twelve apostles carried Christ's baptism to the ends of the earth. This laver was adorned and surrounded by the mirrors of the women, so that those entering the temple could see if there was anything unclean or unseemly about their appearance;* similarly, baptism demands a clear conscience, hatred for sin, and heartfelt contrition.* ***R 16** *1 Kgs 7:23-26 *Exod 38:8 **SHS 12*

It is also prefigured by Naaman the Syrian, a Gentile and leper who immersed himself seven times in the Jordan at Elisha's command and was cleansed of all his leprosy.* These seven washings prefigure the seven kinds of deadly sin taken away in baptism, and just as Naaman's flesh became like that of a child, so those who are baptized are like innocent babes.* *2 Kgs 5:14 **SHS 12*

Finally, baptism is prefigured by the children of Israel crossing the Jordan River to enter the Promised Land; those who desire the Promised Land of heaven must cross the Jordan of baptism.* The ark of the covenant standing in the Jordan while they crossed prefigures Christ, who was baptized in the Jordan. The twelve stones that the people took from the bed of the Jordan River and set up as a perpetual memorial represent the twelve apostles who bore witness to Christ's baptism to the whole world.* *Josh 3–4 **SHS 12*

The Institution of Baptism and the Other Sacraments

*From all that has been said we can see that the Lord intimated, instituted, and confirmed his sacrament of ***R 17** baptism. He insinuated by word and deed what he was later to establish. He suggested it by word when he told Nicodemus, *Unless a man be born again of water and the Holy Spirit, he cannot enter into the kingdom of God.** He suggested it by deed when he was baptized by John. He instituted it by deed when* the disciples baptized by his authority, and by word when he sent them out to preach and to baptize. He confirmed what he had established by deed and word as well: by deed when from his pierced side flowed blood and water, and by word when, after his resurrection, he sent his disciples into the whole world to preach and baptize.[6]‡

*John 3:5

*during his public ministry

‡*Gorran Matt 3:14 approx*

***R 18**

Since we have said something about the grace of this great sacrament, the first instituted by Christ, it might be appropriate to say something about the others. First, we should know that the divine physician, who has come to bring healing to our diseased human race, accomplishes his purpose in the most effective way. The principal illness that afflicts humanity is original sin. While it is true that this sickness has its origin in the consent of reason, the point where the disease gains entrance is the doorways of our senses. If the remedy is to correspond to the illness, therefore, it cannot be simply spiritual but must also include signs perceptible to the senses. Just as our senses are the cause of our sinning, so they are linked to our rising again; hence the salve that heals our wounds is given in the church's sacraments.

**Bonaventure, Breviloquium 6.1 approx*

[6] Following Aquinas, Ludolph understands baptism to be instituted when Christ himself was baptized, and that the disciples did baptize during the lifetime of Jesus, as we read in John 3:22 and 4:1-2. But Aquinas also teaches that it was only after Christ's passion and resurrection that the figurative sacraments became obsolete, and also only then could baptism configure its recipients to Christ's death and resurrection (ST III, q. 66, a. 2).

God instituted these sacraments in various ways. Two of them, matrimony and penance, were instituted before the Lord's coming but were confirmed by Gospel precept and perfected by the Lord himself, at the wedding feast of Cana and when he preached his message of repentance. The other five sacraments were instituted by Christ himself: baptism, by receiving it himself and giving the formula for its conferral; confirmation, when he laid his hands on the children; anointing of the sick, when he sent out his disciples to cure the sick and anoint them with oil; holy orders, when he bestowed the power to hear confessions and to bind and loose; the sacrament of the altar, when on the eve of his passion he gave the sacrament of his Body and Blood to his disciples.*

**Bonaventure, Breviloquium 5.4 approx*

The sacraments were instituted for many reasons. First, to increase our humility: it is a great humiliation for a human being to seek from God the salvation lost by pride through these visible signs that are so inferior to us. Second, to instruct us, so that we can be roused to make progress. Third, because it is fitting for us to receive medicine through our senses because it was through them that we fell into sin. Fourth, to counteract our laziness and preoccupation with useless things by listening attentively at Mass, receiving the Eucharist, and performing other similar exercises. Fifth, to conform to the nature of our physician: because he is both God and Man, the medicine he dispenses should contain something divine, that is, invisible grace, and something human, the visible form of the grace. Sixth, because of the condition of the patient: we are made up of soul and body, and the spiritual nature in our bodies cannot comprehend spiritual realities very well unless they come in a material way. It is helpful to administer spiritual medicine in a material container, like coating a pill with sugar. Seventh, to increase merit, because it is meritorious for us to believe God in matters where there is no human proof.*

**Hugh 6.3*

*R 19

A sacrament consists of material elements, actions, and words. Sacramental elements are water, oil, etc.; actions are immersion, breathing upon, etc.; words, the invocation of the Holy Trinity, etc. A sacrament is a visible sign of invisible grace, so when a person is baptized there is an exterior washing of the body, which we see, and the interior cleansing of the soul by the remission of sins, which we do not see. We are led out of Egypt by baptism, as through the Red Sea, because the consecration by Christ's blood destroys the enemy that is our sin. Baptism draws its efficacy and power from Christ's death and the shedding of his blood, as do all the sacraments, both those antecedent to the law and those from the law. Through his blood Christ forgives the sins we have committed, helps us to avoid sinning again, and leads us to the place where we can never sin any more.

Zachary 1.14 approx; PL 186:102AC

The enumeration of the sacraments can be explained by the fact that they are ordained to combat three kinds of sins and four kinds of punishment. Baptism was instituted to take away original sin; penance, to take away mortal sin; and anointing of the sick, to take away venial sin. Confirmation was instituted to combat weakness; holy orders, to combat ignorance; the Eucharist, to combat evil; matrimony, to combat concupiscence, which it tempers and controls.*

Hugh 6.5

Because sacramental character leaves an indelible mark, it is not given in sacraments that are customarily repeated—penance, matrimony, anointing, and the Eucharist.* On the other hand, baptism, confirmation, and holy orders impress an indelible mark on those who receive them. Baptism distinguishes believers from unbelievers, confirmation the weak from the strong, and holy orders the clergy from the laity; hence they cannot be received more than once.* These three sacraments cannot be administered a second time to the same person without an affront to the sacrament itself, by implying that the earlier celebration was useless or inefficacious.*

Hugh 6.7

Bonaventure, Breviloquium 6.6

Hugh 6.7

✠

Most merciful Jesus, you willed to be baptized by John. I have broken faith with the promises made at the first font by sinning, so I hasten now to the second bath of penance. I confess to you, O God, that I am a guilty sinner; I have offended you in my thoughts and in my words, in what I have done and in what I have failed to do. My transgressions are numberless, and so are those associated with them, for I have not only ensnared myself in sin but have helped others to sin through my suggestion, my example, and my negligence. For their failings and mine I earnestly implore you in your mercy to forgive us and blot out our transgressions. Amen.

CHAPTER 22

The Lord's Fast and Temptation

(Matt 4:1-11; Mark 1:12-14; Luke 4:1-13)

‡R 1
†Latin Diatessaron?
*Luke 4:1
*John 1:16
*Matt 4:1

‡*And* **after his baptism**† *Jesus returned from the Jordan, being full of the Holy Spirit,** with that superabundant *fullness* of which *we all have received.** *Then*, without delay, *Jesus was* hurriedly *led by the spirit into the desert,** and he went willingly to a high mountain called Quarantania, situated about two miles from Jericho and twelve miles from Jerusalem. This wilderness was inhabited by bandits, so the area was known as *Domyn*, meaning *bloodshed*, on account of the violent attacks that took place there.[1]*

*Massa

Specifically, *Domyn* is the hovel where the man going down to Jericho from Jerusalem was set upon by thieves. This took place about halfway between the two cities; the road on which he was traveling went across the southern slope of Quarantania from Jericho up to Bethany, Bethphage, and Jerusalem, crossing the southern slope of Mount Olivet.

Because the man set upon by robbers represents the figure of Adam overcome by demons, it was fitting that Christ overcame the demons literally and in truth at the place where the first man was figuratively defeated.* The text says that the Samaritan was traveling down the same road: the Son of God, the protector of

*Massa

[1] This is *Tal'at ed Dumm* or Addumim ("the red ones"), about halfway between Jerusalem and Jericho.

our race, took on our human nature to experience all our temptations in that desert.

The Lord withdrew into the desert for this combat with the devil to teach us that if we want to vanquish the evil one completely we must distance ourselves (sometimes in body, but always in mind) from the crowd of evil spirits and the company of wicked people. We might take for our model that royal figure who, surrounded by the throngs in his court, said, *I have gone far off flying away, and I abode in the wilderness.** Following the examples of John and Jesus himself, let us be led by the Holy Spirit, and not by the evil spirit of hypocrisy, into the solitude of the wilderness or at least into the interior desert of our heart in contemplation. There, removed from the clamor of the world, we can better make room for God; abandoning the world in our minds, we can learn to hunger for eternal joys alone, like manna in the desert.

*Ps 54:7; Haymo, Hom 28 approx; PL 118:192:BC

Jesus was led by the Spirit because his humanity was the instrument of his divinity, so that in all he did he was moved by the inspiration of the Holy Spirit.*

*Lyra, Matt 4:1

When and Why Christ Chose to Be Tempted

Moved by the Spirit, Jesus went off to a deserted place so that he could offer his spirit to God for us by prayer, and his innocent body by fasting; in this he gives an example to the faithful, that they in turn may give themselves to God by prayer and fasting. He did not go reluctantly; rather, he freely went to fight and *to be tempted by the devil.**

*R 2

*LV 10

*Matt 4:1

This suggests that whoever goes into the wilderness of penitence should be ready to be assailed even more by the enemy, as it says: "*Son, when you come to the service of God, stand in justice and in fear, and prepare your soul for temptation,** to resist what will assault you."‡ This is why he was led by the Holy Spirit, who singled

*Sir 2:1
‡*Lyra Matt 4:1 mor*

him out in baptism; those whom the Spirit fills, he sends out to do battle and he gives them strength.

Christ chose to be led into the desert, to that battleground where the fighting is fierce; Adam had enjoyed the delights of Paradise, but those very delights overcame him. Jesus chose to be tempted so that by overcoming he would empower us to do the same, just as he chose to die so that by his death our death would be destroyed.*

*Massa

This contest took place after Christ's baptism and fast to suggest that after our baptism into new life and the reception of grace, and after we have embraced a life of asceticism and holiness, it is then that the devil immediately appears as a tempter, throwing himself upon us more fiercely, hoping to turn us away from our good course.* He is jealous of those who make progress and lays traps for them, so we must be more on guard than ever; he tempts those who are good more than those who are evil. As Gregory observes, the devil does not bother to tempt those who are already living under his power.‡ Isidore warns, "You are being assailed most fiercely when you are not aware of being attacked."*

*Zachary 1.15; PL 186:103B

‡Mor 24.XI.27; PL 76:301C; CL 143A:1207

*Jer, Ep 14.4; PL 22:349; CS 54:49

These four events were arranged by the Lord in a particular sequence: first, he was baptized; second, he was led into the desert; third, he fasted; fourth, he was tempted. This means that we must first be washed of our sins, then withdraw from worldly attractions, next practice self-denial, and finally fend off the attacks of our enemy. We see a type of these four stages in the history of the Jewish people: first, they crossed the Red Sea; next, they went into the desert; third, they experienced hunger and thirst; last, they repulsed the attacks of their enemies.‡

‡Gorran Luke 4:2 approx

***R 3**

After he had been baptized, the Lord embraced a continual life of solitude and asceticism to encourage his followers to seek perfection and strengthen them to assume arduous duties. He did not go into the desert for his sake but for ours. He went to provide a model of the eremitical life to those who sought to follow him perfectly; but also, as Chrysostom points out, to show all the baptized that they must leave behind worldly desires and bad companions, and seek to follow God's will in all things. The devout faithful observe the Lenten fast in imitation of Christ, as though they were in the desert with him. Christ did not undertake this time of penance because he needed to, but to admonish us to do penance by his example.

*Bede, Com Mark 1:13; PL 92:139D; CL 120:444

Authentic and fruitful penance has three characteristics: first, it must be pure if it is to be pleasing to God, because Jesus undertook his penance immediately after his baptism; second, it must be rigorous if it is to subdue the flesh, because Jesus undertook his penance in a wasteland, not an oasis; third, it must be prudent if it is not be excessive, because Jesus undertook his penance guided by the Holy Spirit. He did not need a guide, but he wanted to show us in this way how important it is to entrust ourselves to a prudent director in matters of asceticism.

***R 4**

*Going into the desert, Jesus *fasted forty days and forty nights,** eating nothing. The evangelist expressly adds *nights*, so that it cannot be thought that he ate at night. This also indicates that we must defend ourselves against demonic attacks both in days of prosperity and nights of adversity, because he never relents in laying siege to us with temptation. Christ fasted to show us how powerful a weapon fasting is in the struggle against temptation; Basil teaches that sobriety is essential if we want to overcome temptation.* But Jesus also wanted to warn us that a life of luxury threatens baptismal innocence: those who belong to Christ by baptism, who have put on Christ and become members of his body, and who have been buried with him must crucify their flesh with its desires and see themselves as dead to the things of this world, mortifying the body with their spirit.

*Matt 4:2

*Ps-Basil, Admonitio 14; PL 103:695C

Chrysostom writes,

> The Lord did not fast because he needed to, but for our instruction. Recall that the sins we committed before our baptismal washing came from serving our bellies; so our Lord wants us to learn that fasting is a great good and serves as a strong shield against the devil, so that after the cleansing bath we will not give ourselves over to luxury, drunkenness, and sumptuous feasts, but to fasting. If you had helped a sick man get better, you would order him to avoid doing whatever had made him ill; so here, he himself introduced fasting after baptism to counteract the vice of gluttony. Adam lost Paradise because of this vice, and it was this greed that brought about the flood in Noah's time and called down fire on Sodom. The Jews* committed great wickedness on account of their feasting and drunkenness. This is why Jesus fasted—to show us the pattern of salvation.*

*in Isaiah's day; Isa 5:11-12

*Hom Matt 13.1; PG 57/58:209

Ambrose says, "He did this for the sake of our salvation, to show us what is useful not only by his teaching, but by his example as well.* But what kind of Christian are you, if you are feasting while your Lord is fasting? He goes hungry for you, and you are afraid to fast for your sins?"‡ And elsewhere, "Nothing is as sly as the danger of worldly sweetness, which while it soothes the spirit overwhelms life and seduces the thoughts of the mind. Quite rightly, then, our Lord Jesus Christ by his fasting in the desert shows us how to resist the siren voice of allurement, and the Lord of all permits himself to be tempted by the devil so that we might learn through him how to avoid all delights."*

*Maximus of Turin, Sermo 19 [50a.1 extra]; PL 57:569C; CL 23:202

‡Maximus, Sermo 26 [50.1]; PL 57:583B; CL 23:197

*Exp Luke 4.3-4; PL 15:1613B–14A; CL 14:106–7

We should understand that Christ took different medicines to heal our various illnesses. He healed us by diet when he *fasted forty days and forty nights*. He healed us by an electuary when he gave his disciples his Body and Blood at the Supper.[2] He healed us by sweating when *his sweat became as drops of blood, trickling down upon the ground*.* He healed us by a plaster when his face was coated with spittle. He healed us by a potion when he tasted the vinegar mixed with gall. He healed us by blood-letting when the nails and spear pierced him.

*Luke 22:44

Here let us consider carefully and observe attentively what the Lord Jesus does, for he exemplifies many virtues. He went into solitude, fasting, praying, keeping vigils; he slept on the bare earth and humbly and peacefully kept company with wild beasts. Share his lot by compassion: always and everywhere, but especially here; his life was painful and his body was afflicted, and we should learn to do what he did.

***R 5**

**Massa; MVC 17; CM 153:84*

Four spiritual exercises are mentioned here, which marvelously support one another: solitude, fasting, prayer, and bodily mortification. By means of these we can attain in the highest degree that purity of heart that is the greatest of our desires, because in a way it embraces all virtues and expels all vices. A pure heart cannot abide vices or defects in virtue. This is why, in the collections of the lives and sayings of the desert fathers, we read that the whole purpose of the monastic life is to gain purity of heart. It is only in this way that a human being can deserve to see God, as the Lord says in the gospel, *Blessed are the clean of heart; they shall see God*.* As Bernard remarks, the brighter you are, the nearer you are to God; to be absolutely bright is to have arrived.*

*Matt 5:8

*SC 31.3; PL 183:941D; SB 1:221; *Massa; MVC 17; CM 153:84–85*

Fervent, constant prayer is very useful for attaining this purity of heart, but prayer accompanied by overindulgence, sloth, or pampering does not avail much. Therefore, fasting and bodily mortification are called for, although they must be done prudently, because

[2] An electuary is a medicine mixed with honey to make it palatable.

indiscretion impedes all good. The consummation of the aforementioned disciplines is found in solitude, for it is not possible to pray very well when surrounded by noise and distractions. It is difficult to see or hear many things without becoming sullied or sinning, because death comes in through the windows of the senses to attack our souls.*

*Massa; MVC 17; CM 153:85

So if you desire to be united with God and behold him with purity of heart, separate yourself from commotion and seek solitude. Flee from useless chatter—and even that which seems to be useful—by keeping silent, as the prophet teaches: *I was mute, and was humbled, and kept silence from good things*.* Do not seek to make new friends, for they will only provide new opportunities for conversation, and so new obstacles. Do not fill your eyes or ears with vain fantasies, and avoid like a poison and the enemy of your soul anything that disturbs your peace of mind and tranquility of spirit. It was not without reason that the desert fathers asked to live as hermits and commanded their followers who continued to live in community to be blind, deaf, and mute, for in this way they could better attain union with God.*

*Ps 38:3

*Massa; MVC 17; CM 153:85

Chrysostom says,

> When the Holy Spirit descended upon our Lord, he immediately drove him out into the desert. When monastics live with their families, if the Holy Spirit descends and comes to rest upon them, he will drive them out of their homes and lead them into solitude. The Holy Spirit does not dwell gladly where there are crowds, noise, arguments, and quarrels; on the contrary, solitude is his true resting place. Our Lord spent the day with his disciples, but when he wanted to pray intently he went off by himself. When we want to pray in a place apart, we have our cell or the fields or the wilderness; in this way we can possess both the strength of our companions and solitude.*

*Jerome, Com Mark 1; CL 78:458

And Augustine writes, "Dearest brethren, let us strive as much as we can to put an end to useless tales, gossip, and banter. Let us devote all our energy to banishing for a few hours the burdens of this world so that we can spend our time in holy reading and prayer for the good of our souls."* *Ps-Augustine, Fratres 56; PL 40:1340

From all this teaching it is clear that we should strive with all our heart to imitate the Lord Jesus by solitude, prayer, fasting, and moderate bodily mortification.* **Massa; MVC 17; CM 153:87*

Beasts and Angels

R 6

**And he was* dwelling peacefully *with beasts*, that is, with lions, bears, and other wild animals; *and the angels ministered to him*.* From this we learn that we should associate humbly with others and deal calmly with those who sometimes seem to be acting irrationally.* Also, those who can keep their sensual nature peacefully under control by their reason will be borne to heavenly realities through the ministry of angels.* It is truly angelic to dwell among savage people in the desert of the human heart; that is, to be able to close one's door and contemplate, pray, and read without getting tainted by their wild behavior. It is difficult to touch pitch and not be defiled.

*Mark 1:13

**Massa; MVC 17; CM 153:87*

**Lyra, Com Mark 1:13 mor*

Bede writes, "The Lord dwelt among beasts as one who is human, but enjoyed the ministrations of angels as God. And if we can put up with the behavior of brutish people and remain unstained in the desert of a holy life, then when we are freed from the bonds of this body we will be carried to the eternal joys of heaven by ministering angels."* And Jerome, "Then the wild beasts dwell in peace with us, when the flesh does not war against the spirit. Afterwards, ministering angels are sent to us to give solace and answers to watchful hearts."*

*Com Mark 1:13; a:140A; CL 120:445

*Cumm Mark 1:13; PL 30:595A

Let us pay frequent visits to the Lord in his solitude, watching carefully all that he does, especially seeing how he sleeps each night on the ground. All devout souls should visit him at least once daily from Epiphany through the forty days he remained there, humbly recommending themselves to Christ.*

Massa; MVC 17; CM 153:87

On this mountain and in the surrounding wilderness many holy people, inspired by the Lord's example, embraced the eremitical life, dwelling in small cells. Performing their service to the Lord most devoutly, they transformed their cells into a veritable hive and, like bees of the Lord, produced the honey of spiritual sweetness. On the side of this mountain, about half a mile from its base, is the place where the Lord retired to do penance. There is a church on this site, and a chapel housing an altar where he stood when he was tempted by Satan.[3]

The Forty Days' Fast

***R 7**

*The Lord *fasted forty days and forty nights* because the number forty is made up of the numbers four and ten (four times ten making forty); four stands for the gospels in the New Testament, ten for the commandments in the Old Testament.* Therefore, to fast for forty days means to observe the precepts of both Testaments and to avoid what both Testaments forbid. To keep the fast it is necessary for the body to abstain from food and the soul to abstain from sin. The Lord

Zachary 1.15; PL 186:103D

[3] Christian ascetics occupied the caves on this mountain in early times, and a monastery was established in the fourth century. It was abandoned in the seventh century after the Persian invasion. Some efforts were made in Crusader times to revive the monastery without success; in the late nineteenth century it was rebuilt by the Russian Orthodox Church and is frequented by pilgrims and tourists today.

fasted forty days and forty nights: his abstinence from food symbolizes for us the bodily fast, the number of days the abstinence of the heart.* The church follows his example in her penitential practice: she does not begin the fast immediately after Epiphany, but around forty days later, showing in this way that her fast is a continuation of the fast undertaken by the Lord.*

**Bruno Com Matt 4:1; PL 165:93C–94A*

**Comestor, Hist ev 35; PL 198:1556C; Massa*

Bede writes, "The forty-day Lenten fast has its roots both in the Old Testament, in the persons of Moses and Elijah, and in the New, by the number of days the Lord himself fasted.[4] This shows that the Gospel does not differ from the law, represented by Moses, and the prophets, represented by Elijah. Christ appeared in glory between them on the mountain to affirm quite clearly the words of the apostle, *being witnessed by the law and the prophets*."* Alcuin agrees: "Just as Moses had done with the law, and Elijah with prophecy, so our Lord consecrated the preaching of the Gospel by fasting for forty days. It is appropriate that the Lenten fast precedes the Lord's passion, because it reminds us that we must break worldly ties if we want to follow God."*

*Rom 3:21; Com Luke 4:2; PL 92:366C; CL 120:94

*Ep 80; PL 100:261C

[4] The Latin name for the Lenten season is *Quadragesima*. The first mention of a penitential season before Easter is at the Council of Nicea, 325. The length of the season and the nature of the fast and abstinence varied from place to place, but the goal of fasting or at least abstaining from certain foods for forty days was widespread. Mitigations were given for various reasons; in Ludolph's time there was some relaxation because of vicissitudes caused by the Black Death. Monastic communities as a rule had stricter requirements for fasting, and the Carthusians practiced perpetual abstinence from meat. The practice was controversial, and in Ludolph's day there was some pressure from Rome for mitigation, but the Carthusians pointed to the longevity of their monks as testimony that such a diet was not deleterious. The first full-length defense of a meatless diet, *De esu carnium*, was written by Arnaldus of Villanova at the beginning of the fourteenth century to defend the Carthusian practice.

Here is what Augustine says:

> Moses, Elijah, and the Lord himself all fasted for forty days so that we can learn a lesson taught in the law, the prophets, and the Gospel itself: we must not conform ourselves to this age or cling to it; rather, we must crucify the old person and not follow the desires of the flesh. It is a fitting expression of devotion if, before celebrating the passion of the crucified Lord, we restrain our earthly desires by crucifying them, as the apostle teaches: *They that are Christ's have crucified their flesh, with the vices and concupiscences.**
>
> The Christian should hang on this cross throughout this life, in which we are led into the midst of temptation. This life is not the time to pull out the nails that were spoken of in the psalm, *Pierce my flesh with your fear.** The flesh is carnal desire, the nails are the precepts of judgment. The fear of God nails these desires to the cross and makes of us an offering acceptable to God. O Christian, live always like this, nailed to the cross! Do not come down from it, lest you sink into the mud.*

*Gal 5:24

*Ps 118:120

*Sermo 205.1; PL 38:1039

Be on guard not to come down from this cross by mingling worldly pleasures into a good life. As Augustine warns, it does no good to fast all the day long if at the end of it you gorge your soul on delicacies and excesses.*

*Ps-Augustine, Sermo 141.4; PL 39:2021

By the forty-day fast we are able to pay our tithes and offer our first fruits. There are three hundred and sixty-six days in the year; setting aside six days, a tenth of the remaining number is thirty-six. A tenth of the remaining six days would be less than one day, but one day must be added, since this is the minimum. By this calculation, a tithe of the year is thirty-seven days. The final three days are in the nature of an offering of first fruits, which in the church finds expression in the three-day fast at the beginning of each season.[5] The law directs us to offer first fruits and tithes, and we fulfill this command by fasting for forty days. We have lived for ourselves throughout the year given to us by our Creator, so we mortify ourselves by offering tithes and first fruits. We fell from Paradise by eating; so far as we can, let us rise back up to it by abstinence. During Lent we should be more attentive than usual to fasting and prayer, so that in this holy season we may purge ourselves and make amends for the other seasons of the year.

The number forty is sacred for many reasons: for forty years the Lord fed the children of Israel with the bread of the angels in the wilderness, for forty months he preached in the world, for forty weeks he was in the womb of the Virgin, for forty days he fasted in the desert, for forty hours he was in the tomb, counting from the hour of his death,* for forty days after his resurrection he was with his disciples in the world. Ambrose also points out that just as the rain fell for forty days to wipe away sinners and that fine weather followed, so by this holy season of fasting sins are washed away and divine mercy shines forth.‡

Gorran Matt 4:2

‡*Exp Luke 4.15–16 approx; PL 15:1617AC; CL 14:111–12*

***R 8**

**And when he had fasted forty days and forty nights, afterwards he was hungry*.* Jesus did not fast longer lest the truth that he had assumed a human body would seem incredible, and to conceal his divine power from the devil, since Moses and Elijah had fasted this long.*

*Matt 4:2

**Lyra, Com Matt 4:2*

[5] Ludolph refers here to the Ember Days, which were prescribed by Pope Gregory VII (1073–1085) for the Wednesday, Friday, and Saturday after the feast of Saint Lucy (Dec. 13), Ash Wednesday, Pentecost, and the Exaltation of the Cross (Sept. 14). The custom of fasting at the beginning of each season goes back to the early centuries of the church: Leo the Great believed that the fasts in winter, summer, and fall were of apostolic origin, and Pope Gelasius (492–496) is the first to mention all four fasts. The idea of offering a tithe for the year by fasting for thirty-six or thirty-seven days goes back to Gregory the Great, 40 Hom 16.5 [14] (PL 76:1137C).

He was not hungry of necessity; he freely willed this fast to manifest the frailty of his human nature and to provide an opportunity for the devil to tempt him, in order to show us how to overcome him. Chrysostom says, "If he did not feel hungry for forty days, he was not human; if he did experience hunger after forty days, he was not divine: so the devil had doubts about Christ and took the occasion to test him."* Moses and Elijah had fasted forty days, but they experienced hunger and thirst while they were fasting; Christ did not feel hungry during the forty days, but afterwards. Christ did not want to fast longer than they, lest the devil suppose he was God; nor did he fast less, lest the devil think he was not truly human.

*Opus imperf 5; PG 56:664

The Three Temptations

***R 9**

*Aware that Jesus was hungry, the devil approached to see if he could entice him to sin, and also to investigate whether this was the Son of God, for he knew that one day the Son would come to take away his power. According to Pope Gregory, the devil tempted the Lord with the same three temptations he used on our first parents: first, gluttony, with the forbidden fruit; next, vainglory, by promising, *You shall be as gods;* and finally greed, by adding, *knowing good and evil,** for the ambition to obtain knowledge for the sake of superiority is a kind of greed.*

*Gen 3:5

*40 Hom 16.2; PL 76:1136A; CL 141:111; *Massa*

This is how he tempted the Lord, but he had to retire defeated. David felled Goliath with three stones from the riverbed; Christ vanquished the devil with three passages from Scripture.* Gregory also points out that temptation is carried out in three ways: by suggestion, by delight, and by consent; but the Lord was only tempted by suggestion, because no delight in sin took hold of his heart, nor did consent master him. Therefore his temptations came from without, not from within; he endured no inconsistency within himself.*

**Zachary 1.15; PL 186:106C*

*40 Hom 16.1; PL 76:1135CD; CL 141:110–11

The Scriptures do not specify whether these temptations all happened at the same time or on different days.

*Satan tempted him first to gluttony, saying, "*If you are* by nature *the Son of God*, and consequently equal to him in power, *command that these stones be made bread*."* He reasoned within himself as follows: "If he can change these stones into bread, he is the Son of God; if he cannot, he is only human." The temptation was well chosen for a man who was famished: seeing the stones, he would be overcome by an immoderate hunger. The devil not only wanted to discover whether Jesus was God, but he also wanted to entice him as Man, because by excessively desiring food he would be guilty of the sin of gluttony. Hilary writes, "The prince of demons wanted to ascertain the nature of his divine power by the changing of stones into bread and to ridicule him as human for enduring hunger by enticing him with food."*

***R 10**

*Matt 4:3

*Com Matt 3.3; PL 9:929B

But he could not trick the Master, who responded in such a way that he could not be accused of gluttony, nor did he reveal his divine power. Jesus did not succumb to temptation, and he did not affirm or deny that he was the Son of God; he countered by appealing to the authority of Scripture:* "*Not in* earthly *bread alone does man live* and endure, *but in every word that proceeds from the mouth of God* when he reveals his will through the Scriptures."* Augustine observes, "You can be very certain, dearest brethren, that the way the body feels after many days without food is how the soul feels when it does not feed regularly on the word of God."*

**Massa*

*Matt 4:4

*Attr. to Augustine in Defensor, Lib Scintillarum; PL 88:623D

This biblical quotation by our Lord is as true for the life of the body as it is of the spiritual life: it is clear that Moses, who fasted for forty days and forty nights, was sustained bodily as well as spiritually by the word of God. It is as if he were saying, "People do not live solely on material bread, but also on the spiritual bread of God's word, the bread of good works, the bread of grace, and, after final victory, on the bread of eternal glory. Therefore, although I am hungry I do not have to turn the stones into bread because the Lord sustains the one who hungers by his word alone. Your suggestion is a temptation, because you speak of physical bread but are silent about spiritual sustenance." Chrysostom notes that Christ responded with a quotation from the Old Testament and taught that when we hunger or suffer any other adversity we should never abandon the Lord.*

*Hom Matt 13.3; PG 57/58:211

Jesus could have turned the stones into bread, but he did not wish to. He did not do it because it was not seemly for several reasons: first, to hide his divinity from the evil one; second, to teach us that we triumph through humility and wisdom more than through power; third, to instruct us to shun ostentation; fourth, to show his disdain for the tempter's desire, because it was not right that the Lord should exercise his power at the devil's invitation, and such a tempter is not vanquished unless he is also despised; fifth, to teach us that the devil should never be given credence or obeyed in anything, even if what he commands seems to be pleasant or useful.

***R 11**

In a moral sense we see that the devil urges us to turn stones into bread when, under the guise of discretion, he suggests that we exchange our hard penance for soft self-indulgence, whispering, "Are you not already a child of God? You have no need of these austere penances." Thus did Jezebel turn Naboth's vineyard into vegetable garden and Lebanon was turned into *Carmel*, a word that means *easy*.[6]* This temptation arises especially on festive occasions or community celebrations, as when the Jews petitioned Pilate not to allow Jesus' body to stay on the cross because it was a feast day. When this suggestion arises, answer the devil with the Lord's response.

*2 Kgs 21
*Isa 29:17

[6] Jerome, Int nom, renders *Carmel* as *mollis*, a word meaning soft, mild, easy, weak, or unmanly (PL 23:803; CL 72:92).

Let us note that the Lord's example teaches us to resist gluttony at the outset if we want to avoid other sins. It seems that those who give in to gluttony find that they are too weak to resist other vices. Bede counsels us,

> You will labor against other temptations in vain unless your appetite is brought under control. The temptation of gluttony appears first here because this is the first temptation to beset us, even in infancy; the others follow upon it. The Lord was tempted while he was fasting so that if you are tempted while fasting you will not say, "I have lost the fruit gained by my fasting." Your fasting would not have borne fruit if you were not tempted, but it will bear fruit if you are not overcome by temptation. If the soul is not to be vanquished by the body, it is necessary to resist the devil's enticements and serve God as your ruler.*

*Laon Matt 4:2 approx; PL 162:1270D

Augustine says, "If you want your body to serve your soul, have your soul serve God. You must be ruled, if you are to rule."‡

‡Sermo 128.5; PL 38:715

***R 12**

When the devil saw that he could not overcome his adversary in this way, Chrysostom suggests that he reasoned to himself, "This appears to be a holy man. Even if holy people are not susceptible to gluttony, they can often be ensnared by vainglory." *Then the devil took him up* ***and carried him*** *into the holy city,* ***Jerusalem.**** Jerusalem was called holy in contrast to other cities, in which idols were worshiped, and it was called holy on account of the temple and the holy of holies located there, since according to the law this was the only place where sacrifices could be offered. Today it is called holy because the great mysteries of our salvation took place there.

*Opus imperf 5; PG 56:665

*Matt 4:5; Latin Diatessaron?

Chrysostom states that Jesus went freely, not because he was too weak to resist.* The Gloss suggests it is very likely that the devil appeared in human form, but that the Lord went in such a way that no one saw

*Opus imperf 5; PG 56:665

*Laon, Matt 4:2; PL 162:1273C

him.* Some people maintain that the devil carried Jesus in his arms, while others suggest that he led him by the hand and that Jesus followed him like an athlete willingly coming forward to enter the contest.*

*Origen in CA Luke 4:9-13

Reflect here on the Lord's great patience and goodness: he allowed himself to be handled and carried by that cruel beast, who thirsted for his blood and the blood of all his friends.* We should not be surprised, Gregory writes, that Jesus permitted himself to be led by the devil, because he let the devil's agents lead him to the cross.*

**Massa*

*40 Hom 16.1; PL 76:1135C; CL 141:110

And he *set him upon the pinnacle of the temple*, to tempt him by vainglory.* Recall that there were three levels to the temple complex: the first story or terrace was about forty-five feet above the pavement; a second terrace rose above the first another forty-five feet; the roof of the temple (which was not domed, but flat) was about seventy feet above the level of the second terrace. Each terrace was surrounded by a large walkway and colonnade; a learned scholar suggests that these colonnades were the pinnacles of the temple.* The devil set Jesus on one of these, either the higher one or the lower one, where the scribes and priests were accustomed to instruct the people about the law. If the latter is correct, the Gloss notes that the devil tempted Christ to commit the sin of pride in the place where many have succumbed to vainglory—the teacher's rostrum.*

*Matt 4:5; *Massa*

**Comestor, His sch 3 Kgs 9; PL 198:1354D*

*Laon Com Matt 4:2; PL 162:1274A

Still probing to discover Christ's identity, he tempted him to vainglory, saying to him, *If you are the Son of God, cast yourself down.** This was as if to say, "By your own power you can cast yourself down without danger, and you also have angels to serve and protect you." He reasoned that if Jesus could leap from the pinnacle unharmed, he was indeed the Son of God. And he urged him to do this because if he cast himself down from the pinnacle unhurt, the people would be amazed and would revere him as God's Son. When everyone was talking about him, this would be an occasion to gain empty praise.

*Matt 4:6

This is truly the devil's voice! He prompts us to descend rather than to rise heavenward, and he tempts us to plummet from the heights of good behavior. It is not enough for him to counsel us not to go higher; he seeks to persuade us to cast ourselves down—he who was the first to experience a fall wants everyone else to share his lot. The devil urges those who are standing to fall down, while God urges those lying down to get up. He betrays his weakness by saying *cast yourself down,* because no one can be hurt unless he throws himself down: the enemy who wants everyone else to fall can only persuade, he cannot push. Chrysostom says, "He did not say, 'I cast you down,' but *cast yourself down*, to show that each of us falls to our death by our own free will and choice of evil. He tries to persuade us, but we can resist his seduction by observing God's commandments."‡

‡Opus imperf 5 approx; PG 56:666

*Because Christ had appealed to Scripture earlier, the devil now invokes the same authority, not to teach and lead to virtue but to deceive and sow error. And thus he adds, "*It is written* in the book of Psalms, *that he has given his angels charge over you* to keep you from harm, *and in their hands shall they bear you up* when falling, *lest perhaps you dash your foot against a stone** and experience misfortune." The *hands of the angels* refers here to their twofold power, protection from evil and assistance in doing good, symbolized by the left and right hand respectively. This text is in fact not apposite to the situation for, as Jerome says, it does not refer to Christ the Head, but to his members, that is, to just persons.* Christ is not carried in the hands of the angels; rather he himself is *upholding* angels and *all things by the word of his power;** he who is greater than the angels has no need of their help.*

***R 13**

*Matt 4:6

*Com Matt 4:6; PL 26:32B; CL 77:21

*Heb 1:3

*Jer (Origen) Hom 31 Luke; PL 26:311A

The Gloss gives this interpretation to the verse: *He has given his angels* as ministering spirits *charge over you*, O just one, whoever you are; *and in their hands shall they bear you up* to raise you on high with their help *lest perhaps you dash your foot* (your heart and soul)

*Laon Com Matt 4:6; PL 162:1274B
‡*lapidem*
†*laedens pedem*
°Ety 16.3.1; PL 82:562B

against a stone (any impediment of sin).* The word *stone*‡ is derived from the words *hurting the foot*,† so that any occasion of sin or ruin that causes the soul to fall may be called a stumbling block.° Thus this passage means that God sends his angels to protect righteous people from sin, not that good people, presuming on angelic protection, should throw themselves into sin at the urging of the devil.

We know that God deputes his angels to safeguard the lives of his holy ones; the devil interprets the Scripture incorrectly and perverts its meaning. His choice of text is both impudent and incomplete: if he wishes to argue that the verse refers to Christ, why does he omit the next line: *You shall walk upon the asp and the basilisk, and you shall trample underfoot the lion and the dragon*?* The devil himself is the asp and the basilisk, he is the lion and the dragon whom Christ tramples underfoot in these temptations. See how in his pride he flaunts the passage that serves his purpose while cleverly concealing the part that tells against him. He speaks of angelic assistance as if Christ needed it but evasively keeps silent about the line that speaks of his being trampled underfoot.

*Ps 90:13

***R 14**

Here again, Jerome points out, the adversary is rebuffed by the words of Scripture, and his purpose is frustrated.[7] In all of these temptations the devil is probing to see if this is indeed the Son of God, but the Lord answers with such reserve that he remains uncertain. So here Christ responds, "*It is written again*, and said to everyone, '*You shall not tempt the Lord your God*,'* so long as any other means of escape is possible. I am a human being, and there is another way for me to come down from here other than by leaping, and so I do not want to test the Lord."

*Com Matt 4:7; PL 26:32B; CL 77:21–22

*Matt 4:7

There are many ways we can tempt God: by unduly putting his power or will to the test, or inquiring ex-

[7] "He shatters the false arrows drawn from the Scriptures by the devil on the true shields of the Scriptures."

cessively into his wisdom, or making improper demands on him. Such things should be avoided so long as we can act on the basis of reason or some other human faculty. The point here is that when it is possible to avoid danger by calling upon reason, counsel, or assistance, we should not neglect to do this, seeking to test divine power. As Augustine says, those who do not avoid danger when they can are not so much hoping in God as testing him.* Hence the Lord, even though he could do all things, instructed his disciples, *When they persecute you in this city, flee to another*.* Christ himself fled and hid at times.

*De civ Dei 16.19; PL 41:498; CL 48:522

*Matt 10:23

This is why the ordeal by fire and the judicial duel are both held to be illicit in law.[8]* If, however, human reason or foresight fail us and we see no avenue of escape, we can certainly turn to God's power and commend ourselves to his providence. This is not testing, but devoutly trusting, and could not be called tempting God.

**Lyra Matt 4:7*

There was a normal way for Jesus to come down from the pinnacle, a fine set of stairs, and this is why he responded that there was no need to tempt God. Chrysostom writes, "He responds very modestly, without indignation or emotion, answering him with the voice of Scripture. In this he shows us that the devil is overcome by patience and longsuffering, not by a great display; the grand gesture only feeds our vainglory." And elsewhere,

***R 15**

*Hom Matt 13.3; PG 57.58:211

> Notice how the Lord, rather than being perturbed, humbly disputes with the evil one from the Scriptures and strives to imitate him as much as possible.

[8] Canon 18 of the Fourth Lateran Council (1215) condemned judicial ordeals such as employing hot irons, plunging someone into freezing water, or engaging in duels. Peter Cantor wrote at length on such procedures, condemning them as unscriptural (citing Matt 4:7) because they tempt God, are ineffective in practice, and are immoral because they involve the clergy in the shedding of blood (PL 205:226–33, 542–48).

> The devil knew the weapons that vanquished him: Christ took him captive by meekness and overcame him by humility. When you see someone who has become like a devil approaching you, subdue him in the same way. Teach your soul to conform your words to Christ's. For as a Roman judge on the bench refuses to hear the response of one who does not know the proper way to address him, so also Christ will not hear you or protect you unless your manner of speech is like his.*

*CA Luke 4:9–13

The moral lesson here is that the devil raises people on high only to make them fall more precipitously, just as a crow will drop a nut from a great height to break it open or a wrestler will pick up his opponent to throw him to the ground. Many who would have remained secure had they stayed in the valley of a simple life are drawn to positions of eminence and fall from them. The strong ones of Israel fell on the mountain of Gilboa.* Augustine warns that whoever is in a high position is in greater danger of falling.[9]* And, according to Chrysostom, exaltation subverts leaders. The Lord allowed himself to be taken up to such a place but did not consent to the devil's temptation to show those in positions of leadership how to resist him.* Sometimes the devil carries us to the pinnacle of the temple when we think we are better than other people and we cast ourselves down by false humility.

*1 Sam 31:1

*Rule of Tarn 23; PL 66:986C

*Opus imperf 5; PG 56:665

***R 16**

Then, according to Bernard, because the Lord had not revealed his divinity the enemy believed he was only human, and tempted him a third time as Man. Leaving the temple precincts, *the devil took him up* ***and***

*Sermo in resurrectione 1.11; PL 183:280B; SB 5:88

[9] The *Rule of Tarn* is believed to have been written in the late sixth century in Gaul and came to be associated with the *Rule of St. Augustine*. The sentiment expressed here is found in a *Rule* composed by Caesarius of Arles (PL 67:1114A), and the exact words cited by Ludolph, *in loco superiori, tanto in periculo majori versatur*, appear in many monastic rules.

carried him *into a very high mountain* two miles from Quarantania towards Galilee. Each site was chosen for its temptation: when Jesus was famished in the desert, the enemy tempted him to gluttony; upon the pinnacle near the teacher's rostrum, he tempted him to vainglory; on the mountain offering a view of temporal realms, he tempted him to avarice.

*Latin Diatessaron?
‡Matt 4:8

*And he showed him all the kingdoms of the world, and the glory of them.** Chrysostom suggests *he showed him* means he did what we do when we find ourselves at a high vantage point: he pointed and said, "There is Africa . . . and that is Palestine . . . over there is Greece . . . and in the distance is Italy."* Or *showed him* can mean that he summarized the histories of all the kingdoms of the world, describing the magnificent display of their rulers, their wealth and power; or all the desirable things in the world—riches, delicacies, and honors—hoping that these would entice Christ to fall down before him.

*Matt 4:8

*Opus imperf 5; PG 56:667

The enemy did this *in a moment of time*.* Now a *moment* is one-tenth of a quarter-hour, or one-fortieth of an hour; that is, 1.5 minutes.* This fact suggests how brief and fleeting are the temporal goods of this world. Ambrose writes, "The temporal and the earthly are rightly shown in a moment of time; the term does not so much express the speed of sight, but the fragility of fleeting power. All the kingdoms pass by in a moment, because worldly honor often disappears before it even arrives."*

*Luke 4:5

**Bede, De tempore ratione 3; PL 90:303A*

*Exp Luke 4.28; PL 15:1620A; CL 14:115

He tempted the Lord of creation with avarice, arrogantly and boastfully making promises he could not keep and lying: *"All these will I give you* to rule over, *if falling down you will adore me** as your superior." It truly *would* be falling down, to worship the devil! Chrysostom says, "Nothing makes us fall under the spell of Satan so much as the desire to acquire wealth and heap up possessions."* And elsewhere, "He promises earthly realms to the one who has prepared

*Matt 4:9

*Hom Matt 13.4; PG 57/58:212

the kingdom of heaven for believers and offers worldly pomp to the Lord of heavenly glory. He who has nothing swears he will give everything to the one who possesses all things, and he commands the one who is worshiped by angels and archangels in heaven to adore him on earth."* The Gloss comments, "Behold the devil's ancient pride! In the beginning he wanted to make himself God's equal, and now he wants to usurp divine worship to himself."*

*Chromatius 14.4; CL 9A:254

*Laon Com Matt 4:9; PL 162:1274D

***R 17**

*We should note that what began as a temptation to greed ended as a temptation to idolatry. They go together well, because the apostle speaks of *covetousness, which is the service of idols*.* Let us consider also that mundane glory, which will pass away with this world, is fittingly symbolized by a high mountain: the devil raises us to the heights only to throw us down and enslave us by persuading us to neglect the righteousness of God and serve him instead. Christ underwent his temptation and his passion to free us from this slavery; he went down onto the lowly plain to overcome the devil by his humility. Nor did he look upon what was displayed to him with a greedy eye, as we would, but more like a physician who can examine the sick without catching their disease.

*Col 3:5

When you seek to be great and exalted and set such things before your eyes, realize that the devil is showing you all the kingdoms of the earth: if you want to possess them, you must fall down and worship him. Worship of the devil precedes a fall, nor can anyone worship him without falling. Ambrose writes, "Ambition carries a secret danger: to rule over others, you must first be a lackey; you must grovel to attain honors; if you seek a promotion you become a slave. All power and order come from God, but ambition is a perversion of power. The power itself is not wicked, but it is made so by a malicious person. We must learn to despise ambition, for by it we become subject to the power of the devil."*

*Exp Luke 4.31; PL 15:1621BC; CL 14:117

Jesus Dismisses Satan

*In truth, that assassin was defeated again and the victorious Lord threatened him with divine authority and commanded him to leave, saying, "*Begone* and retreat from me into the everlasting fire, *Satan*!* You are the enemy of truth and human salvation." With these words, as Chrysostom says, he put an end to the devil's temptations, who ventured no further attempt.* He immediately put him to flight, lest he make any further efforts to traduce him. Elsewhere Chrysostom observes, "When Christ was afflicted by the devil's temptation, *If you are the Son of God, cast yourself down*, he was undisturbed and did not rebuke the devil. Now, however, when the devil seeks to claim divine honors for himself by saying, *All these will I give you, if falling down you will adore me,* he becomes irritated and drives him away, saying, *Begone, Satan*! We learn from his example to endure bravely the injuries visited upon us, but we should not bear to hear offenses directed against God. It is praiseworthy for us to accept patiently injuries directed against us, but it is very impious to ignore those directed at God."* And Jerome writes, "It is not, as the majority think, that Satan is being condemned in the same way as the apostle Peter. It is said to Peter, *Go behind me, Satan,** that is, 'You are opposing my will: follow me.' But here he says, *Begone, Satan*, and *behind me* is not mentioned. This should be understood to mean, 'Go into the eternal fire prepared for you and your angels.' "*

***R 18**
*Matt 4:10
*Hom Matt 13.3; PG 57.58:212
*Opus imperf 5; PG 56:668
*Matt 16:23
*Com Matt 4:10; PL 26:32D; CL 77:22

Then the Lord added, "*For it is written* to every person: *'The Lord your God you shall adore, and him only you shall serve.'** He is *Lord* of all by his power, and *God* by virtue of creation; as *your God*, he is deserving of your special honor: the interior *adoration* of faith, hope, and love, and the exterior *service* of worship." As Augustine points out, this honor does not exclude service due to earthly rulers.* Bede for his part writes, "We

*Matt 4:10
*De civ Dei 10.1.2; PL 41:278; CL 47:272

*Greek: *latreuseis* are commanded here to *serve** God alone with the service of *latria*, the worship due to God alone. Hence those who offer worship to idols are called *idolaters*. But the apostle commands us, *By charity of the spirit*

*Greek: *douloueite* *serve* one another*.‡ This kind of service, *dulia*, is a reverence owed to God, one another, and all creation."† And elsewhere he writes, "When the devil said to the Savior, *if falling down you will adore me*, he heard that on the contrary he should worship Christ as his Lord and God. It is as if Jesus said, 'I should not worship you; you should adore me as your God.' "‡ Worship of the devil is not devotion, it is slavery.

‡Gal 5:13
†Com Luke 4:8; PL 92:368D; CL 120:96
‡Smaragdus, Com Matt 4:10; PL 102:128D

***R 19**

The sequence of the temptations just described demonstrates that the devil begins with relatively trivial temptations, then moves on to more grave ones, and ends with the most serious. The temptation to gluttony, especially when a person is hungry, is rather minor, but he concludes with the temptation to idolatry, the most serious sin of all. Christ overcame these temptations by rejecting them at once: as soon as the devil began to make his wicked suggestions, the Lord rebuffed them. We should follow his example and reject temptation as soon as it appears. Jerome warns, "The ancient serpent is slippery: if he is not grasped by the head he will slide in completely." This infernal reptile has a head, evil suggestion; he has a body, consent; and he has a tail, the action carried out. If he can get his head in (the thought), his body (consent) immediately follows, and right after comes his tail (the act). The head of evil suggestion must be crushed; then he can inflict no harm with his body or tail. When the head of suggestion is cut off, so is the infernal serpent's strength.

*Isidore, Sent 3.5.14; PL 83:663A; CL 111:208

***R 20**

**Then*, having carried out every test he had come to inflict on the Lord without success, at the mention of God's name *the devil* Lucifer *left him*.* He withdrew vanquished and covered with shame, for he had not gained even a foothold with these temptations. But this was only a strategic retreat: the devil would return

*Matt 4:11

to test him again, not through these underhanded deceptions, but by a frontal assault on Jesus and his disciples through their enemies. When the time of the passion drew near, he would persecute them not only himself, but also through the agency of others, the religious leaders of the Jews, thinking he could overcome him by his fear of dying.

Chrysostom is of the opinion that the devil did not depart because he was told to, but that Christ's divinity and the indwelling Holy Spirit drove him away. And he suggests that we should draw comfort from this because it means that the devil cannot tempt God's people as much as he wants, but only so much as God allows. Although God may permit him to tempt us for a time, he will drive him away on account of our weakness; *he will not suffer you to be tempted above that which you are able.** Augustine observes, "If it were possible for the devil to injure us as much as he wished to, none of the just would remain."*

*1 Cor 10:13; Opus imperf 5; PG 56:668

*En Ps 61, 20; PL 36:743; CL 39:788

In the three encounters just described, a campaign that is still waged against Christians, each temptation is pulled out by the roots and overcome. Every kind of temptation is a species of gluttony, vainglory, or greed, and in these three vices is found the matter of every sin. We should be on guard that these seeds do not take root; as John attests, *All that is in the world is the concupiscence of the flesh and the concupiscence of the eyes and the pride of life.** We can protect ourselves from these three darts with a three-pronged shield: we repel the concupiscence of the flesh by fasting, pride by prayer, and greed by almsgiving.

**1 John 2:16; Zachary 1.15 approx; PL 186:106A*

And just as the ancient foe withdrew from the Lord for a time, only to return openly during the passion to attack him, so he interrupts his campaign against us when his temptation is unsuccessful, but when our guard is down he returns and discovers he can gain entry more easily.* We must be circumspect: even if we banish some temptation, we should always be prepared for the devil's assaults.

**Gorran Luke 4:13*

At the time of our Lord's passion Satan was definitively routed and cast into the nether world, from whence he shall be released in the days of the Antichrist, as the book of Revelation says.* This is why Augustine infers that the tempter was Lucifer, the first angel, who overcame our first parents.[10] It must be supposed that the devil took on human form for a time, in which he could speak to the Lord and take him various places.

*Rev 20:7; *Massa*

***R 21**

*Notice that in Matthew's account Christ's temptations follow the sequence of Adam's: "*In what day soever you shall eat thereof* (gluttony), *you shall be as gods* (vainglory), *knowing good and evil* (greed)."* As explained earlier, greed here is not for wealth, but for position and knowledge. Augustine notes that we cannot be sure which temptation was in fact second and which third, because the biblical accounts differ.* The explanation could be that one evangelist emphasizes the temptation of greed and the other the temptation of pride; in practice, however, greed usually leads to pride, and vice versa. Remigius says, "The reason one evangelist places this event first, and another that, is that vainglory and greed give birth to one another."*

*Gen 3:5

*De cons 2.16.33; PL 34:1094; CS 43:134

*Greek catena CA

Luke 4:9–13

First Jesus bested the devil when he tempted him to gluttony, and this was prefigured in the story of Bel and the Dragon.* In Babylon there was an idol of Bel‡ that was worshiped as a god and was said to eat and drink much; Daniel destroyed it and killed its priests. There was also a dragon in that locale that the people worshiped as a god, and a priest fed him at scheduled times; but Daniel made a concoction of pitch, fat, and hair and threw this into the dragon's mouth. As soon

*Dan 14

‡Baal

[10] Jesus was tempted by the prince of demons, De civ Dei 9.21 (PL 41:274); Lucifer was the first angel to fall, Tr John 3.7 (PL 35:1399; CL 36:23–24); he deceived Adam and Eve, causing their spiritual death, Tr John 42.11 (PL 35:1704; CL 36:370).

as he swallowed it, he burst asunder. Thus both these gluttons were destroyed by Daniel through their own voracious appetites, and so Daniel is a type of Christ, who overcame the temptation to gluttony.* **SHS 13*

Next Christ triumphed over the temptation to vainglory, and this was prefigured by David's slaying Goliath.* Goliath boasted of his superb strength, but David felled him with only his sling and killed the warrior with his own sword. The giant Goliath is a figure of Lucifer's pride, and David, the shepherd boy who vanquished him, is a figure of Christ, who overcame the temptation to pride by his humility.* *1 Sam 17 **SHS 13*

Third, Christ's victory over the temptation of greed was prefigured by David's killing a lion and a bear.* The lion and the bear symbolize avarice, because they carried off a sheep for themselves. But David freed the sheep and killed the plunderers, and Jesus, by overcoming the temptation to greed, drove Satan away from him.* *1 Sam 17:34-36 **SHS 13*

*When Satan had been driven away, *angels came and ministered to him** as to a victor. Whoever struggles valiantly and triumphs in combat with the devil will be worthy of the ministrations and companionship of the angels. ***R 22** *Matt 4:11

Concerning the temptation by suggestion, Chrysostom writes, "Now I will briefly summarize the meaning of Christ's temptations. Fasting is abstinence from wrongdoing. However, when you succeed in this you might begin to have grand notions that you are a saint, and you are carried, as it were, onto the roof; the second temptation follows the first, and, glorying in your victory over the first temptation, you fall. Flee, therefore, from all exaltation of the heart, and you will not suffer this fate. To ascend a high mountain is to lose your footing on the heap of worldly possession and honors and so to fall by arrogance."* Bernard says, "If you have not read about the Lord's fourth temptation, you must be ignorant of the Scripture that *Opus imperf 5; PG 56:670

*Job 7:1

says that *the life of man on earth is a warfare.** The apostle also states that Christ was *tempted in all things like as we are, without sin."**

*Heb 4:15; Habitat 14.4; PL 183:240D; SB 4:471

Why Did the Lord Allow Himself to Be Tempted?

***R 23**

Jesus chose to be tempted for many reasons. The first, according to Gregory, is that by his temptation he might deliver us from ours, just as he freed us from death by dying. The second, Hilary says, is to give us warning that none of us, no matter how holy we may be, should think that we are beyond temptation. Christ chose to be tested after he was baptized, and the Holy Spirit descended upon him to show that temptation will strike most forcefully those who have been sanctified.* A third reason, Augustine teaches, is to show us how to fight and train us for the conflict. In this way Christ is our Mediator not only by the help he gives us, but also by the example he presents.* Fourth, Chrysostom writes that he was tempted to give us encouragement, so that when we see that Christ himself was subject to temptation we will not lose heart when such trials come upon us.* Fifth, Pope Leo says this happened so that Christ could vanquish the devil and check his audacity and power.* Sixth, the apostle teaches that the Lord endured temptation so that he might know how to enter into the sufferings of those who are tested and better show them mercy, and thus encourage them to rely on his mercy: a person who has been tested can sympathize more easily with those who are facing temptation, and show mercy to them.*

*40 Hom 16.1; PL 76:1135C; CL 141:110

*Com Matt 3.3; PL 928B

*De Trin 4.13.17; PL 42:899; CL 50:183

*Hom Matt 13.1; PG 57/58:208

*Sermo 39.3; PL 54:265A; CL 38a:215

*Heb 4:14-16; *LV 10*

Again, he chose to be tempted himself to give comfort to others who are tempted. Christ was tempted immediately after his baptism, when he had been called "Son" by the Father and the Holy Spirit had come to rest upon him, when the heavens had opened, and after he had fasted forty days and forty nights. In this he gives us to understand that when we are tempted, we are not on that account less cleansed of sin, less worthy of divine sonship, less filled with the Holy Spirit, less worthy of heaven; nor is our penitence less acceptable to God.‡ ‡*Voragine, Sermo 2 1st Sunday Lent, p. 68*

*Because the Lord himself was probed and tested it should come as no surprise that we are tempted, too. He conquered each time, which gives us cause to hope that, with his help, we also can triumph. We do not trust in any strength of our own but put all our hope and faith in the assistance of the Most High. On each occasion the Savior was victorious over his adversary by relying not on his own power, but on the authority of Scripture, saying, *It is written.* He won through by humility, not force, wanting to give us an example of patience. In the same way, when we suffer at the hands of wicked people we should be aroused by doctrine rather than by vengeance; we will conquer more by patience and humility than by strength and pride. ***R 24**

Attend carefully to the fact that in each of his temptations the Lord had recourse to the Sacred Scriptures, and this he did to enlighten us. Listen to what he said, and when a similar temptation assails you speak as he did, answering with the words of holy Writ. If you are tempted by a desire for honors, respond, "It is written, *Why are earth and ashes proud?"** If it is a thirst for riches, "It is written, *For we brought nothing into this world, and certainly we can carry nothing out,** and, *Naked came I out of my mother's womb, and naked shall I return there."** If you are tempted by carnal pleasures, answer, "It is written, *Flesh and blood cannot possess the kingdom of God."** According to the Gloss, *flesh and blood* here refer to the works of the flesh, gluttony and lust.* And whatever other vices assail you, rely on the shield of Sacred Scripture to defend yourself.*

*Sir 10:9

*1 Tim 6:7

*Job 1:21

*1 Cor 15:50

*Gloss 1 Cor 15:50; PL 114:549D

**Voragine, Sermo 1 1st Sunday Lent, p. 17*

Anselm writes, "After your baptism you went into the desert in the strength of the Spirit so that the example of the solitary life would not be wanting in you. You calmly endured the forty days' fast and solitude, the pangs of hunger, and the testings by evil spirit so that you could enable us to bear with these things, too."* And elsewhere, "After that, the most loving Jesus dedicated for your benefit the solitude of the desert and sanctified fasting to teach you that it is there that you must fight your crafty enemy. Notice carefully that this was done for you and in your stead, and how diligently it was done, and love him who did it."*

*Eckbert Stim [Anselm Med 9]; PL 158:751A

*Aelred, De inst 31 [Anselm Med 15]; PL 159:787B; CM 1:665

So now, disciple of Christ, in the company of your loving Master search out hidden places of solitude, dwell among wild beasts, imitate his secret, silent prayer, his daily fast, his threefold conflict with a hostile foe, and in every kind of temptation learn to have recourse to him. *For we have not a high priest who cannot have compassion on our infirmities, but one tempted in all things like as we are, without sin.** Do not be afraid of temptations or let them raise doubts in you; those whom God loves he chastises often, and *many are the afflictions of the just**—not of just anyone, but of the *just*, who receive the crown after they have been tested.

*Heb 4:15; *LV 10*

*Ps 33:20

Ambrose writes,

> Sacred Scripture teaches us that our struggle is not only against flesh and blood, but also against spiritual enemies. The crown is awarded to those who have endured conflicts; they cannot be crowned unless they have won, and no one can win unless he has fought. And the crowns are greater where the battle has been fiercer. For this reason we should never fear temptation, for it offers an opportunity for victory and provides spoils for our triumph. Far from fearing temptations, we should glory in them, saying with the apostle, *When I am*

> *weak, then am I powerful.** The laurel crown is woven by temptation. Bear the struggles of the martyrs, and you have borne their crowns; endure the suffering, and you have received the blessings. Let us not regard as evils the temptations of this age, which win for us such prizes; rather, let us ask, mindful of the human condition, that we may be able to bear the temptations that come our way.*

*2 Cor 12:10

*Exp Luke 4.37–42 approx; PL 15:1523B–1625B; CL 14:119–21

And Prosper of Aquitaine, "The struggle against temptations is of great benefit to the faithful: holiness will not fall into the sin of pride so long as we are aware of our weakness when the enemy assails us."‡

‡De vocatione omnium 1.8; PL 51:656C

***R 25**

The devil has six weapons in his armory: he tempts the good by pride, the wicked by despair, the lazy by luxury, the diligent by agitation, the just by cruelty, and the merciful by flattery. And although he can launch these attacks in any number of ways, he seems to favor four strategies. First, he encourages good for the sake of evil, as when he persuades an unstable person to enter religious life, one who subsequently abandons it. Second, he entices a person to do evil under the semblance of good, as when someone commits perjury to retain another's goods. Third, he represents the good as something injurious, as when he dissuades a good person from entering religious life by suggesting that he or she will later repent of the decision and depart in great confusion, or when he convinces someone to leave off praying or almsgiving on the pretext that they are sources of vainglory. Fourth, he tempts us to avoid something bad only to lead us into a worse failing, as when he suggests an intemperate abstinence from food or sleep in order to make the person weakened by such indiscretion susceptible to worse failings.

**Hugh 2.27*

From this it is clear that we must exercise great vigilance in all things to avoid the snares and insinuations of the devil, who sets his traps everywhere in various ways. Pope Leo warns,

> The ancient enemy, transforming himself into an angel of light, does not cease from laying his traps of deception everywhere. He knows to which person he should apply the flames of desire, to which he should suggest the enticements of gluttony, to which he should offer the allurements of sensuality, into which one he should pour the venom of envy. He knows which one to depress with sadness, which one to deceive with joy, which one to oppress with fear, and which one to seduce with flattery. He dissects the character of each of us, exposing our cares and prying into our inclinations. Whenever he has observed a person to be excessively taken with something, it is there that he looks for ways to inflict harm.*

*Sermo 27.3; PL 54:218B; CL 38:134

And Bernard cautions, "I want to forewarn you that no one can live in the body without being tempted; as soon as you are delivered from one temptation, expect another to come right on its heels. And if you beg to be freed from this second one, a third will follow it. Frequently the Lord allows us to endure a certain temptation for a long time only to prevent us from having to face a worse one; and sometimes he frees us quickly from one because we are ready now to take on another."*

*Habitat 5.3; PL 183:196D; SB 4:403

Ministering Angels

***R 26**

*When the tempter, vanquished, had withdrawn in confusion, *angels came* back to Jesus *and ministered to him,** paying homage to him for his triumph. They were the Lord's own servants, who did his bidding, and he had asked them to withdraw during the time of his testing, which they watched from a distance. He had asked them to leave to better conceal his divinity from the devil, because this made it easier for the temptations to take place; had the enemy seen Christ surrounded by an angelic retinue he would never

*Matt 4:11

have dared to approach him. Their absence also made Christ's victory more splendid, because he beat the devil single-handed; their assistance might have robbed the Lord's triumph of some of its luster. The temptation went before so that the victory could follow.

Immediately after the devil's rout the angels came to minister to Christ and affirm the excellence of that victory. Their service points to Christ's divinity and makes it manifest, because only the divine nature is higher than the angelic. Pope Gregory points out that this event demonstrates the reality of the two natures possessed by the one Person: it was as Man that Christ was tempted by the devil and as God that he was served by angels.* These angelic ministrations can be understood to be of three kinds: first, they *ministered to him* bodily, coming to his aid by bringing him food to satisfy his hunger; second, they *ministered to him* by adoring him, offering worship to their God; third, they *ministered to him* by praising and congratulating him on his victory.

*40 Hom 16.4; PL 76:1136D; CL 141:112

Here is what Anselm has to say about the Lord's victory and the service of the angels: "When he had completed his forty days' fast and triumphed over the devil's temptations, he was glorified by angelic ministrations. This teaches us that we will be assisted by the angels' protection if throughout our earthly life we strive to shun the temptation of passing delights and crush this world and its prince under our heel."* And Bernard: "Then, when he had overcome the temptations and put the tempter to flight, *angels came and ministered to him*. If you want to be waited on by the angels, flee the consolations of this age and reject the devil's temptations. Refuse to let your heart be comforted by other things if you wish to find your delight in the recollection of God."* Chrysostom for his part writes, "As long as the conflict was being waged he would not allow the angels to appear, lest his prey take flight before he had vanquished him. But

*Elmer 7 [Med 1 Anselm]; PL 158:717A

*Habitat 4.2; PL 183:194B; SB 4:398

after he had routed him at every turn and caused him to flee, then the angels appeared. From this you learn that after you have emerged victorious from your struggle with the enemy, angels will immediately receive you also, applauding you, crowding around you, and honoring you. In just this way the angels carried Lazarus to his place of rest after he endured the furnace of poverty, famine, and all manner of distress."* And elsewhere, "The angels watched Christ's struggle from a distance, lest it seem that the victory was gained by their help. Once the tempter had been routed, they *came and ministered to him*."‡

*Hom Matt 13.4; PG 57/58:213

‡Gloss Matt 4:11; PL 114:86B

*R 27

*The Scriptures do not specify what form these angelic ministrations took, but it is credible to hold that they served the Lord by bringing him something to eat, because we read that he was hungry. Chrysostom points out that they did not serve him because he was powerless to help himself, but to show him reverence and honor his power: the text does not say that they *assisted* him, but that they *ministered* to him.*

*Opus imperf 5; PG 56:671

*R 28

Pause here and lovingly contemplate the Lord as he eats alone, surrounded by angels; ponder this scene carefully, for it contains much that is beautiful and devout. What, we might ask, did the angels serve to Jesus after his lengthy fast? The Scriptures are silent on this point, but we can imagine it must have been quite a victory feast! We might picture the banquet we would order, and when we recall his power we realize that Jesus could create anything he wanted and by his own will have anything he had created.

**MVC 17 approx; CM 153:88–89*

But we do not find that he exercised this power for his own sake, or for that of his disciples, although on two occasions he did feed the multitudes miraculously with a few fish. As to his disciples, we recall that on one occasion when he was present they picked ears of grain and ate them because they were hungry. Similarly, when he was tired out by his journey and sat by the well speaking to the Samaritan woman, it does not say that he created food but that he sent his disciples into the city to obtain it. Nor is it likely here that he performed a miracle to provide himself with food: he did miracles in the presence of other people for their edification, and there were no witnesses here but the angels.* *MVC 17 approx; CM 153:89*

How should we picture this scene? On that mountain there were no human dwellings and no place to prepare food; the angels carried food to him that had been prepared elsewhere, as they once did for Daniel. When the prophet Habakkuk had prepared a stew for his reapers, the angel of the Lord carried him by the hair from Judea to Babylon, to Daniel, so that he could eat; and an instant later brought him back.* *Dan 14:32-38; *MVC 17 approx; CM 153:89*

Let us linger here and rejoice with the Lord Jesus in his meal as the angels serve it to him. His most excellent mother, too, experienced joy at her son's victory. We might devoutly and lovingly picture the following scene: at a signal from the Lord, two of the angels departed and in a moment were in Mary's presence; greeting her reverently, they related her son's condition to her. She gave them some of the stew she had prepared for herself and Joseph, along with some bread and whatever else was at hand, which they carried back and set out on a flat stretch of ground; then they solemnly blessed the meal.* *MVC 17 approx; CM 153:89–90*

Watch him carefully and observe each and every thing he does: he sits calmly on the ground and quietly eats his food; the angels surround him, ministering to their Lord, joyfully singing the songs of Sion, rejoicing and keeping festival with him. But, if it may be permitted to say so, their joy is tinged with sorrow, and we should share in their sadness as well as their rejoicing. They are reverently gazing upon their Lord and God, the Creator of all things *who gives food to all flesh,** so greatly humbled, in need of food to sustain his body just like any other human creature, and they are moved with compassion for him. And I truly believe *Ps 135:25

that if we look upon him in this condition with affectionate hearts we will love him in the same way, and heartfelt compassion will incite tears.*

*MVC 17 approx; CM 153:90

When at last he had finished eating and given thanks for his meal, the Lord Jesus desired to return to his mother and began to climb down the mountain. Watch carefully, now, how the Lord of all, barefoot and alone, makes his way. Enter with all your strength into what he is experiencing and walk the journey with him, dutifully serving him in every way.*

*Massa; MVC 17 approx; CM 153:92

Good Jesus, you were led into the desert by the Spirit and, being hungry after fasting for forty days and forty nights, you overcame the tempter. Mercifully grant me through the virtues of abstinence and self-control the grace to fast from sin and wickedness and to hunger and thirst for righteousness. By your grace and help, O God, may I be able to overcome my tempter—or better, my tempters: the world, the flesh, and the devil. Because temptation is our life and affliction on earth, remember, Lord, our misery and struggle. Do not allow us to fall into temptation, but to conquer it always by the virtue of your testing, until by your mercy we are freed from all temptations. Amen.

CHAPTER 23

John Announces That Christ Is the Lamb of God

(John 1:29-34)

***R 1**

***The next day, after his return from the desert,* *John saw Jesus coming to him, and* pointing at him, *he said* loudly, "*Behold the Lamb of God. Behold him who takes away the sin of the world.*"* In this way he bore double witness to Christ: first, to his true humanity, by which he would offer himself in sacrifice for us, when he said *Behold the Lamb of God*, meaning that he had been sent from God to be a most perfect offering; second, to his true divinity when he added *who takes away the sin of the world*, because God alone can take away sin.*

*Latin Diatessaron?

*John 1:29

**Lyra John 1:29 approx*

This is why Christ had come: to take upon himself the sins of the dying world, so that he could abolish sin and death itself, which could not conquer him.* He had already come, unrecognized; now he is pointed out. This is the one whom the patriarchs had desired, the prophets had foretold, the law had foreordained.* *Behold the Lamb of God. Behold him who takes away the sin of the world*, which is to say, "Behold the Innocent among sinners, the Just among the reprobate, the Reverent among the impious; no sin could be found in him, and that is why he can take away the sins of the world. He is like the lamb sacrificed for the sins of the people because in him is the grace and power to cleanse sinners."*

**Ambrose, Exp Luke 2.40; PL 15:1567B; CL 14:48*

**Aug, Sermo 66.2; PL 38:431; CL 41 Aa:409*

**Haymo, Hom 16; PL 118:115C*

*R 2

It was customary in the law to offer different animals in sacrifice, such as oxen, calves, goats, and so on, but Christ is particularly identified with the lamb rather than any of these other beasts. First, because the paschal lamb prefigures more expressly the innocent Christ who would offer himself in sacrifice, for the lamb was without blemish and through its sacrifice the children of Israel were freed from slavery in Egypt. Similarly, Christ was without sin, and through his sacrifice we are freed from our slavery to the devil. And Christ is likened to the lamb not only because of its innocence, but also because of its simplicity: the lamb was led to the slaughter but did not open its mouth.* Second, because although the other animals were sacrificed in the temple at certain times, only one animal was offered up on a daily basis: every morning and every evening a lamb was sacrificed. This practice never varied, and it was the principal sacrificial offering; other sacrifices supplemented it at different times. This was a continuous offering, symbolizing perpetual blessedness, and Christ is our perpetual blessing.*

*Lyra John 1:29 approx

*Bruno Com John 1:29; PL 165:457C

*Aquinas, Com John 1:29 approx

He is called a *lamb*,* derived from *acknowledgement*, or *acknowledging*.* Christ acknowledged his Father, *becoming obedient unto death** to him; and he acknowledged his mother, whom he commended to the disciple's care.* And he is called the Lamb who by his devotion *takes away the sins of the world* because he did not do this only once but does so every day. Theophylact says, "He did not say *will take away*, but *takes away*, as if he were always doing this. For he not only took sins away when he suffered, but he takes them away from that time to the present, not by being always crucified, for he made one sacrifice for sins, but by ever washing them away by means of that sacrifice."*

*agnus

*agnitione, agnoscendo

*Phil 2:8

*Vor Quad, Sermo 1 Tueday 6th week Lent approx, p. 158

*En John 1:29; PG 123:1171D–73A

He takes away sins by making satisfaction for them and cleansing us from sin by his blood; he takes them away by forgiving the sins we commit daily and helping us to avoid sinning; he takes them away by liberating us from all sin and leading us to eternal life where we can no longer sin.* He did not only wash us when he shed his blood for us, or when we were baptized into the mystery of his passion. No, he cleanses us daily in his blood when the memorial of his blessed passion is repeated: by the ineffable power of the Holy Spirit the created elements of bread and wine are transformed into the sacrament of his Body and Blood, and we are nourished by them.* Because of the power of Christ's blood to take away sin and to help us, we pray twice at Mass, "Lamb of God, have mercy on us," and because of its power to bring us to eternal life, we pray, "Lamb of God, grant us peace." O Lamb of God,* may you acknowledge* me, a poor sinner, among the sheep you will place at your right hand! But first forgive my sins and offenses, so that you may recognize* me even better!

**Martin of Leon, Com 1 John 3:5 approx; PL 209:269B*

**Zachary 1.16; PL 186:107A*

**Agne Dei*

**agnosce*

**agnoscas*

*According to Chrysostom, Jesus came a second time to John after his baptism for two reasons. The first reason is that John's was a baptism of repentance and Jesus had received it along with many others. He came again so that no one would assume that he had been motivated to come to John at the Jordan for the same reason as the others, to confess his sins and be cleansed of them in the river by doing penance. Therefore, he came to provide an opportunity for John to correct this impression; this John did by calling Jesus the Lamb and Redeemer who would take away all the sins of the world. His words, *Behold the Lamb of God. Behold him who takes away the sin of the world*, removed all suspicion: he who was so pure that he could take away the sins of everyone else, the sins of every human being, must be free from any sin whatsoever. So it was evident that he had not come to confess his sins or to be washed clean of them in penance, but rather to provide an occasion for John to bear witness to him.*

***R 3**

*Hom John 17.1; PG 59:108–9

The second reason was so that those who had heard what John said before would be more convinced of what he had said and in turn would hear more about Jesus.* So John continued, "*This is he of whom I said*

**CA John 1:29–31*

before he came to be baptized, *'After me there comes a man*, truly manly in virtue, grace, and maturity, *who is preferred before me because he was before me* in dignity, being prior to me from eternity.' *And I knew him not*, as regards his personal identity before he came to me: *but that he may be made manifest in Israel, therefore do I come baptizing with water** and preaching repentance."

*John 1:30-31

"Therefore," he said, "I left the solitude of the desert and came down to the plain to begin baptizing, so that I could make him known to the people who were coming from all sides to me."* The purpose of John's whole mission of preaching and baptizing was to make Christ known and to testify about him. He himself was commanded by God to baptize in the name of the one who was to come, to proclaim his coming, and to prepare the people to welcome him. John spoke about Christ repeatedly, so that his testimony would spread far and wide.

**Bruno Com John 1:31; PL 165:458A*

John Describes the Descent of the Holy Spirit

***R 4**

And John* again *gave testimony, saying: "I saw the Spirit coming down, as a dove from heaven; and he remained* resting *upon him." This took place when John baptized him. The Holy Spirit dwelt in Christ from the first moment of his conception, not just from his baptism; with others, however, he comes at baptism, and he does not remain where there is sin. Chrysostom teaches, "The Holy Spirit descended and remained on Christ; he descends on others, too, but does not remain. When we are angry or backbiting, when we have that sorrow that leads to death, when we entertain lustful thoughts, we can assume that the Holy Spirit does not remain in us. When we dwell on the thought of good things we can know that the Holy Spirit is with us; when, on the other hand, we dwell on evil thoughts, this is evidence that the Holy Spirit

*John 1:32

has departed."* As long as air‡ remains in a body, even if that body is in the water and is tossed about by the waves, it will not sink; it floats on top of the waves. But if water gets into some part of the body, the air is discharged and the body sinks and is lost. So it is with us, who find ourselves swimming in the water of this world with its temporal delights and riches: if we keep the Spirit within us by love of God and neighbor, we will never sink even if we are buffeted by the waves of trial and tribulation. If we want to preserve the Spirit within us, we must keep our senses shut tight against earthly preoccupations and worldly enjoyments. Water cannot get into a vessel that is carefully sealed, and the Spirit cannot be expelled.

*Jerome, Com Mark 1:12; CL 78:458
‡*spiritus*

*Then John said, *And I knew him not*.‡ According to Chrysostom, John did not recognize Christ by sight when he came to be baptized because John had lived in the wilderness away from his family home from a young age; he did not know Jesus personally before he came to the Jordan. He did know that the Lord Christ who was to baptize in the Holy Spirit was born of the Virgin; when they came face to face on the occasion of Christ's coming to be baptized, he came to know who he was by a divine revelation.* Augustine, however, proposes that *I knew him not* means that John was ignorant of the tremendous power of baptism that Christ had reserved for himself, a power that Christ himself would exercise and not share with another. This is why John says later, *he it is that baptizes*,* meaning that Christ alone bestows this excellent baptism.

***R 5**
‡John 1:31
*Hom John 17.2; PG 59:110
*John 1:33

Let us pause here to consider that the power to baptize can be understood in different ways. First, there is the power of original authority, which God does not share and indeed cannot share, just as he cannot share the power to create. Second, there is the power of delegated authority. In the opinion of the Master of the Sentences, God could share this power but does not; others are of the opinion that he cannot delegate this power because this implies the power to create, as for example, grace. Third, there is the power of alteration, which God could give if he wished, so that baptism could be given in the name of Saint Peter or Saint Paul. But God chose not to do this, lest we assume that our hope has a merely human foundation, and also to avoid schism—for there would be as many kinds of baptism as there were baptizers. Fourth, there is the power of excellence, wherein one person's baptism would be considered more efficacious than another's, but God does not grant this power to anyone. Fifth, there is the power of institution, which Christ alone possesses, because he instituted the sacrament. Sixth, there is the power of preparation, which John possessed because his baptism was a kind of pre-figuration and preparation for the baptism to come. Seventh, there is the power of administration, which has been given to the ministers of the church. John did not know these profound and subtle truths until the Spirit descended upon Christ; then he learned that, as with the other sacraments, so with baptism the Lord has retained the power to himself and does not give it to any servant.[1]

According to Chrysostom, John also learned by Christ's coming for baptism that he was the one whose advent he had been proclaiming.* But Augustine holds that what John learned was that Christ's baptism possesses an excellence and authority that he, Christ, retains, whether living on earth in the body or present through his majesty. John had not known that Christ held the power of baptism himself, but he learned this by means of the descending dove.*

*Hom John 17.3; PG 59:111

*Tr John 5.8; PL 35:1418; CL 36:44–45

[1] Ludolph presents Augustine's teaching (Tr John 5.6–7.11; PL 35:1417, 1419; CL 36:43–44, 46) as interpreted by Peter Lombard. In Sent 4.5.2 (PL 192:851) the Lombard distinguishes between the power of the sacrament, which Christ retains to himself, and the role of the minister of the sacrament. Ludolph gives a summary and codification of the Lombard's text.

John's Testimony

*John continued, "*But he* (God, the undivided Trinity, whose works are indivisible) *who sent me to baptize with water*, not in the Spirit, *said to me* through the agency of an angel or an inspiration, '*He*, among all those you baptize, *upon whom thou shall see the Spirit descending and remaining upon him* in the visible form of a dove, *he* alone *it is that baptizes with the Holy Spirit*,* with power and authority for the forgiveness of sins.'" It pertains to God's power to cleanse souls through the grace of the Holy Spirit; he shares with others the administration of this gift, but the power remains his alone. The minister administers, but Christ baptizes. For this reason when baptism is administered by any cleric, or even in danger of death by a lay person, male or female, it is not repeated. This is why Bede says that when a heretic, a schismatic, or a wicked person baptizes someone by professing the name of the Trinity, that baptism is valid; the person should not be re-baptized by a Catholic, lest the profession and invocation of such a great name would seem to be annulled.* God does not hand over the power to anyone, but the ministry is given to both good and bad people. If you shudder at the wickedness of the minister, consider the power of the Lord; the truth of the sacraments is not diminished by the unworthiness of the minister. ***R 6**

*John 1:33

*Com John 3:4; PL 92:668C

John went on, "*And I saw* the Holy Spirit descending upon Jesus, *and I gave testimony that this is the* only *Son of God*,* a Son not by adoption." From these words it is shown that because of what he saw the Baptist understood that Christ was the true Son of God by nature and for this reason possessed the same power as the Father. Here he calls *Son of God* the one whom earlier he had called a man, so that John gives testimony to both of Christ's natures. The Lord received testimony from four quarters: from the prophets, that

*John 1:34

he was the Messiah; from John, *Behold the Lamb of God;* from the Father, *This is my beloved Son*; and from his works, *If I do not perform the works of my Father, do not believe me.**

*John 10:37

Conclusion

***R 7**

*Consider now how eagerly Jesus was welcomed by John and how he stayed with him for a time, sharing with him the meager diet the desert supplied. As you stand watching them from a distance, stretch out your hand like a beggar seeking alms; imagine that you are dying of hunger, should you have the privilege of being invited to share their meal.

At last, when they have been refreshed and have given thanks for their meal, watch Jesus as he bids farewell to John and leaves him for the time being. Then, follow Jesus—and when you come and when you leave, kneel before John, kiss his feet, and ask a blessing, recommending yourself to him. For he is a man truly excellent and great, who could give such testimony to the Lord.*

**MVC 13; CM 153:59*

✠

Lord God, Lamb of God, Son of the Father, you take away the sins of the world. Through the merits of him who by his testimony revealed you to the world, take away the sins of the world that I committed in the world. Saint John, who made known to the world the one who would take away its sins, by the grace given to you may you obtain mercy for me so that he will take away my sins. O God, you take away the sins of the world; friend of God, you say, "This is he who takes away the sins of the world." See before you both one who is burdened with the sins of the world: God, confirm in me your deed, and you, John, your word. You are great, O God, and you, John, are great before the Lord God, who is merciful forever and blessed above all. Amen.

CHAPTER 24

John's Further Testimony and the Calling of the First Disciples

(John 1:35-51)

*R 1

*Jesus had not left that wilderness area. *The next day* (not necessarily the very next day, but soon thereafter) *again John stood** steadfast on the bank of the Jordan, at the peak of perfection and never wavering from the path of true rectitude: he was eager to carry out his mission of bearing witness to Christ, teaching, and baptizing all who came to him. Formerly he had borne witness to the crowds, but now he did so to his followers. *And two of his disciples** devoted themselves entirely to his teaching.

*John 1:35

*John 1:35

One of these disciples was Andrew, but the Scriptures are silent about the identity of the other. Just as Stephen was the first Christian martyr, so Andrew was the first Christian disciple; of the first two followers of Christ, he was the first to be named. Some suggest that the other disciple was John the evangelist himself who, as the author of the gospel, did not want to draw attention to himself; seeking to avoid the trap of arrogance, he chose to speak of others instead of himself.*

**Lyra John 1:40*

Looking up, John saw *Jesus walking** alongside the Jordan, advancing as it were to win our salvation. Jesus had remained in the area after he was baptized by John and was familiar to him. John spoke frequently about him to others, so Christ was known to

*John 1:36

them as well. John deserves credit for this: he did not mention him only on one occasion but spoke of him many times. He repeated what he had said earlier when he saw Jesus: "*Behold the Lamb of God,** behold the mighty *Ram** who must be followed as the leader of the flock."[1] The evangelist summarizes what John said here, omitting what he had recorded explicitly earlier: *who takes away the sin of the world.**

*John 1:36

**vervex*

*John 1:29

John symbolizes the preacher of the Gospel. When it says he *stood* and saw *Jesus walking* and *said*, "*Behold the Lamb of God,*" this suggests that the preacher must stand firm when proclaiming God's word, study carefully the progress of Jesus' life, and not only study it but proclaim it. Those who listen, for their part, should attend carefully; the Lord Jesus will turn with mercy to those who do so, welcome them with grace, and instruct them in what pertains to their salvation. This is how preaching becomes fruitful.*

**Lyra John 1:36 mor*

Jesus Encounters the Two Disciples Who Are Following Him

*R 2

And the two disciples heard him speak*, and, putting their trust in what their teacher said in commendation of him, *they followed Jesus. John's word urged them on: they preferred to listen now to Jesus rather than John, rejoicing that they had at last found the one about whom the Baptist had spoken so often. Leaving John,

*John 1:37

[1] In standard Latin dictionaries *vervex* is a castrated ram or a stupid person. But in medieval bestiaries (inspired by Isidore's etymology), the root of the word was thought to be *vir*, designating either a male sheep or one stronger than the others (PL 82:426A). The following line appears in an Easter sequence by Adam of St. Victor: *Puer nostri forma risus, pro quo vervex est occisus, vitae signat gaudium* (Isaac, whose name means laughter and in whose stead the ram was slain, was a figure of the joyful mystery that gives us life) (PL 196:1438B).

they *followed Jesus*—not just literally, but also by their hearts' devotion and the imitation of his good works. Jesus was John's master, too, so they wanted to attach themselves to him and listen to his teaching.

Pause to admire the simple, humble, and natural way these disciples followed, without cavil or scrutiny. The merciful Lord was thirsting for their salvation and the salvation of all, so, *turning* with compassion (for he always turns towards those who turn towards him) *and seeing them* with his merciful eyes *following him,* he *said to* encourage *them: "What do you seek?"** This was as if to say, "I am at your service." He did not ask, "Whom do you seek?" because they had been enlightened about his identity by John; rather he asked, *What do you seek?* because he knew that they were anxious to learn things pertaining to their salvation.

*John 1:38; *Massa*

He did not ask out of ignorance, as if he needed to be informed; no, he inquired in order to put them at their ease, and so that he could direct them more fittingly on the basis of their answer.* The fact that the Lord turned and looked at them and spoke with them was a sign of his good will and clemency, but he already knew what prompted them to follow him.

**Lyra John 1:38*

By this meeting we can understand that Christ will give confidence and hope for salvation to those who begin to follow him with a pure heart, pouring out on them his merciful assistance. Chrysostom says, "This demonstrates that, if we begin with good will, he will give us many opportunities for salvation."* And Theophylact: "Observe, then, that it was upon those who followed him that the Lord turned his face and gazed. If you do not follow him by doing good, you will never be able to look upon his face or enter his dwelling."‡

*Hom John 18.3; PG 59:117

‡En John 1:37–40; PG 123:1179C

***R 3**

*John 1:37

They said to him: "Rabbi (which is to say, being interpreted, Master), where do you dwell?" In other words, "We seek your doctrine and your teaching." In this brief question he understood why they were following him, for the wise can understand much from a few words. *Where do you dwell?* It was as if they were asking, "Where are you lodging as you sojourn here?" They asked about his lodging, not his house, because he did not have one: the Son of Man had nowhere to lay his head. In fact, the Lord owned nothing here on earth, except that one title Pilate nailed above his head—and yet we cannot amass titles enough!

On the moral level their question, *Where do you dwell?* means that they desire to know what people must do so that they will be worthy to have Christ come and dwell in them. Whoever seeks this privilege should follow their example.

In a spiritual sense, this is a delightful question that can be understood to refer to the contemplation of that light in which God dwells. As the psalmist says, *I have loved, O Lord, the beauty of your house and the place where your glory dwells.** They are seeking his dwelling as attentive disciples so that they can come there frequently, speak with him often, and be taught by him. Bede writes, "They did not want to receive some passing instruction in the truth; they inquired about where he was staying so that they could be more fully instructed by him. Whenever we call to mind the passover* of his incarnation, we should beg with all our hearts that he may find us worthy to show us his eternal dwelling-place."*

*Ps 25:8; *Albert, Com John 1:37*

**transitum*

*Hom ev 23 [1.16]; PL 94:257D–58A

Graciously responding to their question, *he said to them*: *"Come and see."** *Come*, at John's testimony, from the burden of the law to the fountain of grace; and *see*, with the eyes of faith until you can see face to face. Alcuin suggests that it is almost as if he were saying, "My dwelling place cannot be described in words; it is shown by deeds: *come*, then, by believing and doing good, and *see* by understanding."* Or, as Origen suggests, by saying *come*, Christ calls us to the active life; by saying *see*, to the contemplative.* He did not answer, "I live here," or "I live there," for if he had, they might have thought he was simply pointing the place out to them, rather than inviting them in.

*John 1:39

*Com John 1:39; PL 100:759D

*Com John 1:39; PG 14:179

*R 4

*And he led them to the inn where he was residing for the time being (for he had no house to call his own), *and they stayed with him that day*,* that is, the remainder of that day and through the night, hearing from him the words of life. The evangelist says *day* because there can be no darkness where Christ, the light of virtues and the sun of justice, dwells. O, what a blessed day and night they spent as they listened to him and saw him: many have desired to see and hear him, and have not been able to! Who can tell us what they heard from the Lord? Let us build a dwelling-place in our hearts for him and prepare a home for him so that he can come to us, speak with us, and teach us.*

*John 1:39

**Aquinas, Com John 1:39*

Now it was about the tenth hour,* that is, towards evening, which speaks well for both Jesus and the disciples. The *tenth hour* (4 p.m.) is near sundown, so Christ is praiseworthy for his diligence: he was so anxious to teach that he did not let the lateness of the hour deter him. And the disciples are to be commended for their eagerness to listen to Christ: although the hour was late and perhaps they had not yet broken their fast, they did not hesitate to follow him. At the time of day when most people go to their own homes, they left everything else behind and stayed with Jesus all night long, so anxious were they to hear him.* Chrysostom suggests that this detail shows that any time is a good time to hear the word of God—there is no unseasonable season for this.* Theophylact concurs: "It is not to no purpose that the evangelist mentions the time: this instructs both teachers and learners not to let time interfere with their work."*

*John 1:39

**Aquinas, Com John 1:39 approx*

*Hom John 18.4; PG 59:118

*En John 1:37–40; PG 123:1179B

The lesson for us is to be ready at any hour to invite Christ in to stay with us, because we do not know the hour when he will appear upon the seashore of this world to judge us and condemn the bitter sins we have committed—it could be during the night or during the day, at dusk or dawn, or at cockcrow. So in this night of sin let us look for where Christ lives; let us follow him with true repentance, so that he will look upon us. Let us beseech him with all our hearts that we may deserve to see his eternal dwelling-place and he will invite us to stay there with him. Truly, *blessed are they that dwell in your house.** *Ps 83:5

The *tenth hour* also suggests that these disciples were observers of the Decalogue, which was about to be fulfilled. Augustine teaches, "This number also signifies the law, which was given in the Ten Commandments. The time had come for this law to be fulfilled by love, which the Jews had been unable to fulfill by fear."* Chrysostom states that their only motivation for following Christ was to learn his doctrine; and so captivated were they by what they heard in a single night that both of them set out immediately to capture others.*

*Tr John 7.10; PL 35:1442; CL 36:72

*Hom John 18.3; PG 59:118

Andrew and Peter

Having heard Christ's doctrine, Andrew went immediately to get his brother so that he, too, could hear Jesus Christ. Simon, the man closest to Andrew by the ties of blood, was not at home. Andrew searched diligently for him because he wanted his brother to be as closely related to him in religious faith as he was by birth. In doing this he acted contrary to those who try to dissuade their relatives from entering religious life and those who lead others from the ways of truth and virtue. ***R 5**

**Lyra John 1:42*

He found first his brother Simon and said to him, "We have found, like a precious stone or hidden treasure, *the Messiah* so long promised by the law and the prophets, and so ardently desired, *which is, being interpreted, the Christ."** And well did he say *we have found*, because he had been sufficiently instructed by Jesus to discover that he truly was the Christ. As Bede says, "This is to truly find the Lord: to be aflame with love

*John 1:41

of him, and to look out for a brother's salvation. The Hebrew *Messiah* is *Christ* in Greek and *Anointed One** in Latin. He is called Christ because he has been anointed. All Christians are anointed, too, but Christ was anointed in a singular way by the invisible anointing of the Holy Spirit *above his fellows*."* All the holy ones share in this anointing, for they are anointed with this oil, but Christ was singularly holy, and thus singularly anointed. Cyril of Alexandria writes, "The Savior was anointed by the Holy Spirit as Man, in the form of a servant; as God, he anoints those who believe in him with the Holy Spirit."* In the Old Testament, kings and priests were anointed with oil; but Christ was anointed king and priest, not with a human anointing but with a divine one, because he was anointed with the fullness of grace by God the Father, that is, by the whole Trinity, in the human body he took for our sake, as Alcuin teaches.*

**unctus*

*Ps 44:6; Hom ev 1.23; PL 94:258C [1.16; CL 122:114]

*attr. to Cyril in CA Luke 2:8–12

*Com Rev 1:1; PL 100:1090A

In matters of faith, greater or lesser years mean nothing: Andrew was Simon's younger brother, but he found Jesus first. As soon as he did, he went to tell his brother and to share his good fortune. He wanted them to be brothers in belief as well as in blood. Here is true devotion: he informed his brother of this treasure as soon as he found it, and he led him to Jesus, because he would not begrudge him this good.‡

‡*Zachary 1.16; PL 186:107D–8A*

***R 6**

†John 1:42

**And he brought him to Jesus*† the Savior because he did not think his description would do justice to him. Andrew's example can be observed in the church's custom of having sponsors, called godparents, accompany those who are to receive the sacraments of baptism and confirmation.* Jesus welcomed him with great joy because he was aware of his future destiny. Reflect on Peter's humility and obedience: he did not think it beneath him to be led by his younger brother; he went immediately and without hesitation.

**Albert, Com John 1:42*

And Jesus looking upon him with merciful eyes, and seeing his devotion (for he could look below the surface into the heart), said, *You are Simon the son of Jona.** This was as if he were saying, "You are *Simon*, that is, *truly obedient*. Your name is consonant with your qualities: *son of Jona*, or *Bar-Jonas*, that is, *belonging to one who is graced* or *son of the dove*. Your surname goes well with your name, because the man who is truly obedient is a son of the grace of the Holy Spirit, who is signified by a dove." (The name *Simon Bar-Jona* is very apt: *Simon* means *obedient*; *Joanna*; grace, *Bar*, son; and *Jona*, dove.[2]) "You are an obedient son of grace, or offspring of the dove, that is, the Holy Spirit, because you have received humility by the grace of the Holy Spirit so that, at Andrew's invitation, you wanted to see me." These names are laden with mystery, for they suggest that obedience is needed if one is to be converted to Christ through faith, that people come to faith in Christ through the grace of the Holy Spirit, and that our love for God is strengthened by the Holy Spirit.‡

*John 1:42

‡*Aquinas, Com John 1:42 approx*

***R 7**

**You shall be called Cephas, which is interpreted Peter.*† In Latin this name is related to *rock* and in Greek to *head* or *leader*. There is a spiritual significance to this, because the one who was to be the leader of the others and the Vicar of Christ would have the firmness of rock.* His name was Simon before his call and conversion, but he was given the name Peter afterwards. Similarly, when an adult is baptized or a man is elected pope he takes a new name. Simon became his first name, Peter his second, while his family name was in Hebrew *Bar-Jona*, or *son of Jona*; another evangelist has *son of Joanna*. Some suggest that his father was known as either *Jona* or *Joanna*, and they were variations of the same name—just as we might call someone "Nicholas" or "Nicky." Others are of the opinion that Simon's father had two names, each with its own

†John 1:42

**Aquinas, Com John 1:42*

[2] Jerome renders *Simon* as *listening* (PL 23:1193), *Joanna* as *the Lord's grace or mercy*, and *Jona* as *dove* (PL 23:844; CL 72:140).

significance: *Joanna* means *one who is graced*, and *Jona* means *dove*.[3]

Cephas is Hebrew and Syriac; *Peter* is Greek and Latin, and the root of this name in both these languages is *rock*. He was called Peter because of his strength of mind, the firmness of his faith, and his forceful confession about Christ, when he said, *You are Christ, the Son of the living God*.* He held onto this firmly, as to the most solid rock. We do not know whether Christ gave him this name on this occasion or promised him he would receive it later. It is more likely the latter, because he says *you shall be called*. He may have given it when he said, *You are Peter, and upon this rock I will build my church*,* or when he chose the Twelve, where we read, *And to Simon he gave the name Peter*.* Similarly, he promised Peter the keys of the kingdom before his resurrection, but gave them to him after it. If, on the other hand, he gave him the name now, he confirmed it on those other occasions. These three disciples were the first to be called to the faith; they came and, after getting acquainted with Jesus, they returned home.

*Matt 16:16

*Matt 16:18

*Mark 3:16; *Comestor, Hist ev 36; PL 198:1557B*

Philip and Nathaniel

***R 8**

**On the following day*, after calling Andrew and Peter, *he was to go forth* from the region of Judea, where John was baptizing, *into Galilee*,* the native land of these first disciples and the place where he parted from his mother. *And he found Philip*, who was *of Bethsaida* by the Sea of Galilee, *the city of Andrew and Peter*.* There

*John 1:43

*John 1:43-44

[3] Jerome was aware of these variations. His explanation is that while *Jona* is the correct word, *Ioanna* may have been a scribal error based on John 21:15, *Simon Joannis*; Com Matt 16:18 (PL 26:117B).

is a spiritual meaning to this, because *Bethsaida* means *the home of the hunters*: these men were to hunt souls and call them to eternal life.[4]* **Aquinas, Com John 1:43*

This was not a chance encounter; it was preordained, and Jesus sought Philip out intentionally to illuminate him and call him to faith.* Hence the text then says, *And Jesus said to him, "Follow me."** Alcuin suggests that this means to imitate Christ's teaching and example: the one who follows him imitates his humility and his sufferings, in order to share also in his resurrection and ascension.* Philip immediately followed him, without raising any objections, as a good and obedient man. **Lyra John 1:43* *John 1:43 *Com John 1:43; PL 100:761A

From these words it seems that Philip was the first of the apostles to be called.* These four people (Andrew, Peter, Philip, and the unnamed man) had been John's disciples; seeing the testimony John gave about Jesus, they joined him. **Bruno Com John 1:43; PL 165:460A*

*At Christ's direction Philip went to look for his brother Nathaniel, hoping he would become a brother in faith as well as in family; he was not at home, but after a diligent search he found him sitting under a fig tree. *And* he *said to him, "We have found him of whom Moses, in the law and the prophets, wrote, Jesus,* the author of salvation, *the* putative *son of Joseph of Nazareth."** Jesus had been conceived and reared in Nazareth, and Philip had read in the prophets, *He shall be called a Nazarene.** Philip used the ordinary form of speech because it was assumed that Jesus was the son of Joseph, Mary's husband. Nathaniel was surprised to hear that the prophet had arisen in Galilee rather than Judea, because the prophet Micah had written that the Messiah would be born in Bethlehem. ***R 9** *John 1:45 *Matt 2:23

[4] Jerome, Int nom, renders *Bethsaida* as *home of crops* or *home of the hunters* (PL 23:839; CL 72:135).

*And Nathanael said to him: "Can anything good come from Nazareth?"** Chrysostom suggests that he asked this question to express his doubts, expecting a negative response.* On the other hand, Nathaniel was well versed in the Scriptures: he knew the prophecy *He shall be called a Nazarene,* and perhaps he was aware of the signs that would accompany the Lord's coming. Augustine suggests that when he heard the words *of Nazareth* his hopes were immediately raised, and he said affirmatively and positively, "Something good can come out of Nazareth."[5]*

*John 1:46

*Hom John 20.1; PG 59:125

*Tr John 7.15; PL 35:1445; CL 36:76

Because Philip was not yet fully instructed himself, he invited Nathaniel to come to Jesus and learn the whole truth from him directly. *Philip said to him: "Come and see.** Learn at first hand what virtue is in him." So Philip brought Nathaniel to Jesus, certain, in Chrysostom's opinion, that once he had savored the Lord's words and doctrines his doubts would be dispelled.* *Nathaniel* means *gift of God,* and when anyone is converted to Christ, this certainly is a divine gift.[6]

*John 1:46

*Hom John 20.1; PG 59:125

R 10

Jesus saw* with divine intuition *Nathanael coming to him,* drawing near not only bodily but in his heart as well, *and he said of him* to those standing around, *"Behold an Israelite* (seeing God) *indeed, in whom there is no guile or deception." He was coming without hypocrisy or deception to learn the truth; if he has sins, he acknowledges them. Jesus does not say he is sinless, but he praises Nathaniel's forthright admission of them. Deceitful people, you see, claim that they are good and just when in fact they are evil sinners.*

*John 1:47

**Zachary 1.17; PL 186:109A*

How great Nathaniel is, if the Lord himself gives such a testimony about him! *Israel* means *seeing God,*

[5] Augustine maintains that the statement can be interpreted either as a question or as an affirmation, and he prefers the latter interpretation.

[6] Jerome, Int nom, renders *Nathaniel* as *my God* or *gift of God* (PL 23:795; CL 72:83).

and he is called a true Israelite for two reasons.[7] First, on account of his faith, because he had already begun to see God and to believe in him;* having been instructed in the law through faith and an understanding of the Scriptures, he had at least some vision of God, although it was in a mirror darkly.* Second, by the confession of faith he made by responding to Christ's invitation.

*Bruno Com John 1:47; PL 165:460C

*1 Cor 13:12

Nathaniel realized that Jesus could read the thoughts of his heart, so he asked him how he could do this, saying, "*How do you know me?*" That is, by what power, because this is beyond human ability. *Jesus answered* by revealing something else that was hidden and said to him, "*Before Philip called you* and spoke to you about me, *I saw you when you were under the fig tree*,* that is, I knew you and what was in your heart."

*John 1:48

In the literal sense this could mean that Nathaniel had been sitting under a certain fig tree, perhaps meditating on the future coming of the Savior,* when Philip came along and began, remarkably, to speak to him about the Christ with no one else present.

*Albert, Com John 1:48

*On the basis of these two signs Nathaniel immediately proclaimed Jesus to be the Christ. *Nathanael answered him and said*: "*Rabbi, you are the Son of God, you are the King of Israel*,* the long-awaited ruler and defender of Israel." All the Jews were expecting an earthly Messiah, some future king, and it was in this vein that Nathaniel spoke, for his understanding of Christ's mission was not yet mature. It seems he did not yet grasp that Christ was divine, because he said *you are the King of Israel*, and not of the whole world. Thus, when he said *you are the Son of God* he was not proclaiming that Christ was divine, for he understood this sonship to represent simply some excellence of grace.* Chrysostom says that Nathaniel had not yet

***R 11**

*John 1:49

*Lyra John 1:49

[7] Jerome, Int nom, renders *Israel* as *a man seeing God* (PL 23:853; CL 72:155).

been enlightened by faith in the Trinity, so he believed Jesus to be merely a wise man, who knew secrets by some divine revelation; he professed him to be Son of God not by nature, but by the grace of adoption.* Other interpreters hold that what Nathaniel believed in his heart he confessed with his lips, but the first explanation seems more reasonable, as what follows suggests.

*Hom John 21.1; PG 59:128 approx

The Lord began to deepen Nathaniel's understanding, raising his thoughts to the more profound truth of his divine identity by speaking of the service angels perform on his behalf, as to a being superior to them. The only nature superior to that of the angels is the nature of God himself, and it is of this that Jesus now speaks. *Jesus answered and said to him: "Because I said to you, I saw you under the fig tree, you believe* me to be the Christ on account of some superior grace; *you shall see greater things than these,** knowing the power of the divine substance." Chrysostom writes, "It is as if he were saying, 'What I have said to you seems to be something of great moment, and so you profess that I am the King of Israel. What will you say when you see greater things?' "*

*John 1:50

*Hom John 21.1; PG 59:129

What those greater things are he makes clear in his next sentence, which he addressed to Philip and Nathaniel, enforcing its meaning by the double *Amen* that conveys a sense of absolute certitude. *And he said* ***to them:**** *"Amen, amen, I say to you, you shall see the heaven opened and the angels of God ascending and descending upon the Son of man,** offering worship to the Godhead hidden in his human nature." During Christ's passion *there appeared to him an angel from heaven, strengthening him.** Angels were seen around his tomb after the resurrection. When Jesus ascended into heaven *two men stood by them in white garments.** But even earlier, during his time in the wilderness *angels came and ministered to him,** and they also announced his birth.* Chrysostom asks, "Do you see

*Latin Diatessaron?

*John 1:51

*Luke 22:33

*Acts 1:10

*Matt 4:11

**Aquinas, Com John 1:51 approx*

how, little by little, he raises him above the earth and causes him to imagine no longer that he is only human? If the angels serve him like this, can he be merely human? In this way he persuades Nathaniel to profess him Lord of the angels."* *Hom John 21.1; PG 59:128–29

Although this Nathaniel was most learned and expert in the law, the Lord did not choose him to be one of the apostles; nor did he choose Nicodemus, as will be noted later, although he too was an educated man. Christ chose simple and unlettered men as the apostles and first founders of his church, lest the doctrine of the faith and the initial conversion of people be attributed to human cleverness rather than divine wisdom. He did this to confute worldly wisdom.* **Massa* However, he did call Nathaniel and Nicodemus to the faith at the outset so that the teachings of the faith, which were embraced by simple people, would not be held in contempt; if only the ignorant accepted the Gospel at the beginning, it might be thought that they were deceived. Paul was called to be an apostle after the catholic faith took root, and he was a learned man. Philip and Andrew, who were solicitous for the salvation of their brothers at Christ's instruction, symbolize those who do their best to lead their nearest and dearest to Christ. This is contrary to the behavior of many who not only do not lead one soul to him, but in fact lead many away.‡ ‡*Lyra John 1:51 approx*

*And Jesus returned to Galilee with Philip and came to Nazareth, where his mother welcomed him with great joy. Notice the lesson here: after his baptism and victory over the devil Jesus returned to *Nazareth*, which means *flower*. So when we have been washed clean of sin, overcome temptations, or done good works we should always seek the native soil in which we have blossomed. Jesus remained in Galilee for a year, but the gospels are silent about his activities between his baptism and the wedding feast at Cana. None of the evangelists says anything about what ***R 12** happened after his fast in the desert, his temptations by the devil, the testimony given of him by the Baptist, and the conversion of his first disciples.

✠

O good Jesus, you are the Redeemer of the ruined, the Savior of the redeemed, the hope of exiles, the sweet solace of the poor in spirit, the strength of laborers, the refreshment of the weary, the crown of victors, the only reward and true joy of the citizens of heaven, the august offspring of the supreme God, and the sublime fruit of the Virgin's womb. Because you are that fountain of all graces from whose fullness we have all received, may I be borne toward you as the end of all things in my striving, hoping, and loving. O, longed-for Jesus! May I be led to you and follow you because you alone suffice, you alone save, you alone are good and gracious to those who love you and seek your name. Amen.

CHAPTER 25

Water Changed into Wine

(John 2:1-11)

The following year, when Jesus was thirty-one years old, he began to show the world wondrous signs. To indicate his approval of marriage, the first of these took place when he attended a wedding and changed water into wine. This happened a year to the day after his baptism.[1] By his presence in person and by performing the first of his signs at a wedding the Lord wanted to commend and honor the institution of marriage, which he himself had established, as something both lawful and worthy. This event contradicts those heretics who scorn and condemn the married state.[2] Bede writes, "Because chaste marriage is good, widowed continence is better, and virginal purity is best, he demonstrated his approval of the choice of these states in life, while determining the merits of each: he deigned to be born from the inviolate womb of the Virgin Mary; soon after his birth he was praised by the prophetic voice of the widow Anna; and as a young man he was invited to a

*R 1

*Zachary 2.45; PL 186:167C

[1] The idea that these events took place on the same day in different years is found in the *Golden Legend*. Ludolph finds this useful for the literal meaning of the story because he wants to harmonize the chronology of the synoptic gospels with John's, which does not speak of Jesus' forty days in the wilderness.

[2] Zachary is probably referring to the Cathars, a dualistic sect that held matter to be evil and forbade marriage.

*Hom ev 1.13; PL 94:68B [1.14; CL 122:95]

*John 2:1

wedding, which he honored by the presence of his power."*

And the third day, there was a marriage in Cana, a village or hamlet in the province *of Galilee*.* When the evangelist says *the third day*, he uses the term in reference to the two days mentioned previously, when Jesus came to John after his time in the desert, although many days had passed between those encounters and the wedding feast.

*Massa

*Bede Hom ev 1.8; PL 94:46A [1.9]; CL 122:62

*John 2:1

We are not told whose wedding it was, but we are inclined to hold that it was that of John the Evangelist, as Jerome suggests in his prologue to the gospel of John: Christ called this man from his wedding feast,* and from that time on he was dearer to Christ than the other disciples because of his virginal purity.[3]* This tradition is strengthened by the fact that we do not read of Jesus attending other weddings, and that *the mother of Jesus was there*,* as for the wedding of her nephew. It is not likely that she would have come if she were not a close relative, just as she had gone to her cousin Elizabeth, and we do not read of her visiting anyone else.

Massa; MVC 20; CM 153:97

Therefore our Lady was present, not as an invited guest, but as the firstborn and eldest sister in her sister's house, as if in her own home. When her sister Mary Salome, the wife of Zebedee, wanted to arrange for her son John's wedding, she came to Nazareth (which was only about four miles from Cana) to tell Mary, who arrived ahead of the guests to help in the preparations for the celebration. That is why the text says that *the mother of Jesus was there*, but that Jesus and his disciples were *invited*.* These disciples were

[3] This suggestion is made in a prologue to the gospel of John erroneously attributed to Jerome. Bede refers to it as "a story handed down," and it appeared in medieval commentaries. The first explicit mention is ca. 750 by Ps-Isidore, *De ortu et obitu partum* 43 (PL 83:1288), and it is suggested as a possibility in the Hist ev (PL 198:1559A).

not yet permanently associated with Jesus, but they followed him in order to become better acquainted with him and to learn his doctrine. There is nothing said of the Virgin's husband, Joseph. Some say that he was already dead and that Mary was in her son's care because there is no further mention of him in the gospel; he certainly was dead by the time of Christ's passion, because his wife was commended to the care of another.* **Hist ev 38; PL 198:1559A*

Observe how the Lord Jesus eats with the ordinary people and how he humbly takes the lowest place and is not seated among the honored guests. Later he himself would teach, *When you are invited to a wedding, sit down in the lowest place.** In truth, *he began* first *to do and* then *to teach.** See, too, how helpful our Lady is, taking care that everything is done well and in proper order.* *Luke 14:8, 10 *Acts 1:1 **Massa*

***R 2**

*And when, toward the end of the banquet, she noticed that the wine was running out, Mary **went*** to her son and said, *They have no wine.*‡ Given that the Lord was present at the wedding, it is not possible to think that it was by chance that the wine had run out; rather, it provided an opportunity for him to perform a miracle. The holy Mother of God realized that the time had at last come for him to show the world by his miracles that he was God. Then it would be understood that he was not Joseph's child, but the Son of God and of the Blessed Virgin.* So she said, *They have no wine,*‡ that is, not enough. It was as if she said, "My son, there is not sufficient wine." She indicated the deficiency but did not ask him to do anything: for the one who loves it is enough to point out the need without making a request. *Latin Diatessaron? ‡John 2:3; *Massa* **Haymo Hom 18; PL 118:129B* ‡John 2:3

She did not say, "Give them wine," because she maintained reverence for her son; putting her trust in his mercy and generosity, she simply mentioned the need.* Moved by her compassionate heart, she brought the problem to his attention, urging him to save the hosts from embarrassment by using the power she **Albert, Com John 2:3* knew he had. She was filled with the Holy Spirit and knew what miracle her son would perform. What he was planning to do, she urged him to do.*

**Bruno Com John 2:3; PL 165:461C*

Jerome observes, "It is fitting that the wine of worldly pleasure should run out when God is invited. The saints do not enjoy this vintage, because under its influence a person forgets God and is incited by concupiscence."* There is no doubt that Christ does not take part in gatherings where the wine of earthly delight is served, and it stands to reason that there would be none of this wine at the nuptial feast of the saints.

*Attr. to Jerome by Albert *Com John 2:3*

The Response of Jesus and Mary's Trust

Jesus answered, "*Woman, what is that to me and to you?** Why are you troubling me?" According to Augustine, Mary was addressed as *Woman* here, not because she was no longer a virgin, but because of her gender. This term is used for everyone of the female sex in the Hebrew tongue: the virgin Eve was spoken of in this way while she was still in Paradise, when Adam said, *The woman whom you gave me.** Origen says that Mary was addressed as *Woman* both because of her sex and because of the tenderness of heart she showed on this occasion: she was sensitive to the embarrassment the bridal party would feel if the lack of wine were to become known.‡

*John 2:4

*Sermo 51.11.18; PL 38:343; CL 41Aa:30

‡Attr. to Origen in Albert, Com John 2:4

*And Jesus added, "*My hour is not yet come,*† since those present are not aware that the wine has run out." He wanted to wait, because people value a benefit more when they know they need it. Chrysostom says that the Blessed Virgin, moved with pity, sought to anticipate the time determined for Jesus to perform the miracle.* This first of Jesus' miracles was intended to confirm the faith of his disciples, so it was fitting that it should be done in their presence because they were among the invited guests.

***R 3**

†John 2:4

*Hom John 21.1; PG 59:130

The mother of Jesus was hoping that this miracle would be done immediately, before the wine ran out. Now Jesus knew better than his mother the opportunity this situation presented, so he said, to restrain her, *Woman, what is that to me and to you?* This was as much as to say, "The right moment for the sign to be done is not to be determined by you and me together; I alone decide." This is why he added, "*My hour* to do this miracle *is not yet come*; only I know the time." Alternatively, Augustine explains that Christ's power to perform miracles came from his divine nature, which he had not received from his mother, and that he answered her in this way to show her that he owed her no obedience in this regard. He had not received his divine nature from her, so she had no claim over it. When he said, *Woman, what is that to me and to you?* he meant, "You want a miracle to be performed. Have I received that power from you? It is not from our shared human nature that I have this power, but from the nature I have in common with the Father." But because Jesus had received the human nature in which he was able to suffer from his mother, he then added, "*My hour is not yet come*, the hour freely determined by me, not by fate. The hour for suffering is one we share by virtue of the human nature I have received from you; at that hour I will recognize you and submit to you." When the hour had come for him to die as Man, Jesus acknowledged his mother and commended her to the care of the disciple he loved above all others.* Chrysostom's interpretation, that by his answer Jesus was not denying his mother's request but simply deferring it, seems more reasonable in light of what the text describes next.

*Tr John 8.9; PL 35:1455–56; CL 36:87–88; *Hist ev 38; PL 198:1559B*

*In any event, Mary did not take these words as a refusal. Relying on her son's kindness, she returned to the waiters who were serving the wedding banquet and confidently sent them to him, saying to them, *Do whatever he shall tell you.** She presumed that her son would fulfill her request at a moment of his choosing; ***R 4**

*John 2:5; *Massa; MVC 20; CM 153:99*

it was as if she were saying, "Although he seems to refuse, he will do it." She understood by his words that the Lord was not annoyed, so she confidently ordered the waiters to carry out her son's bidding. She knew that he was kind and merciful, especially to those in need, and he would do what she asked even though he had spoken brusquely and seemed to deny her request. The Virgin Mary offers sound teaching here: we should always obey Christ, and we are admonished that we should not despair of the Lord when we seem to receive a stern answer to our prayers. Together with the Virgin Mary, we should confidently await his mercy.

Given the great reverence Christ had for his mother, we might be surprised at the curt nature of his reply, as if she were not even related to him. But this is instructive, in Augustine's opinion, because it shows that the things that pertain to God demand a higher loyalty even than that we owe to a mother.*

*Attr. to Augustine in Albert, Com John 2:4

Bernard agrees that there is an important lesson here:

> What is that to you and her, Lord? Is it not to a son and a mother? Why do you ask what you have to do with her, when you are the blessed fruit of her immaculate womb? Did she not conceive you with her modesty intact and bring you to birth without corruption? Did you not rest in her womb for nine months and nurse at her virginal breast? When you had reached twelve years of age, did you not go down with her from Jerusalem and become subject to her?
>
> You say, *What is that to me and to you?* Much in every way. Now I see clearly that it was not that you were indignant or wished to disturb the Virgin Mother's tender modesty when you said, *What is that to me and to you?* When the servants came to you at her bidding, you did not hesitate for a moment to do what she had asked. Why then, brethren, did he initially respond as he did? Certainly

for our sake, and for the sake of those like us who have turned to the Lord, so that we would not be preoccupied with the concerns of our earthly relatives, and their needs would not hinder our spiritual training. As long as we are in the world, it is right that we should be responsible for our relatives. But once we have left our own concerns behind, so much the more should we be delivered from theirs.

So we read of a certain man who went to live in the desert. When his brother came to ask him for some help he answered that he should apply instead to another brother of theirs, even though that brother was deceased. The astonished visitor pointed out that the brother was already dead, and the hermit replied, "So am I."* *quoting Cassian, Conf 24.9; PL 49:1247C

When the Lord answered his mother—and such a mother!—*What is that to me and to you, Woman?* he was teaching us in the most effective way possible that we should not be more concerned for our relatives than religion requires. So too, in another place, when someone told Jesus that his mother and brothers were outside and wanted to speak with him, he responded, *Who are my mother and my brethren?** Where in this response are to be found those who are accustomed to expend so much earthly and useless anxiety on their relatives as if they were still living with them?‡

*Mark 3:33

‡Sermo 2.5, Sunday after Octave Epiphany; PL 183:160A; SB 4:322–23; *Massa; MVC 20; CM 153:98-99*

The Miracle

***R 5**

Now there were set there six waterpots of stone, according to the manner of the purifying* rites *of the Jews, among whom it was customary for the guests and servants to wash themselves and their vessels. The Jews frequently washed their hands and purified utensils at banquets, and if they came into contact with something considered ritually unclean they would not eat until they had washed. These stone jars contained *two or three measures apiece.** According to Isidore,

*John 2:6

*John 2:6

*metron in Greek
‡Ety 26.9–10; PL 82:595A

a *measure** is so called because it contains ten *sextarii;* a *sextarius* contains two pounds, and two of them together are called a *bilibris*.[4‡]

*John 2:7
*Lyra John 2:7
*John 3:7

*Jesus said to them: "Fill the waterpots with water."** Some of the water previously stored in the jars had been used for the ritual purifications, so Jesus ordered them to be refilled.* Going out, the waiters drew water from a well (which it is said can still be seen at the outskirts of the village), *and they filled them up to the brim.** The water in these jars was turned into wine by the divine will—not by any spoken word, as in the transubstantiation of bread and wine into the Body and Blood of Christ—but simply by unseen divine power. The water was changed into very good wine by the Lord's willing it to happen without a word spoken, although on other occasions he performed miracles by speaking, or touching a body, or on occasion by weeping.

***R 6**
*John 2:8
‡*Massa; MVC 20; CM 153:99*
*Acts 10:34
*Tr John 30.8; PL 35:1636; CL 36:293

And Jesus said to them: "Draw out now and carry to the chief steward of the feast." There are two points to be noted here. First, we see the Lord's discretion, because he sent the wine immediately to the most honored person.‡ However, he was not a *respecter of persons,** for, as Augustine observes, when we do not treat people differently because of their rank then we need not fear that we are acting with partiality.*

*architriclinus
Massa; MVC 20; CM 153:99–100

Second, we see the Lord's humility: it is clear that he was seated at some distance from the chief steward when he instructed the waiters to carry the jars to him; this steward* must have occupied a place of honor, so it can be assumed that Jesus had chosen not to sit there, but rather chose the lowest place for himself.*

A *triclinium* is a dining room where there are three ranked arrangements of tables, from lower to higher, as is customary in refectories of religious. It is called a *triclinium* because of the arrangement of couches

[4] The *sextarius* was about one pint; the waterpots held between 2.5 and 4 gallons each.

upon which the diners reclined to eat (*kline* in Greek is *lectum* in Latin). In antiquity it was customary to dine in this manner so that the diner's body could relax; this explains the biblical references to people reclining at table. The *architriclinus* held the highest rank of those present and occupied the place of honor among the diners. It is likely that in those days this personage was a priest of some kind who had been invited to bless the feast and to instruct the guests how to observe the dictates of the law and the statutes of the elders on such an occasion. Our Lord wanted him, as the most honored guest, to be the first to taste that wine so he could give his judgment as the one presiding that it was even better wine; by his commendation the miracle would be more apparent. Similarly, we should submit all of our actions to our superiors for their approval.[5]

***R 7**

And when the chief steward had tasted the water made wine and knew not where it came from*, that is, by Christ's power, *the chief steward called the bridegroom* as if to accuse him *and said to him*, "Acting with prudence and reason, *every man at first sets forth good wine* when the guests are alert and can savor a fine vintage, *and when men have well drunk, then* ***he serves up* that which is worse*, because their inebriation prevents them from discerning good wine from bad. *But* on the contrary *you have kept the good wine until now*,* when the guests' palates cannot appreciate it." It was if he were complaining to him, "You have done the opposite, which is imprudent and irrational." He said this because he was ignorant of what had happened. But the waiters who brought the wine to him and others who were

*Latin Diatessaron?

*John 2:9-10

[5] Ludolph's explanation of the dining arrangements is taken, with some additions, from Comestor, Hist ev 38 (PL 198:1559C), Aquinas, *Com John 2:8*, and CA John 2:5–11. Aquinas mentions that for Chrysostom the *architriclinus* was the person responsible for overseeing the banquet, while for Augustine he was the guest of honor.

aware of what had occurred revealed to him the miracle that had taken place.

The chief steward praised the quality of the wine, and after this everyone present commented on the surprising wonder. No doubt, this wine was superior to anything found in nature. Chrysostom says, "He turned the water into wine—and not simply wine, but the best wine. The effect of Christ's miracles is always to make something better than what is found in nature itself; this is seen elsewhere, when he restored defective limbs, he made them more than sound. Generally speaking, in all of Christ's miracles the final state is superior to what is found in nature."‡

‡Hom John 2.3; PG 59:136; CA John 2:5–11

*R 8

Jesus performed this first miracle to show the truth of the divine nature hidden within him and to confirm the disciples' faith. Hence we read, *This beginning of miracles Jesus did,** because before this the wonders were done around him by the Father. Clearly the claims we read in the *Book of the Savior's Infancy* and the *Gospel of the Nazarenes* that the boy Jesus performed miracles are false.[6] He performed this miracle *in Cana,* a certain village in the province *of Galilee.** In that village there can still be seen the location of the stone water jars and the dining room where the tables stood; these places are in a crypt many steps below street level, as in other holy places, because so much destruction has taken place there over time.‡

**Lyra John 2:11*

*John 2:11

*John 2:11

‡*Burchard, pp. 38–39*

And Jesus *manifested his glory** by this sign, the glory of the divine nature hidden in his flesh. The divine power with which he wrought this deed is truly glorious and reveals to the world that he is the Lord of Hosts, the King of Glory, and the Bridegroom of the church. He who was able to create out of nothing also

*John 2:11

[6] *The Book of the Savior's Infancy* is also known as the *Gospel of Pseudo-Matthew,* which was in turn based on the *Protoevangelium of James,* an early apocryphal work. The subject matter treated in the *Gospel of the Nazarenes,* also known as the *Gospel of Nicodemus,* is Christ's passion, not his childhood.

has the power to change created elements at will. Chrysostom points out that he himself pours water on the vines and gradually changes the rainwater into wine as it is absorbed by the roots and taken into the plants; what he does over time in nature, he did in a moment at the wedding feast.‡ ‡Hom John 22.2; PG 59:135

*R 9

*John 2:11

And*, having seen the miracle, *his disciples believed in him more strongly and perfectly than they had before. Like John the Baptist, Jesus had some disciples whom he taught familiarly, but they were not yet permanently attached to him; nor did they have perfect faith in him until after this miracle. We do not know who they were. They are called *disciples* because they were acquainted with him and followed him, and on account of the mutual affection between Christ and themselves. Or they were given this name because they became his disciples later: on the basis of John's testimony many people listened to him privately who followed him later. It can also be said that some came to believe him for the first time now, whereas some, like Andrew and the others, became more firm in their faith.* As Augustine says, "Scripture refers not only to the Twelve as his disciples, but also to all those believers who were instructed by his teaching about the kingdom of heaven."*

**Lyra John 2:11 this sent.*

*De cons 2.17.40; PL 34:1096; CS 43:140

Spiritual Meanings of Cana

*R 10

*Note that the wedding has four meanings according to the four senses of Scripture: literally, it refers to the conjugal union of man and woman; allegorically, to the divine incarnation; tropologically, to the spiritual nuptials of the soul; anagogically, to the fruition of beatitude. This gospel passage refers to the literal sense of marriage. The wedding was attended by the mother of Jesus, Jesus himself, and his disciples, and these represent the three goods of marriage: chaste conjugal fidelity, signified by the chaste Mother of

God; the sacrament, signified by the conjunction of divinity and humanity in Christ, or the union of Christ and the church, the sacred realities that Christ symbolized and effected by attending the wedding; and the rearing of children and their education in Christian faith, signified by Christ's disciples.

Second, in an allegorical sense marriage refers to the divine incarnation: in this case, the bridegroom is the Son of God, the bride is his human nature. The mother of Jesus and Jesus himself assist at this wedding, as do his future disciples whom he chose in himself before the foundation of the world. The children of this union are all those who believe in him. Or the allegory refers to the marriage between Christ and his bride the church, and the offspring again are all believers.

Third, in a tropological sense the wedding stands for the spiritual union between God and the soul: the three goods of this spiritual marriage are faith, offspring, and sacrament. Fourth, in an anagogical sense we think of the heavenly wedding in which our joy will be complete. As we read in the book of Revelation, *Let us be glad and rejoice and give glory to him. For the marriage of the Lamb is come, and his wife has prepared herself.** Only the blessed who are called to the wedding feast of the Lamb are permitted to attend this nuptial banquet. These are the prudent virgins who went in with the bridegroom, *and the door was shut*.*

*Rev 19:7

*Matt 25:10

Just as human marriage entails the bodily union of man and woman, so in the nuptials of the incarnation there is a joining of two natures and the union of a created spirit and an uncreated spirit, and similarly in the realms of grace and glory. The first union between God and Man occurred when the divine nature and a human nature were united in one Person. The second is a spiritual union between God and human beings in the grace of mutual charity. The third union between God and human beings takes place in glory, when the faithful soul is led into the bridal chamber of her husband in the hidden recesses of divine splendor. In every one of these cases, the tasteless water of earthly consolations is transformed into the wine of eternal joy, savored in God's company.

*We can also say that marriage, which we are considering here in its literal sense, can be understood as the union of Christ and the church. This marriage was contracted in the Virgin's womb when God the Father united a human nature to his Son's divine nature in the unity of the Son's Person; the bridal chamber of these nuptials was the womb of the Virgin. It was proclaimed publicly when the church was united to the Son by faith. And it will be consummated when the bride, that is, the church, is brought into the Son's bridal chamber in the glory of heaven. ***R 11**

Bede writes that it was not without a spiritual meaning that the marriage took place *on the third day*. The first day refers to the era of the law of nature, exemplified by the patriarchs; the second day, the time of the Mosaic Law, written by the prophets; the third day is the era of grace when the Lord appeared as one born in the flesh and celebrated his nuptials; by the preaching of the evangelists this has shone out through the world as the light of the third day. As the prophet Hosea says, *He will revive us after two days, on the third day he will raise us up*.* This wedding took place *in Cana of Galilee*, that is, in the *zeal* of *emigration*, to signify that those who are aflame with devout zeal and know how to turn from vices to virtues and move from earthly concerns to heavenly ones are deserving of God's grace.*

*Hos 6:3

*Com John 2:1 approx; PL 92:657A

Augustine says, "Let us see the mysteries hidden in that miracle of the Lord. It was necessary for all that had been written about him to be fulfilled in Christ; those Scriptures were the water, and he turned them into wine when he opened the minds of his disciples and explained their meaning to them. What was tasteless now has flavor; what could not intoxicate now inebriates."* Alcuin compares the waiters to the teachers of the New Testament who carry the spiritual

*Tr John 9.5; PL 35:1460; CL 36:93

meaning of the Scriptures to others; the chief steward is an expert in the Law, like Nicodemus, Gamaliel, or Saul, to whom the word of the Gospel is hidden within the letter of Scripture. He is given the first drink, as the chief steward was the first to taste the water made wine. The three levels of tables in the banquet room, or three degrees of honor pertaining to those reclining at the wedding feast, represent the three orders of the faithful that comprise the church: the married, the celibate, and teachers.* Christ has saved the best wine, the Gospel, till last, keeping it until the sixth age of the world.

*Com John 2:8; PL 100:771–72A

Although others have avoided reflecting on the tropological meaning of the wedding for the sake of avoiding prolixity, let us consider at least briefly the moral lessons contained in this event. *In a spiritual sense, then, the wedding feast at Cana is celebrated in holy church whenever faithful souls unite themselves to Christ by good deeds or fervor. *Cana* signifies fervent *zeal* and *Galilee*, meaning *emigration* to another land, signifies the church. This interpretation suggests that those who want to share joyfully in this wedding feast and be found worthy to recline at table with Christ will learn by fervent love and zeal for God to reject evil deeds and love the good; they will abandon vices for virtues, a guilty condition for the state of grace, earthly attractions for heavenly desires, and self-love for love of God. As members of the holy church, let us love the good by abhorring wickedness and living a spiritual life in charity; setting aside passing goods, let us seek those that are lasting.*

***R 12**

**Allegoriae NT 1.1 approx; PL 175:752A*

Apropos of this, we should note that the extraordinary marriage of the annunciation, when the blessed Virgin was wedded to the architect of the heavens, took place in Galilee. This suggests that the soul prepared for spiritual marriage ought to be on the move. In this wedding Jesus the Savior, the one who *saves his people from their sin,** turns water into wine when a wicked person becomes devout or when guilt is taken

*Matt 1:21

away and grace is given. The water jars are filled in answer to the prayer of the Blessed Virgin, who is always compassionate to those who suffer; the water of tears is changed into the wine of consolation and eternal dedication.

The six jars represent our five bodily senses and our sense of understanding; they are described as being made of stone because our senses are hardened by sin before the gift of grace. We fill these jars with water when our tears of compunction wash our senses entirely clean of all the guilt we have contracted. By this water the Jews were purified, that is, those who truly confess Christ not only by the words on their lips but also by the works of their hands and the truth in their hearts. These jars hold two or three measures: two, when we weep over the delight or consent with which we sin; three, when we shed tears over the sins themselves. The water is turned into wine when pleasant grace follows guilty tears, or else when the human mind, which through spiritual neglect found the work of God to be insipid, now savors divine sweetness.*

**Allegoriae NT 1.1 approx; PL 175:753BC*

Every man at first sets forth good wine because so many love and pursue a vintage prized in the present age, only to find and receive an inferior wine in the life to come. Thus, for example, the devil advances a temptation under the guise of an apparent good: when we have been captivated and become tipsy, he produces the lesser vintage, that is, various contemptible deeds, and leads us into sin. Christ, on the other hand, withholds the best wine at first and reserves it for later; at the outset he proposes things that are bitter and difficult. Christ says, *Strait is the way that leads to life.** Elsewhere we read that *all that will live godly in Christ Jesus shall suffer* bitter trials and *persecution*‡ in the present age, but joy and delights will follow in the age to come. The goods of this world are as nothing compared with the blessings we will receive in the life to come.

*Matt 7:14; *Aquinas, Com John 2:10 approx*
‡1 Tim 3:12

A good doctor never administers unadulterated wine to patients who are sick or convalescent until they have fully recovered their health; he prescribes wine diluted with water. Similarly, in the hospital ward of this world we are still too weak from sin to drink pure wine, so the Lord gives us wine that is cut by the water of tribulation. At the end, when our health is restored, then he will administer the pure wine of eternal consolation.

***R 13** *Here is what Bernard says about the water jars:

> Six water jars are set out for those who fall into sin after baptism. The first water jar and the first purification is compunction, about which we read, *But if the wicked man does penance for all his sins which he has committed I will not remember all his iniquities that he has done.*[7]* The second is confession—everything is washed clean in confession. The third is almsgiving, as we read in the gospel, *Give alms, and behold, all things are clean unto you.** The fourth is forgiveness of others, which is why we say when we pray, "Forgive us our trespasses as we forgive those who trespass against us." The fifth is bodily asceticism, and so we ask, *Once purified by abstinence, may we sing God's glory.*[8] The sixth is obedience to the precepts, so that we might deserve to hear what the disciples heard: *You are clean, by reason of the word which I have spoken to you.** When they heard his word they obeyed, so that they were not like those to whom Jesus said, *My word has no place in you.**
>
> These are the six water jars set out for our purification, but they are empty and hold only air if we use them for the sake of vainglory. They are filled with water if they are safeguarded by the fear of God, for *the fear of the Lord is a fountain of life.** Yes,

*Ezek 18:21, 22

*Luke 11:41

*John 15:3

*John 8:37

*Prov 14:27

[7] Ludolph cites the Vulgate, but Bernard's version is more to the point: "In whatever hour a sinner groans in compunction, I shall not remember his iniquities."

[8] From a sixth-century hymn formerly sung at Prime, *Iam lucis ordo sidere*; it is now used at Lauds on the second and fourth Thursday.

the fear of the Lord is water: not very tasty, but the best source of refreshment for one who burns with harmful desires. This is the water that can extinguish the enemy's fiery darts. By divine power water is turned into wine, because *perfect charity casts out fear*.* They are described as stone water jars not because of their hardness but because of their stability. *1 John 4:18

They hold two or three measures each. The two measures are the double fear of being deprived of glory and being cast into Gehenna. Now these results lie in an uncertain future, so there is a danger that the soul might delude itself and say, "After you have lived in pleasure for awhile you can do penance; then you will not be deprived of the first or cast into the second." That is why it is good to add a third measure, which is known to spiritual people and is more useful because it pertains to the present. Those who are familiar with spiritual food fear that at some time they could be deprived of it: this is the bread of angels, living bread, daily bread.

This is the hundredfold we have been promised we will receive in this age. Just as workers receive a daily ration of bread, but their payment comes only at the end, so the Lord will give us eternal life at the end, but in the meantime he promises—and delivers—a hundredfold. It is not surprising that we should fear losing the grace we have already received. This is the third measure, which he has purposely distinguished from the other two; it does not belong to everyone, because the hundredfold is not promised to everyone, but only to those who have left everything.*

*Sermo 1.3–5 Sunday after Octave Epiphany; PL 183:156A; 156C–57C; SB 4:316–18

In another sermon Bernard exhorts us,

Let us seek those two or three measures that the water jars contained. The Savior poured out water three times, and one who is perfect will have all three measures. First, he wept for Lazarus and for Jerusalem; this was the first measure. Second, he perspired profusely, even sweating blood, as his passion drew near; this came not just from his eyes, but from his whole body. Third, water and blood flowed from his pierced side.

We have the first measure if we water the bed of our conscience with the tears of compunction. We have the second if we earn our bread by the sweat of our brow and chasten our body with penitential labors. This water is tinged red either because of the labor involved or because of the fire of concupiscence that it extinguishes. We receive the third measure if we are able to attain to the grace of devotion: then we can drink the water of the Savior's grace and the water of the Holy Spirit, which is sweeter than honey, as the Lord says, *The water that I will give him shall become in him a fountain of water, springing up into life everlasting*.* Keep in mind that this water flowed from Christ's side after he was dead, so it caused him no discomfort; it is necessary for us to be dead to this world if we want to savor this grace.

*John 4:14

The first measure of water purifies our conscience from past sins; the second extinguishes the fire of concupiscence and makes us capable of receiving future benefits;* the third, should we deserve to attain it, satisfies all the desires of our thirsting soul.[9]*

**capias*

*Sermo for St. Clement 5–6; PL 183:501C–2C; SB 5:416–17

The Call of John the Evangelist

***R 14**

When the banquet was over Jesus drew John apart from the others and said to him, "Leave your wife and follow me." Having witnessed the miracle Jesus performed at the wedding feast, John immediately parted from his wife and followed the Lord. This was the first call of John, by which he came to be familiar with Christ. His wife, named Anachita (others hold that it

**Massa; MVC 20; CM 153:100*

[9] Where Ludolph has *capias*, Bernard has *caveas*: "extinguishes the fire . . . to avoid future sins."

was Mary Magdalen), likewise freely abandoned the married state and followed the Lord in company with the other holy women. The works of God are perfect: because he had called one of the spouses, it was fitting that Jesus should also call the other.[10]

Jesus showed his approval for the married state by his attendance at the wedding, but by calling John away from marriage he clearly demonstrated the superiority of spiritual marriage.* This is why the church allows a spouse to enter religious life if the marriage has not been consummated.

*Massa; MVC 20; CM 153:100

✠

Lord Jesus Christ, on the third day, the time of grace, you attended the marriage feast to celebrate in the flesh your nuptial union with the church. You changed water into wine: you revealed the spiritual meaning hidden in the stone jars of the Old Testament, which were filled to the brim because their prefigurations are now fulfilled. I ask you to change my cold soul by the warmth of your charity, my insipid soul by the savor of your sweetness, my wavering and unsteady soul by the constancy of your virtue and grace. Turn the water of my lack of devotion entirely into the wine of fruitful compunction for me, a poor sinner, to drink always and become inebriated, so that at length in your mercy you will deign to change it into the wine of heavenly joy. Amen.

[10] There is a Greek tradition that the bridegroom was the apostle Simon. Ludolph may be the source of the name Anachita. There is an eastern legend that Mary Magdalen was the bride. In the story she is jilted, not invited to become a follower of Jesus, and this leads her to turn to a life of prostitution.

CHAPTER 26

The First Cleansing of the Temple and the Visit of Nicodemus

(John 2:12–3:21)

***R 1** *The miracle at Cana took place in January, and Jesus stayed on in Galilee until the month of April, when the Jewish Passover was celebrated. First *he went down from Cana to Capharnaum, he and his mother and his brethren* (that is, the relatives of his mother and his putative father Joseph, who made up his earthly
*John 2:12 family) *and his disciples,** who were being taught by him. He desired to come to Capharnaum, the largest town in Galilee, to begin to manifest his glory. But *they*
*John 2:12 *remained there not many days** because the residents of Capharnaum were very corrupt and had no interest in learning Christ's doctrine, and also because the approaching feast of Passover made it necessary to start out for Jerusalem. *And the pasch of the Jews was at hand,*
*John 2:13 *and Jesus* and his disciples *went up to Jerusalem,** the capital of Judea, in accordance with the dictates of the law.

***R 2** **And he found in the temple them that sold oxen and*
*John 2:13 *sheep and doves, and the changers of money sitting.** The word *temple* here does not refer to the Lord's house itself, in which the altar of incense and the lampstand stood, nor to the court of the priests where the altar of holocausts was located; rather, it was a certain atrium where the people prayed, the doctors taught, and animals were sold for sacrifice. Because these animals

could not be brought over long distances, the priests (who in their greed were always looking for ways to make money off the people) stationed men there to sell these animals so that those who had traveled a long distance would have no excuse for forgoing the offerings required by the law. Some of the pilgrims had no money, so money changers were also stationed there, who loaned them money under a bond; they did not take their fee in money (so as to avoid breaking the law that forbade usury) but received gifts in kind.* **Lyra John 2:13*

And when he had made, as it were, a scourge of little cords, he drove them all out of the temple, the vendors and the money changers, *the sheep also and the oxen; and the money of the changers he poured out* and scattered, *and the tables* piled high with coins *he overthrew. And to them that sold doves he said: "Take these things out of here, and do not make* by your trading *the house of my Father*, which should be a house of prayer, *a house of traffic** and commerce." We read that Jesus went up to Jerusalem twice: on the occasion of the Passover at the beginning of his public ministry and again in the year he died. Here, at the beginning of his public signs, he expelled the sellers from the temple; the second time, as his passion approached, he drove out both the sellers and the buyers. His action on the second occasion was more forceful because there were more buyers than sellers. This time his rebuke was rather mild: *Do not make the house of my Father a house of traffic*. Later, his words were more damning: *You have made it a den of thieves*.* He made *a scourge of little cords* because, according to Augustine, the Lord collects the material to punish us from our own sins. This whip is woven of sin added onto sin. As it says in the Book of Proverbs, *He is fast bound with the ropes of his own sins*.‡

*John 2:15-16

*Mark 11:17

‡Prov 5:22; Tr John 10.5; PL 35:1469; CL 36:103

***R 3**

*Alcuin tells us that in a spiritual sense God enters his church daily to observe how all are conducting themselves. Accordingly, we must take care to be free of chatter, laughter, hatred, or greed when we go into

God's house; otherwise, when he comes he will scourge us and drive us out of the church.* Augustine says that the merchants in the church are those who *seek the things that are their own, not the things that are Jesus Christ's*;* they do not wish to be redeemed, but they have everything for sale.*

*Com John 2:15; PL 100:773D

*Phil 2:21

*Tr John 10.6; PL 35:1469; CL 36:103

Note that the innocent sheep, whose white wool symbolizes works of piety and purity, are sold by those who cloak their hypocrisy with fleece to win human praise; truly, such hypocrites are wolves in sheep's clothing. The oxen that pull the plow represent those* who have proclaimed heavenly doctrine; they are sold by those who preach for personal gain, not from love of God. These oxen can also represent those who perform great labors for God's sake, and so deserve to be promoted in the church. The sellers of doves are those who, having received freely the grace of the Holy Spirit (symbolized by a dove), do not give it freely but sell it for a price—if not for money, then to gain a popular following. They seek not a virtuous life, but favor. The money changers are those in the church who, under the guise of spiritual concerns, devote themselves to worldly gain and *seek the things that are their own, not the things that are Jesus Christ's*. These are not the only kinds of people who turn the Lord's house into a marketplace; the same is true of those who gain some position or office in the church with selfish intent, seeking thereby their own reward.*

*the apostles

**Bede, Com John 2:15 approx; PL 92:664BC; and Allegoriae NT 1.3 approx; PL 175:754D–55A*

Christ drives all such people out of the temple to show that they will be expelled from the temple of God's holy glory. Those who do not want to be driven out of the church and their heavenly home upon the Lord's return should themselves banish all such conduct from their own behavior, forsaking the buying and selling of greed and simony.* People who do evil when placed in sacred positions, either openly or under cover of good, cannot share in the lot of the saints. The Lord will fashion a rope from their sins to correct them by scourging; if they resist correction,

**Ivo of Chartres, Panormia 3.124; PL 161:1157C*

then at the end they will be bound with the rope and sent to perdition.* **Bede, Com John 2:15 approx; PL 92:664D*

The Lord effected this remedy by word and deed to teach those who exercise an office in the church that they must correct those under their care by word and deed. Now, if even in the figurative temple, and, indeed, the place of prayer in its outer court, he forbade the legitimate buying and selling of temple offerings, how much more will he prohibit revelry, laughter, quarrelling, idle talk, and other such behavior in the church of God.* Because every action of Christ offers us a precept and rule of conduct, it is not permissible to sell candles or any other offerings for God in the church, nor should any business be carried out, unless it is solely pertaining to the church. **Gloss John 2:14 approx; PL 114:365B*

***R 4**

And his disciples remembered that it was written* about Christ by the psalmist, "*The zeal of your house has eaten me up and inflamed me." These words about the Messiah were recorded in Scripture and fulfilled in Christ. Healthy zeal is fervor for the good in the soul by which a person sets aside human fear and is incited to defend the truth. Augustine writes, *John 2:17; Ps 68:10

> Brethren, let each and every Christian among the members of Christ be consumed with zeal for God's house. Who is consumed with zeal for God's house? The one, perhaps, who sees everything that is wicked and works to correct, desires to improve, and does not keep quiet. If you cannot improve the situation, then tolerate it, weep, sigh, put up with the chaff. For example, what if you see brothers or sisters hurrying off to the theater? Stop them, admonish them, show that you are saddened by them. In this way, zeal for the God's house consumes you. Do you see others rushing off to get drunk? Stop those you can, restrain those you can, frighten those you can; those you cannot, cajole—but do not keep silent.
>
> What if you were to remain coldly unconcerned, languid, looking to yourself alone? And, as if

> sufficient to yourself alone, you were to say in your heart, "Why is it my business to worry about another's sins? My soul is enough to worry about, that I keep it whole for God." What? Does this not suggest to you the story of the servant who hid the talent and refused to use it? Was he condemned because he lost it, or because he kept it without gain? Listen, brethren, so that you will not remain quiet. Do not cease trying to gain *for* Christ, because you were gained *by* Christ.*

*Tr John 10.9; PL 35:1471–72; CL 36:105–6

From this it can be seen that zeal is an intense love for God, such that we cannot endure anything contrary to that love. We have this virtue when we can abide nothing detrimental to the honor of the God whom we deeply love. Let us strive to love the house of God so dearly that we are consumed with zeal for it. If we see something unworthy of it, even if done by those who are dear to us, let us make it our business to remove it; nor should we fear to suffer evil for this.* We can appreciate how worthwhile zeal for the house of God is, and indeed any healthy zeal, when we find it among the very first works that Christ performed. By such zeal Phinehas received the sacred priesthood for ever,* Mattathias defended the law,‡ and Elijah killed the prophets of Baal.†

**Aquinas, Com John 2:17 approx*

*Num 25:13
‡1 Macc 2:26
†1 Kgs 18:40; *Albert, Com John 2:17*

The Jews Ask for a Sign

***R 5**

*John 2:18

The Jews, therefore, answered, and said to him: "What sign can you show us, seeing you do these things? You have driven these people out with great power and authority, but you hold no official position, and we do not think you are within your rights; so give us a sign that we can rely on." Although what Jesus did was in itself a good thing, it did not pertain to just anyone to act in this way, but only to someone who had authority to correct the wrongdoings of the priests. Ordinary people did not have this right, because the priests were their superiors, except on occasion when God commissioned prophets to do this. Since Christ was not a descendent of Aaron and thus not a priest according to the law, nor was he held to be a king by the people, they could not understand by what authority he had driven out the sellers and overturned their tables, unless he had been sent as a great prophet. So they demanded that he produce a sign to show he had been sent, not daring to lay a hand on him. They asked for a sign so that they could put faith in his power. It was customary for the Jews to look for signs because this was how they had been called to the law and to faith.

But on this occasion they asked for a sign, not so that they could believe in him and honor him, but in the vain hope that he would not be able to produce a sign, and then they could mock him and attack him. This becomes clear when we see how they responded to what he said. *He gave them the sign of his divine might when he raised his body from the dead by his own power. But because they were asking with an obtuse spirit he did not give them the sign openly, but in a hidden way, speaking figuratively about his resurrection.* ***R 6**

**Aquinas, Com John 2:18 approx*

They did not deserve to have him foretell openly the resurrection of his body. So *Jesus answered and said to them: "Destroy this temple, and in three days I will raise it up."** He was speaking in a spiritual sense about the temple of his body, referring to his body by the word *temple*, because Christ's humanity was the special dwelling place of God himself.* A temple is a place inhabited by God: because the divinity dwelt in Christ's body, his body as well as his soul was truly God's temple.

*John 2:19

**Lyra John 2:19*

In saying what he did, Christ was not directing them to do something, or suggesting it, or exhorting them; he was merely foretelling and declaring what in fact they would do. This was no inducement, but rather a statement of the wicked deed that would be done by some of the Jews. Christ could not lead people to commit wrongdoing. By his words he was simply announcing what they would do, so that their desires would not remain hidden. It was as if he were saying, "You will *destroy this temple,*" when, in his passion, Christ's soul would be separated from his body, his blood from his flesh, and the integrity of his members would be shattered by the nails and spear: *"And I,* by the divine power hidden within me, *will raise it up* as if from a dream, this temple you have destroyed." He gave them the sign of his future resurrection because this was the greatest manifestation of divine power and strength that he could show them. No mere human being could raise himself from the dead; only Christ, who was *free among the dead,** could do this by his divine power and strength. This was also a sign of repentance and the remission of sins, which would be relevant to sinners.

*Ps 87:6

He gave them this sign figuratively, meaning by *temple* his body. Because they could only think in earthly terms, they did not understand, and they assumed that he was speaking of the actual building. So they began to ridicule him, seeking to allege that his words referred to the material temple.

They asked, *It took forty-six years to build this temple, and you will raise it up in three days?** They said this in derision, as if such a thing would be impossible. But they would have ridiculed him even more if he had openly predicted his bodily resurrection, because it would be more difficult to bring a dead body back to life than to build such an edifice.*

*John 2:20

**Lyra John 2:20*

They were not speaking of Solomon's temple, which had been built and furnished in seven years, only to be destroyed later by Nebuchadnezzar. Rather, they were referring to the temple rebuilt by Zerubbabel and Nehemiah after the Babylonian captivity, which took forty-six years to complete because the Jews were frequently prevented from building the temple by the nations that surrounded them.[1]* *Lyra John 2:20*

***R 7**

Many* began to have faith and *believed in his name, seeing his signs which he did that gave evidence of his divine power, and they followed him. From this it is apparent that their faith was still not very strong, because they believed on account of the great signs and not from inner conviction. *But Jesus did not trust himself to them, for that he knew all men, and because he did not need anyone to give testimony of man: for he knew what was in man.** To read human hearts is the prerogative of God alone, because he alone has shaped the human heart, so Jesus knew that they were inconstant and would abandon him in time of trial.* Bede cautions us that these words admonish us not to be self-confident but to remain on guard: what is hidden from us cannot be hidden from the eternal Judge.*

*John 2:23

*John 2:24-25

**Attr. Chrys CA John 2:23–25*

*Attr. Bede CA John 2:23–25

It is uncertain what signs they saw Jesus perform; we do not read of any wonders he did in Jerusalem at that time. For one thing, it can be said that Jesus performed many signs that are not described here. The evangelists intentionally omitted many miracles Christ performed because they could not be easily recorded. In the second place, it can be said that the action of a single individual, and an obscure one at that, expelling so many people from the temple with the aid of a single whip, holds pride of place among the wonders Jesus performed at this time.*

**Aquinas, Com John 2:23 approx*

[1] Many scholars today hold that the Jews are speaking of Herod's temple, which was still being built in Jesus' lifetime. Taking the number forty-six to refer literally to the building of the second temple after the exile created problems as far back as Origen; he and other fathers chose to focus instead on various spiritual interpretations of the number. Curiously, in this instance Ludolph does not mention these, although he certainly would have been familiar with them from his patristic sources and the Catena Aurea.

Divine power was at work in that deed, a strength that he could call upon at will. Christ's body was like an instrument linked to his divinity: a wondrous and overpowering splendor must have streamed from his face and eyes, frightening them with divine majesty; the terrified priests, Levites, and others had neither the will nor the power to resist him. Similarly, at the time of the passion Christ's voice was an instrument that gave expression to his divinity, and we read that it made a great band of soldiers fall prostrate.

Jerome says,

> Most people think that the greatest sign was that Lazarus was raised from the dead, or a man blind from birth received sight, or the Father's voice was heard at the Jordan, or that in his transfiguration on the mountain he showed the glory of his triumph. But in my opinion, of all the signs he performed this was the most remarkable: that one man, and a man who was then held in such contempt that he would later be crucified, could, with a single crack of the whip, expel such a large number of people and overturn their tables and chairs, wreaking more havoc than a vast army, while the scribes and Pharisees raged against him. Some sort of heavenly fire flashed from his eyes, and divine majesty shone in his face.*

*Com Matt 21:15; PL 26:152B; CL 77:189

*R 8

*Augustine suggests that those who believed in his name only because of the works he did represent those, such as catechumens, who have not yet received baptism: because they do not yet have the fullness of faith in Christ and his sacraments, *Jesus does not trust himself to them* and so the church does not give them the Body of Christ.* Just as a man must be a priest in order to consecrate the Body of Christ, so those who receive the Eucharist must be baptized.*

*Tr John 11.3; PL 35:1476; CL 36:111

**Aquinas, Com John 2:24*

According to Chrysostom, those who believed in his name because of the signs he performed did not believe in him strongly and perfectly, so he would not trust himself to them; it was a different matter with his disciples, whose faith in him was much stronger.* *Hom John 24.1; PG 59:143 Jesus did not invite the former to stay with him continually in perfect intimacy; nor did he convey to them all of his doctrines and secrets; nor did he reveal to them the higher mysteries of faith. This was because their faith was not strong, but was based on the mere suspicion that he might be the Messiah because of the signs he worked. They did not think that he was God, but that he was merely a human being sent from God as a teacher of the truth.

To make this perfectly clear the evangelist does not say that they believed in *him*, because they did not yet believe in his divinity; rather, that they believed in *his name*, that is, in some quality they could name about him, such as that he was just or something of that sort.* **Aquinas, Com John 2:24*

Nicodemus

R 9

A man of the Pharisees*, who were religious teachers, *named Nicodemus, a ruler of the Jews, came to Jesus by night *John 3:1 because he was in the darkness of error, although he sought to come to the light. He was still in darkness, not light, because he had not been born again. So he came from darkness to light to be enlightened, but because he was one of the leaders of the people, who were governed at that time by priests and teachers, he was fearful of offending his colleagues.

He did not dare to come openly, for fear that he would be recognized and might be expelled from the synagogue.* **Lyra John 3:1* Also, he was embarrassed to be seen in the position of a student because he was a teacher in Israel, so he came alone, apart from the crowds, to be fully instructed by Jesus himself. He is praiseworthy for the zeal and desire to learn the truth beyond what had been written down that prompted him to come by night.

Bede writes, "He *came to Jesus by night*, longing to learn more fully by speaking with him in secret about the mysteries of faith, the rudiments of which he had already perceived by the clear disclosure of Jesus' signs. Because he had prudently observed the open and manifest signs, he deserved to receive a full explanation of the mysteries of the faith."* The Lord instructed him about the second, spiritual birth of baptism and about entering the kingdom of God. He spoke of his divinity and twofold birth, about his passion, resurrection, ascension, of his first and second coming, and about many other things necessary for salvation.* Thus it is fitting that on Trinity Sunday the gospel is read that speaks about baptism being conferred in the name of the Trinity.*

*Hom ev 2.12; PL 94:197C [2.18; CL 122:311]

**Comestor, Hist ev 39; PL 198:1560B*

*Matt 28:18-20

This sacrament of baptism is necessary and should be received in fact if possible and by desire when it is not possible. Those who hold baptism by water in contempt will not be able to enter into the reign of God, and neither baptism of desire nor baptism by blood of martyrdom will avail them.[2]* Only those who are members of the Body of Christ can attain heaven, and it is only by spiritual regeneration that they are united with him. They become members of his Body and ascend to heaven by his power. *No man has ascended*, that is, can ascend, *into heaven* by his own power, *but he that descended from heaven*,* leaving it not by local movement, but by uniting flesh to himself *de novo*. All who ascend do so by his power; he alone ascends by his own power. If the objection is made that many people in the Old Testament were saved without baptism, it must be said that there was no commandment to baptize in those days: they acquired spiritual life through faith in the Christ who was to come and so had the underlying reality* of baptism;

**Aquinas, Com John 6:53*

*John 3:13

**res*

[2] This probably refers to Albigensians, Cathars, and similar groups that held matter to be evil and disparaged the sacraments.

furthermore, they had a figurative baptism that corresponded in some way with the sacrament, by which original sin was taken away.[3]

The conclusion of Matthew's gospel is read on the Feast of the Most Holy Trinity because each of the three Persons is clearly spoken of there. They appear in the meeting with Nicodemus also: it is the Person of the Son who speaks, the Person of the Father is mentioned when Nicodemus says, *We know that you are come a teacher from God,** and the Person of the Holy Spirit is mentioned when Jesus says, *Unless a man be born again of water and the Holy Spirit, he cannot enter into the kingdom of God.** The attributes of each Person are also expressed: the power of the Father, when Nicodemus says, *No man can do these signs which you do, unless God be with him*, because miraculous signs can only be performed with divine power; the wisdom of the Son, when he says, *Rabbi, we know that you are come a teacher from God,** because he looks to him as a Master to teach wisdom; the goodness of the Holy Spirit, when Jesus says, *The Spirit breathes where he wills,** because it is not because of our merits but of his goodness that he fills us.*

*John 3:2

*John 3:5

*John 3:2

*John 3:8

**Voragine, Sermo 1 Trinity Sunday, 154*

It is true that the Father, Son, and Holy Spirit possess the same power, wisdom, and goodness. However, because the name *Father* carries the connotation of advanced age, and accordingly feebleness, the attribute of power is attributed to him as a corrective to the misunderstanding of the ignorant. Similarly, the word *Son* might suggest the inexperience of youth, so wisdom is attributed to him. And likewise, the name *Holy Spirit* could suggest to the unlettered some kind

[3] Aquinas taught that circumcision was a sacrament of the old law that took away original sin because it was an outward sign expressive of faith and it united the recipient to the community of believers (ST III, q. 70, a. 1). In scholastic theology, the *sacramentum* was the visible sign, the *res* the underlying reality it signified.

of fury, as when the prophet Isaiah says, *Turn therefore from the man, whose breath is in his nostrils,** so goodness is attributed to the Holy Spirit to correct this wrong impression.*

*Isa 2:22

**Voragine, Sermo 1 Trinity Sunday, 154*

Among other things, faith in and confession of the Holy Trinity, if expressed with devotion, can dispel danger. Saint John Damascene tells of an occasion when a terrible plague broke out in the city of Constantinople. A boy in the crowd was caught up in a heavenly rapture and learned from the angels a hymn to the Trinity: "Holy God, Holy Strong One, Holy and merciful Savior, have mercy on us." Coming back to earth, he began to sing this hymn in the midst of the people, and the pestilence immediately abated.[4]*

*Orthodoxa 3.10; PG 94:1022B

Nicodemus, who came to Jesus to learn fully everything pertaining to the faith, can represent humble and diligent students who come to their teacher for instruction. Teachers, for their part, should welcome students warmly and with gentleness, speaking serenely with them, as Jesus did with Nicodemus.* His example also teaches us how to deal with the irascible, who tend to speak with much noise and fury: a useful remedy with such is to speak softly without raising your voice, as the Sage suggests: *A mild answer breaks wrath, but a harsh word stirs up fury.** Chrysostom

**Lyra John 3:1*

*Prov 15:1

[4] The *Trisagion* is mentioned as far back as the Council of Chalcedon in the fifth century and is sung in the Byzantine liturgy as the Gospel Book is carried in. It served a similar purpose in the Gallican Liturgy and is used in the Roman Rite during the adoration of the cross on Good Friday, when it is chanted antiphonally in Greek and Latin. There is a Coptic tradition that links the acclamation with Nicodemus: it is said he heard the angels singing it as Christ's body was taken down from the Cross. The original version has as its third phrase *Holy Immortal One*; Ludolph's variation (*Holy and merciful Savior*) comes from a medieval adaptation of the *Trisagion* in the antiphon *Media Vita,* which was part of the office of Compline in the Dominican Rite. Cranmer translated this into English and included it in the burial service in the *Book of Common Prayer*.

writes, "If our servants bear with meek silence our rough treatment when we are annoyed with them because they fear us, what excuse will we have and what mercy can we expect if we cannot put up with the same—or rather, *will not* put up with it—for fear of God?"*

*Hom 1 Tim 16; PG 62:590

✠

Lord of all things, to whom nothing is wanting, you chose to erect your temple within us. Cast out from my heart and my body all things that are offensive or displeasing to you. Cleanse me from all taint and blemish in mind and body, and make of me a temple worthy of you and in which you will delight to dwell, for your delight is to be with the sons of men. O Wisdom who came forth from the mouth of the Most High, O Master who has come from God, teach me, I beseech you, to avoid evil and do good, to despise the things of earth and love the things of heaven. Then, by putting off the old person with its practices and putting on the new, I shall be found worthy as one born again to enter your kingdom and behold you. Amen.

CHAPTER 27

John Is Imprisoned

(Matt 14:1-9; Mark 6:24-29; Luke 3:19-20; John 3:22-30)

*R 1

*When the feast of Passover was concluded in Jerusalem, which is in one part of Judea, *Jesus and his disciples* and believers *came into* another region of *the land of Judea,** near the Jordan. The territory allotted to the two tribes* was called the kingdom of Judah after its principal tribe; this whole area inhabited by the children of Israel was known as Judea. *And there he stayed with them and baptized** by means of his disciples, and many became believers and disciples. *Judea* means *confession*, and Jesus went there because many came to see him to confess their sins or God's praise, *and he stayed with them*, because their sojourn was not brief, *and there he baptized*, that is, cleansed them from their sins.[1] Alcuin writes, "By Judea are meant those who confess, whom Christ visits; for wherever there is confession of sins or the praise of God, Christ comes there accompanied by his disciples, that is, his doctrine and enlightenment, and there he abides, cleansing people from their sins and wickedness by the baptism of the Holy Spirit."*

*John 3:22

*Benjamin and Judah

*John 3:22

*Attr. Alcuin CA John 3:22–26; Gloss on John 3:22; PL 114:368D–69A

According to Augustine Christ first baptized his disciples in water and the Holy Spirit, and then entrusted to them the office of baptizing so that he could

[1] Jerome renders *Judaea* as *confession* (PL 23:1230).

concentrate on preaching and teaching.* Similarly, the apostle Paul baptized only a few people so that he could carry out the task of preaching more assiduously. From this time on, only Jesus' disciples baptized, and he occupied himself with teaching profound truths. In this he provides an example to prelates in the church, who should delegate what they can to subordinates in order to devote themselves to higher things. So Jesus did not baptize with his own hands but through the ministry of his apostles, although he was baptizing by the presence of his majesty. The sacrament of baptism remained his, carried out through the ministry of the disciples. He is the one who baptizes, and up to our own day whenever any of us are baptized, we are baptized by Jesus. Augustine writes, "It is equally true to say he baptized and he did not baptize: he baptized, because he was the one who cleansed; he did not baptize, because he was not the one who washed. His disciples performed the bodily ministry, he provided the assistance of his majesty; that is why it was said of him, *He it is that baptizes with the Holy Spirit*."*

*John Scotus Eriugena, Com John 3:22; PL 122:322C

*John 1:33; Tr John 15.3; PL 35:1511; CL 36:151

The Consternation of John's Disciples

*R 2

**And John also was baptizing in Aenon near Salim*, a town near the Jordan, *because there was much water there*.* The Hebrew word *Aenon* means *water*, or *much water*.[2] Some people confuse *Salim* with *Salem* and say that this was where Melchizedek reigned, but they are mistaken. Salem, where Melchizedek ruled, was on the future site of Jerusalem. Melchizedek built the first city there and called it *Salem*, *peaceful*, because there was peace throughout his reign. Later it came to be

*John 3:23

[2] Jerome, Int nom, renders *Aenon* as *eye* or *their fountain* (PL 23:844; CL 72:142).

called *Jerusalem*, from the occasion when Abraham wanted to offer his son there and called the place *The Lord sees*. And so *Jerusalem* means *vision of peace*, because *vision* was added to the original name *peace*.*

*Lyra John 3:23

John sent to Jesus those who were coming to him for baptism; but those coming to Jesus were not sent to John. Before Christ's baptism, John was baptizing in the name of the Messiah who was arriving; after Christ's baptism, he sent those he baptized to Christ and in this way confirmed his testimony about Christ. This disturbed John's disciples and created jealousy; with excessive zeal, some preferred their master's baptism to Christ's. They grumbled because they were protective of their teacher's reputation, and they feared that his teaching and the authority of his baptism were being diminished.

And there arose a question between some of John's disciples and the Jews, concerning purification,* that is, baptism. Some of John's disciples defended their teacher's baptism and held that he was greater than Christ because they had seen Jesus receive baptism from John. *The Jews*, that is, Christ's disciples and others coming to Christ for baptism, were hurrying to him because of his miracles and were saying that Christ was superior, and that people should come to him because his baptism was something greater. They pointed out that John was sending those he baptized to Jesus, while Jesus was not sending those he baptized to John. *The issue was referred to John by his disciples, who complained that, now that Christ was baptizing, more people were hastening to him than to John. With more zeal than discretion, they said, "*Rabbi*, although you excel as a teacher of all and are deserving of a reputation as such, *he that was with you* as with a superior *beyond the Jordan*, where you baptized him as a disciple, bestowing a benefit on him, *and to whom you gave testimony*, pointing him out clearly and giving him great honor: *behold, he* has separated from you and

*John 3:25

*R 3

now *baptizes*, daring to usurp your office. *And* to our great surprise, *all men come to him*,* forsaking you who baptized him." *John 3:26

It was as if they were saying, "We have been abandoned; there are only a handful of us left.* The crowds ignore you and run after him, and your fame is fading. Should we not stop them, so they will come instead to you?" **Jer, Com Matt 11:2; PL 26:72C; CL 77:77*

Chrysostom comments, "Although Christ himself was not baptizing, those who said this wanted to stir up the envy of their hearers.* Why? Because vainglory is the source of all evils. It leads to jealousy, which drives those under its influence to do evil deeds and keeps them from doing good ones; jealousy forces people to work hard and robs them of their reward."* *Hom John 29.2; PG 59:168 *De superbia 16; PG 63:675

John wished to allay his disciples' rivalry and envy, so he commended Christ and praised him highly. He said that he, John, was not the Messiah, but his herald, that he was not the bridegroom, but the friend of the bridegroom,* that Christ should increase, not in himself but in others' estimation of his reputation and authority, and that the impact of his miracles and works should become greater and greater, and that he, John, should become smaller and abased both in himself and in the estimation of others,* like the morning star that fades with the rising of the sun, or the authority of the herald that yields to that of the judge, or the office of the legate at the arrival of the emperor.* *John 3:28-29 *John 3:30 **Lyra John 3:30 from "morning star" on*

Naturally Christ was becoming more important in the people's eyes because it was known that he was the Messiah, whereas before they thought he was just a prophet. And John for his part was growing less and less, because he stopped saying what he was not and the people who previously thought he was the Christ now regarded him as a prophet. And this comparative increase and diminishment is illustrated by the fact that after the feast of John's birth the days grow shorter, while after the feast of Christ's birth they grow longer. And John was diminished in death by being decapitated, while Christ increased by being stretched on the cross.[3]

We should apply this statement to ourselves in a moral sense. Christ should grow in us by our knowing and loving him more and more. The more we are able to perceive by love and knowledge, the more Christ increases in us, just as the longer a person sees in one and the same light, the brighter the light appears. Similarly, we should continually decrease in our self-estimation, because the more we know of divine realities, the smaller and more humble we will be in our own eyes.*

Aquinas, Com John 3:30

*R 4

Those disciples of John who showed intemperate zeal for their master and complained about Christ are like many religious today who abandon truth itself and cling to the opinions they learn from their friends. The Philosopher teaches that where both are friends, it is right to prefer truth, and Plato said of his teacher, "Socrates is my friend, but truth is a better friend."* John's correction of his carping followers offers a salutary lesson for good teachers to reject the flattery of their disciples.* Also, those who eagerly listen to detractors and become angry at those they criticize should meditate on the way John immediately checked his disciples' complaints about Christ by singing Christ's praises and lowering himself. He restrains the detractors by his example of self-abasement, he praises those who are the object of calumny, and he silences the critics with a forbidding look. As the wise man teaches, *The north wind drives away rain, as does a frown a backbiting tongue.**

*Aristotle

*Nich ethics 1096a15

**Lyra John 3:25 mor*

*Prov 25:23

[3] Gloss on John 3:30: *Christus in cruce exaltatur, Joannes in capite minuitur* (PL 114:369D). Ludolph adds to the image by substituting *extenditur* for *exaltatur*.

John Is Arrested

*John's preaching mission lasted a year and three months; he converted many people, but he also castigated Herod. So *Herod* the tetrarch *himself had sent* servants *and apprehended John, and bound him,* who had been freely proclaiming the word of God, and brought John to him in Galilee and put him *in prison for the sake of Herodias the wife of Philip his brother, because he had* taken him from his brother and unlawfully *married her.** According to the law that he had accepted, a man could not marry his brother's wife if the brother were still living. (Thus does the devil attract a soul by temptation, bind her by consent, and imprison her by habit in order to separate her from Christ her spouse and marry her to another.) Herod was a proselyte who had accepted circumcision so that he would be more acceptable to the Jews and could reign over them. He was as obligated by the Law of Moses in this matter as much as anyone else. And he was also bound by the law of common decency not to make known his brother's disgrace, nor in the event of his brother's death to marry his wife, except for the sake of raising up progeny for him.

*R 5

*Mark 6:17

John, that resolute defender of the truth, had said to Herod, *It is not lawful for you to have your brother's wife.** In this he showed great constancy: he preferred to risk Herod's enmity rather than to win his praise at the expense of God's law. Having come in the power and spirit of Elijah, who had accused Ahab and Jezebel, John did not hesitate to attack Herod and Herodias.* He would not keep silent about the truth in spite of Herod's power and Herodias' treachery, and in this he gives an example to preachers of the Gospel not to let such things shake their resolve to preach the truth.*

*Mark 6:18

**Jer, Com Matt 14:4; PL 26:97B; CL 77:117*

**Lyra Matt 14:4*

Herod had John imprisoned for several reasons. First, he had reproached him about Herodias, whom he had taken from his brother, and she had suggested that he be arrested. Second, John was preaching justice and baptism, and many people were coming to John from all sides to hear him and be baptized. Herod feared that his people, following John, would turn against him as a foreigner and banish him from the kingdom because of his incest. So he had John taken away and chained in prison to keep him from interfering. Third, John had been announcing that a great king was to come after him. The Romans had decreed that no one could be appointed as a king without the approval of the Senate, so Herod was afraid to offend Caesar, and had John incarcerated.*

Voragine, Sermo 1 3rd Sunday Advent, 12

Finally, Herod had John imprisoned at the instigation of the Pharisees, who were jealous of John's success at preaching to the crowds. They persuaded Herod to arrest him, encouraging him to put John to death.*

Aquinas, Com John 4:1

***R 6**

Now the adulteress *Herodias laid snares for him.** She feared that John's preaching would cause Herod to repent for his sin and send her back to her husband, who might kill her.* Herodias *was desirous to put him to death and could not. For Herod feared John,* with a worldly fear, *knowing him to be a just and holy man, just* in the sight of men and *holy* in the sight of God, *and kept him,** so that Herodias could not kill him. For this reason, Herod left himself open to loss and damnation: it was only fear that stayed his hand from killing John. He knew that all the people regarded John as a holy man, so he did not execute him, only because this could cause an insurrection. *And when he heard him,* Herod *did many things, and he heard him willingly.**

*Mark 6:19
Lyra Mark 6:19
*Mark 6:19-20
*Mark 6:20

Herod consulted John about some trivial matters and feigned interest in him, but this was all done as a ruse to keep the people from rising up against him. Herod feared the people's sedition, but love for the woman overcame his caution, and it drove him to disregard God himself. Chrysostom says, "It is easy to deviate from justice when hesitation is prompted by human considerations, not by God. The fear of God corrects; the fear of other people postpones evil but does not take it away. The desire remains, only awaiting an opportunity. Then those who have been delayed in wrongdoing are more eager than ever to act, and they seethe until they can carry out the evil they contemplate. Only the fear of God reforms the sinner, banishes the sin, delivers the innocent, and confers a lasting peace."* *Chrysologus?; CL 24B:785

Herod seized and threw into a prison a man who in all charity was confronting him with his evil actions. Those who act like Herod can be likened to madmen who try to strike and kill a devoted doctor.* *Lyra Luke 3:19 mor

Conclusion

*Reflect now on how John greatly preferred to please God rather than human beings, and feared offending God more than people. Imitate him by always regarding God rather than others; do everything to please God and avoid offending him in any way. Chrysostom counsels us, ***R 7**

> When we suffer anything from wicked people, let us look to *the author and finisher of faith** and consider that we are being made to suffer by evil people for the sake of truth and for Christ. For if we reflect on these things, everything becomes easy and tolerable. If you are proud to suffer for those you love, what feeling will you have if you suffer for the sake of God? Christ called that shameful thing, the cross, glory; much more should we be disposed to do so. When you are about to endure anything unpleasant, think not of the effort but of the crown. If something evil seems attractive to you, recall that God does not wish it and it will immediately lose its appeal. For if fear of others diverts us from unseemly things, much more should the love of Christ.*

*Heb 12:2

*Hom John 77.4 approx; PG 59:418

Lord Jesus Christ, good Teacher, teach me true life, righteousness, and doctrine. May fear or human favor never drive these realities from my heart, my lips, or my deeds, nor may the weakness of carnal love or dread succeed in overpowering the fulfillment of my spiritual love. Through the sin of our first parents, our courage has been weakened, our reason has been darkened, and our desire for good has been perverted.[4] *Send the Paraclete to defend me against attacks, enlighten me to oppose errors, and enflame me to resist evil desires, so that I may always be able to do what pleases you and avoid what offends you. Amen.*

[4] Ludolph uses the technical terms taken from Platonic thought to describe the powers of the soul: *vis irascibilis, vis rationabilis*, and *vis concupiscibilis*.

CHAPTER 28

The Lord Jesus Begins His Public Ministry

(Matt 4:12-17)

*R 1

*Matt 4:12

*Opus imperf 6; PG 56:671

And when Jesus had heard that John was delivered up, he retired into Galilee. Chrysostom notes that John was delivered up by God, for no one can do anything against a holy person unless God allows it.* Jesus was told that the Pharisees had heard that he was baptizing and making more disciples than John had done (although Jesus himself did not perform the baptismal washing, but this was done by the disciples he had previously baptized), so he left Judea, where there were many Pharisees. These Pharisees were not believers: they were jealous of Jesus' growing success in baptizing, and they feared that his teaching would empty the law of its meaning and thereby provide an opportunity for the Gentiles to be taught. They had encouraged John's arrest, and now they planned to go after Jesus. So *he retired* again *into Galilee.*

Jesus *retired*: first, to provide an example of patience and gentleness in yielding to wickedness; second, so that his absence would cool the jealousy of his adversaries and bring them to a better frame of mind; third, to teach us by example to flee from persecution and danger; fourth, so that he could proclaim the Good News to others; fifth, because the time of his passion had not yet come; sixth, to prefigure the passage of the word of God from the Jews to the Gentiles and in this way instruct his disciples on how they should act in the future. His move signifies the spread of the Gospel to the Gentiles and that this would be brought about by the hostility of his own people.

Jesus returned to Galilee in the power of the Spirit, performing signs and wonders. He had always been filled with the Holy Spirit, but from this time on his power became more evident in the proclamation of his teaching and the performance of miracles. His fame spread throughout the region, and he was received with honor in Galilee because of what the people had seen or learned of what he had done in Jerusalem during the feast of Passover, and because Nicodemus had come to believe in him.

Jesus Settles in Capharnaum

*R 2

And leaving the city Nazareth*, where he had been conceived and raised, *he came* into Galilee to preach, *and* he *dwelt in Capharnaum on the sea coast, in the borders of Zabulon and of Nephthalim.* *From that time Jesus began to preach* openly, *and to say*, because the fullness of time had come, the moment for the redemption of the human race, *"Do penance, for the kingdom of heaven is at hand." In other words, "Do penance and believe the Good News while you still have time, because *without* penance and *faith it is impossible to please God.* *The kingdom of heaven is at hand*, and the gates of heaven have been opened by Christ." Bede says, "The gates of heaven draw near to those who will enter them by doing penance."* And Jerome: "Do penance if you wish to cling to the eternal good, that is, the kingdom of God. Whoever wants the nut must crack the shell; the sweetness of the apple compensates for the bitterness of the root; the hope of wealth makes the dangers of the sea a delight; the prospect of recovery makes sour medicine agreeable."*

*Matt 4:13

*Matt 4:17

*Heb 11:6

*Com Luke 9:6; PL 92:447D; CL 120:196

*Cumm Mark 1:15–16; PL 30:595D

In a spiritual sense, from the fact that Jesus came to Galilee before he began his public ministry we can gather that a preacher of the Gospel must first pass from carnal matters to spiritual ones, and from meditation on earthly concerns to those of heaven; for *Galilee* means *emigration*.[1] And he settled in Capharnaum, a large and populous city where by his preaching and miracles he would enlighten more people; Remigius suggests that this provides an incentive for preachers to carry out their mission in places where the greatest number of people will benefit.* *CA Matt 4:12–16

Jesus Begins Preaching

*They say that Capharnaum is on the border between Judea and the Gentile lands. It was *from that time* that Jesus began to preach, to signify the calling of both Jews and Gentiles, for he had come to save both peoples. Jews and Gentiles lived together in Galilee, so it was there that the cornerstone was laid that would make one people of them, for he would bring together in himself the two walls of Jews and Gentiles. Later the priests would tell Pilate, *He stirs up the people, teaching throughout all Judea, beginning from Galilee to this place.** *R 3 *Luke 23:5

There were in fact two Galilees, one of the Jews and another of the Gentiles. Galilee was divided in the time of Solomon: he gave twenty cities to Hyram, the King of Tyre, who settled Gentiles in them.* This was known as "Galilee of the Gentiles," while the remainder was of the Jews.* It is noteworthy that Jesus began his preaching in that region, where many Jews and Gentiles flocked to hear him preach. *1 Kgs 9:11 **Lyra Matt 4:13*

[1] Jerome, Int nom, renders *Galilee* as *roll, wheel*, or *emigration accomplished* (PL 23:844; CL 72:140).

Or, *from that time* can be understood to mean after his baptism, by which the fullness of grace was manifested in him by the testimony of the Trinity; after his temptation, by which the holiness of his life was manifested by his victory over temptation; after John's testimony, by which was manifested his qualification as a preacher; and after John had been handed over, by which was manifested the fading of the law and the beginning of the Gospel, just as the sun rises after the dawn.

*Matt 4:17 *Jesus began to preach, and to say: "Do penance."** He did not say, "Discuss doing penance," to correct those who talk but do not act. He did not say, "Plan on doing penance," to correct those who procrastinate. He did not say, "Remember to do penance," to correct the negligent. He did not say, "Do not undo penance," to correct those who return to their sins. No, he said simply, *Do penance*—as a medicine to heal sickness, as armor for going into battle, as a key to open heaven. And then he added, *For the kingdom of heaven is at hand.*

**Gorran Matt 4:17* What sin drives off, penance attracts.*

***R 4**

It was fitting that the Lord began to preach after John had been handed over: with the waning of the law, the grace of the Gospel could appear, which alone can be called the Good News. The law promised earthly, passing benefits; the Gospel promised earthly and heavenly benefits alike. Theophylact says, "The Old Testament guaranteed length of days to those who observed it, but the Gospel promises eternal life."

*En John 3:15–17; PG 123:1211D

And Chrysostom: "For this reason he did not preach before John was thrown into prison, lest by his preaching the multitude should be divided. This is also why John did not perform a single miracle, so that he could cede the multitude to Christ, who would draw them by his signs."*

*Hom Matt 14.1; PG 57/58:218

Augustine writes,

> John preceded—the voice before the Word, the dawn before the sunrise, the herald before the

> Judge, the servant before the Master, the friend before the Bridegroom. And because the whole world was shrouded in the dark night of infidelity and could not look upon the Sun of Justice, blessed John went ahead as a lamp. Eyes grown bleary by sin were unable to gaze upon the true, great light, so the lamp's glimmer shone first to gradually accustom them. Little by little the cloudiness of sins was dispersed, the fluid of infidelity drained away; when Christ arrived people could rejoice in the heavenly light, where before they had to turn away.* *Ps?-Augustine, Sermo 197.3; PL 39:2114

Note here that evangelical perfection consists of three things: works of piety, counsels of humility, and precepts of charity. The Lord stressed these three things in his preaching of the Gospel. And the Lord began as John had done, preaching the same message John had proclaimed before him. He did this for several reasons: to show that the disciple and the Master were of one mind in their teaching, to ratify and confirm what John had taught, to humble the pride of those who refused to accept their teaching, and to demonstrate that he was the Son of the same God whose prophet John was. This Word cried out through the voice of John and through all the prophets, proclaiming the kingdom of God and inviting people to undertake penance, because it is impossible to enter the kingdom of heaven without baptism and fitting penance; hence he did not begin by preaching justice, but penance.

Chrysostom asks, "Who would dare to say, 'I want to be good, but I can't be?' Repentance involves the amendment of the will. If the fear of punishment does not move you to do penance, perhaps the attraction of the good will, *for the kingdom of heaven is at hand*, that is, the blessedness of the heavenly kingdom. And this is as much as to say, 'Prepare yourself through penance, for the time of eternal reward will draw near.'"* The Lord preached a message calling people to repent because the kingdom of heaven and the end *Opus imperf 6; PG 56:673–874 of the world were at hand, so that a young world might perhaps feel a sense of dread. Now that the kingdom of heaven approaches and the kingdom of this world is *in extremis*, it is a better time than ever to convert.

The Lord taught such things covertly in private places from the time of his baptism up till John's arrest, but thereafter he taught publicly and in synagogues. John was Christ's Forerunner, and his preaching prepared the way for Christ's; this was why Christ did not preach openly before John had been imprisoned and his preaching career finished. Here Christ gives us a remarkable example of humility: he deferred meekly in the task of preaching and teaching to his servant John, far beneath him in dignity. But today, alas! How many religious there are who do not defer—I will not say, to their inferiors, but to their equals and their betters—and who prefer themselves to God the Son and push in front of him!

Christ's Age When He Began to Preach

***R 5** *The perfect age is a requirement for preaching and teaching. That age is thirty years, so Christ did not begin to preach and teach until after he was thirty years old. It is evident from this fact that this is a mature age for preaching. It is also an apt age for leadership, as is clear from Joseph, who was made overseer of Egypt at this age.* It is an apt age for ruling, as is clear from David, who was thirty years old when he began to rule.* It is an apt age for a man to be made a bishop—but oh! Today mere boys are appointed, unequal to the position and far from worthy.

*Gen 41:46

*2 Sam 5:4

Three years and a little more (the period of time from Epiphany to Easter) elapsed between Christ's baptism and his death, so his preaching mission was rather short. Christ changed the water into wine one year to the day from his baptism. The following Passover, when Jesus was thirty-one, John was imprisoned. John was beheaded at Passover of the following year; and one year later, at the age of thirty-three, the Lord was put to death. Jesus lived for thirty-two complete years, and about half of his thirty-third year, the length of time between his birth and Passover.[2]* In the thirtieth year of Jesus' life, Passover fell on Thursday, March 28; the following year, on Wednesday, April 16; the next year, Jesus' thirty-second, on Sunday, April 5; and in his thirty-third year, on Friday, March 25.[3]

**Comestor, Hist ev 33; PL 198:1554CD*

*There are three reasons that Christ preached for such a short time: first, to show his power, because he was able to transform the whole world in such a brief period; second, to enflame the disciples' fervor, because they would desire him more ardently if he sojourned for only a little while with them in the body; third, to assist their spiritual progress, because Christ's humanity is the road that takes us to God. He himself said, *I am the way*,* so we should not treat his humanity as an end in itself, but go through it into God. Christ took away his bodily presence quickly so that the hearts of the disciples would not halt at merely human affection for him. The apostle writes, "*And if we have known Christ according to the flesh*, when he was with us bodily, *now we know him so no longer*."‡

***R 6**

*John 14:6

‡2 Cor 5:16; *Aquinas, Com John 7:33*

On the eve of his passion, among other things the Lord said, *If I go not, the Paraclete will not come to you.**

*John 16:7

[2] The visit of the Magi, the Lord's baptism, and the miracle of Cana are associated liturgically; this may be the origin of the idea that the baptism and miracle took place on the same day.

[3] As far back as the early third century Tertullian said that Jesus died on March 25 (Adv Iud 8; PL 2:616B). Ludolph assumes the chronological understanding of his time. Modern scholars differ on the computation of Passover in the first century and recognize that the synoptic gospels and John preserve different traditions on the relationship between Passover and the events in the final week of Jesus' life.

In other words, for the disciples to become capable of receiving the Spirit it was expedient that he be taken away from them in the flesh in the form of a servant, lest they continue to love him simply in human terms. The Lord, who had overcome the world, wanted his disciples to direct all their affection heavenward so that it would be possible for them also to conquer the world with ease. It is the same for us: if we aim the desires of our heart to heaven and, with our eyes fixed on the author of our faith, seek to follow in his footsteps, it will be easy for us to disdain worldly adversity and prosperity, and we can conquer the world itself.

✠

Lord Jesus Christ, you have compassion on our misery, and as a good physician you prescribe the medicine needed by our souls. You began your preaching by calling us sinners to repent and enjoined us to do penance while we still had time. You have shown great patience with me in my wanderings, and for this I thank you; grant this poor sinner the opportunity and the will to do penance. In this way, may the kingdom of heaven, far removed and barred by sin, be at hand and unlocked for me by true repentance and contrite sorrow. Grant that I may possess at the hour of death the innocence you gave me at my baptism, so that I may be fit to enter the kingdom of heaven. Amen.

CHAPTER 29

The Second and Third Calls of the Disciples

(Luke 5:1-11; Mark 1:16-20)

*Upon his return to Galilee from Judea the Lord Jesus preached and performed many deeds. *And it came to pass one day that when the multitudes pressed upon him to hear the word of God, he stood by the lake of Genesareth,* which is also called the Sea of Galilee or of Tiberias, *and saw two ships standing by the lake;* one belonged to Simon and his brother Andrew, and the other to James and John. *But the fishermen were gone out of them* onto land *and were washing their nets** to remove the dirt so they could fold them up, for they had caught no fish that night. *And going into one of the ships, which was Simon's, he desired him to draw back a little from the land** so that he could more easily teach the people from the boat. He wanted to get just enough distance from the shore that the people could hear him without crushing him. ***R 1**

*Luke 5:1-2

*Luke 5:3

And sitting like a teacher having authority, *he taught the multitudes* on land *out of the ship.** Marvel at the Lord's great humility and gentleness! As a teacher, he could have commanded, but he preferred to ask. In this he gives an example to leaders: they should seek to advise rather than command, and desire to be loved rather than feared. As Seneca teaches, "A noble soul

*Luke 5:4

is more easily led than dragged."[1] The opposite approach is taken by foolish leaders, whom Ezekiel condemns with these words: *You ruled over them with rigor, and with a high hand.**

*Ezek 34:4

***R 2**

In a mystical sense the lake can represent the old law: the Lord was outside of this because its legal prescriptions were beginning to cease. The two boats he saw are the Jews and the Gentiles: he saw them both, because in his mercy he called many to faith from both peoples. The fishermen represent the preachers and teachers in the church who draw us in by the nets of faith and preaching and drag us ashore to the land of the living. They are brought down from the heights of oratory by the consideration of their own fragility and must wash their nets clean of the filth of the failings they incur by their preaching.

**Zachary 1.9; PL 186:1212B*

The proclamation of the Gospel is sometimes sullied by greed, vainglory, or deceptive praise, all of which are washed away by the water of contrition. It can be said that those who cast out worldly gain, intellectual pride, and the desire for applause wash their nets.* Simon's boat, into which the Lord climbed through faith to teach the crowds, is the primitive church of the Jews, of which Peter was the first preacher; the authority of his church to teach the nations continues to this day. The other boat is the church of the Gentiles, to whom Paul was sent to preach because not all the believers predestined to eternal life come from Judea.

**St Cher Luke 5:2*

Jesus taught from a boat very close to shore, which suggests that when explaining heavenly realities we ought to do so in a way that ordinary folk can apprehend or understand through faith. In preaching to the crowd we should avoid on the one hand such common language that the subject seems banal, and on the other hand language that is so high-flown that our

[1] *Generosus animus facilius ducitur, quam trahatur*. This is a paraphrase of *De clementia*, 1.24.1, cited often in medieval works.

listeners feel that these spiritual matters are simply beyond them.*

*Aug, Quaest Ev 2.2 approx; PL 35:1333; CL 44B:42

The lake, or sea, can also be taken as an image of the world, which swells with pride, roils with greed, and foams with luxury. In order to make his way through this world Jesus saw, that is, approved, two boats: the owner of one is unnamed, and stands for the common road of the commandments that all people without distinction must observe; the other belonged to Simon, whose name means obedient and stands for the way of the evangelical counsels and religious life, and of these the vow of obedience is the most important.*

*St Cher Luke 5:2 approx

Christ got into this second boat, sat in it, taught from it, and asked that it put off a little distance from shore; similarly, he comes through grace into the hearts of dedicated religious who observe the counsels, takes his seat there through contemplation, and instructs them through the influence of the gifts of the Holy Spirit. He wants religious to move out a little distance from the land, in heart though not in body, because the heart cannot be preserved if it is cut off entirely from this life. Holy people cannot separate themselves completely from this world because they must make provision for the needs of the body. Those in Simon's boat, religious life, should however be some distance from land, but many entering religious life today, far from separating themselves from worldly concerns, are in fact closer to them than they were before they got into the boat.

The two boats Jesus saw can also remind us of the two paths he has approved for us to enter into life: innocence and penitence.* An inheritance can be obtained by succession or by purchase.[2] The heavenly inheritance can be received by the way of innocence

*St Cher Luke 5:2

[2] The *emptio hereditatis* in Roman law allowed someone to purchase another's inheritance.

as a sort of legacy, and this is the boat Christ got into, *who did no sin, neither was guile found in his mouth.** There is also the way of purchase, or penitence, and Christ climbed into that boat for our sake when he did not disdain to accept death itself. Chrysostom writes, "The ship is the church, the rudder is the cross, the steersman is Christ; the net is the Father, the wind is the Spirit, the sail is grace, the sailors are the apostles, the navigators are the prophets, the two boats are the Old and New Testaments. Let us set sail on the open sea, searching everywhere in the depths of holy Scripture for the pearls that lie hidden there."*

*1 Pet 2:22

*Chromatius 42.5 approx; CL 9A:402

The Miraculous Catch of Fish

***R 3**

Now when he had ceased to speak,* Jesus chose to confirm his teaching with a miracle. So *he said to Simon, "Launch out into the deep* where the fishing is better *and let down your nets for a catch* of fish." *And Simon answering said to him,* "Jesus, *Master* whom we should obey, *we have labored all the night and have taken nothing*, although we have expended much effort, *but at your word I will let down the net*, trusting in your power." *And when they had done this* in obedience to the Master, *they enclosed a very great multitude of fishes, as many as the Lord of land and sea wanted. This was not surprising: since the birds of the air and the fishes of the sea obey him, these creatures were delivered up by his power over them. Anselm says, "There is no law that God's creatures need fear to break by their wicked actions."*

*Luke 5:4-6

*Eadmer, De exc 10; PL 159:576C

Here the disciples provide religious with a good example of obedience: they acted quickly at a word from Jesus, not waiting for a command or threat. Notice also that, although the order to let down the nets of preaching was given to the others associated with Simon's submissiveness, only to Peter were the words addressed, *Launch out into the deep*, that is, into the profound depths of Scripture and doctrine. And what could be deeper than to know the Son of God? This was as if to say, "The lower clergy know enough to preach the basic beliefs, but when questions arise in the church they should be brought to the bishops to be resolved." In a spiritual sense this scene suggests the three qualities preachers should possess: first, they should speak about sublime matters, as when the Lord said, *Launch out into the deep*; second, their discourse should be thorough and plain, as when he added, *let down your nets*; finally, they should be acting for a good purpose, as when the Lord specifies, *for a catch* of fish. That is, preachers should be motivated by a desire to edify their flock, not by a thirst for adulation, fame, or worldly profit.

***R 4**

And their net broke‡ from the weight of so many fish. So it seems that a double miracle took place: not only had they caught a huge number of fish, far beyond what was usual or possible by human means, but this huge catch was held by nets that were broken.* *And they beckoned to their partners that were in the other ship*, the sons of Zebedee, *that they should come and help them*.* Theophylact writes, "He summoned them by a sign because the large catch of fish left him speechless. *And they came and filled both the ships, so that they were almost sinking*."* The church rides on the swells and is battered by the waves, but she cannot sink. Simon Peter and his companions were thunderstruck and could barely grasp the remarkable deed Christ had done.

‡Luke 5:6

**Lyra Luke 5:6*

*Luke 5:7

*Luke 5:7; En Luke 5:1–11; PG 123:758D

When Simon Peter saw that no mere mortal could have done this, *he fell down* humbly *at Jesus' knees*, as if he recognized that he was the Lord, saying, "*Depart from me, for I am a sinful man* unworthy to be in your company, *O Lord*.* Depart from me, because I am only human and you are the God-Man; I am a sinner and you are holy; I am a slave and you are the Lord." It

*Luke 5:8

was as if he were saying, "Let me be separated from you by location, because I am already far from you on account of my fragile nature, my great sins, and my weak powers!" He felt unworthy to be in the presence of such a holy man. He teaches us that we who are sinful should handle sacred objects, stand around Christ's altar, and approach the Eucharist with holy dread.

The Lord consoled Peter and explained to him that the catch of fish signified that through Christ he was going to catch people. He said, "*Fear not*, and do not be astounded; rather, believe and rejoice, because you are destined for a much greater haul than this, and you will be given a different boat and other nets.* Up until now you have used these nets to catch fish, but *from henceforth*,* in the near future, *you shall catch men*‡ by your words. By the office of preaching you take on, you will draw them to eternal life by sound doctrine."

*Bruno Com Luke 5:10

*ex hoc

‡Luke 5:10

The word of God may be likened to the fisherman's hook: just as the hook does not catch a fish unless the fish takes hold of it, so the word of God does not catch people and reel them in to eternal life unless they take the word into their heart.*

*Lyra Luke 5:10

*ex hoc

Or, *from this** can mean, "From this event that has taken place is signified that *you shall catch men*." Or, "From this event that has humbled you, you will receive the office of catching men and women." Humility is an attractive virtue, and it is fitting that those placed in authority over others should not vaunt their pride.

He is not chosen to be an apostle now, but his future election is foretold; this whole event illustrates the place he will have in the church.*

*Bonaventure, Com Luke 5:10

Peter, together with his companions, had labored all night long without success, but at the word of Christ he let down his nets and took in a huge catch of fish. However, he knew that the only thing he could take credit for was his sins, so he said, "*Depart from me, for I am a sinful man."* He is a good model for a preacher of the Gospel, who realizes that any success he enjoys comes from the Lord's power and not from his talents. And just as Peter fell on his knees before Jesus after the great catch of fish, so the preacher who has won over many souls should humble himself before God, attributing all the success to the Lord and claiming only the failings for himself.* Then the Lord will comfort him, saying, *"Fear not,"* adding the promise, *"from henceforth you shall catch* even more *men* and women." **Lyra Luke 5:10 mor*

***R 5**

***R 5** *And having brought their ships to land,* they carefully arranged their equipment, planning to come back later. *Leaving all things* for the time being, *they followed him** at a respectful distance. Peter, Andrew, James, and John associated themselves with Jesus but returned later to their homes and boats to ply their trade. Clearly they had not left all their possessions for good, nor had they yet perfectly answered Christ's call. *Luke 5:11

***R 6**

*Now this Sea of Galilee, or Tiberias, also called the Lake of Gennesaret, is situated between Jerusalem and Damascus, about a three-day journey from each city. Measuring twelve miles long and five miles wide, it is a very picturesque site, surrounded by forests and having sandy beaches. There are many fish of various kinds to be found in it, and the water is very good to drink. Although it is a freshwater lake, it is called a sea because in the Hebrew tongue any large body of water, whether fresh or salt, is called *tharsis*, or *sea*, as it says in the book of Genesis: *and the gathering together of the waters, he called Seas.** *Gen 1:10

It is called the Sea of Galilee because it is situated in the province of Galilee (the Galilee of the Jews, not Galilee of the Gentiles), or the Sea of Tiberias from the city of that name on its shore that Jesus visited frequently in his youth. It is also called a *lake** because its water is still; the only current comes from the Jordan river flowing into it and out of it, nor are there **stagnum* riverbeds that allow the water to flow out of it into streams. The name *Gennesaret* is given to it from the nature of the lake itself: it comes from a Greek word meaning *making a breeze for itself*. Winds blowing down from the passes of the hills surrounding the lake frequently stir up gusts on the water, and these can generate great waves and create such a tempest that occasionally small boats capsize and sink.

*Jewish Wars 3.10.7
‡*lacus salinarum*

Josephus, however, says the lake receives this name from its proximity to Genezar, a very lush and temperate valley that is home to a great variety of trees; so its name is interpreted as garden of princes.* Occasionally it is called the *lake of the salt-pans*‡ because of the wells there from which salt is taken. The source of the Jordan River is in the mountains of Lebanon near Caesarea Philippi, where there are two springs, called the Jor and the Dan. The river flows down into the Lake of Gennesaret, passes through it, and flows out at the other end. After irrigating a good part of the region, the Jordan passes into the celebrated valley known as the Valley of the Salt Sea and empties into the Dead Sea not far from Jericho, and thence disappears into the depths of the earth.[3]

The Final Call of the First Disciples

***R 7**

*Mark 1:16

And* sometime after the disciples had returned to their fishing after the aforementioned call, *passing by the sea of Galilee, he saw Simon and Andrew his brother, casting nets into the sea, for they were fishermen. He was seeing them spiritually rather than just bodily, studying their hearts more than their faces. They were earn-

[3] Ludolph has taken this description from Zachary 1:19 (PL 186:112A), Comestor, Hist ev 40 (PL 198:1560CD), medieval guide books, and a passage attributed to Bede in Glosses (e.g., PL 102:375A; CA Luke 5:1–3).

ing their living as fishermen and, as the Gloss notes, it was appropriate that the Fisherman went down to the docks to find fishermen.* *And Jesus said to them: "Come after me* by affection and imitation, walk the road I will walk, *and I will make you to become fishers of men."** He said, "fishers of *men*"—not of benefices or of tithes, but of souls. With the nets of sacred preaching they were to catch men and women swimming in the depths of infidelity and drag them to the light of faith as onto the shore of salvation. Theophylact writes, "Wonderful indeed is this fishing! Fish die as soon as they are caught, but when people are captured by the word of preaching, they live."* Chrysostom notes that Jesus called them while they were at work to show that following him should take precedence over all other occupations.* Those who are chosen to be pastors or preachers in the church should be solicitous to follow the Lord completely. This means, *Let him deny himself and take up his cross.** *And immediately leaving their nets, they followed him.** They followed not only with their feet but also with their hearts and wills, leaving behind for ever their trade and home.

*Gloss Matt 4:19; PL 114:87D

*Mark 1:17

*Attr. to Remigius CA Mark 1:16–20

*Hom Matt 14.2; PG 57/58:219

*Luke 9:23

*Mark 1:18

R 8

And going on from there* a little farther, *he saw other two brothers, James the son of Zebedee, and John his brother, in a ship with Zebedee their father*, who as an old man was holding an oar, and they were *mending their nets, which suggests that they were very poor. Chrysostom writes,

*Matt 4:21

> See how careful the evangelist is to describe their poverty: he found them *mending their nets*. So great was their poverty that they had to repair and restore their old nets because they lacked the means to buy new ones. And they provide an example of filial piety, too, in the midst of their poverty. They took care of their elderly father and brought him along in the boat, not to help them in their work but so that they could console him with their company. This is no small lesson for us: they bear poverty with

ease, supporting themselves with their labors and being bound together in mutual love, keeping their poor father with them and working for him.*

*Hom Matt 14.2; PG 57/58:219

So it is good to take a break occasionally—from preaching as from fishing—to repair your nets. If, for example, you have mended your nets by gathering together biblical citations to strangle greed, then leave off preaching for a time and repair your nets again by collecting other authoritative texts to attack other vices and root them out. Jesus called them to himself so that they would stop searching for fish and start fishing for men and women. According to Chrysostom, he called fishermen on purpose so that their work would suggest the grace of the dignity of their future office. By a marvelous transformation, they were to abandon their earthly trade and become heavenly fishermen, drawing the human race like fish to salvation from the deep sea of error.‡

‡Chromatius 16.2; CL 9A:264

***R 9**

*Matt 4:22

And they forthwith left their nets and father, and followed him by every means of imitation and following of perfection. They changed their purpose, not their profession: they exchanged their nets for doctrine, their ambition for a love of souls, the sea of this world for the ship of the church, the fish for people good and bad alike. In this they gave an example to anyone who wants to follow Christ.

By abandoning nets, boats, and father as soon as Christ asked them to follow him, Peter, Andrew, James, and John show us that neither carnal desires, worldly gain, nor family ties should prevent us from following Christ.* Perfect followers leave behind the nets of sin, the boat of possessions, and even their parents (at least so far as worldly affections go) in order to follow Christ with an eager spirit.*

**Lyra Mark 1:18 mor*

**Lyra Matt 4:22*

Nets, boats, and father symbolize three things a follower of Christ must leave behind: sinful actions, which ensnare us like a net; earthly possessions, the boats; and family affection, represented by the father. Chrysostom says, "Whoever comes to Christ must abandon three things: sins of the flesh, worldly goods, and family, which are signified by the fishing nets, the boats, and the father. They left behind their boats to become steersmen on the bark of the church, their nets to draw people to heaven rather than fish to an earthly city, and one father to become the spiritual fathers of everyone."* *Opus imperf 7; PG 56:676

Notice also that the text says that Peter and Andrew were casting their nets into the sea, whereas James and John were mending theirs. Chrysostom suggests that an explanation of this is that Peter cast his words while John repaired his—by which he means that Peter preached the Gospel but did not write one, but John both preached and wrote.* This may also refer to the active and contemplative life, because the word used of Peter speaks of action, while that used of John suggests contemplation. Peter was the most ardent and zealous of the apostles, but John was the most excellent theologian. *Opus imperf 7; PG 56:676

Consider here the remarkable obedience of these four blessed disciples, who at one word of command left all things, even their own will and way of life, to follow Christ. Chrysostom says that by this willingness they show themselves to be true sons of Abraham: imitating his example, they followed as soon as they heard God's voice. They immediately gave up the quest for worldly profit to gain eternal wealth, and they left their earthly father to have a heavenly Father. This shows that they were worthy to be chosen. ***R 10** *Chromatius 16.2; CL 9A:264

Elsewhere he writes,

> Assess carefully the faith and obedience of the men who were called. You know how avidly they plied their trade as fishermen; although they were busy about their work when the Lord's command came, they did not hesitate or delay for a moment, nor

> did they say, "Let's go home and talk this over with the family." No, as Elisha did at Elijah's command, they left everything behind immediately. This is the kind of hair-trigger response Christ demands of us: we should not temporize or see if there is any pressing business to attend to. On another occasion he called someone to follow him, and the man asked leave to bury his father; his request was refused, to show that Christ takes priority even over the most necessary duties.*

*Hom Matt 14 Anianus, Cratandri 1:72

Pope Gregory teaches, "You have heard that at the sound of one command they followed the Redeemer, at one order from the Lord they forgot all they possessed. What are we going to say at the Judgment, we who have disdained his call to follow and are not turned away from love of the present world by his commands or corrected by his chastisement?"* Those who walk in his footsteps imitate his works, those who cling to his virtues follow the Lord; this is what it means to march behind Christ and to follow him. It is not enough for our feet to follow—our hearts and minds must do the same. From these disciples we learn, as Hilary teaches, that to follow Christ means to let go of the anxieties of the worldly life and the customs of our paternal home.*

*40 Hom 5.1; PL 76:1092D; CL 141:33

*Hom Matt 3.6; PL 9:931B

While these disciples did not own much, they gave up a great deal, because they strove to keep nothing and love nothing of this world. Gregory says,

> In this matter we should consider their natural feeling rather than how much they abandoned. Someone who has left everything behind, no matter how little that is, has left much; whoever has kept nothing has abandoned a great deal. The one who surrenders the hunger to possess gives up a lot; the one who forsakes not only property but the desire for it has left much. Christ's followers give up as much as those who refuse to follow crave. The Lord

considers the heart, not the substance; he does not measure the amount we sacrifice to him, but the effort we make to do it. The kingdom of God has no assessed value; it is worth everything we have. In God's eyes no hand is ever empty of a gift if the ark of the heart is full of good will. Nothing more precious can be offered to God than good will.*

*40 Hom 5.2–3; PL 76:1093B–94B; CL 141:34–35

✠

Lord Jesus Christ, make me seize the nets of preaching, love, and good works by eagerly listening to God's word. May I wash them clean of all greed, flattery, and vainglory, and return them from earthly concerns to the ship of religious devotion. There may I sit in peace, teaching others by my example and guiding them to the heights of contemplation and preaching. At an inspiring word from you may I lower them into the waters of tribulation and collect therein a wealth of interior consolations. Call me and draw me, a miserable sinner, to holy discipleship, so that by renouncing all things and following you I may deserve to be numbered among your poor. Amen.

CHAPTER 30

Conclusion of the Call of the Disciples; Christ's Zeal to Preach

*R 1 *In the preceding chapters you have read about three different calls of the disciples. The first is related by John: on that occasion, they were simply called to faith and to gain some familiarity with Jesus. Luke describes the second call: then they began to follow him in spirit and to learn something of his doctrine, but they returned to their own homes. The third call is narrated by Matthew and Mark: then they came and stayed with him continuously, imitating his perfection. The first two calls are repeated in the novitiate in religious life when candidates come to be instructed and tested, and return home from time to time. The third call is repeated in religious profession, because then the candidates bind themselves to Christ inseparably through the Christian religion. The same pattern will be seen later in the call of Matthew the tax collector. The call of the other disciples is not described in any detail. Chrysostom asks, "Why are we told nothing about the call of the other disciples, and only about Peter, Andrew, James, and John, and Matthew? Because they represent the most ordinary and the most base ways of life. There is no profession more ignoble than the tax collector's, nor one more ordinary than being a fisherman."*

*Hom Matt 30.1; PG 57/58:363

*R 2 *Pause here to consider with a keen eye the Lord Jesus as he invites these disciples to be his companions.

With what gentleness he calls them! He shows himself to be friendly, at ease, kind, and compliant with them. He attracts them both inwardly and outwardly, taking them to his mother's house or wherever he was staying temporarily, and going willingly to their homes, too. He patiently instructs them and lavishes special attention upon them, like a mother with her only child. It is said that blessed Peter used to relate how once, when Jesus was sleeping with them in some place, he got up during the night to cover them, so tender was his affection for them. He knew what he intended to make of them: they were men of rough manners and low birth, true, but he was going to establish them as princes of the world and the leaders of all the faithful in the spiritual combat.* **Massa; MVC 19; CM 153:95–96*

Consider also the praiseworthy obedience of those called. Their obedience was prompt, because they responded immediately and without delay as soon as they were called; it was total, because they left all things; it was direct, because they followed the Lord Jesus. The first quality is perfect, the second more perfect still, the third most perfect of all. But why did they leave all things? Chrysostom gives this answer: "The apostles did this to teach us that no one who has earthly possessions can hasten perfectly to heavenly ones. The atmosphere placed between the heavens and the earth shows that there is no union between earthly and heavenly things: celestial things, being spiritual and light, rise upward, while those of earth, being heavy and burdensome, fall downward."* But, you might object, did not the apostles resume their fishing later? If so, was their leaving imperfect? In answer it should be said that their leaving was perfect because, although they fished later on, they did not do it as an occupation to make money, but only for their own subsistence. *Opus imperf 7; PG 56:675

*Consider, finally, who and what kind of persons he chose to bring his church to birth. The Lord did not ***R 3** wish to choose as the first founders of the church men who were wise, powerful, or noble in the world's estimation, lest the faith of the Gospel, the power of belief, and the great works that they were to accomplish could be credited to their own wisdom, power, or nobility. This he reserved to himself, for he redeemed us with his own power, wisdom, and goodness.* Had he chosen someone who was learned, powerful, or noble, it is possible that the person would think he deserved to be chosen because of these qualities. Desiring to crush human pride, he chose unlettered men whom the world disdained and made doctors of them, sending them out to preach. He subjected the rulers of the world to him through them, so that the faith of believers would be ascribed to the power of God and not to human wisdom or strength.

**Massa; MVC 19; CM 153:96*

Gregory writes, "Choosing the foolish, he left the wise; choosing the weak, he left the strong; choosing the poor, he left the rich.* He wanted his faithful people and the mighty to be gathered together by preachers who were weak and common. With messengers such as these there could be no temptation to self-congratulation: it would be obvious that anything they accomplished was due simply to the truth itself and not to any talent of theirs."* Chrysostom exclaims,

*Mor 33.XVI.32; PL 76:693A; CL 143B:1701

*Mor 33.XVI.32; PL 76:693D; CL 143B:1702

> O those blessed fishermen, whom the Lord first chose among so many worldly wise doctors of the law and scribes for the office of preaching and the grace of the apostolic office! Such a choice was worthy of our Lord and appropriate to the mission of preaching: the proclamation of his name would receive greater glory when preached by humble men of no worldly standing. He would not capture the world by wise words: the human race was to be liberated from death's deception by a simple proclamation of the faith. He did not choose the rich or the powerful of this world, lest their preaching be admired; he did not choose the wise of this

age, lest it be thought that the human race was won over by human wisdom.

Instead he chose illiterate fishermen, ignorant and simple men, so that the Savior's grace would be more evident. They were of no account in the world's eyes, even as regards the skill of their art, but pre-eminent in faith and humble submission to God, worthless in the world's eyes, but noble in Christ's. Their names were not inscribed in the ranks of earthly senators, but they were listed in the rolls of the heavenly senate. They were despised on earth, but most dear in heaven; poor to the world, but rich to God. God, who reads the depths of the heart, knew the ones he chose: these men certainly were not seeking human wisdom, but the wisdom of God; they longed for heavenly treasure, not worldly riches.*

*Chromatius 16.1; CL 9A:263

Let the noble, the powerful, and the rich of this world attend carefully and know that the common, the weak, and the poor have been chosen in their stead—and from this let them be confounded and blush, so as to counteract their pride. *Following the example of our captains and leaders, let us abandon all things and follow Jesus, in whom we possess everything. Chrysostom exhorts us well in these words: ***R 4**

The monk desires to imitate the apostolic life. Do you wish, O monk, to be Christ's disciple? Or better, to be a disciple of his disciples? Do what Peter, James, and John did: they had an eye that was a source of scandal, by which I mean father, boats, and nets. Jesus said to them, "Come, follow me," and they plucked out their eye and followed Jesus. Monks are imitators of the apostles, but we cannot imitate them unless we do what they did. Let no monk therefore say, "I have a father, I have a mother, I have others I hold dear." I answer, "You have Jesus—why do you seek those who are dead?" Whoever has Jesus has father and mother, sons, and all relations.

Why do you look for the dead? Follow the living one, forget the dead, and let the dead bury the dead. One disciple said to him, *Allow me first to go and to bury my father.** He did not say, "Let me go and stay with my father," but, "Let me go for an hour." What did the Lord say in answer? "In an hour you can be lost. See that while desiring to bury the dead you yourself do not die."*

*Luke 9:59

*Jer, Hom Matt 18:7–9; CL 78:505; *Massa*

***R 5** *Jerome has this to say about the summons of the four disciples to leave their fishing:

In a mystical sense, we are carried up to heaven like Elijah, drawn by these fishermen like four horses. They are the four cornerstones upon which the first church is built. By these four letters, as in the Hebrew *tetragrammaton*, the name of the Lord is known by us. We are commanded, following their example, to hear the voice of the Lord and forget the people of wickedness and the house of our paternal ties, which is foolishness to God. We are to abandon the nets on the seashore, those webs that seem to hang on nothing and in which, like gnats in the air, we were all but snared. And let us forget the boats of our earlier way of life.

Again, *Simon* means *obedient*, *Andrew* means *strong*, *James* means *supplanting*, and *John* means *grace*. By these four names we are transformed into the image of God: obedient, that we may listen; strong, by which we do battle; overthrowing, that we may persevere; and graced, that we may be preserved. These are the four cardinal virtues: by prudence we obey, by justice we act manfully, by temperance we crush the serpent underfoot, and by fortitude we earn the grace of God.*

*Cumm Mark 1:16–20; PL 30:595D

Christ Teaches and Heals in Galilee

***R 6** **And Jesus went about all Galilee, teaching in their synagogues, and preaching the Gospel of the kingdom, and heal-*

ing all manner of sickness and every infirmity among the people.* Chrysostom says, "Because their weakness made it impossible for the sick to come to the physician, Jesus, like a zealous doctor, went about visiting the sick."* Here Christ gives a good example to teachers, pastors, and preachers of the Gospel: they should not be lazy or indolent, but ardent and diligent, for the evangelist says *Jesus went about*. They should teach doctrine to everyone regardless of station and not court favorites, for he adds *all*. They should not seek sinecures or prestigious posts, for he specifies *Galilee*, a poor and insignificant province. They should not be idle or engage in frivolous matters, for he adds *teaching*. Their message should be useful to many and above suspicion, so the evangelist mentions *in their synagogues*, which is where the crowds and the teachers were to be found. They should preach without error about matters that pertain to salvation and avoid useless discussions and fabulous stories, so he says *preaching the Gospel of the kingdom*, that is, they should point out the sure path heavenward. Finally, they should confirm their teaching by their virtues and attend to their listeners' temporal needs as well as their spiritual ones, so the evangelist concludes *healing all manner of sickness and every infirmity among the people*, that is, among the crowds of poor and unimportant people.

*Matt 4:23

*Opus imperf 8; PG 56:677

In sum, Jesus taught diligently, *going about;* widely, *all*; unselfishly, *Galilee*; manifestly, *in synagogues*; usefully, *teaching* virtues and moral life and *preaching the Gospel of the kingdom* through the precepts of the faith and the mysteries; wondrously, *healing all manner of sickness*; enduringly, *and every infirmity*; and attractively, because those who were not persuaded to believe by his words were won over by his deeds. Jesus did not teach with words only; he confirmed his message by his actions through the various miracles that he alone could do because of his divine power.

Or *sickness* could be understood to refer to bodily passions and *infirmity* to spiritual passions, to show that he is the Creator of both natures. A real physician cures all ailments, bodily and spiritual. The prophet foretold this when he wrote, *He bore our illnesses and carried our infirmities.**[1] Chrysostom says, "Christ the Lord had come as the teacher of life and the heavenly physician so that by his instruction he could teach people the way to life and heal their bodily and spiritual ills with heavenly medicine. He freed their bodies from demonic possession and restored full health to those laboring under various illnesses. By divine power he brought healing to sick bodies by a mere word, and with the medicine of heavenly teaching he cured their spiritual wounds. He was a true and perfect physician who restored bodily health and gave spiritual salvation."‡

*Isa 53:4

‡Chromatius 16.4; CL 9A:266

***R 7**

†Matt 4:24

**And his fame went throughout all Syria,*† a spacious territory embracing Palestine, where the Jews lived, and other provinces surrounding it. The eastern border of Syria is the Euphrates River, and it stretches west to the Mediterranean Sea at Acre; to the north it is bordered by Armenia and Cappadocia and on the south by Egypt and the Arabian Gulf.* This is Syria in the broader sense, whereas the term is also used more narrowly for the region whose capital is Damascus, and this does not include Judea. Jesus' fame had spread beyond Judea to the surrounding provinces on account of the miraculous works he performed. This is why King Abgar, whose kingdom was on the banks of the Euphrates, wrote a letter to the Savior, as we read in the *Ecclesiastical History* of Eusebius.[2]*

**Zachary 1.22; PL 186:118B*

*Hist 1.13

[1] The text Ludolph uses here is not from the Vulgate, but is a verse from Matins of Holy Thursday (PL 78:764C). Unlike the Vulgate, this text parallels exactly the terms *illnesses* and *infirmities*.

[2] Eusebius relates that King Abgar V of Edessa was suffering from an incurable illness and, having heard stories of Jesus'

*And they presented to him all sick people that were taken with various diseases and torments, and such as were possessed by devils, and lunatics, and those that had the palsy, and he cured them.** He cured their bodies to dispose them to receive spiritual healing, since it would be pointless to restore to health those who were about to die. Chrysostom says of this passage, "Notice the moderation of the evangelist, who does not describe every healing in detail: he summarizes an abundance of miracles in a few words."* *R 8 *Matt 4:24 *Hom Matt 14.3; PG 57/58:220

In a spiritual sense *those possessed by devils* can represent fortune-tellers and those who dabble in superstition; *lunatics* those inconstant in doing good; *paralytics* the lazy who are practically powerless to do good works. Such as these can be healed by a sound preacher and a prudent confessor.

And many people followed him from Galilee (passing over), *and from Decapolis* (the region of the ten cities), *and from Jerusalem* (peaceful), *and from Judea* (confession), *and from beyond the Jordan* (the river of judgment).[3]* Spiritually this suggests that those who follow Christ pass over from vice to virtue, obey the Ten Commandments, live peaceably with others, humbly confess their sins, and fear divine Judgment. *Matt 4:25

Those who followed him hailed from many different regions; as they were diverse in appearance, so they also were diverse in intention. Some, like the disciples,

---

miraculous healings, wrote him a letter asking him to come to Edessa. Jesus wrote a response in which he declined to do this but promised to send a disciple endowed with power after his ascension. Thaddeus (or Addai) went, the king was healed, and he became a Christian. Eusebius quoted the texts of the letters in his history and said that the original letters were still in the archives of Edessa. In fact, the story was probably written down in the early third century, since it quotes the second-century *Diatessaron*. In a later version of the legend Jesus sent his portrait to Abgar (either painted by a court artist sent for the purpose or created by Jesus holding a towel to his face).

[3] Jerome renders *Jordan* as *river of judgment* (PL 25:479A).

followed him to learn heavenly truths; the sick followed in the hope of being healed; the hungry, because they wanted to be fed; the curious followed because they wanted to see miracles and find out if he really was who he claimed to be; and some of the Jewish leaders were motivated by jealousy—they were following to see if by word or deed Jesus would give them an excuse to seize and accuse him.* These motivations are summed up in a verse:

**Massa*

> Five are the reasons the crowds pursued our Lord:
> Sickness, wonders, food, slander, and hunger for the word.[4]*

*Peniteas 471

Whenever the word *crowd* is used in the gospel it signifies a diversity of people, as different in intention as they are in appearance, for people followed Jesus for a variety of reasons. Whether their motives were good or bad, the Lord bestowed benefits on all alike by his teaching, feeding, and cures.

***R 9**

*The five locations mentioned correspond to the five motivations for following. From Galilee, meaning *whirling around*, come the curious, of whom it is said, *Men of Galilee, why do you stand looking up to heaven?** The sick come from the Decapolis because they are healed by observing the Ten Commandments, as it says, *If you will enter into life, keep the commandments.** Those who are watching with a jealous eye come from Jerusalem, as it says, *Jerusalem, that kills the prophets.** The hungry come from Judea to be fed by Gospel doctrine, and they confess their sins and give thanks. The disciples come from beyond the Jordan to be instructed and washed, so that they in turn can instruct and wash others.*

*Acts 1:11

*Matt 19:18

*Luke 13:34

**St Cher Matt 4:25*

[4] *Morbus, signa, cibus, blasphemia, dogma fuere / Causae, cur Dominum turba secuti fuit*. This distych is n. 1373 in the *Versarius* of William of Montibus.

The five locations also stand for the five states of life of those who follow Christ: by Galilee, meaning *turning about*, penitents; by the Decapolis, meaning *devotion to the Decalogue*, those in the active life; by Jerusalem, meaning *vision of peace*, contemplatives; by Judea, meaning *confession*, prelates; by *beyond the Jordan*, those who are innocent, having been restored to holiness by baptism, of which the Jordan is a symbol.

Chrysostom urges us:

> Let us follow him, too: we have various ailments of the soul, and it is these that he most wants to heal. Let us approach him and beg forgiveness for our sins. He will be prompt to grant this if we are not slow to request it. Now if we have bodily pain we make every effort and pay any price to obtain relief; but when it is our soul that is sick we ignore the symptoms and put the matter off. And so we are not delivered from our bodily ailments either, because we are treating as essential what is secondary while putting what really matters in second place. We ignore the fountain from which our sickness flows and devote all our energy to disinfecting the streams that pour from it, forgetting that many bodily illnesses are due to spiritual wickedness. If we clean out the evils in the fountain all the streams of sickness will dry up.
>
> And if you do not suffer when you sin, do not think you are safe! You should weep all the more if you do not feel pain when you sin: this happens not because the sins do not sting, but because your soul is too deadened to feel them. The best thing is not to sin at all, but the next best is to feel it when we have sinned and grieve. But if we do not have this sense of compunction, how will we entreat God? How can we ask God to forgive sins if we are not even aware of them? If you transgress but make it your business to remain ignorant of the fact, will you ask God's forgiveness for sins you

are unaware of? And how, then, will you ever know the greatness of the divine favor?

Strive to know well your sins, so that you may learn what mercy can be extended for them and be grateful to your Benefactor. The fact that we feel no pain when we sin angers God and provokes his wrath more than the sin itself. For all these reasons let us ask God to unite our will with his so that we will zealously desire what is good. In this way we will be delivered in a short time from the evils that oppress us, come to understand our previous condition, and lay claim to truly worthy freedom.*

*Hom Matt 14.5–6 Anianus; Cratandri 1:72–73

✠

Lord Jesus Christ, as a zealous physician you went in search of the sick and healed their infirmities of body and soul. I beseech you to heal me from the illnesses that afflict my body and soul. Draw me after you so that I may follow you by passing over from virtues to vices, observing the Ten Commandments, living at peace with others, humbly confessing my sins, and fearing the divine judgments. Lead me out of the lake of misery and the mire of filth. Direct my steps into the path of salvation so that they make progress in the way of your precepts, hasten to their blessed homeland, and arrive there without hindrance. Amen.

CHAPTER 31

The Call of Matthew and His Feast

(Matt 9:9-17; Mark 2:14-22; Luke 5:27-39)

*Jesus returned and came to the Sea of Galilee, to the place where taxes were paid, especially on goods taken from the sea. With his merciful and insightful gaze *he saw a man sitting in the custom house** *collecting taxes named Matthew*, the son of Alpheus, who was also called Levi before his call. (*Telos* is the Greek word for tax or tribute.) He was sitting because all his attention was directed to the work of making as much money as he could. *And he said to him: "Follow me."** It was as if he were saying, "Do not sit any longer, but from now on follow. And do not pursue worldly concerns or chase after wealth; follow me with your heart's affection and serve me with your bodily labors."

***R 1**

**telonium*

*Matt 9:9

Jesus called him from this despised profession so that no one would ever despair of God's grace, no matter how vile his occupation had been.*

**Lyra Matt 9:9*

And leaving all things, he rose up both from the customs post and from a love of earthly goods in order to seek heavenly ones, *and followed him*.* He left all things, both what was his own and what he had plundered by his collecting. He who had stolen from others (for Chrysostom says this kind of taxation was simply robbery under the cloak of law) now left behind even what was his own.* He followed him without a moment's hesitation, with the eager step of a disciple

*Luke 5:28

*Hom Matt 30.1; PG 57/58:362

following his teacher, a traveler following his guide, a servant following his Lord, or a sheep following his shepherd. He did not untie the rope: he cut it in two, as Jerome advises.*

*Ep 53.10; PL 22:549; Ep 53.11; CS 54:464

He followed without delay because divine power was at work within him, enflaming and instructing. The one who called him externally also kindled a spark of fervor within, attracting him and teaching him, so that he would follow immediately. Jerome says, "The splendor and majesty of his hidden divinity that shone forth on his face could draw at first glance those who looked upon it. If a magnet has the power to attract iron, how much more was the Lord of all creatures able to draw to himself those whom he wanted?"* And Chrysostom comments, "You have seen the power of the one calling; learn further the obedience of the one called. He did not resist or hesitate, but obeyed at once. He did not even ask leave to go home and tell his family."*

*Com Matt 9:9; PL 26:56A; CL 77:56

*Hom Matt 30.1; PG 57/58:363

The Feast at Matthew's House

***R 2**

*Matthew followed the Lord joyfully, and he showed his gratitude by inviting Jesus and his disciples into his home for a festive meal. By this splendid repast he expressed appreciation for the heavenly benefits he had received, he gave earthly possessions to the one who had sown the seeds of spiritual possessions in his soul, and he bestowed passing goods on him from whom he hoped to gain eternal ones. Moved by devotion and delight at the arrival and presence of such a guest, he provided a *great feast*, so great in fact that its leftovers refreshed the angels themselves, because *there shall be joy before the angels of God upon one sinner doing penance*.* It was only fitting that the banquet should be so sumptuous for, as Ambrose says, whoever welcomes Christ into the inner dwelling-place feeds on the greatest delights of abundant pleasures.*

*Luke 15:10

*Exp Luke 5.16; PL 15:1640B; CL 14:140

The Lord gladly went into the house and reclined at table in true friendship. Chrysostom writes, "As soon as the Lord said to him, *Follow me*, he arose immediately and followed him without delay. He showed his trust in God and also that he was a true son of Abraham, who had similarly acted promptly when the Lord spoke to him. And, that he might be a worthy son of Abraham in every way, he also welcomed the Lord into his home and gave him a feast."* *Chromatius 45.1; CL 9A:417

In a spiritual sense we can understand that just as Matthew prepared a great feast in his home for Christ after his conversion, so whenever we turn to the Lord we should honor him with a spiritual banquet in the home of our heart and conscience. There let us serve Christ holy thoughts, meditations, and desires. Jesus says in the book of Revelation, *Behold, I stand at the gate and knock. If any man shall hear my voice and open to me the door, I will come in to him and will sup with him and he with me.** *Rev 3:20

***R 3**

And it came to pass as he sat at meat in his house, many publicans and sinners* and other people of this kind who had come together for the meal *sat down together with Jesus and his disciples. These were Matthew's colleagues and others in his profession; since he was leaving them to follow Christ, he wanted to give a dinner for them, as Elisha had done for his companions when he chose to follow Elijah as his teacher.* And there were many other sinners who were following Jesus as penitents, hoping to receive forgiveness for their sins. Jerome says, "Because they had seen a tax collector turn away from sin and make room for repentance, they did not despair about their own situation. They came as penitents and *sat down together with Jesus and his disciples.*"* Perhaps Matthew himself invited them, so that as he had had companions in sinning he would now have companions in repenting. The Gloss hails this as a most happy presage: he who was to become an apostle and a teacher of the nations drew a flock of sinners after him on the very day of his conversion.

*Mark 2:15

*1 Kgs 19:21; *Lyra Matt 9:10*

*Com Matt 9:10; PL 26:56B; CL 77:56

What he was to do later by his words he was already accomplishing by his example.*

*Laon, Matt 9:10; PL 162:1330C

Chrysostom writes,

> After having approved the tax collector Matthew's faith, the Lord rightly sat at table with tax collectors and sinners. They came to Matthew as a colleague who shared their station; for his part, Matthew rejoiced in Christ's visit and invited them all to join him.
>
> Christ employed every avenue for healing people, not just by speaking, by healing, and by rebuking his adversaries—he led no small number from the wrong path also by eating. In this he shows us that every work and every season may be turned to our profit. For the sake of the good result that would follow he did not avoid the company of tax collectors, just as a good physician must come in contact with pus if he is going to heal the patient.*

*Hom Matt 30.2; PG 57/58:363–64

Jerome says, "The Lord went to the meals of sinners because they gave him an opportunity to teach and to give spiritual sustenance to his imitators.[1] Indeed, when he is described as frequenting banquets nothing else is related except what he said and did there. Both his humility in entering the homes of sinners and the power of his teaching to summon people to repentance are demonstrated."* For this same reason we may eat with sinners, acting for another's benefit rather than our own. This does not hold true for usurers and thieves, however, because what they would serve us should be returned to its rightful owners.

*Com Matt 9:13; PL 26:56C; CL 77:56

***R 4**

*But *the Pharisees*, who held tenaciously to the justice of the law and the traditions of their ancestors but declined to be merciful, were indignant. They murmured and complained *to his disciples: "Why does your*

[1] Where Ludolph has imitators (*imitatoribus*) Jerome has hosts (*invitatoribus*).

*master eat with publicans and sinners?"** It was as if they were saying, "What he is doing is contrary to the law, and you are foolish to be following such a teacher."* It is the practice of detractors to speak to others about someone behind his back. On other occasions the Pharisees talk to the teacher when in their opinion his disciples have sinned; here, they talk to the disciples about the teacher, but it is always the teacher who is their target, because the failings of the disciples are the disgrace of their teacher. Detractors do the same thing these days when they criticize the good deeds done by members of the Body of Christ.

*Matt 9:11

**Lyra Matt 9:11*

The error of these Pharisees is twofold: they believe they are just when in fact they are proud, and they condemn others as sinners who are already doing penance, as the Pharisee did who justified himself but condemned others.* True justice is marked by compassion, false justice by contempt. It is customary for the just to be indignant with sinners, but there is a great difference between indignation fueled by pride and that which is motivated by the desire to correct.* These Pharisees are like those people who prefer their traditions to God's precepts and works of mercy; they sedulously foster and carefully execute them, straining at the gnat of punctilious customs while swallowing the camel of God's commandments, putting them aside like something bitter to the taste.

**Zachary 2.56; PL 186:186A*

**Bede, Com Luke 15:1; PL 92:519D; CL 120:285*

*In stark contrast to the grumbling of the Pharisees we have the Lord's mercy inviting sinners to repent. His food and drink, his travels, and all his works called them to salvation; his every word and action provide lessons for our instruction. The teacher *by whose stripes you were healed** showed himself to be also the physician. He responded to the Pharisees on behalf of his disciples, first making an argument from reason: "*They that are in health do not need a physician* except to remain healthy, *but they that are ill** do, so a doctor should be more attentive to those who need healing than to those who do not."

***R 5**

*1 Pet 2:24

*Matt 9:12

Because Christ is the true physician of souls, he had to devote more time to those who were laboring under spiritual illnesses. It is as if he were saying, "You believe that you are in good health and do not need my ministrations, but these people know that they are sinners. Very well, I will not call on you, since you have no need of me—but I will visit them, because by doing penance they are making room for grace in their lives."* According to Chrysostom this shows that those who give themselves a clean bill of health, deeming themselves to be just, reject the Lord's medicine and do not deserve to obtain spiritual healing; on the other hand, those who know they are sick on account of their sins seek the cure given by heavenly grace by believing with complete faith.* As Augustine succinctly put it: "None of us receives strength from God unless we feel that we are weak in ourselves."*

*Zachary 2.56; PL 186:186C

*Chromatius 45.2; CL 9A:418

*Sermo 76.6; PL 38:481

‡R 6

‡Next he responded to them by appealing to the authority of what was written by the prophet Hosea, reproaching them for their ignorance of Scripture: "*Go then*, to curb your rashness and correct your ignorance, *and learn what this means* that the Lord said through the prophet Hosea: '*I will have mercy* through forgiving sins *and not sacrifice** through the offering of holocausts.'" As we read in the book of Proverbs, *To do mercy and judgment pleases the Lord more than victims.**

*Matt 9:13; Hos 6:6

*Prov 21:3

It is as if he were saying, "Go and consider diligently what was written in the prophet Hosea; if you do, you will see that I am acting according to what he said.* I prefer mercy even without sacrifice, if it comes with humility of heart, to sacrifice without mercy accompanied by a boastful spirit." God prefers lowly sinners who are aware of their condition and who submit to God's grace by repentance to people who presume on their own righteousness, condemning others and criticizing any mercy shown to them.

*Lyra Matt 9:13

According to Chrysostom, the scribes and the Pharisees believed that they could wipe away their sins by means of sacrifices offered according to the law; they disdained all other power, putting all their trust in sacrifices. The Lord preferred mercy to sacrifices to make it clear that sins are taken away by works of mercy, not by ritual sacrifices.* The Gloss makes this distinction: "It is not that God despises sacrifice, but sacrifice without mercy. The Pharisees offered sacrifices in order to appear to be righteous in the sight of the people, but they did not perform the acts of mercy that demonstrate true righteousness."* And Rabanus Maurus writes, "He admonishes them to seek out the reward of divine mercy by their deeds and not presume that they can please God through offering sacrifices while at the same time ignoring the needs of the poor."‡

*Chromatius, Trac in Matt 45.1; CL 9A:419

*Laon Com Matt 9:13; PL 162:1331B

‡Com Matt 9:13; PL 107:876A; CM 174:266

***R 7**

*Next Jesus proposed his own example of mercy to them: "*I have not come to call the just* to repentance, but to make greater progress in virtue; *but sinners** I do call to change their lives by doing penance." Or, "*I have not come to call the just*, that is, those who think they are righteous and who, ignoring God's justice, seek self-justification (whereas converted sinners do not perceive themselves to be just), *but sinners*, who are aware of their sins and evil deeds and recognize their need for healing, and so submit to God's grace by doing penance." Or again, "*I have not come to call the just*, because no one is just, *but sinners, for all have sinned and do need the glory of God*."* Gregory of Nyssa says, "It is as if he were saying, 'So far am I from hating sinners that I came to bring them grace, so that they would not remain sinners but be converted and become good.'"* And the apostle teaches, *Christ Jesus came into the world to save sinners*.*

*Matt 9:13

*Rom 3:23

*CA Luke 5:27–32

*1 Tim 1:15

See what great hope there is for sinners: the Son of God himself came into this world for their sake! Augustine writes, "The sole reason Christ came was to save sinners. Take away the sickness, take away the wounds, and there is no need for the medicine. The great physician came down from heaven because a great illness was afflicting the whole earth—the sinful human race. The one who is sinless came to save the multitude from sin. He came from heaven not to take on our merits, but our misery."* Therefore, as Ambrose says, "The usurpers of justice are not called to grace: because grace comes from repentance, those who scorn penitence renounce grace."*

*Sermo 175.1; PL 38:945; CL 41 Bb:526

*Exp Luke 5.22; PL 15:1642A; CL 14:142

‡R 8

‡The word *publican* was used of those who were publicly stigmatized for crimes, or those who collected taxes or revenue, or those who oversaw such transactions and controlled the public purse, or, finally, for all those who earned money through financial transactions, such as money changers. The term was used mainly for tax collectors, and it is said that the name comes from the Roman king Publius, the first to collect taxes. And because, as Gregory teaches, this was an occupation that it was practically impossible to exercise without sinning, the greatness of God's mercy is seen in the fact that he called Matthew from his tax collector's booth to be an apostle.[2]*

*40 Hom 24.1; PL 76:1184C; CL 141:197

All Christ's words and deeds proclaim that God will gently welcome back every sinner who returns to him, just as Jesus showed such tenderness in receiving Matthew the tax collector. According to Jerome, the other evangelists were unwilling to call him by the common name *Matthew*, but called him *Levi*. But Matthew identifies himself and his profession, in accord with the command of Solomon, *The just is first accuser of himself*.* In this he shows us that none of us should despair of salvation if we are called to better things, for he

*Prov 18:17

[2] Ludolph's sources for his definition are Bede, Com Mark 2:18 (PL 92:150C) and Aquinas, Com Matt 5:46; the association with Publius is also found in Gloss Matt 5:46 (PL 114:98C). Although the Vulgate uses the term *publicanus* for Matthew, in fact the *publicani* were wealthy members of the equestrian class who bought the rights to collect taxes, putting a deposit in the treasury (*in publicam*) as a guarantee, and this is the origin of their name. They were assisted by regional managers (Zacchaeus may have been one of these) who oversaw the *portitores*, who, like Matthew, actually collected the taxes.

himself was suddenly changed from a tax collector into an apostle.* Another lesson we learn here is that we should conceal and hide the sins of others to the best of our ability and not betray them with so much as a word or a glance; instead, following Matthew's example, let us accuse ourselves and confess our own most disgraceful sins.

*Com Matt 9:9; PL 26:55C; CL 77:55

According to Bede the choice of Matthew and the calling of the tax collectors prefigure the faith of the Gentiles: formerly they coveted worldly riches, but now they are restored spiritually by the Lord. The arrogance of the Pharisees, on the other hand, suggests the envy of the Jews, who are tormented by the salvation being extended to the Gentiles. Or Matthew can stand for worldly people intent only on earthly riches; Jesus looks upon them with merciful eyes and calls them—either through a preacher, or a biblical admonition, or an inner inspiration, or a tribulation, or in some other way.* The call of Matthew to be an apostle can also represent the call for someone to leave the world and enter religious life; the carping Pharisees are the wicked persons who disparage religious life. To such as these it is best to say, *Go then and learn what this means, I will have mercy and not sacrifice*,* for it is indeed a great work of mercy to call sinners to repentance.

***R 9**

*Com Matt 9:11; PL 92:47A

**Laon Com Matt 9:11; PL 162:1331C*

*Matt 9:13; Hos 6:6

The Question of Fasting

**Then came to him the disciples of John*‡ and the Pharisees, asking why they fasted often but his disciples did not. The Pharisees did fast frequently, and up until that point John's disciples had also observed this Jewish custom. Earlier the Pharisees had approached the disciples to criticize their Master for eating with sinners; now they come to the Master to criticize his disciples for not fasting, hoping by these maneuvers to create dissension between Jesus and the disciples.* They were wrong on two counts: first, because they

***R 10**

‡Matt 9:14

**CA Mark 2:18*

were boasting about their abstinence, which should have been carried out in secret; second, because they tried to lay the blame for the disciples' shortcomings in the matter of fasting at the feet of their Master. These men who bragged about their fasting and felt that this made them better than Christ's disciples are an image of those hypocrites who make much of their own religiosity while holding others in contempt, saying with the Pharisee, *I give you thanks that I am not as the rest of men; I fast twice in a week*,* and so on.

*Luke 18:11-12

***R 11**

*But Jesus confounded them and gave reasonable explanations for his disciples' behavior: because he was still bodily with them and because, as beginners in the way of discipleship, they should not be overtaxed with new and onerous duties. He offered them three images: the bridegroom at his wedding, a patch on a piece of cloth, and wine and wineskins.

Jesus first asked, "*Can you make the children of the bridegroom*, that is, these disciples, who have been born of me, the bridegroom, and my spouse, the church, through faith, *fast* and mourn *while the bridegroom is with them*?"* According to Jerome, there are different kinds of fasting.* One is a fast of expectation, to be better prepared to welcome someone; this was the fasting of the Old Testament. The disciples were not bound by this, because Christ had arrived. Then there is fasting as a spiritual discipline, which aims at abstaining from earthly goods to dispose oneself for contemplation; a person rejects carnal delights in order to be filled with spiritual ones. The disciples did not need to observe this kind of fast, either, because Christ was with them: his presence and his teaching enabled them to resist selfish desires far more effectively than the austerity of a fast would in others. They could not fast or mourn so long as the bridegroom was present in person with his bride; they should rejoice in his presence, not fast.

*Luke 5:34

*source unknown

There is another kind of fasting that derives from the fullness of perfect contemplation; this was the fast of Moses on the mountain. In this case, the higher the soul is lifted up in contemplation, the less need is felt for nourishment. The disciples were not ready for this kind of fast, because they were still unseasoned beginners. First they needed to be renewed through the charity of the Holy Spirit, which was to happen at Pentecost; reborn in the grace of the Holy Spirit, they would begin to live in a new way.* **Lyra Matt 9:14*

*Then Jesus added, *"But the days will come* (that is, the days of the passion and ascension) *when the bridegroom shall be taken away from them* in his bodily form: *then shall they fast* because of their grief and tribulation *in those days."** As the apostle says, *in hunger and thirst, in fastings often.** Augustine interprets Christ's words in this way: "Then they will be forsaken and plunged into grief and mourning, until joys and consolations are restored to them by the Holy Spirit."* And Bede writes, "Note that this sorrow over the absent spouse was felt not only after his death and resurrection, but also through all the ages before his incarnation. In the first ages of the church, before the Virgin gave birth, there were holy people who longed for the coming of Christ incarnate. And in the time after his ascension into heaven there have also been holy people who longed for his return to judge the living and the dead. Indeed, the only time the church did not experience this sense of mourning was in the short time that Christ dwelt in the flesh with his disciples."*

***R 12**

*Luke 5:35

*2 Cor 11:27

*Quaest Ev 2.18; PL 35:1340; CL 44B:60

*Com Luke 5:34; PL 92:391B; CL 120:125

Although Christ was speaking of his bodily presence, in a moral sense we can interpret the days when Christ is taken away from us to mean the days when we sin and thereby shut out of the house of our conscience Christ, the soul's true bridegroom, and let in the adulterous devil. On that day we will fast and abstain from the spiritual food of consolation, and endure days of sorrow and weeping. Therefore, let us cling to our spouse lest our nourishment be lost! When the bridegroom is taken away by mortal sin, then we must fast with efficacious and sincere mourning.

Sometimes the spouse absents himself so that we will more eagerly call him back and hold onto him more tightly. When in answer to our longing and our sighs he returns, then we truly rejoice, because as long as the bridegroom is with us we cannot fast or mourn. Ambrose writes, "Those who are without Christ fast: those, I mean, who are lacking in an abundance of good works. But when we find that the strength of our own will is sufficient because we have received Christ into our home, then we set out a luxurious banquet. This is the spiritual feast of good works, at which the rich man starves but the pauper dines sumptuously. No one can take Christ away from you unless you take yourself away; be on guard that your boasting and arrogance do not carry you off."‡

‡Exp Luke 5.19–20; PL 15:1641AB; CL 14:141

***R 13**

*In a spiritual sense, the soul is the bride with whom Christ wishes to dwell. This bridegroom has all the qualities looked for in a spouse. He is extremely rich, for otherwise he could not provide his bride with a dowry. As he says in Proverbs, *With me are riches*.* He is very wise, for otherwise he would squander all he possessed. Hence the apostle says, *in whom are hid all the treasures of wisdom*.* He is extremely handsome, for otherwise he would displease his bride. We read in the Psalms, *You are beautiful above the sons of men*.* He is very noble, for otherwise he would be held in contempt. This is why Wisdom praises his generosity. He is all-powerful, for otherwise he would be thrown down. Hence it says in Sirach, *There is one most high Creator Almighty*.* He is the best, for otherwise he would not be loved. The bride says in the Song of Songs, *My beloved is chosen out of thousands*.* The apostle speaks of all these qualities in the Letter to the Hebrews: "God *has spoken to us by his Son* (see the excellence of his nobility), *whom he has appointed heir of all things* (see the abundance of his wealth), *by whom also he made the world* (see the wonder of his wisdom), *who is the brightness of his glory and the figure of his substance* (see the elegance of his form) *and upholds all*

*Prov 8:18

*Col 2:3

*Ps 44:3

*Sir 1:8

*Song 5:10

things by the word of his power (see his infinite power), *making purgation of sins* (see his immense goodness)."* Truly the bride of such a spouse and the children of such a bridegroom cannot mourn so long as he is with them.* *Heb 1:2-3 *Gorran Matt 9:17

Notice that Christ sometimes calls himself Lord, sometimes Father, and sometimes Bridegroom. Pope Gregory explains, "When the Lord wants to be feared, he calls himself Lord; when he wants to be honored, he calls himself Father; when he wants to be loved, he calls himself Bridegroom. Attend to the order: honor customarily grows from fear, and love customarily grows from honor."* Bernard says, *Exp in Cantica, Proem 8; PL 79:476A

> God asks, *If I be a master, where is my fear? If I be a father, where is my honor?** But if he declares himself to be a spouse, I think he would change his tone and ask, "If I be a bridegroom, where is my love?" God then requires that he be feared as Lord, honored as Father, and loved as Bridegroom. Which of these is highest or most lofty? Surely it is love. Without love, fear brings pain and honor has no grace. Fear is the lot of slaves unless they are set free by love. Honor without love is not honor, but flattery. *To the only God be honor and glory**—but God will accept neither if they are not sweetened with the honey of love. Love is sufficient to itself, pleases itself and for its own sake. It is its own merit and its own reward. Love needs no cause beyond itself and produces no fruits beyond itself: the fruit of love is love itself.* *Mal 1:6 *1 Tim 1:17 *SC 83.4; PL 183:1183A; SB 2:300

Bernard also says, "The soul is called the spouse of God because she is affianced to him by the gifts of grace, united with him in chaste love, and gives birth to the progeny of virtues."‡ ‡Hugh of Saint Victor, De amore sponsi; PL 176:987C

*Then Jesus proposed a second image to them: "*No man* acting wisely and with discretion *puts a piece* or patch *from a new*, unused *garment upon an old garment*,* because the new cloth is rough and not broken in." ***R 14** *Luke 5:36

The new garment is deformed, robbed of its beauty and uniformity, and its heaviness pulls at the old cloth and makes an even larger tear in it. (The word *piece** here means one thing joined to another or a patch put on something: it comes from *cum*, that is, *together with*, and *mittere*, *to thrust*; items that are conjoined are thrown together.[3])

*commissuram

***R 15**

*Finally, Jesus offered a third image: "*No man* acting with prudence *puts new wine*, which is still fermenting, *into old bottles: otherwise* the pressure from *the new wine will break the bottles** and the wine will run out. *And no man drinking old has presently a desire for new,** because he is accustomed to the old." Similarly, it is not wise to impose immediately a serious regimen of fasting on those who have recently converted and are still receiving initial formation, because it is not easy for them to give up something they have grown used to.

*Luke 5:37

*Luke 5:39

From all of these images the good teacher implied that inasmuch as his disciples were as yet mere beginners it would not be wise for them to embrace an austere program of fasting; they would fast later, after they had been renewed and more firmly established by the Holy Spirit. He wishes to teach us that those who have been recently converted should not be burdened with difficult penances, lest the harshness cause them to lose heart and give up altogether. Rigorous practices that lead to greater perfection should not be imposed on people until they have left behind their former way of life because novices are not accustomed to labors that are difficult or onerous; it is better and easier if they become used to such things gradually. Whoever wishes to lead others to a life of virtue and perfection should first persuade them to make small changes and make progress gradually.

[3] Isidore of Seville defines *commissura* as the joining together of two panels (PL 82:681C).

Chrysostom says, "In saying this, Christ lays down a rule for his disciples: they should welcome those who come to them from the whole world with gentleness."* We do not expect everyone to gain the same prizes, but if we reach for what is possible, we will go farther and faster. Those who make laws and confessors who impose penances should attend particularly to this truth. Following the Lord's example, it is better to assign a lighter penance that penitents will be able to do, rather than lay upon them a heavy penance that they cannot carry out. Better an easier penance that is embraced joyfully than a burdensome one that is received under compulsion and with resentment. It is the same with sentences given or laws decreed: mercy and leniency should outweigh harsh judgment.

*Hom Matt 30.4; PG 57/58:367

✠

Lord Jesus Christ, you call and admonish me in many ways to follow you. Enkindle my heart with your divine inspiration so that by your grace I may answer your call; let nothing separate me from your love. Grant that I may serve you with holy thoughts, feelings, and affections, with good deeds and virtues. Allow me to provide you with a banquet of great delight and devotion of spirit. You who desire mercy rather than sacrifice and have come to call sinners and not the just, graciously grant that this poor sinner may deserve to experience your mercy. Amen.

CHAPTER 32

The Choosing of the Twelve Apostles

(Matt 10:1-4; Mark 3:13-19; Luke 6:12-16)

*R 1

*After the Lord had called many disciples, he withdrew to escape from the clamor of the crowds that followed him. *He went out into the mountain* of Tabor *to pray** alone, because to pray well we must raise our mind above earthly distractions and possess bodily tranquility. This mountain stands in the plain of Galilee; at its base is shown the location where it is said Melchizedek met Abraham upon his return from slaughtering the kings, and from its foot flows the brook Cison.* Tabor is about four miles east of Nazareth; at one time there was a Benedictine abbey on the mountain under the authority of the Metropolitan of Nazareth.* Others are of the opinion that Jesus went up onto another mountain overlooking the Sea of Galilee.

*Luke 6:12

**Burchard p. 43*

**de Vitry, Hist Orient, 58*

*Luke 6:12

And he passed the whole night in the prayer of God.* He offered *the prayer of God*, not of the world. He did not pray for himself as one who was weak and in need; he prayed for us as one who is loving and merciful. There is the prayer of God, which asks for true spiritual goods. Then there is the prayer of the world, which seeks temporal benefits, and this can also be of the devil if it is motivated by greed. Then there is the prayer of the devil, which seeks to have carnal desires satisfied.

Ambrose says, "*And he passed the whole night in prayer*. A form is given to you, a model is prescribed that you must imitate. What should you do for your salvation, when Christ spent the whole night in prayer for you? What should you do to undertake the duty of piety, when Christ prayed before he sent out his apostles? And he prayed alone—in fact, unless I am mistaken it is nowhere recorded that he prayed with his apostles. Everywhere he entreats alone, for human prayers do not grasp the counsels of God, nor can anyone share with Christ in the inner mysteries."* Bernard writes, "He said, *When you pray, enter into your room, and having shut the door, pray*,‡ and what he said, he did. He passed whole nights alone in prayer, hiding not only from the crowds but also from his disciples and familiar friends. He did take three friends with him when the hour of his death was approaching, but the urge to pray drew him apart even from them. You too must act in this way when you want to pray."*

*Exp Luke 5.43; PL 15:1648A; CL 14:150
‡Matt 6:6

*SC 40.4; PL 183:984A; SB 2:27

Chrysostom counsels us,

> Get up to pray during the night. The soul is purer then, and the darkness and profound silence are enough to lead us to compunction. At that hour vainglory does not assail us; neither sloth nor agitation overtakes us. Fire does not so thoroughly destroy the rust of iron as much as nocturnal prayer wipes away the blight of sin. The person oppressed by the noonday sun finds refreshment at night, but nightly tears are more soothing than any evening dew and are proof against desire and fear. If you are not refreshed by this dew, you will wither during the day. For this reason, pray at night and show that the night restores the soul as well as the body!*

*CA Luke 6:12–16

To seek God by prayer you must silence the cacophony of vices and press on to higher things. Ascend to the height of the heavenly courts, and when the tumult of outside distractions has subsided you can converse with God about your inmost desires in the secret sanctuary of your heart.* If you want to speak with God and be worthy to receive divine consolation, leave human consolations behind and embrace solitude.

*Zachary 2.70; PL 186:223C

Saint John the Evangelist provides us with a wonderful example: everyone knows how beneficial and fruitful solitude was to him. Having been exiled to the island of Patmos and deprived of human companionship, he was privileged to enjoy the company of angels and was found worthy to receive a revelation from the Lord about the present and future condition of the church, a revelation he recorded with his own hand. Of this matter Bede writes, "It is well known that John was exiled to that island by the order of the Emperor Domitian on account of the Gospel. He could not leave the confines of the island in body, but fittingly it was given to him to penetrate the secrets of the heavens."* The same thing is said of many others: they gained far more in a short space of time alone than they had in all the time spent with others.

*Com Rev 1:1; PL 93:135B

When Christ prayed, he instructed us about the contemplative life; when he taught, he informed us about the active life. From this we learn not to let attention to our neighbor deaden contemplation, nor to allow our contemplative life, although in itself superior, to lead to the neglect of our neighbor's needs. Anselm writes, "Jesus spent his days among the people, proclaiming the kingdom of God and edifying the assembled crowds by his miracles and preaching; he passed his nights on the mountain alone in prayer. By this pattern he teaches us that at some times we should show our neighbors the way to live by word and example, and at other times we should seek out spiritual solitude by climbing the mountain of virtues to breathe in the pure air of heavenly contemplation, directing all our thoughts to higher things."* Bernard concurs with this, addressing these words to himself:

*Elmer 8 [Med 1 Anselm]; PL 158:717A

*"Come and let us go up to the mountain of the Lord, and to the house of the God of Jacob, and he will teach us his ways.** Longings, thoughts, desires, affections, and all that is within me, *come and let us go up to the mountain*, to the place where the Lord sees and is seen! Worries, anxieties, cares, labors—you all must stay behind here with this donkey (my body) while I and the boy (my mind) hasten up the mountain, and wait here until we return. We will come back to you. Alas! We will return all too soon."‡ *Isa 2:3 ‡William of Saint Thierry, De contemplando 1.1

And when day was come, he called his disciples*, who perhaps were still sleeping; *and he chose twelve of them* to be the principal disciples with him, *whom also he named apostles*,* because they were to be sent to proclaim the kingdom of God. He had formerly called them to be disciples, now he named them apostles. ***R 2 *Luke 6:13

Notice here how Christ prayed at great length when he was about to choose the apostles: he spent the whole night in prayer, and indeed had passed an entire day and night praying before he chose them. This suggests that bishops should be chosen in the church only after much prayer, and that the candidates themselves should devote themselves to prayer, and not to intrigues or making deals.* **Lyra Luke 6:12 mor*

The Gloss says, "The Lord went up onto the mountain and called to himself and chose those whom he wanted; the call to the apostolate is not based on human merits and abilities, but on divine grace and honor. He himself said, *You have not chosen me, but I have chosen you*."* The Lord excludes questions such as human desire, ambition, gain, wealth, and family background when choosing shepherds. Divine grace alone should be the operative means by which a candidate is chosen. We read in the book of Psalms, *The mountains ascend, and the plains descend into the place* of leadership *which you have founded for them*.* Grace and canonical election, not money and human affection—but these latter are the ruin of the church in many places today, to the great offense of God. *John 15:16; Gloss Luke 6:13; PL 114:361C *Ps 103:8

Christ called the apostles on the mountain to signify that the bishops, as successors of the apostles, hold the highest position of leadership in the church. This is why they are called *episcopi*, from *epi* (above) and *skopos* (careful regard). They are set over the Lord's flock to keep watch over it and guide it heavenwards.* But, alas! How many of them today are unworthy of this trust. Useless to others as well as themselves, they empty the name of meaning.

**Lyra Mark 3:13 mor*

***R 3**

If grace shines out in the call of the apostles, so too there is fittingness to the number called: the number of the twelve apostles was prefigured in many ways. First, by the twelve patriarchs, for the apostles give birth spiritually to the whole Christian people. Second, by the twelve springs of Elim, for their teaching irrigates the church and the world. Third, by the twelve precious stones decorating the high priest's breastplate, for they adorn the church by their example.* Fourth, by the twelve loaves placed on the table of proposition, for they nourish souls with the word of life.* Fifth, by the twelve leaders of the tribes, for they lay down salutary precepts and beneficially guide the church. Sixth, by the twelve scouts who explored the Promised Land, for by contemplation they scrutinize the future life and bring news of it to the faithful.* Seventh, by the twelve stones set up in the Jordan river, for they oppose the currents of the world.* Eighth, by the twelve stones of the altar, for they bear Christ's sacrifice within themselves.* Ninth, by the twelve calves offered in sacrifice, for they endured martyrdom for Christ.* Tenth, by the twelve oxen supporting the sea of bronze, for they herald and minister the grace of baptism.* Eleventh, by the twelve small carved lions around Solomon's throne, for they vanquish worldly tyrants and threaten the obstinate with the punishments of hell.* Twelfth, by the twelve prophets, for they admonish the church regarding the end times. Thirteenth, by the twelve hours of the day, for they regulate the times of the Christian life. Four-

*Exod 15:27

*Exod 28:17-19

*Num 4:7

*Num 13:1-2

*Josh 4:9

*1 Kgs 18:31

*Num 29:17

*1 Kgs 7:25

*1 Kgs 10:20

teenth, by the twelve gates of the city, for they open the kingdom of heaven by the power of the keys.* *Rev 21:12 Fifteenth, by the twelve foundation stones of the city, for they support the church by their merits and prayers.* *Rev 21:14 Sixteenth, by the twelve stars in the bride's crown, for they illuminate the church by their teaching and miracles.* *Rev 12:1; *Zachary 1.22 approx; PL 186:119AC*

According to Bede, the Lord chose this number of apostles to symbolize mystically the salvation of the whole world: their number signified what they were to accomplish by their preaching. Three times four equals twelve, and this number of apostles was sent out because faith in the Trinity was to be proclaimed to the four corners of the world; they carried the faith of the Holy Trinity to the four points of the compass. This is why it is said of the holy city of Jerusalem coming down out of heaven from God, *On the east, three gates: and on the north, three gates: and on the south, three gates: and on the west, three gates.** *Rev 21:13 Figuratively, this suggests that through the preaching of the apostles and their successors peoples of all the nations of the world will come into the church by faith in the holy Trinity.* *Com Mark 3:14; PL 92:159AB; CL 120:469–70

According to Jerome, Jesus made twelve men apostles because one day they would *sit upon thrones, judging the twelve tribes of Israel.** *Luke 22:30; Cumm Mark 3:14; PL 30:600A Or, because six is a perfect number and two times six equals twelve, Christ may have wished to suggest that those who hold the apostolic office should possess a twofold perfection, of life and knowledge, or of words and deeds.

*The names of those he chose to be apostles are as follows: ***R 4** *Simon whom he surnamed Peter, and Andrew his brother; and James the son of Zebedee, and John the brother of James, whom he named Boanerges, which is the sons of thunder,* because they often heard the Father's voice thundering in the cloud to announce his Son; *Philip and Bartholomew; Thomas and Matthew* the tax collector; *James of Alphaeus,* who was also called James the Just because of the holiness of his life, or James the Less because he was called later, or James the brother of the Lord because he resembled Jesus, *and his brother Simon, who was called the Cananean* because he came from the village of Cana in Galilee, or Simon the Zealot, because *Cana* means *zeal*, and *Cananean* means *one who jealously loves; and Thaddeus*, another brother of James the Less, also called Jude of James; *and Judas Iscariot*, so designated because of his native town in Judea.[1]*

*Matt 10:2-4; Mark 3:16-19; Luke 6:14-16

Judas was included among those chosen both to show that David's prophecy that a disciple would betray the Lord Jesus was fulfilled and to give good people an excuse when they discover a bad person in their company. Augustine says, "I dare not claim that my home is better than the Apostolic College."* In another place he suggests that Jesus chose Judas to bring good out of evil by putting into effect the plan for his passion and teaching his church to be patient with evildoers.* Ambrose for his part says that Judas was chosen to show that the truth is so powerful that not even a hostile minister can weaken it.‡ Christ chose to be deserted, betrayed, and handed over by his own apostle so that when you are betrayed by a friend you will be able to bear it well and gain some benefit from your error in judgment. And finally Theophylact says that we learn from this choice that God does not reject

*Ep 78.8; PL 33:272; CL 31A:91

*Breviculus conl cum Don; 3.8.11; PL 43:630

‡Exp Luke 5.45; PL 15:1648B; CL 14:151

[1] Ludolph combines the lists of apostles given by the various evangelists. There are variations in these lists, even in the two given by the same author, Luke (see Acts 1:13). In all four lists, Peter is always first and Judas Iscariot is always last. The lists are given in three groups of four, and in all the New Testament accounts Peter leads the first group, Philip the second, and James of Alphaeus the third. The names in the first two groups (Peter, Andrew, James, John; Philip, Bartholomew, Matthew, Thomas) are the same, but the order changes. The third group is more fluid: Simon the Cananean and Simon the Zealot are generally thought to be the same person; there is less certainty about Thaddeus (Lebbaeus) and Jude.

us because of a future sin, but welcomes us on account of our present virtue.*

*En Mark 3:13–19; PG 123:523D

The apostles were called by their proper names to exclude false claimants to the title of apostle who would appear later, so that all the faithful would shun them and no one would dare to add a name to the list of apostles.* Also, they are given by name to show the faithful that they, too, will be recorded in the Book of Life by name. They are listed in pairs as a testimony to their mutual love and the bonds that united them: they strengthened one another in bearing witness to the faith before the wicked and enduring the torments the preaching of the Gospel entailed.

**Lyra Matt 10:1*

Augustine says of them, "He chose his apostles, as he had his disciples, from those of humble birth, dishonorable and illiterate, so that whatever greatness they attained or performed, it would be clear that he had in fact done these things in them."* Ambrose agrees: "Observe the heavenly strategy: he did not choose men who were learned, wealthy, or aristocratic; he chose fishermen and tax collectors whom he could direct, lest they seem to have won people by their wisdom, or enticed them with riches, or attracted them by some innate nobility and authority. In this way the victory would be gained by the presentation of the truth rather than the power of human eloquence."‡

*De civ Dei 18.49; PL 41:611; CL 48:647

‡Exp Luke 5.44; PL 15:1648B; CL 14:150

***R 5**

*The Lord went up onto the mountain to escape from the tumult of the crowd, to pray quietly, and to choose and converse familiarly with his apostles. He would have liked to take the multitudes up there, too, but they were unable to ascend those heights, so only these disciples followed him. He wanted to climb to the summit of the mountain to teach there the highest truths he had come to impart. He had given the lesser precepts of the law to the children of Israel on a mountain, and now he chose to deliver the greater law to his angelic disciples on a mountain to show that the same God had given the law and the Gospel pattern of life. After he had chosen the apostles, Christ wanted to instruct them in the works of perfection because those promoted to a higher grade should have greater understanding.

Bede writes, "In a mystical sense the mountain on which the Lord chose the apostles signifies the loftiness of justice in which they needed to be instructed and later would proclaim to the human race. By the altitude of the place Christ wanted to admonish those chosen to preach the Gospel of the kingdom of God that they should not indulge their lower desires but on the contrary always long for and seek heavenly realities. In this same way the Lord had appeared on the mountain earlier when he gave his people the law, and from the mountain he made known to them what they were to do."* And we read in the Gloss, "The Mountain himself ascended the mountain so that he could make known the highest peaks of virtue, and to show that the church, upon which he sits proclaiming God's law, should be raised up on high, and that he would teach this same sublime doctrine to her until the end of time."*

*Com Mark 3:13; PL 92:158C; CL 120:469

*Gloss Matt 5:1; PL 114:89A

Jesus could just as easily have taught this where he was, but he went up the mountain to signify that those who desire to preach or teach God's justice must themselves climb the mountain of virtue. Chrysostom says, "Whoever wants to hear or teach justice must stand in the truth. No one can linger in the valley and talk about the mountain. Speak where you stand, or stand where you speak. If your mind is on earth, how can you speak about heaven? If you speak about heaven, then take your place in heaven. And if you do not want to act justly, how can you hear the Teacher of righteousness? How can you call him 'Teacher' if you do not want to be his disciple?"* Richard of Saint Victor echoes this counsel: "Jesus went up on the mountain to teach his apostles so that we would understand that those who preach the word of sacred doctrine should

*Opus imperf 9.1; PG 56:679

not dwell in the valley of evil works or the field of unbridled dissipation. No, they should climb the mountain of a spiritual way of life by the exercise of virtues and the doing of good works, just as it is written, *Get up upon a high mountain, you that bring good tidings to Sion.*"*

*Isa 40:9; Allegoriae NT 2.1; PL 175:763B

✠

Lord Jesus Christ, your inestimable mercy prompted you to come into this world to call erring sinners to repentance, and from among these you have chosen many deputies and special disciples. Merciful God, call me back, miserable sinner that I am, embrace me upon my return, comfort me in sorrow, and instruct my ignorance. Although I am unworthy, at length count me among your disciples; lift me up completely from earthly desires and carry my spirit wholly to divine realities. Grant that I may hear and understand your words and put all your commands into action. Amen.

CHAPTER 33

The Sermon on the Mount: The Beatitudes

(Matt 5:1-12; Luke 6:17-26)

***R 1**

After choosing the apostles, the Lord Jesus delivered that long and very beautiful discourse that, as Augustine says, gives to those who study it devoutly and calmly the perfect model of Christian life and all the precepts that should shape the behavior of a follower of Christ.

*Sermone monte 1.1.1; PL 34:1231; CL 35:2

Matthew and Luke recount this sermon in different ways. Some are of the opinion that the Lord first spoke these words to his disciples alone on the mountain top seated as a doctor, as Matthew reports, and later preached a similar sermon to his disciples and the crowds together standing on the side of the mountain, as Luke says. Others hold that the Lord sat for a time with his chosen Twelve and some other disciples and afterward descended to a plateau or open meadow where he delivered this sermon only once to both his disciples and the crowds.*

**Massa; Comestor Hist ev 48 approx; PL 198:1564B*

The evangelists' accounts of this discourse vary in particulars but are in substantial agreement. The first explanation seems more likely to me and has a ring of truth to it. It also explains the custom in the church that a preacher stands when he preaches a sermon to the faithful, as it were exhorting them to take arms and act, but he sits when giving a discourse to clergy and religious, as it were inviting them to quiet contemplation.* *Gorran Matt 5:1

*At the outset of his sermon the Lord Jesus proposed eight beatitudes, or virtues, and attached an appropriate reward to each of them. He introduces the virtue in each sentence with the word *blessed*, and the reward with the word *for*: the first half pertains to the beatitude of merit and second half to the beatitude of reward. Whoever wishes to obtain the reward must strive first to possess the virtue. Augustine says, "It is impossible to find someone who does not desire to be blessed. But, O! If people desire to receive the recompense, let them not refuse to do the work for which the reward is given! Who would not come running when told they will be blessed? Should they not also listen attentively when they are told what to do? If you long for the prize, do not shirk the battle. Let us be eager to perform the deeds to which the reward is attached."* ***R 2**

*Sermo 53.1; PL 38:365; CL 41 Aa:88–89

There are two sides to beatitude: it is experienced here below in hope and in our heavenly homeland in reality. Those who excel in virtue are blessed here by grace, and they will be blessed in heaven with the beatitude of glory. As Augustine comments, they are not blessed because they are *poor in spirit*, but because *theirs is the kingdom of heaven*, and so on with all of the other beatitudes.[1]‡

‡Sermo 61.6.7; PL 38:411; CL 41 Aa:269

And opening his mouth he taught them, saying: "Blessed are the poor in spirit, that is, by their own free choice and not from necessity or by deceit, *for theirs is the kingdom of heaven,** which is the reward that corresponds to their merit." It must be understood that here poverty of spirit signifies avoiding love of the world, that is, of those things that the lover of this world ***R 3**

*Matt 5:2-3

[1] Augustine's sermon actually has *Blessed are they that hunger and thirst after justice*, but Ludolph applies his point to the first beatitude as representative of all of them.

seizes and holds onto. This means a total renunciation of all the delights to be found in riches, luxury, and honors.*

**Zachary 1.22; PL 186:120B*

This beatitude should be understood in a twofold sense: first, contempt for wealth and carnal pleasure; second, disregard for yourself and your own talents, so that although you are good you still consider yourself useless and inferior to others. Contempt for riches is born from contempt of self. If you truly and humbly look down on yourself for the sake of God, you can disparage worldly goods for your own sake; nor will you be captivated by external goods if you take no notice of yourself. Therefore poverty of spirit suggests both voluntary poverty for Christ's sake and true humility.

This beatitude holds first place when understood in either way. In the first sense, poverty is the first perfection of one who wants to follow Christ and the foundation of the whole spiritual edifice. One who is weighed down by possessions cannot follow Christ, the mirror of poverty, unencumbered; one whose heart is set on the passing things of this world is not free, but a slave. Whatever I love, I freely serve—and this is why nothing should be loved but God himself, and anything else only for his sake.*

**Massa*

Ambrose writes, "Both evangelists placed this beatitude first. It is the first in order, the birth-giver and parent of the virtues, as it were, because those who despise passing things will deserve eternal ones. Nor will one who is unable to escape the pull of worldly desires deserve to attain the kingdom of heaven."* In the second sense this beatitude enjoys primacy because humility opposes pride, which is the root of all other vices and holds first place among them. Augustine says, "The poor in spirit are rightly understood to be those who are humble and God-fearing, that is, those who do not have an inflated ego. It is placed first among the beatitudes because humility is the first step on the path to the highest wisdom.

*Exp Luke 5.50; PL 15:1650A; CL 14:152

Scripture says, *The fear of the Lord is the beginning of wisdom,** and on the contrary, *Pride is the beginning of all sin.*"* And Chrysostom teaches, "Just as all vices, but especially pride, lead to hell, so all virtues, but especially humility, lead to heaven."‡

*Prov 1:7

*Sir 10:15; Sermone monte 1.1.3; PL 34:1232; CL 35:4

The greedy and proud lust after earthly dominions; but *blessed are the poor in spirit,* that is, poor by choice and in their own estimation, *for theirs is the kingdom of heaven*, now in hope and later in reality. The reward suits the virtue well: abundance and exaltation succeed indigence and humiliation. By *kingdom* is meant every sort of sufficiency and excellence, which is promised in heaven to those who despise such things on earth.

‡Opus imperf 9.4; PG 56:681

*Then follows the second beatitude: *Blessed are the meek, for they shall possess the land.*[2]* Meekness follows logically upon poverty because the poor endure many indignities and must of necessity be meek and gentle. These two words express two facets of the same reality: it is meek not to cause offense and gentle to put up with wrongs inflicted by others. *Gentle** comes from the words *manu assuetus*, meaning *accustomed to the hand,** and such persons can easily put up with ill treatment, not returning evil for evil. The *meek* are those who maintain equanimity of spirit and persevere in doing good. According to this understanding, meekness refers to inner disposition and gentleness to outward conduct. The meek are thus the gentle, modest, lowly, and simple in faith, who bear patiently with injuries and who feel no bitterness of spirit. When provoked they neither plan nor carry out evil. They give way to the wicked, not resisting evil but overcoming evil by good.*

***R 4**

*Matt 5:4

**mansuetus*

*Ety 10.169; PL 82:385A

**Gorran Matt 5:4 approx*

Truly, *blessed are the meek, for they shall possess the land*: this means both the land of the body they direct

[2] Ludolph follows the Vulgate, which reverses the second and third beatitudes. This order is also found in Clement, Origen, Hilary, Basil, Gregory of Nyssa, and other fathers.

and the land of Paradise they seek. The land, I say, refers to their own bodies because the meek have self-control, unlike the hot-tempered, who have not subjected their emotions to the rule of their reason. It also refers to the land of Paradise: because the Lord quietly and peacefully possesses the meek in the land of the dying, they will possess the Lord in the land of the living.* It says in the Gloss that those who possess themselves in the present will possess the inheritance of the Father in the future.*

**Gorran Matt 5:4 approx*

*Laon Com Matt 5:1–11; PL 162:1289C

Augustine writes, "You will truly possess the earth when you cling to the one who made heaven and earth. This is what it means to be meek: not to resist your God, so that when you do well you will be pleasing to him, not to yourself, and when you suffer ill justly, you will be displeased with yourself and not with him. For it is no small matter to be pleasing to God when you are displeased with yourself, whereas if you are pleased with yourself, you will be displeasing to him."*

*Sermo 53.2; PL 38:365; CL 41Aa:89

Cruel people quarrel violently and squabble over transitory, worldly things, but *blessed are the meek, for they shall possess the land* of eternal blessedness as their permanent inheritance.* Fierce people wage war and prosecute tendentious lawsuits in a futile effort to carve out some little territory from which their enemies are vanquished; but the possession of peace in the land of the living, a possession that their enemies cannot take away, is promised fittingly to those who are untroubled by any violent emotion. Augustine suggests that *the land* stands for something solid, the stability of a perpetual heritage where the soul rests in a state of well-being in its own proper place, just as the body rests on the earth, and from which the soul draws its food, just as the body receives nourishment from the earth. This is the rest and the life of the saints.* Bede asks: if the kingdom of heaven is promised to the poor, and the earth is promised to the meek, what is left for the proud and contentious, except hell?*

**Lyra Matt 5:4*

*Sermone monte 1.2.4; PL 34:1232; CL 35:4

*Isaac of Stella, Sermo 2; PL 194:1694A

*The third beatitude is *Blessed are they that mourn, for they shall be comforted.** This beatitude follows logically upon the first and second: after having gained contempt for the world through poverty and calmed our soul through meekness, we enter into ourselves and consider our condition.* We find nothing in ourselves or in anything else except matter for mourning and lamentation, and so we begin to grieve. But these tears should be shed for spiritual damage, not temporal losses. Truly, *blessed are they that mourn,* because *God shall wipe away all tears from their eyes.** Bernard exclaims: "Happy tears, found worthy to be wiped away by a loving God!"* And as Maximus of Turin says, "The tears do not ask for pardon, but they earn it; they do not speak, but they obtain mercy. Words do not always express our needs clearly, but tears manifest our state of mind."*

*R 5
*Matt 5:5
**Gorran Matt 5:5 approx*
*Rev 21:4
*Gaufrid 34.40; PL 184:459C
*Ps-Maximus, Sermo 53; PL 57:351B

Those who mourn will be comforted both here and hereafter. Penitents receive spiritual consolation now from the Holy Spirit, who is called the *Paraclete*, that is, the *Consoler*. They will receive consolation in the future when they are led to glory, where they will obtain joy and gladness. Chrysostom says that the Lord will compensate present mourning with never-ending joy.* Elsewhere he writes, "If there is ever a time to mourn, it is in this present life, so full of the dishonor of evils, and in which we behold daily such an accumulation of shameful deeds that were we to consider them one by one we could not hold back our tears. If a stranger came from a distant land and saw the way we flout Christ's teaching by our way of life, he would conclude that we were God's enemies, opposed to Christ's precepts. Indeed, it would seem to him that we made a special study of how to act contrary to his commands in every way we could."*

*Chromatius 3.3; PL 20:334B
*Compunctione 1.1; PG 47:395

*There are five reasons to mourn. The first two concern our guilt and the guilt of others; the next two concern present and future punishment; the fifth concerns heavenly glory. We mourn in this life first

*R 6

for our own sins and miseries, second for the sins and miseries of others, third because the sufferings of this life continue, fourth on account of the possibility of eternal punishment, and fifth because glory is deferred.*

*Gorran Matt 5:5 approx

Therefore, *blessed are they that mourn* now, *for they shall be comforted* completely later for each of the five causes of grief: by the forgiveness of sins and the salvation of the good, the punishment of the wicked, the end of earthly exile, deliverance from eternal punishment, and the attainment of glory. Then we can say with the psalmist, *According to the multitude of my sorrows in my heart, your comforts have given joy to my soul.** Gregory agrees with this sentiment: "There are four ways in which the minds of the righteous are forcefully moved to compunction: when they call to mind their sins and consider where they have been; when, fearing the sentence of God's Judgment and examining themselves, they consider where they will be; when they observe the evils of this world and sorrowfully consider where they are; or when they contemplate the blessings of their heavenly homeland and, because they do not yet enjoy them, regret where they are not."*

*Ps 93:19

*Mor 23.XXI.41; PL 76:276A; CL 143B:1175

Frivolous people rejoice in this world; but *blessed are they that mourn, for they shall be comforted* in heaven. It is fitting that those who mourn receive the promise that eternal consolation awaits them: those who are sad now will be happy later, and those who let go of passing joys will enjoy lasting ones.

***R 7**

*Matt 5:6

*The fourth beatitude is *Blessed are they that hunger and thirst after justice, for they shall have their fill.** This rightly follows upon the first three: those who despise worldly pleasures, conduct themselves with gentleness, and weep over their shortcomings can then hunger and thirst for justice. They could not do this before because, as Ambrose points out, a seriously ill person has no appetite.* The first three beatitudes disengage us from a depraved world: poverty casts away

*Exp Luke 5.56; PL 15:1651C; CL 14:154

riches, gentleness makes us unaffected by injuries, mourning washes away the sins we have committed. The beatitudes that follow raise us heavenwards.* **Gorran Com Matt 5:6 approx*

The first of these beatitudes is not justice itself, but a hunger or desire for justice, because in this world we cannot possess perfect justice, although we can long for it. This is why it says *blessed are they that hunger and thirst after justice*, that is, yearn for justice with the longing of a ravenous person for food and drink. Bede says that we should never feel that we have become truly just, but we should burn with the desire to become more just each day.* Jerome writes, "It is not enough for us to desire justice; we must truly *hunger* for it. From this we understand that we are never sufficiently righteous; we must always hunger for the works of justice."*

*Com Luke 6:21; PL 92:401C; CL 120:138

*Laon Com Matt 5:6; PL 26:34C; CL 77:25

Justice is here understood as a virtue common to all people by which they avoid evil and do good. People are called righteous because they practice justice; for, as Chrysostom observes, to hunger for justice means that you desire to shape your life in accord with God's justice.* But we should thirst to find this justice and right living not only in ourselves but also in everyone else. Justice means giving each his or her due—be it God, neighbor, or self. We owe God three things: honor as our Creator, love as our Redeemer, fear as our Judge. We owe our neighbors three things: obedience to superiors, peace with our equals, kindness to inferiors. And we owe ourselves three things: purity of heart, custody of speech, discipline of body.*

*Opus imperf 9.6; PG 56:682

**Gorran Com Matt 5:6 approx*

Truly *blessed are they that hunger and thirst after justice, for they shall have their fill*, that is, their hunger and thirst for justice here below will be rewarded with an abundance of glory later. What they endured to become righteous will be repaid a hundredfold in that blessed life of which the psalmist says, *I shall be satisfied when your glory shall appear*.* But they are also rewarded in this life: greedy people hunger and thirst for the property of others, but the righteous are satiated

*Ps 16:15

by justice, so they are content with what they have and do not lust after the possessions of others. The righteous are not only those who act justly but also those who hunger and thirst for justice, that is, those who ardently want to act justly but are not in a position to do so. They too are blessed, because their desire takes the place of the act itself, and they will be satisfied when all their desires are fulfilled. Augustine says, "Those who know and love justice perfectly are already righteous, even if they lack the means or the opportunity to show it."* It is foolish to desire anything else, for nothing else truly satisfies. *Blessed are they that hunger and thirst after justice, for they shall have their fill*, in some small measure now, but fully in the future.

*De Trin 9.9.14; PL 42:968; CL 50:305

***R 8**

*The fifth beatitude is *Blessed are the merciful, for they shall obtain mercy*.* Mercy rightly follows on the heels of justice, for one virtue should not be exercised without the other. Mercy without justice degenerates into weakness, justice that is not tempered with mercy becomes harsh; the two virtues together strike a balance.* Mercy (*misericordia*) means a heart moved by the evils endured by another (*miseria cordis*). The merciful are moved with pity for those who suffer; they consider the misfortune of others to be their own, and feel it as if they themselves were enduring it. It is merciful to forgive without rancor or hatred the injuries inflicted by another and to offer whatever help one can, whether spiritual or temporal.

*Matt 4:7

**Gorran Com Matt 5:7 approx*

There is a certain order to be observed in the exercise of mercy. In the first place we should be merciful to ourselves after we sin, as it says in the book of Sirach, *Have pity on your own soul, pleasing God*.* Next we should be merciful to our neighbors, putting up with their faults and even going so far as to lay down our lives for them, as Christ did when he surrendered himself to death out of mercy for us. We show mercy to ourselves by doing penance, mercy to our neighbor by doing good. We can also show mercy toward God

*Sir 30:24

as his children, experiencing compassion for the sufferings of Christ, but, alas! So many *are not concerned for the affliction of Joseph.** The first kind of mercy brings about the forgiveness of every sin. The second kind lessens our punishment and multiplies our intercessors: those who alleviate the suffering of another deserve to have their own punishment reduced. The third kind leads to the attainment of glory because, as the apostle says, *If we suffer with him, we may be also glorified with him.**

*Amos 6:6

*Rom 8:17; *Gorrran Com Matt 5:7 approx*

However, Ambrose warns us that such compassionating with Christ should not be a mere lip service: rather, we should fill up in our bodies what is lacking in Christ's sufferings, as Paul did.*

*Com Ps 118, 8.13; PL 15:1299A

Let us devote ourselves assiduously to being merciful because we are so in need of God's mercy. So great is this virtue that God attributes it to himself as his distinctive attribute. This is why we pray, "God, whose nature it is always to forgive and show mercy."[3] God condemns the absence of this virtue in the reprobate and praises its presence in the elect. On the Day of Judgment, how effectively those deeds of mercy will rush to the aid of those who performed them! But James warns of *judgment without mercy to him that has not done mercy.**

*Jas 2:13

Augustine says, "Christ calls blessed those who come to the aid of the needy because they will be repaid by being freed from distress.* Do it, and it will be done; do this to another, and it will done to you. The way you treat your petitioner is the way God will treat his."* And Hilary teaches, "God so treasures our kindness toward others that he will extend his mercy only to the merciful."‡ Chrysostom for his part says,

*Sermone monte 1.2.7; PL 34:1232; CL 35:5

*Sermo 53.5; PL 38:366; CL 41 Aa:91
‡Com Matt 4.6; PL 9:933A

[3] This opening line of a collect has appeared in various prayers over the centuries, in recent times as part of the Litany for Rogation Days and in the Requiem Mass on the day of burial. Many medieval authors incorporated the phrase into their writings.

"The Lord of mercies pronounces the merciful blessed, showing that each of us cannot hope to find mercy unless we are merciful ourselves."* And again, "There seems to be parity between the virtue and its reward, but in fact the reward is much greater: human mercy cannot hope to compare with God's mercy."*

*Chromatius 3.6; PL 20:335D

*Hom Matt 15.6; PG 57/58:227

Tyrants who rage in their cruelty do not receive mercy and will be lost, but *blessed are the merciful, for they shall obtain mercy* in the future when they will be lifted out of all guilt and punishment. But they are also blessed in this age: their sins are forgiven, grace is lavished upon them, temporal blessings are given them, and they are delivered from many misfortunes to the extent that this allows for spiritual growth in their present condition.

***R 9**

*The sixth beatitude is *Blessed are the clean of heart: they shall see God*.* This beatitude is most appropriate for the sixth place because through it God's image in us is repaired, that is, our capacity to know and love God. Humankind lost this image six days after our creation, and it was restored* in the sixth age of the world.* It is also fitting that it follows the beatitude about mercy, for, as Ambrose observes, even those who are merciful forfeit the reward unless they are merciful with a pure heart: they lose the fruit if they seek praise.*

*Matt 5:8

*by Christ

**Gorran Matt 5:8 approx*

*Exp Luke 5.57; PL 15:1652A; CL 14:154

Christ says, *Blessed are the clean of heart.* He does not say, *clean of appearances*, like false hypocrites who clean only the exterior, or *clean of body*, like the rich who lavish so much attention on their ablutions. No, he says, *clean of heart*, those whose conscience cannot convict them of sin, who turn away from evil of every kind, and who do all the good they can with a virtuous and right intention.

Truly the pure of heart are blessed because *they shall see God*, for the greatest purity is united to the highest beatitude, and only the pure of heart can behold Purity himself.* The pure heart is one that the conscience cannot charge with any sin; it is God's holy temple

**Gorran Matt 5:8*

because no evil thoughts arise from it. If our hearts are free from sinful thoughts, our whole person is cleansed of wickedness: sins sprout up where they take root, and when pulled up they cannot grow.* **Bruno Com Matt 5:8; PL 165:99C*

*God is a spirit,** so he cannot be seen with the bodily eye but only with the eyes of the heart and the mind. Just as our physical eyes must be pure and clean in order to see the sun, in the same way—and even more so—the eye of the heart must be pure to be able to behold God, who *dwells in light inaccessible,** in whom all our needs are met and all our desires fulfilled. *John 4:24 *1 Tim 6:16

Augustine says, "This is the goal of our love: whatever we do well, whatever we find praiseworthy, whatever we desire for a good reason, none of these will we long for when we attain the vision of God. We want to see God, but see what he says: *Blessed are the clean of heart: they shall see God*. We must provide what is required to enable us to see: we cannot behold with impure hearts what only pure hearts can see."* Ambrose counsels us, "Cleanse your hearts. Expel all base thoughts and let nothing pollute your soul. Let your mind be integrated and your sincerity be genuine, for it is to such as these that God deigns to reveal himself once we have left behind the physical limitations of this world."* *Sermo 53.6; PL 38:366; CL 41 Aa:91 *Com Ps 118, 8.21; PL 15:1303B

The impure of heart wallow in their vices up to this very moment, but *blessed are the clean of heart*, for *they shall see God* in this world by faith as his friends and in the world to come by the vision of his glory. Hereafter we will see God to a greater or lesser degree according to how much we have avoided evil and done good; where the cleansing has been more thorough, the vision will be clearer and stronger.

*Then follows the seventh beatitude: *Blessed are the peacemakers, for they shall be called the children of God.** The beatitude of peace is given the seventh place because in the Sabbath of the seventh age peace will be given fully to those who possess the beatitudes mentioned previously. This beatitude follows fittingly ***R 10** *Matt 5:9

after the one dealing with purity of heart: one who has been purified advances in the way of peace. Indeed, peace is only nurtured by those of good will.* Ambrose writes, "When you empty your inner self of every stain of sin you begin to have peace within yourself; then you can give peace to others."*

**Gorran Matt 5:9 approx*

*Exp Luke 5.58; PL 15:1652B; CL 14:155

The Lord says, *Blessed are the peacemakers*, not "Blessed are the tranquil of spirit," because the latter pertains to the meekness spoken of in the second beatitude. Peacemakers make peace first within themselves, courageously expelling all evil thoughts, words, or deeds as soon as they detect them.* Nor do they allow any kind of commotion to disturb their inner realm; if adversity befalls them they preserve their peace of mind and appraise everything with a calm spirit. Then they are not content to treasure this peace within themselves, but seek to restore peace among other contending parties. Whether for themselves or for others, they vigilantly strive to make peace, restore peace, and preserve peace.

**Gorran Matt 5:8*

Such peace has five enemies: wars, lawsuits, rebellion, disorder, and annoyance. Peacemakers end wars, resolve lawsuits, quell rebellions, calm disorders, and alleviate annoyances. This was the work of the Son of God: possessing peace in himself, he restored peace to others; hence it is well said of peacemakers that *they shall be called the children of God*.* It is also said of peacemakers that they unite themselves heart and soul with God as the highest good and desire nothing apart from him; they find their peace and tranquility in him. They deserve to be called children of God because sonship from God suggests likeness to God, and it is characteristic of God to rejoice and take his rest in what is like him.

**Gorran Matt 5:8 approx*

Let us be peacemakers so that we can truly deserve to have the God of peace himself dwelling in us, as it is written, *And his place is in peace*.*

*Ps 75:3; *Chromatius 3.7; PL 20:337A*

Augustine says,

> The kingdom of God is made up of those who are at peace with themselves: they quell all the passions of their souls and subject them to reason, that is, to the mind and spirit, and keep their carnal feelings under control. In this kingdom everything is so ordained that the noblest and most excellent elements in a person control without opposition the other elements we share with animals. Moreover, what is pre-eminent in human beings, mind and reason, is itself subject to a higher power, the only-begotten Son of God, who is Truth himself. Nor can the mind control what is lower unless it in turn serves what is higher. This is the peace that is given *on earth to men of good will;** this is the life of one who has achieved perfect wisdom.*

*Luke 2:14

*Sermone monte 1.2.9; PL 34:1233; CL 35:6

Litigious people are quarrelsome, imitating their father, the devil; but *blessed are the peacemakers* who make peace both internally and fraternally, *for they shall be called the children of God*, and his true imitators. They possess a likeness to God the Father because God is the highest peace and perfect rest, and he disposes all things with tranquility.

*The eighth beatitude is *Blessed are they that suffer persecution for justice's sake, for theirs is the kingdom of heaven.** Chrysostom suggests that this follows the previous beatitude so that no one will imagine that peace is the only good to be sought.*

***R 11**

*Matt 5:10

*Hom Matt 15.4; PG 57/58:228

This beatitude helps us suffer well, just as the previous beatitudes help us act well; virtue entails enduring as well as doing. The preceding beatitudes were aimed at perfecting our actions; this one perfects our sufferings. Just as in our heavenly homeland there are two kinds of rewards, the golden crown* that all receive and the laurel of victory or little crown* awarded to some, so on our pilgrimage the first seven beatitudes are a kind of image of the crown and the eighth

**aurea*

**aureola*

corresponds to the laurel wreath, the regal prize that Jerome suggests can be gained through martyrdom.[4]*

*Gorran Matt 5:10 approx

Therefore, Christ says, "*Blessed are they that* not only act virtuously but *suffer persecution* patiently, not on account of their sins and misdeeds, but *for justice's sake*." This lawful justice embraces every virtue; that is, according to Chrysostom, truth, godliness, and the defense of others.* This is why it is customary to use the term *righteousness* for all the soul's virtues. Those who suffer are truly blessed in hope, and they will be blessed later in reality, *for theirs is the kingdom of heaven*, in which they will receive both the crown and the laurel of victory.

*Hom Matt 15.4; PG 57/58:228

Does this promise include risking death to safeguard the liberty of the church? Certainly, and for other spiritual causes as well. But this does not extend to the church's temporal goods: all too often the defense of these is motivated more by greed than by justice. Here is what Ambrose wrote about this subject*: "If the emperor asked for what was mine, such as my estates or my money, let him know that I would not refuse to hand it over, even though all I possess belongs to the poor. But what belongs to God is not subject to imperial power. If you want my patrimony, take it; if you want my self, I will go at once. If you

*when the emperor demanded that he surrender one of the churches in Milan

[4] Jerome says that the eighth beatitude of the true circumcision is terminated with martyrdom (Com Matt 5:10; PL 26:35A). ST Suppl., q. 96, a. 1 explains *aurea* and *aureola*. The crown is our essential reward, the soul's perfect union with God; the "little crown" is an additional reward added to the joy of union with God that virgins, martyrs, and doctors receive because of their victory over the flesh, the world, and the lies of the devil. The Supplement of the ST cites Bede's commentary on Exod 25:25, *and over the same another little golden crown*—"This crown denotes the new hymn that the virgins alone sing in the presence of the Lamb" (PL 91:410A)—and comments, "Wherefore apparently the aureole is a crown awarded not to all, but especially to some whereas the aurea is awarded to all the blessed. Therefore the aureole is distinct from the aurea." The last chapter of the *Vita Christi* describes the aureole at greater length.

want to lock me up or kill me, I willingly comply; I won't defend myself against the mob, nor will I cling to the altar and beg to be spared. But I will gladly sacrifice myself rather than betray the altars and the spiritual goods of the church."* *Ep 20.8; PL 16:996B

*This eighth beatitude fills out the list and sums up all the preceding rewards: when we have been perfected by the other beatitudes, we are prepared to suffer adversity. Chrysostom writes, ***R 12**

> In enumerating the beatitudes Christ has each depend on the one that went before, weaving them together into a kind of golden chain. It follows that those who are humble will be meek, that the meek will weep over their sins, that those who weep over sins will hunger and thirst for justice, that just people will also be merciful, that those who are just and merciful will feel remorse and be clean of heart, and from this comes peace. Having been perfected to this point, there is no doubt that they will be prepared for dangers, able to endure insults of any kind and a thousand evil deeds.* *Chrysostom Hom Matt 15.6; Caillau Chrys 5:419

Those who have the aforementioned virtues are blessed, but more blessed are those who do not waver in exercising these virtues while enduring adversity. The first seven virtues perfect us, but the eighth displays and magnifies this perfection. *Patience has a perfect work*:* through this beatitude the others are perfected and we are brought back to the beginning of the list.* The eighth beatitude returns to the first to test it for impurities and purify it: "Blessed are the poor, if they suffer persecution for justice's sake." Then on to the second, for the same purpose: "Blessed are the meek, if they suffer persecution for justice's sake." And so on with the rest, probing, purifying, perfecting. This final beatitude should be applied to all the others to test them. *Jas 1:4 **Massa*

If a scorpion is not disturbed, it lies still and does not thrust out its tail; but as soon as you touch it, it stings. It is the same for people without virtue: when provoked by an unkind word or afflicted with some injury, they are riled up and immediately strike out at the one who has offended them, stinging with the venom of angry and hateful words. In this they clearly show that they lack virtue. The saints, on the other hand, turn the other cheek, love their enemies, and pray for them. Bernard suggests the image of the stars that shine at night but are not visible in the daytime; he says that virtues that do not appear in seasons of prosperity shine out in troubled times.*

*SC 27.8; PL 183:917C; SB 1:187

Viewed in this way, the eighth beatitude is not properly speaking distinct from the other seven, but it confirms and illuminates them. This beatitude is given the eighth place because this number symbolizes the general resurrection that will take place in the eighth age; it also suggests the octaves of saints.[5]* It might also be compared with our Lord's circumcision on the eighth day and his resurrection, for this beatitude removes what spoils our other virtues and perfects them. Just as in the general resurrection we will be transformed and perfected by glory, so through this beatitude we are changed here below by grace and merit.

**Gorran Matt 5:10 approx*

***R 13**

*And notice that the reward attached to the last beatitude is the same as the first: *the kingdom of heaven*. Those who are treated with contempt experience the greatest persecution in this world; those who are mocked by many are truly poor in spirit. The same great reward is appropriate in both cases, because voluntary poverty is a kind of martyrdom. In both

[5] Beginning in the seventh century it became customary to celebrate an octave for important saints such as Peter, Paul, Agnes, or the patron saint of a particular locale or religious order. Originally this celebration was held eight days after the feast, but from the twelfth century on the intervening days were included. The number of these saints' octaves was reduced by Pius V in the sixteenth century, and again by Leo XIII and Pius X. They were finally suppressed altogether by Pius XII in 1955.

cases, our spirit must overcome its attachment to the delights of this world. The word *kingdom* suggests both riches and power. It is promised to the poor in relation to riches: those who renounce worldly possessions for the sake of Christ will rejoice in eternal ones. It is promised to those who suffer in relation to the Lord: those who are crushed for the sake of Christ will rule with him over their oppressors.* **Gorran Com Matt 5:10 approx*

Some might say that the prize is not the same in either case: that the kingdom of heaven as a reward for the first beatitude refers to the crown, while for the eighth beatitude it is the laurel of victory.[6] But in fact in either case the reward is the same, the kingdom of heaven, designated by different names. Chrysostom says, "Do not be sad because you do not hear the kingdom of heaven promised as a reward for each of the beatitudes. Although the recompense is called by different names, these all lead back to the same thing: the kingdom of heaven. The various rewards promised all refer to nothing other than the heavenly reign."* *Chrys? Hom Matt 15.5; Caillau Chrys 5:416

As you hear Christ speaking, consider what is contained in the beatitudes. If you find something of yourself in them, be assured that you will be blessed. Truth himself has spoken, and he cannot lie.* **Bruno Com Matt 5:10; PL 165:100C*

Persecution and Its Reward

*After speaking these words to everyone, Christ turned to his apostles and addressed them specifically. He predicted that they would be persecuted in three ways, by heart, by word, and by deed: "*Blessed shall you be when men shall revile you and hate you* (persecution from the heart), *and when they shall persecute you and separate you* by excluding you from the synagogue as unclean and unworthy even to be seen (persecution ***R 14**

[6] Gorran does say this.

by deeds), *and speak all that is evil against you* to blacken your reputations, *and shall reproach you* with insults and mockery, *and cast out your name as evil*, that is, the name *Christian*, slandering it, cursing it, and seeking to banish it completely (persecution by words)."*

*Matt 5:11 and Luke 6:22

These words should not be taken to suggest that we ought to court such treatment, rather, that the prospect of it should not cause us to abandon the truth of life, justice, or sound doctrine. Because persecution comes our way on three fronts, from hearts, words, and deeds (and this last takes three forms: loss of property, persecution of friends, bodily injury), so our patient endurance of heartfelt hatred, insulting words, and bodily punishment also takes three forms: forgiving every injury, feeling sorrow for our neighbors' sins, and praying that they will turn from their evil ways so that their sins can be wiped away. This threefold enemy assails the church, and she continually meets these attacks with this threefold patient endurance.

***R 15**

*Up to this point Christ had been speaking to everyone, but he addressed these last words to his apostles. Although they could apply also to others, he wanted to warn them of what they would have to suffer for the sake of his name, and how they would be persecuted with particular vehemence. He spoke to them directly because he knew that he was sending them out as sheep in the midst of wolves and that they would need special encouragement. Bede exclaims, "How different we are from those apostles who *went from the presence of the council, rejoicing that they were accounted worthy to suffer reproach for the name of Jesus*!"*

*Acts 5:41; Ps-Bede, Hom 69; PL 94:449C

Not every persecution makes us blessed, but only one that is joyfully endured for justice's sake, that is, for the Virgin's son, Christ. This is why he adds, *untruly*, and, *"for my sake*,* the sake of the Son of Man." For a persecution to produce blessedness, it must be one that is prompted by lies and so is unjust, and one that we suffer on account of Christ. The sorrow brought about by this kind of persecution will be

*Matt 5:11

turned to joy when God gives his holy ones the reward for their labors. Any other kind of persecution produces only misery, not blessedness; it brings no reward, only suffering. Augustine says,

> If you endure suffering because you have sinned, you sustain it for your own sake, not God's. But if you experience it because you have obeyed God's commandments, then you truly bear it for God's sake and your reward will be eternal.* This reward is already felt in the hearts of those who endure such sufferings and can say, *We glory also in tribulation*.* The reward comes not simply from enduring such things, but bearing them for the name of Christ, and with an unperturbed and even joyful spirit.*

*En Ps 68 1.12; PL 36:850; CL 39:912

*Rom 5:3

*Sermone monte 1.5.13; PL 34:1236; CL 35:13

When he had concluded saying this, Jesus added a word about the recompense, in this way encouraging them to accept the suffering. Jerome suggests that a task becomes easy to perform when we contemplate the prize, and the expectation of reward makes effort seem small. Christ said, "*Be glad* in your heart *and rejoice* with every fiber of your being, manifesting to others the happiness you feel as much for the goodness of the virtue of patience itself as for the hope of a glorious recompense: *for your reward is* not only as great as that received by others, but is *very great in heaven*,* far beyond what you deserve." ***R 16**

*Pelagius, Ad Dem 28; PL 30:43A

*Matt 5:12

The heavenly prize is proportionate to what you have suffered here below. This reward is great, manifold, precious, and enduring: it is so great that it cannot be comprehended, so manifold that it cannot be counted, so precious that it cannot be estimated, so enduring that it cannot end.* The reward is more fruitful according to the degree that faith was more joyfully zealous in time of trial. God does not reward us for the amount of our labor or the multitude of our works, but for the generosity with which we do good and endure evil. He is concerned not with *how much*,

**Allegoriae NT 2.1; PL 175:766D*

but with *how*: he treasures the widow's mite more than half the wealth of Zacchaeus.

Augustine observes that those who rejoice in spiritual goods already experience this reward, but that they will be perfected in every respect after death when *this mortal must put on immortality*.*

*1 Cor 15:53; Sermone monte 1.5.15; PL 34:1237; CL 35:15

But we, alas, deceive ourselves! We rejoice and exult when worldly delights please us and the praise of the crowd lifts us up, although we really should be weeping and mourning: prosperity is more dangerous than adversity, and praise than insults. Instead, let us rejoice and exult with the apostles, who learned from Christ that healthful joy and delight were to be found in slander and persecution.*

**Allegoriae NT 2.1; PL 175:766D*

Jerome says, "I do not know who among us can fulfill the command that we should rejoice in the Lord when our reputation is torn to shreds by disgraceful speech. The one who pursues empty fame cannot fulfill this. Therefore, we should rejoice and exult so that a reward will be prepared for us in heaven. We find this idea elegantly stated in a certain book: 'Do not seek glory, and you will not grieve when you are deprived of it.' "* And Chrysostom writes, "To the extent that you lap up praise, to that extent you are depressed by criticism. But whoever longs for glory in heaven has no fear of reproaches on earth."* And Seneca teaches, "You are not yet happy if the crowd does not yet ridicule you.* If you wish to be happy, decide first to contemn contempt.[7]* If you wish to be happy, if you wish in good faith to be a good person, let one person think you a fool and another despise you; allow anyone to do you wrong—nevertheless, if you are virtuous, you will suffer nothing."*

*Com Matt 5:12; PL 26:35B; CL 77:26

*Opus imperf 9.11; PL 56:684

*Syrus 23

*Moribus 2; PL 72:29C

*Lucilium 71.7

***R 17**

*To urge the apostles to embrace suffering and to temper the rigor of their tribulations, after speaking of a reward Jesus sought to comfort them by appealing

[7] Ludolph has *contemnere contemptum*; the original is *contemnere et contemni*, "scorn and be scorned."

to the example of the prophets who had undergone such terrible sufferings before them; their companionship would console them and persuade them to endure. He said, "*For so they persecuted the* true *prophets,* like Jeremiah, Isaiah, and others, *that were before you,** who endured persecution for the sake of the truth, and to give you both the example and the courage to endure." It was as if he were saying, "Do not be surprised if you have to suffer, for such a lot is neither novel nor unusual. If their blessedness and joy delight you, let their example instruct you. Their example should incite you, lest fear lead you to grow weak in defense of truth. They had to suffer, and they had no example to inspire them." *Matt 5:12

Along this same line, just as it is customary to wave a cloth dyed red in front of an elephant to provoke it to charge into battle, so the examples of Christ and the martyrs are held up to us to comfort us in time of persecution.* **Gorran Com Matt 5:12*

Contemplating the great rewards promised, let us be ready to embrace all that we suffer with fortitude and sincere faith, so that we may be found worthy to share in the glory of the prophets and apostles. Let no one abandon the cause of truth from fear of persecution; on the contrary, let us desire persecution when the cause of Christ calls for it. The apostle says, *All that will live godly in Christ Jesus shall suffer persecution.** If you are persecuted, take it as a good indication that you *are living godly in Christ,* because if you do not suffer persecution you do not *will to live godly in Christ.* Ambrose warns, "It could be that an absence of persecution is a sign of reprobation because we do not want *to live godly in Christ.* The apostle's words are very explicit: *All that will live godly in Christ Jesus shall suffer persecution.* It seems that those who do not experience persecution have been disinherited because they are lacking in love of Christ. Warfare follows upon faith's devotion."* *2 Tim 3:12

*Com Ps 118, 11.21; PL 15:1357B

But suppose someone were to object, "No one can attain blessedness by means of persecution nowadays because peace is widespread and the church is free from persecution in most places." I would answer that temptations and persecutions are all around us, because daily in the very heart of the church Cain attacks Abel, Ishmael attacks Isaac, Esau attacks Jacob; in a word, the unjust attack the just. And even if someone avoids persecution from without, nonetheless he is betrayed by false brethren. *All that will live godly in Christ Jesus shall suffer persecution*. And if there are no persecutions from other people, there are the inner attacks by wicked spirits. Because the persecutions are relentless, patience is essential to us if we are to receive what is promised. Woe to those who lose patience, because they also forfeit the crown of patience. Let us not grumble if we are vexed by a few trials; we will be allotted many blessings.*

**Allegoriae NT 2.1; PL 175:765D–66A*

Luke's Account

***R 18**

Whereas Matthew recounts eight beatitudes, Luke records only four. But, according to Ambrose, those four are in these eight, and these eight are in those four. Meekness and peace refer to patience; purity of heart, to poverty of spirit; mercy, to hunger for justice.‡

*Exp Luke 5.49; PL 15:1649C; CL 14:152
‡Vincent of Beauvais, Speculum hist 7.13

The Lord had challenged the people previously by means of rewards to strive for faith and virtue, so it follows that he would likewise seek to turn them away from wickedness and sin by warning them of future punishments.* Hence he says, "*But woe*, eternal woe, *to you that are rich*; not all the rich, but *for you* who *have your consolation*‡ now from your wealth, squandering it on self-indulgence."

*Ambrose, Exp Luke 5.72; PL 15:1655C; CL 14:159
‡Luke 6:25

It is as if Christ were saying, "You have your wealth, but you won't have mine; not now, and not later."* By the rich he means those whose lives are absorbed with

**Gorran Com Luke 6:24*

their possessions; it is not so much wealth as the love of it and the abuse of it that are sinful.* Just as earlier he had said that the kingdom of heaven belongs to the poor, so by contrast it is obvious that those are excluded from that kingdom who use their riches not for their basic necessities and to remedy the misery of others and bring them relief, but simply for their own delectation. When they seek consolation, they will hear the just Judge say, *Son, remember that you received good things in your lifetime*.* Ambrose comments, "Those who enjoyed the consolation of the present life forfeited the reward of eternal life."*

**Gloss Luke 6:24; PL 114:262D*

*Luke 16:25

*Exp Luke 5.69; PL 15:1655A; CL 14:158

Next he says, "*Woe to you that are filled*, idly passing your days in carousing, drunkenness, and high living; *for you shall hunger** in the future, not only from a shortage of food but from the lack of all good things." Recall the rich man who was accustomed to feast splendidly, living in luxury; later, when he was ravenous, he had to sustain the dreadful blow of this *Woe!* when he begged for a drop of water from the fingertip of the man Lazarus whom he had despised.* Those who gorge themselves at banquets will be punished with the strictest fasting; their sin of gluttony will be punished by its opposite. Contraries are punished by their contraries, so when doing penance we should embrace the discipline opposed to our weakness. Bede writes, "If those who hunger and thirst for justice are called blessed, it follows that those are wretched who only satisfied their own selfish desires and in this thought themselves to be well off, never experiencing a pang of hunger for truly good things or voluntarily depriving themselves of anything, even for a season."*

*Luke 6:25

**Zachary 1.23; PL 186:123A*

*Com Luke 6:25; PL 92:404A; CL 120:141

Then Christ says, "*Woe to you that now laugh* inordinately, making frivolous sport of inane pleasures; *for you shall mourn* with inner grief *and weep** with outer anguish." Or perhaps, "*You shall mourn* because of the absence of any good thing, *and weep* because of the presence of every punishment in the eternal flames,

*Luke 6:25

*Matt 8:12 *where there shall be weeping and gnashing of teeth."** If those who mourn will be blessed and consoled, it only makes sense that those who laugh will suffer agony as evildoers.

*Prov 14:13 Solomon teaches, *Laughter shall be mingled with sorrow, and mourning takes hold of the ends of joy.** Basil says, "Since the Lord rebukes those who laugh, it is clear that there will never be a time for the faithful to laugh, especially because a multitude of them will die in sin and we must mourn for them."* And Chrysostom asks, "Tell me, why are you frittering away your life when you will have to stand before the awful Judgment and give an account of the things done here?"*

*Regula monachos Interr 53; PL 103:515C

*CA Luke 6:24–26

Last Christ says, "*Woe to you when men shall bless you*, praising and extolling you, feeding your wickedness with their applause, so that you become blind to your failings and forget the words of the apostle, *If I yet pleased men, I should not be the servant of Christ.** *For this is how their fathers treated the false prophets,** praising those who prophesied untruthfully because their hearts were moved, not by the Holy Spirit or the mouth of the Lord, but by a desire to please the crowd and win its favor." The psalmist complained of this: *For the sinner is praised in the desires of his soul: and the unjust man is blessed.**

*Gal 1:10

*Luke 6:26

*Ps 9:24 [10:3]

Woe also to those who offer this kind of praise; the flatterer's tongue is more lethal than the enemy's sword.* Those who praise evildoers are placing pillows under their heads as they sleep so that they can rest comfortably in their sins.* If those who are spoken ill of by others are blessed, it follows that those who are praised by others deserve to be considered cursed. It is a great sign of God's wrath and vengeance if sinners are praised rather than corrected for doing wrong: the adulation feeds their wrongdoing, and their punishment will be all the greater.

**Augustine, En Ps 69.5; PL 36:869; CL 39:934*

**Gregorgy, Mor 18.IV.8; PL 76:42A*

Luke records these sentences so that the truth of the preceding four beatitudes may be put in relief against the background of the opposing condemnations.

✠

Lord Jesus Christ, you ascended the mountain with your disciples to teach the loftier heights of holiness; you announced there the sublime virtues of the beatitudes and promised corresponding rewards. As I listen to your voice, grant that I, frail creature that I am, may strive to put those virtues into practice and so deserve with your mercy to obtain their recompense. In view of the reward may I not refuse the work it requires; let the prospect of eternal salvation sweeten the bitterness of the medicine in this present life and spur me on to act cheerfully. Make me blessed now with the beatitude of grace on my pilgrimage and blessed later with the beatitude of glory in my heavenly homeland. Amen.

CHAPTER 34

The Sermon on the Mount, Continued: Pastors Should Enlighten by Preaching and Works; Christ Has Come to Fulfill the Law

(Matt 5:13-37)

***R 1** *Having exhorted his apostles to bear with tribulations, the Lord now offers four images to help them appreciate the importance of standing firm in the face of persecutions: they are salt, light, a city, and a lamp. It is as if he were saying to them, "Do not give up in time of trial, because your failure would be the cause of ruin to many others." He tells them, "*You are the salt of the earth, you are the light of the world,** you are a city on a mountain top, you are a candle placed on a candlestick. I say you *are*; that is to say, you *ought to be*." The first two images are positive, describing what they should do: season hearts and enlighten minds. The second two describe what they should not do: hide either themselves or their doctrine from other people.

*Matt 5:13-15

Apostles and pastors are called the salt of the earth by virtue of their irreproachable way of life, which seasons and instructs the minds of those who are still captivated by earthly values. For what is salt? It sterilizes soil, seasons food, cures meat, prevents putrefaction; it is made from fire and water; it is offered in every sacrifice. Similarly, the example of a holy life tempers worldly desires, rendering them unfruitful; it adds spice to holy longings, it cures the flesh by mortification, it keeps our desires from rotting. Holiness comes from tears of devotion and fire of love heated in the furnace of repentance; it is offered when it guides and moderates every work.* But above all, in Scripture salt signifies the discretion that pastors must exercise in directing and seasoning the works of those under their care so that they will be more palatable to God, just as salt makes food more pleasant to taste. **Gorran Matt 5:13*

*Christ warns the apostles and other pastors in the church that they must persevere in living a virtuous life, "*But if the salt*, that is, a leader or teacher, *lose its savor* on account of fear of persecution or adversity, or love of pleasures and wealth, or pride and vainglory, or the desires of the flesh, or neglect of responsibilities, or erroneous doctrines imparted by word or example to those under his care, *wherewith shall it be salted,** to help this feeble flock that ought to be seasoned by the life and teaching of its shepherd?" What other doctor can restore or season salt itself, that is, the one who should be seasoning others? *Who will pity an enchanter struck by a serpent*?* To such a one it must be said, *Physician, heal yourself.** ***R 2** *Matt 5:13 *Sir 12:13 *Luke 4:23

Similarly, if the discretion that should flavor our good works is lacking, these deeds will not be acceptable to God; here the image of salt's being included in every sacrifice is apt. When salt loses its savor it is useless in itself and useless for anything else: *it is profitable neither for the land nor for the dunghill.** It is useless for the land because it sterilizes the soil; it is useless for the dunghill because when mixed with the manure it robs it of its ability to fertilize.[1] *Luke 14:35

[1] In ancient times salt was spread on manure to keep it from decomposing and so used when dung was burned for fuel.

It is as if Jesus were saying, "Such a leader is good for nothing. He is unproductive in himself, because his land does not bring forth the fruits of good works; nor does he improve the fruitfulness of others by making their souls fertile or invigorating their growth as manure does. He is *good for nothing anymore but to be cast out** of office and returned to the lay state: he is hurting himself and not helping anyone else."

*Matt 5:13

Such a one should be removed so that the dignity of the pastoral office is not brought into disrepute.* He deserves to be deposed from ecclesiastical office, or separated from the community of those who by right belong to the unity of the church, or even excluded from the glory of the saints. He should be trodden underfoot in this world by human scorn, at the Judgment by angelic separation from the good, in hell by demonic torment.

**Lyra Matt 5:13*

***R 3**

*Matt 5:14

*Jesus also calls apostles and pastors light: *You are the light of the world,** that is, to people who live in the world, on account of the word of their teaching, which should enlighten the ignorant about what they must believe and how they must behave. Just as the sun and the moon give light to our bodily eyes, so apostles and teachers give light to the eyes of our minds. But it is more important for the pastors to live well than to teach well. Christ had said that by living wisely the apostles were the salt of earth; afterwards he says that by enlightening those in darkness they are the light of the world. It follows that a pastor should be *salt* by living rightly and *light* by teaching well—*salt* by example and *light* by doctrine. The proper order is first to live virtuously and then to teach effectively. According to the Gloss, God is the light that enlightens but does not receive light; the apostles and apostolic men are the light that receives light and gives light; ordinary believers are the light that receives light but does not impart light. The first can be compared to the light of the sun, the second to the light of the moon, and the third to the light of the stars.*

**Gorran Matt 5:14 approx*

*After the savor of salt and the ray of light come the protection of the city and the illumination of a lamp, because the apostles and pastors should not hide themselves away, nor conceal the lamp of God's word under the basket of human respect or the bed of tranquil worldly prosperity. Rather, they should be a fortified city on a mountain top that offers refuge to those who are unjustly oppressed and a lamp placed on a stand so that the example of a holy life will shine forth in the darkness. *R 4

The images of the city on a mountain and the lamp in its stand admonish apostles and leaders to let their light shine out before others so that others, seeing their good works, will be drawn by their fragrance and shaped by admiration of them in such a way as to glorify not them, but God the Father, from whom every good and praiseworthy gift comes. They should shine in both word and deed.

Jesus did not say, "that they may hear your good talk," but *that they may see your good works, and glorify your Father who is in heaven*.* Actions speak louder than words and example moves people more than talk, because deeds shine more brightly than words.* Those who use only words preach for only one hour a week; but those who act preach with their whole life and at every moment. Elsewhere it says, *The just shall shine, and shall run to and fro like sparks among the reeds*.* Gregory says of this verse: "The reeds signify the lives of the worldly, who outwardly rise to great heights but inwardly lack any solidity."* On the other hand, to preach without practicing is a form of vanity and does little good. Bernard teaches that it is a monstrous thing to possess an eloquent tongue and an idle hand, or to combine brilliant doctrine and a shady life.*

*Matt 5:16

**Bruno, Com Matt 5:16; PL 165:101D–2A*

*Wis 3:7

*Mor 33.III.7; PL 76:673B; CL 143B:1675

*De consideratione 2.7.14; PL 182:750C; SB 3:421

However, the reason to have these good acts shine out is to glorify God, not human beings: we should not seek glory for ourselves but for God, and strive to edify our neighbors so *that they may see your good works, and glorify your Father** by whom they are accomplished

*Matt 5:16

in us, ascribing everything to him as the author of all good. What Christ is saying here need not contradict what he says a little further on: *Take heed that you do not your justice before men.** The present passage exhorts us to seek to do good works for the glory of God; the latter passage exhorts us to flee from adulation for ourselves.

*Matt 6:1

Christ Has Come to Fulfill the Law, Not Destroy It

***R 5**

*Then Jesus begins to inform them concerning a wrong idea they may have gotten on the basis of what he was saying. It was as if the apostles asked, "Look, we do not want to hide your doctrine, but what exactly is it that you have forbidden us to conceal? Is it possible that you are going to teach different truths, contrary to what is written in the law and the prophets?" He denied this: "*Do not think* erroneously *that I have come to destroy the law, or the prophets** by prohibiting their spiritual fulfillment." Augustine says that everything written in the Old Testament is a type or image of what is found in the New Testament.* "*I have not come to destroy* the law, *but to fulfill*."‡ According to Augustine, this statement of the Lord carries a twofold meaning. For *fulfill the law* can mean either adding something it lacks or carrying out what it says. When the Lord adds what is missing he certainly does not destroy what he finds there; on the contrary, he strengthens it by bringing it to perfection.*

*Matt 5:17

*Ps-Augustine, Sermo 2; PL 39:1741
‡Matt 5:17

*Sermone monte 1.8.20; PL 34:1239; CL 35:20

Even now what the law and the prophets had promised concerning him has already been fulfilled in part; *and before heaven and earth pass,** and their elements are transformed from their changeable form to one that is immutable, that is before this world (as regards its shape, not its material) is finished, everything that was written concerning him will be fulfilled in its spiritual sense. Nor can *one jot, or one tittle,** that is, even the

*Matt 5:18

*Matt 5:18

tiniest precept of the law, fail to be fulfilled and remain useless and empty. The jot* is the smallest letter in the alphabet, made with one stroke; the tittle* is a tiny mark made above a letter to distinguish it from others. The meaning of Christ's words is that the smallest precept, even the tiniest part of a precept *of the law shall not pass away** until it is fulfilled in due season in Christ, either in his Head or in his Body.

*iota

*apex

*Matt 5:18

*Having shown how the law is to be fulfilled in himself and in his teaching, Christ goes on to show how it must be fulfilled by teachers, and how their doctrine concerning him should be proven. Here he distinguishes between two kinds of doctors. There are some who live badly but teach well, as the scribes and Pharisees were doing. Concerning them he says, "*He therefore that shall break* by his evil way of life *one of these least commandments* (that is, the Ten Commandments, which are called least because they are the initial laws to be followed on the way to perfection), *and shall so teach men* by their bad example *shall be called the least in the kingdom of heaven.*"* The kingdom of heaven here means the church militant: according to Pope Gregory teachers who break a commandment remain in the church but are called least because their life is contemptible and thus their teaching is despised.*

***R 6**

*Matt 5:19

*40 Hom 12.1; PL 76:1119A; CL 141:82

O how many in the church today are among these least, who in their own eyes are very great! Augustine warns, "It follows that those who are least in the kingdom of heaven, such as the church is now, will not enter the kingdom of heaven, such as the church will then be, because by teaching what they destroy they will not belong to the company of those who do what they teach."* And Chrysostom, "To preach without practicing not only does no good; it causes great harm. Those who labor over their sermons but ignore their own behavior will be judged severely."*

*Tr John 122.9; PL 35:1965; CL 36:675

*Compunctione 1.10; PG 47:410

There are others who both teach well and live properly, and these are worthy to be leaders in the church.

Of them Christ says, *But he that shall do and teach, he shall be called great in the kingdom of heaven.** Chrysostom observes that it is easy to show true wisdom in words, but to prove it by deeds is the mark of one who is noble and great.* People who act but do not teach are also great, although less so: those who fulfill the law are justified in the sight of God. They are credited with having fulfilled the whole law when what they have neglected to do has been forgiven, which is why we must pray, "Forgive us our trespasses."

*Matt 5:19

*Hom John 80.1; PG 59:433

Jesus then confirms what he had said to the effect that, far from destroying the law, he desires to fulfill it very abundantly. He goes on to say that he wants his disciples to fulfill it in the same manner, so that *their justice abounds more than that of the scribes and Pharisees,** who talk but do not act. They will fulfill the law more abundantly when their actions match their words: sound doctrine without virtuous living is not sufficient for salvation. Augustine teaches that no one will enter the kingdom of heaven unless he fulfills not only the least prescriptions of the law, but also those added to it by Christ; the justice that comes from the law alone is not enough to admit one into the kingdom of heaven.*

*Matt 5:20

*Sermone monte 1.9.21; PL 34:1239; CL 35:22

Although justice ordinarily refers to the cardinal virtue by which we give all their due, it has a broader meaning in this context; according to Jerome all virtues are included under the name *justice*.* Augustine says that justice contains two parts, avoiding evil and doing good, and this is how justice can be contrasted with sin.* It should also be understood that just as there are various kinds of grace given by God, so there are diverse human states and conditions. It can be said aptly of those who hold a higher position in respect to others, "*Unless your justice abounds more than that* of those in lower positions, *you shall not enter into the kingdom of heaven*."

*Pelagius, Ad Dem 1.5; PL 30:19D

*De correptione 1; PL 44:917; see ST II-IIa, q. 79, a. 1 contra

***R 7**

*Next we should see that the Savior reviews the Ten Commandments and exhorts people to follow them,

explaining their true meaning and excluding certain ideas of his own people concerning them. For the Jewish teachers interpreted the Decalogue in a negative sense, holding that the commandments simply prohibited certain actions and not their underlying motivations, and that an evil will was not sinful unless it was expressed in a deed.* Thus, in speaking of the commandment *Thou shalt not kill*, they said that this prohibited the act of killing, but not the intent. It is to this that Jesus refers when he says, *You have heard that it was said to them of old: Thou shalt not kill.** But the Savior teaches that it is wrong to limit this prohibition to the act; the commandment forbids us to be angry without cause. Not to commit murder pertains to the justice of the law. Whoever kills another will be liable to the death penalty according to the law, that is, will be accused and condemned to death, following the principle of the law of retribution.*

**Lyra Matt 5:17 mor*

*Matt 5:21

**lex talionis*

To be perfect we must go further: this commandment forbids us from harboring anger against another in our heart without cause, or showing this anger by our tone of voice, saying, *Raca*, which expresses indignation, or blaspheming or otherwise insulting another and inflicting injury by using an epithet like, "Fool!" which is more hurtful than a word like *raca*.[2] So three things are prohibited: first, the emotion of anger in the soul; second, the indignation in the expression; third, the insult in the word.

Different punishments are assigned to each of these three sins: the first sin is anger or hatred hiding in the heart; the second sin is anger finding expression in one's general demeanor; the third sin is the insulting

[2] Concerning *raca*, Augustine comments that it is an interjection expressing emotion, and that it is not easy to translate these from one language to another: "When I asked a certain Hebrew about it, he said that the word does not signify anything in particular, but expresses the feelings of an indignant person" (PL 34:1241).

Zachary 1.26; PL 186:137D

behavior itself.* And Christ proposes three corresponding punishments. First, *whoever is angry* inwardly *with his brother*, not from zeal but because he hates him and would do him harm if the opportunity presented itself, *shall be in danger of the judgment*,* that is, deserving of accusation before God in the court of the great Judge, albeit not before other people because it is not possible to accuse someone in a human court concerning his or her will. Next, *whoever shall say to his brother, Raca*, out of indignation and contempt, *shall be in danger of the council*,* that is, the verdict of the judges who must pass sentence and determine punishment because the fault has come to light. Finally, *whoever shall say, You fool*, out of contempt for a person and not from a desire to correct a fault, *shall be in danger of* the predetermined sentence of *hell fire*.* The Gloss explains that it is no minor transgression to call someone a fool whom God has seasoned with the salt of wisdom.*

*Matt 5:22

*Matt 5:22

*Matt 5:22

*Paschasius Radbertus, Com Matt 5:22; PL 120:240B; CM 56:319

Moses and the law applied the ax to the branch by forbidding homicide. Christ, that wise farmer, and the Gospel laid the ax to the root by forbidding anger, so that the cause of sin could be taken out of our hearts; it is anger that leads eventually to murder. And he did well to begin with anger, because, as the Gloss says, wrath is the gateway of all the vices: if that door is closed, all the virtues will rest peacefully within; if it is open, the soul will be roused by every sort of crime.* Jerome defines anger as any evil emotion that leads us to harm another.*

*Rabanus, Com Prov 3.29; PL 111:773B

*Gloss Matt 5:22; PL 114:93B

This emotion can arise spontaneously, in which case the sin is venial, or it can be fostered by deliberation and consent, and then the sin is mortal. It must be said that not every kind of anger is sinful: for example, vengeance is a kind of anger, but it is not sinful to desire vengeance if the cause is just.

There are four ways vengeance can be unjust: either we want to punish someone who does not deserve it, or we want to punish him more than he deserves, or our desire for vengeance is exaggerated, or our intent is not to serve justice but simply to take revenge.* By pulling up the roots of hostility and sealing off the fountain that extinguishes the fire of charity, Christ strives to tie together the bonds of mutual charity that unite us. But, O! we pay so little attention to this! **Lyra Matt 5:22*

Chrysostom says,

> We put up with all kinds of insults and injuries when it comes to those who are more powerful or greater than ourselves, fearing that otherwise we will suffer even more at their hands. But sometimes we get angry with our equals or inferiors even if they have not hurt us. In this way we give preference to human fear over the fear of God. The Lord told us not to be angry with our brother without cause; how much easier this is when the other person has not given us cause to be angry. Why do you accept greater outrages out of human fear and will not endure much lighter ones out of fear of God?*

*Compunctione 1.3; PG 47:397

And if Christ forbids fresh anger, how much more does he condemn nursing a grudge? Augustine warns, "If it is not lawful to be angry with another or to say '*Raca*' or 'Fool,' much less lawful is to retain in the mind anything that may turn anger into hatred."*

*Sermone monte 1.10.26; PL 34:1242; CL 35:27

The Need to Be Reconciled

*From what has been said it can be concluded that if you want to *offer* by thought, word, or deed *at the altar* of your faith and heart some *gift*, be that a sacrifice, or alms, or teaching, or prayer, or a hymn, or a psalm, or indeed any kind of spiritual or bodily offering, then you must *go first to be reconciled to your brother** whom you have offended or hurt by word or deed, bodily or spiritually. Your gift will not be accepted until you have driven this discord from your ***R 8**

*Matt 5:24

heart. God does not reject the gift, but he looks for our love of neighbor; so if we long to have our gift be pleasing to God, we must first extend charity to our neighbor.

A gift offered to God does not benefit its donor unless it is made in charity, and we do not possess charity if we do not desire to make amends with someone we have offended. If we know that the person we have offended is nearby, we must go in person to make satisfaction and beg forgiveness. If it is not convenient to do this, it suffices to go to the person mentally, prostrating ourselves at his or her feet, humbly promising to make satisfaction at an appropriate time and place. This is the custom of the Roman Church: a penitent is absolved from guilt at the moment of confession, but then a penance is imposed to make amends for the harm done to another.* Understand that if your sin is known to the person offended, you must beg that person's forgiveness. But if it is not, you are not required to make it known to the person lest his or her anger be stirred up, but you must ask God's forgiveness and reveal it to the priest in confession.

Lyra Matt 5:24

Chrysostom counsels, "If you offended in thought, be reconciled in thought; if you offended in words, be reconciled with words; if you offended in deed, be reconciled by deed. The manner of repentance should correspond to the nature of the sin."* So, for example, if you have hurt someone by detraction, you must be reconciled by restoring that person's reputation.

*Opus imperf 11.24; PG 56:692

We should pay careful attention to this matter because here the greatness of God's mercy shines out all around us. He cares more for what is useful to us than what gives honor to him, and he loves harmony among the faithful more than the gifts we offer him. This leads Chrysostom to exclaim, "O the admirable goodness and ineffable love of God toward humanity! He disdains his own honor while requiring that we love our neighbor. He desires nothing so much as that we be united in the bonds of mutual charity. This is why he made all things; this is why he became Man; this is why bore so much: that he might bring us together as one flock."*

*Ps-Chrys Com Matt 16:9; Caillau Chrys 5:451, 453

But no less dramatic is God's harsh severity when he refuses the vows and gifts of those who are quarrelling. Gregory says, "Behold, he does not want to accept the sacrifice offered by contentious parties; he refuses their holocaust. Weigh carefully, therefore, how evil discord is: because of it, what frees us from guilt is cast aside."* Here is what Cyprian has to say about the sin of discord: "Quarrelsome and dissident people who are not at peace with the community will not escape the charge of fraternal dissension, even if they were to be killed for the name of Christ. How great is the sin that cannot even be washed away by the baptism of blood? How terrible is the crime that even martyrdom cannot expiate?"*

*Hiez 1.8.9; PL 76:858B; CL 142:106

*Orat Dominica 24; PL 4:536B

Chrysostom writes, "Abel's offerings were accepted by God and Cain's were rejected because Abel made his offering to the Lord with a pure and simple heart, but Cain harbored hatred against his brother. Abel's gift was pleasing because his heart was pleasing. But alas! Many are like Cain today, approaching the altar with hearts full of treachery and discord."* And elsewhere, "God has such great concern for our reconciliation that he is willing to allow our service to him to be interrupted until we forsake hatred for our brother or sister. And yet we do not blush or feel ashamed about this; on the contrary, we allow many days to pass in this state of animosity, playing out our disagreements like a long rope, unaware that the lengthier our discord is, the lengthier the punishment for it will be."*

*Hom Genesis 18.5; PG 53:156

*Compunctione 1.3; PG 47:398

*Because this harmony with an offended party must be re-established, Christ urges us to make amends with our adversary and to be in accord while we are on the way in this present life, which is the place for grieving and doing penance. We should act today and not put this off till tomorrow. Any delay brings danger ***R 9** with it, and none of us knows the length of our days. Chrysostom gives this caution: "Nothing is so able to ruin our lives as continually to ignore opportunities to do good works, and always to delay putting them into effect. Often this is enough to cause the loss of all the good we have done."* Quickly, I say, you should *be at agreement with your adversary, lest perhaps the adversary deliver you to the judge* at the Last Judgment, *and the judge deliver you to the officer* or tax collector, that is, to an evil spirit for retribution, *and you be cast into* the *prison** of hell to pay the penalty for your sins.

*Ps-Chrysostom, Hom Matt 16.10; Caillau Chrys 5:455

*Matt 5:25

The Lord warns, *You shall not go out from there till you repay the last penny.** That is, we must make amends for even the slightest and smallest transgressions; nothing will go unpunished. The word *till* here carries the connotation of *never*, suggesting the negative of all time, for, as Augustine suggests, the word does not signify the end of punishment, but the continuation of misery.*

*Matt 5:26

*Sermone monte 1.11.30; PL 34:1244; CL 35:32

Those in Gehenna suffer punishment eternally even for their slightest transgressions because these are linked to their mortal sins; they cannot expiate them or obtain forgiveness for them. There is no place of pardon there, so they can never obtain that last penny, but must always be paying it. They can never leave because they are in hell—and where there is no place of pardon, there is no avenue of escape.

The word *adversary* here does not refer to the devil, because we must never *be at agreement* with him and always resist him; here the *adversary* is the neighbor we have offended or injured, with whom we should have agreed to make amends, or some opponent to whom we should have extended good will and kindness. Or the *adversary* can be self-evident moral truth* and our conscience, which quietly rebuke our evil wishes and bad actions and accuse us with their testimony; we should *be at agreement* with them by doing good. In a mystical sense the *adversary* when we sin is

**synderesis*

God, because he stands in opposition to us when we move away from him by sinning; we can *be at agreement* with him by repenting and doing his will. Or it can be the word of God, which contradicts our sinful desires and blames and accuses wrongdoing; we ought to obey it by avoiding sin and humbly following its precepts.* **Aquinas, Com Matt 5:25 approx*

Christ Refutes Wrong Interpretations of Other Commandments

*To confirm that he has *not come to destroy, but to fulfill* the Law, Christ gives an explanation of how some of the other commandments are to be interpreted. The Jews understood the commandment *Thou shalt not covet thy neighbor's wife** to forbid certain actions, such as passionate touches, kisses, and other such things; *thou shalt not covet* meant "you shall not perform lustful deeds." Similarly, they interpreted the commandment *Thou shalt not commit adultery** to condemn certain kinds of behavior; inner longings and desires of the heart of any kind, provided that they were not expressed by some gesture or act, were not held to be sinful. ***R 10** *Deut 5:21 *Exod 20:14

But this is an unreasonable interpretation: gestures and acts are sinful only insofar as they are voluntary. Therefore the Savior dismisses this understanding: "*But I say to you, that whosoever shall look on a woman to lust after her*, that is, with the express purpose of lusting after her and fully consenting to this desire, *has already committed adultery with her in his heart*."* Chrysostom says, "If I lust after a woman I will be numbered among the adulterers even if I do not act on my desire."* Self-indulgence in deed is condemned by the law, but the author of purity condemns self-indulgence in thought as well. The law forbids adultery; the Gospel punishes lust, which is the root of *Matt 5:28 *Opus imperf 12.27; PG 56:694

adultery. This is why John was bound about the loins, while Christ was bound around his chest.[3]

It should be understood that there are two kinds of lustful thoughts. The first is called a *pre-passion*: it arises spontaneously, without consideration of a good or evil deed or consent, and is a venial sin. The second is called a *passion*: this is marked by deliberation in the will and consent in impure thoughts or deeds and is a mortal sin.[4] The Lord is speaking here of intentional lust, which suggests consent in thought or deed.*

**Gorran Matt 5:28 approx*

Therefore, to consent intentionally to lust in the heart is a mortal sin, even if it is not expressed in act or gesture. Because seeing is a provocation to lust, Ambrose counsels us to avert our eyes from sources of temptation: "What the eye sees, the heart desires."* And Gregory warns us, "We must take precautions, because it is not fitting to look upon what we should not lust after. If the mind is to be kept pure in thought, the eyes must be forced away from their wanton pleasure, which is a kind of sinful ravishing."* Chrysostom says, "Whoever gazes intently upon beautiful faces lights the furnace of passion within himself, which in turn leads to action. What answer to this can be given by those who live in cohabitation with virgins? By the tenor of this law, they must commit adultery ten thousand times a day, because they are looking upon them daily with desire.[5]* Those who are

*Com Ps 118, 5.27; PL 15:1260C

*Mor 21.II.4; PL 76:190B; CL 143A:1066

*Hom Matt 17.2; PG 57/58:256–57

[3] This refers to a passage from Jerome's *Com Mark 1:4* that sees John the Baptist's leather belt as an allegory of the law and the golden belt around Christ's breast (Rev 1:13) as an allegory of the Gospel (CCL 78:453).

[4] In CA Matt 5:27–28 Aquinas traces this distinction back to Jerome (PL 26:38C), and it is frequently mentioned by medieval authors. Ludolph follows Aquinas again on this point when speaking of Christ's agony in the garden.

[5] Chrysostom is referring to a "spiritual marriage" in which a couple lived together, but not as husband and wife; he inveighed against this arrangement in *Contra eos qui subintroductas habent virgines* (PG 47:1858).

always running off to the theater should pay attention to this: they are plunging daily into a veritable cesspool, committing adultery a hundred times a day and creating ten thousand occasions to lose their immortal souls."* *Hom Matt 17.3; PG 57/58:259

On the other hand, listen to this useful advice from Pope Gregory: "When the flesh attracts you, think about what it will be like when it is lifeless, and understand what you are loving. Nothing is so effective at countering carnal desires as imagining what that thing we love will be like when it is dead."‡ ‡Mor 16.LXIX.83; PL 75:1162A; CL 143:848

***R 11**

*Because the Lord had said that a man could commit adultery simply by looking at a woman, he also teaches that we must avoid the occasions that encourage us to make this consent: "*If your right eye* or hand *scandalize you*, that is, cause you to give your consent, *pluck it out* or cut it off *and cast it from you*,* totally annihilating it." He does not mean, of course, literally sacrificing your eye or hand, but refraining from the wrongful use of your faculties for illicit ends. "*For it is expedient for you that one of your members should perish* (in the aforementioned sense of forsaking the sinful use of it, even though the object is attractive), *rather than that your whole body* and soul *go into hell*."* As Gregory says, "It is not proper to look at what you should not desire."* And Bernard comments, "A man who takes a woman's hand is chained to the devil."[6]‡

*Matt 5:29

*Matt 5:30

*Mor 21.II.4; PL 75:189B; CL 143A:1065
‡Alcuin, Com Eccl 7:27 approx; PL 100:698A

The many people who gaze with lustful intent on the beautiful visages of women or young men, or caress their faces and fondle them, or engage in intimate conversations, should attend very carefully here: in the opinion of many learned doctors of the church and

[6] Alcuin expresses this idea without the pithy directness found here. He is commenting on the verse, "And I have found a woman more bitter than death, who is the hunter's snare, and her heart is a net, and her hands are bands. He that pleases God shall escape from her: but he that is a sinner shall be caught by her."

masters of the spiritual life, their behavior is a sign of interior corruption and gives evidence of a certain weakness and degradation. According to Augustine, the Lord is not instructing us literally to cut off a part of our body, but to cut off the occasion of sin. Such occasions can come from looking, in which case the eye is a cause of scandal, and when looking is done with a good intention, it is the right eye that is the cause. Such occasions can also arise from touching; if undertaken for a good purpose, it can be said that it is the right hand that is the source of scandal.* Whatever is a source of scandal must be cut out, because we must flee from the occasions of sin.

*Attr. to Augustine in Hugh 5.70.8

Perhaps an example will illustrate this lesson: suppose that you are engaged in some good work at a convent, preaching to the nuns or giving them spiritual direction, or you are giving alms to a woman, and you recognize that this is a proximate occasion of temptation that may lead you into sin. You ought to forgo a good work of this kind, lest the whole edifice of your good works should collapse.*

**Lyra Matt 5:29, 30*

Alain of Lille gives this advice:

> If you want to avoid fornication,
> Flee from a tempting situation:
> Times and places fuel inclination.*

*De planctu naturae, 6; PL 210:456B

Other authors propose the same remedy. Seneca writes, "If you want to destroy the worldly desires that lust provokes, close your eyes and ears to what you have forsaken."* And this candid admission of his makes the point as well: "Whenever I have been out in the company of others I return home more lascivious, more ambitious, more avaricious, indeed more vicious."*

*Lucilium 7.69.3

*Lucilium 1.7.3

We can also understand the right eye and hand to refer to our inner being and the left eye and hand to refer to our body, which is more frail. And if the right hand scandalizes the left, what is to be done? Jerome says, "We must beware that what is best in us does not fall into vice. For if your right eye or hand are an occasion for falling, what will be the chance that your left eye or hand will avoid sin? If the spirit slips, what of the body, which is more prone to sin?"* Finally, Chrysostom writes, "The eye and the hand here do not refer to parts of the body, but to the eye and hand of the heart, that is, to the attraction of evil desires and lustful thoughts. He commands us to cut these out and throw them away through divine faith, because all wicked deeds proceed from them. The Lord tells us to exterminate the wicked members of depraved thoughts for the sake of the kingdom of heaven, lest our vices come to dominate us and our whole being, body and soul, be found deserving of the eternal flames."*

*Com Matt 5:29; PL 26:39B; CL 77:31

*Chromatius 23.2.1-2

Christ's Teaching on Divorce

Having taught that it was wrong to desire another man's wife, Christ next teaches that it is wrong to send one's own wife away, and he gives the correct meaning to a permission given in the law that allowed a bill of divorce. The Jews simply assumed that this was licit, but they were wrong: divorce was not permitted because it was lawful, but to avoid the even greater wrong of a man murdering his wife. It cannot be denied that it would be far worse to kill one's wife than to send her away, but still (excepting the case of a woman committing fornication) it is not lawful to repudiate her. *Moses permitted to write a bill of divorce** on account of the *hardness of* a husband's *heart,** who felt such hatred for his wife that he wanted to kill her. This was not granting divorce, it was preventing homicide; better to allow this lesser evil than to shed blood.

***R 12**

**Zachary 1.29; PL 186:131A*

*Mark 10:4

*Mark 10:5

Christ, however, commanded that a man must not repudiate his wife at all, *excepting the cause of fornication,** because in that case it is the wife who first violated the conjugal vow. In such circumstances he may

*Matt 5:32

send her away in the sense of not living with her and denying her right to marital relations. However, the marriage bond itself remains so long as they are both living: if he sends her away to marry another woman he commits adultery, as does a man who marries her.

Whoever wants to dismiss his wife for *the cause of fornication* should first be innocent of fornication himself. Jerome teaches, "A commandment given to men logically applies to women also: it cannot be that, while an adulterous wife can be put away, a fornicating husband must be retained."*

*Ep 77.3; PL 22:691; CS 55:39; *Zachary 1.29; PL 186:131B*

Christ's Teaching on Oaths

***R 13**

Having taught that we must avoid anger and lust so as not to injure our neighbor, the Lord now forbids the taking of oaths and perjury so that we will not offend God, and he gives the proper interpretation to a precept in the old law forbidding perjury. The Jews were of the opinion that this commandment simply forbade lying under oath, but that an illicit oath must still be honored and that a rash oath, for which there is no need, is nonetheless licit. But the Savior says we should not swear for any reason; this does not include oaths that are required, but all useless oaths.

**Lyra Matt 5:33*

Justice according to the Pharisees meant not committing perjury. The Lord confirms this by forbidding swearing: this is the justice of those who are to enter into the kingdom of heaven. Just as a person who keeps silent cannot speak falsely, so one who does not swear cannot commit perjury.* We read that *in the multitude of words there shall not want sin*,‡ so in the multitude of swearing there shall not want perjury. The Lord had commanded the Jews to offer him sacrifices according to the law, not because these were pleasing to him, but so that they would not offer them to idols, as had been their custom in the past. Similarly, as a concession to their weakness he allowed them to

*Augustine, Sermone monte 1.17.51; PL 34:1255; CL 35:57
‡Prov 10:19

swear by God, not because this was pleasing to him, but because it was less wicked for them to swear by him than by some creature. Jerome writes, "The Law required his people to swear by God alone; not that this was a good thing, but it was better than their custom of swearing by creatures, thereby offering them the homage due to God. The Gospel does not admit of oaths, because every statement of a faithful Christian should be like sworn testimony."*

*Com Matt 5:34; PL 26:40B; CL 77:33; *Zachary 1.30; PL 186:132C*

According to Chrysostom,

> Swearing of any kind is not permitted to us. Why is it necessary to swear, since we are not permitted to lie for any reason? Should not all our words always be so true that they can be trusted as absolutely as if we had sworn an oath? The Lord forbids not only perjury but the taking of an oath so that it cannot be thought that an oath is needed to guarantee the veracity of what we say, and that we might be suspected of lying if we are not speaking under oath. An oath is taken for one reason: to guarantee the truthfulness of what we say. But the Lord does not choose to distinguish between what we say under oath and anything else we say. Just as what we say under oath should be devoid of treachery, so what we speak should be free of falsehood. Both perjury and lying will be punished by divine Judgment. Whoever speaks swears to be truthful, as it is written: *A faithful witness will not lie.** It is not without reason that the holy Scriptures frequently exhort us not to swear: God is truthful and knows what we say, so every word we speak should be uttered as if under oath.*

*Prov 14:5

*Chromatius 10.2; PL 20:352A

Seneca writes, "There is no difference between swearing an oath and making an affirmation: you should know that religion and faith are involved whenever the truth is handled."* Augustine points out that people who swear call God to be their witness, but it is laughable to think that they have not sworn because they did not say "by God," but rather, *for God*

*Martin Braga 4 [5]; PL 72:27B

*Rom 1:9
‡Gal 1:20
#2 Cor 11:31; Sermone monte 1.17.51; PL 34:1255; CL 35:58
†Matt 5:34; *non iurare omnino*

is my witness, behold, before God, I do not lie,‡* or *God knows that I do not lie.*[7]#

Therefore the Lord commanded us *not to swear at all,†* that is, not to swear on every occasion or in every case because this would be a rash oath, but he did not exclude taking an oath when this is required. Here the negative precedes the universally affirmative statement, which is equivalent to its contradiction; if it came after the statement, it would be equivalent to its contrary. He did not say *omnino non iurare*: this would mean that there is no situation in which an oath should be taken, which is false: there are occasions when we should take an oath and other occasions when we should not. He said *non iurare omnino*, that is, do not take an oath on every occasion. His meaning is not that there is no occasion for swearing, but that it should be done only when absolutely necessary; needless swearing constitutes a rash oath.[8]* Therefore, Augustine says, the Lord did not command us *not to swear at all* because to do so is unlawful, but to curb those who think that oaths are good in themselves and swear easily, and by force of habit fall into false swearing.*

Lyra Matt 5:34

*Sermone monte 1.17.51; PL 34:1255; CL 35:58

There are three requirements for an oath to be proper. The first pertains to the matter about which the oath is taken, that is, the truth; otherwise, there is nothing suitable to be confirmed. The second pertains to the motivation for swearing, that is, to reach a judgment; if this is not the purpose, there is no need to take an oath. The third pertains to the person swearing, that is, the need for justice or discretion; if this is lack-

[7] Augustine is dealing with the objection that certain phrases of Paul seem to violate Christ's prohibition of oaths; he rejects the technicality that we only swear when we say, "*by* God."

[8] Lyra applies two principles regarding "equipollence" (equivalent meanings) laid down by Peter of Spain in his *Summulae logicales*, an important thirteenth-century textbook on logic.

ing there is the danger of swearing falsely. Hence the prophet Jeremiah says, *And you shall swear: As the Lord lives, in truth, and in judgment, and in justice.** *Jer 4:2; *ST II-II, q. 89, a. 2 approx*

It is not only unlawful to swear rashly by God; it is also wrong to swear by creatures, inasmuch as divine power shines out through them. Hence Christ adds, "*neither by heaven, for it is the throne of God,* and it is from there above all that his glory shines out; *nor by the earth, for it is his footstool,* because it is his humblest creation; *nor by Jerusalem, for it is the city of the great king,** that is of God, the King of Kings, and the place chosen by him as the center of worship." To underscore this divine element he adds, "*Neither shall you swear by your head, because you cannot make one hair white or black,** for this is God's work, not yours." *Matt 5:34-35 *Matt 5:36

What Jesus is saying here is that just as we should not swear by God, so we should not swear by creatures: because any creature is God's creation, to swear by the creature is to swear by God.* We are also forbidden to swear by creatures lest we give divine honors to what is God's handiwork, and also to avoid committing perjury by taking a false oath by creatures. (Some believe that swearing by created things is tantamount to swearing by nothing, and the oath is not binding.) Sometimes people swear on the cross or on the gospels, that is, by him to whom these objects are dedicated. This also holds true for swearing on the relics of the saints: in this case we are honoring God's power rather than a saint's because he is their Maker, and all the good they possess comes from him.* **Lyra Matt 5:33* *see ST II-II, q. 89, a. 6

He who forbids us to swear tells us what to do instead: "*But let your speech be yes, yes, no, no*:* simply affirm what is true and deny what is false." His repetition of *yes* and *no* suggests that our mouth expresses externally what is in our heart. We fulfill this gospel precept of *yes, yes, no, no* when we affirm or deny with both our lips and our heart.* Therefore, let what is in our conscience be on our lips, let what is real be in our mouth, and let what is in our mouth also be in our *Matt 5:37 **Zachary 1.30; PL 186:133B* works. Let us prove by our deeds what we affirm in our speech, and not profess by action what we deny in speech.

*Matt 5:37

Christ goes on to say, "*That which is over and above these*, to swear, *is of evil*,* that is, comes from weakness and suspicion because the person will not be believed unless he swears." He does not say, "It is evil," because you do not do evil if you make use of an oath properly—not because it is good in itself, but because it is required to persuade others when proposing something helpful to them. He says, "*It is of evil*," that is, it manifests the weakness of another party who compels you to take an oath, when you see that he or she is slow to believe what will be of use to them, and they will not credit it unless you so swear.*

*Augustine, Sermone monte 1.51 approx; PL 34:1255–56

There is always an element of evil here, either on the part of person who swears unnecessarily or on the part of the one who demands it. It is either an evil done* when an oath is insisted on unnecessarily, or an evil suffered* because of a weakness inherent in the human race that we do not take one another at our word without an oath.[9]*

**malum culpae*

**malum poenae*

**Lyra Matt 5:37*

Let us speak the truth and commend it by the probity of our conduct rather than a torrent of oaths. And when talking, let us speak plainly and not send other messages by gesture or expression, for such behavior also *is of evil*. We read in Proverbs, *A man that is an apostate, an unprofitable man, walks with a perverse mouth, he winks with the eyes, presses with the foot, speaks with the finger*.* It is foolish to imitate this unprofitable man and *speak with the finger*; more foolish still to speak with the hand, because this has five fingers, and it follows that someone who speaks with arms and shoulders is most foolish of all. Moreover, those wild

*Prov 6:12-13

[9] In *De malo* 1.4 Aquinas distinguishes between the *malum poenae* (the evil of penalty) due to the Fall, such as sickness and pain, and the *malum culpae* (the evil of fault), which is a morally evil action.

gesticulations and tremors of the head make a person look possessed. It is expedient for us restrain all bodily movements when speaking so as not to give others occasion for scandal.

✠

Lord Jesus Christ, you promised worldly benefits to our ancestors, but to us you have promised eternal blessings so that our righteousness may be greater. Grant that I may shine before you and my neighbor by word and deed in such a way that I will not abolish your law but fulfill it more abundantly. Safeguard me from feeling anger or offending my neighbor; then the gifts of my heart, speech, and actions that I offer to you will be acceptable in your sight. Most merciful God, grant that I may avoid lustful and wicked glances and all oaths. May I be able to abstain from injuring either you or my neighbor, and always please you in all things. Amen.

CHAPTER 35

The Sermon on the Mount, Continued: Love of Enemies

(Matt 5:39-48; Luke 6:27-36)

*R 1

After teaching that we should not injure others or show irreverence toward God, the Lord now goes on to teach how Christians should respond to those who injure them. In a few words, he forthrightly commends and encourages patience and generosity toward everyone, saying that this suffices for perfection.

**Bruno Com Matt 5:39; PL 165:110A*

He begins by giving a correct understanding of a judicial precept about which the Jews were mistaken. They considered vengeance a good in itself, but this is false. To punish someone is not an absolute good; it only becomes a good when it is pursued to attain some other end: to preserve a just order, or to correct the offender, or to dissuade others from doing the same evil when they see how it is punished, or for a similar reason. When it appears that no good will come from punishing a person, but rather it is likely that such a course of action will cause scandal or lead to worse evils, then we must restrain ourselves from seeking vengeance. In such situations, this is a necessity; but in other circumstances, the refusal to seek vengeance goes beyond the call of duty.*

**Lyra Matt 5:38*

*Matt 5:39

In some circumstances the teaching *not to resist evil** is a commandment, and in others a counsel, and it can even be wrong not to resist evil, if as a result wicked people oppress ordinary folk and can carry out their evil without fear of retribution.* The evil of sin must always be opposed; but the evil of injury should never be wantonly vindicated, but only pursued through the agency of a judge, and out of a love for justice, for the sake of the good of the church or the correction of a neighbor, lest he or she become accustomed to wrongdoing. **Lyra Matt 5:39*

The *lex talionis* in the law was applied to killing, beating, and mutilation: offenders would suffer punishment equivalent to what they had inflicted and *render life for life, eye for eye, tooth for tooth.** People are prone to injure their neighbors, even without cause, and can be fierce in vindicating wrongs done to them far beyond a just punishment. Because of the rashness of both perpetrators and victims, the law established a measure and limit to retribution that no one was to exceed, that is, the *lex talionis.* A foreordained surety provided the measure: the impudence of the offender would be checked by fear, and the vengeance by the injured party would not go beyond proper limits. *Exod 21:23-24

But of Christ it is said, his *mercy exalts itself above judgment,** and this is the justice of his Gospel: "*I say to you not to resist evil** with evil, but conquer an evil injury by patient goodness." Nor, what is more, should we respond to injuries, but be prepared to bear them patiently when they beset us. Retribution is in the law because it directs that a wrong be adjudicated with justice. Grace is in the Gospel because it teaches the power of patience, even at the expense of our members. Chrysostom says, "If you pluck out another's eye, you do not recover your own, but you forfeit your patience along with your member. The devil strikes at your body in order to injure your soul. If you do not retaliate, it may seem in human terms that you have been vanquished—but you have vanquished the devil. If you do not return evil for evil, even though you lose part of your body you acquire a wealth of patience. But if you take revenge, you suffer both *Jas 2:13 *Matt 5:39

bodily loss and the loss of your soul: you are less injured by the harm done by an enemy than you are by the loss of your constancy and goodness."*

*Opus imperf 12 approx; PG 56:699

Turning the Other Cheek

*R 2

*There are four degrees of maintaining peace with our neighbors. First, to do no more evil to them than they do to us. Second, to do less to them than they deserve; this was the practice of the Pharisees, who prescribed forty lashes less one. Third, to return no evil at all. Fourth, to be prepared to accept even more evil at their hands. The first two degrees are found in the law; the third marks the beginning of the Gospel, which says *not to resist evil.** The fourth is the fulfillment of the Gospel, about which Christ goes on to speak. He says that evil must not be resisted, but, lest someone think that this refers to the evil of sin and not of injury, he adds, *But if someone strike you on your right cheek, turn to him also the other.**

**Gorran Matt 5:38*

*Matt 5:39

The other here means the inner right cheek of the soul: you remain silent under the blow and are ready to receive another, and even several harsh blows, sooner than resist evil in a way that scandalizes or encourages an offense against charity. Augustine says, "It is not enough to refrain from retaliating; you must be willing to receive a blow on the other cheek, should he wish to give it."* And Chrysostom, "If you strike back, you fulfill the mandate of the law, but not the mandate of Christ. You might say, 'He deserves to be struck back.' Perhaps—but you do not deserve to do the striking, because you are the disciple of the one who did not speak evil of others when they spoke evil of him."*

*Gloss Matt 5:39; PL 114:97A

*Opus imperf 12 approx; PG 56:699

The Lord confirms in every way the lessons of patience and humility by the Gospel precepts. He not only forbids us to strike those who strike us; he also enjoins us to be prepared to accept further blows and not resist the evil of injuries that can still be inflicted. Bede exclaims, "What could be greater than to turn the other cheek to those who strike us? Does this not shatter the fury of their indignation and allay their wrath? Will not our patience move them and urge them to repent? By doing this the commandment is fulfilled, we conform ourselves to Christ, the devil is defeated, and total peace is attained among people."* And Chrysostom: "Meditation on this kind of forbearance led to the passion of the martyrs. It is easy to put up with bodily punishment in time of persecution if we are practiced beforehand in gladly sustaining injuries with equanimity."*

*Gloss Luke 6:29; PL 114:263D

*Chromatius 11.1; PL 20:354A

Augustine points out that this precept does not rule out vengeance that has a corrective purpose, but such retribution is inappropriate unless it overcomes hatred by love: parents do not hate the child they punish. Those who mete out punishment should act to correct from love, not hot-blooded hostility; they should possess the appropriate authority to punish, as a child is corrected by its parents, and they should be prepared, if necessary, to tolerate calmly further injury from those they desire to improve.* This loving vengeance is in fact a great mercy. Blessed indeed are those who are ready to embrace wholeheartedly all that they suffer for God and can truly say and sing with the prophet, *My heart is ready, O God, my heart is ready.**

*Sermone monte 1.20.63; PL 34:1261–62; CL 35:72

*Ps 107:2

Give Away Your Coat as Well as Your Shirt

The Lord not only commands us to turn the other cheek; he also enjoins us to accept the loss of property. According to Chrysostom, along with enduring physical injury the Lord wishes us also to disdain earthly goods: we are to show patience regarding our possessions as well as our persons. So Christ continues, "*Do not prevent someone from taking your coat** by fighting back or contending with him." The Lord

***R 3**

*Hom Matt 18.2; PG 57/58:266

*Luke 6:29

himself exemplified this principle when he allowed his garments to be taken from him and divided among the soldiers. While you might be able to reclaim your bodily clothing, you forfeit the far more valuable garment of your soul.*

*last sentence: Ps-Chrysostom, Opus imperf 12; PG 56:700

"And if a man will contend with you argumentatively *in judgment*, causing you distress by dragging you before the judge, *and take away your shirt*, that is, whatever is truly essential, *let him also have your coat*,* giving him also what is superfluous, and never act in anger." This was as if to say, "If someone wants to take what is necessary from you by arguing, before you fight it out in court it would be better to put up with this and give him everything else, too." According to Augustine, this should be understood to mean readiness of heart, not the doing of works.* We can also draw the lesson that if someone wishes to take our shirt, that is, our soul or interior goods, we should give instead the coat of our external goods.

*Matt 5:40

*Ps-Rufinus, Com Ps 5:2; PL 21:662C

Chrysostom advises, "If a lawsuit is pending, you should not participate: it is better to be free from strife than to keep your belongings with contention. It is difficult to give up your possessions, but it is more difficult to go to court without sinning."* And elsewhere, "The Lord not only says that you should tolerate injury without being moved to anger at those who hurt you, but if they take something from you, let it go freely. When they find that you act in this way, they will be stung to the quick and mortified."* And Bede writes, "What is said about the shirt and coat applies not only to those two items, but to all things that we speak of as temporal goods. If this is what must be done as regards necessities, how much more should we disregard superfluous goods?"* The law says that we should not take what belongs to another, nor are we obligated to give; grace says that we should not take what belongs to another, but we are to give what is our own.*

*Opus imperf 12 approx; PG 56:700

*Compunctione 1.3.4; PG 47:399

*Com Luke 6:29; PL 92:406C; CL 120:144

*Chrys, Opus imperf 12; PG 56:701

Augustine holds that if people, either spontaneously or when requested, refuse to repay the money that they owe us, we should let them keep it. The rule is that a servant of God should not engage in lawsuits; while that rule remains in force, we should be mentally prepared to forfeit what is owed to us. We may strive by gentle persuasion to have it returned, not so much for the sake of the money itself but to reform the other parties—for it is doubtless destructive if they have the means of paying but do not. In doing this, not only are we not sinning, but we are also performing a great service by trying to prevent those who want to profit from our expense from making shipwreck of the faith. This is an incomparably more serious matter.*

*Sermone monte 2.8.28; PL 34:1281; CL 35:117–18

Note here that there are two ways we can try to recover what belongs to us. The first is to bring the matter before a judge who is not a believer; Christians are not permitted to do this, especially in places where the church enjoys freedom. The second way is to submit the case to a judge who is a believer. This can be done in two ways: contentiously and fraudulently, and no one is allowed to do this, or modestly and justly, and this is permitted to the weak and imperfect. Anyone acting without contention or fraud is allowed to reclaim what is his directly without recourse to a judge. As regards religious, who do not own anything, there are also two ways of recovering something: either for their own use, which is not allowed to the perfect, or for the common use of the community, and this is permitted even to the perfect, who possess nothing themselves but are seeking the restoration of property in the name of the community. And if they do not have ownership either in their own name or that of the community, the use of the property is delegated to them. However, it is better in such matters to consult with a judge privately rather than bring the matter to court.*

**Gorran Matt 5:40*

Going the Extra Mile

*R 4
*angariaverit
*Matt 5:41

*Jesus continued, *"And whosoever will force* you one mile, go with him another two."** That is, bear it patiently when someone asks you to go farther. *Angaria* means compulsory service that a person must provide personally, or any unjust constraint; *angariare* means to constrain someone to do something unjust or expend personal effort that is very inconvenient and burdensome.[1] The sense of this instruction is: if someone wants to coerce you to perform a service that is not required and is not sinful, you should be so ready that you are willing to do even more than they ask.

*mille passus = a thousand paces

*One mile** is a Sabbath's journey, so this is not contrary to the Sabbath of the law; thus, to endure an offense of this sort is not contrary to the Sabbath of the heart. Or, a *thousand* signifies spiritual perfection, because it suggests the complete fulfillment of this precept. And, since a *thousand* is a number of perfection, the *other two* added to the first implies a threefold perfection of patience, in body, reason, and will.*

*Zachary 1.31; PL 186:134BC

Chrysostom exclaims, "See the superabundance of philosophy, the pinnacle of wisdom! After giving your cheek, your shirt, and your coat, Christ says that if your enemies want to use your body, naked as it is, to perform laborious tasks, even then you should not prevent them. He wants us to share all things in common, both our bodies and our goods, not only with those in need, but with those who wrong us. The former is mercy, the latter, long-suffering."* And elsewhere: "The Lord commands us to be ready and energetic for every work of devotion. He wants our good conduct to be prompted by our own desire rather than

*Hom Matt 18.3; PG 57/58:268

[1] The word comes through Greek to Latin from a Babylonian word meaning "mounted courier." The supply and maintenance of the horses used for this imperial communication system was a compulsory duty. The word came to be used for animals that pulled transport vehicles, and later a service forcibly or unjustly demanded.

necessity. If we do more than the other person demands, we will receive a greater reward. An act of perfect charity and devotion consists in spontaneously doing more than you are asked."* According to Augustine, the Lord is not telling you to walk a certain number of steps, but to be ready in spirit.*

*Chromatius 11.3; PL 20:354C

*Sermone monte 1.19.61; PL 34:1261; CL 35:71

To avoid wrangling, you should make not only your goods available to the person who demands them but your very self; you should be prepared to do more than you are asked, not so much with feet and works as with your soul and compassionate affection.* What has been said here should be understood to refer to your interior disposition in such situations. It does not apply to circumstances where, by following this commandment, the person who takes or demands or offends is encouraged in evil or iniquity. On the contrary, to bear with such behavior would not be good, except to avoid scandal or some greater evil. For, as Augustine bears witness, when freedom is taken away from those who abuse it by doing wrong, they are vanquished to their own advantage. Nothing is more a misfortune than the good fortune of sinners by which a punishing impunity is maintained and an evil disposition is strengthened like an enemy inside the gates.*

**Zachary 1.31; PL 186:134B*

*Ep 138.2.14; PL 33:531; CL 31B:284

Augustine also observes that these three examples cover every kind of injury. All matters in which we tolerate wickedness can be divided into two kinds. Restitution cannot be made for the first kind. Wounded pride seeks the solace of revenge, but a healthy and firm mind chooses to bear with another's infirmity. Nor is retribution for the sake of correction forbidden, as we saw earlier. Complete restitution can be made for the second kind of injury, and the recompense can take two forms, money or labor. The example of the shirt and coat is applicable to the first, the compulsory service of the miles to the second: a garment can be returned, and someone you have helped by your labor can help you in turn. But sometimes, as with bodily

R 5

*Sermone monte 1.20.62; PL 34:1261; CL 35:71

injury, complete restoration is impossible. In every kind of injury, the Lord teaches the highest degree of mercy and patience; Christian souls should be eagerly prepared to bear with even more injuries right to the end, encouraged by hope of eternal recompense.*

*Sermone monte 1.20.66; PL 34:1263; CL 35:75–76

Liberality Toward Our Neighbor

***R 6**

*It is a small matter not to inflict harm unless you bestow a benefit when you can, so the Lord added the following: *Give to every one that asks you.** In other words: "You should be patient in bearing your own injuries, but also compassionate toward the injuries of others." He does not specify what to give, because sometimes you may not have the wherewithal to provide material assistance, but you are still obliged to give, even if it is only a word of encouragement. When those in need ask you for something material or spiritual, give a gift or a word. If their request is reasonable, you should give them what they ask for. If you are in a position to do this and they are in extreme need, this is a matter of precept; it is only a counsel if they can also turn to someone else, as in the case of almsgiving.

*Luke 6:30; *Augustine, Sermone monte 1.20.67; PL 34:1263*

And if you are lacking material means, give an affectionate and good disposition, a kind answer and prayer. If their request is unreasonable, talk with them and give a just cause for your refusal, explaining why what they ask is not feasible, so that you do not send them on their way as fools. Instruction of this kind is a work of justice and spiritual almsgiving. They may not have received what they asked for, but they received something better: improvement.* *Give to every one that asks you*; give something, even if it is not what they asked. Christ said to give to everyone who asks, but not everything they ask; you should give what can be given honestly and justly.*

**Lyra Matt 5:42*

**last sentence: Augustine, Sermone monte 1.20.67; PL 34:1263*

Ambrose writes, "It is no less a crime to take from others who have than to have an abundance of goods and not share with those in need. The bread you keep belongs to the hungry; the clothing in your closet belongs to the widow; the money you bury is the deliverance and ransom of the poor. You should be aware that you unjustly possess many things when you do not share them."* As Chrysostom notes, our wealth is not our own: it belongs to God, and he wants us to be the dispensers of his riches, not its masters.‡

*Attr. to Ambrose, Gratian, Concordia, Dist 47.8; PL 187:248A
‡Opus imperf 12; PG 56:701

So give, do not sell! You sell when you must be badgered, you sell when you postpone a benefit, you sell when you insult the poor, you sell when you give with a sad face, you sell when you expect something in exchange. Paupers who possess nothing are not bound to hand over a material gift, but they should give the gift of compassion from their heart, consolation from their mouth, and the assistance of their labor for the place and time. We read in the Gloss, "If you lack means, give service, or affection, or a word."* These are the four things Magdalen gave Christ: the tears of compassion, the hair of assistance, the kiss of service, and the ointment of consolation.‡

*Gloss Matt 5:42; PL 114:97C
‡*Gorran Matt 5:42 approx*

*The words that follow should be understood in the same way: *"And do not turn away from him that would borrow from you** by refusing, postponing, or giving less than he asks." If the request is reasonable, make the loan; if it is not, explain why. Lend gladly, *for God loves a cheerful giver;** and with genuine charity, not hoping for something in return or receiving interest, labor, or some other commodity in exchange. We should not lend with the aim of gaining, except for the reward that comes from God. Be merciful, and set your hopes not on human recompense but on God, for he can pay you greater interest than what you spend in doing what he commands. Augustine teaches, "Do not alienate your goodwill from those who appeal to it, as if God will not pay you back for

***R 7**
*Matt 5:42
*2 Cor 9:7

what you have given them. When you act because of God's precept it cannot be unfruitful with the one who commands this."*

*Sermone monte 1.20.68; PL 34:1264; CL 35:77

When the Lord says, *Give to every one that asks, and do not turn away from him that would borrow from you,* he includes two kinds of beneficence: we either give outright, or lend hoping for a return.* And we should be prepared to do both. Whether we give alms or lend them, we are bound to give to those who ask. If we are perfect, we will do this even for an enemy; but if we are imperfect, we are only bound to do this for an enemy in desperate need. Chrysostom says, "When someone appeals to our mercy, let us give what we can; with this service going before us, it will be easier for us to ask God for those things we want him to give us. But if we treat with contempt those who ask something of us, what confidence makes us believe that God will give us what we ask of him? We are commanded to safeguard the religion of piety and faith in all things in such a way that we view the tribulations of another as if they were our own and do not prize possessions more than persons. Our hope is for a return that is eternal."*

**Zachary 1.31; PL 186:134C*

*Chromatius 11.4; PL 20:354D–55A

What has been said here does not pertain only to almsgiving, but to the money that never fails, wisdom and doctrine. This kind of wealth scornfully rejects the one who hoards it, but it increases and enriches its distributor when it is given away. For love of God, dispense these riches to whoever asks for them, and do not turn from those who would borrow from you. Do not refrain from teaching others, for what you give to others in instruction will be repaid with high interest by God.* Both kinds of wealth, material and spiritual, must be given away—the material without interest, the spiritual with interest.

**Zachary 1.31 approx; PL 186:134CD*

Then follows this admonition, *"And of him that takes away your goods* of money or anything else, *do not ask to get them back* by contentious lawsuits in court."* It is not permitted to demand something back by litiga-

*Luke 6:30

tion when this is prompted by anger and inner turmoil or from inordinate desire, rather than for the improvement of the offending parties or to curb their avarice, in which case their loss benefits them.

Love of Enemies

*Having said that we should offer no resistance to those who harm us, but on the contrary be prepared to accept even greater injuries, Christ now exhorts us to have a heartfelt charity that expresses itself in deeds. The works of justice are fruitless without charity, so he adds a word about perfect charity. He presents a correct interpretation of the precept to love our neighbor, about which his contemporaries held erroneous views. It says in the law, *Thou shalt love thy neighbor/friend as thyself.*[2]* From this teaching they drew the conclusion that if they should love their friends, they ought to hate their enemies. But this is not true: every human being should be loved in charity because he or she is made in God's image and has the capacity to know and love God.* ***R 8**

*Lev 19:18

**Lyra Matt 5:43*

So Jesus says, "*You have heard that it has been said* ***in the law,**** '*Thou shalt love thy neighbor* with your heart, a commandment binding on everyone, and in your actions, which is true for the perfect, as occasion allows; *and hate thy enemy.*' "* The commandment to hate your enemy is not written in the law itself but was a tradition handed down by the scribes in their other writings. According to Augustine, this precept should not be understood as a commandment given to a righteous person, but as a concession made to a weak one.*

*Latin Diatessaron?

*Matt 5:43

*Sermone monte 1.21.70; PL 34:1265; CL 35:79

[2] The Vulg has *friend* (*amicum*) for the Leviticus passage and *neighbor* (*proximum*) for Christ's citation of it in Matthew. Several Latin fathers have *friend* in their version of the gospel, and it has been suggested that this goes back to the Latin translation of Tatian's *Diatessaron*; *neighbor* and *friend* are equivalent in Syriac.

*Matt 5:44
*Bruno, Com Matt 5:44; PL 165:110B
*Prosper 2; PL 45:1859

Christ goes on, *"But I say to you, 'Love your enemies** with goodwill: love sinners, but not their sins; their nature, not their faults.' "* Augustine teaches us to love other people, but not their errors.* We should love our enemies by wanting them to receive the goods of grace and glory, because a person cannot misuse these. As to goods of nature or fortune, we should not wish them to have these, except in a very general way and only to the extent that they contribute to their salvation. Temporal blessings can be used well or sinfully, and only God knows the use to which an individual will put them, so it is better not to make specific petitions about such matters.* Note that we have even greater cause to love our friends, and the Lord will see to it that such love does not go unrewarded. However, all things being equal, love of enemies is more meritorious: such love is more difficult, because it demands more good will; it is more selfless, because it is relies on grace rather than on our natural inclination; it is more generous, because it is not based on the pre-existing merits of the recipient.*

*Lyra Matt 5:44
*Gorran Matt 6:3

***R 9**

*It is not enough to love in our hearts: we must demonstrate this love in action when circumstances allow. Accordingly Jesus adds, "*Do good to them that hate you** in what pertains to their salvation, assisting them to attain these blessings whenever possible, because doing good in this way is a sure sign of love." If we desire the good of our enemies as regards grace and glory, then we must contribute to their salvation by what we do.* All of us must love our enemies in a general way inasmuch as they share our human nature, and the commandment is, *love thy neighbor*, but to love our enemies with a special affection is not a commandment, it is a counsel of perfection.

*Matt 5:44
*Lyra Matt 5:44

We are not commanded to love everyone with a special affection, because this is not possible; similarly, we are not commanded to lavish special affection on an enemy, but simply to have the love that springs from our common humanity. Exterior benefits are proportionate to interior charity: therefore, we are all obligated not to exclude our enemies from the good we do for the community at large or the prayers we offer for all people. To exclude them would be an expression of hate, not love. Similarly, we all have a responsibility as human beings to help others in an emergency, and this holds true for our enemies, too (provided that this does not worsen the situation or attack the faith). But we are not required apart from such circumstances to offer signs of special affection to our enemies; this is a counsel for those seeking perfection.

Charity is both interior and exterior. The inner charity sufficient for salvation, which even the imperfect can attain, is to love our enemies; exterior manifestations of love for our enemies, such as going out of our way to do them a good turn, is required only of those who are striving for perfection. Even imperfect Christians must root out rancor towards enemies and wish them well whether they ask for this or not. And we must be willing to greet them and speak with them should they request it; however, we are not bound to lavish temporal blessings upon a foe. But those who seek to be perfect must also do good to their enemies and serve their needs, whether or not they ask.

If we find it necessary to exclude enemies from our company, this must also be done for their benefit: the purpose should be to call them back from their sinful ways. We read in the Gloss, "Do good by providing nourishment to the soul, that is, by instruction and corporal punishment. All such discipline in the church, even excommunication, is aimed at making people into friends and kin."*

*Gloss Matt 5:44; PL 114:97D

There is a certain kind of service that even a poor person can provide for the spiritual benefit of others, and that is to pray for the salvation of their souls. Accordingly the Lord adds, "*Bless them,* that is, call down the goods of grace and glory on them *that curse you* either openly or behind your back, *and pray for them*

*Luke 6:28

*that calumniate you** by accusing you falsely of wrong-doing." The Lord himself exemplified this on the cross, as did Stephen when he was being stoned and David when Shimei cursed him.*

**last sentence: Gorran Luke 6:28*

Here we should note that injuries can be inflicted in three ways: in the heart, by harboring rancor and hatred; in the mouth, by detraction or cursing; and in action, by physical violence. The Lord offers a remedy for each: against the first, *Love your enemies*; against the second, *Bless them that curse you and pray for them that calumniate you*; against the third, *Do good to them that hate you.** The Gloss says, "The church is attacked in three ways: hatred, wicked speech, and actual persecution. And she opposes these by loving, praying, and doing good."* Therefore, if we wish to be perfect we should do good to those who injure us by loving them in our hearts, praying for them with our lips, and performing works of mercy for them with our hands.

**Gorran Matt 5:44*

*Gloss Matt 5:44; PL 114:97D

***R 10**

*Christ gives a challenging commandment, but he promises a great reward. He says, "Love your enemies, pray for them, and do good to them, *that you may be the children of your Father* most high *who is in heaven.** You are his sons and daughters by the imitation of his goodness, by the grace of adoption, and by the training that leads to your inheritance. As you are God's children through creation and nature, so may you be by grace and the imitation of his most characteristic trait, which is to be merciful." Bede writes, "There can be no greater reward for those born of earthly parents than that they should become children of the Most High *who is in heaven*. We receive the power to become God's children to the extent that we do what he commands."*

*Matt 5:45

*Com Luke 6:35; PL 92:408A; CL 120:146

The Lord adds, "*who makes his sun to rise upon the good and bad, and rains upon the just and the unjust,** on the grateful and ungrateful, doing good to enemies as well as friends." God cares for his enemies as well as his friends, sending sunshine and life-giving rain

*Matt 5:45

upon them both. He does not withhold his common largesse from the wicked, although they are his enemies, but bestows the blessings of this life indiscriminately upon everyone. Jerome expresses it nicely: "Do not deny what God denies to no one,* even the impious blasphemer.* Let us give to everyone without distinction, not asking to whom we are giving, but why."*

Noli negare quod Deus nulli negat

*Com Rom 12:20; PL 30:703D

*Com 2 Cor 9:11; PL 30:796B

As was stated previously, all are bound by the precept to include their enemies in the prayers and good wishes they offer for the community in general; however, to do good for them especially is not a commandment but a counsel of perfection. Chrysostom lays down nine steps to be mounted in fulfilling this counsel:

> You have seen the steps the Lord climbed toward perfection and how he established us on the pinnacle of truth, gradually leading us to the heavenly heights. The initial step is not to injure an enemy first; the second is not to seek vengeance greater than the injury received; the third is not to seek revenge at all; the fourth is to make yourself vulnerable to injuries; the fifth is to be disposed to receive even greater injuries than those inflicted; the sixth is not to hate the perpetrator; the seventh is to love the person who injures you; the eighth is to do good freely to your enemy; the ninth is to pray to God for your adversary. Here you can observe the height of philosophy. The prize is so remarkable because the commandment is so great.*

*Hom Matt 18 Anianus; Cratandri 1:100

Christ offers us a reward formerly unheard of: to become like God to the extent that our human nature allows. Let us then do good to everyone, for, as Seneca observes, no one has benefited the neighbor who has not also benefited himself.* There is no more perfect form of charity than love of one's enemies, so Christ adds, *Be therefore perfect, as also your heavenly Father is perfect*.* It is his commandment of love that we also

*Lucilium 81.19

*Matt 5:48

extend charity to our enemies; he who bestows his gifts even on the wicked invites us to follow his example. Chrysostom notes that children resemble or imitate their parents according to the flesh, so children should strive to resemble their heavenly Father by their holiness.* Nothing makes us more like God than to forgive those who hurt us and to pray for them.

*Opus imperf 13.45; PG 56:703

*R 11

*To illustrate his point Christ uses the example of tax collectors and pagans who love their friends and do good for them. If we want to receive the reward promised us, out of love for God we must do more than they do and extend charity to our enemies. He asks, *"For if you love those that love you, what reward shall you have** for this from God in eternal life?" His implied answer is, "None." Of such people it could be said: *They have received their reward.** This kind of love is merely natural; it is not meritorious because it does not proceed from charity, which embraces all people. We should carry out the latter without omitting the former. To love those who love you is natural; to love those who do not love you is grace; not to love those who love you is a great perversity; not to love those who do not love you is a human imperfection.*

*Matt 5:46

*Matt 6:16

**last sentence: Gorran Matt 5:46*

"And if you salute your brethren only, desiring their salvation and showing them love and affection simply because they are related to you, *what more are you doing* to reach perfection? *And if you do good to those who do good to you,* which is only natural in light of what they have done for you, *what thanks* are due to you,* that is, what merit of grace is there in that before God?"* Again, the answer is, "None." He drives his point home: *"Do not even the publicans and heathens do this?"** (*Publicans* were tax collectors, who took their name from one Publius; *heathens* refers to the Gentiles, who lived in sin.) *"And if you lend to those from whom you hope to receive, what thanks are due to you** before God?" Yet again, "None."

**gratia*

*Matt 5:47; Luke 6:33

*Matt 5:46-47

*Luke 6:34

It says in the Gloss, "You do not give for God if you give only to get."* Those who lend in the hope of

*Gloss Luke 6:34 approx; PL 114:264B

human recompense *have received their reward.* "*For sinners* who do not possess God's grace *also lend to sinners, in order to receive as much** without interest." This suggests that those who lend money at interest are worse than sinners. Bede asks, "If people like these, guided only by nature, know how to be generous, how much greater is your obligation to be even more generous because of your Christian profession and to extend your charity to those who hate you?"* Chrysostom asks, "What punishment will we deserve, we who are commanded to shape our lives according to God and are not even on a par with the pagans?"* And elsewhere he says,

*Luke 6:34

*Com Luke 6:34; PL 92:407A; CL 120:145

*Ps-Chrysostom, Hom Matt 18.6; Caillau Chrys 5:486

> Should we not grieve and beat our breast if we cannot do better than tax collectors and pagans in this regard? Far from loving our enemies, we do not even show charity to our friends; on the contrary, we hate those who love us. In this, we are not like the tax collectors and pagans—we are far beneath them! Christ not only wants us to forgive our enemies but also to love them and pray for them. Perhaps you do not hurt those who have injured you, but you avoid them and will not speak with them. Without doubt, this shows that you still nurse your wound and that resentment is growing in your heart. Suppose God were to treat you in this way: not doing you harm, but turning away from you, clinging to the recollection of your sins, and not wishing to see you? If you want God to be gracious to you and forgive your failings when you ask, act in the same way toward those who have offended you.*

*Compunctione 1.4–5; PG 47:400

*Such actions can be the fruit of natural affection, caused by motives that are honest, useful, or attractive, grounded in the ethics of friendship; however, these cannot merit eternal life. But when they are prompted by habitual charity, then they are the source of merit with God, because it is charity that distinguishes the ***R 12** children of his kingdom from the children of perdition. To love on the basis of reciprocal affection is natural; to love on the basis of a benefit hoped for or received is mercenary; to love on the basis of mutual lust is wicked; to love on the basis of consensual sin is malicious; to love on the basis of a good turn is gratuitous. But if you love your neighbors because they are good, or so that they might become good, or because you and they are members of the Body of Christ and children of the same heavenly Father—that can truly be called love. This kind of love is spiritual and thus is unfailing; carnal love withers away, as does the body itself.

Tax collectors and pagans love one another, but such love is shaped by nature alone, not grace: they love those who love them, and as soon as they realize that others do not love them, they do not love them either. But we should love everyone without exception, desire the salvation of all, do good to all; we should show charity to all, not seeking to know for whom we express charity, but why. In this way love and harmony increase.

We should seek our recompense, not from one another but from God. Just as God is the origin of all good, so he also desires to be its goal. As he says, *I am Alpha and Omega, the Beginning and the End.**

*Rev 21:6; *Gorran Luke 6:34*

Hence Augustine writes, "Someone who loves a friend for profit is guilty of loving the profit, not the friend. Therefore God, than whom nothing is greater or better, should be loved for himself and is loved perfectly when loved for himself. But if he is loved because of what he bestows, then he is not loved freely: the benefit for which he is loved is impiously preferred to him."* And elsewhere, "Let us love God for his own sake and not for the rewards he gives to those who serve him. Out of love for Jesus we should be seeking nothing other than his sweet presence."* And Bernard writes, "Love for God never goes

*Pomerius, Vita Contemplativa 3.25; PL 59:508A

*Tr John 51.11 approx; PL 35:1767; CL 36:443–44

unrewarded, although he should be loved without thought of reward. Genuine lovers do not seek a reward, but they merit it."*

*De diligendo 7.17; PL 182:984C; SB 3:133–34

Concluding Exhortation

*Let us love our enemies and do good to them, so that we might *be perfect* in the way we can be, by the perfection of grace, as our *heavenly Father is perfect* by the perfection of nature. The perfect Lord desires servants who are good and perfect. Let us at least attain the sufficient perfection of charity toward God and neighbor, and strive for the more perfect summit of generosity by loving our enemies and praying for them, as Christ did. Chrysostom says, ***R 13**

> Not only are we not harmed when our enemies hurt us, but we also benefit because the constancy of our goodness does not retreat before their wicked intentions.* Therefore, do not hate those who harm you and do not revile the troublesome—rather, love them all the more, as if they were so many good counselors who are leading you to greater honors. Otherwise you will lose the fruit of your labors, you will pay the price but forfeit the reward. It is the height of insanity to endure great trials but refuse to put up with minor ones.
>
> Perhaps you ask, "How can I do this?" I answer: You have seen God become Man! He came down for your salvation and endured great suffering for your sake. And still you ask and wonder how you can forgive the injuries of your fellow servants? But you have done more harm than they have! How do your sufferings compare with those endured by the Lord of all? However seriously you have been offended, to that extent return a blessing: you will be forging a more glorious crown for yourself and releasing your neighbor from a very severe punishment.*

*Opus imperf 24.17; PG 56:758

*Ps-Chrysostom, Matt Hom 18.4; Caillau Chrys 5:482–83

Lord Jesus Christ, so very meek and the teacher of humility and patience, grant to me, the least and simplest of your servants, that I may desire to be disregarded and despised by everyone. By bearing patiently with physical and temporal injuries may my soul be prepared to accept even more, and to the best of my ability may I come to the spiritual and material aid of those who ask my help. Grant also that I may love my enemies as well as my friends in my heart and by my words and deeds. May I love those who persecute me, speaking well of them, doing good for them, and praying for them, so that by your grace I may deserve to be numbered among your chosen sons and daughters. Amen.

CHAPTER 36

The Sermon on the Mount, Continued: Do Not Seek Human Praise for Good Works

(Matt 6:1-8, 16-18)

*After instructing his hearers about the great way of perfection, the Lord cautions them not to brag foolishly about their good deeds; for indeed it is very difficult to avoid vainglory completely. He says, "*Take heed that you do not your justice*, that is to say, works of justice and all good deeds, *before men, to be seen by them; otherwise you shall not have a reward from your Father who is in heaven*."* In other words, "You must be extremely vigilant and on guard to avoid the trap of pride, because this vice can seep even into your good works and poison them. Do not perform good works to impress others or to make a name for yourself, but to glorify God and help your neighbor; otherwise you shall not have a reward from God, because you have not acted from love of him." ***R 1**

*Matt 6:1

God rewards only the worker whose incentive is love or obedience to his command. If God is not our sole motivation, we are playing false by expecting recompense from him: we have sought to receive favor from other people and our reward will be but the light breath of human adulation. We find our reward where we seek it. If our intention is to be rewarded by other people, it is unjust to expect anything from God: he rewards not our works, but the purpose for our works.

People are compensated by the love that prompted them to act; if the desire is for human approval, so also is the reward. What is worse, our faulty intention not only deprives us of our true reward; it also paves the way for vainglory, which will always precede or follow such actions—and, since this is a mortal sin, its reward is eternal punishment. The hunger for human applause also dulls conscience. Boethius says, "Every time we receive the recompense of fame when we advertise our good works, we diminish in some degree the secret reward of a good conscience."* And elsewhere, "Wise people measure their good not by popular repute but by the truth of inner conviction."*

*Cons I Prosa 4; PL 63:627A; CL 94:10

*Cons III Prosa 6; PL 63:745A; CL 94:46

We should also consider, Chrysostom suggests, that the Lord commands us not only not to advertise our good works, but even to conceal them; there is a difference between not seeking publicity and making an effort to conceal.* Naturally this does not prohibit us from doing good in the sight of others for God's glory and the edification of our neighbor, for this is good and meritorious in God's eyes.* Gregory, however, observes that although those who are well advanced can seek their Maker's glory by letting their works be shown and will not congratulate themselves privately when others praise them, those who are weaker cannot avoid vainglory, and so they should keep hidden the good they do.*

*Hom Matt 19:4; PG 57/58:276

*Lyra Matt 6:1

*Mor 8.XLVIII.84; PL 75:853D; CL 143:448

Almsgiving

*R 2

Having spoken of justice in general terms, the Lord goes on to speak of its constituent elements and to caution against boasting in connection with almsgiving, prayer, and fasting, because vainglory often attends these three activities. These are three works of satisfaction: in almsgiving we make amends for sins against our neighbor, in prayer for sins against God, and in fasting for sins against ourselves. They are also powerful bulwarks against the three roots of sin, which draw their nourishment from the three evils that exist in the world: almsgiving as an act of justice counteracts the concupiscence of the eyes, prayer opposes the pride of life, and fasting reins in the concupiscence of the flesh. **Gorran Matt 6:1*

*So Jesus says, "*Therefore when you give alms*, either bodily or spiritual, *do not sound a trumpet before you, as the hypocrites do.*"* That is, do not be conspicuous or seek to draw attention to yourself in order to win praise. The visible act itself is not what displeases God, but doing it in such a way that others will be sure to see it. Those who are intent on fleeting marks of esteem thereby forsake the honor that is true and eternal. And so Jesus adds, "*Amen I say to you, they have received their reward*,* human praise, which was the aim of their almsgiving—but they can look forward to the punishment due to their wicked intention." ***R 3** *Matt 6:2 *Matt 6:2

"*But when you give alms*, or indeed perform any work of mercy, *let not your* perverse *left hand know what your* holy *right hand is doing*."* The left signifies the hunger for human acclaim or worldly advantage; the right signifies the desire to fulfill the divine precepts, love God, or receive a heavenly recompense. The sense of this is: do not mingle evil intentions with good when you fulfill God's precepts.* *Matt 6:3 **Zachary 1.33 approx; PL 186:137D*

What is hidden is not known, and he clarifies that this is what he means by your left hand *not knowing*: "*That your alms may be in secret*."* Even if what you do is not *in secret*, your intention for doing it should be; let this remain hidden in your mind. A good conscience cannot be manifest to human eyes; it should be enough for you that the one who can look into the conscience gives a reward.* *Matt 6:4 **Sermone monte 2.2.9; PL 34:1274; CL 35:100*

Hence he continues, "*And your Father*, that is, God, who is the Father of everyone by creation and of the just by the grace of adoption, *who sees in secret will*

*Matt 6:4

*repay you."** He who alone can read the human heart will reward good people according to the secret intentions of their hearts, either here or hereafter. We should not be concerned whether or not others see the good we do, but let us examine ourselves to make sure that we are not acting to win human applause.

In all our deeds, the left hand will not know what the right is doing if we do what we do for love of God and justice, and not for admiration. When giving alms or doing any other good deed in the synagogues, or in the streets and squares, you act secretly if your wish is that your action will be seen by God and not by other people. On the other hand, even if you perform a good deed in secret, if your wish is that people will notice it and praise you, it is as if you ostentatiously performed it in public. Chrysostom teaches, "One person might give alms in the presence of others but is not doing it to be seen. Another gives alms secretly but hopes that the largesse will become known. God rewards or punishes the desire, not the deed; the recompense, good or bad, depends on the motivation of the donor, not the gift itself. Virtue consists not in the alms alone, but in the intention for which they are given."*

*Hom Matt 19.2; PG 57/58:275

Prayer

***R 4**

Similarly Christ teaches us to shun vainglory in prayer, warning us against praying in public to attract attention. This is to act like hypocrites who, according to Chrysostom, want not to be heard, but seen. Because their intention is skewed, condemnation follows: *they have received their reward*,* the reward of momentary praise, but at the end they shall receive eternal punishment. From this we can draw an important lesson: since vainglory is a mortal sin, any deeds done out of vainglory are also mortal sins, deserving

*Attr. to Chrysostom, St Cher Matt 6:5

*Matt 6:5

of eternal punishment.[1] This is how hypocrites act. *"But when you pray, enter into your chamber* or hidden place, *and having shut the door* so that people will not interrupt the lifting of your mind to God and distract you from your purpose, *pray to your heavenly Father in secret."** According to Remigius, the meaning of this is: It should be enough for you that he who alone can read the human heart knows your prayer, for he who sees will listen.*

*Matt 6:6

*CA Matt 6:5-6

"And your Father, whom you seek to honor and *who sees in secret, will repay you** the reward for your prayer openly." Chrysostom says, "Those who pray in secret so that people will see that they are praying in secret do not look at God but at the people. And those who intend to pray sincerely in the synagogue are deserving of double praise because they pray, and they pray in secret. If they have their eyes on God alone when praying, even though they are praying in the synagogue they seem to pray secretly all by themselves. Moreover, such people do nothing novel, or cry out, or beat their breast, or stretch out their hands to attract attention to themselves."*

*Matt 6:6

*Opus imperf 19; PG 56:709

It should be understood that there are two kinds of prayer. Liturgical prayer is offered by the ministers of the church, and this prayer should be made publicly in church in the presence of the people because it is offered for the whole community. The people should also enter into this prayer, entreating God in a way proper to them. Private prayer should be offered in secret for two reasons: first, because prayer is the mind's elevation to God, and the mind can be raised to God more quickly and effectively when a person is in a place apart, removed from distractions; second, to

[1] *Vana gloria* is one of the traditional capital vices, and was listed first by Thomas Aquinas and Bonaventure. Following Augustine's lead, medieval writers abhorred vainglory because it corrupted even charitable works or service to God.

avoid vainglory, which can be aroused in a public setting.* Christ gives the sound advice that when we want to pray we should go into our room, the secret chamber of the heart, and close the door of our bodily senses, through which external distractions shamelessly intrude and disturbing images create a cacophony. With the mind's door closed, we should concentrate the powers of our soul and speak from the depths of our heart, offering fervent prayer to our Father in secret.* The more we disregard what is outside us, the more we can marshal our energies within; the more recollected we become interiorly, the easier it is to ascend to God in contemplative prayer.

**Lyra Matt 6:6*

**Zachary 1.34 approx; PL 186:138B*

In the matter of prayer, Jesus corrects an error made by pagans: *"And when you are praying, do not speak much, as the heathens do. For they think that in their much speaking*, and lofty speaking, and sweetly speaking, *they may be heard*. They think that by their words they can win God over, like an orator persuading a judge. But *your Father knows what is needful for you, before you ask him*,* for he reads the dispositions of every heart." He added these final words to remove a false impression held by these pagans, that God needed to be informed of things afresh; he knows everything from all eternity.

*Matt 6:7-8

The Lord is not prohibiting the multiplication of words in prayer *tout court*, because he himself spent whole nights in prayer, and, *being in an agony, he prayed the longer*.* Rather, he forbids us to use a multitude of words in our prayer for the reasons the idolatrous pagans did.* These were three: first, they were praying to demons, who would not know what they were asking for unless they were informed by external words and gestures, for they cannot penetrate the secrets of the human heart; second, they imagined that these demons were like human beings, and could be won over by a torrent of words and persuasive suggestions, and so they used many words to excite their pity; third, because they thought that the demons to whom

*Luke 22:43

**Lyra Matt 6:7*

they were praying were absent, and could be summoned by such prayers. Such notions are wicked and have no place in the prayers of believers.

Similarly, there are three reasons that we should make vocal prayers. First, so that we can serve God with our lips as well as with our heart and our hands; for we should offer to God the threefold sacrifice of voice, heart, and actions. Second, to remember what it is we are asking for, and to rouse our lazy nature by means of vocal prayer; if we were to pray only silently, we could easily fall asleep and forget what we are begging for. Third, so that by means of vocal prayer we can instruct our neighbor and encourage him to pray, too. God wants us to pray so that we will not take for granted what he gives us; but also so that we will adore him, and desire him more, and so deserve to receive more from him.

Nor is it a waste of breath to pray to one who already knows what we need, for, as Jerome observes, in prayer we are not narrators, but beggars: it is one thing to report to one who is ignorant, and a different thing to make a request of one who knows.* Chrysostom says we should pray, not to instruct God, but to prevail with him, to grow more intimate with him by continued supplication, and to be humbled by the remembrance of our sins.*

*Com Matt 6:8; PL 26:42C; CL 77:36

*Hom Matt 19.4; PG 57/58:278

Note, too, that it is possible to use many words in prayer, and by means of these devout expressions the soul lifts itself up to God more effectively. And not the soul only; a person's body can also be raised up by vocal prayer, as we read: *My heart and my flesh have rejoiced in the living God.**

*Ps 83:3; *Lyra Matt 6:7*

There is no hard and fast rule in this matter. If you find that using vocal prayers stirs up feelings of devotion, use them. If, on the other hand, you find that they are a distraction because a multitude of words hinders devotion, then stop speaking and pray to God with your heart's affection.* According to Augustine, "When we pray to God, we need piety more than

**Lyra Matt 6:7*

prattling; lengthy talk is very different from lasting affection. The business of prayer consists more in groaning than in speaking and is expressed more with tears than with words."* What is said here pertains to private, voluntary prayers; obligatory public prayers should be said aloud so that others can hear them.

*Ep 130.10.19, 20; PL 33:501; CL 31B:226–27

Fasting

*R 5

*The Lord then instructs us to avoid hypocrisy in the matter of fasting: *"And when you fast*, as is necessary at certain times, *be not as the hypocrites, sad."** When he says *be not*, Christ does not forbid us to be sad; he forbids us from wanting to be sad, for the root of reward and punishment is found in the will.* According to Chrysostom, the Lord knows that someone may feel unhappy, so he does not say, "Do not be sad," but, "Do not become sad." It is one thing to be dismal, and another to become dismal. A person who is fasting rigorously naturally feels sadness, while someone who appears pale through some ruse is not sad, but merely looks sad.*

*Matt 6:16

**St Cher Matt 6:16*

*Opus imperf 15; PG 56:716–17

Such people are *as hypocrites*, because their sorrowful demeanor displays a false and empty fast. *For they disfigure** *their faces* by distorting them beyond all bounds, and their bodies with clothing covered with filth, *that they may be seen to be fasting*.[2]* They are

**exterminant*

*Matt 6:16

[2] "Distorting them beyond all bounds" is an attempt to capture something of Ludolph's interpretation of *exterminant*: *"quasi extra proprios terminos ponunt et adducunt."* In *Com Matt 6:16* (PL 26:44A), Jerome writes: "The word *exterminant*, which is common in the church's Scriptures, by a fault of the translators, signifies something far different from what is commonly understood. For exiles are banished who are sent beyond the borders (*extra terminos*). Therefore, in place of this word, we ought always to use *demoliuntur* (they disfigure)."

always moping about, bewailing the sins of others, exhibiting by their sorrowful expression and singular appearance a pretense of penitential rigor. They seem to be more religious than everyone else, and for this they are praised by others.

O, what insane vanity! They do not want to be in truth what they appear to be!* For this reason, the Lord threatens them with no slight punishment: "*Amen* (that is, *in truth*) *I say to you, they have received their reward*,* the human praise for which they long; but in the future they will be condemned for their pretense, which they do not fear." He expressly states *they have received*, not *they are receiving*: so brief is human praise, it is as if it has already slipped away. As we read in the book of Job, *The praise of the wicked is short, and the joy of the hypocrite but for a moment*.* The Lord does not forbid the true sadness of repentance for sin, but the counterfeit sadness that aims at gaining praise. Similarly, he does not forbid a fasting person to be seen, but he does forbid a person from wanting to be seen fasting. The Lord does not prohibit virtue; he condemns deceit. Chrysostom asks, "If those who fast and make themselves look sad are hypocrites, how much more reprehensible are those who give their face a cosmetic pallor by some kind of trick to feign fasting?"*

Ps-Chrysostom, Opus imperf 13; PG 56:709

*Matt 6:16

*Job 20:5

*Opus imperf 15; PG 56:717

Christ then goes on to explain how a fast should be undertaken: "*But when you fast*, do not imitate the hypocrites, but *anoint your head, and wash your face*."* It would be absurd to interpret this to mean literally pouring oil on our heads. Jerome proposes the text be read metaphorically: in Palestine it was customary for people to anoint their heads on feast days; so when we fast, we should show ourselves to be joyful and festive.*

*Matt 6:17

*Com Matt 6:17; PL 26:44B; CL 77:38

Thus: *anoint your head* by appearing joyful, and *wash your face* literally so that it is clean. Jesus counteracts the sadness of hypocrites with the oil of gladness, and the disfigurement of their faces with the water of cleansing.*

**Gorran Matt 6:17*

Or Jesus is referring to the two elements of righteousness. First, *wash your* inward *face*, your conscience, clean of evil by confession, so that it is unsoiled in God's sight. Just as people find a clean face pleasing, so a pure conscience is precious in God's eyes. Then, *anoint your head*, that is, the mind or reason (which is the pre-eminent part of your soul, guiding thoughts and everything else in a person) with the glad oil of devotion, so that while fasting you can show God a joyful countenance. Spiritual joy is essential to fasting, as it is to almsgiving: just as *God loves a cheerful giver*,* so he loves a cheerful faster.

*2 Cor 9:7

Augustine writes, "This precept must be understood as referring to the inner self. To anoint the head pertains to joy, to wash the face pertains to cleanness. Those who rejoice inwardly in their mind or reason anoint their heads; they do not seek their joy in external things by basking in human praise. They wash their faces in the same way, cleansing their hearts so they can see God, with no veil intervening on account of a weakness contracted from uncleanness."*

*Sermone monte 2.12.41; PL 34:1287; CL 35:132

Or according to Chrysostom, *anoint your head*, Christ, with the oil of mercy by welcoming the poor; *wash your face*, that is, your intention, by doing this for God.*

*Opus imperf 15 approx; PG 56:718

And, to remove all perverse motives, Christ adds, "*So that you will not appear to men to be fasting* and in this way seek glory from them, *but to your heavenly Father*, whose glory alone you should seek in your works, *who is in secret*."* He *is in* the *secret* depths of the heart, for he is *the searcher of hearts and reins*.* Or his reward *is in secret*, either because he hides it for those who fear him or because God cannot be seen in this present life although he is everywhere.

*Matt 6:18

*Ps 7:10

"*And your Father*, who never forgets his children and *who sees in secret*, approving your **hidden and** proper intentions, *will repay you* **a reward*** for this kind of

*Matt 6:18; Latin Diatessaron?

fasting." Truly, *God rewards the labors of his holy ones*.* Remigius suggests that it is enough for you that the one who sees your conscience should be your rewarder.* Listen to what Augustine has to say about the efficacy of fasting: "Fasting purifies the mind, sharpens perception, subjects the flesh to the spirit, makes the heart contrite and humble, dispels the mists of desire, extinguishes lust, and kindles the flame of charity."* He also urges that particular attention be paid to the fact that we can fall into the sin of vainglory not only when surrounded by splendor and pomp, but also in filthy sackcloth. This is more dangerous because it masquerades as service to God; the deception is revealed by the rest of our behavior.* The Christian should steer a middle course between splendor and squalor.

*Responsory based on Wis 10:17

*CA Matt 6:17–18

*Chrysologus? *Sermo* 6; PL 52:678C

*Sermone monte 2.12.41; PL 34:1287; CL 35:131–32

Conclusion

From what has been said it is clear that we should strive to be virtuous for God's sake and our own, and not on account of other people. Chrysostom says, "There is no small profit to be had in disregarding human praise, for this frees us from an onerous servitude. We become true doers of virtue who love it for itself and not for the sake of others."

***R 6**

*Hom Matt 20.4; PG 57/58:288

Notice that our Lord joins almsgiving and fasting to prayer: prayer is like a small bird that soars to heaven on the two wings of almsgiving and fasting. He speaks first of almsgiving and last of fasting, with prayer between them; prayer is, as it were, borne aloft by the wings on either side, reaching heavenward and flying up to God himself.* It says in the book of Tobit, *Prayer is good with fasting and alms*.* In all our works, then, let us flee from human praise, for, as Boethius teaches, "Wise people estimate their goodness from the truth of conscience, not popular opinion."*

**Massa*

*Tob 12:8

*Cons III Prosa 6; PL 63:745A; CL 94:46

We should avoid human applause for our rest as well as for our works. Here is the counsel of Seneca:

> Retire and conceal yourself in repose. There is no need to call what you are doing philosophy. Give your purpose some other name; call it ill-health, or bodily weakness, or laziness. To boast of retirement is self-seeking. Certain animals hide themselves from discovery by confusing the footprints around their lairs. You should do the same, or you will be plagued with visitors. It is best not to vaunt your seclusion. "That one has hidden himself"; "That one has locked herself up"; "That other one has not crossed the threshold of his house for years"—to advertise your retirement is to draw a crowd. When you withdraw from the world, your business is to talk with yourself, not to have people talk about you.
>
> But what shall you talk about? I am trying to cure my own sores. If I were to show you a swollen foot, or an inflamed hand, or some shriveled sinews in a withered leg, you would allow me to lie quietly in one place and treat the diseased member. But my trouble is greater than any of these, and I cannot show it to you. Do not praise me, do not say, "What a great person! You have learned to despise all things; condemning the madness of human life, you have made your escape!"
>
> I have condemned nothing except myself. You are mistaken if you think that you will get any help from this quarter: it is not a physician living here, but a patient. I would rather have you say when you leave, "I used to think he was fortunate and learned. I pricked up my ears to listen to him, but I was misled. I have seen nothing, heard nothing that I desired, or that I would come back to hear." If you feel thus, and speak thus, some progress has been made. I prefer you to pardon rather than to envy my retirement.*

*Lucilium 68.1–8

✠

Lord Jesus Christ, in all your works you have shown us a model of humility and you have taught us to flee from vainglory. Guard me, I beseech you, within and without against the snares of pride so that there may be no opening available to the enemy of my soul. Grant that in almsgiving, prayer, and fasting, and in all good works, I may seek solely God's glory and my neighbor's good and not human praise and the world's favor. May I never foolishly take pride in them lest, having received my reward here, I deserve to be deprived of my true reward and consigned to eternal perdition. Amen.

CHAPTER 37

The Sermon on the Mount, Continued: The Lord's Prayer

(Matt 6:9-15; Luke 11:2-4)

*R 1

The Lord's Prayer is included in what Christ said about prayer in the Sermon on the Mount because it excels all other prayers for many reasons: by virtue of the authority of its source, for it was spoken by the mouth of the Savior himself; by virtue of its brevity, for it is easy to learn and to say; by virtue of the adequacy of its petitions, for it contains all that is needful in life; and by virtue of the profundity of its meaning, for it enshrines an immense number of mysteries.

**Durandus, 4.47.4 approx; CM 140:506*

Chrysostom writes,

> The Lord gave to his disciples a brief formula of prayer containing a full summary of everything we should ask for to attain blessedness and all other gifts both here and hereafter. It is a short set of words, but it embraces all that is most spiritual and holy that we should seek, both because it comes from the mouth of the Most High and because it includes all the petitions found in every other prayer. O, how trustworthy and blessed this prayer is to us, for it was set down in order for us by the Doctor of life and heavenly Teacher! And how blessed we will be if we are not content merely to recite the Lord's Prayer, but put it into practice very faithfully! The Lord taught this prayer to his disciples to offer the hope of salvation to humanity.

All that is necessary for our salvation is found in the few words of the Lord's Prayer.* *Chromatius 14.1 partial; PL 20:359

Regarding the sufficiency of this prayer, Augustine for his part says, "Whatever other words we may say, if we pray rightly and as becomes our desires, we say nothing but what is already contained in the Lord's Prayer. If you study the words of all holy prayers you will find nothing that is not found in the Lord's Prayer. Whoever prays anything not found in this gospel prayer is praying in a carnal way, and I do not know how such prayer can be legitimate, because the Lord instructed those who were reborn to pray only spiritually."* Cyprian holds that by his teaching Christ condensed all our prayer into the one saving sentence of the Lord's Prayer.‡ *Ep 130.12.22; PL 33:502; CL 31B:228–29 ‡Orat Dom 28; PL 4:588A

There are seven reasons that this prayer is so brief and consists of only a few words: first, so that it can be learned very quickly; second, so that it can be retained very readily; third, so that no one could claim he did not know it; fourth, so that it can be said very frequently; fifth, so that reciting it would not be tiresome; sixth, so that we may believe that what is asked will be given quickly; seventh, to encourage a devout heart rather than a multiplicity of words.*[1] **Gorran Matt 6:1; Jordan, Exp Or Dom 3 lines 5–9*

The prayer contains seven petitions because the number seven signifies universality; everything that can reasonably be asked for is contained in these seven

[1] Ludolph draws extensively on the *Expositio Orationis Dominice* of Jordan of Quedlinburg. His citations will be given where possible, but at times he re-works the text considerably. The text, with English translation, has been published by Eric Leland Saak, *Catechesis in the Later Middle Ages I: The* Exposition of the Lord's Prayer *of Jordan of Quedlinburg, OESA (d. 1380)* (Leiden: Brill, 2014), and line numbers refer to that text. Saak offers a thorough presentation on the relationship between Jordan and Ludolph's works.

petitions. So it is fitting that the petitions should be organized into seven.*

*Exp Or Dom 3.26–28

Our Father

*R 2

*However, the Lord's Prayer has eight parts. The first part is a *captatio benevolentiae*, with the seven petitions following.* The introductory address seeks the good will of our hearer in three ways: first, on the part of those asking, because we call him *Father*, whose children we are by faith; second, on the part of the one addressed, because we say *our*, and he has been given to us in love; third, on the part of those we associate with our petition, the saints, because we say *who art in heaven*, thereby seeking their assistance in hope. So, we say *Father*, in whom we believe; *our*, whom we love; *who art in heaven*, from whom we hope; and these constitute the three proper motives for prayer—faith, love, and hope.

*Comestor, Hist ev 49; PL 198:1554C

We call the Lord *Our Father* for three reasons, based on the three gifts we have received from him: nature, grace, and glory. He gave us nature by creating us, grace by re-creating or redeeming us, glory by accompanying us to his kingdom.* He can be called *Father* by everyone by virtue of creation, but he is the Father of believers in a particular way by virtue of adoption. The title *Father* here should be understood to refer to the entire Trinity, Father, Son, and Holy Spirit.

*Exp Or Dom lines 94–96

O, with what faith and trusting audacity does the handiwork address its Maker, the creature its Creator, the human being his God and Father! Did anyone dare such presumption under the old law? No! According to the Gloss, in ancient times people used the title *Lord*, as servants; now we say *Father*, because we serve him in love rather than fear.* Augustine says, "Nowhere is a command given to the people of Israel to say *Our Father*; it was their custom to use the word *Lord*, as servants. But as those who have been made children

*Gloss Matt 6:9; PL 114:99D

by adoption through the blood of Christ, we can confidently cry out, '*Abba* Father.' "* And again,

*Sermone monte 2.16; PL 34:1276; CL 35:105–6; *Exp Or Dom lines 59–68*

> This name stirs up the ardor of love, for what should be dearer to children than their father? And a suppliant spirit, too, when we say *Our Father*, almost presuming that we will receive what we ask for. Indeed, what would he not give to the children who ask him, since he has already given them the great gift of their being his children? Last, what care must that soul take who says *Our Father*, not to be unworthy of such a Father! Here we need to caution the rich and those whom the world esteems as noble that when they have become Christians they are not to lord it over poor and lowly. They say *Our Father* together with them—and this they cannot do honestly and devoutly, unless they recognize that they are truly their brothers and sisters.*

*Sermone monte 2.4.16; PL 34:1276; CL 35:106–7

And Chrysostom exclaims,

> What great love the Lord has for us, how great his mercy and care, that he granted us the gift of such grace that we servants could freely dare to call the Lord God our Father! By this word he shows that we are not so much servants but sons and daughters of God. Having received the grace of such a gift, we must strive to behave as his children. Let us confirm what we say by our spiritual deeds; if we do not live as God's sons and daughters, we have usurped the title.
>
> He also instructs us to pray for our brothers and sisters: he did not say *my Father*, but *our Father*, so we should pray for the needs of the whole body, and everywhere prayers are to be offered not only for ourselves, but for our neighbors. This destroys enmity, checks pride, drives away envy; it brings in charity, the mother of all good things, utterly abolishes all distinction of persons, showing that the king and pauper enjoy equality of honor. We are all united in the great and necessary things

> pertaining to eternal life. God has conferred on us all the same identical nobility, when he allowed everyone to address him as Father.*

*Chromatius Matt 14.1 partial; PL 20:359

Here we are urged to foster fraternal love and unity: we are born of one heavenly Father by grace, and we are created and molded by this same supreme heavenly Father. We are formed from the same clay, so let none of us think more highly of ourselves, as if birth made one person more illustrious than another.

Who Art in Heaven

***R 3**
‡Matt 6:9

**Who art in heaven.*‡ *Heaven* signifies the saints and the just, who are God's temple, for God dwells in them as in a temple. It is true that God is in everyone by virtue of his divinity, but he is present in the just in a special way by virtue of indwelling grace,* and his presence shines out pre-eminently in the saints by virtue of his glory.* Augustine teaches, "The words *Our Father, who art in heaven* are rightly understood to mean *in the hearts of the just as his holy temple*. As we pray, we express as well the hope that he whom we invoke will dwell in us also. When this is our desire, we will cling to righteousness; by means of this duty, God is invited to make the soul his home."*

**inhabitantem gratiam*

**Zachary 1.34; PL 186:138D*

*Sermone monte 2.5.18; PL 34:1277; CL 35:108–9

Or, *who art in heaven* means *in your hidden majesty*, for this majesty is still concealed from us. As Isaiah says, *Truly you are a hidden God,** and these words encourage us to imitate the example of the saints and aim at living a hidden life. Or, *in heaven* can mean the direction where eternal blessedness lies. Fearing any delay in the earthly pilgrimage that separates us from our heavenly Father, we acknowledge that we seek to abide in that realm with him, and so we press on with all our strength toward our heavenly homeland. We are also admonished to refuse anything that will deprive us of our paternal inheritance.

*Isa 45:15

Now by saying *in heaven* we do not deny the truth that he is indeed present everywhere and in every place; but although he is everywhere in his essence, his presence, and his power, we pray *who art in heaven* to acknowledge that the heavenly Father desires to have heavenly sons and daughters. As Chrysostom notes, those who have a heavenly Father should blush to yield themselves to earthly things.* Also, by praying in this way we ask for heavenly things, and this leads us to ponder our heavenly inheritance as the sons and daughters of God.*

*Opus imperf 14; PG 56:711

**Exp Or Dom 2.74–77 approx*

Again, the power and virtue of the divine works shines forth more brightly *in heaven*, so God's power is thought to be there more than elsewhere—just as the soul is present in the whole body, but is thought to be more intensely concentrated in the heart, or, as others say, in the head, because its more noble operations seem to emanate from these two parts of the body.

Hallowed Be Thy Name

*Now let us consider what we long for. First of all we pray *hallowed be thy name*; that is, we ask that your name, always venerable and holy in itself, may be glorified, renowned, and sanctified in us. We pray that your name will appear as holy in our life and behavior: in our heart by belief and love, in our mouth by praise and proclamation, and in our works by a good life. So we are asking that it be hallowed, glorified, and magnified, not in itself but in us. ***R 4**

We do not ask that some new kind of holiness may accrue to God, for that is impossible, but that his eternal sanctity may shine out more brilliantly in creatures, and first and foremost in the works of human beings. As the apostle instructs, *Do all to the glory of God*.*

*1 Cor 10:31; *Lyra Matt 6:9*

Chrysostom says, "No more fitting prayer can be made by one who calls God Father than to beg first for him to be glorified. It is fitting that we should live in such purity that you are glorified through us in everything.* Whenever someone gazes upon the beauty of the heavens, he says, 'Glory to you, God.' In the same way, when he sees virtue in another person he glorifies God, for human virtue is much greater than the skies."*

*Hom Matt 19.4 approx; PG 57/58:279

*Hom 1 Cor 18.3; PG 61:148

Or, may *your name* by which you are called Father *be hallowed*, that is, confirmed in us through constancy and perseverance, lest we do anything inconsistent with the holiness of your name. Rather, may we manifest the Father's name by showing in our manner of living that we are his sons and daughters, so that we will never separate ourselves through sin from the gift of adoption and forfeit the grace of sonship. May we remain your children through grace and truly be your sons and daughters because you have deigned to be our Father.

Or may *your name*, that is, the knowledge of you, *be hallowed*, that is, confirmed in us through true faith. In that way you, O God, who are holy in yourself, may be revered as holy by human beings and be so renowned to them that they will consider nothing to be holier than you, whom they will greatly fear to offend and more diligently strive to honor.

Thy Kingdom Come

***R 5**

*The second petition follows: *thy kingdom come*, that is, may the kingdom of the church be revealed to humanity. In this way you who now reign, and have always reigned, on earth will be acknowledged as reigning by those who are ignorant of you. Although the kingdom of God has never been absent from the earth, it has seemed so to them, just as the light seems absent to those who are blind or shut their eyes.*

**last sentence: Zachary 1.34; PL 186:139B*

Or, *thy kingdom come*, that is, the kingdom of grace that reigns daily in the lives of the saints. This happens when, with vice extinguished and Satan's empire banished from our hearts, virtue is enkindled and you begin to reign in us. The devil, the world, and mundane attractions hold no sway, nor does any sin—you rule supreme without them.

Or, *thy kingdom come*, that is, the kingdom of glory, determined in advance for the perfect at the end of time, and promised generally to the sons and daughters of God. With these words let us stir up our desire for that future reign, so that it will come to us and in us and we will be found worthy to reign in it. It will definitely come, whether we want it to or not.* May it find us ready at its coming! **Zachary 1.34 approx; PL 186:139B*

Chrysostom writes, "This is what he finds most pleasing in his servants, that we be detached from present realities and put no store in what is seen, but rather press on toward the Father and aim always toward the future. This produces the best conscience, stripping the mind of all worldly preoccupations. Whoever is aflame with this love and cherishes this desire will neither be puffed up by prosperity and wealth nor crushed by humiliation and adversity. It is as if they are already dwelling in heaven, and neither circumstance will affect them."* And elsewhere, "It is a sign of great confidence and an untroubled conscience to wish boldly for the kingdom to come. And since we are always praying that the reign of God will come, we should show ourselves to be so faithful to God and his commandments that we will be found worthy of his coming kingdom."* **Hom Matt 20 Anianus; Cratandri 1:106* **Chromatius 14.3; PL 20:360B*

Thus the kingdom of God has a threefold meaning: in the church, in the soul, and in eternal life. We are unable to come to God through glory unless God first comes to us through grace.

Thy Will Be Done, on Earth as It Is in Heaven

*There follows the third petition: *thy will be done, on earth as it is in heaven*,* meaning that, just as the angels ***R 6** *Matt 6:10

and the elect who are in heaven have thoroughly done your will, conforming themselves to your commandments, holding fast to you in everything, and serving you blamelessly, and thus possess you completely, so may it be done by human beings who are of the earth and dwell upon the earth.‡

‡Zachary 1.34 approx; PL 186:139B; Exp Or Dom 5.9–11

Or, *thy will be done, on earth as it is in heaven*, meaning in sinners as it is in the just:* may they turn to you, the one true God, and do your will, not their own, in everything,* and may they believe that you arrange all things, favorable and adverse, for our benefit. There is as vast a difference spiritually between the righteous and sinners as there is physically between the earth and the heavens, and this is because of their different dispositions: the affections of the just are directed heavenward, while those of sinners are earthbound.

*Zachary 1.34; PL 186:139B

*Exp Or Dom 5.33–35 approx

Or, *thy will be done, on earth as it is in heaven*, meaning in body as well as in soul.* May the desires of the body not be in conflict with those of the spirit so that, just as a good spirit does not resist you, so the body will not resist the spirit, and consequently not resist you.* May our soul and body together hate everything that you hate, and love what you love, and may we fulfill what you command.

*Zachary 1.34; PL 186:139B

*Exp Or Dom 5.35–39 approx

This is what Cyprian says about the will of God in his treatise on the Lord's Prayer:

> The will of God is what Christ did and taught. Humility in conduct, steadfastness in faith, modesty in conversation, justice in deeds, mercy in actions, self-control in behavior; a refusal to harm others and a readiness to endure harm ourselves; peace with others; wholehearted love for the Lord by which we fear him as God and love him as Father; preferring nothing to Christ because he preferred nothing to us; clinging tenaciously to his love; standing by his cross with loyalty and courage whenever there is any conflict involving his honor and his name; manifesting in our speech the constancy of our profession, under torture the

> courage with which we do battle, in dying the endurance by which we are crowned. This is what it means to want to be a coheir with Christ. This is what it means to keep Christ's commandment. This is what it means to fulfill the Father's will.*

*Orat Dom 15; PL 4:529BC

Give Us This Day Our Daily Bread

***R 7**

*The fourth petition then follows: *Give us this day our daily bread,** meaning the daily food required by our body; this is designated as *bread,* and it is understood that by this that we are requesting all things needed for life. Augustine comments, "Therefore we ask for a sufficiency by specifying a very important part, for by the name *bread* we signify the totality."* The Lord says *bread,* not meat or fish, that is, not something superfluous, but something required by nature. This is symbolized well by bread, as we read in Sirach, *The chief thing for man's life is water and bread.**

*Matt 6:11

*Ep 130.11.21; PL 33:502; CL 31B:228

*Sir 27:28; *Exp Or Dom 6.1–15 approx*

And he specifies *our,* so that no one will appropriate material things to oneself alone. According to Chrysostom, everything God bestows, be it to those who pray or to those who serve under his banner, he gives not only to us, but also to others through us, so that we will share with the weak some of what God has given us.* Therefore, those who do not share the fruits of their labor with those in need eat not only their own bread, but also the bread of another. Furthermore, those who eat bread gained honestly eat their own bread, but those who gain their bread by sin eat the bread of another:* God gives bread to the one who gains it justly, while the devil gives bread to the one who gains it by sin. Gregory notes that we call this *our* bread, but we pray that it will be given to us; it is God's gift, because it is given by him and it only becomes ours when we receive it.*

*Opus imperf 14; PG 56:713

**Exp Or Dom 6.17–20 approx*

*Mor 24.VII.13; PL 76:293B; CL 143B:1196

Jesus specifies *daily* bread—not a year's supply, or several years' stored up. Matthew uses the word *supersubstantialem*, that is, added to our substance to sustain us.* Cyril suggests that by commanding us to ask for daily food, Christ seems to imply that we should possess nothing and practice an honorable poverty; those who are oppressed by want seek bread, not those who already have it.*

*Exp Or Dom 6.29

*CA Luke 11:1–4

Christ adds, *Give us this day*, because we will not possess even the least thing unless he *who gives food to all flesh* bestows it on us.* Devout souls should eat their food with the idea that God himself is literally present, feeding them with his own hand. He specifies *this day*, meaning the present, or what is needed simply for this day, so that we will give no thought to the morrow, because we do not know if we will even be here tomorrow.

*Ps 135:25; *Exp Or Dom 6.36–38*

O, the true wisdom and divine providence that instructs us to ask only for *bread* and specifies only for *this day*! By this one phrase, gluttony and greed are banished, and we are reminded of the uncertainty of human life.*

**Ps-Augustine, Sermo 65.3; PL 39:1870*

Or *give us this day our daily bread* can refer to the spiritual bread of the divine precepts, upon which we should both meditate and act each day. The Lord himself said of these precepts, *Labor not for the food which perishes, but for that which endures unto life everlasting*.* This bread is called *daily* because it lasts only as long as the day of this earthly life. And *give us this day* can be understood to mean for the duration of our earthly life; in the future, those who deserve it will receive bread that cannot be taken away from them, because they will be satisfied eternally by spiritual food.

*John 6:27

Or *give us this day our daily bread* can refer to the living, sacramental Bread that comes down from heaven. This bread is *supersubstantial* because it is beyond every living thing and surpasses every creature.* This Bread of ours is on the altar and is offered daily for the health/salvation of the faithful; it nourishes our spiritual nature, which transcends the body. This

**Jerome, Com Matt 6:11; PL 26:43C; CL 77:37*

Bread strengthens us in our weakness, because we are prone to slip or fall every day.

It is also called *our daily bread* because we obtain it daily through the ministers of the church, who receive this sacrament for themselves and for the entire community.* Chrysostom says, "Not without reason are we urged to pray always that we may deserve to receive this heavenly bread, lest sin intervene and we be separated from the Lord's Body."*

**Lyra Matt 6:11*

*Chromatius 14.5; PL 20:361C

Finally, we can distinguish three kinds of bread: the first is the bread of doctrine or understanding, the second is the bread of affliction or grief, the third is the bread of heaven or glory. Of the first it is written, *With the bread of life and understanding, she shall feed him.** Of the second, *How long will thou feed us with the bread of tears?** And of the third, *Blessed is he that shall eat bread in the kingdom of God.** The final beatific enjoyment is fittingly called bread: just as material bread satisfies the hunger of those who eat it, so that enjoyment satisfies the desires of those who behold it. As the psalmist says, *I shall be satisfied when your glory shall appear.**

*Sir 15:3

*Ps 79:6

*Luke 14:15

*Ps 16:15; *Exp Or Dom 6.91–130 approx*

Forgive Us Our Trespasses

*The fifth petition follows, *forgive us our trespasses,*‡ that is, the sins that make us debtors to you and for which we are obliged to do penance, making satisfaction here or in purgatory or in hell.* We owe recompense for whatever sins we have committed against you, our neighbors, or ourselves; also against you the Father, or you the Son, or you, the Holy Spirit; also for sins committed in our thoughts, in our words, or in our deeds. Cyprian says, "Lest any of us should flatter ourselves that we are innocent, and by exalting ourselves come to a worse condition, we are instructed that we sin daily by being directed to make daily entreaty for our sins."*

***R 8**

‡*debita;* Matt 6:12

**Gorran Luke 11:2*

*Orat Dom 22; PL 4:534C

And Jesus adds, *as we forgive those who trespass against us*. Behold the rule proposed to us: if we want to be forgiven our sins, we must forgive the sins committed against us by our neighbor! According to Gregory, the good that we seek from God with a contrite heart we must first bestow on our neighbor.* Cyprian writes, "He who taught us to pray for our sins has promised his paternal mercy; but he has clearly added a law, binding us with a clear stipulation, that we ask for our sins to be forgiven in the same way that we forgive those who offend us."* Chrysostom warns, "He did not say that God would first forgive us, and afterwards we would forgive those who trespass against us. God knows that people are liars: even if they receive forgiveness for their sins, they do not forgive those who sin against them. So he instructs us to forgive first, and only then to ask to be forgiven."* And elsewhere: "Considering these things, we should be merciful to those who wrong us. If we are wise, they can become the cause of our greatest pardon; by producing only a few things, we will receive a great many. After all, we owe the Lord many large debts, and if he were to exact payment from us for the least of them we would soon perish."*

*Mor 10.XV.30; PL 75:938A; CL 143:559

*Orat Dom 22–23; PL 4:535A

*Opus imperf 14; PG 56:715

*Attr. to Chrysostom, CA Luke 11:5–8

What should we do in the case of someone who is able to make satisfaction but does not want to or who does not ask forgiveness when unable to make satisfaction? A fundamental distinction must be made here. If you are striving to be perfect, you must forgive in every circumstance, even if the other party does not request it. You should not only banish all animosity from your soul, but you should forgive everything even when there is no satisfaction made for the offense, or restitution of property, or prayerful entreaty, and you must love with a pure heart. This is a counsel of perfection. If you have not yet made a vow of perfection, you are still required to banish all animosity from your soul, not desiring an increase of evil or a diminution of good for your foe; other than that, you should be satisfied with any sort of recompense offered for the harm done you. This is a precept, not a counsel, and applies to everyone. In sum, we must forgive wrongs, because we are all bound in charity to love everyone; excusing injuries goes beyond the call of duty.*

Innocent III, De sacro altaris 5.22 approx; PL 217:902A

Someone who has taken your money does not get to keep it but must return it if possible; similarly, it is fair to request some restitution to make amends for an injury—this is in the order of justice. But here, Augustine says, it is not a financial debt or something in the order of justice that is being spoken of, but uprooting rancor from our hearts.* There are, however, offenses that it would be remiss not to punish: we can pardon offenses against us, but we should punish offenses against God and our neighbor. Jerome writes, "If our brother or sister sins against us and injures us in some way, we have the power—more, the obligation—to forgive them. If someone sins against God, it no longer depends on our choice. But we do the opposite: we are mild about an injury done to God but moved to hatred by insults to ourselves!"*

*Sermone monte 2.8.28; PL 34:1281; CL 35:117; *Exp Or Dom* 7.93–97

*Com Matt 8:15–17; PL 25:131B

Those whose hearts are full of hatred or envy will be more troubled than pleased by this prayer. It is as if they were saying, "Do not forgive my sins, because I do not want to forgive the sins of others." See how much the Lord detests fraternal hatred: he makes our willingness to forgive the indispensable condition for our being forgiven ourselves! Anselm says, "You will not have forgiveness unless you give it away."* And Seneca counsels, "Forgive others always, yourself never."*

*Ps-Anselm, Ad contemptum; PL 158:682A

*Moribus 111

And Lead Us Not into Temptation

*Then the sixth petition follows: *and lead us not into temptation*:* of the flesh, lest its pleasures overwhelm us; of the world, lest its riches consume us; or of the

***R 9**

*Matt 6:13

devil, lest his malice destroy us. There are two kinds of temptation/trial.[2] The first is a probationary trial: God tests his holy ones, not so that he can learn something about them (for everything is known to him beforehand), but so that they can prove themselves to themselves and become aware of something about themselves that they did not know. The second kind of temptation is deception. This never comes from God: it comes from the flesh, the world, and the devil, which suggest self-indulgence, vanity, and bitterness. God merely permits this kind of temptation. Thus the meaning of *lead us not into temptation* is "**Do not allow us to be tempted*** beyond our ability. Grant with the trial a way of escape so that we may be able to bear it and not be entangled in its meshes or overpowered by its force." It is as if we were saying, "Even though to test us you allow us to be induced by our senses, do not allow us to be seduced by our consent to succumb."

*Latin Diatessaron?

God does not directly cause someone to be led into temptation; he permits it to happen by withdrawing his help. Thus, when we read, *Pharaoh's heart was hardened,** this means God allowed it to be hardened, and when Amos asks, *Shall there be evil in a city, which the Lord has not done?** this means evil God has permitted to be done. Cyprian observes, "These words show that an adversary can do nothing against us unless God has previously permitted it, so that all our fear and devotion will be turned towards God."*

*Exod 8:19

*Amos 3:6

*Orat Dom 25; PL 4:536C

It is one thing to be led *to* temptation and another to be led *into* temptation.* We are led to temptation when we are assailed by it but do not give in; we are led into temptation when we yield and are conquered. *Inducti = intus duci** and thus means to succumb.‡ This suggests that we are not praying that there be no temptation, because to be tempted is not an evil. On

**aliud est in tentationem duci et aliud induci*

*to be led inside

‡*Augustine, Sermone monte 2.9.30 approx; PL 34:1282; CL 35:119*

[2] *Tentatio* means both a trial and a temptation.

the contrary, it is very useful: virtue is only strengthened by exercise, and without temptation no one can prove his mettle to himself or others. Rather, we pray that when temptation comes, either with pleasant charm or bitter adversity, we will not be deprived of God's help, for otherwise we will consent to what deceives us or bow before what afflicts us, and so be overcome utterly.

If we are not fooled by what is alluring, we will not be routed by what is harsh, for, in the words of Augustine, "No one is broken down by the troubling appearance of adversity who does not succumb to the lure of prosperity."* Elsewhere he writes, "Pleasure must be shunned first, pain after. How can you withstand the world's blows if you cannot resist its caresses?"* And again, "God wants us to ask him that we may not be led into temptation, although he could have granted this without our prayer, to remind us who it is from whom we receive all benefits."* By this, Cyprian says, we are reminded of our infirmity and weakness, lest anyone should insolently vaunt himself or herself; when a humble and submissive confession comes first and all is attributed to God, he may grant it by his own loving-kindness.*

*Sermone monte 2.9.34; PL 34:1284; CL 35:125

*Ps-Maximus of Turin, Sermo 89; PL 57:711B

*Dono persever 7.15; PL 45:1002

*Orat Dom 26; PL 4:537B

But Deliver Us from Evil

*Then comes the seventh and final petition, *but deliver us from evil** **of every kind**,‡ whether it is the innate evil we inherit, original sin; or the additional evil we commit, actual sin; or the inflicted evil we endure, the punishment meted out for our sins. Or *from* all *evil*, visible and invisible, that is, offense and punishment; or *from evil* past, present, and future. Note that this petition should not be understood as referring to the evil of sins we have already committed, because then it would be equivalent to the fifth petition.* Rather, it speaks of the evil of sins we could

***R 10**

*Matt 6:13

‡Latin Diatessaron?

**Exp Or Dom 9.15–19*

commit here and now; by praying to be delivered from evil, we are evidently praying not to sin.

Again, this petition does not refer to future punishment, because then it would be equivalent to the second petition.* Rather, it speaks of present punishment to the extent that this could be the cause and occasion for a fall. We can apply this petition in one way to the evil of future punishment: we pray to be delivered from present evil so as not to incur the evil of future punishment. In asking to be delivered from all present evils, we are praying and speaking in the person of the church. But if we want to be delivered from evils, we should strive to sympathize with the evils sustained by our neighbor; if we seek to beg mercy from God, we must show mercy to our neighbor.

*Exp Or Dom 9.19–20

Amen

*R 11

*Then follows the conclusion to the whole prayer: *Amen*, that is, "May all that has been asked for come about." This word expresses the longing of the one praying for the blessings that have been named, and the hope that all his petitions will be fulfilled. This word was added by John because it is an angelic word, like *Alleluia*, and no one would presume to translate it into another language.[3] The word is Hebrew, and no one dares to translate it into Greek or Latin out of reverence for the Savior, who often used this word to confirm the truth of his statements. It stands untranslated to honor it with a veil of secrecy, not so that it

[3] The *Amen* and the doxology *for thine is the kingdom* were additions to early texts of the gospels reflecting liturgical usage. It is not clear why Ludolph attributes the addition to John; perhaps he was influenced by the text of Augustine, who is explaining why John did not translate the Hebrew word in his gospel.

will be negated, but so that it will not be rendered meaningless by being stripped bare.*

*Aug, Tr John 41.3; PL 35:1694; CL 36:359

Sometimes the word is used as a noun, as in the book of Revelation, where it says, *The Amen says these things,** that is, Truth himself. Other times it is used as a verb, as frequently in the Psalms, where we read, *Amen, Amen*! that is, "May it be so, may it be so!" This use appears at the end of a prayer, as here. And it can be used as an adverb, as is often the case in the gospels, where Christ says: "*Amen* I say to you," that is, "truly and surely."*

*Rev 3:14

**Exp Or Dom 10.4–8*

When placed at the end, this word *Amen* has a threefold efficacy and power. First, it concludes a prayer; Jerome calls it a seal on the prayer.* Just as the final word *Amen* seals the entire Bible, so it closes this prayer. Second, it recollects our intentions: by saying *Amen*, we express our desire for all spoken previously in the prayer; if through human weakness we have become distracted in prayer, our purpose is recovered by saying *Amen*. Third, it represents a final appeal that our prayer will be heard and answered favorably. Rabanus Maurus says, "By having said *Amen*, the Lord shows that without doubt he will bestow all things that are rightly asked, provided that we do not fail to observe the added condition that we forgive those who have sinned against us."*

*Com Matt 6:13; PL 26:33C; CL 77:37

*Com Matt 6:13–14; PL 107:823A; CM 174:188; *Exp Or Dom 10.12–23 approx*

O Lord, it matters little if I say *Amen*, hoping that it will be,‡ unless you say *Amen*, commanding it to be! O, that magnificent and efficacious word, *fiat*! By that word, Father most high, you created all things in the beginning through your Word: you spoke and they were made. By that same word you renewed us who were lost, when our most holy Reparatrix said to the angel, *Be it done* to me according to your word*!‡ O, that saving word *fiat*, O *Amen*, O *fiat*, O word all-powerful and of marvelous efficacy! Come on, my good Lord Jesus, Word of the Father, finish my prayer, bring about the words you yourself have given and I have

‡*fiat*

**fiat*

‡Luke 1:38

spoken with my lips, accomplish them and say *Amen*, say *Fiat*, say to me what you said to that Canaanite woman, *Let it be done to you as you will.** O Jesus, sweet love, O sweet Truth, O sweet *Amen*, O sweet word *fiat*: *Be it done to me according to your word. Fiat*! *Amen*!

*Matt 15:28

Saint Luke's Version

*R 12

*It should be noted that Luke omits two petitions of the Lord's Prayer, the third and the sixth, because the third is contained in the previous two petitions, and the seventh is contained in the sixth. In the first petition we pray for the sanctification of the soul, in the second for the resurrection of the flesh, and these are fulfilled in the divine will, for which we pray in the third petition. Or, if we seek primarily the glory of God and a share in his kingdom, which are contained in the first two petitions, we will strive to do God's will and it will be fulfilled in us, the third petition: his will aims principally at our knowing his holiness and reigning with him. Similarly, the seventh petition is contained in the sixth, for we are delivered from evil if we are not led into temptation. If we are not led *into* temptation by succumbing to it, but instead prevail by resisting it, we are quite rightly delivered from evil. Luke includes implicitly what Matthew makes explicit.*

**Exp Or Dom 3.16–24 approx*

The Importance of Forgiving Others

*R 13

*Augustine writes, "We must not negligently overlook the fact that among all those texts in which the Lord commanded us to pray, he has declared that special emphasis should be given to the petition that has to do with the forgiveness of sins. In this way he wanted to show that our being merciful was the one and only counsel for avoiding misery. In no other prayer do we enter into a contract with him, as it were. We say, *Forgive us as we forgive those who trespass against us*. If we lie in that contract, the whole prayer is fruitless."* *Sermone monte 2.11.39: PL 34:1287; CL 35:130

When speaking about prayer on another occasion Jesus said, *And when you shall stand to pray, forgive, if you have anything against any man, so that your Father also, who is in heaven, may forgive you your sins.** *Mark 11:25 Chrysostom comments, "Therefore he makes mention of heaven and of the Father to capture our attention: nothing makes us so like God as forgiving those who injure us. It is entirely unsuitable for the son or daughter of such a Father to be cruel, or for one who is called to heaven to nurture an earthbound frame of mind."* *Hom Matt 19.7; PG 57/58:283

Following the Lord's Prayer, Christ adds, "*For if you will forgive men their offences,* not harboring resentment or seeking revenge for offenses **committed against you**,* *Latin Diatessaron? *your heavenly Father will forgive you also your offences. But if you will not forgive men, neither will your Father forgive you your offenses.*"* *Matt 6:14-15 Quite properly does he say *your* offenses—sin is the only thing we can boast of doing completely by our own power. We can do evil by ourselves, but not good. See the law the Lord has laid down for you: if you forgive, you will be forgiven; if you do not forgive, you will not be forgiven.* **Gorran Matt 6:15*

Cyprian warns, "You will have no excuse on the Day of Judgment when you are condemned by the same sentence you meted out, and you suffer what you yourself inflicted on others."* *Orat Dom 23; PL 4:535B Chrysostom writes,

> Having given the formula of prayer, he emphasizes only one commandment, the one where he tells us to forgive: *For if you will forgive men their offenses, your heavenly Father will forgive you also your offenses.* This is the fundamental principle from which everything flows, and the power of our fu-

ture Judgment rests in our own hands. Now unless you are insane you must lament God's Judgment on you for your sins, be they great or small, but God allows the guilty parties to determine their own sentence. He says, "I will judge you as you have judged. If you have forgiven your fellow servant, you will receive the same grace from me."

But how unequal are the circumstances! You forgive, needing forgiveness yourself; the God who forgives you needs no pardon from anyone. You forgive an equal, God forgives a slave. You are guilty of a thousand sins, God is utterly sinless. And notwithstanding all this, he shows us an abundance of mercy. What punishment will we deserve, if God has given us such great power and we become the traitors of our own salvation? How can we dare ask him to hear us when we pray for anything, if we will not give ourselves what is in our power?

Nothing makes us so similar to God as to be kind to those who malign and injure us. This is why every one of the petitions of the Lord's Prayer is in the plural: *Our* Father, etc. The plural wording is meant to teach us that we should be kindly disposed to our neighbors in all things and not harbor any resentment toward them. If we decided to tally up just the sins we commit in a single day, we would learn very well how much evil we are guilty of. Who of us has not neglected prayer? Who has not been swelled up by pride or borne aloft by vainglory? Who has not maligned another? Who has not entertained impure thoughts or looked lustfully at someone? Who has not nursed bitter resentment against an enemy? Who has not been envious or tormented by another's success, or taken delight in his adversity?

And in the face of this litany of offenses, God offers us a quick and easy way to free ourselves, a way that requires no work. Really, how hard is it to pardon a grieving brother or sister? Forgiving requires no effort, but holding grudges demands

> a great deal. Letting go of anger brings great peace of mind, and it is easy for those who want to do it. It is enough to want to do this, and all our sins are immediately forgiven.[4]*

*Hom Matt 19.7 approx; PG 57/58:283

Augustine suggests that we should welcome with open arms such a mild stipulation, that we wash away our own offenses by forgiving others theirs.* He also argues that there are many works of charity we can practice to help take away our sins, but none is greater than when we forgive from our heart someone who has sinned against us.*

*Prosper 359; PL 45:1892

*Ps-Augustine, Sermo 304.3; PL 39:2329

Let us then not be slow to forgive others. As Chrysostom says, if you forgive your neighbors, you free yourself of guilt before you free them.* Gregory writes, "If we were to reflect that we are benefitting ourselves more than the person who afflicts us, we would quickly expel the venom of resentment.* When we forgive another it is necessary to restrain our anger, which often urges us to be vengeful."‡

*Hom 23.2; PG 57/58:309

*Attr. to Chrysostom in Ps-Bonaventure, Pharetra 2.40
‡Augustine, Sermo 315.6.9; PL 38:1430

And Augustine again:

> My friends, exert yourselves to the best of your ability to show gentleness even toward your enemies. Rein in the anger that is prodding you to avenge yourselves.* If you want to avenge yourself on an enemy, direct your attention to your own anger, because that is the enemy who can kill your soul. You are going to pray to God; you are coming to that verse, *forgive us our trespasses*. What follows? *As we forgive those who trespass against us*. That enemy, anger, stands up against you, blocking the way to your prayer. It has built a wall you cannot pass beyond. If you want to rage against an enemy, rage against this one. *Better is one who overcomes*

*Augustine, Sermo 315.6.9; PL 38:1430

[4] This citation varies in places from Chrysostom's text, and some of it comes from a different Latin translation: Roland 2:44.

*Prov 16:32

*Sermo 315.7.10; PL 38:1430

wrath than one who conquers a city.[5]* You cannot destroy anger, but you can restrain it. If you are brave, conquer anger and spare the city.*

Our Father—supreme in creation, delightful in love, rich in inheritance—who art in heaven the mirror of eternity, the crown of joy, the treasury of happiness, hallowed be thy name, which is like honey in our mouth, a lyre in our ear, and ardent affection in our heart. Thy kingdom come: unalloyed joy, undisturbed tranquility, and untroubled security. Thy will be done on earth as it is in heaven, so that we will detest what you hate, embrace what you love, and do what pleases you. Give us this day our daily bread of doctrine, of penance, and of virtues. Forgive us our trespasses committed against you, our neighbor, or ourselves, as we forgive those who trespass against us by speech or who injure us in our persons or in our possessions. And lead us not into temptation of the world, the flesh, or the devil. But deliver us from evil past, present, or yet to come. Amen.[6]

[5] *Melior est qui vincit iram quam qui capit civitatem*. Augustine's text differs from the Vulgate.

[6] Ludolph uses phrases from Jordan's work in composing this prayer.

CHAPTER 38

The Sermon on the Mount, Continued: Treasure in Heaven

(Matt 6:19-34; Luke 12:22-34)

*Next, to teach disregard of worldly wealth for love of God, Jesus lays down a prohibition against storing our treasure in insecure places: *where the rust* can corrode man-made riches like gold, silver, and other metals, *and* the worm of *the moth consume* natural possessions like grain, wine, clothing, and similar items, *and where thieves break through, and steal** the precious jewels that rust and worms cannot ruin.* Chrysostom asks, "What can I say about that commandment not to store up treasure on earth? It seems that very few observe it. Many act as though they were ordered to do just the opposite: 'Amass as much worldly wealth as you can.' Abandoning the things of heaven, they cling to those of earth, and go mad in their effort to make money."*

***R 1**

*Matt 6:19

**Lyra Matt 6:19*

*Grimlaicus 28; PL 103:616A

Christ goes on to tell us where we can safely store our wealth: "*But lay up to yourselves treasures in heaven, where neither the rust nor moth consume,* because there is no passage of time or decay, *and where thieves do not break through, nor steal,** because there is no fraud or violence." The most excellent means of amassing wealth is to put to good use the passing goods of this world, converting them into spiritual and eternal goods that are not subject to decay.* Let us then not store up our worldly wealth here on earth, where

*Matt 6:20

**Lyra Matt 6:20*

things hidden away rot or get mislaid, and which we must leave one day. Instead, let us invest in the gain of heavenly merit, for what is hidden away there is secure and multiplies, and we will live there for ever.

Jerome counsels, "How foolish it is to keep your treasure in a place you must leave so soon and not forward it on ahead to your eternal dwelling place. Store your wealth where your permanent home is."* Gregory writes, "The righteous do not bother about amassing wealth here, where they are sojourners and visitors. They want to rejoice in their own true home and so turn down the passing joys of a foreign land."* And Chrysostom, "People who keep their treasure on earth have nothing to hope for in heaven. Why should they look up to heaven, where they have laid nothing up for themselves?"*

*Ps-Chrysostom, Opus imperf 15; PG 56:719

*Paterius, Expos Vet et Novi Test 1.1.32; PL 79L676D

*Opus imperf 15; PG 56:719

Where Your Treasure Is, There Will Your Heart Be

*R 2

*Everyone desires to reach the place where they know their riches are kept. You will be blessed if you have stored yours in heaven: your mind will always be centered there, and you will continually strive wholeheartedly to be there. Hence the Lord adds, "*For where your treasure is*, that is, what you love and desire, *there is your heart* and affection *also*."* Where your treasure has preceded, the thoughts of your heart must of necessity follow. For, according to Augustine, love is the weight of the soul, carrying it wherever it goes,* and the soul is present more where it loves than where it lives.[1] Fulgentius urges, "Let us store up treasure in heaven, let us love heavenly things. If you want to

*Matt 6:21

*Conf 13.9.10; PL 32:849; CL 27:246

[1] *Anima verius est ubi amat quam ubi animat*. The idea is taken from Bernard, but the expression was coined by Bonaventure, with the play on *anima/animat*; Soliloquium 2.2.12. Aquinas attributes the line to Augustine, as did many later writers.

know what you value, pay attention to what you love; if you want to know what you love, pay attention to what you think about. You will know what your treasure is when you know what you love, and you will know what you love by attending to what you think about."* Pope Gregory says that the heart is divided into as many parts as there are things it loves.‡

*Sermo 1.8; PL 65:724A
‡Dial 4.1.4; PL 77:176C; Reg past 1.4; PL 77:17C both approx

Chrysostom writes,

> Do not lay up treasure on earth, for you simply amass it for moths, worms, and thieves. Even if you avoid these nuisances, your heart will be reduced to servitude by its attachment to such ephemeral things, and anxiety will build a prison for your mind. You experience no small loss by your attachment to passing things. You exchange freedom for slavery, and, plummeting from heavenly goods, you will not be able to think about anything of higher importance.*

*Hom Matt 20.3; PG 57/58:290; Latin differs

> This is why the pagans do not believe what we tell them: they look for evidence of future things from our deeds, not our words. At present they see us building splendid mansions, purchasing fields, supplying baths and gardens with all the amenities; how can they believe that we are looking forward to a more perfect city? "If that were true," they say, "these Christians would be selling forthwith everything they possess here and sending the proceeds on ahead." Weighing all this very carefully, let us break the fetters of so great an error. Those who are enslaved to money bind themselves in chains now and forge links for the future. But those immune to greed obtain a double liberation: they free themselves from the weighty irons of avarice and are lifted up to the heights of heaven.*

*Hom Matt 12.5; PG 57/58:207–8; Latin follows Roland, 2:27

And Anselm, "Let the world be worthless to you; view all carnal love as ignoble. Forget that you are in this world, for you have turned your heart's intent and purpose to those who are in heaven and live in God. *Where your treasure is, there is your heart also.* Do not lock your heart in your purse with your worthless silver; you can never soar up to heaven carrying such a heavy weight."*

*Med 16; PL 158:704D

According to Jerome, what is said here does not concern only money, but all the passions and possessions. The glutton's god is the belly, banquets are the treasure of the luxurious, parties of the lascivious, lust of the amorous, money of the avaricious. *For by whom a man is overcome, of the same also he is the slave.** Where our heart is, there is our treasure, so it follows that if our heart turns to such things it must distance itself from God. If your heart is in heaven it will be clean, for the heavens are pure, but if you wallow in the mud, concerning yourself only with these earthly things, how can it remain clean? Augustine writes, "A thing becomes adulterated when it is mixed with something inferior, however pure that other thing may be in itself. Thus gold is adulterated even by pure silver when mixed with it. So our soul becomes tarnished through our desire for earthly things, even though the earth is clean in its own way."* Therefore, Richard of St. Victor counsels, "Spend liberally whatever you desire or fear for in this world to purchase freedom of heart."‡ As Augustine says, those who lay up treasure for themselves in heaven ought to ignore the whole world.†

*2 Pet 2:19; Com Matt 6:21; PL 26:44C; CL 77:38–39

*Sermone monte 2.13.44; PL 34:1289; CL 35:135
‡Gratia contemplat 3.5; PL 196:115C
†Sermone monte 2.13.44; PL 34:1289; CL 35:135

Trust in God; Generosity

***R 3**

*Concerned that his disciples would feel uneasy regarding the necessities of life, Christ excluded a lack of trust by saying, "*Fear not, little flock,* that is, community of the humble, *for it has pleased your* heavenly *Father to give you a kingdom,* not because of your merits, but merely because of his liberality and divine goodness."* It is as if he were saying, "Such a great heavenly kingdom is being prepared for you that you need not trouble yourself about earthly matters. Those who

*Luke 12:32; *Lyra Luke 12:32 mor*

have been promised such a kingdom of life, containing a sufficiency of everything, need not doubt that they will also be provided with the necessities of life here."* *Lyra Luke 12:32

He calls them a *flock* because of the obedience of faith, and *little* by virtue of the dedicated humility and voluntary poverty by which they will come into possession of the heavenly reign.* *Lyra Luke 12:32* Or, they are the *little flock* of the elect compared to the great number of the condemned: there are few believers in comparison to unbelievers, and few elect in comparison to the reprobate.* *Zachary 1.35; PL 186:143C* May we deserve to be numbered among the least in that little flock, and so be able to reign with them!

*R 4

*The way to the riches of that kingdom is the path of the evangelical counsels, which leads to perfection. So Jesus goes on to say, "*Sell what you possess*, even what is necessary, and give alms, for that is the road to this kingdom. *Make to yourselves* places to store the reward of your good work of almsgiving, *bags which grow not old* and fall apart. That is, put your money into the hands of the poor: they will carry it past your enemies and any thieves and bring it to where it will be safe. None of it will be lost, and you will have an eternal *treasure in heaven which does not fail*."* *Luke 12:33 Money given to the poor earns the profit of merits, which are kept in the unfailing treasury of our homeland.* *Zachary 1.35; PL 186:143D* If, through almsgiving, we have merits in heaven, our hearts will long to reach that treasure-house of rewards.

Good and Bad Intentions

*R 5

Then Christ teaches us to have a "single eye" through which we should appraise all our works. *Massa* He says, *The light of your body is your eye*.* *Matt 6:22 This is metaphorical language, by which the moral body is seen as an ensemble of operations, as the physical body is made up of diverse members. Just as the physical eye governs the whole physical body and directs the workings of its members, so the moral eye, or intention, governs the moral body and directs its various operations toward their goal.* Thus he adds, *"If your eye be single,* that is, if you have a right intention without a wrinkle of error or deceit, *your whole body shall be full of light."** That is to say, all your doings will be good and meritorious, even if they are not seen as such by others. Of course the actions themselves must be by their very nature good, or at least morally neutral and licit, for otherwise they could not be done with a right intention. Seneca teaches, "It does not matter with what spirit you have done something vicious. The deed can be seen, although the spirit cannot."*

*Lyra Luke 11:34

*Matt 6:22

*Moribus 3

Christ continues, *"But if your eye be evil,* that is, your intention is perverse, *your whole body shall be full of darkness."** That is, your combined operations are darkened by sin and wickedness, even if the actions are good in themselves and others judge them to be right; a work good in itself becomes bad by reason of an evil intention.* See to it that your intention is not bad, for this corrupts every good thing. *"If then the light that is in you be darkness,* that is, if an action is good in itself, and is thus a kind of light, but becomes evil by virtue of an evil intention, *how great the darkness of it shall be!"** This is as much as to say that an intrinsically evil action is all the darker when it is done for an evil purpose; this makes it even blacker than it is in itself. When a deed is evil *per se* and it is done for an evil end, this doubles the darkness: it is a perverse deed done for a perverse purpose.

*Matt 6:23

*Zachary 1.36; PL 186:145A

*Matt 6:23

With this in mind, we must examine not only what we do but why we do it.* We must strive to act with purity of intention, for without this, whatever we do has no value. If you do a good deed for a good reason and there is no shadow troubling your conscience, your action itself will shine when it makes its appearance. And it will shine on you as well, shedding light on you—the splendor of grace here, and the splendor of glory hereafter.* On the other hand, if you do some-

*Aug, Sermone monte 2.13.46; PL 34:1289; CL 35:137

*Bede, Com Luke 11:34 approx

thing good in itself, but without a right and clear conscience, you will be condemned, not for the good you did, but for the evil you intended.* Let us then be on guard that the heart's intention, which is the soul's lamp, be not obscured by the darkness of evil. In this way, the simple eye can give light to the whole body. Let us do everything for God. Then the grace will return to its origin and flow again to us.

Aug, Sermone monte 2.13.46; PL 34:1290; CL 35:138

No One Can Serve Two Masters

*Some people imagine that it is possible to pursue both earthly and heavenly things with a right and simple intention, and to benefit both here and hereafter by what they do. To dispel this idea the Lord speaks about two competing rulers: "*No man can serve two* different and incompatible *masters* without subordinating one to the other."* Bede says, "It does not work to love passing and eternal things simultaneously."* And Augustine, "A single eye cannot look at both heaven and earth."[2] And Cyprian, "Love of God and love of the world cannot dwell equally together in one place, just as the eyes cannot look at the heavens and the earth at the same time."* In his *De animalibus*, the Philosopher observes, "Birds close their eyes with their lower lids, but larger animals use their upper lids."* We can take birds to symbolize spiritual people, who close their eyes to lower, earthly matters, and the larger animals to stand for worldly types, who close their eyes to heavenly realities and keep them open to worldly concerns.

***R 6**

*Matt 6:24

*Com Luke 16:13; PL 92:531D; CL 120:300

*Ps-Cyprian, De duodecim 7; PL 4:876A

*De animalibus 14.4.11

Chrysostom comments that Christ is speaking here of two masters who issue contradictory orders. If they

[2] *Unus oculus non potest videre in coelo et in terra*. The source of the wording unknown, but the idea is taken from a 7th-century Irish work often attributed to Augustine or Cyprian, *De duodecim abusivis* 7 (PL 40:1084).

command the same thing, then they are not several but one, for mutual agreement makes many one.* The two masters who cannot be served simultaneously are vice and virtue, heavenly and earthly matters, God and the devil, flesh and spirit. They command contrary things, so it follows that to obey one necessitates disobeying the other.

*Hom Matt 21.1; PG 57/58:294

As if to make this clear, the Lord adds, *You cannot serve God and mammon.** *Mammona* is a Syriac word for riches; the masculine form *Mammon* is the name of a demon who controls riches and tempts people with the vice of greed.[3] It is not that he really possesses riches, for they can only be given or withheld when God allows: he simply uses them to entice people and entangle them in his snares. Although we cannot serve both God and riches, we can use riches to serve God. We serve riches when we are tempted and deceived by our desire for wealth, when we see riches as the ultimate end in themselves, and when we greedily amass them, tenaciously cling to them, and guard them like a slave. But if we spend our wealth on good works, then we are not serving riches—rather, they are serving us, because we distribute them as the Lord does, and we are using them as a means to acquire virtue.

*Matt 6:24

Ambrose teaches that just as riches are obstacles for the wicked, so they are aids to virtue for the good.* Chrysostom writes, "Two masters are set before us: God and mammon, that is, the devil, who is the source of mammon. The first master urges us to be merciful, the second to be greedy; one leads toward life, the other toward death; one to salvation, the other to damnation. Which of the two should we serve? Surely the one who invites us to life, not the one who drags us to death.* What could be worse than to fall away from

*Exp Luke 8.85; PL 15:1791B; CL 14:330

*Chromatius 17.4; PL 20:368C

[3] Jerome, *Com Matt 6:24* (PL 26:44D) gives the Syriac derivation; the source for the attribution to a demon is St Cher *Com Matt 6:24*.

the service of Christ for the sake of riches? And what could be more desirable than to be joined to him entirely, heart and soul, by despising wealth?"* *Hom Matt 21.1; PG 57/58:295

From what has been said it should be evident that *no man can serve two masters*. And yet there are many who try to accomplish this foolish impossibility! They are like the people we read about in the book of Kings who feared the Lord but served idols.* *2 Kgs 17:41 Clearly it is impossible to love wealth for itself and God for himself, and to make both an ultimate end. It is possible to seek one and then the other in proper order, that is, to seek wealth for the sake of God. Bodily effort can be made for a temporal end, provided that the temporal is then referred to God. But it is utterly perverse to make God our proximate end and temporal things our ultimate end. Something that is desired for the sake of something else is inferior to what is ultimately desired. It is very acceptable to set two goals, one temporal and the other eternal, provided that the temporal is subordinate to the eternal. One intention shapes many actions, but you cannot have different goals, unless one is referred to the other.* **Hugh 5.14 approx*

We Are Not to Worry about Food or Clothing

***R 7**

Having concluded this topic, the Lord then began to teach that we should not be solicitous about food or clothing. He addressed his disciples, whom he encouraged particularly to condemn the world. And he spoke especially to the apostles and their successors, as well as others who desire to attain the heights of perfection; they should give no thought to earthly goods but be content simply to have food and clothing. **Bruno Com Matt 6:25; PL 165:122B* What he says can be applied also to all preachers of the Gospel, to take from them all unnecessary solicitude about the necessities of the present life. Lest his hearers object, "How can we live if we give up everything?" he resumed what he had been saying earlier and continued, "*Therefore I say to you, be not solicitous for your* physical *life* and its need for food, *what you shall eat* or drink, *nor for your body, what you shall put on*."* It was as if he said, "If you want to serve God, you must renounce the mammon of the obsession about temporal concerns."

*Matt 6:25

Christ did not say, "You may not work for, care about, or seek food, drink, or clothing," but *be not solicitous*, that is, while conceding what is necessary, he prohibits the anxious concern that disturbs our mind and distracts us from eternal realities. Bede says, "He commands us not to be solicitous about what we eat; however, we must work because we have to earn our bread by the sweat of our brow. But we must guard against anxiety."* And Chrysostom, "Bread must be acquired not by spiritual worries but by bodily labors. Just as bread abounds, with God's assistance, as a reward for the diligence of those who work for it, so, by God's permission, it is taken away as a punishment for the negligent."*

*Com Luke 12:22; PL 92:492C; CL 120:252

*Opus imperf 16; PG 56:723

Notice, too, that he did not tell us to be unconcerned about whether we eat, or drink, or have clothing, but about *what* we are to eat, or drink, or wear. Food, drink, and clothing are necessary for survival; solicitude concerns elegance, expense, and delight and pertains to the vices of gluttony, vainglory, and even avarice.* Bede suggests that here our Lord condemns those who spurn communal food and clothing, seeking instead items that are either richer or poorer than the food and drink of those with whom they live.[4]* In a spiritual sense, we can understand food as referring to the gluttonous, clothing to the proud, and both to the avaricious. Elsewhere the Lord describes *a certain rich man* (greed) *who was clothed in purple and fine linen*

Lyra Matt 6:25 mor

*Com Luke 12:29; PL 92:493D; CL 120:253–54

[4] Bede's comment may be inspired by chap. 49 of the Rule of Saint Benedict, which instructs monks that any additional practice of austerity undertaken by a monk during Lent should be approved by the abbot, to avoid the sin of vainglory.

(vanity) *and feasted sumptuously every day* (gluttony).* Whoever you may be, if you have spurned worldly glory and have elected to serve God, do not be solicitous about food and clothing in your life; such anxiety is vain. *Luke 16:19

The Lord strengthens our hope by descending from greater to lesser things: since we need not be solicitous about the greater gifts, we can trust God for lesser things, too. If he gives us the greater gifts out of love, he will not neglect the lesser ones out of necessity. God has given us the great blessings of soul and body; he will certainly provide food and clothing.* The soul was not created for the sake of food, nor was the body created for the sake of clothing, but the other way round, so the soul should not fear that it will not procure what has been created for its use.* Chrysostom says, "God would not have created something unless he intended to keep it in existence. If he has created the soul, he will give it food; if he has fashioned the body, he will supply it with clothing."* He gave us life without our solicitude; he will certainly provide in the same way what we needed to maintain life. It would be foolish indeed to lose what is greater, soul and body, for the sake of what is far less valuable, food and clothing.

**Gorran Matt 5:25*

**Gloss Matt 6:25; PL 114:105D*

*Opus imperf 16 approx; PG 56:723

The Birds of the Air, the Lilies of the Field

*Christ now addresses the concerns of food and clothing individually. He first speaks of food, strengthening our hope now by ascending from lesser things to greater ones, convincing us of the latter by means of the former. He begins with irrational creatures, the birds that fly through the air: "*They neither sow, nor do they reap* to obtain food, *nor gather into barns* to preserve it, *and your heavenly Father feeds them** without their solicitude, for our use." How much more will he feed human beings, who are dearer to him, without ***R 8**

*Matt 6:26

our needless worry. Human beings, which are rational animals, undoubtedly have greater value in God's sight than irrational animals.* Birds are animals created for our sake, and the creature for whose sake something else has been made possesses greater worth.

*Zachary 1.37–38; PL 186:146A

God feeds the birds in a way suited to their nature, and he will feed us in a way suited to ours, in harmony with the rule of right reason, but we must make an effort to use our reason in agreement with his commands. Just as it is natural for birds to live according to their nature, so it is natural for human beings to live in accord with the dictates of right reason. From this it follows that we should exercise prudent concern to obtain the food and clothing that nature does not provide.*

*Lyra Matt 6:26 approx

This is why the Lord did not say about birds that they do not fly into fields to find food: he condemns anxiety and avarice, not industry and prudence.* Chrysostom observes, "God made all the birds for the sake of human beings, but he made human beings for his own sake. If he attends to the animals he made for our sake, how can he not attend to the human creatures he made for his own sake?"‡

*Gorran Matt 6:26

‡Opus imperf 16; PG 56:723

*R 9

*Turning to the question of clothing, Christ gives two examples. The first concerns a person's height, which God gives without any attention or care on our part: *And which of you by taking thought can add to his stature one cubit?** Now, since clothing must be larger or smaller, depending on the size of the body, and this size is given to us without any concern on our part, it follows that clothing will also be provided without our undue anxiety.*

*Matt 6:27

*Lyra Matt 6:27

His second example is drawn from nature around us: the plants such as lilies and grass are born from the earth and grow without any attention on our part and are decorated by God according to their various kinds: "*They labor not* to adorn themselves with colors, *neither do they spin** to weave raiment for themselves."

*Matt 6:28

Yet they are painted by God's providence with the most splendid hues, for the colors of flowers excel those of any vesture, even the robes of royalty. The Lord underscores this by referring to Solomon, who, although he was the most powerful of kings, was not arrayed as the wildflowers. Art imitates nature but cannot equal it in beauty.* Jerome asks, "Truly, what silk, what royal purple, what weaver's embroidery can be compared with flowers? What is as red as a rose? What gleams as white as a lily? No purple dye surpasses the purple of a violet. This is a judgment more of the eyes than of words."* And Chrysostom asks, "Why did he make the grass so beautiful? To display his wisdom and the greatness of his power, so that from everything we might learn his glory. For not only *the heavens show forth the glory of God,** but the earth too."*

**Lyra Matt 6:29*

*Com Matt 6:28; PL 26:46A; CL 77:41

*Ps 18:2

*Hom Matt 22.1; PG 57/58:301

From this example Christ concludes that God will clothe us without undue anxiety on our part: *"And if the grass of the field, which is* here *today and tomorrow is cast into the oven* (for in some places it is customary to burn straw and such things instead of wood in a furnace), *God so clothes* with charming, attractive, and varied colors, *how much more* will he clothe *you* with no anxiety on your part, *O you of little faith*?"* It was as if he were saying, "If God shows such concern for the flowers, which bloom and fade almost immediately, how much more will he care for human beings, who are made in the image of God and called to eternal life?" He describes those who are preoccupied with these concerns as *you of little faith,* for their anxiety is born of a want of trust; this is not true of those whose concern is reasonable and moderate.‡

*Matt 6:30

‡*this sentence: Lyra Matt 6:30*

In a moral sense, the Gloss suggests it would not be out of place to compare the saints to birds: they own nothing of this world, they do not labor, and in their contemplation they despise the things of earth and long only for those of heaven. They are already like the angels. Look, there are three characteristics

***R 10**

*Gloss Matt 6:26; PL 114:106A

that distinguish the saints: voluntary poverty, for they have nothing; contemplative repose or holy leisure, for they do not labor; and elevation of the mind toward higher things, for they desire eternal realities.* The birds of the air thus symbolize contemplatives,* who *neither sow, nor do they reap, nor gather into barns* by involving themselves in worldly affairs, and the Lord takes care of them, supplying what they need. By the lilies of the field we can understand those who are truly chaste:* the splendid whiteness of purity and the fragrant virtue in which they thrive is not due so much to their work as it is to God's gift. We who observe such holy people closely should both praise and imitate the abundance of their good works, the repose of their holy contemplation, and the attractiveness of their upright way of life.

**Gorran Luke 12:24*

**Lyra Matt 6:26 mor*

**Lyra Matt 6:28*

Confidence in God's Providence

***R 11**

From this teaching we learn that we should not entertain doubts about the necessities of life, which God will provide in due season if we do what he commands. If we lack confidence about temporal goods, how can we hope for eternal ones? Faith fears not famine.[5] Those of little faith, who are uncertain about lesser things, will also not hope for lasting things. If we understand what humanity is, we will never despair of God, but if we despair of God, then we do not really understand what humanity is, because God is in us and we are in God. If we put our trust in creatures, we have despaired of the Creator. Anselm counsels, "Do not let the prospect of a lack of productivity

**this sentence: Opus imperf 16; PG 56:724*

[5] *Fides famem non timet*. The author of this lapidary sentence is Tertullian, who urged Christians to give up occupations contrary to their faith: *De idolatria* 12 (PL 1:678B). Jerome applied it to the ascetical life in Ep 14.10 (PL 22:354), and it became a commonplace in later monastic texts.

alarm you, or the thought of future hunger weigh on your mind. Put all your trust in the one who feeds the birds and clothes the lilies. Let him be your barn, your storehouse, your purse, your wealth, your delight. Let him alone be your all in all."* *Med 16; PL 158:795A

The Lord mentions the three gifts God has given to us: our soul, our body, and our possessions. The soul should be subject to its superior, God, by obedience; the body should be subject to its superior, the soul, by complying with its dictates. And we should make our possessions subject to their superiors: to God, by distributing them to the poor; to the soul, by loving them with discretion; and to the body, by using them to serve its needs. But the rich pervert this whole order: their possessions are not subject to God, because they give the poor nothing; or to their soul, because they love them inordinately; or to their body, because they consume them foolishly.* **Voragine, Sermo 1 15th Sunday after Trinity, 240*

To bring home his lesson more forcefully, the Lord repeats it, saying, *Be not solicitous therefore, saying: "What shall we eat, or what shall we drink, or how shall we be clothed?"** According to Chrysostom, when he says *be not solicitous* this is not the same as saying, "Do not work"; he does not put an end to all labor, but to anxiety about it, so that our mind will not be vexed by worldly concerns.* And he asks, "If we are not to be anxious about necessities, what will the punishment be for those who lose sleep over what is superfluous, or who take other people's belongings?"* *Matt 6:31 *Hom Matt 22.1; PG 57/58:300 *Hom Matt 22.2; PG 57/58:301

The Lord continues, "*For after all these things*, food, clothing, and the like, *do the heathens seek** with blameworthy greed." The pagans have an excessive preoccupation with such things because they deny that divine providence directs human affairs.* They are completely absorbed in the pursuit of things in this present life and give absolutely no thought to the world to come, nor do they cherish any promises about it.* Or, *after all these things do the heathens* excessively *seek* can refer to worldly Christians who strive *Matt 6:32 **Lyra Matt 6:32* **Chrys, Hom Matt 22.3; PG 57/58:303; Latin Anianus* for things in the present more than those in the future; such behavior makes them like pagans. For what advantage does a Christian have over a nonbeliever, if our lack of trust makes us anxious and the concerns of this life exhaust us? Alas! Many of us surpass the heathens in our rapacity for the things of this world! I say, if you seek what is not necessary, you are seeking with anxiety.

***R 12**

*The Lord goes on, "*For your Father*, who does not close the depths of his heart to his children, *knows that you have need of all these things** that are required." You cannot live or serve God without these things, so he will certainly give them—unless your lack of faith interferes. What loving father does not give his children what is necessary when he knows what they require? Because God is truly a Father, he desires to give; because he is the heavenly Father, he is able to give; since he wants to and he can, have no doubt that he will give us whatever is helpful to our health/ salvation.

*Matt 6:32

Rabanus Maurus asks, "What king would not provide supplies to his devoted soldiers? What master would not allot rations to his servants? What father would not give food to his children?"* And Chrysostom writes, "To lead them to a greater hope, he did not say, 'God knows,' but, 'Your Father knows.' For if he is a Father, and such a Father, then he will not be able to ignore his children in the extremity of evil, seeing that even human fathers cannot do this. It is very clear that God knows nature itself, for he is its Creator and he formed it to be as it is; evidently he knows its needs even more than you do, who are constrained by them. It is by his decree that your nature has these needs. Therefore, he will not oppose himself to what he has willed, nor deprive you of receiving what is necessary."* And Augustine also says, "The heavenly physician knows what to give us for our consolation, and what to take away for our training; not even a human being withholds fodder from a beast

*Attr. to Rabanus in Gorran Matt 6:26

*Hom Matt 22.2; PG 57/58:302; Latin Anianus

without a reason."* If God knows, as was said, and if he wills, because he is a Father, and if he is able, because he is all-powerful, we should have no fear that he will provide for us. *Sermone monte 2.17.58; PL 34:1296; CL 35:154

*There are many reasons that we are sometimes allowed to experience a want of the necessities of life: first, because of our sins; second, to strengthen our virtue; third, to counteract our greed, for sometimes by seeking unnecessary earthly goods we lose what is essential; fourth, to chasten us for our attachment to what is superfluous, for it is fitting that we who chase after luxuries should sometimes need what is essential; fifth, it is right that sometimes what is needful is taken away because of our abuse of God's creatures; sixth, because of our ingratitude, for it is appropriate for God to withdraw some of his benefits from those who are ungrateful; seventh, so that we will believe that temporal goods come from God, not from ourselves, and that he does not have to give them to us; by withholding them he shows that he is the Master. ***R 13**

*Therefore, the Lord allows us to be concerned about work and the need to provide, but he prohibits anxiety that is fearful or faithless. He forbids disordered and overly solicitous concern, for this impedes or delays spiritual goods; he permits moderate and necessary concern that is guided by the rule of right reason, for this is an aspect of prudence. If we expect to receive everything we need from God without doing what we humanly can, we are testing God. ***R 14**

We can love two kinds of temporal goods, those that are superfluous and those that are necessary. In opposition to the first, God forbids us to store up treasure; in opposition to the second, a choking anxiety.* **Hugh 3.19*

Note, too, that there are three kinds of solicitude. The first is from nature and might more truly be called the effort to provide what we need; this is given to us so that we will not test God, provided that we still prefer God to all else. Thus it was said to Adam, *In the sweat of your face shall you eat bread.** And we read in *Gen 3:19

the gospel that the Lord had a money box. The second kind of solicitude is culpable and consists in amassing a lot more than we really need. This concern is the child and companion of avarice; it is also accompanied by a desire for what is most elegant and luxurious, or such an excessive anxiety to provide what is necessary that spiritual matters are neglected. This kind of solicitude is considered a vice and is always prohibited. Third, there is a solicitude born of grace, which consists in doing works of righteousness and having compassion on our neighbor. Hence the apostle speaks of *my daily concern, the solicitude for all the churches*.* This kind of solicitude is commanded because it is recognized as pertaining to charity. The first kind of solicitude is permissible, the second is censured, and the third is praiseworthy.

*2 Cor 11:28

Seek First the Kingdom of God

***R 15**

Finally the Lord concludes by speaking about what should concern us, the things of eternity. He mentions three kinds of goods here: heavenly, spiritual, and temporal—the goods of glory, grace, and prosperity. The first is the greatest, the second less great, and the third least. Heavenly goods should hold first place in our intentions, as a reward; spiritual goods come second in our works, as merit; and temporal blessings are added in third place, for our sustenance. He teaches, "*Be not solicitous* to pursue worldly gain. *Seek therefore first* in your attention and affection *the kingdom of God*, that is, eternal life and heavenly goods, as the principal source of your happiness before everything else, and as the ultimate end to be sought for its own sake. *And*, to avoid error in this quest, seek in the second place *his justice* as the right path by which you can deserve to obtain the kingdom of God, fulfilling his precepts and doing works of righteousness. *And* in the third place *all these things* necessary for life, that

**Gorran Matt 6:31*

is, all temporal goods (signified by food, drink, and clothing) *shall be added unto you.*"* *Matt 6:31, 33

They are *added unto you* as collaborators and cooperators, who work with appropriate concern to gain them: just as the fruits of the earth are taken away because of evil works, so they are added for good works. However, if present goods are removed, this can be for our training and testing; if they are taken away entirely, we can be found worthy of a martyr's crown; if they are bestowed, this is for our comfort and is a cause for thanksgiving. *To them that love God all things work together unto good.** The divine Physician knows what is best for us.* *Rom 8:28 **Zachary 1.37–38 approx; PL 186:146D*

Something is designated as *first* in relation to something else, so it is obvious that Christ does not rule out any solicitude for the necessities of life. Rather, he shows that we should be concerned first about spiritual matters, and only secondarily about temporal ones,* because these *shall be added unto* us, provided we set up no impediment and do not, in our concern for what is secondary, ignore what is primary or set up two competing ends. According to Augustine, in using the word *first* in relation to the kingdom of God, Christ indicates that temporal goods are sought second, not in point of time but in worth; the kingdom is sought as our good, other things as necessary in view of that good.* To seek first the kingdom of God and temporal goods afterwards is simply to have our priorities right: we ought to seek temporal goods for the sake of the kingdom of God and not vice versa. He clearly teaches that we should not strive eagerly for temporal things, nor do good for their sake, even though they are necessary; rather, we are taught to do everything for the sake of the kingdom of God. **Lyra Matt 6:31* *Sermone monte 2.16.53; PL 34:1292; CL 35:144

So even when we do good works we should be thinking of our eternal welfare, not our temporal well-being; longing for the kingdom of God should hold first place in our intentions and affections. The early saints sought first the kingdom of God and therefore, in the time of Constantine, God added unto them an earthly kingdom. But today there are many who first and foremost seek earthly domains instead of the kingdom of God, and they are more anxious about property and riches than they are for souls and the church. I fear for them, that they will forfeit the kingdom of God and also their earthly realms.

Have No Anxiety about the Future

*R 16
*Matt 6:34

*Then the Lord forbids us to fret about the future, saying, "*Be not therefore solicitous for tomorrow*,* that is, for the future." We should not be excessively worried about the cares of the morrow, anticipating them today. According to Jerome, he concedes that those who are forbidden to worry about the future should be attentive to the present.* It is enough for us to be concerned about present matters; future ones, which are uncertain, we should leave to God.

*Com Matt 6:34; PL 26:46B; CL 77:41

Peter Cantor writes,

> Above, the Lord forbade anxious concern about the present, which we can interpret as a period of one year, because we sow, reap, and gather in crops annually. Now he forbids solicitude about the future, which can be taken to mean the following year. It is not right to be preoccupied about the things divine providence bestows. If your foresight extends beyond one year, it is turning excessive—like the case of that abbot who stored up three years' worth of grain. How can we call such people prudent, when they are acting contrary to the Lord's prohibition, who allows us only to concern ourselves with the present? This is how people act when they do not trust God, and they are very miserable.*

*Com Matt 6:34

Chrysostom says, "The Lord directs us to give no thought to tomorrow, but no one listens and no one puts his words into practice. God does not command us to pray for temporal goods, but we expend all of our effort on them, and we are consumed with thinking about them. The more we attend to worldly matters, the more we neglect spiritual ones—indeed, we are far removed from them."* The Lord does not want us to be anxious about the future, as if we were certain of days to come, when we cannot even be secure about the present. Anselm counsels, "Imagine you are going to die today, and you will not think about tomorrow."* And Seneca: "Every day should be planned as if it were the last."*

*Compunctione 1.4.5; PG 47:401

*Med 16; PL 158:794D

*Lucilium 12.8

Therefore it is sufficient for us to give thought to the present and let go of anxiety about the future, which is uncertain. The Lord says, "*For the morrow will be solicitous for itself,** that is, it will bring its own cares with it." The future will have its own cares. Different times bring different challenges, and it suffices to deal with each as it comes.* It is as if he were advising us, "Be concerned about the future when it arrives, and not before. Just as I do not forbid concern about the present day, so I do not forbid concern about tomorrow—when it comes."* As was noted earlier, the word *solicitous* means avaricious anxiety, which should always be avoided; prudent attention to present matters is necessary.

*Matt 6:34

**Lyra Matt 6:34*

**Bruno Com Matt 6:34 approx; PL 165:124C*

And to emphasize that our concern should be limited to the day at hand, he adds, *Sufficient for the day is the evil thereof.** That is, each day has its own time of labor and effort, misfortune and contrition, sorrow and grief, anguish and affliction, cares and concerns. The word *evil* here does not refer to the evil of wrong that we commit, but to the evil of punishment that we endure. (Our first parents did not experience this anxiety in their state of innocence.)

*Matt 6:34

It is as if he is saying, "There is no need to anticipate the needs of tomorrow, because today has enough of its own. Today has cares enough, do not add to them. Why do you want to pile evil upon evil, work upon work, care upon care?" Thus the word *evil* here refers to effort and misery, not wickedness. Are we not accustomed to say, "I've had a very bad day," when we have been worn out by labor or suffering?*

**Bruno Com Matt 6:34 approx; PL 165:124C–25A*

Chrysostom writes,

> By *evil* here he means effort and distress, not wickedness. Similarly, when in another place he says, *Shall there be evil in a city, which the Lord has not done?** this refers, not to greed or robbery or such things, but to punishments visited by God. Elsewhere he says through the prophet, *I make peace, and create evil.** Again, this is not understood to mean wickedness, but things like pestilence, famine, and similar catastrophes that many call evil. So here, he uses the word *evil* to mean affliction, saying, *Sufficient for the day is the evil thereof,* because nothing so drags down the soul as anxious preoccupation.*

*Amos 3:6

*Isa 45:7

*Hom Matt 22.4; PG 57/58:304; Anianus

Labor and foresight are not condemned, but stifling anxiety is. This is why Augustine warns:

> Here we must be scrupulously on our guard, lest when we see some servants of God making provision for their own needs or the needs of those in their care, we judge them to be acting contrary to the Lord's precept by being solicitous for the morrow. For the Lord himself, whom the angels served, set an example for the sake of his church because he deemed it proper to have a money box, so that no one would be scandalized by such behavior. It is amply apparent that the Lord did not disapprove of people procuring things in the ordinary way but only when someone enlists under his standard for the sake of plunder and not for the kingdom of God.
>
> The whole precept can be reduced to this: we should keep our minds on the kingdom of God even when we are providing for such things, but when serving in the ranks of the kingdom of God

we should not think of them.* With undivided heart we should work good to all because of the kingdom of God, and in so doing, we should not have our minds on temporal rewards, either alone or together with God's kingdom.* Thus, if at times these things should be lacking—a situation that God often permits for our training—this not only does not weaken our resolve, but it also strengthens it through testing.*

*Sermone monte 2.17.58; PL 34:1296; CL 35:153

*Sermone monte 2.17.56; PL 34:1295; CL 35:148–49

*Sermone monte 2.17.58; PL 34:1296; CL 35:153

✠

Lord Jesus Christ, grant that I may not lay up the treasure of wealth on earth, but the reward of merits in heaven. Since no one can serve two masters issuing contradictory orders, free me from my servitude to the dominion of the world, the flesh, and the devil, so that I may gaze in contemplation upon the things of heaven rather than those of earth. Add to the stature of my nature a cubit now of grace, and hereafter of glory, so that I may consider the lilies of the field, the faithful members of your church clothed in radiant virtues, rather than the rich of this world, who are destined to be cast into the oven of hell. May I seek first the kingdom of God and its justice so that, equipped with the needed provisions for the journey, I may come by the path of virtues to the kingdom of heaven.

CHAPTER 39

The Sermon on the Mount, Continued: The Need to Be Merciful; the Importance of Prayer

(Matt 7:1-12; Luke 6:36-49; 11:5-13)

***R 1** *Luke 6:36

*Next the Lord exhorts us to be merciful to our neighbor: *Be merciful, as your Father also is merciful.** God alleviates our misery, moved solely by his own goodness and expecting nothing in return; just so, we should be moved to relieve the sufferings of our neighbors, not for our advantage or gain, but for their health/salvation and from love of the divine goodness. If we look out for others or do them good with an eye to our own benefit, this is not charity: we are seeking what is useful to ourselves, not loving them as we love ourselves. The Lord wants us to imitate the Father in being merciful—we, who stand in such need of his mercy ourselves. We should not strive to imitate him in power, for such pride caused the demon to be cast into hell. Nor should we seek to imitate his wisdom, for by desiring that, our first parents lost Paradise and were deprived of the glory of immortality. But his praise of mercy is great, for this imprints upon our souls certain signs of a heavenly nature.

It is natural for animals of the same species to look out for one another. How much more should human beings, who are made in God's image, be compassionate with others who share that image? We ought to feel others' misery in our own hearts; this is the rule of mercy. Jerome says this about works of piety, "I have never read anywhere of those who generously performed works of mercy dying a bad death; they have many intercessors, and it is impossible that the prayers of so many should not be heard."*

*Ps-Augustine, Fratres 44; PL 40:1319

The First Kind of Mercy: Not to Judge Others

*R 2

*The Lord then specifies three expressions of mercy, the first being not to judge others. It is difficult to know with certainty in what spirit many actions are done, whether they are performed from a pure heart or by duplicity; so he wisely adds, "*Judge not* your neighbor **rashly or unjustly**,* *and you shall not be judged*."* That is, you will not commit a sin for which you deserve to be judged by God. And if, on account of human weakness, you suspect that someone is deserving of judgment, then, *Condemn not, and you shall not be condemned*.* That is, do not declare that someone merits condemnation, and you yourself will not be condemned for this sin. The wickedest person today might be a good person tomorrow.

*Latin Diatessaron?

*Luke 6:37

*Luke 6:37

It should be understood that there is judgment involved when a civil or ecclesiastical court renders a verdict, but that is not what is under discussion here. Another form of judgment is to judge that another person is wicked on the basis of certain actions; this is what is forbidden by the words *Judge not*.

However, there are many ways we can judge that another is evil. There is a judgment made on the basis of factual evidence: for example, if you see one man kill another, you could judge that he is a murderer. Such a judgment is not a sin. Then there is a judgment made on the basis of very strong circumstantial evidence: for example, if you see a man and a woman lying alone together naked, you could judge that they are committing the sin of fornication. Again, this judgment is not a sin.*

*Lyra Matt 7:1

Then there is a judgment made on the basis of slight evidence. There are three degrees of judgment here. The first is when you begin to doubt another person's goodness on the basis of trifling evidence. This is a venial sin because it emerges from human weakness; properly speaking, it is not a judgment, but a suspicion. The second degree is when, on the basis of trifling evidence, you are firmly convinced in your heart that a person is wicked. This is judgment properly so called, because judgment consists in a definite sentence. This is a mortal sin if, on the basis of trifling evidence, you determine that the individual is guilty of mortal sin, for this is an offense against charity. The third degree is when, on the basis of trifling evidence, you not only judge another but punish the person as if the offense were a matter of fact. This is more serious still: it offends not only charity but the equity of justice. It is of judgments of this last kind that the prohibitions to *judge not* and *condemn not* apply.*

*Lyra Matt 7:1

The Lord forbids us to judge or condemn rashly. Wicked people often give an evil interpretation to what they see and hear. Good people, however, interpret everything in a positive light: they do not doubt that everything happens according to the will of God, or is at least justly permitted by him, and so they gain in every circumstance.*

*MVC 43 approx; CM 153:157

Augustine says, "The behavior of good people consists of three things: thinking well of everyone, doing good to everyone, enduring evil from everyone."* And Bernard warns, "Refrain from curiosity about other people's conduct and shun rash judgment. Even if you should see your neighbor doing what is wrong, refuse to pass judgment; excuse instead. Excuse the intention even if you cannot excuse the act, which

*source unknown

might have been the fruit of ignorance or surprise or chance. Even if you are so certain that to dissemble is impossible, you must still endeavor to convince yourself by saying, 'It was an overwhelming temptation; what should become of me if it attacked me with the same force?' "*

*SC 40.5; PL 184:984B; SB 2:27

The Lord thoroughly reproves those who rush to judgment in doubtful cases and condemn on the basis of mere suspicion. In doubtful matters it is advisable always to give the best and most benign interpretation. Augustine comments,

> I think this text enjoins one thing on us: that we must put the best construction on actions where the motivation is in doubt.* Some actions are neutral; we do not know with what intention they were done, because it could have been with either a good or a bad one; it is rash to judge them, and especially to condemn.* Now there are two situations in which we must guard against rash judgment: when we are unsure about the disposition with which something is done, or when we are uncertain what a person will be like in the future who appears to be good or bad now. Let us not, therefore, pronounce a verdict of guilty in matters whose motivations we do not know, nor denounce what is obviously wrong as if we despaired of a remedy. In this way we will avoid the sentence pronounced here: *Judge not, and you shall not be judged.**

*Sermone monte 2.18.59; PL 34:1296; CL 35:154

*Sermone monte 2.18.60; PL 34:1297; CL 35:156

*Sermone monte 2.18.61; PL 34:1297; CL 35:157

Chrysostom writes, "We should not harshly censure the sins of others or crush the guilty with opprobrium, but gently reprove them. Do not overwhelm them with invective, but assist them with advice. Otherwise, you will condemn yourself, not them: truly terrible will be the Judgment you bring upon yourself, and you will experience the most exacting punishment for even your smallest failings. Your sins will be weighed with the same severe measure you used when judging

*Hom Matt 23.1; PG 57/58:309; Latin Anianus
‡Attr. to Chrysostom CA Luke 6:37–38

your neighbor.* This is a snare of the devil, for if you severely examine others, you will never deserve forgiveness for your own sins."‡ And elsewhere he warns, "If we committed no other sin, this would be sufficient, and more than sufficient, to make us worthy of Gehenna: to pass a severe and harsh verdict on others' failings. We ignore the beam stuck in our own eye while scrupulously surveying even the slightest imperfections of others, spending our whole lives condemning them. You will not easily find anyone who is free of this defect, either in the world or in the cloister."*

*Grimlaicus 28; PL 103:616C

Christ continues, "*For with what judgment you judge others*, just or unjust, merciful or harsh, *you shall be judged by God; and with what measure you mete out* to others, *it shall be measured to you again** in Judgment." In other words, the intensity of your punishment will match the rashness of your judgment,* and the length of your future retribution will equal the perverseness of your will. Two things are threatened: judgment and measure. Judgment refers to the nature of the sin and its retribution, measure refers to quantity.

*Matt 7:2

**Lyra Matt 7:2*

However, Augustine cautions, this should not be interpreted to mean that if we judge rashly, God will judge us rashly; or that if we employ an unjust measure, God will use an unjust measure on us. No, the force of the statement is that the temerity with which we punish others will punish us in turn.* Unfairness is not proportioned to unfairness; punishment is proportioned to sin. If through our fault we have judged rashly, God's just Judgment will punish us according to the gravity of our offense, and the measure of our sin will determine the measure of our penalty. We can apply here another word of Jesus: *All that take the sword shall perish with the sword.** If we strike someone with the sword of unjust judgment, we will be pierced justly by the sword of the divine verdict and suffer eternal death.

*Sermone monte 2.18.62; PL 34:1297; CL 35:157

*Matt 26:52

The Second Kind of Mercy: To Forgive Others

*Then the Lord specifies the second kind of mercy, which consists in forgiveness: "*Forgive* the injuries done to you by others and the debts owed you by the poor, *and you shall be forgiven** by God for your sins, by which you have injured him and incurred a debt to him." *R 3 *Luke 6:37

The Third Kind of Mercy: To Give to the Poor

*He then specifies the third kind of mercy, which consists in giving: "*Give* temporal goods to those in need, *and it* (eternal life), *shall be given to you*."* *To forgive* and *to be forgiven* are inseparable companions, as are *to give* and *to be given*. Augustine writes, "There are two works of mercy that free us: *Forgive, and you shall be forgiven; Give, and it shall be given to you. Forgive, and you shall be forgiven* refers to pardon. *Give, and it shall be given to you* refers to giving benefits. If you want to be pardoned, pardon: *Forgive, and you shall be forgiven*. If you want to receive, give: *Give, and it shall be given to you*."* Augustine also observes that there are two wings attached to prayer that carry it up to God: forgiving wrongdoers and giving to the poor.* Bede comments, "He commands us to forgive injuries and give benefits, so that we may be forgiven our sins and be given eternal life. In one brief but excellent sentence he includes everything he has taught about how to treat our enemies."* *R 4 *Luke 6:38 *Sermo 83.2; PL 38:515 *Sermo 205.3; PL 38:1040 *Com Luke 6:37–38; PL 92:409A; CL 120:147

Because, as James says, *For judgment without mercy will be meted to him that has not done mercy*,* the Lord is very insistent that we show mercy to others in their need so that we may receive help in time of need, too. As Augustine says, "Everyone will receive the same *Jas 2:13

*Ps-Augustine, Sermo 304.2; PL 39:2329

pardon from God that he gave to others."* And again, "This is the one way to evade evils: put up with the weaknesses of others, help them to the best of our ability (just as we desire divine help), and forgive as we wish to be forgiven. *Blessed are the merciful,** because God will be merciful to them."*

*Matt 5:7

*Sermone monte 1.4.11 approx; PL 34:1235; CL 35:10

Here we might recall a story from the lives of the Desert Fathers. There was once a very prosperous monastery whose monks gave generously to those in need. However, as soon as they stopped giving alms they found themselves in want. They referred the matter to a holy man, who said, "There were two companions living in that monastery: *Give* and *It will be given to you*. You expelled the first companion, so the second one no longer wanted to remain."*

*source unknown

The Lord encourages us to be generous in showing mercy and giving benefits, for we will be rewarded for this liberality. If we give someone even a glass of cold water, God will give us the reward of eternal blessedness because of the intercession of those we have helped and because of our merits. He describes the reward in these words: *Good measure and pressed down and shaken together and running over shall they pour into your lap.** The measure is *good*, because it is just and given according to our merits; it is *pressed down*, that is, full, because it is more than we merit; it is *shaken together*, because it surpasses our desires; and it is *running over*, because it exceeds even what surpasses our desires.

*Luke 6:38; *sinum*

Or we can understand the reward for being merciful in this way: it is a *measure*, because God distributes rewards according to each one's deserts; it is *good*, because the reward of beatitude is good, for that beatitude is Goodness itself, containing within it all goodness; it is *pressed down*, that is, full, for heavenly beatitude is such that the soul is completely saturated with glory; it is *shaken together*, that is, firm, for just as we shake things together to make them firm, so the reward of the blessed is stable and secure; and it is *running over*, that is, superabundant, for it exceeds our merits: we have given temporal, worldly goods and we receive eternal, divine ones. And *they pour into your lap* because, according to Gregory, there is nothing more beloved and more secure than that which we place *in the bosom*.* *source unknown; *in sinu*

Then Christ specifies the equity of recompense: "*For with the same measure that you shall mete out* in merit, *it shall be measured to you again** in reward." He says *with the same measure*, that is, with a like measure: if you do good, good will be done to you. But he also says *running over*, because God does a thousand times more good to you than you do to others. God rewards us more abundantly and punishes us less severely than we deserve. We can apply these words in a general way to everything we do in thought, word, and deed: God gives to each according to our deserts. If our works of piety are greater, so will the divine recompense be. However, this greatness is not to be measured always by our external deeds, but by our interior disposition.* As the Savior said, the widow who put two small coins into the temple treasury gave more than many rich people, whose actual donations were much greater. *Luke 6:38 **this sentence: Lyra Luke 6:38*

Blind Guides

**R 5*

And he spoke also to them a similitude: "Can the blind lead the blind? Do they not both fall into the ditch and perdition?" That is, "Can a fool guide a fool in the way of righteousness? Will they not both fall into sin, and later into Gehenna?" As Gregory teaches, "If the shepherd walks on precarious paths, the flock will follow him to the precipice."* It is as if the Lord is saying, "Do what I have said, so that you can illumine those you govern by word and example, unlike the blind guides of the synagogue, not the church." It is ridiculous, and worse, very dangerous, to have a blind *Luke 6:39 *Reg past 1.2; PL 77:15C guide, an ignorant teacher, a lame forerunner, a negligent leader, a mute herald.[1] To avoid danger, do not entrust leadership to someone who is ignorant. If you judge someone else but commit the same sins yourself, you are like a blind person leading another blind person. Can he be led by you into goodness, when you, who consider yourself to be a teacher and doctor, are also sinning?

R 6

*Then he presented another image: *"And why do you see the mote in your brother's eye*, a tiny and insignificant sin that does not completely blind him, and which could be consumed in the fire of charity like a wisp of straw; *but the beam* of a grave sin *that is in your own eye* of intention and conscience *you do not consider*?"* In other words: "How can you have your eyes wide open to judge the least failings of another, but close them when it comes to judging your own great offenses?* How can you scrupulously examine others' mistakes, while neglecting your own?" This criticism applies to everyone, but especially to teachers who punish the least infractions committed by their subjects and leave their own unpunished.

*Luke 6:41; *Gorran Matt 7:3*

**St Cher Com Matt 7:3*

"*Or how* in good conscience *can you* dare *say to your brother* who has sinned less or is even innocent, '*Brother* (feigning affection), sit still and *let me pull the mote* of a minor failing *out of your eye* by rebuking your conscience and intent,' *when you do not see the beam in your own eye?"** The point is, "You cannot rightly say such a thing." Chrysostom warns, "Not everyone can see a mote and remove it, but only those who are learned and holy."* And he also cautions that any priest who wants to teach the people should first instruct himself.*

*Luke 6:42; *Gorran Matt 7:4*

*Opus imperf 17 approx; PG 56:725

*Opus imperf 17; PG 56:726

"*Hypocrite*, that is, one who poses or plays a part (for often the wicked accuse the good to appear righteous and attack others to extol themselves), *cast first*

[1] These oxymorons are attributed to Gilbert in Durandus, 1.7.15; CM 140:88.

the beam of serious sin *out of your own eye* of conscience with the eye salve of penitence: because you know yourself better than you know another, because you can see greater sins more easily than smaller ones, because you are dearer to yourself than your neighbor is, and because serious sins are more dangerous than venial ones. *And then*, when your own eye is cleansed, *you shall see clearly to take out the mote* of minor sins *from your brother's eye** by confronting him." When the eye of conscience is cleansed, it can see; but if it is blinded by the clouds and obscurity of sin, it cannot. This is what you should do, so that you will correct your neighbor more by example than by words. Otherwise, it will be said to you, *Physician, heal yourself,** and, in the words of the apostle, *You that teach others do not teach yourself.** The order of charity dictates that we begin with ourselves; that is, we should correct our own erring conduct before we amend another's.

*Luke 6:42; *Gorran Matt 7:5 approx*

*Luke 4:23

*Rom 2:21

Fraternal Correction

There are several points to be made regarding fraternal correction. The sequence is to amend our own lives before we correct someone else; the mode, gentleness; the motivation, fervent charity. Times and circumstances should be taken into account, as well as the likely outcome of our intervention. It is fairly common, and only natural, for us to minimize our own sins and exaggerate those of others. Hilary states that it is nearly impossible to find someone free of this weakness, because everyone is quick to reproach others while excusing his own conduct. **R 7**

*Gloss Matt 7:3; PL 114:108B; see Hilary, Com Matt 5:15; PL 9:951A

Augustine teaches:

> We must be scrupulously careful when circumstances require us to correct or reproach someone. First, we must consider whether the fault is one that we have had. If we have never had it, we should

reflect that we are only human and might have had it. If we formerly did have it but no longer do so, the recollection of that weakness should be impressed upon our memory; in that way, mercy will be a herald preparing the way for our reproach. But if upon reflection we find the same fault in ourselves as in the one we were planning to correct, then let us not reproach or rebuke that one. Instead, let us sigh deeply and invite that one not to conform himself or herself to us, but to join with us in a common endeavor.* Rarely, therefore, and only under the force of great necessity, should we resort to scolding, and then only in such a way that in these instances, too, we strive to serve God and not ourselves.*

*Sermone monte 2.19.64; PL 34:1298; CL 35:160–61

*Sermone monte 2.19.66; PL 34:1299; CL 35:162

Basil for his part cautions that it is very difficult to judge others because we must first honestly look at ourselves and judge our own behavior, and this is the most important thing of all. While our attention is directed outward on all that is happening around us, we are not keeping an eye on ourselves. When our mind is busy correcting the faults of others, it is hard to see our own defects.*

*Hom in Hexaemeron 9.6; PG 29:203

It should also be noted that someone can offer a rebuke publicly or privately. If done in public, the rebuke is sinful both on account of presumption and scandal; if administered privately, it is only a sin of presumption. But if the person who offers correction first does penance and then speaks with genuine humility, he or she does not sin.*

**Lyra Matt 7:3*

***R 8**

*Because there are some who, in their desire to obey God's precepts, explain them in a way that is beyond the understanding of their hearers (and in this way do more harm than they would had they kept them hidden), the Lord rightly adds, "*Give not that which is holy*—the mysteries of sacred Scripture, the secrets of the faith, or even the sacraments of the church—*to dogs*, by preaching the mysteries or distributing the sacraments to barking detractors or attackers of the truth. *Neither cast your pearls*, that is, what is holy, *before swine, lest perhaps they*, the mockers and despisers, *trample them* with disdain and contempt of mind or heart *under their feet* like pigs, *and turning upon you, they tear you** like dogs after they hear you, blaspheming, criticizing, and assailing the simplicity and truth of the faith."* Augustine says, "There are two reasons that people reject what is of manifest importance: contempt and hatred. The first is symbolized by swine, the second by dogs. We must, therefore, beware of revealing something to those who cannot receive it. It would be better for them to seek what is hidden away than what has been revealed, lest they viciously attack it, like a dog, or contemptuously neglect it, like a pig."*

*Matt 7:6

**Gorran Matt 7:6 approx*

*Sermone monte 2.20.69 approx; PL 34:1300–301; CL 35:165–66

The Necessity of Prayer

Some people, conscious of their ignorance, might say, "How can you tell me not to give what is holy to dogs, or cast pearls before swine, when as yet I do not even have these things?" So the Lord suitably adds, "*Ask* in faith and by praying, *and it shall be given you; seek* in hope and by right living, *and you shall find; knock* in charity and by perseverance, *and it shall be opened to you.*"*

***R 9**

**Zachary 1.40; PL 186:151B*

*Matt 7:7; *Gorran Matt 7:7 approx*

Chrysostom writes, "Because the commandments that he gave earlier are beyond human strength, he sends them to God, with whose grace nothing is impossible, saying, *Ask, and it shall be given you*. What cannot be accomplished by human power can be fulfilled through God's grace. God armed other animals with the ability to run or fly swiftly, or with talons, horns, or teeth. Only in the case of us human beings did he arrange it that he himself would be our strength, so that, compelled by the necessity of our own weakness, we would always rely on our Lord."* And Jerome comments, "If the one who asks receives, and the one who seeks finds, and it is opened to the one

*Opus imperf 18; PG 56:729–30

who knocks, it follows that if people do not receive, find, or have the door opened it is because they have not sought, asked, or knocked well."* And Chrysostom makes this observation: "Where the mercy of the Giver is beyond doubt, the fault lies with the negligence of the petitioner."* Augustine writes, "The Lord Jesus Christ, who unites himself to our asking, unites himself to the Father in giving; he certainly would not exhort us to ask if he were not willing to give. Human laziness should blush for shame—God is anxious to give more than we are anxious to receive, he wants to show mercy more than we want to be freed from misery. He exhorts us here to do something that is for our own good. Let us be attentive and believe that he will do what he has promised; let us pray, so that we can give joy to the Giver."*

*Com Matt 7:7; PL 26:47BC; CL 77:42

*Opus imperf 35; PG 56:825

*Sermo 105.1–2; PL 38:619

***R 10**

Note that prayer must possess three characteristics if it is to be heard. First, it should be devout and just, that is, it should pertain to salvation; in other matters, it may not always be advantageous for our prayer to be answered. Second, it should be constant and not interrupted by things contrary to prayer; however, a person who does not cease doing good does not cease praying. Third, the prayer should concern ourselves: we can pray devoutly and persistently for another, but the efficacy of the prayer might be impeded by the other's defects. If these three conditions are all present, our prayer will always be heard. This is brought out by the three words used here: *ask*, devoutly; *seek*, with perseverance; *knock and it shall be opened to you*, which clearly suggests praying for ourselves.

**Lyra Luke 11:5 mor approx*

Prayer of this kind is unfailing, but so that we would not despair of having our prayer heard, he continues, "*For every one that asks* as he should by believing, *receives; and he that seeks* as he should by hoping, *finds; and to him that knocks* by working, *it shall be opened.*"* Therefore, perseverance is needed if we are to receive what we ask, find what we seek, and have the door

*Matt 7:8

opened when we knock. By this threefold repetition of words the Lord emphasizes that he wants us to be insistent, anxious, bothersome, and shameless in our asking. Someone has said, "Unrelenting effort conquers all."[2] When we ask for something that concerns our salvation, it is not always given immediately; it may be deferred and given at a more opportune time. This delay makes the gift more highly prized because things that are longed for are sweeter when they are granted, whereas things that are given immediately are considered worthless.

And, if we want our prayer to be heard, we must avoid idle prattling. Gregory says that the omnipotent God is less likely to hear our prayers the more we defile our tongue with foolish chatter.* If we hope to be heard, we should also strive ourselves to understand what we are asking for. Ambrose states that God will not attend to the prayer of those who are not themselves attentive to what they are praying about.* God earnestly desires to give what he disposes us to pray for. Bernard writes, "God wishes to be asked for what he has promised. And perhaps he promised many things that he has predetermined to bestow so that the promise may stir up our devotion: what he had determined to give *gratis*, we may merit to receive by devout prayer."*

*Dial 3.15; PL 77:256C

*Hugh of Saint Victor, Reg Augustini 3; PL 176:892B

*Laudibus 4.11; PL 183:86A; SB 4:57

The Lord did not specify what we will receive when we ask, seek, and knock: sometimes we are heard according to our desire and are given what we have asked for; at other times, we are heard according to our merit and will be given something equivalent, or even better. Sometimes holy people do not get what they asked for—they receive more. Augustine cautions,

[2] *Labor improbus omnia vincit* (Virgil, *Georgics*, 1.145–47); the motto adapts Virgil's words.

> Do not think it is such a great thing when God gives you what you want. Sometimes it almost seems that God is angry when he gives you what you ask, and well-disposed to you when he refuses to. The Physician knows what is beneficial to us.* Although God does not give according to our will, he does give for our salvation. What if the thing you ask for will be to your detriment, and the Physician knows this; what then? Brethren, learn to petition God the way you would consult a doctor. Let him do what he knows is best. Confess the disease and let him apply the healing medicine. He does not heed your desire, but your salvation; not what you wish to be done, but what is advantageous.*

Zachary 3.132; PL 186:419B

*Ep John 6.8; PL 35:2024

And Bernard counsels, "Let none of you think little of your prayers, because the one to whom we pray does not think little of them: he will give us either what we ask or something more useful."*

*Sermo 5.3 in Lent; PL 183:180A; SB 4:373

The Lord frequently exhorted his disciples to pray, he often confirmed this instruction by example, and he proposed many lessons to them about this. All of this was done to convince us of the efficacy of prayer. Obviously prayer possesses an inestimable and effective power to obtain what is good and beneficial, and to repel what is evil and harmful. So, if you want to bear patiently with adversity, pray. If you want to crush underfoot corrupt desires, pray. If you want to know Satan's stratagems and evade his lies, pray. If you want to live joyfully in the works of God, never giving way in the midst of labors and affliction, pray. If you want to live a spiritual life and make no provision for the cares of the flesh, pray. If you want to drive away the gnats of vain thoughts, pray. If you want to build up your spirit with holy, good thoughts and fervent desires, pray. If you want to make your heart firm with a valorous spirit, living in a way that is pleasing to God, pray. If you want to expel vice and be imbued with virtue, pray. If you want to rise up to contemplation and enjoy the Bridegroom's embrace, pray. If you want to savor heavenly sweetness and the other great blessings of God, pray. In a word, prayer serves in any necessity: it drives from us the spirit of evil and calls good things to us.* *Massa; MVC 36; CM 153:135–36

Bede writes, "Just as the thief runs away and the neighbors come to help when a cry goes up, so at the cry of prayer the devil flees and all the saints and angels are summoned to our aid."* And Bernard again: "There is a most trustworthy messenger between Babylon and Jerusalem, known to the king and his retinue. This is prayer, which, in the secret silence of the night and on unknown paths, makes its way into the hidden heart of heaven and approaches the king's bedchamber. With timely importunity, it convinces the loving king to dispatch needed help."‡

*cited in St Cher Com Luke 22:40

‡Parabola 2.6; PL 183:764A; SB 6:2:271

***R 11**

You can see how great is the power of prayer. Leaving aside the proofs found in Scripture, evidence is offered every day by what we see and hear, through the experience of simple, unlettered people who receive through prayer what we have been talking about, and indeed even more and greater things. It is certainly a great sign of God's grace to make time frequently for prayer. Augustine says, "When you see that your supplication is not turned away from you, be secure, for his mercy is not turned away from you."*

*MVC 36; CM 153:136

*En Ps 65, 24; PL 36:801; CL 39:856

I would briefly sum up the usefulness of prayer by saying that it is very necessary for salvation. Augustine, again, says, "We believe that no one would come to salvation unless God summoned him or her, no one would be summoned unless with God's help he or she did good works, and no one can receive God's help without praying."*

*Gennadius, Eccles dogmatibus 26; PL 42:1218

Give yourself over to prayer and let nothing but the most necessary tasks keep you from it; let nothing give you such pleasure as prayer, for nothing is sweeter than to abide with God, which is what we do in prayer.* Chrysostom writes, "Consider what happiness is given you, what glory to converse with God, to hold conversation with Christ, to desire what you would, and to ask for what you desire."*

*MVC 36; CM 153:136

*Cited in ST II-II, 83.2, ad tertium

Examples to Encourage Prayer

***R 12**

Then, to foster the trust of those who pray, the Lord confirms what he promised above by giving examples, arguing from lesser things to greater ones. First he tells the parable of a man who gets up at midnight and supplies bread to an importunate friend who asks for it. If a human being gives out of weariness when another asks persistently, how much more will God do so from friendship? Bede writes, "The comparison is from something less: If someone will get out of bed to give to another, not from friendship but from weariness, how much more will God give generously without being pestered; but he wants to be asked, so that those who petition will have the capacity to receive what they ask for." Augustine says, "Although he was a friend, he did not do this for friendship's sake, but because of the man's importunity—he kept knocking and would not go away if refused. The man did not want to do what the other asked but did so because he would not stop asking. How much more will the good Father give: he exhorts us to ask him, and he is displeased if we do *not* ask."*

*Com Luke 11:8; PL 92:473D; CL 120:228

*Sermo 61.5.6; PL 38:411; CL 41 Aa:269

And Ambrose for his part comments,

> He came at midnight so that prayer would be offered at every moment, by night as well as by day. Attentive to the Scriptures, therefore, let us be constant in prayer night and day, asking forgiveness for our sins. A very holy man, occupied with the needs of his realm, offered praise to God *seven times a day*,* always intent on morning and evening sacrifices. How much more frequently must we

*Ps 118:164

> ask, we who offend more frequently through the weakness of body and mind, so *that* the restoring *bread* that *strengthens man's heart** be not lacking to us who are exhausted on the winding path of our journey through the course of this age? The Lord teaches us that we should be vigilant not only at midnight, but almost always. We must keep awake, for many snares surround us: the mind loses the strength of its vigor if it begins to succumb to the body's heavy drowsiness. Rise from your sleep so that you can knock on Christ's door!*

*Ps 103:15

*Exp Luke 7.87–89; PL 15:1721AD; CL 14:242–43

Next he tells the parable of the earthly father who gives his children what they need when they ask him. He mentions three items so that we will understand what kinds of things we should ask for from God. The first is bread, signifying charity. Just as every table without bread is considered destitute, so without charity every virtue is vain and empty, and every good work is wasted. The opposite of this is hardness of heart, symbolized by a stone. We should pray for both these things: to have our hardness of heart taken away and to be given charity.

***R 13**

**Bonaventure, Com Luke 11:11–12 approx*

The second item is a fish, signifying faith. The fish is born in water, and, far from perishing in the waves, it is purged and strengthened by them. Similarly, faith is born in baptism, and it is not extinguished by the waves of adversity in this world; rather, it is purified. The contrary here is a serpent, because of the venom of infidelity. Let us ask for this faith from God, so that he will not give us a serpent—that is, lack of faith or the perverse teachings of the heretics, which are symbolized by the serpent.*

**Bonaventure, Com Luke 11:11–12 approx*

The third item is an egg, signifying hope. The egg is not yet a formed animal but holds the promise of one, and hope consists in anticipation, not possession. We expect a chick to hatch once the egg is warmed by the mother hen, and we await eternal beatitude to be born of hope if that hope is warmed by the heat of charity. To this is opposed the scorpion, whose venom is in its tail. Let us ask Christ to give us this hope instead of a scorpion, which stings with its tail, and kills, and leads to eternal death. We must beg God for these three virtues, for there is no salvation without them.*

**Bonaventure, Com Luke 11:11–12 approx*

If human beings, *being evil* (both because we are prone to evil and by comparison with divine mercy and clemency, in respect to which no one is good) give their children the good material things they have received from God, *how much more will your Father from heaven*, whose very nature is goodness itself, *give the good Spirit*, that is, the spiritual goods of grace and glory, *to them that ask him*?* He calls every spiritual good *the good spirit* because, according to Augustine, the Holy Spirit is the first gift, in whom everything is given.[3] Augustine also says, "He who gives himself freely to those who do not ask will not refuse himself to those who do."*

*Luke 11:13

*Paschasius Radbertus, Com Matt 7:8; PL 120:319D; CM 56:436

And more than this, how could *he that spared not even his own Son, but delivered him up* to death *for us all*‡ not give us everything we ask for? He will give what we ask if we do what he commands. Elsewhere Augustine teaches, "If you want God to listen to you, you must first listen to God.* How can you have the audacity to demand what God promised if you do not do what God commanded? First hear his admonitions and then examine his promises. Those who turn away from God's precepts do not deserve to receive what they ask for in prayer."*

‡Rom 8:32

*Sermo 17.4; PL 38:126; not in CL

*Ps-Augustine, Sermo 382.1; PL 39:1685

The Golden Rule

***R 14**

*Then Jesus indicates what behavior will make our prayer deserving of a positive response: *"All things therefore whatsoever* that are reasonable and in accord with charity *that you would that men should do to you*

[3] De Trin 15.19.34 (PL 42:1084): "Through the Gift, which is the Holy Spirit, common to all the members of Christ, gifts proper to each are divided."

usefully and properly, *do you also to them** according to time and place." How can you dare to petition your God when you ignore your equal? In other words: "If you want to receive what you ask for, find what you seek, or enter by knocking, then do to others what you wish them to do to you, and do not hope to receive from them what you have not done." Chrysostom writes, "It is as though he were saying, 'If you want to be heard concerning the things about which I spoke, then likewise do this. You have certainly seen that the practice of virtue must accompany prayer. Display in your dealings with others what you want to be done to you.' What precept could be easier or more just than this?"*

*Matt 7:12

*Hom Matt 24.5; PG 57/58:314; Latin Anianus

The righteous do all these things; this is why *the continual prayer of a just man avails much.** Just people are truly a strong tower and wall in adversity, protecting both themselves and others. There is a figure of this in the book of Numbers, where it says that Aaron stood praying between the dead and the living; the plague ceased and he delivered the people from the destroying fire.* And, in reference to the words in Genesis, *I will not destroy it for the sake of ten,** Ambrose says, "From this we learn what a bulwark the just are to their homeland. Their faith protects us, their righteousness defends us from divine wrath."[4]* And Gregory advises, "Better to go into battle with one righteous person praying than with numberless soldiers. The prayer of the just pierces the heavens; how can it not vanquish enemies on earth?"*

*Jas 5:16

*Num 16:48

*Gen 18:32

*De Abraham 2.5.48; PL 14:439C

*Rabanus Maurus, Com Num 31:8; PL 108:795C

Note that when he says *all things*, the Lord means that this commandment is not fulfilled if we omit something, especially if we are able to do it, unless exempted for a greater good. What then of those who not only neglect to do these things but afflict others, doing to them what they would not want done to themselves, and so break this commandment? It can

[4] Ludolph has *odio divino*; Ambrose has *excidio* (destruction).

be said that the perfect are bound to observe both parts of this rule, omitting no good and not doing what they would not have done to themselves. The imperfect are bound only by the second half, except in case of necessity: the second half is obligatory, the first goes beyond the call of duty.

There is a twofold aspect of the natural law. The first is negative, and it is expressed by Tobit: *See you never do to another what you would hate to have done to you by*
*Tob 4:16 *another*.* The other aspect is positive and is stated here: it includes the negative prohibition within it. Hence Chrysostom says, "Since there are two ways that lead to virtue, namely abstaining from evil and doing good,
CA Luke 6:27–31 he names one, signifying by it the other also." This positive precept calls for greater perfection than the negative one; so it is reasonable that the affirmative is stated in the new law, which leads to greater perfection.

Formerly we were forbidden to do evil; here we are commanded to do good, even to the wicked. *Charity*
*1 Cor 13:4 *is patient, is kind*;* it does not only bear with injuries from another; it also kindly anticipates these with grace, so as to derive the benefits of charity. Weigh carefully how perfect this rule is, to draw the blessings of love from one who does not love. Therefore, Christ did not say, "Do unto others as they do unto you," but
**Zachary 1.31 approx; PL 186:134D* "Do unto others as you *would have them do* unto you."* If we think about doing unto others as we hope they would do unto us, we will doubtless do good to those who are evil, and do even more for those who are good.

This Fulfills the Law and the Prophets

***R 15** *In praise of this rule, the Lord adds, *For this is the*
*Matt 7:12 *law and the prophets*.* That is, it fulfills the natural law that is inscribed in the human heart, the innate ability we possess to distinguish between virtue and vice, and it fulfills the Law of Moses and the preaching of

the prophets that is summed up in the commandment to love your neighbor as yourself out of love for God. It is as if he were saying, "Everything taught in the law, the prophets, and sacred Scriptures is fulfilled in this one commandment, leads to it, and was pronounced for its sake. All precepts governing behavior toward others are simply conclusions drawn from this rule." This is why the apostle can say, *For he that loves his neighbor has fulfilled the law.** *Rom 13:8

Chrysostom says, "The Lord has summed up in one brief phrase everything necessary for our faith and salvation, so that we will treat others the way we would like to be treated ourselves. He clearly states that all the precepts in the law and the prophets are contained in this one mandate: *For this is the law and the prophets*. Whatever things the law and the prophets have commanded here and there in all the Scriptures are summed up in this one comprehensive commandment, just as the countless branches of a tree all derive from one root."* If we wish to receive from others only what is good and useful, we for our part should act with grace and love toward them; in this we will fulfill the law and the prophets and receive a reward for our faith from the Lord. Truly the Lord's *yoke is sweet and burden light*:* all of the precepts regarding our neighbor are contained in one brief rule. *Chromatius 33.8; CL 9A:363 *Matt 11:30

In another place, when speaking of the twofold commandment to love God and neighbor, the Lord did not just say, "On these two commandments depends the law and the prophets," but he added, *On these two commandments depends the whole law and the prophets.** But by not making the same addition here he left room for the precept pertaining to the love of God. Some people suggest, however, that what Christ says here embraces also the love of God, without which charity towards our neighbor cannot be fulfilled—we cannot love God without loving our neighbor, and vice versa.* Reflect upon the precept taught here by the Lord and consider how rare it is for anyone to observe it. *Matt 22:40 **Gloss Matt 7:12; PL 114:109D*

As to the positive rule laid down here in the gospel (*All things therefore whatsoever you would that men should do to you, do you also to them*), I do not know if we could find anyone today who keeps this. Regarding the negative rule enunciated in the book of Tobit (*See you never do to another what you would hate to have done to you by another*), if there are any observing it, they are few indeed, for, as Chrysostom notes, on the contrary we do to others what we do not want them to do to us.* And we see this not only among people in the world, but even among some religious, who harm their brethren by taking away persons or things that are necessary or procuring for them what is useless. In these and many other ways people act contrary to the Lord's command by doing what they would not want done to them—and it will not be a cause for wonder if in the future they must endure what they will not want done to them.

*Compunctione 1.6; PG 47:403

✠

Lord Jesus Christ, you have taught us to be merciful to everyone and to judge no one. Grant that I may carry out your teaching so that with your help I may please you. You have exhorted us to pray, and you are certainly willing always to give what you inspire us to ask for. Therefore I ask, because you command it; I seek, because you order it; I knock, because you enjoin it. Since you have made me ask, make me receive; since you have given me to seek, grant that I may find; since you have taught me to knock, open so that I may enter. My desire comes from you; so may its fulfillment. Give what I offer and protect what you exact, so that you will crown what you give. Amen.

CHAPTER 40

The Sermon on the Mount: Conclusion

(Matt 7:13-29; Luke 6:46-49; 13:24)

*The Lord taught many and wonderful things, but he also admonished his disciples to free themselves of immoderate passions. And, lest someone object that what he enjoined was difficult and the way he laid out was so demanding that his teaching could not be followed, he added this warning: "*Strive to enter by the narrow gate*, not the broad one."* In other words, "Although what has been said is difficult and restricting, it is meritorious and gains entrance to heavenly things." Note that he says *strive*, because *the kingdom of heaven suffers violence, and the violent bear it away.** The resident on earth can become a citizen of heaven only with great effort. This is a good and holy struggle, as is evidenced by the Theban Legion, whose members vied with one another in their longing for a glorious death.[1] But the combat is very different these days: people struggle for prestige, wealth, revenge, and similar things.

*R 1

*Luke 13:24

*Matt 11:12

[1] The Theban Legion were Christian soldiers serving under a pagan Roman emperor executed for refusing to sacrifice to the emperor. The earliest account of their martyrdom dates back to ca. 450, in a description by Saint Eucherius of Lyons (PL 50:824–32). Saint Maurice and his companions were popular saints in the Middle Ages, and the *Golden Legend* has a lengthy description of their martyrdom.

The Lord explains the reason for this warning: *Enter in at the narrow gate, for wide is the gate, and broad is the way that leads to destruction, and many there are who go that way. How narrow is the gate, and strait is the way that leads to life, and few there are that find it!** The *gate*, or entrance, applies to beginners; the *way*, or progress, to the proficient. And what he says is very true: the way that leads to life is narrow and difficult, while the alternative is spacious and easy. Who of us does not find it difficult to fast, keep vigil, abstain from delightful pleasures, and not do what we like? On the other hand, what could be easier than to enjoy fine food and drink, hearken to pleasures of the flesh, and never contradict our own whims? Alas! Almost all of us march down the broad road, and few take the narrow path.*

*Matt 7:13-14

**Bruno Com Matt 7:13 approx; PL 165:129C*

Chrysostom has this to say about the Lord's directive:

> We are commanded to enter through the narrow gate, and yet we are always strolling down the broad highway. Now it is no great surprise that worldly people should take such an easy road, but you should marvel that those who want to take up their cross and follow Christ choose this wide path. Worse still, there are monks who, in seeking out a monastery, inquire first about whether there is repose to be found there, an abundance of amenities, and plenty of running water. And when looking for a hermitage, their primary concerns seem to be whether there is leisure and every bodily comfort. Or, if you are chosen to fill some position in the sacred ministry, and your first questions are, "Will I be able to relax? Is there a lot of property?" is this any different from those who insist on following the broad and easy road?
>
> What are you doing, what are you saying? You have been commanded to take the hard, narrow path; why are you lingering on the highway? You have been told to enter through the narrow gate; why do you demand a wide portal? Can there be

a worse change, a more harmful perversion? Even those who serve worldly princes do not preoccupy themselves with these things—they only ask for a billet and pay for their military service. Facing the prospect of being alone, they refuse no work, they evade no danger, they beg off from no humiliating service that they are asked to perform, no matter how demeaning. They do not spurn long and dangerous journeys, they bear with insults, torture, and changing circumstances, all for the hope of gain. They have no fear when, perhaps, their miserable hopes are dashed, nor at the prospect of a premature death in a foreign land. They put up with separation from their wife and children, their homeland, and their creature comforts. Their thirst for wealth makes them frantic, and so great is their greed that they are insensible to work and pain alike.

We, on the other hand, seek wisdom, not wealth, we strive for heaven, not earth, and we hasten to heavenly riches *that eye has not seen, nor ear heard, neither has it entered into the heart of man.** We, I say, who should be storming heaven in our search for these things, are preoccupied instead with bodily comfort! We are weaker and more miserable than worldly people. What is that you are saying? What are you doing? You are preparing to ascend to heaven and invade the very kingdom of God, and you inquire whether the road is steep and there might be some obstacles on the way? And you do not blush for shame to bury yourself in the ground!

*1 Cor 2:9

If every evil were to befall you, every danger threaten you—insults, injuries, dishonor, calumnies, swords, weapons, fire, fierce beasts, precipitous heights, hunger, sickness—in a word, if every calamity I can describe or imagine were to descend upon you, all these things should provoke nothing more than a scornful smile in view of the great things to be gained. Such fear is effeminate, the spirit of an old lady. There is something base, unhappy, and ignoble about a soul who wants to ascend to heaven but ponders earthly rest: to long for something and also expect to receive it here and now is the piety of the Old Testament. I do not see, my beloved, any of us aflame with a true and perfect desire for heaven; if we were, all these things that seem burdensome would be mere shadows that make us laugh.*

*Compunctione 1.6–7; PG 47:403–4; Latin differs

Concerning the narrow way, Gregory writes,

The strict constraint of right living is not a broad road; it is a narrow path in which we are strictly hemmed in by our careful observance of the commandments. Is this not, as it were, a very narrow way: to live in this world with no desire for this world, neither to covet others' possessions nor cling to one's own, to despise the praises of the world and to love reproaches for God's sake, to avoid praise and court contempt, to despise flatterers and honor our despisers, to banish from our hearts the wrongs of those who hurt us and retain the unchanging grace of heartfelt affection for them? All of these are paths, but in fact great ones: the narrower they are in this life as they regulate our conduct, the wider they spread out as regards our eternal reward. It is indeed perfect wisdom for you to do all these things and to know that you can do none of them by your own strength.‡

‡Mor 27.XXXVII.61–62; PL 76:435D–36A; CL 143B:1379–80; *Massa*

And Abbot John* of Sinai cautions,

*Climacus

Let us attend to ourselves, lest we keep running along the broad and spacious road even though we say we have taken the hard and narrow path. Here are the signposts that will indicate the narrow way and illuminate it for you: stomach ache, standing in prayer throughout the night, small portions of bread and water, mockery, derision, jeers, curbing self-will, the cup of dishonor, patience in sustaining inward and outward attacks, silence in the face of contempt, bearing wounds bravely, not resenting detractors, not meeting contempt with rage, and humbling yourself in judgment. Blessed are those who enter upon this narrow path, *for theirs is the kingdom of heaven*.* *Matt 5:10; Scala paradisi 2.7; PG 88:658AB; *Massa*

A Narrow Path, but an Easy Yoke

*Do not be disturbed that the Lord says, *How narrow is the gate, and strait is the way that leads to life*, for he also says, *My yoke is sweet and my burden light*.* Just as a burden may be heavy in itself but is called light in comparison to its reward, so present realities are troublesome in relation to future glories. In a sense this way can be called *wide*, because reflection on the love of heavenly things causes the heart to expand: *the sufferings of this time are not worthy to be compared with the glory to come that shall be revealed in us*.* But it is *narrow* because it chokes the love of earthly things and estranges us from them. *R 2 *Matt 11:30 *Rom 8:18

Chrysostom says, "The way is narrow and close, but it is also light and easy because the adversity of this life is passing and leads to a good end, eternal life. For a time there is sweat on the brow; in eternity, a crown. And we can gain great solace from our efforts because the labor comes first, only to give way to glorious things that abide. Although we are commanded to do what is difficult in itself, it must be done so that we can deserve to attain glory."* *Hom Matt 23.5 approx; PG 57/58:314; Latin Anianus in part

If we do not suffer with Christ we will not reign with him, and he *is not crowned, except he strive lawfully*.‡ Chrysostom continues, "If you find the way laborious, blame your own indolence. The tempestuous waves seem light and tolerable to sailors, the wounds and slaughters to soldiers, the winters and storms to farmers, the blows and injuries to boxers; they endure all these things for rewards that are temporary and fleeting. How much more should we disregard present difficulties when heaven is the prize? Do not think how hard the path is; think where it leads, and recall where the wide road ends."* ‡2 Tim 2:5 *Hom Matt 23.5 approx; PG 57/58:314; Latin Anianus in part

This same Chrysostom teaches us how the Lord's precepts can seem light and easy, rather than difficult and burdensome:

> Regarding what has been said, let us not fuel disobedience by contention, for these precepts carry a great reward with them and are also desirable in themselves. And if they appear troublesome and difficult to you, and the effort needed to carry them seems immoderate, recall that you have undertaken them for the sake of Christ; then you will judge that what seems to be sad in fact is most joyful. If we maintain this attitude at all times, nothing will seem burdensome, but we will draw pleasure from every quarter. Work will no longer feel like work; the more effort we put into it, the pleasanter and sweeter it will seem.
>
> When the love of wealth and the draw of wicked habits threaten to take possession of you, say to your soul, "You are sad because I defraud you of bodily pleasure, but you should rejoice because I am making provision for the kingdom of heaven. You are working not for a creature's sake, but for God's. Wait a little while, and you will see what great things are being prepared for you. Learn to bear the burdens of this present life with a generous spirit, and you will rejoice at the liberality with which God rewards your trust in him."
>
> If we could consistently drive home this message to ourselves we would quickly be delivered from our defects. God requires only one thing of you: undertake to fight your foe fiercely for the honor of the king and your own salvation. If you give him just this, he will decisively win every battle. Then even those things that we consider unbearable now we will find to be very easy; we will think them light and even lovable. We think every kind of virtue is difficult and arduous so long as we remain in our vices; wickedness is what seems sweet and desirable. But let us step back for a moment: we will see that vice is disgraceful and awful, while virtue is easy and attractive. And we

> can easily learn this from the example of those who have changed their lives for the better.* *Hom Matt 16.11; PG 57/58:253–54; Latin Anianus

As Seneca says, "It is not that we do not dare because things are difficult; they are difficult because we do not dare."* *Lucilium 104.26.5

Beware of False Prophets

*The Lord stated that there are few who enter by the narrow gate. Heretics and other perverse people who hide their deceit under a cloak of virtue mislead simple folk who are walking in the way of God by claiming that these words refer to them, because they are few in number. Thus he immediately adds, *Beware of false prophets*.* That is, be aware of them and studiously avoid them. Hilary says, "Because they are few who enter by the narrow way, Christ exposes the deceit of those who lie and say that they are the ones who go in, lest they keep us from entering: *Beware*, he says, *of false prophets*."* He means deceiving heretics, posing hypocrites, false brethren, those feigning the appearance of religion, and such like. ***R 3** *Matt 7:15 *Hom Matt 6.4; PL 9:952B

In a moral sense, the three false prophets are the flesh, the world, and the devil. A *false prophet* is so called because he foretells or promises one thing but delivers another; in this way he deceives and beguiles people. The first false prophet is carnal desire, which promises delight but delivers eternal affliction; the second is material greed, which promises a sufficiency but delivers final destitution; the third is the devil, or worldly pride, which promises fame but delivers future disgrace: *every one that exalts himself shall be humbled*.* This warning can also be applied to all those demons who transform themselves into angels to deceive the righteous. Hence John warns, *Believe not every spirit, but try the spirits if they be of God*.* *Luke 14:11; *Gorran Matt 7:15 approx* *1 John 4:1; *Lyra Matt 7:15 mor*

He continues, "These deceivers *come to you in the clothing of sheep.*"* They appear before people in the guise of religion, resembling ministers of righteousness: with humble clothing, lengthy prayers, strict fasts, generous almsgiving, smooth words, and the other signs of piety. They feign simplicity, simulate gentleness, and parade a false humility before their people, having, in the words of the apostle, *an appearance indeed of godliness but denying the power thereof.** Christ goes on to say, "*Inwardly,* in their deceptive hearts and wills, *they are ravening wolves.*"* They are clothed in the robes of virtue, but their lives are corrupted by depravity. They must be avoided, lest by their destructive charms and pretenses they tear you to pieces.

*Matt 7:15

*2 Tim 3:5

*Matt 7:15

Chrysostom warns, "Nothing is more fatal to goodness than the pretense of goodness: when evil is disguised as good, it is not guarded against so long as it is not known."* And Jerome says, "To be sure, this can be understood to refer to all those who promise one thing by their dress and speech but who show something else by their actions. But it should be understood primarily of heretics, who appear to wrap themselves in a kind of garment of piety with their continence, chastity, and fasting, but within they have venomous spirits, and they deceive the hearts of their simpler brethren."*

*Opus imperf 19; PG 56:736

*Com Matt 7:15; PL 26:48B; CL 77:43

By Their Fruits You Shall Know Them

***R 4**

*False prophets cannot be detected by appearances, so the Lord indicates how they can be known: by their works and fruits. They are difficult to recognize because they appear to be one thing, but their inner attitude is different: "*By their fruits you shall know them* eventually."* They will not be seen for what they are by everyone, since their works will seem good and laudable to others; but some will recognize them, es-

*Matt 7:16

pecially because of their impatience in times of adversity or persecution. Those who feign righteousness cannot bear oppression, and *in time of temptation they fall away*.* Augustine warns, "Not only is there no remedy for those who wear the religious habit without good works, but they will also have to endure God's just judgment."* As Seneca observes, evil is worst when it masquerades as good.‡ He also teaches that what matters is what you are, not what you have.†

*Luke 8:13

*Ps-Augustine, Sermo 249.6; PL 30:2208

‡Syrus, Sent 395

†Moribus 1.2

The Lord then proposes an image to illustrate his teaching. Just as thorns, thistles, vines, and figs are known by their different fruits, so it is with people: *Do men gather grapes of thorns, or figs of thistles?** Chrysostom says, "Truly, he is saying that there is nothing gentle, meek, or sweet about such people; they are sheep only to the depth of their wool. This makes them easy to recognize; of this there can be no doubt."*

*Matt 7:16

*Hom 23.7; PG 57/58:316; Latin Anianus in part

We can understand *thorns* to symbolize desires of the flesh, which always burn but are never consumed; *thistles*, spiritual evils, which are full of the nettles of sin; *grapes*, the fervor of the active life; *figs*, the sweetness of the contemplative life. A good act cannot blossom from carnal desires, because it requires the body to be subject to the spirit; nor can contemplation be produced by an evil heart, for it needs a heart that is devout and at peace. *Wisdom will not enter into a malicious soul*, as regards the contemplative life, *nor dwell in a body subject to sins*,* as regards the active life, which is expressed bodily.

*Wis 1:4

He reaffirms his lesson by speaking in general terms: just as each kind of tree can be identified by its fruit, so each human being can be identified by the works he or she produces. Notice that he did not say *leaves*, that is, words, but *by their fruits you shall know them*,* that is, by their works. If we listen to words, it may be hard to distinguish good people from bad ones. But what words can disguise, deeds will reveal: if they are faithful, meek, patient, humble, and chaste, if they despise avarice, and if they have other virtues

*Matt 7:20

too numerous to list. False prophets can be known by their fruits. For a time they may seem to be doing good through their almsgiving, fasting, prayer, and similar things, but they are motivated by greed, or vainglory, and their pretense cannot remain hidden for long.* True, the human heart is inscrutable, but it can be known to human judgment by its actions and works, especially over a long time.

**Bruno Com Matt 7:20; PL 165:130BC*

These are called *fruits*, because what we are will be made known by what we say and do. Although malicious people can conceal their wickedness for a time by doing good works, they will not be able to avoid acting according to their wicked desires for long. Seneca writes, "No one can wear the mask for very long; pretense soon relapses to its true nature. Anything that grows from the solid ground of truth becomes better with the passage of time."* Deception is exposed in trial or difficulty. Some feign humility and good works in times of prosperity, when they are honored, but their pride becomes evident when they are touched by adversity and honor is taken away. It can also make itself known in the case of those who do good works for honors and such things—simply by the fact that once they have gained them, they stop doing the good works.

*De clementia 1.1.6

Augustine says, "Whatever fails to reveal itself through words or deeds is made evident through temptations. Now temptation is twofold: it is present either in the hope of gaining some temporal advantage or in the fear of losing it.* It becomes apparent that a person is not a sheep, but a wolf in sheep's clothing, when some circumstance denies or takes away the very things he has, or hopes to have, by donning his disguise."*

*Sermone monte 2.25.82; PL 34:1306; CL 35:182

*Sermone monte 2.12.41; PL 34:1287; CL 35:132

In addition, they can be known from the following traits: they oppress the simple, disparage their superiors, criticize the smallest things, spurn correction, do not do what they say, stand on ceremony, give up after a good beginning, and complain in adversity.*

**Gorran Matt 7:20*

Their impatience in time of trial is the clearest way to recognize these hypocrites, as was said above. Recall that we never speak more clearly and rightly than when we speak with our own voice. There are some people who are like a caged bird that changes its voice to mimic human speech or the calls of other birds. It does this when all is well, but if someone hurts its foot, causes pain, or does something to annoy the bird, it immediately screeches in its own voice. In the same way, there are many people who adopt an artificial voice with which they praise God with fawning adulation when all is well and they are prosperous, but should they find themselves in some difficulty or crossed in any way, they quickly recover their own voice: ingratitude, impatience, and so on.

*Christ rightly says that people are known by their fruits, for *every good tree brings forth good fruit, and the evil tree brings forth evil fruit.** That is, a good person with a good will produces good works, and so merits eternal life; someone with a depraved will produces evil actions and deserves punishment. Ambrose teaches, "Your intention shapes your acts."* And, according to Chrysostom, it is the will that is rewarded for doing good and punished for doing evil, but the deeds bear witness to the will.* ***R 5**

*Matt 7:17

*De officiis 1.30.147

*Opus imperf 46; PG 56:891

What the Lord says is true: "*A good tree*, so long as it remains good, *cannot bring forth evil fruit; neither can an evil tree bring forth good fruit* as long as it remains evil."* This must be correctly understood: so long as a tree remains good it cannot produce the bad fruit deserving of reprobation, and so long as a tree remains evil it cannot produce the good fruit deserving of eternal life. If good people produce bad fruit, they are no longer good; if bad people want to produce good fruit, let them begin to be good.

*Matt 7:18

Truly, *every good tree brings forth good fruit, and the evil tree brings forth evil fruit* because, as he says elsewhere, "*A good man out of a good treasure* of his good intention and will, which is like a treasure hidden within, *brings forth* into the mind *good things* in speech and action, *and an evil man out of an evil treasure* of a wicked will *brings forth* into the mind *evil things** in speech and action." Contrary causes produce contrary effects.*

*Matt 12:35

**Lyra Matt 12:35*

According to Bede, the treasure of the heart is like the root of the tree: as the root brings forth a certain fruit, so particular actions are produced from the heart.* Remigius writes, "The treasure of the heart is the intention, from which God judges the works, so that sometimes a small reward is given for great deeds, or a great reward for little ones. A good will is a great gift of God, surpassing all earthly things."* Augustine teaches, "A good will is what makes us strive to live an honest, upright life, and so attain to the highest wisdom.* Whoever has a good will possesses a treasure far greater than any earthly realm or any bodily delights. Consequently, whoever is without it lacks the one essential thing, for the will gives in itself something greater than all goods."* And elsewhere he says, "If deeds be lacking, look no further than the will."‡

*Com Luke 6:45; PL 92:411C; CL 120:150

*Attr. to Remigius, Zachary 2.62; PL 186:203B

*Libero arbitrio 1.12.25; PL 32:1234

*Libero arbitrio 1.12.26; PL 32:1235

‡Gloss John 6:29; PL 114:382A

The good tree's root is the will informed by divine grace; its leaves, thoughts; its flowers, words; its fruit, deeds. The bad tree's root is the will devoid of God's grace; its leaves fall, its flowers wilt, its fruit spoils—none of which happens to the good tree.

It is right to say that good or bad fruit can be judged to come from a good or bad heart, *for out of the abundance of* goodness or evil hidden within *the heart, the mouth speaks* externally by words and deeds.* The outward effect of speech or act proceeds from the inner person, and words and actions testify to the inner concept.*

*Matt 12:34

**Gloss Matt 12:34; PL 114:266C*

By the word *mouth* the Lord wishes to signify every thought, word, or deed that comes from the heart. It is customary in Scripture to use the term *word* at times for what is done or made. For example, when Hezekiah showed the Chaldean ambassadors all his treasures, we read, *For there was nothing** *in his house, nor in all his dominion that Hezekiah did not show them,** and cer-

**non fuit verbum*

*Isa 39:2

tainly it was things and not words that he showed them.* The *mouth* does have a special meaning here, because the heart is especially revealed through the mouth, and words hold the first place among signs.

**Bede, Com Luke 6:46 approx; PL 92:412AB; CL 120:151*

Augustine says, "God judges all hearts from the mouth, because he is not ignorant of the intention that produces the words. He expressly says, *Out of the abundance of the heart the mouth speaks. Abundance*, because there is more within than what emerges—like smoke wafting up from the fire or a pot boiling over."* And Chrysostom comments, "It is a natural consequence that when wickedness abounds within, wicked words should pour out of the mouth. So when you hear people speak evil words, do not suppose only so much wickedness to be in them as the words display, but conjecture that the fountain must be much more abundant. What is spoken outwardly is the overflow of what is within. Through shame, the tongue often refrains from pouring forth all its wickedness at once, but the heart, having no human witness, freely gives birth to whatever evils it wishes. It does not have much regard for God."* Christ spoke these words and used the image of the tree here in opposition to hypocrites, especially the scribes and the Pharisees. Later he will use it again against wicked blasphemers who said that Christ cast out demons by the power of Beelzebub.

*Gloss Luke 6:45 approx; PL 114:266C

*Hom Matt 42:1; PG 57/58:452; Latin differs

*Some lukewarm people may believe that they will be spared punishment because they have refrained from evil, have not stolen, and have lived at peace with others. But they have not shown compassion to their neighbors or helped those in need, so the Lord adds, *Every tree that does not bring forth good fruit shall be cut down, and shall be cast into the fire.** That is, they shall be cut off from association with good things and separated from the number of the faithful; then the sentence will be executed by the harvesting angels and they shall be cast into the eternal flames of Gehenna. The Lord threatens the unfruitful with the punishment of damnation because they are cut off

***R 6**

*Matt 7:19

from the land of the living, and with the punishment of the senses because they are cast into never-ending fire. The Lord will not reproach them for doing evil, but for neglecting to do good, saying, *I was hungry and you gave me not to eat,** and so on.

*Matt 25:42

Know that the fruits of the heart are contrition, meditation on the law of God, recollection of God's blessings, remembrance of death, and compassion toward others. The fruits of speech are prayer, preaching, thanksgiving, counsel, correcting one in error, instructing the ignorant. The fruits of action are penitence, almsgiving, obedience, attentiveness to duties, putting up with adversity.*

**St Cher Gloss Matt 21:41*

Faith Must Be Lived

Lest we think that it is enough to say, "Lord, Lord!" for us to be trees that bear good fruit, Jesus adds, *Why do you call me, "Lord, Lord" and do not do the things which I say?** It as if he wanted to tell hypocrites, especially the scribes and the Pharisees, "You are trees with leaves but no fruit, words but no deeds. You will be cursed like branches with leaves that look like olives but are barren of fruit."* There is as much difference between saying and doing as there is between leaves and fruit.

*Luke 6:46

**Gorran Luke 6:46*

***R 7**

*He then goes on to show that a mere formula of words cannot save us; we must do God's will. "*Not every one that says to me, 'Lord, Lord,'* simply mouthing a profession of the Catholic faith, *shall enter into the kingdom of heaven.*"* To profess faith without living it is insufficient for salvation. Such *faith is dead in itself,** for there are people who confess God with their lips, *but in their works they deny him.** Many people continually parrot the words, "*Lord, Lord,*" in their prayers, *but their heart is far** from God, and hypocrites do the same by striking a pious pose before others. Rather, the Lord says, *He that does the will of my Father who is in heaven, he shall enter into the kingdom of heaven.**

*Matt 7:21

*Jas 2:17

*Titus 1:16

*Matt 15:8

*Matt 7:21

Such people are the good trees that bear good fruit by doing God's will, as Jesus himself did, and in so doing he deigned to give us an example. What is the point of merely saying, *"Lord, Lord"* to the Lord? Would he not be the Lord if we did not say he was?* To say in truth, "Lord, Lord," or, "Lord Jesus," means to believe in our hearts, to speak with our mouths, and to show by our deeds; to have one without the others is to deny he is Lord. Augustine says, "To believe in God means by believing to love and cherish, by believing to go to him and be incorporated in his members."*

Hilary, Com Matt 7:21; PL 9:952C

*Tr John 29.6; PL 35:1631; CL 36:191

It should be noted here that certain signs immediately demonstrate that people are doing God's will: they seek to do everything, have everything, and bear with everything in conformity with his will, and from this they draw inner peace; they see the face of God in all things, so that they gaze upon him constantly, and from this they draw reverence, shame, and discipline, both inwardly and outwardly; they frequently reflect upon the goodness of God's grace and generosity, and from this they draw gratuitous love and confidence in the future, and they always seek to build up their neighbor, carefully weighing their words and calculating their actions, reflecting frequently upon themselves.

*So that we will not be taken in, not only by those who speak Christ's name but do not act, but also by those who even add some works and miracles to their proclamation, the Lord continues, *Many will say to me in that day: "Lord, Lord, have not we prophesied in your name, and cast out devils in your name, and done many miracles in your name?"** *That day* is the renowned and remarkable day of the Last Judgment, a day of terror to the impious but of joy to the devout. On that day, Chrysostom says, hearts will speak and tongues will be silent; the person will not be questioned but the conscience will be examined, and there will not be flattering witnesses but truth-telling angels.* Many ***R 8**

*Matt 7:22

*Opus imperf 19; PG 56:742

will ask then, "Have we not proclaimed the prophetic word and denounced hidden sins by the invocation of your powerful name? Have we not freed those who were possessed by demons and performed miraculous feats?" These will be the words of those who teach well but live badly.* Chrysostom writes, "Certainly they will see that their end is contrary to their expectations: they were renowned here for performing miracles, but there they will understand that they are to be punished. In their astonishment and wonder, they will say, '*Lord, Lord, have not we prophesied in your name?* How is it that things are now against us?' Who could wish for this new and unforeseen end?"*

**this sentence: Lyra Matt 7:22 mor*

*Hom Matt 24.1; PG 57/58:521-522; Latin Anianus

In answer, the Judge hands down his sentence for these rejected reprobates: "*And then will I state clearly to them, 'I never knew you** beforehand with the knowledge of approval, but only of disapproval.'" It can be said that he *knows* those whom he approves; those he does not know are those he does not commend in his love.* Augustine says, "He knows the condemned, and his knowledge is their judgment; he does not acknowledge their will, which opposes his."* And Bede, "It is not in accord with the wisdom of the Scriptures that those whose works are unworthy of God's gaze can be said to be known by him."*

*Matt 7:23

**Zachary 1.42; PL 186:155C*

*Bede, Com Luke 13:25; PL 92:508C; CL 120:272

*Com Luke 13:27; PL 92:509A; CL 120:272

Finally, rejecting those people because of their wicked deeds, the Lord says, "*Depart from me*, thereby magnifying the elect, *you that work iniquity*."* He separates them and tells them to *depart* into iniquity, to be consigned to eternal damnation. God only knows those who act justly; he commands these others to depart from him, for, although he is everywhere by virtue of his divinity, he is not present to them as the object of the beatific vision. And he uses the present tense, *you that work iniquity*, because evil effects still remain in them.

*Matt 7:23

Jerome explains, "He did not say, 'You who have worked iniquity,' lest he should seem to be taking away repentance, but '*you that work*,' that is, up to this present hour of judgment. Although you no longer have the ability to sin, you still have the affection for it."* Chrysostom agrees: "He did not say 'you who were evildoers,' but, 'you evildoers,' because the wicked do not cease to be wicked after death. Even if they can no longer sin, they do not lose the desire to sin. Death, to be sure, separates the soul from the body, but it does not change the soul's intention."* This same father says elsewhere, "The Lord wanted to assert here that faith without the works of holiness has no value. And not only faith—even if someone were to perform miracles, these have no value if the person does not possess virtue. Neither faith nor miracles are of any avail without the testimony of life."* And elsewhere yet again, "In no way is blessedness to be found in doing signs and wonders, but in fulfilling the commandments and perfection.* Those who seek approval by appealing to the evidence of their wondrous works cannot be seen to be good. A good life and honest works, even without miracles, merit a crown; unjust conduct, even if accompanied by prodigious signs, cannot escape punishment."*

*Com Matt 7:23; PL 26:49D; CL 77:46

*Opus imperf 19; PG 56:743

*Hom Matt 24.1; PG 57/58:521; Latin Anianus in part

*Compunctione 1.8; PG 47:407; Latin differs

*Compunctione 1.9; PG 47:407–8; Latin differs

Here it should be noted that a miracle can occur for many reasons: sometimes because of the worthiness of the one who performs it; sometimes because of the worthiness of the one who receives it; sometimes because of neither of them, but for the benefit of the bystanders, so that seeing it, they will honor God and believe in Christ; sometimes for the condemnation of those involved and those who witness it, so that seeing, they may not see and become blind; and sometimes even to increase vainglory or for some other harmful reason.

Do not be surprised, then, if wicked people sometimes prophesy and perform miracles. These gifts are *gratiae Dei gratis datae,* which are given primarily for the common good of the church, and rarely for that of the individual. Sometimes these are given to us from God through wicked people, not because of the merit of the one who asks but to show forth Christ's power and confirm the faith, even though the ones who pray for the miracle are evil. In the same way, alms can be distributed by a good master through the hands of a wicked servant.[2]*

*Lyra Matt 7:22 approx

[2] Ludolph presents the mature teaching of Aquinas: "Now gratuitous grace [*gratia gratis data*] is ordained to the common good of the church, which is ecclesiastical order, whereas sanctifying grace is ordained to the separate common good, which is God" (ST 1a 2ae, q. 111.5, a. 1). The theology of grace developed in several stages, even in Aquinas's own writings. For Peter Lombard, *gratia gratis data* was justification, to be distinguished from *gratia gratis dans*, the uncreated grace that is God himself. At the beginning of the thirteenth century the distinction began to be drawn between *gratia gratum faciens* (sanctifying grace), a supernatural habit in the human being, and *gratia gratis data* (actual grace), any direct or indirect divine assistance. Albert the Great listed eight senses of the term, of which one is "inspiration, thaumaturgy, and similar gifts." Because *gratia gratis data* are given for the good of the community, they are not dependent on the holiness of their recipient. Regarding miracles performed by wicked people, Aquinas writes, "True miracles cannot be wrought save by the power of God, because God works them for human benefit, and this in two ways: in one way for the confirmation of truth declared, in another way in proof of a person's holiness, which God desires to propose as an example of virtue. In the first way miracles can be wrought by any one who preaches the true faith and calls upon Christ's name, as even the wicked do sometimes. In this way even the wicked can work miracles. Hence Jerome commenting on Matt 7:22, 'Have not we prophesied in your name?' says, 'Sometimes prophesying, the working of miracles, and the casting out of demons are accorded not to the merit of those who do these things, but to the invoking of Christ's name, that people may honor God, by invoking whom such great miracles are wrought.' In the second way miracles are not wrought except by the saints, since it is in proof of their holiness that miracles are wrought during their lifetime or after death, either by themselves or by others. . . . In this way indeed there is nothing to prevent a sinner from working miracles by invoking a saint, but the miracle is ascribed not to the individual, but to the one in proof of whose holiness such things are done" (ST II-II, q. 178, resp.).

Let us, then, pursue the good, avoid every evil, and wholeheartedly fulfill the heavenly precepts; in this way, we can be known by God. Let us pride ourselves on doing what God wants done, rather than what can be done.*

Hilary, Com Matt 7:22; PG 9:953A

A House Built on Rock

*The Lord spurns those who confess him with their lips but do not do what he commands. He concludes that it is useless to listen if action does not follow, and he admonishes us to carry out Christ's teaching, lest we depart from him with other evildoers. Again, it is useless to hear the law but not put it into practice. This is how he ends his whole sermon, with a conclusion that is extremely sobering and deserving of our full attention: "*Every one therefore*, without exception, *that hears these my words* with the inner ear of understanding, *and does them* by doing works with heartfelt charity, *shall be likened to a wise man*, provident about his future, *that built his house upon a rock*,* that is, Christ, doing all he does for the sake of Christ." Two things are essential to good actions: they must be good in themselves and they must be performed with the correct intention. No one is confirmed in what they have heard or understood unless they put it into practice. ***R 9**

*Matt 7:24

And, because the rock is Christ, they build on Christ who do what they have heard from Christ. "*And the rain fell* (carnal temptations and lustful desires), *and the floods came* (avarice and a thirst for worldly possessions), *and the winds blew* (pride and diabolical vainglory), *and* impetuous and forceful temptations *beat upon that house* raised upon the solid virtues of Christ, *and it fell not* from virtue by succumbing to temptation, *for it was founded* purposefully, radically, and unfailingly through faith, hope, and charity *on a rock*,* Christ himself."* Three different kinds of temptation are sug-

*Matt 7:25

**Zachary 1.43; PL 186:155D*

gested here, which embrace every kind of temptation: there are the desires of the flesh, signified by the *rain*, which falls drop by drop and softens; there are trials and adversities, signified by the *floods*, which strike with great force; finally, there are enticements, signified by the *winds*, which can be stirred up by threats, flattery, or diabolical suggestion.

All of these temptations can be brought on by either seductive prosperity or crushing adversity. We need not fear any of them if we have built our house on the solid rock of Christ and it is supported by the observance of his precepts; again, not only hearing what he commands but putting it into practice. But we will be exposed to all these dangers if we hear but do not act, for we will not have a sure foundation or be strengthened by doing what the Lord commands.‡

‡*Aug, Sermone monte 2.25.87; PL 34:1308; CL 35:187*

***R 10**

*Consequently, the Lord paints this contrasting picture: *"And every one that hears these my words and does not do them,* but disdains them, *shall be like a foolish* and evil *man that built his house,* that is, the edifice of his works, *upon the sand** of earthly love, a shifting and unstable foundation." Everyone does this who, despising heavenly realities, continues to covet those of earth; these are given priority in his thoughts over God himself. Every creature is changeable. *Sand* is a good image of earthly desires, because it is sterile, and those who love riches produce no fruit; it is fluid, passing over everything like a shadow; and it is tossed about by the waves, like those who are overwhelmed by worldliness. It is also a fitting image of bad company, which is beyond counting in its multiplicity, fragmented in its quarrels, and sterile as regards any increase in good works. And so there is a fall into sin.

*Matt 7:26

The wicked temptations mentioned earlier came, and they *beat upon that* badly founded *house* with sudden impetuosity, *and it fell* through sin, *and great was the fall thereof,** for it collapsed into Gehenna. First there is the fall into the pit of sin, and afterwards the fall into the pit of hell; this is the great fall, because it

*Matt 7:27

is irreparable.* Every conscience that does not remain fixed in God with firm hope cannot withstand temptations; the more we are separated from the higher things and are caught up in the things of this world, the more violent the tremor will be. *Lyra Matt 7:27*

Bede comments, "It is very clear that when some temptation assails those who are really evil and those who only appear to be good, they immediately worsen until they fall into final, perpetual punishment."* And Chrysostom, *"And great,* he says, *was the fall thereof.* The risk did not concern mere trifles, but the crisis of the soul, everlasting punishment, and the loss of the heavenly realm."* *Com Luke 6:49; PL 92:4141A; CL 120:153 *Hom Matt 24.4; PG 57/58:326; Latin Anianus

It does not always happen that someone who hears the word of God and does not act on it falls into this catastrophic ruin. Two distinctions must be made. The first concerns the hearers: if they omit to do God's will out of contempt, then this fate awaits them, but if they fail to do it out of weakness, no. The second concerns what God says: if the message concerns what is essential to salvation, such as the Gospel precepts, then this end awaits those who hear but do not act, but if the teaching concerns evangelical counsels or other matters that go beyond the call of duty, then they pertain only to those called to perfection.

*In a moral sense, the just one's house, whose edifice is a good conscience, rises up to the perfection of good works; its excavation is poverty and contempt for worldly possessions; its foundations are love and meditation on heavenly things; the elements battering it are the assaults of temptations; its steadfastness, final perseverance. The home of the wicked is a bad conscience, about which Micah says, *As yet there is a fire in the house of the wicked.** Its mundane structure rises up to the love of worldly things; its lack of foundations creates mental instability; the floods inundating it are the waves of carnal pleasures; its rapid fall, the inclination to sin; the greatness of its ruin, eternal damnation.* Furthermore, such a house is shaken by ***R 11** *Mic 6:10 *Gorran Luke 6:49 approx* temptation, it leans by enjoyment, and it falls by consent. The collapse is great in giving consent, for there is a fall from grace; it is greater in actions, because there is a fall from life; and it is greatest in obstinacy, because there is a fall from mercy.

If we are wise, we will put into practice and complete what we have heard and so build a sturdy structure. Through the accumulation of good works God gives us grace, which strengthens and confirms our merits, and without which the house will collapse. By doing good through grace, we merit final perseverance in good; thus our spiritual house is founded on the rock of faith, constructed through hope, and reinforced by charity. So long as Christ gives his grace, neither rain nor flood nor wind can cause the house to fall. On the other hand, fools who hear but do not act (or pretend not to have heard), become forgetful hearers and build their house upon sand, as it were. Because they do not build their dwelling on the foundation of what they have heard, it collapses and disappears as soon as temptations arrive. *For not the hearers of the law are just before God: but the doers of the law shall be justified.**

*Rom 2:13

There are three kinds of human builders. First, there are those who love God alone. These build with gold, silver, and precious stones: gold is love of virtue, silver is knowledge of the truth, and precious stones are cooperation in good works. Next are those who love other things besides God, but nothing contrary to God and nothing more than God. Because their love of God is not demolished, their foundation remains; however, their divided love makes for a somewhat unstable underpinning. These build with wood, hay, and straw: wood is the sin of illicit deeds, hay is the sin of illicit desires not acted on, and straw is the sin of illicit thoughts. Finally, there are those who love something in opposition to God, and in this way they utterly destroy any foundation: the love of God cannot exist where he is not loved alone or as the highest of loves.

The first are praiseworthy and will be saved; the second must be corrected but can be liberated; the third must be accused and condemned.* *Allegoriae NT 2.15; PL 175:789CD

Again, some build on the foundation of faith with the gold of contemplation, others with the silver of preaching, and others with the precious stones of good works; these will all be saved on account of the foundation and the good works. Others, however, build with the wood of a burning desire for possessions, or the hay of the muck of carnal delights, or the straw of empty words and irresolute deeds. These latter will also be saved on account of the foundation, *yet so as by fire,** which will utterly destroy everything unworthy of this foundation.* *1 Cor 3:15 *Bonaventure, Sermo 1 Nov 2 approx

The Admiration of the Crowd

*Finally, by way of conclusion to all that had gone before, we read, *"And it came to pass when Jesus had fully ended** *these words, the people were in admiration at his doctrine** and the superiority of his wisdom, for no man had ever spoken like this." Quite rightly the evangelist says *consummasset*, because the Sermon on the Mount lacked nothing and contained everything necessary for salvation.[3] And it is right that they *were in admiration*, for, as Chrysostom says, "We marvel at whatever we cannot adequately praise."* That *the people were in admiration* testifies to the superiority of Christ's teaching: he pointed out the pre-eminent virtues, supplied what was lacking in the law, promised not only earthly but also heavenly benefits, and confirmed his teaching marvelously. ***R 12** *consummasset *Matt 7:28 *Opus imperf 20; PG 20:746

The reason for their astonishment is given: *For he was teaching them as one having power.** He taught *as one having power* by instructing them in his own name, giving preference to his counsels over the precepts of *Matt 7:29

[3] *Consummare* means to finish off, end, or bring to perfection.

the law, adding to that law where it seemed deficient, explaining its more obscure elements, correcting it, changing it, and revoking parts of it, all at his pleasure as its Author and Originator, subject to no one. Or, *as one having power* to heal the sick and perform miracles. Or, *as one having power* to make an impression and turn the hearts of his listeners to him. *And not as the scribes and Pharisees*, who gave the law to the people as they had learned it themselves and permitted no alteration in it. Even Moses could only say what the Lord had commanded him to, omitting or changing nothing.

Chrysostom writes, "Among other things, they were astonished especially by his authority. Unlike Moses and the prophets, he did not present his decrees as coming from another, but everywhere indicated himself to be the one who had the power to command. In enacting his laws, he frequently said, *But I say to you.* In making mention of the terrible Day of Judgment, he showed himself to be the Judge who will award both punishments and prizes."*

*Hom Matt 25.1; PG 57/58:327; Latin Anianus

Conclusion

***R 13**

*Now watch the Lord Jesus as he delivers this sermon, and contemplate him. How affectionately, kindly, and persuasively he addresses his hearers and leads them to acts of virtue! Study the disciples, too, and see how reverently and humbly they devote their entire attention to Christ, listening to his marvelous discourse and committing it to memory. What pleasure they take at rejoicing in his words as much as his appearance! Truly it can be said of him, *You are beautiful above the sons of men: grace is poured abroad in your lips.** Contemplation of this scene should bring joy to you, too, as you watch and listen—it is as if you were really seeing him and hearing him speak and drawing near to them if, perchance, invited, so that you could linger there should the Lord give this to you.*

*Ps 44:3

**Massa; MVC 21; CM 153:103*

Then observe Jesus as he walks down from the mountain with his disciples, conversing familiarly with them on the path. See how that flock of ordinary folk follows, not carefully regimented but crowding around like chicks behind a mother hen, striving to get close so that they can hear him better. Follow that precious treasure, even if at a distance, and see if you can catch some stray phrases as the words come to you over the shoulder of this loving Teacher.

✠

Most merciful Lord Jesus Christ, grant that I may enter the royal court of salvation and the life of glory through the narrow road of righteousness and the narrow gate of penitence. Teach me to avoid the falsehood of deceivers and help me imitate the simplicity and innocence of spiritual sheep. May I root my heart in heaven, not earth, so that I will be found faithful in the fruit of good works rather than merely the leaves of words. Grant that I may do the heavenly Father's will and act on your words when I hear them. With you as my firm foundation, may no temptation separate me from you. Amen.